T0386380

THE SARACENS:

THEIR HISTORY,

AND THE

RISE AND FALL OF THEIR EMPIRE.

BY

EDWARD GIBBON AND SIMON OCKLEY.

LONDON:

DARF PUBLISHERS LIMITED

1984

First published 1885
New impression 1984

ISBN 1 85077 484

Printed by A. Wheaton & Co. Ltd, Exeter, Devon

THE

RISE AND FALL

OF THE

SARACEN EMPIRE.

In the vacant space between Persia, Syria, Egypt, and Æthiopia, the Arabian peninsula may be conceived as a triangle of spacious but irregular dimensions. From the northern point of Beles on the Euphrates, a line of 1500 miles is terminated by the straits of Babelmandel and the land of frankincense. About half this length may be allowed for the middle breadth, from east to west, from Bassora to Suez, from the Persian Gulf to the Red Sea. The sides of the triangle are gradually enlarged, and the southern basis presents a front of 1000 miles to the Indian ocean. The entire surface of the peninsula exceeds in a fourfold proportion that of Germany or France ; but the far greater part has been justly stigmatized with the epithets of the *stony* and the *sandy*. Even the wilds of Tartary are decked by the hand of nature with lofty trees and luxuriant herbage ; and the lonesome traveller derives a sort of comfort and society from the presence of vegetable life. But in the dreary waste of Arabia, a boundless level of sand is intersected by sharp and naked mountains ; and the face of the desert, without shade or shelter, is scorched by the direct and intense rays of a tropical sun. Instead of refreshing breezes, the winds, particularly from the S.W., diffuse a noxious and even deadly vapour ; the hillocks of sand which they alternately raise and scatter, are compared to the billows of the ocean, and whole caravans, whole armies, have been lost and buried in the whirlwind. The common benefits of water are an object of desire and contest ; and such is the scarcity of wood, that some art is requisite to preserve and propagate the element of fire. Arabia is destitute of navigable rivers, which fertilize the soil, and convey its produce to the adjacent regions : the torrents that fall from the hills are imbibed by the thirsty earth : the rare and hardy plants, the tamarind or the acacia, that strike their roots into the clefts of the rocks, are nourished by the dews of the night : a scanty supply of rain is collected in cisterns and aqueducts :

the wells and springs are the secret treasure of the desert ; and the pilgrim of Mecca,* after many a dry and sultry march, is disgusted by the taste of the waters, which have rolled over a bed of sulphur or salt. Such is the general and genuine picture of the climate of Arabia.   The experience of evil enhances the value of any local or partial enjoyments. A shady grove, a green pasture, a stream of fresh water, are sufficient to attract a colony of sedentary Arabs to the fortunate spots which can afford food and refreshment to themselves and their cattle, and which encourage their industry in the cultivation of the palm-tree and the vine.   The high lands that border on the Indian ocean are distinguished by their superior plenty of wood and water : the air is more temperate, the fruits are more delicious, the animals and the human race more numerous ; the fertility of the soil invites and rewards the toil of the husbandman ; and the peculiar gifts of frankincense and coffee have attracted in different ages the merchants of the world. If it be compared with the rest of the peninsula, this sequestered region may truly deserve the appellation of the *happy :* and the splendid colouring of fancy and fiction has been suggested by contrast and countenanced by distance.   It was for this earthly paradise that nature had reserved her choicest favours and her most curious workmanship : the incompatible blessings of luxury and innocence were ascribed to the natives : the soil was impregnated with gold and gems, and both the land and sea were taught to exhale the odours of aromatic sweets.   This division of the *sandy*, the *stony*, and the *happy*, so familiar to the Greeks and Latins, is unknown to the Arabians themselves ; and it is singular enough, that a country whose language and inhabitants have ever been the same, should scarcely retain a vestige of its ancient geography.   The maritime districts of *Bahrein* and *Oman* are opposite to the realm of Persia.   The kingdom of *Yemen* displays the limits, or the situation, of Arabia Fœlix : the name of *Neged* is extended over the inland space ; and the birth of Mahomet has illustrated the province of *Hejaz* along the coast of the Red Sea.

The measure of population is regulated by the means of subsistence ; and the inhabitants of this vast peninsula might be out-numbered by the subjects of a fertile and industrious province.   Along the shores of the Persian Gulf, of the ocean, and even of the Red Sea, the *Icthyophagi*, or fish-eaters, continued to wander in quest of their precarious food. In this primitive and abject state, which ill deserves the name of society, the human brute, without arts or laws, almost without sense or language, is poorly distinguished from the rest of the animal creation. Generations and ages might roll away in silent oblivion, and the helpless savage was restrained from multiplying his race, by the wants and pursuits which confined his existence to the narrow margin of the sea-coast.   But in an early period of antiquity the great body of the Arabs

* In the 30 days, or stations, between Cairo and Mecca, 15 are destitute of good water.

had emerged from this scene of misery; and as the naked wilderness could not maintain a people of hunters, they rose at once to the more secure and plentiful condition of the pastoral life. The same life is uniformly pursued by the roving tribes of the desert, and in the portrait of the modern *Bedouins*, we may trace the features of their ancestors, who, in the age of Moses or Mahomet, dwelt under similar tents, and conducted their horses, and camels, and sheep, to the same springs and the same pastures. Our toil is lessened, and our wealth is increased, by our dominion over the useful animals; and the Arabian shepherd had acquired the absolute possession of a faithful friend and a laborious slave. Arabia, in the opinion of the naturalist, is the genuine and original country of the *horse :* the climate most propitious, not indeed to the size, but to the spirit and swiftness, of that generous animal. The merit of the Barb, the Spanish, and the English breed, is derived from a mixture of Arabian blood : the Bedouins preserve, with superstitious care, the honours and memory of the purest race. The males are sold at a high price, but the females are seldom alienated; and the birth of a noble foal was esteemed, among the tribes, as a subject of joy and mutual congratulation. These horses are educated in the tents, among the children of the Arabs, with a tender familiarity, which trains them in the habits of gentleness and attachment. They are accustomed only to walk and to gallop : their sensations are not blunted by the incessant abuse of the spur and the whip : their powers are reserved for the moments of flight and pursuit; but no sooner do they feel the touch of the hand or the stirrup, than they dart away with the swiftness of the wind; and if their friend be dismounted in the rapid career, they instantly stop till he has recovered his seat. In the sands of Africa and Arabia, the *camel* is a sacred and precious gift. That strong and patient beast of burthen can perform, without eating or drinking, a journey of several days; and a reservoir of fresh water is preserved in a large bag, a fifth stomach of the animal, whose body is imprinted with the marks of servitude : the larger breed is capable of transporting a weight of a thousand pounds; and the dromedary, of a lighter and more active frame, outstrips the fleetest courser in the race. Alive or dead, almost every part of the camel is serviceable to man : her milk is plentiful and nutritious : the young and tender flesh has the taste of veal : a valuable salt is extracted from the urine : the dung supplies the deficiency of fuel; and the long hair, which falls each year and is renewed, is coarsely manufactured into the garments, the furniture, and the tents, of the Bedouins. In the rainy seasons they consume the rare and insufficient herbage of the desert : during the heats of summer and the scarcity of winter, they remove their encampments to the sea-coast, the hills of Yemen, or the neighbourhood of the Euphrates, and have often extorted the dangerous license of visiting the banks of the Nile, and the villages of Syria and Palestine. The life of a wandering Arab is a life of danger and distress ; and though sometimes, by rapine or exchange, he may appropriate the fruits of industry, a private citizen in Europe is in the possession of more solid and pleasing luxury than the proudest emir, who marches in the field at the head of 10,000 horse.

Yet an essential difference may be found between the hordes of Scythia and the Arabian tribes, since many of the latter were collected into towns, and employed in the labours of trade and agriculture. A part of their time and industry was still devoted to the management of their cattle : they mingled, in peace and war, with their brethren of the desert ; and the Bedouins derived from their useful intercourse, some supply of their wants, and some rudiments of art and knowledge. Among the 42 cities of Arabia, enumerated by Abulfeda, the most ancient and populous were situate in the *happy* Yemen : the towers of Saana, and the marvellous reservoir of Merab, were constructed by the kings of the Homerites ; but their profane lustre was eclipsed by the prophetic glories of MEDINA* and MECCA, near the Red Sea, and at the distance from each other of 270 miles. The last of these holy places was known to the Greeks under the name of Macoraba ; and the termination of the word is expressive of its greatness, which has not indeed, in the most flourishing period, exceeded the size and populousness of Marseilles. Some latent motive, perhaps of superstition, must have impelled the founders, in the choice of a most unpromising situation. They erected their habitations of mud or stone, in a plain about two miles long and one mile broad, at the foot of three barren mountains : the soil is a rock ; the water even of the holy well of Zemzem is bitter or brackish ; the pastures are remote from the city ; and grapes are transported above 70 miles from the gardens of Tayef. The fame and spirit of the Koreishites, who reigned in Mecca, were conspicuous among the Arabian tribes ; but their ungrateful soil refused the labours of agriculture, and their position was favourable to the enterprises of trade. By the sea-port of Gedda, at the distance only of 40 miles, they maintained an easy correspondence with Abyssinia ; and that Christian kingdom afforded the first refuge to the disciples of Mahomet. The treasures of Africa were conveyed over the peninsula to Gerrha or Katif, in the province of Bahrein, a city built, as it is said, of rock salt, by the Chaldean exiles : and from thence, with the native pearls of the Persian Gulf, they were floated on rafts to the mouth of the Euphrates. Mecca is placed almost at an equal distance, a month's journey, between Yemen on the right, and Syria on the left hand. The former was the winter, the latter the summer, station of her caravans ; and their seasonable arrival relieved the ships of India from the tedious and troublesome navigation of the Red Sea. In the markets of Saana

---

* The distances from Medina are reckoned by Abulfeda in stations, or day's journey of a caravan (p. 15.) : to Bahrein, 15 ; to Bassora, 18 ; to Cufah, 20 ; to Damascus or Palestine, 20 ; to Cairo, 25 ; to Mecca, 10 ; from Mecca to Saana (p. 52.) ; or Aden, 30 ; to Cairo, 31 days, or 412 hours (Shaw's Travels, p. 477.) ; which, according to the estimate of d'Anville (Mesures Itiner. p. 99.), allows about 25 English miles for a day's journey.

and Merab, in the harbours of Oman and Aden, the camels of the Koreishites were laden with a precious cargo of aromatics ; a supply of corn and manufactures was purchased in the fairs of Bostra and Damascus ; the lucrative exchange diffused plenty and riches in the streets of Mecca ; and the noblest of her sons united the love of arms with the profession of merchandise.

The perpetual independence of the Arabs has been the theme of praise among strangers and natives ; and the arts of controversy transform this singular event into a prophecy and a miracle, in favour of the posterity of Ishmael. Some exceptions, that can neither be dissembled nor eluded, render this mode of reasoning as indiscreet as it is superfluous : the kingdom of Yemen has been successively subdued by the Abyssinians, the Persians, the sultans of Egypt, and the Turks ; the holy cities of Mecca and Medina have repeatedly bowed under a Scythian tyrant ; and the Roman province of Arabia embraced the peculiar wilderness in which Ishmael and his sons must have pitched their tents in the face of their brethren. Yet these exceptions are temporary or local ; the body of the nation has escaped the yoke of the most powerful monarchies ; the arms of Sesostris and Cyrus, of Pompey and Trajan, could never achieve the conquest of Arabia ; the present sovereign of the Turks may exercise a shadow of jurisdiction, but his pride is reduced to solicit the friendship of a people, whom it is dangerous to provoke and fruitless to attack. The obvious causes of their freedom are inscribed on the character and country of the Arabs. Many ages before Mahomet, their intrepid valour had been severely felt by their neighbours in offensive and defensive war. The patient and active virtues of a soldier are insensibly nursed in the habits and discipline of a pastoral life. The care of the sheep and camels is abandoned to the women of the tribe ; but the martial youth, under the banner of the emir, is ever on horseback and in the field, to practise the exercise of the bow, the javelin, and the scymetar. The long memory of their independence is the firmest pledge of its perpetuity, and succeeding generations are animated to prove their descent and to maintain their inheritance. Their domestic feuds are suspended on the approach of a common enemy ; and in their last hostilities against the Turks, the caravan of Mecca was attacked and pillaged by 80,000 of the confederates. When they advance to battle, the hope of victory is in the front ; in the rear, the assurance of a retreat. Their horses and camels, who in 8 or 10 days can perform a march of 400 or 500 miles, disappear before the conqueror ; the secret waters of the desert elude his search ; and his victorious troops are consumed with thirst, hunger, and fatigue, in the pursuit of an invisible foe, who scorns his efforts, and safely reposes in the heart of the burning solitude. The arms and deserts of the Bedouins are not only the safeguards of their own freedom, but the barriers also of the happy Arabia, whose inhabitants, remote from war, are enervated by the luxury of the soil and climate. The legions of Augustus melted away in disease and lassitude ; and it is only by a naval power that the reduction of Yemen has been successfully attempted. When Mahomet erected his holy standard, that kingdom was a province of the Persian empire ; yet seven princes of the Homerites still reigned in the mountains ; and the vicegerent of Chosroes was tempted to forget his distant country and his unfortunate master. The historians of the age of Justinian represent the state of the independent Arabs, who were divided by interest or affection in the long quarrel of the East : the tribe of *Gassan* was allowed to encamp on the Syrian territory : the princes of *Hira* were permitted to form a city about 40 miles to the southward of the ruins of Babylon. Their service in the field was speedy and vigorous ; but their friendship was venal, their faith inconstant, their enmity capricious : it was an easier task to excite than to disarm these roving Barbarians ; and, in the familiar intercourse of war, they learned to see, and to despise, the splendid weakness both of Rome and of Persia. From Mecca to the Euphrates, the Arabian tribes were confounded by the Greeks and Latins, under the general appellation of SARACENS,* a name which every Christian mouth has been taught to pronounce with terror.

The slaves of domestic tyranny may vainly exult in their national independence ; but the Arab is personally free ; and he enjoys, in some degree, the benefits of society, without forfeiting the prerogatives of nature. In every tribe, superstition, or gratitude, or fortune, has exalted a particular family above the heads of their equals. The dignities of sheich and emir invariably descend in this chosen race ; but the order of succession is loose and precarious ; and the most worthy or aged of the noble kinsmen are preferred to the simple, though important, office of composing disputes by their advice, and guiding valour by their example. Even a female of sense and spirit has been permitted to command the countrymen of Zenobia. The momentary junction of several tribes produces an army ; their more lasting union constitutes a nation ; and the supreme chief, the emir of emirs, whose banner is displayed at their head, may deserve, in the eyes of strangers, the honours of the kingly name. If the Arabian princes abuse their power, they are quickly punished by the desertion of their subjects, who had been accustomed to a mild and parental jurisdiction. Their spirit is free, their steps are unconfined, the desert is open, and the tribes and families are held together by a mutual and voluntary compact. The softer natives of Yemen supported the pomp and majesty of a monarch ; but if he could not leave his palace without endangering his life, the active powers of government must have been devolved on his nobles and magistrates. The cities of Mecca and

---

* The name which, used by Ptolemy and Pliny in a more confined, by Ammianus and Procopius in a larger, sense, has been derived, ridiculously, from *Sarah*, the wife of Abraham, obscurely from the village of *Saraka* (μετα Ναβαταιουϛ.) The appellation cannot therefore allude to any *national* character ; and, since it was imposed by strangers, it must be found, not in the Arabic, but in a foreign language.

Medina present, in the heart of Asia, the form, or rather the substance, of a commonwealth. The grandfather of Mahomet, and his lineal ancestors, appear in foreign and domestic transactions as the princes of their country ; but they reigned, like Pericles at Athens, or the Medici at Florence, by the opinion of their wisdom and integrity ; their influence was divided with their patrimony ; and the sceptre was transferred from the uncles of the prophet to a younger branch of the tribe of Koreish. On solemn occasions they convened the assembly of the people ; and since mankind must be either compelled or persuaded to obey, the use and reputation of oratory among the ancient Arabs is the clearest evidence of public freedom. But their simple freedom was of a very different cast from the nice and artificial machinery of the Greek and Roman republics, in which each member possessed an undivided share of the civil and political rights of the community. In the more simple state of the Arabs, the nation is free, because each of her sons disdains a base submission to the will of a master. His breast is fortified with the austere virtues of courage, patience, and sobriety ; the love of independence prompts him to exercise the habits of self-command ; and the fear of dishonour guards him from the meaner apprehension of pain, of danger, and of death. The gravity and firmness of the mind is conspicuous in his outward demeanour : his speech is slow, weighty, and concise, he is seldom provoked to laughter, his only gesture is that of stroking his beard, the venerable symbol of manhood ; and the sense of his own importance teaches him to accost his equals without levity, and his superiors without awe. The liberty of the Saracens survived their conquests : the first caliphs indulged the bold and familiar language of their subjects : they ascended the pulpit to persuade and edify the congregation : nor was it before the seat of empire was removed to the Tigris, that the Abbassides adopted the proud and pompous ceremonial of the Persian and Byzantine courts.

In the study of nations and men, we may observe the causes that render them hostile or friendly to each other, that tend to narrow or enlarge, to mollify or exasperate, the social character. The separation of the Arabs from the rest of mankind, has accustomed them to confound the ideas of stranger and enemy ; and the poverty of the land has introduced a maxim of jurisprudence, which they believe and practise to the present hour. They pretend, that in the division of the earth the rich and fertile climates were assigned to the other branches of the human family ; and that the posterity of the outlaw Ishmael might recover, by fraud or force, the portion of inheritance of which he had been unjustly deprived. According to the remark of Pliny, the Arabian tribes are equally addicted to theft and merchandise ; the caravans that traverse the desert are ransomed or pillaged ; and their neighbours, since the remote times of Job and Sesostris, have been the victims of their rapacious spirit. If a Bedouin discovers from afar a solitary traveller, he rides furiously against him, crying, with a loud voice, " Undress thyself, thy aunt (*my wife*) is without a "garment." A ready submission entitles him to mercy ; resistance will provoke the aggressor, and his own blood must expiate the blood which he presumes to shed in legitimate defence. A single robber, or a few associates, are branded with their genuine name ; but the exploits of a numerous band assume the character of a lawful and honourable war. The temper of a people, thus armed against mankind, was doubly inflamed by the domestic licence of rapine, murder, and revenge. In the constitution of Europe, the right of peace and war is now confined to a small, and the actual exercise to a much smaller, list of respectable potentates ; but each Arab, with impunity and renown, might point his javelin against the life of his countryman. The union of the nation consisted only in a vague resemblance of language and manners ; and in each community, the jurisdiction of the magistrate was mute and impotent. Of the time of ignorance which preceded Mahomet, seventeen hundred battles are recorded by tradition : hostility was embittered with the rancour of civil faction ; and the recital, in prose or verse, of an obsolete feud was sufficient to rekindle the same passions among the descendants of the hostile tribes. In private life, every man, at least every family, was the judge and avenger of its own cause. The nice sensibility of honour, which weighs the insult rather than the injury, shed its deadly venom on the quarrels of the Arabs : the honour of their women, and of their *beards*, is most easily wounded ; an indecent action, a contemptuous word, can be expiated only by the blood of the offender ; and such is their patient inveteracy, that they expect whole months and years the opportunity of revenge. A fine or compensation for murder is familiar to the Barbarians of every age ; but in Arabia the kinsmen of the dead are at liberty to accept the atonement, or to exercise with their own hands the law of retaliation. The refined malice of the Arabs refuses even the head of the murderer, substitutes an innocent to the guilty person, and tranfers the penalty to the best and most considerable of the race by whom they have been injured. If he falls by their hands, they are exposed in their turn to the danger of reprisals, the interest and principal of the bloody debt are accumulated ; the individuals of either family lead a life of malice and suspicion, and fifty years may sometimes elapse before the account of vengeance be finally settled. This sanguinary spirit, ignorant of pity or forgiveness, has been moderated, however, by the maxims of honour, which require in every private encounter some decent equality of age and strength, of numbers and weapons. An annual festival of two, perhaps of four, months, was observed by the Arabs before the time of Mahomet, during which their swords were religiously sheathed, both in foreign and domestic hostility ; and this partial truce is more strongly expressive of the habits of anarchy and warfare.

But the spirit of rapine and revenge was attempered by the milder influence of trade and literature. The solitary peninsula is encompassed by the most civilized nations of the ancient world : the merchant is the friend of mankind : and the annual caravans imported the first seeds of knowledge and politeness into the cities, and even the camps of the desert. Whatever may be the pedigree of the Arabs, their language is derived from the same original stock with the Hebrew, the Syriac, and the Chaldean tongues ; the independence of the tribes was marked by their peculiar dialects ; but each, after their own, allowed a just preference to the pure and perspicuous idiom of Mecca. In Arabia, as well as in Greece, the perfection of language outstripped the refinement of manners ; and her speech could diversify the 80 names of honey, the 200 of a serpent, the 500 of a lion, 1000 of a sword, at a time when this copious dictionary was entrusted to the memory of an illiterate people. The monuments of the Homerites were inscribed with an obsolete and mysterious character ; but the Cufic letters, the ground-work of the present alphabet, were invented on the banks of the Euphrates ; and the recent invention was taught at Mecca by a stranger who settled in that city after the birth of Mahomet. The arts of grammar, of metre, and of rhetoric, were unknown to the freeborn eloquence of the Arabians ; but their penetration was sharp, their fancy luxuriant, their wit strong and sententious, and their more elaborate compositions were addressed with energy and effect to the minds of their hearers. The genius and merit of a rising poet was celebrated by the applause of his own and the kindred tribes. A solemn banquet was prepared, and a chorus of women, striking their tymbals, and displaying the pomp of their nuptials, sung in the presence of their sons and husbands the felicity of their native tribe ; that a champion had now appeared to vindicate their rights ; that a herald had raised his voice to immortalise their renown. The distant or hostile tribes resorted to an annual fair, which was abolished by the fanaticism of the first Moslems ; a national assembly that must have contributed to refine and harmonise the Barbarians. Thirty days were employed in the exchange, not only of corn and wine, but of eloquence and poetry. The prize was disputed by the generous emulation of the bards ; the victorious performance was deposited in the archives of princes and emirs ; and we may read in our own language, the seven original poems which were inscribed in letters of gold, and suspended in the temples of Mecca. The Arabian poets were the historians and moralists of the age ; and if they sympathised with the prejudices, they inspired and crowned the virtues, of their countrymen. The indissoluble union of generosity and valour was the darling theme of their song ; and when they pointed their keenest satire against a despicable race, they affirmed in the bitterness of reproach, that the men knew not how to give, nor the women to deny. The same hospitality, which was practised by Abraham and celebrated by Homer, is still renewed in the camps of the Arabs. The ferocious Bedouins, the terror of the desert, embrace, without enquiry or hesitation, the stranger who dares to confide in their honour and to enter their tent. His treatment is kind and respectful; he shares the wealth or the poverty of his host; and, after a needful repose, he is dismissed on his way, with thanks, with blessings, and perhaps with gifts. The heart and hand are more largely expanded by the wants of a brother or a friend; but the heroic acts that could deserve the public applause, must have surpassed the narrow measure of discretion and experience. A dispute had arisen, who, among the citizens of Mecca, was entitled to the prize of generosity; and a successive application was made to the three who were deemed most worthy of the trial. Abdallah, the son of Abbas, had undertaken a distant journey, and his foot was in the stirrup when he heard the voice of a suppliant, " O son of the uncle of the apostle of God, I am a traveller and in distress." He instantly dismounted to present the pilgrim with his camel, her rich caparison, and a purse of 4000 pieces of gold, excepting only the sword, either for its intrinsic value, or as the gift of an honoured kinsman. The servant of Kais informed the second suppliant that his master was asleep; but he immediately added, " Here is a purse of 7000 pieces of gold (it is all we have in the house), and here is an order, that will entitle you to a camel and a slave:" the master, as soon as he awoke, praised and enfranchised his faithful steward, with a gentle reproof, that by respecting his slumbers he had stinted his bounty. The third of these heroes, the blind Arabah, at the hour of prayer, was supporting his steps on the shoulders of two slaves. " Alas!" he replied, " my coffers are empty! but these you may sell; if you refuse, I renounce them." At these words, pushing away the youths, he groped along the wall with his staff. The character of Hatem is the perfect model of Arabian virtue; he was brave and liberal, an eloquent poet and a successful robber : forty camels were roasted at his hospitable feasts; and at the prayer of a suppliant enemy, he restored both the captives and the spoil. The freedom of his countrymen disdained the laws of justice : they proudly indulged the spontaneous impulse of pity.

The religion of the Arabs, as well as of the Indians, consisted in the worship of the sun, the moon, and the fixed stars, a primitive and specious mode of superstition. The bright luminaries of the sky display the visible image of a Deity : their number and distance convey to a philosophic, or even a vulgar eye, the idea of boundless space : the character of eternity is marked on these solid globes, that seem incapable of corruption or decay : the regularity of their motions may be ascribed to a principle of reason or instinct; and their real or imaginary influence encourages the vain belief that the earth and its inhabitants are the object of their peculiar care. The science of astronomy was cultivated at Babylon; but the school of the Arabs was a clear firmament and a naked plain. In their nocturnal marches they steered by the guidance of the stars : their names, and order, and daily station, were familiar to the curiosity and devotion of the Bedouin ; and he was taught by experience to divide in 28 parts, the zodiac of the moon, and to bless the constellations who refreshed, with salutary rains, the thirst of the desert. The reign of the heavenly orbs could not be extended beyond the visible sphere ; and some metaphysical powers were necessary to sustain the transmigration of souls and the resurrection of bodies : a camel was left to perish on the grave that he might serve his master in another life ; and the invocation of departed spirits implies that they were still endowed with consciousness and power. I am ignorant, and I am careless, of the blind mythology of the Barbarians ; of the local deities, of the stars, the air, and the earth, of their sex or titles, their attributes or subordination. Each tribe, each family, each independent warrior, created and changed the rites and the object of his fantastic worship ; but the nation, in every age, has bowed to the religion, as well as to the language, of Mecca. The genuine antiquity of the CAABA ascends beyond the Christian æra : in describing the coast of the Red Sea, the Greek historian Diodorus has remarked, between the Thamudites and the Sabæans, a famous temple, whose superior sanctity was revered by *all* the Arabians : the linen or silken veil, which is annually renewed by the Turkish emperor, was first offered by a pious king of the Homerites, who reigned 700 years before the time of Mahomet. A tent or a cavern might suffice for the worship of the savages, but an edifice of stone and clay has been erected in its place ; and the art and power of the monarchs of the East have been confined to the simplicity of the original model. A spacious portico encloses the quadrangle of the Caaba ; a square chapel, 24 cubits long, 23 broad, and 27 high : a door and a window admit the light ; the double roof is supported by three pillars of wood ; a spout (now of gold) discharges the rain-water, and the well Zemzem is protected by a dome from accidental pollution. The tribe of Koreish, by fraud or force, had acquired the custody of the Caaba : the sacerdotal office devolved through four lineal descents to the grandfather of Mahomet ; and the family of the Hashemites, from whence he sprung, was the most respectable and sacred in the eyes of their country. The precincts of Mecca enjoyed the rights of sanctuary ; and, in the last month of each year, the city and the temple were crowded with a long train of pilgrims, who presented their vows and offerings in the house of God. The same rites, which are now accomplished by the faithful Mussulman, were invented and practised by the superstition of the idolaters. At an awful distance they cast away their garments : seven times, with hasty steps, they encircled the Caaba, and kissed the black stone : seven times they visited and adored the adjacent mountains : seven times they threw stones into the valley of Mina ˙ and the pilgrimage was achieved, as at the present hour, by a sacrifice of sheep and camels, and the burial of their hair and nails in the consecrated ground. Each tribe either found or introduced in the Caaba their domestic worship : the temple was adorned, or defiled, with 360 idols of men, eagles, lions, and antelopes ; and most conspicuous was the statue of Hebal, of red agate, holding in his hand seven arrows, without heads or feathers, the instruments and symbols of profane divination.   But this statue was a monument of Syrian arts : the devotion of the ruder ages was content with a pillar or a tablet ; and the rocks of the desert were hewn into gods or altars, in imitation of the black stone of Mecca, which is deeply tainted with the reproach of an idolatrous origin. From Japan to Peru, the use of sacrifice has universally prevailed ; and the votary has expressed his gratitude, or fear, by destroying or consuming, in honour of the gods, the dearest and most precious of their gifts.   The life of a man is the most precious oblation to deprecate a public calamity ; the altars of Phœnicia and Egypt, of Rome and Carthage, have been polluted with human gore : the cruel practice was long preserved among the Arabs ; in the third century, a boy was annually sacrificed by the tribe of the Dumatians ; and a royal captive was piously slaughtered by the prince of the Saracens, the ally and soldier of the emperor Justinian.   A parent who drags his son to the altar, exhibits the most painful and sublime effort of fanaticism : the deed, or the intention, was sanctified by the example of saints and heroes ; and the father of Mahomet himself was devoted by a rash vow, and hardly ransomed for the equivalent of an hundred camels.   In the time of ignorance, the Arabs, like the Jews and Egyptians, abstained from the taste of swine's flesh ; they circumcised their children at the age of puberty : the same customs, without the censure or the precept of the Koran, have been silently transmitted to their posterity and proselytes.   It has been sagaciously conjectured, that the artful legislator indulged the stubborn prejudices of his countrymen.   It is more simple to believe that he adhered to the habits and opinions of his youth, without foreseeing that a practice congenial to the climate of Mecca, might become useless or inconvenient on the banks of the Danube or the Volga.

Arabia was free : the adjacent kingdoms were shaken by the storms of conquest and tyranny, and the persecuted sects fled to the happy land where they might profess what they thought, and practise what they professed.   The religions of the Sabians and Magians, of the Jews and Christians, were disseminated from the Persian Gulf to the Red Sea.   In a remote period of antiquity, Sabianism was diffused over Asia by the science of the Chaldeans and the arms of the Assyrians. From the observations of 2000 years, the priests and astronomers of Babylon deduced the eternal laws of nature and providence.   They adored the seven gods or angels who directed the course of the seven planets, and shed their irresistible influence on the earth.   The attributes of the seven planets, with the twelve signs of the zodiac, and the twenty-four constellations of the northern and southern hemisphere, were represented by images and talismans ; the seven days of the week were dedicated to their respective deities ; the Sabians prayed thrice each day ; and the temple of the moon at Haran was the term of their pilgrimage. But the flexible genius of their faith was always ready either to teach or to learn : in the tradition of the creation, the deluge, and the patriarchs, they held a singular agreement with their Jewish captives ; they appealed to the secret books of Adam, Seth, and Enoch ; and a slight infusion of the gospel has transformed the last remnant of the Polytheists into the Christians of St. John, in the territory of Bassora. The altars of Babylon were overturned by the Magians ; but the injuries of the Sabians were revenged by the sword of Alexander ; Persia groaned above 500 years under a foreign yoke ; and the purest disciples of Zoroaster escaped from the contagion of idolatry, and breathed with their adversaries the freedom of the desert. Seven hundred years before the death of Mahomet, the Jews were settled in Arabia : and a far greater multitude was expelled from the holy land in the wars of Titus and Hadrian. The industrious exiles aspired to liberty and power : they erected synagogues in the cities and castles in the wilderness, and their Gentile converts were confounded with the children of Israel, whom they resembled in the outward mark of circumcision. The Christian missionaries were still more active and successful : the Catholics asserted their universal reign ; the sects whom they oppressed successively retired beyond the limits of the Roman empire ; the Marcionites and the Manichæans dispersed their *phantastic* opinions and apocryphal gospels ; the churches of Yemen, and the princes of Hira and Gassan, were instructed in a purer creed by the Jacobite and Nestorian bishops. The liberty of choice was presented to the tribes : each Arab was free to elect or to compose his private religion ; and the rude superstition of his house was mingled with the sublime theology of saints and philosophers. A fundamental article of faith was inculcated by the consent of the learned strangers ; the existence of one supreme God, who is exalted above the powers of heaven and earth, but who has often revealed himself to mankind by the ministry of his angels and prophets, and whose grace or justice has interrupted, by seasonable miracles, the order of nature. The most rational of the Arabs acknowledged his power, though they neglected his worship ; and it was habit rather than conviction that still attached them to the relics of idolatry. The Jews and Christians were the people of the *book ;* the Bible was already translated into the Arabic language, and the volume of the Old Testament was accepted by the concord of these implacable enemies. In the story of the Hebrew patriarchs, the Arabs were pleased to discover the fathers of their nation. They applauded the birth and promises of Ishmael ; revered the faith and virtue of Abraham ; traced his pedigree and their own to the creation of the first man, and imbibed with equal credulity, the prodigies of the holy text, and the dreams and traditions of the Jewish rabbis.

The base and plebeian origin of Mahomet (A.D. 569—609) is an unskilful calumny of the Christians, who exalt instead of degrading the merit of their adversary. His descent from Ishmael was a national privilege or fable ; but if the first steps of the pedigree are dark and doubtful, he could produce many generations of pure and genuine nobility : he sprung from the tribe of Koreish and the family of Hashem, the most illustrious of the Arabs, the princes of Mecca, and the hereditary guardians of the Caaba. The grandfather of Mahomet was Abdol Mottalleb, the son of Hashem, a wealthy and generous citizen, who relieved the distress of famine with the supplies of commerce. Mecca, which had been fed by the liberality of the father, was saved by the courage of the son. The kingdom of Yemen was subject to the Christian princes of Abyssinia : their vassal Abrahah was provoked by an insult to avenge the honour of the cross ; and the holy city was invested by a train of elephants and an army of Africans. A treaty was proposed ; and in the first audience, the grandfather of Mahomet demanded the restitution of his cattle. "And why," said Abrahah, "do you not rather implore my clemency in favour of your temple, which I have threatened to destroy ?" "Because," replied the intrepid chief, "the cattle is my own : the Caaba belongs to the gods, and *they* will defend their house from injury and sacrilege." The want of provisions, or the valour of the Koreish, compelled the Abyssinians to a disgraceful retreat ; their discomfiture has been adorned with a miraculous flight of birds, who showered down stones on the heads of the infidels ; and the deliverance was long commemorated by the æra of the elephant. The glory of Abdol Motalleb was crowned with domestic happiness, his life was prolonged to the age of one hundred and ten years, and he became the father of six daughters and thirteen sons. His best beloved Abdallah was the most beautiful and modest of the Arabian youth. Mahomet, or more properly Mohammed, the only son of Abdallah and Amina, of the noble race of the Zahrites, was born at Mecca, four years after the death of Justinian, and two months after the defeat of the Abyssinians, whose victory would have introduced into the Caaba the religion of the Christians. In his early infancy, he was deprived of his father, his mother, and his grandfather ; his uncles were strong and numerous ; and in the division of the inheritance, the orphan's share was reduced to five camels and an Æthiopian maid-servant. At home and abroad, in peace and war, Abu Taleb, the most respectable of his uncles, was the guide and guardian of his youth ; in his twenty-fifth year he entered into the service of Cadijah, a rich and noble widow of Mecca, who soon rewarded his fidelity with the gift of her hand and fortune. The marriage contract, in the simple style of antiquity, recites the mutual love of Mahomet and Cadijah ; describes him as the most accomplished of the tribe of Koreish; and stipulates a dowry of twelve ounces of gold and twenty camels, which was supplied by the liberality of his uncle. By this alliance, the son of Abdallah was restored to the station of his ancestors; and the judicious matron was content with his domestic virtues till, in the fortieth year of his age, he assumed the title of a prophet, and proclaimed the religion of the Koran.

According to the tradition of his companions, Mahomet was distinguished by the beauty of his person, an outward gift which is seldom despised, except by those to whom it has been refused. Before he spoke, the orator engaged on his side the affections of a public or private audience. They applauded his commanding presence, his majestic aspect, his piercing eye, his gracious smile, his flowing beard, his countenance that painted every sensation of the soul, and his gestures that enforced each expression of the tongue. In the familiar offices of life he scrupulously adhered to the grave and ceremonious politeness of his country : his respectful attention to the rich and powerful was dignified by his condescension and affability to the poorest citizens of Mecca : the frankness of his manner concealed the artifice of his views; and the habits of courtesy were imputed to personal friendship or universal benevolence. His memory was capacious and retentive, his wit easy and social, his imagination sublime, his judgment clear, rapid, and decisive. He possessed the courage both of thought and action; and, although his designs might gradually expand with his success, the first idea which he entertained of his divine mission bears the stamp of an original and superior genius. The son of Abdallah was educated in the bosom of the noblest race, in the use of the purest dialect of Arabia; and the fluency of his speech was corrected and enhanced by the practice of discreet and seasonable silence. With these powers of eloquence, Mahomet was an illiterate Barbarian : his youth had never been instructed in the arts of reading and writing; the common ignorance exempted him from shame or reproach, but he was reduced to a narrow circle of existence, and deprived of those faithful mirrors, which reflect to our mind the minds of sages and heroes. Yet the book of nature and of man was open to his view; and some fancy has been indulged in the political and philosophical observations which are ascribed to the Arabian *traveller*. He compares the nations and the religions of the earth; discovers the weakness of the Persian and Roman monarchies; beholds, with pity and indignation, the degeneracy of the times; and resolves to unite, under one God and one king, the invincible spirit and primitive virtues of the Arabs. Our more accurate inquiry will suggest, that instead of visiting the courts, the camps, the temples of the East, the two journeys of Mahomet into Syria were confined to the fairs of Bostra and Damascus; that he was only thirteen years of age when he accompanied the caravan of his uncle, and that his duty compelled him to return as soon as he had disposed of the merchandise of Cadijah.

2

In these hasty and superficial excursions, the eye of genius might discern some objects invisible to his grosser companions ; some seeds of knowledge might be cast upon a fruitful soil ; but his ignorance of the Syriac language must have checked his curiosity ; and I cannot perceive in the life or writings of Mahomet, that his prospect was far extended beyond the limits of the Arabian world. From every region of that solitary world, the pilgrims of Mecca were annually assembled, by the calls of devotion and commerce : in the free concourse of multitudes, a simple citizen, in his native tongue, might study the political state and character of the tribes, the theory and practice of the Jews and Christians. Some useful strangers might be tempted, or forced, to implore the rights of hospitality ; and the enemies of Mahomet have named the Jew, the Persian, and the Syrian monk, whom they accuse of lending their secret aid to the composition of the Koran. Conversation enriches the understanding, but solitude is the school of genius ; and the uniformity of a work denotes the hand of a single artist. From his earliest youth, Mahomet was addicted to religious contemplation : each year, during the month of Ramadan, he withdrew from the world, and from the arms of Cadijah : in the cave of Hera, three miles from Mecca, he consulted the spirit of fraud or enthusiasm, whose abode is not in the heavens, but in the mind of the prophet. The faith which, under the name of *Islam,* he preached to his nation, is compounded of an eternal truth, and a necessary fiction, THAT THERE IS ONLY ONE GOD, AND THAT MAHOMET IS THE APOSTLE OF GOD.

It is the boast of the Jewish apologists, that while the learned nations of antiquity were deluded by the fables of polytheism, their simple ancestors of Palestine preserved the knowledge and worship of the true God. The moral attributes of Jehovah may not easily be reconciled with the standard of *human* virtue : his metaphysical qualities are darkly expressed ; but each page of the Pentateuch and the Prophets is an evidence of his power : the unity of his name is inscribed on the first table of the law ; and his sanctuary was never defiled by any visible image of the invisible essence. After the ruin of the temple, the faith of the Hebrew exiles was purified, fixed, and enlightened by the spiritual devotion of the synagogue ; and the authority of Mahomet will not justify his perpetual reproach, that the Jews of Mecca or Medina adored Ezra as the son of God. But the children of Israel had ceased to be a people ; and the religions of the world were guilty, at least in the eyes of the prophet, of giving sons, or daughters, or companions, to the supreme God. In the rude idolatry of the Arabs, the crime is manifest and audacious : the Sabians are poorly excused by the pre-eminence of the first planet, or intelligence in their celestial hierarchy ; and in the Magian system the conflict of the two principles betrays the imperfection of the conqueror. The Christians of the seventh century had insensibly relapsed into a semblance of paganism ; their public and private vows were addressed to the relics and images that disgraced the temples of the East : the throne of the Almighty was darkened by a cloud of martyrs, and saints, and angels, the objects of popular veneration ; and the Collyridian heretics, who flourished in the fruitful soil of Arabia, invested the Virgin Mary with the name and honours of a goddess. The mysteries of the Trinity and Incarnation *appear* to contradict the principle of the divine unity. In their obvious sense, they introduce three equal deities, and transform the man Jesus into the substance of the son of God : an orthodox commentary will satisfy only a believing mind : intemperate curiosity and zeal had torn the veil of the sanctuary ; and each of the Oriental sects was eager to confess that all, except themselves, deserved the reproach of idolatry and polytheism. The creed of Mahomet is free from suspicion or ambiguity ; and the Koran is a glorious testimony to the unity of God. The prophet of Mecca rejected the worship of idols and men, of stars and planets, on the rational principle that whatever rises must set, that whatever is born must die, that whatever is corruptible must decay and perish. In the author of the universe, his rational enthusiasm confessed and adored an infinite and eternal being, without form or place, without issue or similitude, present to our most secret thoughts, existing by the necessity of his own nature, and deriving from himself all moral and intellectual perfection. These sublime truths thus announced in the language of the prophet, are firmly held by his disciples, and defined with metaphysical precision by the interpreters of the Koran. A philosophic theist might subscribe the popular creed of the Mahometans : a creed too sublime perhaps for our present faculties. What object remains for the fancy, or even the understanding, when we have abstracted from the unknown substance all ideas of time and space, of motion and matter, of sensation and reflection? The first principle of reason and revelation was confirmed by the voice of Mahomet : his proselytes, from India to Morocco, are distinguished by the name of *Unitarians;* and the danger of idolatry has been prevented by the interdiction of images. The doctrine of eternal decrees and absolute predestination is strictly embraced by the Mahometans ; and they struggle with the common difficulties, *how* to reconcile the prescience of God with the freedom and responsibility of man ; *how* to explain the permission of evil under the reign of infinite power and infinite goodness.

The God of nature has written his existence on all his works and his law in the heart of man. To restore the knowledge of the one and the practice of the other, has been the real or pretended aim of the prophets of every age : the liberality of Mahomet allowed to his predecessors the same credit which he claimed for himself ; and the chain of inspiration was prolonged from the fall of Adam to the promulgation of the Koran. During that period, some rays of prophetic light had been imparted to 124,000 of the elect, discriminated by their respective measure of virtue and grace ; 313 apostles were

sent with a special commission to recall their country from idolatry and
vice ; 104 volumes have been dictated by the holy spirit ; and six legislators of transcendent brightness have announced to mankind the
six successive revelations of various rites, but of one immutable religion. The authority and station of Adam, Noah, Abraham, Moses,
Christ, and Mahomet, rise in just gradation above each other ; but
whosoever hates or rejects any one of the prophets is numbered with
the infidels. The writings of the patriarchs were extant only in
the apocryphal copies of the Greeks and Syrians : the conduct of
Adam had not entitled him to the gratitude or respect of his children ;
the seven precepts of Noah were observed by an inferior and imperfect class of the proselytes of the synagogue ; and the memory of
Abraham was obscurely revered by the Sabians in his native land
of Chaldea : of the myriads of prophets, Moses and Christ alone lived
and reigned ; and the remnant of the inspired writings was comprised
in the books of the Old and the New Testament. The miraculous
story of Moses is consecrated and embellished in the Koran ; and the
captive Jews enjoy the secret revenge of imposing their own belief on
the nations whose recent creeds they deride. For the author of Christianity, the Mahometans are taught by the prophet to entertain an
high and mysterious reverence. " Verily, Christ Jesus, the son of
Mary, is the apostle of God, and his word, which he conveyed unto
Mary, and a Spirit proceeding from him : honourable in this world,
and in the world to come ; and one of those who approach near to
the presence of God." The wonders of the genuine and apocryphal gospels are profusely heaped on his head ; and the Latin church
has not disdained to borrow from the Koran the immaculate concep-
tion of his virgin mother. Yet Jesus was a mere mortal ; and, at
the day of judgment, his testimony will serve to condemn both the
Jews, who reject him as a prophet, and the Christians, who adore him
as the Son of God. The malice of his enemies aspersed his reputation, and conspired against his life ; but their intention only was
guilty, a phantom or criminal was substituted on the cross, and the
innocent saint was translated to the seventh heaven. During 600
years the gospel was the way of truth and salvation ; but the Christians insensibly forgot both the laws and the example of their founder ;
and Mahomet was instructed by the Gnostics to accuse the church,
as well as the synagogue, of corrupting the integrity of the sacred
text. The piety of Moses and of Christ rejoiced in the assurance of
a future prophet, more illustrious than themselves : the evangelic
promise of the *Paraclete*, or Holy Ghost, was prefigured in the name,
and accomplished in the person, of Mahomet, the greatest and the
last of the apostles of God.

The communication of ideas requires a similitude of thought and
language : the discourse of a philosopher would vibrate without effect
on the ear of a peasant ; yet how minute is the distance of *their* un-

derstandings, if it be compared with the contact of an infinite and a
finite mind, with the word of God expressed by the tongue or the pen
of a mortal? The inspiration of the Hebrew prophets, of the apostles
and evangelists of Christ, might not be incompatible with the exercise
of their reason and memory; and the diversity of their genius is
strongly marked in the style and composition of the books of the Old
and New Testament. But Mahomet was content with a character,
more humble, yet more sublime, of a simple editor : the substance of
the Koran, according to himself or his disciples, is uncreated and
eternal ; subsisting in the essence of the Deity, and inscribed with a
pen of light on the table of his everlasting decrees. A paper copy in
a volume of silk and gems, was brought down to the lowest heaven by
the angel Gabriel, who, under the Jewish economy, had indeed been
dispatched on the most important errands ; and this trusty messenger
successively revealed the chapters and verses to the Arabian prophet.
Instead of a perpetual and perfect measure of the divine will, the
fragments of the Koran were produced at the discretion of Mahomet ;
each revelation is suited to the emergencies of his policy or passion ;
and all contradiction is removed by the saving maxim, that any text
of Scripture is abrogated or modified by any subsequent passage. The
word of God, and of the apostle, was diligently recorded by his disciples
on palm-leaves and the shoulder-bones of mutton ; and the pages,
without order or connection, were cast into a domestic chest in the
custody of one of his wives. Two years after the death of Mahomet,
the sacred volume was collected and published by his friend and successor Abubeker : the work was revised by the caliph Othman, in the
thirtieth year of the Hegira ; and the various editions of the Koran
assert the same miraculous privilege of an uniform and incorruptible
text. In the spirit of enthusiasm or vanity, the prophet rests the
truth of his mission on the merit of his book, audaciously challenges
both men and angels to imitate the beauties of a single page, and
presumes to assert that God alone could dictate this incomparable
performance. This argument is most powerfully addressed to a
devout Arabian, whose mind is attuned to faith and rapture, whose
ear is delighted by the music of sounds, and whose ignorance is incapable of comparing the productions of human genius. The harmony
and copiousness of style will not reach, in a version, the European infidel : he will peruse with impatience the endless incoherent rhapsody
of fable, and precept, and declamation, which seldom excites a sentiment or an idea, which sometimes crawls in the dust, and is sometimes
lost in the clouds. The divine attributes exalt the fancy of the Arabian
missionary ; but his loftiest strains must yield to the sublime simplicity
of the book of Job, composed in a remote age, in the same country
and in the same language. If the composition of the Koran exceed
the faculties of a man, to what superior intelligence should we ascribe
the Iliad of Homer or the Philippics of Demosthenes? In all reli-

gions, the life of the founder supplies the silence of his written revelation : the sayings of Mahomet were so many lessons of truth ; his
actions so many examples of virtue ; and the public and private me-
morials were preserved by his wives and companions.   At the end of
200 years, the *Sonna* or oral law was fixed and consecrated by the
labours of Al Bochari, who discriminated 7275 genuine traditions,
from a mass of 300,000 reports, of a more doubtful character.   Each
day the pious author prayed in the temple of Mecca, and performed
his ablutions with the water of Zemzen : the pages were successively
deposited on the pulpit, and the sepulchre of the apostle ; and the
work has been approved by the four orthodox sects of the Sonnites.

The mission of the ancient prophets, of Moses and of Jesus, had
been confirmed by many splendid prodigies ; and Mahomet was repeatedly urged, by the inhabitants of Mecca and Medina, to produce
a similar evidence of his divine legation ; to call down from heaven
the angel or the volume of his revelation, to create a garden in the
desert, or to kindle a conflagration in the unbelieving city.   As often
as he is pressed by the demands of the Koreish, he involves himself
in the obscure boast of vision and prophecy, appeals to the internal
proofs of his doctrine, and shields himself behind the providence of
God, who refuses those signs and wonders that would depreciate the
merit of faith and aggravate the guilt of infidelity.   But the modest or
angry tone of his apologies betrays his weakness and vexation ; and
these passages of scandal establish, beyond suspicion, the integrity of
the Koran.   The votaries of Mahomet are more assured than himself of his miraculous gifts, and their confidence and credulity increase as they are farther removed from the time and place of his
spiritual exploits.   They believe or affirm that trees went forth to meet
him ; that he was saluted by stones ; that water gushed from his
fingers ; that he fed the hungry, cured the sick, and raised the dead ;
that a beam groaned to him ; that a camel complained to him ; that a
shoulder of mutton informed him of its being poisoned ; and that
both animate and inanimate nature were equally subject to the apostle
of God.   His dream of a nocturnal journey is seriously described as
a real and corporeal transaction.   A mysterious animal, the Borak,
conveyed him from the temple of Mecca to that of Jerusalem : with
his companion Gabriel, he successively ascended the seven heavens,
and received and repaid the salutations of the patriarchs, the prophets, and the angels, in their respective mansions.   Beyond the
seventh heaven, Mahomet alone was permitted to proceed ; he passed
the veil of unity, approached within two bow-shots of the throne, and
felt a cold that pierced him to the heart, when his shoulder was touched
by the hand of God.   After this familiar though important conversation, he again descended to Jerusalem, remounted the Borak, returned
to Mecca, and performed in the tenth part of a night the journey of
many thousand years.   According to another legend, the apostle

confounded in a national assembly the malicious challenge of the
Koreish. His resistless word split asunder the orb of the moon : the
obedient planet stooped from her station in the sky, accomplished the
seven revolutions round the Caaba, saluted Mahomet in the Arabian
tongue, and suddenly contracting her dimensions, entered at the
collar, and issued forth through the sleeve, of his shirt. The vulgar
are amused with these marvellous tales ; but the gravest of the Mussulman doctors imitate the modesty of their master, and indulge a lati-
tude of faith or interpretation. They might speciously allege, that in
preaching the religion, it was needless to violate the harmony, of
nature ; that a creed unclouded with mystery may be excused from
miracles ; and that the sword of Mahomet was not less potent than
the rod of Moses.

The polytheist is oppressed and distracted by the variety of superstition : a thousand rites of Egyptian origin were interwoven with the
essence of the Mosaic law : and the spirit of the gospel had evaporated
in the pageantry of the church. The prophet of Mecca was tempted
by prejudice, or policy, or patriotism, to sanctify the rites of the
Arabians, and the custom of visiting the holy stone of the Caaba.
But the precepts of Mahomet himself inculcate a more simple and
rational piety : prayer, fasting, and alms, are the religious duties of a
Mussulman ; and he is encouraged to hope, that prayer will carry him
half-way to God, fasting will bring him to the door of his palace, and
alms will gain him admittance. I. According to the tradition of the
nocturnal journey, the apostle, in his personal conference with the
Deity, was commanded to impose on his disciples the daily obligation
of fifty prayers. By the advice of Moses, he applied for an alleviation
of this intolerable burthen ; the number was gradually reduced to five ;
without any dispensation of business or pleasure, or time or place :
the devotion of the faithful is repeated at daybreak, at noon, in the
afternoon, in the evening, and at the first watch of the night ; and, in
the present decay of religious fervour, our travellers are edified by the
profound humility and attention of the Turks and Persians. Cleanli-
ness is the key of prayer : the frequent lustration of the hands, the
face, and the body, which was practised of old by the Arabs, is
solemnly enjoined by the Koran ; and a permission is formally granted
to supply with sand the scarcity of water. The words and attitudes of
supplication, as it is performed either sitting, or standing, or prostrate
on the ground, are prescribed by custom or authority, but the prayer
is poured forth in short and fervent ejaculations ; the measure of zeal
is not exhausted by a tedious liturgy ; and each Mussulman, for his
own person, is invested with the character of a priest. Among the
theists, who reject the use of images, it has been found necessary to
restrain the wanderings of the fancy, by directing the eye and the
thought towards a *kebla*, or visible point of the horizon. The prophet
was at first inclined to gratify the Jews by the choice of Jerusalem ;

but he soon returned to a more natural partiality; and five times every day the eyes of the nations of Astracan, at Fez, at Delhi, are devoutly turned to the holy temple of Mecca. Yet every spot for the service of God is equally pure : the Mahometans indifferently pray in their chamber or in the street. As a distinction from the Jews and Christians, the Friday in each week is set apart for the useful institution of public worship : the people is assembled in the mosque and the imaum, some respectable elder ascends the pulpit, to begin the prayer and pronounce the sermon. But the Mahometan religion is destitute of priesthood or sacrifice; and the independent spirit of fanaticism looks down with contempt on the ministers and the slaves of superstition. II. The voluntary penance of the ascetics, the torment and glory of their lives, was odious to a prophet who censured in his companions a rash vow of abstaining from flesh, and women, and sleep; and firmly declared that he would suffer no monks in his religion. Yet he instituted, in each year, a fast of thirty days; and strenuously recommended the observance, as a discipline which purifies the soul and subdues the body, as a salutary exercise of obedience to the will of God and his apostle. During the month of Ramadan, from the rising to the setting of the sun, the Mussulman abstains from eating, and drinking, and women, and baths, and perfumes; from all nourishment that can restore his strength, from all pleasure that can gratify his senses. In the revolution of the lunar year, the Ramadan coincides by turns with the winter cold and the summer heat; and the patient martyr, without assuaging his thirst with a drop of water, must expect the close of a tedious and sultry day. The interdiction of wine, peculiar to some orders of priests or hermits, is converted by Mahomet alone into a positive and general law; and a considerable portion of the globe has abjured at his command, the use of that salutary, though dangerous liquor. These painful restraints are, doubtless, infringed by the libertine and eluded by the hypocrite; but the legislator, by whom they are enacted, cannot surely be accused of alluring his proselytes by the indulgence of their sensual appetites. III. The charity of the Mahometans descends to the animal creation; and the Koran repeatedly inculcates, not as a merit, but as a strict and indispensable duty, the relief of the indigent and unfortunate. Mahomet, perhaps, is the only lawgiver who has defined the precise measure of charity : the standard may vary with the degree and nature of poverty, as it consists either in money, in corn or cattle, in fruits or merchandise; but the Mussulman does not accomplish the law, unless he bestow a *tenth* of his revenue; and if his conscience accuses him of fraud or extortion, the tenth, under the idea of restitution, is enlarged to a *fifth*. Benevolence is the foundation of justice, since we are forbid to injure those whom we are bound to assist. A prophet may reveal the secrets of heaven and of futurity; but in his moral precepts he can only repeat the lessons of our own hearts.

The two articles of belief, and the four practical duties of Islam, are guarded by rewards and punishments ; and the faith of the Mussulman is devoutly fixed on the event of the judgment and the last day. The prophet has not presumed to determine the amount of that awful catastrophe, though he darkly announces the signs, both in heaven and earth, which will precede the universal dissolution, when life shall be destroyed, and the order of creation shall be confounded in the primitive chaos. At the blast of the trumpet new worlds will start into being ; angels, genii, and men, will arise from the dead, and the human soul will again be united to the body. The doctrine of the resurrection was first entertained by the Egyptians, and their mummies were embalmed, their pyramids were constructed, to preserve the ancient mansion of the soul during a period of 3000 years. But the attempt is partial and unavailing ; and it is with a more philosophic spirit that Mahomet relies on the omnipotence of the Creator, whose word can reanimate the breathless clay, and collect the innumerable atoms, that no longer retain their form or substance. The intermediate state of the soul it is hard to decide ; and those who most firmly believe her immaterial nature are at a loss to understand how she can think or act without the agency of the organs of sense.

The re-union of the soul and body will be followed by the final judgment of mankind ; and, in his copy of the Magian picture, the prophet has too faithfully represented the forms of proceeding, and even the slow and successive operations of an earthly tribunal. By his intolerant adversaries he is upbraided for extending, even to themselves, the hope of salvation, for asserting the blackest heresy, that every man who believes in God, and accomplishes good works, may expect in the last day a favourable sentence. Such rational indifference is ill adapted to the character of a fanatic ; nor is it probable that a messenger from heaven should depreciate the value and necessity of his own revelation. In the idiom of the Koran, the belief of God is inseparable from that of Mahomet : the good works are those which he has enjoined ; and the two qualifications imply the profession of Islam, to which all nations and all sects are equally invited. Their spiritual blindness, though excused by ignorance and crowned with virtue, will be scourged with everlasting torments ; and the tears which Mahomet shed over the tomb of his mother, for whom he was forbidden to pray, display a striking contrast of humanity and enthusiasm. The doom of the infidels is common : the measure of their guilt and punishment is determined by the degree of evidence which they have rejected, by the magnitude of the errors which they have entertained : the eternal mansions of the Christians, the Jews, the Sabians, the Magians, and the idolaters, are sunk below each other in the abyss ; and the lowest hell is reserved for the faithless hypocrites who have assumed the mask of religion. After the greater part of mankind has been condemned for their opinions, the true believers only will be judged by their actions. The good and evil of each Mussulman will be accurately weighed in a real or allegorical balance, and a singular mode of compensation will be allowed for the payment of injuries : the aggressor will refund an equivalent of his own good actions for the benefit of the person whom he has wronged ; and if he should be destitute of any moral property, the weight of his sins will be loaded with an adequate share of the demerits of the sufferer. According as the shares of guilt or virtue shall preponderate, the sentence will be pronounced, and all, without distinction, will pass over the sharp and perilous bridge of the abyss ; but the innocent, treading in the footsteps of Mahomet, will gloriously enter the gates of paradise, while the guilty will fall into the first and mildest of the seven hells. The term of expiation will vary from 900 to 7000 years ; but the prophet has judiciously promised, that *all* his disciples, whatever may be their sins, shall be saved, by their own faith and his intercession, from eternal damnation. It is not surprising that superstition should act most powerfully on the fears of her votaries, since the human fancy can paint with more energy the misery than the bliss of a future life. With the two simple elements of darkness and fire, we create a sensation of pain which may be aggravated to an infinite degree by the idea of endless duration. But the same idea operates with an opposite effect on the continuity of pleasure ; and too much of our present enjoyments is obtained from the relief or the comparison of evil. It is natural enough that an Arabian prophet should dwell with rapture on the groves, the fountains, and the rivers of paradise ; but instead of inspiring the blessed inhabitants with a liberal taste for harmony and science, conversation and friendship, he idly celebrates the pearls and diamonds, the robes of silk, palaces of marble, dishes of gold, rich wines, artificial dainties, numerous attendants, and the whole train of sensual and costly luxury, which becomes insipid to the owner, even in the short period of this mortal life. Seventy-two *Houris*, or black-eyed girls, of resplendent beauty, blooming youth, virgin purity, and exquisite sensibility, will be created for the use of the meanest believer ; a moment of pleasure will be prolonged to a thousand years, and his faculties will be increased an hundred fold, to render him worthy of his felicity. Notwithstanding a vulgar prejudice, the gates of heaven will be open to both sexes ; but Mahomet has not specified the male companions of the female elect, lest he should either alarm the jealousy of their former husbands, or disturb their felicity, by the suspicion of an everlasting marriage. This image of a carnal paradise has provoked the indignation, perhaps the envy, of the monks : they declaim against the impure religion of Mahomet ; and his modest apologists are driven to the poor excuse of figures and allegories. But the sounder and more consistent party adhere, without shame, to the literal interpretation of the Koran : useless would be the resurrection of the body, unless it were restored to the possession and exercise of its worthiest faculties ; and the union of sensual and intellectual enjoyment is requisite to complete the happiness of the double animal, the perfect man. Yet the joys of the Mahometan paradise will not be confined to the indulgence of luxury and appetite : and the prophet has expressly declared, that all meaner happiness will be forgotten and despised by the saints and martyrs, who shall be admitted to the beatitude of the divine vision.

The first (A.D. 609) and most arduous conquests of Mahomet were those of his wife, his servant, his pupil, and his friend ; since he presented himself as a prophet to those who were most conversant with his infirmities as a man. Yet Cadijah believed the words, and cherished the glory, of her husband ; the obsequious and affectionate Zeid was tempted by the prospect of freedom ; the illustrious Ali, the son of Abu Taleb, embraced the sentiments of his cousin with the spirit of a youthful hero ; and the wealth, the moderation, the veracity of Abubeker, confirmed the religion of the prophet whom he was destined to succeed. By his persuasion, ten of the most respectable citizens of Mecca were introduced to the private lessons of Islam ; they yielded to the voice of reason and enthusiasm ; they repeated the fundamental creed, " there is but one God, and Mahomet is the apostle of God ;" and their faith, even in this life, was rewarded with riches and honours, with the command of armies and the government of kingdoms. Three years were silently employed in the conversion of fourteen proselytes, the first fruits of his mission ; but in the fourth year he assumed the prophetic office, and resolving to impart to his family the light of divine truth, he prepared a banquet, a lamb, as it is said, and a bowl of milk, for the entertainment of forty guests of the race of Hashem. " Friends and kinsmen," said Mahomet to the assembly, " I offer you, and I alone can offer, the most precious of gifts, the treasures of this world and of the world to come. God has commanded me to call you to his service. Who among you will support my burthen ? Who among you will be my companion and my vizir ?" No answer was returned, till the silence of astonishment, and doubt, and contempt, was at length broken by the impatient courage of Ali, a youth in the fourteenth year of his age. " O prophet, I am the man : whosoever rises against thee, I will dash out his teeth, tear out his eyes, break his legs, rip up his belly. O prophet, I will be thy vizir over them." Mahomet accepted his offer with transport, and Abu Taleb was ironically exhorted to respect the superior dignity of his son. In a more serious tone, the father of Ali advised his nephew to relinquish his impracticable design. " Spare your remonstrances," replied the intrepid fanatic to his uncle and benefactor ; " if they should place the sun on my right hand and the moon on my left, they should not divert me from my course." He persevered ten years in the exercise of his mission ; and the religion which has overspread the East and the West, advanced with a slow and painful progress within the walls of Mecca. Yet Mahomet enjoyed the satisfaction of beholding the increase of his infant congregation of Unitarians, who revered him as a prophet, and to whom he seasonably dispensed the spiritual nourishment of the Koran.   The number of proselytes may be estimated by the absence of 83 men and 18 women, who retired to Æthiopia in the seventh year of his mission : and his party was fortified by the timely conversion of his uncle Hamza, and of the fierce and inflexible Omar, who signalized in the cause of Islam the same zeal which he had exerted for its destruction.   Nor was the charity of Mahomet confined to the tribe of Koreish or the precincts of Mecca : on solemn festivals, in the days of pilgrimage, he frequented the Caaba, accosted the strangers of every tribe, and urged, both in private converse and public discourse, the belief and worship of a sole Deity.   Conscious of his reason and of his weakness, he asserted the liberty of conscience, and disclaimed the use of religious violence : but he called the Arabs to repentance, and conjured them to remember the ancient idolaters of Ad and Thamud, whom the divine justice had swept away from the face of the earth.

The people of Mecca was (A.D. 613—622) hardened in their unbelief by superstition and envy.   The elders of the city, the uncles of the prophet, affected to despise the presumption of an orphan, the reformer of his country : the pious orations of Mahomet in the Caaba were answered by the clamours of Abu Taleb.   " Citizens and pilgrims, listen not to the tempter, hearken not to his impious novelties. Stand fast in the worship of Al Lâta and Al Uzzah."   Yet the son of Abdallah was ever dear to the aged chief ; and he protected the fame and person of his nephew against the assaults of the Koreishites, who had long been jealous of the pre-eminence of the family of Hashem.   Their malice was coloured with the pretence of religion : in the age of Job, the crime of impiety was punished by the Arabian magistrate ; and Mahomet was guilty of deserting and denying the national deities.   But so loose was the policy of Mecca, that the leaders of the Koreish, instead of accusing a criminal, were compelled to employ the measures of persuasion or violence.   They repeatedly addressed Abu Taleb in the style of reproach and menace.   " Thy nephew reviles our religion ; he accuses our wise forefathers of ignorance and folly ; silence him quickly, lest he kindle tumult and discord in the city.   If he persevere, we shall draw our swords against him and his adherents, and thou wilt be responsible for the blood of thy fellow-citizens."   The weight and moderation of Abu Taleb eluded the violence of religious faction ; the most helpless or timid of the disciples retired to Æthiopia, and the prophet withdrew himself to various places of strength in the town and country.   As he was still supported by his family, the rest of the tribe of Koreish engaged themselves to renounce all intercourse with the children of Hashem, neither to buy nor sell, neither to marry nor to give in marriage, but to pursue them with implacable enmity, till they should deliver the person of

Mahomet to the justice of the gods. The decree was suspended in the Caaba before the eyes of the nation; the messengers of the Koreish pursued the Mussulman exiles in the heart of Africa: they besieged the prophet and his most faithful followers, intercepted their water and inflamed their mutual animosity by the retaliation of injuries and insults. A doubtful truce restored the appearances of concord; till the death of Abu Taleb abandoned Mahomet to the power of his enemies, at the moment when he was deprived of his domestic comforts by the loss of his faithful and generous Cadijah. Abu Sophian, the chief of the branch of Ommiyah, succeeded to the principality of the republic of Mecca. A zealous votary of the idols, a mortal foe of the line of Hashem, he convened an assembly of the Koreishites and their allies, to decide the fate of the apostle. His imprisonment might provoke the despair of his enthusiasm; and the exile of an eloquent and popular fanatic would diffuse the mischief through the provinces of Arabia. His death was resolved; and they agreed that a sword from each tribe should be buried in his heart, to divide the guilt of his blood and baffle the vengeance of the Hashemites. An angel or a spy revealed their conspiracy; and flight was the only resource of Mahomet. At the dead of night (A.D. 662), accompanied by his friend, Abubeker, he silently escaped from his house: the assassins watched at the door; but they were deceived by the figure of Ali, who reposed on the bed, and was covered with the green vestment of the apostle. The Koreish respected the piety of the heroic youth; but some verses of Ali, which are still extant, exhibit an interesting picture of his anxiety, his tenderness, and his religious confidence. Three days Mahomet and his companion were concealed in the cave of Thor, at the distance of a league from Mecca; and in the close of each evening, they received from the son and daughter of Abubeker, a secret supply of intelligence and food. The diligence of the Koreish explored every haunt in the neighbourhood of the city, they arrived at the entrance of the cavern; but the providential deceit of a spider's web and a pigeon's nest, is supposed to convince them that the place was solitary and inviolate. "We are only two," said the trembling Abubeker. "There is a third," replied the prophet; "it is God himself." No sooner was the pursuit abated, than the two fugitives issued from the rock, and mounted their camels: on the road to Medina, they were overtaken by the emissaries of the Koreish; they redeemed themselves with prayers and promises from their hands. In this eventful moment, the lance of an Arab might have changed the history of the world. The flight of the prophet from Mecca to Medina has fixed the memorable æra of the *Hegira*,[*] which, at the end of twelve centuries, still discriminates the lunar years of the Mahometan nations.

[*] The *Hegira* was instituted by Omar, the second caliph, in imitation of the æra of the martyrs of the Christians (d'Herbelot, p. 444.); and probably commenced sixty-eight days before the flight of Mahomet, with the first of Moharren, or first day of that Arabian year, which coincides with Friday, July 16th, A.D. 622.

The religion of the Koran might have perished in its cradle, had not Medina (A.D. 622) embraced with faith and reverence the holy outcasts of Mecca. Medina, or the *city*, known under the name of Yathreb, before it was sanctified by the throne of the prophet, was divided between the tribes of the Charegites and the Awsites, whose hereditary feud was rekindled by the slightest provocations : two colonies of Jews, who boasted a sacerdotal race, were their humble allies, and without converting the Arabs, they introduced the taste of science and religion, which distinguished Medina as the city of the book. Some of her noblest citizens, in a pilgrimage to the Caaba, were converted by the preaching of Mahomet ; on their return they diffused the belief of God and his prophet, and the new alliance was ratified by their deputies in two secret and nocturnal interviews on a hill in the suburbs of Mecca. In the first, ten Charegites and two Awsites united in faith and love, protested in the name of their wives, their children, and their absent brethren, that they would for ever profess the creed, and observe the precepts, of the Koran. The second was a political association, the first vital spark of the empire of the SARACENS. Seventy-three men and two women of Medina held a solemn conference with Mahomet, his kinsmen, and his disciples ; and pledged themselves to each other by a mutual oath of fidelity. They promised in the name of the city, that if he should be banished, they would receive him as a confederate, obey him as a leader, and defend him to the last extremity, like their wives and children. " But if you are recalled by your country," they asked with a flattering anxiety, " will you not abandon your new allies ?" " All things," replied Mahomet with a smile, " are now common between us ; your blood is as my blood, your ruin as my ruin. We are bound to each other by the ties of honour and interest. I am your friend, and the enemy of your foes." " But if we are killed in your service, what," exclaimed the deputies of Medina, " will be our reward ?" " PARADISE," replied the prophet. " Stretch forth thy hand." He stretched it forth, and they reiterated the oath of allegiance and fidelity. Their treaty was ratified by the people, who unanimously embraced the profession of Islam ; they rejoiced in the exile of the apostle, but they trembled for his safety, and impatiently expected his arrival. After a perilous and rapid journey along the sea-coast, he halted at Koba, two miles from the city, and made his public entry into Medina, sixteen days after his flight from Mecca. Five hundred of the citizens advanced to meet him : he was hailed with acclamations of loyalty and devotion ; Mahomet was mounted on a she-camel, an umbrella shaded his head, and a turban was unfurled before him to supply the deficiency of a standard. His bravest disciples, who had been scattered by the storm, assembled round his person : and the equal, though various, merit of the Moslems was distinguished by the names of *Mohagerians* and *Ansars*, the fugitives of Mecca, and the auxiliaries of Medina. To

eradicate the seeds of jealousy, Mahomet judiciously coupled his principal followers with the rights and obligations of brethren, and when
Ali found himself without a peer, the prophet tenderly declared, that
he would be the companion and brother of the noble youth. The
expedient was crowned with success ; the holy fraternity was respected
in peace and war, and the two parties vied with each other in a generous emulation of courage and fidelity. Once only the concord was
slightly ruffled by an accidental quarrel ; a patriot of Medina arraigned
the insolence of the strangers, but the hint of their expulsion was heard
with abhorrence, and his own son most eagerly offered to lay at the
apostle's feet the head of his father.

From his establishment at Medina, Mahomet assumed (A.D. 622—
632) the exercise of the regal and sacerdotal office ; and it was impious
to appeal from a judge whose decrees were inspired by the divine wisdom. A small portion of ground, the patrimony of two orphans, was
acquired by gift or purchase ; on that chosen spot, he built an house
and a mosque more venerable in their rude simplicity than the palaces
and temples of the Assyrian caliphs. His seal of gold, or silver, was
inscribed with the apostolic title ; when he prayed and preached in the
weekly assembly, he leaned against a trunk of a palm-tree ; and it
was long before be indulged himself in the use of a chair or pulpit of
rough timber. After a reign of six years, 1500 Moslems, in arms and
in the field, renewed their oath of allegiance ; and their chief repeated
the assurance of protection till the death of the last member, or the
final dissolution of the party. It was in the same camp that the
deputy of Mecca was astonished by the attention of the faithful to the
words and looks of the prophet, by the eagerness with which they collected his spittle, an hair that dropt on the ground, the refuse water of
his lustrations, as if they participated in some degree of the prophetic
virtue. " I have seen," said he, " the Chosroes of Persia and the
Cæsar of Rome, but never did I behold a king among his subjects like
Mahomet among his companions." The devout fervour of enthusiasm
acts with more energy and truth than the cold and formal servility of
courts.

In the state of nature every man has a right to defend, by force of
arms, his person and his possessions ; to repel, or even to prevent, the
violence of his enemies, and to extend his hostilities to a reasonable
measure of satisfaction and retaliation. In the free society of the
Arabs, the duties of subject and citizen imposed a feeble restraint ;
and Mahomet, in the exercise of a peaceful and benevolent mission,
had been despoiled and banished by the injustice of his countrymen.
The choice of an independent people had exalted the fugitive of Mecca
to the rank of a sovereign ; and he was invested with the just prerogative of forming alliances, and of waging offensive or defensive war.
The imperfection of human rights was supplied and armed by the
plenitude of divine power : the prophet of Medina assumed, in his new

revelations, a fiercer and more sanguinary tone, which proves that his former moderation was the effect of weakness ; the means of persuasion had been tried, the season of forbearance was elapsed, and he was now commanded to propagate his religion by the sword, to destroy the monuments of idolatry, and, without regarding the sanctity of days or months, to pursue the unbelieving nations of the earth. The same bloody precepts, so repeatedly inculcated in the Koran, are ascribed by the author to the Pentateuch and the Gospel. But the mild tenor of the evangelic style may explain an ambiguous text, that Jesus did not bring peace on the earth, but a sword ; his patient and humble virtues should not be confounded with the intolerant zeal of princes and bishops, who have disgraced the name of his disciples. In the prosecution of religious war, Mahomet might appeal with more propriety to the example of Moses, of the judges and the kings of Israel. The military laws of the Hebrews are still more rigid than those of the Arabian legislator. The Lord of hosts marched in person before the Jews : if a city resisted their summons, the males, without distinction, were put to the sword : the seven nations of Canaan were devoted to destruction ; and neither repentance nor conversion could shield them from the inevitable doom, that no creature within their precincts should be left alive. The fair option of friendship, or submission, or battle, was proposed to the enemies of Mahomet. If they professed the creed of Islam, they were admitted to all the temporal and spiritual benefits of his primitive disciples, and marched under the same banner to extend the religion which they had embraced. The clemency of the prophet was decided by his interest, yet he seldom trampled on a prostrate enemy ; and he seems to promise, that, on the payment of a tribute, the least guilty of his unbelieving subjects might be indulged in their worship, or at least in their imperfect faith. In the first months of his reign, he practised the lessons of holy warfare, and displayed his white banner before the gates of Medina ; the martial apostle fought in person at nine battles or sieges ;* and fifty enterprises of war were achieved in ten years by himself or his lieutenants. The Arab continued to unite the professions of a merchant and a robber ; and his petty excursions for the defence or the attack of a caravan insensibly prepared his troops for the conquest of Arabia. The distribution of the spoil was regulated by a divine law : the whole was faithfully collected in one common mass ; a fifth of the gold and silver, the prisoners and cattle, the movables and immovables, was reserved by the prophet for pious and charitable uses ; the remainder was shared in adequate portions, by the soldiers who had obtained the victory or guarded the camp : the rewards of the slain devolved to their widows and orphans ; and the increase of cavalry was encouraged by

* The private arsenal of the apostle consisted of nine swords, three lances, seven pikes or half-pikes, a quiver and three bows, seven cuirasses, three shields, and two helmets, with a large white standard, a black banner, twenty horses, &c.

the allotment of a double share to the horse and to the man. From all sides the roving Arabs were allured to the standard of religion and plunder : and the enjoyment of wealth and beauty was a feeble type of the joys of paradise prepared for the valiant martyrs of the faith. " The sword," said Mahomet, " is the key of heaven and of hell ; a drop of blood shed in the cause of God, a night spent in arms, is of more avail than two months of fasting or prayer : whosoever falls in battle, his sins are forgiven : at the day of judgment his wounds shall be resplendent as vermilion and odoriferous as musk ; and the loss of his limbs shall be supplied by the wings of angels and cherubim." The intrepid souls of the Arabs were fired with enthusiasm : the pic- ture of the invisible world was strongly painted on their imagination ; and the death which they had always despised, became an object of hope and desire. The Koran inculcates, in the most absolute sense, the tenets of fate and predestination, which would extinguish both in- dustry and virtue, if the actions of man were governed by his specula- tive belief. Yet their influence in every age has exalted the courage of the Saracens and Turks. The first companions of Mahomet advanced to battle with a fearless confidence : there is no danger where there is no chance ; they were ordained to perish in their beds ; or they were safe and invulnerable amidst the darts of the enemy.

Perhaps the Koreish would have been content with the flight of Mahomet had they not been provoked and alarmed by the vengeance of an enemy, who could intercept their Syrian trade as it passed and repassed through the territory · of Medina. Abu Sophian himself, with only thirty or forty followers, conducted a wealthy caravan of 1000 camels : the fortune or dexterity of his march escaped the vigi- lance of Mahomet : but the chief of the Koreish was informed that the holy robbers were placed in ambush to await his return. He dispatched a messenger to his brethren of Mecca, and they were roused by the fear of losing their merchandise and their provisions, unless they hastened to his relief with the military force of the city. The sacred band of Mahomet was formed of 313 Moslems, of whom 77 were fugitives, and the rest auxiliaries : they mounted by turns a train of 70 camels (the camels of Yathreb were formidable in war) ; but such was the poverty of his first disciples, that only two could appear on horseback in the field. In the fertile and famous vale of Beder, three stations from Medina, he was informed by his scouts of the caravan that approached on one side ; of the Koreish, 100 horse, 850 foot, who advanced on the other. After a short debate, he sacri- ficed the prospect of wealth to the pursuit of glory and revenge ; and a slight intrenchment was formed to cover his troops, and a stream of fresh water that glided through the valley. " O God," he ex- claimed, as the numbers of the Koreish (A.D. 623) descended from the hills, " O God, if these are destroyed, by whom wilt thou be worshipped on the earth ?—Courage, my children, close your ranks ; discharge your arrows, and the day is your own." At these words, he placed himself, with Abubeker, on a throne or pulpit, and instantly demanded the succour of Gabriel and 3000 angels. His eye was fixed on the field of battle : the Mussulmans fainted and were pressed : in that decisive moment the prophet started from his throne, mounted his horse, and cast a handful of sand into the air ; " Let their faces be covered with confusion." Both armies heard the thunder of his voice : their fancy beheld the angelic warriors : the Koreish trembled and fled : 70 of the bravest were slain ; and 70 captives adorned the first victory of the faithful. The dead bodies of the Koreish were despoiled and insulted : two of the most obnoxious prisoners were punished with death ; and the ransom of the others, 4000 drams of silver, compensated in some degree the escape of the caravan. But it was in vain that the camels of Abu Sophian explored a new road through the desert and along the Euphrates : they were overtaken by the diligence of the Mussulmans ; and wealthy must have been the prize, if 20,000 drams could be set apart for the fifth of the apostle. The resentment of the public and private loss stimulated Abu Sophian to collect a body of 3000 men, 700 of whom were armed with cuirasses, and 200 were mounted on horseback : 3000 camels attended his march ; and his wife Henda, with fifteen matrons of Mecca, incessantly sounded their timbrels to animate the troops, and to magnify the greatness of Hobal, the most popular deity of the Caaba. The standard of God and of Mahomet was upheld by 950 believers : the disproportion of numbers was not more alarming than in the field of Beder ; and their presumption of victory prevailed against the divine and human sense of the apostle. The second battle was fought (A.D. 623) on mount Ohud, six miles to the north of Medina : the Koreish advanced in the form of a crescent : and the right wing of cavalry was led by Caled, the fiercest and most successful of the Arabian warriors. The troops of Mahomet were skilfully posted on the declivity of the hill ; and their rear was guarded by a detachment of 50 archers. The weight of their charge impelled and broke the centre of the idolaters ; but in the pursuit they lost the advantage of their ground : the archers deserted their station : the Mussulmans were tempted by the spoil, disobeyed their general, and disordered their ranks. The intrepid Caled, wheeling his cavalry on their flank and rear, exclaimed, with a loud voice, that Mahomet was slain. He was indeed wounded in the face with a javelin : two of his teeth were shattered with a stone ; yet, in the midst of tumult and dismay, he reproached the infidels with the murder of a prophet ; and blessed the friendly hand that staunched his blood, and conveyed him to a place of safety. Seventy martyrs died for the sins of the people : they fell, said the apostle, in pairs, each brother embracing his lifeless companion : their bodies were mangled by the inhuman females of Mecca ; and the wife of Abu Sophian tasted the entrails of Hamza, the uncle of Mahomet. They might applaud their superstition and satiate their fury ; but the Mussulmans soon rallied in the field, and the Koreish wanted strength or courage to undertake the siege of Medina. It was attacked the ensuing year by an army of 10,000 enemies ; and this third expedition is variously named from the *nations,* which (A.D. 625) marched under the banner of Abu Sophian, from the *ditch* which was drawn before the city, and a camp of 3000 Mussulmans. The prudence of Mahomet declined a general engagement : the valour of Ali was signalized in single combat ; and the war was protracted twenty days, till the final separation of the confederates. A tempest of wind, rain, and hail, overturned their tents : the private quarrels were fomented by an insidious adversary ; and the Koreish, deserted by their allies, no longer hoped to subvert the throne, or to check the conquests, of their invincible exile.

The choice of Jerusalem for the first kebla of prayer discovers the early propensity of Mahomet in favour of the Jews ; and happy would it have been for their temporal interest, had they recognized, in the Arabian prophet, the hope of Israel and the promised Messiah. Their obstinacy converted his friendship into implacable hatred, with which he pursued (A.D. 623—627) that unfortunate people to the last moment of his life : and in the double character of an apostle and a conqueror, his persecution was extended to both worlds. The Kainoka dwelt at Medina under the protection of the city : he seized the occasion of an accidental tumult, and summoned them to embrace his religion, or contend with him in battle. "Alas," replied the trembling Jews, "we are ignorant of the use of arms, but we persevere in the faith and worship of our fathers ; why wilt thou reduce us to the necessity of a just defence?" The unequal conflict was terminated in fifteen days ; and it was with extreme reluctance that Mahomet yielded to the importunity of his allies, and consented to spare the lives of the captives. But their riches were confiscated, their arms became more effectual in the hands of the Mussulmans ; and a wretched colony of 700 exiles was driven with their wives and children to implore a refuge on the confines of Syria. The Nadhirites were more guilty, since they conspired in a friendly interview to assassinate the prophet. He besieged their castle three miles from Medina, but their resolute defence obtained an honourable capitulation ; and the garrison, sounding their trumpets and beating their drums, was permitted to depart with the honours of war. The Jews had excited and joined the war of the Koreish : no sooner had the *nations* retired from the *ditch,* than Mahomet, without laying aside his armour, marched on the same day to extirpate the hostile race of the children of Koraidha. After a resistance of twenty-five days, they surrendered at discretion. They trusted to the intercession of their old allies of Medina : they could not be ignorant that fanaticism obliterates the feelings of humanity. A venerable elder, to whose judgment they appealed, pronounced the sentence of their death :

3—2

700 Jews were dragged in chains to the market-place of the city : they descended alive into the grave prepared for their execution and burial ; and the apostle beheld with an inflexible eye the slaughter of his helpless enemies. Their sheep and camels were inherited by the Mussulmans : 300 cuirasses, 500 pikes, 1000 lances, composed the most useful portion of the spoil. Six days' journey to the north-east of Medina, the ancient and wealthy town of Chaibar was the seat of the Jewish power in Arabia ; the territory, a fertile spot in the desert, was covered with plantations and cattle, and protected by eight castles, some of which were esteemed of impregnable strength. The forces of Mahomet consisted of 200 horse and 1400 foot : in the succession of eight regular and painful sieges they were exposed to danger, and fatigue, and hunger ; and the most undaunted chiefs despaired of the event. The apostle revived their faith and courage by the example of Ali, on whom he bestowed the surname of the Lion of God : perhaps we may believe that an Hebrew champion of gigantic stature was cloven to the chest by his irresistible scymetar ; but we cannot praise the modesty of romance which represents him as tearing from its hinges the gate of a fortress, and wielding the ponderous buckler in his left hand. After the reduction of the castles, the town of Chaibar submitted to the yoke. The chief of the tribe was tortured, in the presence of Mahomet, to force a confession of his hidden treasure : the industry of the shepherds and husbandmen was rewarded with a precarious toleration : they were permitted, so long as it should please the conqueror, to improve their patrimony in equal shares, for *his* emolument and their own. Under the reign of Omar, the Jews of Chaibar were transplanted to Syria ; and the caliph alleged the injunction of his dying master, that one and the true religion should be professed in his native land of Arabia.

Five times each day the eyes of Mahomet were turned towards Mecca, and he was urged by the most sacred and powerful motives to revisit, as a conqueror, the city and the temple from whence he had been driven as an exile. The Caaba was present to his waking and sleeping fancy : an idle dream was translated into vision and prophecy ; he unfurled the holy banner ; and a rash promise of success too hastily dropped from the lips of the apostle. His march from Medina to Mecca displayed the peaceful and solemn pomp of a pilgrimage : 70 camels chosen and bedecked for sacrifice, preceded the van ; the sacred territory was respected, and the captives were dismissed without ransom to proclaim his clemency and devotion. But no sooner did Mahomet descend into the plain, within a day's journey of the city, than he exclaimed, " they have clothed themselves with the skins of tigers ;" the numbers and resolution of the Koreish opposed his progress ; and the roving Arabs of the desert might desert or betray a leader whom they had followed for the hope of spoil. The intrepid fanatic sunk into a cool and cautious politician : he waved in the treaty his title of

apostle of God, concluded with the Koreish and their allies a truce of
ten years, engaged to restore the fugitives of Mecca who should embrace his religion, and stipulated only, for the ensuing year, the humble privilege of. entering the city as a friend, and of remaining three
days to accomplish the rites of the pilgrimage. A cloud of shame
and sorrow hung on the retreat of the Mussulmans, and their disappointment might justly accuse the failure of a prophet who had
so often appealed to the evidence of success. The faith and hope of
the pilgrims were rekindled by the prospect of Mecca : their swords
were sheathed ; seven times in the footsteps of the apostle they encompassed the Caaba : the Koreish had retired to the hills, and Mahomet,
after the customary sacrifice, evacuated the city on the fourth day.
The people was edified by his devotion ; the hostile chiefs were awed,
or divided, or seduced ; and both Caled and Amrou, the future conquerors of Syria and Egypt, most seasonably deserted the sinking
cause of idolatry. The power of Mahomet was increased by the submission of the Arabian tribes : 10,000 soldiers were assembled for the
conquest of Mecca, and the idolaters, the weaker party, were easily
convicted of violating the truce. Enthusiasm and discipline impelled
the march and preserved the secret, till the blaze of ten thousand fires
proclaimed to the astonished Koreish, the design, the approach, and
the irresistible force of the enemy. The haughty Abu Sophian presented (A.D. 629) the keys of the city, admired the variety of arms and
ensigns that passed before him in review ; observed that the son of
Abdallah had acquired a mighty kingdom, and confessed under the
scymetar of Omar, that he was the apostle of the true God. The return of Marius and Sylla were stained with the blood of the Romans :
the revenge of Mahomet was stimulated by religious zeal, and his
injured followers were eager to execute or to prevent the order of a
massacre. Instead of indulging their passions and his own, the victorious exile forgave the guilt, and united the factions of Mecca. His
troops in three divisions marched into the city ; eight and twenty of
the inhabitants were slain by the sword of Caled ; eleven men and six
women were proscribed by the sentence of Mahomet ; but he blamed
the cruelty of his lieutenant ; and several of the most obnoxious victims were indebted for their lives to his clemency or contempt. The
chiefs of the Koreish were prostrate at his feet. " What mercy can
you expect from the man whom you have wronged ?" " We confide
in the generosity of our kinsman." "And you shall not confide in
vain : begone ! you are safe, you are free." The people of Mecca
deserved their pardon by the profession of Islam ; and after an exile
of seven years, the fugitive missionary was enthroned as the prince and
prophet of his native country. But the 360 idols of the Caaba were
ignominiously broken : the house of God was purified and adorned ;
as an example to future times, the apostle again fulfilled the duties of

a pilgrim ; and a perpetual law was enacted that no unbeliever should dare to set his foot on the territory of the holy city.

The conquest of Mecca determined the faith and obedience of the Arabian tribes ; who, according to the vicissitudes of fortune, had obeyed or disregarded the eloquence or the arms of the prophet. Indifference for rites and opinions still marks the character of the Bedouins ; and they might accept, as loosely as they hold, the doctrine of the Koran. Yet an obstinate remnant still adhered to the religion and liberty of their ancestors, and the war of Honain derived a proper appellation from the *idols*, whom Mahomet had vowed to destroy, and whom the confederates of Tayef had sworn to defend. Four thousand pagans advanced with secrecy and speed to surprise the conqueror ; they pitied and despised the supine negligence of the Koreish, but they depended upon the wishes, and perhaps the aid, of a people who had so lately renounced their gods, and bowed beneath the yoke of their enemy. The banners of Medina and Mecca were displayed by the prophet ; a crowd of Bedouins increased the strength or numbers of the army, and 12,000 Mussulmans entertained a rash and sinful presumption of their invincible strength. They descended without precaution into the valley of Honain ; the heights had been occupied by the archers and slingers of the confederates ; their numbers were oppressed, their discipline was confounded, their courage was appalled, and the Koreish smiled at their impending destruction. The prophet, on his white mule, was encompassed by the enemies ; he attempted to rush against their spears in search of a glorious death : ten of his faithful companions interposed their weapons and their breasts : three of these fell dead at his feet: " O my brethren," he repeatedly cried with sorrow and indignation, " I am the son of Abdallah, I am the apostle of truth ! O man, stand fast in the faith ! O God, send down thy succour !" His uncle Abbas, who, like the heroes of Homer, excelled in the loudness of his voice, made the valley resound with the recital of the gifts and promises of God : the flying Moslems returned from all sides to the holy standard ; and Mahomet observed with pleasure, that the furnace was again re-kindled ; his conduct and example restored the battle, and he animated his victorious troops to inflict a merciless revenge on the authors of their shame. From the field of Honain, he marched without delay to the siege of Tayef, 60 miles S.E. of Mecca, a fortress of strength, whose fertile lands produce the fruits of Syria in the midst of the Arabian desert. A friendly tribe, instructed (I know not how) in the art of sieges, supplied him with a train of battering-rams and military engines, with a body of 500 artificers. But it was in vain that he offered freedom to the slaves of Tayef ; that he violated his own laws by the extirpation of the fruit trees ; that the ground was opened by the miners ; that the breach was assaulted by the troops. After a siege of twenty days, the prophet sounded a retreat, but he retreated with a song of devout triumph, and affected to pray for the repentance

and safety of the unbelieving city. The spoil of this fortunate expedition amounted to 6000 captives, 24,000 camels, 40,000 sheep, and 4000
ounces of silver : a tribe who had fought at Honain, redeemed their
prisoners by the sacrifice of their idols ; but Mahomet compensated
the loss, by resigning to the soldiers his fifth of the plunder, and wished
for their sake, that he possessed as many head of cattle as there were
trees in the province of Tehama. Instead of chastising the disaffection of the Koreish, he endeavoured to cut out their tongues (his own
expression), and to secure their attachment by a superior measure of
liberality : Abu Sophian alone was presented with 300 camels and 20
ounces of silver ; and Mecca was sincerely converted to the profitable
religion of the Koran. The *fugitives* and *auxiliaries* complained, that
they who had borne the burthen were neglected in the season of victory. "Alas," replied their artful leader, "suffer me to conciliate these
recent enemies, these doubtful proselytes, by the gift of some perish-
able goods. To your guard I entrust my life and fortunes. You are
the companions of my exile, of my kingdom, of my paradise." He was
followed by the deputies of Tayef, who dreaded the repetition of a
siege. "Grant us, O apostle of God ! a truce of three years, with the
toleration of our ancient worship." "Not a month, not an hour."
"Excuse us at least from the obligation of prayer." "Without prayer
religion is of no avail." They submitted in silence ; their temples
were demolished, and the same sentence of destruction was executed
on all the idols of Arabia. His lieutenants on the shores of the Red
Sea, the Ocean, and the Gulf of Persia, were saluted by the acclamations of a faithful people ; and the ambassadors who knelt before the
throne of Medina, were as numerous (says the Arabian proverb) as the
dates that fall from the maturity of a palm-tree. The nation submitted
(A.D. 632) to the God and the sceptre of Mahomet : the opprobrious
name of tribute was abolished : the spontaneous or reluctant oblations
of alms and tithes were applied to the service of religion : and 114,000
Moslems accompanied the last pilgrimage of the apostle.

When Heraclius returned in triumph from the Persian war, he entertained, at Emesa, one of the ambassadors of Mahomet, who invited
the princes and nations of the earth to the profession of Islam. On
this foundation the zeal of the Arabians has supposed the secret conversion of the Christian emperor : the vanity of the Greeks has feigned
a personal visit to the prince of Medina, who accepted from the royal
bounty a rich domain, and a secure retreat, in the province of Syria.
But the friendship of Heraclius and Mahomet was of short continuance : the new religion had inflamed rather than assuaged the rapacious spirit of the Saracens ; and the murder of an envoy afforded a
decent pretence for invading, with 3000 soldiers, the territory of Palestine, that extends to the eastward of the Jordan. The holy banner
was entrusted to Zeid ; and such was the discipline or enthusiasm of
the rising sect, that the noblest chiefs served without reluctance, under

the slave of the prophet. On the event of his decease, Jaafar and Abdallah were successively substituted to the command; and if the three should perish in the war, the troops were authorized to elect their general. The three leaders were slain in the battle of Muta (A.D. 629), the first military action which tried the valour of the Moslems against a foreign enemy. Zeid fell, like a soldier, in the foremost ranks: the death of Jaafar was heroic and memorable; he lost his right hand; he shifted the standard to his left; the left was severed from his body; he embraced the standard with his bleeding stumps, till he was transfixed to the ground with fifty honourable wounds. "Advance," cried Abdallah, who stepped into the vacant place, "advance with confidence; either victory or paradise is our own." The lance of a Roman decided the alternative; but the falling standard was rescued by Caled, the proselyte of Mecca: nine swords were broken in his hand; and his valour withstood and repulsed the superior numbers of the Christians. In the nocturnal council of the camp he was chosen to command: his skilful evolutions of the ensuing day secured either the victory or the retreat of the Saracens; and Caled is renowned among his brethren and his enemies by the glorious appellation of the *Sword of God*. In the pulpit, Mahomet described, with prophetic rapture, the crowns of the blessed martyrs; but in private he betrayed the feelings of human nature: he was surprised as he wept over the daughter of Zeid: "What do I see?" said the astonished votary. "You see," replied the apostle, "a friend who is deploring the loss of his most faithful friend." After the conquest of Mecca the sovereign of Arabia affected to prevent the hostile preparations of Heraclius; and solemnly (A.D. 630) proclaimed war against the Romans, without attempting to disguise the hardships and dangers of the enterprise. The Moslems were discouraged: they alleged the want of money, or horses, or provisions; the season of harvest, and the intolerable heat of the summer: "Hell is much hotter," said the indignant prophet. He disdained to compel their service; but on his return he admonished the most guilty, by an excommunication of fifty days. The desertion enhanced the merit of Abubeker, Othman, and the faithful companions who devoted their lives and fortunes; and Mahomet displayed his banner at the head of 10,000 horse and 20,000 foot. Painful indeed was the distress of the march: lassitude and thirst were aggravated by the scorching and pestilential winds of the desert: ten men rode by turns on the same camel: and they were reduced to the shameful necessity of drinking the water from the belly of that useful animal. In the midway, ten days' journey from Medina and Damascus, they reposed near the grove and fountain of Tabuc. Beyond that place, Mahomet declined the prosecution of the war; he declared himself satisfied with the peaceful intentions, he was more probably daunted by the martial array, of the emperor of the East. But the active and intrepid Caled spread around the terror of his name; and the prophet received the submission of the tribes and cities, from the Euphrates to Ailah, at the head of the Red Sea. To his Christian subjects, Mahomet readily granted the security of their persons, the freedom of their trade, the property of their goods, and the toleration of their worship. The weakness of their Arabian brethren had restrained them from opposing his ambition : the disciples of Jesus were endeared to the enemy of the Jews ; and it was the interest of a conqueror to propose a fair capitulation to the most powerful religion of the earth.

Till the age of sixty-three years, the strength of Mahomet was equal to the temporal and spiritual fatigues of his mission. His epileptic fits, an absurd calumny of the Greeks, would be an object of pity rather than abhorrence ; but he seriously believed that he was poisoned at Chaibar by the revenge of a Jewish female. During four years, the health of the prophet declined ; his infirmities increased ; but his mortal disease was a fever of fourteen days, which deprived him by intervals of the use of reason. As soon as he was conscious of his danger, he edified his brethren by the humility of his virtue or penitence. " If there be any man," said the apostle from the pulpit, " whom I have unjustly scourged, I submit my own back to the lash of retaliation. Have I aspersed the reputation of a Mussulman ? let him proclaim *my* faults in the face of the congregation. Has any one been despoiled of his goods ? the little that I possess shall compensate the principal and the interest of the debt." " Yes," replied a voice from the crowd, " I am entitled to three drams of silver." Mahomet heard the complaint, satisfied the demand, and thanked his creditor for accusing him in this world rather than at the day of judgment. He beheld with temperate firmness the approach of death ; enfranchised his slaves (seventeen men, as they are named, and eleven women) ; minutely directed the order of his funeral, and moderated the lamentations. of his weeping friends, on whom he bestowed the benediction of peace. Till the third day before his death, he regularly performed the function of public prayer : the choice of Abubeker to supply his place, appeared to mark that ancient and faithful friend as his successor in the sacerdotal and regal office ; but he prudently declined the risk and envy of a more explicit nomination. At a moment when his faculties were visibly impaired, he called for pen and ink, to write, or more properly to dictate, a divine book, the sum and accomplishment of all his revelations : a dispute arose in the chamber, whether he should be allowed to supersede the authority of the Koran ; and the prophet was forced to reprove the indecent vehemence of his disciples. If the slightest credit may be afforded to the traditions of his wives and companions, he maintained in the bosom of his family, and to the last moments of his life, the dignity of an apostle and the faith of an enthusiast ; described the visits of Gabriel, who bade an everlasting farewell to the earth, and expressed his lively confidence, not only of the mercy, but of the favour, of the Supreme Being. In a familiar discourse he had mentioned his special prerogative, that the angel of death was not allowed to take his soul till he had respectfully asked the permission of the prophet. The request was granted; and Mahomet immediately fell into the agony of his dissolution: his head was reclined on the lap of Ayesha, the best beloved of all his wives; he fainted with the violence of pain; recovering his spirits, he raised his eyes towards the roof of the house, and, with a steady look, though a faltering voice, uttered the last broken, though articulate, words: "O God ! . . . . . pardon my sins . . . . . Yes, ... I come, ... among my fellow-citizens on high :" and thus peaceably expired (A.D. 632. June 7) on a carpet spread upon the floor. An expedition for the conquest of Syria was stopped by this mournful event: the army halted at the gates of Medina; the chiefs were assembled round their dying master. The city, more especially the house, of the prophet was a scene of clamorous sorrow or silent despair : fanaticism alone could suggest a ray of hope and consolation. "How can he be dead, our witness, our intercessor, our mediator, with God ? By God, he is not dead; like Moses and Jesus he is wrapt in a holy trance, and speedily will he return to his faithful people." The evidence of sense was disregarded; and Omar, unsheathing his scymetar, threatened to strike off the heads of the infidels who should dare to affirm that the prophet was no more. The tumult was appeased by the weight and moderation of Abubeker. "Is it Mahomet," said he to Omar and the multitude, "or the God of Mahomet, whom you worship ? The God of Mahomet liveth for ever, but the apostle was a mortal like ourselves, and according to his own prediction, he has experienced the common fate of mortality." He was piously interred by the hands of his nearest kinsman, on the same spot on which he expired; Medina has been sanctified by the death and burial of Mahomet; and the innumerable pilgrims of Mecca often turn aside from the way, to bow in voluntary devotion, before the simple tomb of the prophet.

At the conclusion of the life of Mahomet, it may perhaps be expected, that I should balance his faults and virtues, that I should decide whether the title of enthusiast or impostor more properly belongs to that extraordinary man. Had I been intimately conversant with the son of Abdallah, the task would still be difficult, and the success uncertain : at the distance of twelve centuries, I darkly contemplate his shade through a cloud of religious incense; and could I truly delineate the portrait of an hour, the fleeting resemblance would not equally apply to the solitary mount of Hera, to the preacher of Mecca, and to the conqueror of Arabia. The author of a mighty revolution appears to have been endowed with a pious and contemplative disposition : so soon as marriage had raised him above the pressure of want, he avoided the paths of ambition and avarice; and till the age of forty, he lived with innocence, and would have died without a name. The unity of God is an idea most congenial to nature and reason; and a slight conversation with the Jews and Christians would teach him to despise and detest the idolatry of Mecca. It was the duty of a man and a citizen to impart the doctrine of salvation, to rescue his country from the dominion of sin and error. The energy of a mind incessantly bent on the same object, would convert a general obligation into a particular call ; the warm suggestions of the understanding or the fancy, would be felt as the inspirations of heaven ; the labour of thought would expire in rapture and vision ; and the inward sensation, the invisible monitor, would be described with the form and attributes of an angel of God. From enthusiasm to imposture, the step is perilous and slippery : the dæmon of Socrates affords a memorable instance, how a wise man may deceive himself, how a good man may deceive others, how the conscience may slumber in a mixed and middle state between self-illusion and voluntary fraud. Charity may believe that the original motives of Mahomet were those of pure and genuine benevolence ; but a human missionary is incapable of cherishing the obstinate unbelievers who reject his claims, despise his arguments, and persecute his life ; he might forgive his personal adversaries, he may lawfully hate the enemies of God ; the stern passions of pride and revenge were kindled in the bosom of Mahomet, and he sighed, like the prophet of Nineveh, for the destruction of the rebels whom he had condemned. The injustice of Mecca, and the choice of Medina, transformed the citizen into a prince, the humble preacher into the leader of armies ; but his sword was consecrated by the example of the saints ; and the same God who afflicts a sinful world with pestilence and earthquakes, might inspire for their conversion or chastisement the valour of his servants. In the exercise of political government, he was compelled to abate of the stern rigour of fanaticism, to comply in some measure with the prejudices and passions of his followers, and to employ even the vices of mankind as the instruments of their salvation. The use of fraud and perfidy, of cruelty and injustice, were often subservient to the propagation of the faith ; and Mahomet commanded or approved the assassination of the Jews and idolaters who had escaped from the field of battle. By the repetition of such acts, the character of Mahomet must have been gradually stained ; and the influence of such pernicious habits would be poorly compensated by the practice of the personal and social virtues which are necessary to maintain the reputation of a prophet among his sectaries and friends. Of his last years, ambition was the ruling passion ; and a politician will suspect, that he secretly smiled (the victorious impostor !) at the enthusiasm of his youth and the credulity of his proselytes. A philosopher will observe, that *their* cruelty and *his* success, would tend more strongly to fortify the assurance of his divine mission, that his interest and religion were inseparably connected, and that his conscience would be soothed by the persuasion, that he alone was absolved by the Deity from the obligation of positive and moral laws. If he retained any vestige of his native innocence, the sins of Mahomet may be allowed as an evidence of his sincerity. In the support of truth, the arts of fraud and fiction may be deemed less criminal ; and he would have started at the foulness of the means, had he not been satisfied of the importance and justice of the end. Even in a conqueror or a priest, I can surprise a word or action of unaffected humanity ; and the decree of Mahomet, that, in the sale of captives, the mothers should never be separated from their children, may suspend or moderate the censure of the historian.

The good sense of Mahomet despised the pomp of royalty ; the apostle of God submitted to the menial offices of the family ; he kindled the fire, swept the floor, milked the ewes, and mended with his own hands his shoes and his woollen garment. Disdaining the penance and merit of an hermit, he observed, without effort or vanity, the abstemious diet of an Arab and a soldier. On solemn occasions he feasted his companions with rustic and hospitable plenty; but in his domestic life, many weeks would elapse without a fire being kindled on the hearth of the prophet. The interdiction of wine was confirmed by his example ; his hunger was appeased with a sparing allowance of barley-bread ; he delighted in the taste of milk and honey ; but his ordinary food consisted of dates and water. Perfumes and women were the two sensual enjoyments which his nature required and his religion did not forbid. Their incontinence was regulated by the civil and religious laws of the Koran : their incestuous alliances were blamed, the boundless licence of polygamy was reduced to four legitimate wives or concubines ; their rights both of bed and of dowry were equitably determined ; the freedom of divorce was discouraged, adultery was condemned as a capital offence, and fornication, in either sex, was punished with an hundred stripes. Such were the calm and rational precepts of the legislator : but in his private conduct, Mahomet indulged the appetites of a man, and abused the claims of a prophet. The youth, the beauty, the spirit of Ayesha, gave her a superior ascendant : she was beloved and trusted by the prophet ; and, after his death, the daughter of Abubeker was long revered as the mother of the faithful. During the twenty-four years of the marriage of Mahomet with Cadijah, her youthful husband abstained from the right of polygamy, and the pride or tenderness of the venerable matron was never insulted by the society of a rival. After her death, he placed her in the rank of the four perfect women, with the sister of Moses, the mother of Jesus, and Fatima, the best beloved of his daughters. " Was she not old ?" said Ayesha, with the insolence of a blooming beauty ; "has not God given you a better in her place ?" " No, by God," said Mahomet, with an effusion of honest gratitude, "there never can be a better ! she believed in me, when men despised me : she relieved my wants, when I was poor and persecuted."

In the largest indulgence of polygamy, the founder of a religion and empire might aspire to multiply the chances of a numerous posterity

and a lineal succession. The hopes of Mahomet were fatally disappointed. The four sons of Cadijah died in their infancy. Mary, his
Egyptian concubine, was endeared to him by the birth of Ibrahim.
At the end of fifteen months the prophet wept over his grave ; but he
sustained with firmness the raillery of his enemies, and checked the
adulation or credulity of the Moslems, by the assurance than an eclipse
of the sun was *not* occasioned by the death of the infant. Cadijah had
likewise given him four daughters, who were married to the most
faithful of his disciples : the three eldest died before their father ; but
Fatima, who possessed his confidence and love, became the wife of
her cousin Ali, and the mother of an illustrious progeny. The merit
and misfortunes of Ali and his descendants will lead me to anticipate,
in this place, the series of the Saracen caliphs, a title which describes
the commanders of the faithful as the vicars and successors of the
apostle of God.

The birth, the alliance, the character of Ali, which exalted him
above the rest of his countrymen, might justify his claim to the vacant
throne of Arabia. The son of Abu Taleb was, in his own right, the
chief of the family of Hashem, and the hereditary prince or guardian
of the city and temple of Mecca. The light of prophecy was extinct ;
but the husband of Fatima might expect the inheritance and blessing
of her father ; the Arabs had sometimes been patient of a female reign ;
and the two grandsons of the prophet had often been fondled in his
lap, and shown in his pulpit, as the hope of his age, and the chief of
the youth of paradise. The first of the true believers might aspire to
march before them in this world and in the next ; and if some were of
a graver and more rigid cast, the zeal and virtue of Ali were never
outstripped by any recent proselyte. He united the qualifications of a
poet, a soldier, and a saint : his wisdom still breathes in a collection
of moral and religious sayings ; and every antagonist, in the combats
of the tongue or of the sword, was subdued by his eloquence and
valour. From the first hour of his mission to the last rites of his
funeral, the apostle was never forsaken by a generous friend, whom
he delighted to name his brother, his vicegerent, and the faithful
Aaron of a second Moses. The son of Abu Taleb was afterwards reproached for neglecting to secure his interest by a solemn declaration
of his right, which would have silenced all competition, and sealed his
succession by the decrees of heaven. But the unsuspecting hero confided in himself : the jealousy of empire, and perhaps the fear of
opposition, might suspend the resolutions of Mahomet ; and the bed
of sickness was besieged by the artful Ayesha, the daughter of Abubeker,
and the enemy of Ali.

The silence and death of the prophet restored the liberty of the
people ; and his companions convened an assembly to deliberate on the
choice of his successor. The hereditary claim and lofty spirit of Ali,
were offensive to an aristocracy of elders, desirous of bestowing and

resuming the sceptre by a free and frequent election : the Koreish
could never be reconciled to the proud pre-eminence of the line of
Hashem ; the ancient discord of the tribes was rekindled ; the *fugitives* of Mecca and the *auxiliaries* of Medina asserted their respective
merits, and the rash proposal of choosing two independent caliphs
would have crushed in their infancy the religion and empire of the
Saracens. The tumult was appeased by the disinterested resolution
of Omar, who (A.D. 632. June 7) suddenly renouncing his own pretensions, stretched forth his hand, and declared himself the first subject of the mild and venerable Abubeker. The urgency of the moment
and the acquiescence of the people, might excuse this illegal and precipitate measure ; but Omar himself confessed from the pulpit, that if
any Mussulman should hereafter presume to anticipate the suffrage of
his brethren, both the elector and the elected would be worthy of death.
After the simple inauguration of Abubeker, he was obeyed in Medina,
Mecca, and the provinces of Arabia ; the Hashemites alone declined
the oath of fidelity ; and their chief, in his own house, maintained,
above six months, a sullen and independent reserve ; without listening
to the·threats of Omar, who attempted to consume with fire the habitation of the daughter of the apostle. The death of Fatima, and the
decline of his party, subdued the indignant spirit of Ali : he condescended to salute the commander of the faithful, accepted his excuse
of the necessity of preventing their common enemies, and wisely rejected his courteous offer of abdicating the government of the Arabians.
After a reign of two years, the aged caliph was summoned by the angel
of death. In his testament, with the tacit approbation of the companions, he (A.D. 634. July 24) bequeathed the sceptre to the firm and
intrepid virtue of Omar. " I have no occasion," said the modest candidate, " for the place." " But the place has occasion for you," replied
Abubeker ; who expired with a fervent prayer, that the God of Mahomet would ratify his choice, and direct the Mussulmans in the way of
concord and obedience. The prayer was not ineffectual, since Ali*
himself, in a life of privacy and prayer, professed to revere the superior
worth and dignity of his rival ; who comforted him for the loss of empire, by the most flattering marks of confidence and esteem. In the
twelfth year of his reign, Omar received a mortal wound from the hand
of an assassin : he rejected with equal impartiality the names of his
son and of Ali, refused to load his conscience with the sins of his successor, and devolved on six of the most respectable companions, the
arduous task of electing a commander of the faithful. On this occasion, Ali was again blamed by his friends for submitting his right to
the judgment of men, for recognizing their jurisdiction by accepting a
place among the six electors. He might have obtained their suffrage,
had he deigned to promise a strict and servile conformity, not only to
the Koran and tradition, but likewise to the determinations of two
seniors. With these limitations, Othman, the secretary of Mahomet,

accepted (A.D. 644. Nov. 6) the government; nor was it till after the third caliph, twenty-four years after the death of the prophet, that Ali was invested, by the popular choice, with the regal and sacerdotal office. The manners of the Arabians retained their primitive simplicity, and the son of Abu Taleb despised the pomp and vanity of this world. At the hour of prayer, he repaired to the mosque of Medina, clothed in a thin cotton gown, a coarse turban on his head, his slippers in one hand, and his bow in the other, instead of a walking staff. The companions of the prophet and the chiefs of the tribes saluted their new sovereign, and gave him their right hands as a sign of fealty.

The mischiefs that flow from the contests of ambition are usually confined to the times and countries in which they have been agitated. But the religious discord of the friends and enemies of Ali has been renewed in every age of the Hegira, and is still maintained in the immortal hatred of the Persians and Turks. The former, who are branded with the appellation of *Shiites* or sectaries, have enriched the Mahometan creed with a new article of faith; and if Mahomet be the apostle, his companion Ali is the vicar, of God. In their private converse, in their public worship, they bitterly execrate the three usurpers who intercepted his indefeasible right to the dignity of Imaum and Caliph; and the name of Omar expresses in their tongue the perfect accomplishment of wickedness and impiety. The *Sonnites,* who are supported by the general consent and orthodox tradition of the Mussulmans, entertain a more impartial, or at least a more decent, opinion. They respect the memory of Abubeker, Omar, Othman, and Ali, the holy and legitimate successors of the prophet. But they assign the last and most humble place to the husband of Fatima, in the persuasion that the order of succession was determined by the degrees of sanctity. An historian who balances the four caliphs with a hand unshaken by superstition, will calmly pronounce that their manners were alike pure and exemplary; that their zeal was fervent, and probably sincere; and that, in the midst of riches and power, their lives were devoted to the practice of moral and religious duties. But the public virtues of Abubeker and Omar, the prudence of the first, the severity of the second, maintained the peace and prosperity of their reigns. The feeble temper and declining age of Othman were incapable of sustaining the weight of conquest and empire. He chose, and he was deceived; he trusted, and he was betrayed: the most deserving of the faithful became useless or hostile to his government, and his lavish bounty was productive only of ingratitude and discontent. The spirit of discord went forth in the provinces, their deputies assembled at Medina, and the Charegites, the desperate fanatics who disclaimed the yoke of subordination and reason, were confounded among the free-born Arabs, who demanded the redress of their wrongs and the punishment of their oppressors. From Cufa, from Bassora, from Egypt, from the tribes of the desert, they rose in arms, encamped about a league from Medina, and dispatched an haughty mandate to their sovereign, requiring him to execute justice, or to descend from the throne. His repentance began to disarm and disperse the insurgents; but their fury was rekindled by the arts of his enemies: and the forgery of a perfidious secretary was contrived to blast his reputation and precipitate his fall. The caliph had lost the only guard of his predecessors, the esteem and confidence of the Moslems; during a siege of six weeks his water and provisions were intercepted, and the feeble gates of the palace were protected only by the scruples of the more timorous rebels. Forsaken by those who had abused his simplicity, the helpless and venerable caliph expected the approach of death: the brother of Ayesha marched at the head of the assassins; and Othman, with the Koran in his lap, was (A.D. 655. June 18) pierced with a multitude of wounds. A tumultuous anarchy of five days was appeased by the inauguration of Ali; his refusal would have provoked a general massacre. In this painful situation he supported the becoming pride of the chief of the Hashemites; declared that he had rather serve than reign; rebuked the presumption of the strangers and required the formal, if not the voluntary, assent of the chiefs of the nation. He has never been accused of prompting the assassin of Omar; though Persia indiscreetly celebrates the festival of that holy martyr. The quarrel between Othman and his subjects was assuaged by the early mediation of Ali; and Hassan, the eldest of his sons, was insulted and wounded in the defence of the caliph. Yet it is doubtful whether the father of Hassan was strenuous and sincere in his opposition to the rebels; and it is certain that he enjoyed the benefit of their crime. The temptation was indeed of such magnitude as might stagger and corrupt the most obdurate virtue. The ambitious candidate no longer aspired to the barren sceptre of Arabia: the Saracens had been victorious in the East and West; and the wealthy kingdoms of Persia, Syria, and Egypt, were the patrimony of the commander of the faithful.

A life of prayer and contemplation had not chilled the martial activity of Ali; but in a mature age, after a long experience of mankind, he still betrayed in his conduct the rashness and indiscretion of youth. In the first days of his reign (A.D. 655—660) he neglected to secure, either by gifts or fetters, the doubtful allegiance of Telha and Zobeir, two of the most powerful of the Arabian chiefs. They escaped from Medina to Mecca, and from thence to Bassora; erected the standard of revolt; and usurped the government of Irak, or Assyria, which they had vainly solicited as the reward of their services. The mask of patriotism is allowed to cover the most glaring inconsistencies; and the enemies, perhaps the assassins, of Othman now demanded vengeance for his blood. They were accompanied in their flight by Ayesha, the widow of the prophet, who cherished, to the last hour of her life, an implacable hatred against the husband and the posterity of Fatima. The most reasonable Moslems were scandalized, that the mother of the faithful should expose in a camp her person and character; but the superstitious crowd was confident that her presence would sanctify the justice, and assure the success, of their cause. At the head of 20,000 of his loyal Arabs, and 9000 valiant auxiliaries of Cufa, the caliph encountered and defeated the superior numbers of the rebels under the walls of Bassora. Their leaders, Telha and Zobeir, were slain in the first battle that stained with civil blood the arms of the Moslems. After passing through the ranks to animate the troops, Ayesha had chosen her post amidst the dangers of the field. In the heat of the action, seventy men, who held the bridle of her camel, were successively killed or wounded; and the cage or litter in which she sat, was stuck with javelins and darts like the quills of a porcupine. The venerable captive sustained with firmness the reproaches of the conqueror, and was speedily dismissed to her proper station, at the tomb of Mahomet, with the respect and tenderness that was still due to the widow of the apostle. After this victory, which was styled the Day of the Camel, Ali marched against a more formidable adversary; against Moawiyah, the son of Abu Sophian, who had assumed the title of caliph, and whose claim was supported by the forces of Syria and the interests of the house of Ommiyah. From the passage of Thapsacus, the plain of Siffin extends along the western banks of the Euphrates. On this spacious and level theatre, the two competitors waged a desultory war of 110 days. In the course of 90 actions or skirmishes, the loss of Ali was estimated at 25,000, that of Moawiyah at 45,000, soldiers; and the list of the slain was dignified with the names of five and twenty veterans who had fought at Beder under the standard of Mahomet. In this sanguinary contest, the lawful caliph displayed a superior character of valour and humanity. His troops were strictly enjoined to await the first onset of the enemy, to spare their flying brethren, and to respect the bodies of the dead, and the chastity of the female captives. He generously proposed to save the blood of the Moslems by a single combat; but his trembling rival declined the challenge as a sentence of inevitable death. The ranks of the Syrians were broken by the charge of a hero who was mounted on a pyebald horse, and wielded with irresistible force his ponderous and two-edged sword. As often as he smote a rebel, he shouted the Allah Acbar, " God is victorious ;" and in the tumult of a nocturnal battle, he was heard to repeat four hundred times that tremendous exclamation. The prince of Damascus already meditated his flight, but the certain victory was snatched from the grasp of Ali by the disobedience and enthusiasm of his troops. Their conscience was awed by the solemn appeal to the books of the Koran which Moawiyah exposed on the foremost lances; and Ali was compelled to yield to a disgraceful truce and an insidious compromise. He retreated with sorrow and indignation to Cufa; his party was dis-

4

couraged; the distant provinces of Persia, of Yemen, and of Egypt, were subdued or seduced by his crafty rival : and the stroke of fanaticism which was aimed against the three chiefs of the nation, was fatal only to the cousin of Mahomet. In the temple of Mecca three Charegites or enthusiasts discoursed of the disorders of the church and state : they soon agreed, that the deaths of Ali, of Moawiyah, and of his friend Amrou, the viceroy of Egypt, would restore the peace and unity of religion. Each of the assassins chose his victim, poisoned his dagger, devoted his life, and secretly repaired to the scene of action. Their resolution was equally desperate : but the first mistook the person of Amrou, and stabbed the deputy who occupied his seat; the prince of Damascus was dangerously hurt by the second; the lawful caliph, in the mosque of Cufa, received a mortal wound from the hand of the third. He expired in the sixty-third year of his age, and mercifully recommended to his children, that they would dispatch the murderer by a single stroke. The sepulchre of Ali was concealed from the tyrants of the house of Ommiyah ; but in the fourth age of the Hegira, a tomb, a temple, a city, arose near the ruins of Cufa. Many thousand of the Schiites repose in holy ground at the feet of the vicar of God ; and the desert is vivified by the numerous and annual visits of the Persians, who esteem their devotion not less meritorious than the pilgrimage of Mecca.

The persecutors of Mahomet usurped (A.D. 655, or 661—680) the inheritance of his children ; and the champions of idolatry became the supreme heads of his religion and empire. The opposition of Abu Sophian had been fierce and obstinate ; his conversion was tardy and reluctant; his new faith was fortified by necessity and interest ; he served, he fought, perhaps he believed ; and the sins of the time of ignorance were expiated by the recent merits of the family of Ommiyah. Moawiyah, the son of Abu Sophian, and of the cruel Henda, was dignified in his early youth with the office or title of secretary of the prophet : the judgment of Omar entrusted him with the government of Syria ; and he administered that important province above forty years either in a subordinate or supreme rank. Without renouncing the fame of valour and liberality, he affected the reputation of humanity and moderation : a grateful people was attached to their benefactor ; and the victorious Moslems were enriched with the spoils of Cyprus and Rhodes. The sacred duty of pursuing the assassins of Othman was the engine and pretence of his ambition. The bloody shirt of the martyr was exposed in the mosque of Damascus : the emir deplored the fate of his injured kinsman ; and 60,000 Syrians were engaged in his service by an oath of fidelity and revenge. Amrou, the conqueror of Egypt, himself an army, was the first who saluted the new monarch, and divulged the dangerous secret, that the Arabian caliphs might be created elsewhere than in the city of the prophet. The policy of Moawiyah eluded the valour of his rival ; and, after the death of Ali, he negotiated the abdication of his son Hassan, whose mind was either above or below the government of the world, and who retired without a sigh from the palace of Cufa to an humble cell near the tomb of his grandfather. The aspiring wishes of the caliph were finally crowned by the important change of an elective to an hereditary kingdom. Some murmurs of freedom or fanaticism attested the reluctance of the Arabs, and four citizens of Medina refused the oath of fidelity; but the designs of Moawiyah were conducted with vigour and address; and his son Yezid, a feeble and dissolute youth, was proclaimed as the commander of the faithful and the successor of the apostle of God.

A familiar story is related of the benevolence of one of the sons of Ali. In serving at table, a slave had inadvertently dropt a dish of scalding broth on his master: the heedless wretch fell prostrate, to deprecate his punishment, and repeated a verse of the Koran: "Paradise is for those who command their anger :"—"I am not angry :"—"and for those who pardon offences :"—"I pardon your offence :"—"and for those who return good for evil :"—"I give you your liberty, and four hundred pieces of silver." With an equal measure of piety, Hosein, the younger brother of Hassan, inherited a remnant of his father's spirit, and served with honour against the Christians in the siege of Constantinople. The primogeniture of the line of Hashem, and the holy character of grandson of the apostle, had centered in his person, and he was at liberty to prosecute his claim against Yezid, the tyrant of Damascus, whose vices he despised, and whose title he had never deigned to acknowledge. A list was secretly transmitted from Cufa to Medina, of 140,000 Moslems, who professed their attachment to his cause, and who were eager to draw their swords as soon as he should appear on the banks of the Euphrates. Against the advice of his wisest friends, he resolved to trust his person and family in the hands of a perfidious people. He traversed the desert of Arabia with a timorous retinue of women and children; but as he approached the confines of Irak, he was alarmed by the solitary or hostile face of the country, and suspected either the defection or ruin of his party. His fears were just; Obeidollah, the governor of Cufa, had extinguished the first sparks of an insurrection; and Hosein, in the plain of Kerbela, was encompassed by a body of 5000 horse, who intercepted his communication with the city and the river. He might still have escaped to a fortress in the desert, that had defied the power of Cæsar and Chosroes, and confided in the fidelity of the tribe of Tai, which would have armed 10,000 warriors in his defence. In a conference with the chief of the enemy, he proposed the option of three honourable conditions; that he should be allowed to return to Medina, or be stationed in a frontier garrison against the Turks, or safely conducted to the presence of Yezid. But the commands of the caliph, or his lieutenant, were stern and absolute; and Hosein was informed that he must either submit as a captive and a criminal to the commander of the faithful, or expect the consequences of his rebellion. " Do you think," replied he, " to terrify me with death ? " And, during the short respite of a night, he prepared with calm and solemn resignation to encounter his fate. He checked the lamentations of his sister Fatima, who deplored the impending ruin of his house. " Our trust," said Hosein, " is in God alone. All things, both in heaven and earth, must perish and return to their Creator. My brother, my father, my mother, were better than me ; and every Mussulman has an example in the prophet." He pressed his friends to consult their safety by a timely flight : they unanimously refused to desert or survive their beloved master ; and their courage was fortified by a fervent prayer and the assurance of paradise. On the morning of the fatal day, he mounted on horseback, with his sword in one hand and the Koran in the other : his generous band of martyrs consisted only of thirty-two horse and forty foot ; but their flanks and rear were secured by the tent-ropes, and by a deep trench which they had filled with lighted faggots, according to the practice of the Arabs. The enemy advanced with reluctance ; and one of their chiefs deserted, with thirty followers, to claim the partnership of inevitable death. In every close onset, or single combat, the despair of the Fatimites was invincible ; but the surrounding multitudes galled them from a distance with a cloud of arrows, and the horses and men were successively slain : a truce was allowed on both sides for the hour of prayer ; and the battle at length expired by the death of the last of the companions of Hosein. Alone, weary, and wounded, he seated himself at the door of his tent. As he tasted a drop of water, he was pierced in the mouth with a dart ; and his son and nephew, two beautiful youths, were killed in his arms. He lifted his hands to heaven, they were full of blood, and he uttered a funeral prayer for the living and the dead. In a transport of despair his sister issued from the tent, and adjured the general of the Cufians, that he would not suffer Hosein to be murdered before his eyes : a tear trickled down his venerable beard ; and the boldest of his soldiers fell back on every side as the dying hero threw himself among them. The remorseless Shamer, a name detested by the faithful, reproached their cowardice ; and the grandson of Mahomet was (A.D. 680. Oct. 10) slain with three and thirty strokes of lances and swords. After they had trampled on his body, they carried his head to the castle of Cufa, and the inhuman Obeidollah struck him on the mouth with a cane : " Alas," exclaimed an aged Mussulman, " on these lips have I seen the lips of the apostle of God ! " In a distant age and climate the tragic scene of the death of Hosein will awaken the sympathy of the coldest reader. On the annual festival of his martyrdom, in the devout pilgrimage to his sepulchre, his Persian votaries abandon their souls to the religious frenzy of sorrow and indignation.

When the sisters and children of Ali were brought in chains to the throne of Damascus, the caliph was advised to extirpate the enmity of a popular and hostile race, whom he had injured beyond the hope of reconciliation. But Yezid preferred the counsels of mercy ; and the mourning family was honourably dismissed to mingle their tears with their kindred at Medina. The glory of martyrdom superseded the right of primogeniture ; and the twelve IMAUMS, or pontiffs, of the Persian creed are Ali, Hassan, Hosein, and the lineal descendants of Hosein to the ninth generation. Without arms, or treasures, or subjects, they successively enjoyed the veneration of the people, and provoked the jealousy of the reigning caliphs : their tombs at Mecca or Medina, on the banks of the Euphrates, or in the province of Chorasan, are still visited by the devotion of their sect. Their names were often the pretence of sedition and civil war ; but these royal saints despised the pomp of the world, submitted to the will of God and the injustice of man, and devoted their innocent lives to the study and practice of religion. The twelfth and last of the Imaums, conspicuous by the title of *Mahadi*, or the Guide, surpassed the solitude and sanctity of his predecessors. He concealed himself in a caravan near Bagdad : the time and place of his death are unknown ; and his votaries pretend that he still lives, and will appear before the day of judgment to overthrow the tyranny of Dejal, or the Antichrist. In the lapse of two or three centuries the posterity of Abbas, the uncle of Mahomet, had multiplied to the number of 33,000 : the race of Ali might be equally prolific ; the meanest individual was above the first and greatest of princes ; and the most eminent were supposed to excel the perfection of angels. But their adverse fortune, and the wide extent of the Mussulman empire, allowed an ample scope for every bold and artful impostor, who claimed affinity with the holy seed : the sceptre of the Almohades in Spain and Afric, of the Fatimites in Egypt and Syria, of the Sultans of Yemen, and of the Sophis of Persia, has been consecrated by this vague and ambiguous title. Under their reigns it might be dangerous to dispute the legitimacy of their birth ; and one of the Fatimite caliphs silenced an indiscreet question, by drawing his scymetar : "This," said Moez, "is my pedigree ; and these," casting an handful of gold to his soldiers, "and these are my kindred and my children." In the various conditions of princes, or doctors, or nobles, or merchants, or beggars, a swarm of the genuine or fictitious descendants of Mahomet and Ali is honoured with the appellation of sheiks, or sherifs, or emirs. In the Ottoman empire, they are distinguished by a green turban, receive a stipend from the treasury, are judged only by their chief, and, however debased by fortune or character, still assert the proud pre-eminence of their birth. A family of three hundred persons, the pure and orthodox branch of the caliph Hassan, is preserved without taint or suspicion in the holy cities of Mecca and Medina, and still retains, after the revolutions of twelve centuries, the custody of the temple and the sovereignty of their native land. The fame and merit of Mahomet would ennoble a plebeian race, and the ancient blood of the Koreish transcends the recent majesty of the kings of the earth.

The talents of Mahomet are entitled to our applause, but his success has perhaps too strongly attracted our admiration. Are we surprised that a multitude of proselytes should embrace the doctrine and the passions of an eloquent fanatic? In the heresies of the church, the same seduction has been tried and repeated from the time of the apostles to that of the reformers. Does it seem incredible that a private citizen should grasp the sword and the sceptre, subdue his native country, and erect a monarchy by his victorious arms? In the moving picture of the dynasties of the East, an hundred fortunate usurpers have arisen from a baser origin, surmounted more formidable obstacles, and filled a larger scope of empire and conquest. Mahomet was alike instructed to preach and to fight, and the union of these opposite qualities, while it enhanced his merit, contributed to his success : the operation of force and persuasion, of enthusiasm and fear, continually acted on each other, till every barrier yielded to their irresistible power. His voice invited the Arabs to freedom and victory, to arms and rapine, to the indulgence of their darling passions in this world and the other ; the restraints which he imposed were requisite to establish the credit of the prophet, and to exercise the obedience of the people ; and the only objection to his success, was his rational creed of the unity and perfections of God. It is not the propagation but the permanency of his religion that deserves our wonder : the same pure and perfect impression which he engraved at Mecca and Medina, is preserved, after the revolutions of twelve centuries, by the Indian, the African, and the Turkish proselytes of the Koran. If the Christian apostles, St. Peter or St. Paul, could return to the Vatican, they might possibly inquire the name of the Deity who is worshipped with such mysterious rites in that magnificent temple : at Oxford or Geneva, they would experience less surprise ; but it might still be incumbent on them to peruse the catechism of the church, and to study the orthodox commentators on their own writings and the words of their Master. But the Turkish dome of St. Sophia, with an increase of splendour and size, represents the humble tabernacle erected at Medina by the hands of Mahomet. The Mahometans have uniformly withstood the temptation of reducing the object of their faith and devotion to a level with the senses and imagination of man. " I believe in one God, and Mahomet the apostle of God," is the simple and invariable profession of Islam. The intellectual image of the Deity has never been degraded by any visible idol : the honours of the prophet have never transgressed the measure of human virtue ; and his living precepts have restrained the gratitude of his disciples within the bounds of reason and religion. The votaries of Ali have indeed consecrated the memory of their hero, his wife, and his children, and some of the Persian doctors pretend that the divine essence was incarnate in the person of the Imaums; but their superstition is universally condemned by the Sonnites; and their impiety has afforded a seasonable warning against the worship of saints and martyrs. The metaphysical questions on the attributes of God, and the liberty of man, have been agitated in the schools of the Mahometans, as well as in those of the Christians; but among the former they have never engaged the passions of the people or disturbed the tranquillity of the state. The cause of this important difference may be found in the separation or union of the regal and sacerdotal characters. It was the interest of the caliphs, the successors of the prophet and commanders of the faithful, to repress and discourage all religious innovations: the order, the discipline, the temporal and spiritual ambition of the clergy, are unknown to the Moslems; and the sages of the law are the guides of their conscience and the oracles of their faith. From the Atlantic to the Ganges, the Koran is acknowledged as the fundamental code, not only of theology but of civil and criminal jurisprudence; and the laws which regulate the actions and the property of mankind, are guarded by the infallible and immutable sanction of the will of God. This religious servitude is attended with some practical disadvantage; the illiterate legislator had been often misled by his own prejudices and those of his country; and the institutions of the Arabian desert may be ill-adapted to the wealth and numbers of Ispahan and Constantinople. On these occasions, the Cadi respectfully places on his head the holy volume, and substitutes a dexterous interpretation more apposite to the principles of equity, and the policy of the times.

His beneficial or pernicious influence on the public happiness is the last consideration in the character of Mahomet. The most bitter or most bigoted of his Christian or Jewish foes, will surely allow that he assumed a false commission to inculcate a salutary doctrine, less perfect only than their own. He piously supposed, as the basis of his religion, the truth and sanctity of *their* prior revelations, the virtues and miracles of their founders. The idols of Arabia were broken before the throne of God; the blood of human victims was expiated by prayer, and fasting, and alms, the laudable or innocent arts of devotion; and his rewards and punishments of a future life were painted by the images most congenial to an ignorant and carnal generation. Mahomet was perhaps incapable of dictating a moral and political system for the use of his countrymen: but he breathed among the faithful a spirit of charity and friendship, recommended the practice of the social virtues, and checked, by his laws and precepts, the thirst of revenge and the oppression of widows and orphans. The hostile tribes were united in faith and obedience, and the valour which had been idly spent in domestic quarrels, was vigorously directed against a foreign enemy. Had the impulse been less powerful, Arabia, free at home, and formidable abroad, might have flourished under a succession of her native monarchs. Her sovereignty was lost by the extent and rapidity of conquest. The colonies of the nation were scattered over the East and West, and their blood was mingled with the blood of their converts and captives. After the reign of three caliphs, the throne was transported from Medina to the valley of Damascus and the banks of the Tigris ; the holy cities were violated by impious war ; Arabia was ruled by the rod of a subject, perhaps of a stranger ; and the Bedouins of the desert, awakening from their dream of dominion, resumed their old and solitary independence.

The revolution of Arabia had not changed the character of the Arabs : the death of Mahomet was the signal of independence ; and the hasty structure of his power and religion tottered to its foundations. A small and faithful band of his primitive disciples had listened to his eloquence, and shared his distress ; had fled with the apostle from the persecution of Mecca, or had received the fugitive in the walls of Medina. The increasing myriads, who acknowledged Mahomet as their king and prophet, had been compelled by his arms, or allured by his prosperity. The polytheists were confounded by the simple idea of a solitary and invisible God : the pride of the Christians and Jews disdained the yoke of a mortal and contemporary legislator. Their habits of faith and obedience were not sufficiently confirmed : and many of the new converts regretted the venerable antiquity of the law of Moses, or the rites and mysteries of the Catholic church, or the idols, the sacrifices, the joyous festivals, of their Pagan ancestors. The jarring interests and hereditary feuds of the Arabian tribes had not yet coalesced in a system of union and subordination ; and the Barbarians were impatient of the mildest and most salutary laws that curbed their passions, or violated their customs. They submitted with reluctance to the religious precepts of the Koran, the abstinence from wine, the fast of the Ramadan, and the daily repetition of five prayers ; and the alms and tithes, which were collected for the treasury of Medina, could be distinguished only by a name from the payment of a perpetual and ignominious tribute. The example of Mahomet had excited a spirit of fanaticism or imposture, and several of his rivals presumed to imitate the conduct and defy the authority of the living prophet. At the head of the *fugitives* and *auxiliaries*, the first caliph was reduced to the cities of Mecca, Medina, and Tayef ; and perhaps the Koreish would have restored the idols of the Caaba, if their levity had not been checked by a seasonable reproof. " Ye men of Mecca, will ye be the last to embrace and the first to abandon the religion of Islam ?" After exhorting the Moslems to confide in the aid of God and his apostle, Abubeker resolved (A.D. 632), by a vigorous attack, to prevent the junction of the rebels. The women and children were safely lodged in the cavities of the mountains : the warriors, marching under eleven banners, diffused the terror of their arms ; and the appearance of a military force revived and confirmed the loyalty of the faithful. The inconstant tribes accepted, with humble repentance, the duties of prayer, and fasting, and alms : and, after some examples of success and severity, the most daring apostates fell prostrate before the sword of the Lord and of Caled. In the fertile province of Ye-manah, between the Red Sea and the Gulf of Persia, in a city not inferior to Medina itself, a powerful chief, his name was Moseilama, had assumed the character of a prophet, and the tribe of Hanifa listened to his voice. A female prophetess was attracted by his reputation : the decencies of words and actions were spurned by these favourites of heaven. An obscure sentence of his Koran, or book, is yet extant ; and, in the pride of his mission, Moseilama condescended to offer a partition of the earth. The proposal was answered by Mahomet with contempt ; but the rapid progress of the impostor awakened the fears of his successor : 40,000 Moslems were assembled under the standard of Caled ; and the existence of their faith was resigned to the event of a decisive battle. In the first action, they were repulsed with the loss of 1200 men ; but the skill and perseverance of their general prevailed : their defeat was avenged by the slaughter of 10,000 infidels : and Mo-seilama himself was pierced by an Ethiopian slave with the same javelin which had mortally wounded the uncle of Mahomet. The various rebels of Arabia, without a chief or a cause, were speedily sup-pressed by the power and discipline of the rising monarchy ; and the whole nation again professed, and more stedfastly held, the religion of the Koran. The ambition of the caliphs provided an immediate exer-cise for the restless spirit of the Saracens : their valour was united in he prosecution of an holy war ; and their enthusiasm was equally confirmed by opposition and victory.

From the rapid conquests of the Saracens a presumption will natur-ally arise that the first caliphs commanded in person the armies of the faithful, and sought the crown of martyrdom in the foremost ranks of the battle. The courage of Abubeker, Omar, and Othman, had in-deed been tried in the persecution and wars of the prophet ; and the personal assurance of paradise must have taught them to despise the pleasures and dangers of the present world. But they ascended the throne in a venerable or mature age, and esteemed the domestic cares of religion and justice the most important duties of a sovereign. Ex-cept the presence of Omar at the siege of Jerusalem, their longest ex-peditions were the frequent pilgrimage from Medina to Mecca ; and they calmly received the tidings of victory as they prayed or preached before the sepulchre of the prophet. The austere and frugal measure of their lives was the effect of virtue or habit, and the pride of their simplicity insulted the vain magnificence of the kings of the earth. When Abubeker assumed the office of caliph, he enjoined his daughter Ayesha to take a strict account of his private patrimony, that it might be evident whether he were enriched or impoverished by the service of the state. He thought himself entitled to a stipend of three pieces of gold, with the sufficient maintenance of a single camel and a black slave; but on the Friday of each week, he distributed the residue of his own and the public money, first to the most worthy, and then to the most indigent, of the Moslems. The remains of his wealth, a coarse garment and five pieces of gold, were delivered to his successor, who lamented with a modest sigh his own inability to equal such an admirable modeL. Yet the abstinence and humility of Omar were not inferior to the virtues of Abubeker; his food consisted of barley-bread or dates; his drink was water; he preached in a gown that was torn or tattered in twelve places; and a Persian satrap who paid his homage to the conqueror, found him asleep among the beggars on the steps of the mosques of Medina. Economy is the source of liberality, and the increase of the revenue enabled Omar to establish a just and perpetual reward for the past and present services of the faithful. Careless of his own emolument, he assigned to Abbas, the uncle of the prophet, the first and most ample allowance of 25,000 drams or pieces of silver. 5000 were allotted to each of the aged warriors, the relics of the field of Beder, and the last and meanest of the companions of Mahomet was distinguished by the annual reward of 3000 pieces. One thousand was the stipend of the veterans who had fought in the first battles against the Greeks and Persians, and the decreasing pay, as low as 50 pieces of silver, was adapted to the respective merit and seniority of the soldiers of Omar. Under his reign, and that of his predecessor, the conquerors of the East were the trusty servants of God and the people: the mass of the public treasure was consecrated to the expences of peace and war; a prudent mixture of justice and bounty, maintained the discipline of the Saracens, and they united, by a rare felicity, the dispatch and execution of despotism, with the equal and frugal maxims of a republican government. The heroic courage of Ali, the consummate prudence of Moawiyah, excited the emulation of their subjects; and the talents which had been exercised in the school of civil discord, were more usefully applied to propagate the faith and dominion of the prophet. In the sloth and vanity of the palace of Damascus, the succeeding princes of the house of Ommiyah were alike destitute of the qualifications of statesmen and of saints. Yet the spoils of unknown nations were continually laid at the foot of their throne, and the uniform ascent of the Arabian greatness must be ascribed to the spirit of the nation rather than the abilities of their chiefs. A large deduction must be allowed for the weakness of their enemies. The birth of Mahomet was fortunately placed in the most degenerate and disorderly period of the Persians, the Romans, and the Barbarians of Europe: the empires of Trajan, or even of Constantine or Charlemagne, would have repelled the assault of the naked Saracens, and the torrent of fanaticism might have been lost in the sands of Arabia.

In the victorious days of the Roman republic, it had been the aim of the senate to confine their counsels and legions to a single war, and completely to suppress a first enemy before they provoked the hostilities of a second. These timid maxims of policy were disdained by the magnanimity or enthusiasm of the Arabian caliphs. With the same vigour and success they invaded the successors of Augustus, and those of Artaxerxes ; and the rival monarchies at the same instant became the prey of an enemy whom they had been so long accustomed to despise. In the ten years of the administration of Omar, the Saracens reduced to his obedience 36,000 cities or castles, destroyed 4,000 churches or temples of the unbelievers, and erected 1,400 mosques for the exercise of the religion of Mahomet. One hundred years after his flight from Mecca, the arms and the reign of his successors extended from India to the Atlantic Ocean, over the various and distant provinces, which may be comprised under the names of, I. Persia ; II. Syria ; III. Egypt ; IV. Africa ; and, V. Spain. Under this general division, I shall proceed to unfold these memorable transactions ; dispatching with brevity the remote and less interesting conquests of the East, and reserving a fuller narrative for those domestic countries, which had been included within the pale of the Roman empire. Yet I must excuse my own defects by a just complaint of the blindness and insufficiency of my guides. The Greeks, so loquacious in controversy, have not been anxious to celebrate the triumphs of their enemies. After a century of ignorance, the first annals of the Mussulmans were collected in a great measure from the voice of tradition. Among the numerous productions of Arabic and Persian literature, our interpreters have selected the imperfect sketches of a more recent age. The art and genius of history have ever been unknown to the Asiatics ; they are ignorant of the laws of criticism ; and our monkish chronicles of the same period may be compared to their most popular works, which are never vivified by the spirit of philosophy and freedom. The *Oriental library* of a Frenchman would instruct the most learned mufti of the East ; and perhaps the Arabs might not find in a single historian, so clear and comprehensive a narrative of their own exploits, as that which will be deduced in the ensuing sheets.

I. In the first year (A.D. 632) of the first caliph, his lieutenant Caled, the sword of God, and the scourge of the infidels, advanced to the banks of the Euphrates, and reduced the cities of Anbar and Hira. Westward of the ruins of Babylon, a tribe of sedentary Arabs had fixed themselves on the verge of the desert ; and Hira was the seat of a race of kings who had embraced the Christian religion, and reigned above 600 years under the shadow of the throne of Persia. The last of the Mondars was defeated and slain by Caled ; his son was sent a captive to Medina ; his nobles bowed before the successor of the prophet ; the people was tempted by the example and success of their countrymen ; and the caliph accepted as the first fruits of foreign conquest, an annual tribute of 70,000 pieces of gold. The conquerors, and even their historians, were astonished by the dawn of their future greatness: "In the same year," says Elmacin, "Caled fought many signal battles; an immense multitude of the infidels was slaughtered; and spoils, infinite and innumerable, were acquired by the victorious Moslems." But the invincible Caled was soon transferred to the Syrian war : the invasion of the Persian frontier was conducted by less active or less prudent commanders : the Saracens were repulsed with loss in the passage of the Euphrates ; and, though they chastised the insolent pursuit of the Magians, their remaining forces still hovered in the desert of Babylon.

The indignation and fears of the Persians suspended for a moment their intestine divisions. By the unanimous sentence of the priests and nobles, their queen Arzema was deposed ; the sixth of the transient usurpers, who had arisen and vanished in three or four years, since the death of Chosroes and the retreat of Heraclius. Her tiara was placed on the head of Yezdegerd, the grandson of Chosroes ; and the same æra, which coincides with an astronomical period, has recorded the fall of the Sassanian dynasty and the religion of Zoroaster. The youth and inexperience of the prince, he was only fifteen years of age, declined a perilous encounter ; the royal standard was delivered into the hands of his general Rustam ; and a remnant of 30,000 regular troops was swelled in truth, or in opinion, to 120,000 subjects, or allies, of the great king. The Moslems, whose numbers were reinforced from 12,000 to 30,000, had pitched their camp in the plains of Cadesia : and their line, though it consisted of fewer *men*, could produce more *soldiers* than the unwieldy host of the infidels. I shall here observe what I must often repeat, that the charge of the Arabs was not like that of the Greeks and Romans, the effort of a firm and compact infantry : their military force was chiefly formed of cavalry and archers ; and the engagement, which was often interrupted and often renewed by single combats and flying skirmishes, might be protracted without any decisive event to the continuance of several days. The periods of the battle (A.D. 636) of Cadesia were distinguished by their peculiar appellations. The first, from the well-timed appearance of 6,000 of the Syrian brethren, was denominated the day of *succour*. The day of *concussion* might express the disorder of one, or perhaps of both, of the contending armies. The third, a nocturnal tumult, received the whimsical name of the night of *barking*, from the discordant clamours, which were compared to the inarticulate sounds of the fiercest animals. The morning of the succeeding day determined the fate of Persia ; and a seasonable whirlwind drove a cloud of dust against the faces of the unbelievers. The clangour of arms was re-echoed to the tent of Rustam, who, far unlike the ancient hero of his name, was gently reclining in a cool and tranquil shade, amidst the baggage of his camp, and the train of mules that were laden with gold and silver. On the sound of danger he started from his couch ; but his flight was overtaken by a valiant Arab, who caught him by the foot, struck off his head, hoisted it on a lance, and instantly returning to the field of battle, carried slaughter and dismay among the thickest ranks of the Persians. The Saracens confess a loss of 7500 men ; and the battle of Cadesia is justly described by the epithets of obstinate and atrocious. The standard of the monarchy was overthrown and captured in the field—a leathern apron of a blacksmith, who, in ancient times, had arisen the deliverer of Persia ; but this badge of heroic poverty was disguised, and almost concealed, by a profusion of precious gems. After this victory, the wealthy province of Irak or Assyria submitted to the caliph, and his conquests were firmly established by the speedy foundation of Bassorah, a place which ever commands the trade and navigation of the Persians. At the distance of 80 miles from the Gulf, the Euphrates and Tigris unite in a broad and direct current, which is aptly styled the river of the Arabs. In the mid-way, between the junction and the mouth of these famous streams, the new settlement was planted on the western bank ; the first colony was composed of 800 Moslems ; but the influence of the situation soon reared a flourishing and populous capital. The air, though excessively hot, is pure and healthy : the meadows are filled with palm trees and cattle ; and one of the adjacent valleys has been celebrated among the four paradises or gardens of Asia. Under the first caliphs, the jurisdiction of this Arabian colony extended over the southern provinces of Persia : the city has been sanctified by the tombs of the companions and martyrs ; and the vessels of Europe still frequent the port of Bassorah, as a convenient station and passage of the Indian trade.

After the defeat of Cadesia, a country intersected by rivers and canals might have opposed an insuperable barrier to the victorious cavalry ; and the walls of Ctesiphon or Madayn, which had resisted the battering-rams of the Romans, would not have yielded to the darts of the Saracens. But the flying Persians (A.D. 637. March) were overcome by the belief, that the last day of their religion and empire was at hand : the strongest posts were abandoned by treachery or cowardice ; and the king, with a part of his family and treasures, escaped to Holwan at the foot of the Median hills. In the third month after the battle, Said, the lieutenant of Omar, passed the Tigris without opposition ; the capital was taken by assault ; and the disorderly resistance of the people gave a keener edge to the sabres of the Moslems, who shouted with religious transport, " This is the white palace of Chosroes, this is the promise of the apostle of God !" The naked robbers of the desert were suddenly enriched beyond the measure of their hope or knowledge. Each chamber revealed a new treasure secreted with art, or ostentatiously displayed ; the gold and silver, the various wardrobes and precious furniture, surpassed (says Abulfeda) the estimate of fancy or numbers ; and another historian defines the untold and almost infinite mass, by the fabulous computation of three thousands of thousands of thousands of pieces of gold.   Some minute though curious facts represent the contrast of riches and ignorance.   From the remote islands of the Indian Ocean, a large provision of camphire had been imported, which is employed with a mixture of wax to illuminate the palaces of the East.   Strangers to the name and properties of that odoriferous gum, the Saracens, mistaking it for salt, mingled the camphire in their bread, and were astonished at the bitterness of the taste.   One of the apartments of the palace was decorated with a carpet of silk, sixty cubits in length, and as many in breadth : a paradise or garden was depictured on the ground ; the flowers, fruits, and shrubs were imitated by the figures of the gold embroidery, and the colours of the precious stones ; and the ample square was encircled by a variegated and verdant border.   The Arabian general persuaded his soldiers to relinquish their claim, in the reasonable hope that the eyes of the caliph would be delighted with the splendid workmanship of nature and industry.   Regardless of the merit of art and the pomp of royalty, the rigid Omar divided the prize among his brethren of Medina : the picture was destroyed, but such was the intrinsic value of the materials, that the share of Ali alone was sold for 20,000 drams. A mule that carried away the tiara and cuirass, the belt and bracelets of Chosroes, was overtaken by the pursuers ; the gorgeous trophy was presented to the commander of the faithful, and the gravest of the companions condescended to smile when they beheld the white beard, hairy arms, and uncouth figure of the veteran, who was invested with the spoils of the great king.   The sack of Ctesiphon was followed by its desertion and gradual decay.   The Saracens disliked the air and situation of the place, and Omar was advised by his general to remove the seat of government to the western side of the Euphrates.   In every age the foundation and ruin of the Assyrian cities has been easy and rapid ; the country is destitute of stone and timber, and the most solid structures are composed of bricks baked in the sun, and joined by a cement of the native bitumen.   The name of *Cufa* describes an habitation of reeds and earth ; but the importance of the new capital was supported by the numbers, wealth, and spirit of a colony of veterans ; and their licentiousness was indulged by the wisest caliphs, who were apprehensive of provoking the revolt of 100,000 swords : " Ye men of Cufa," said Ali, who solicited their aid, "you have been always conspicuous by your valour.   You conquered the Persian king, and scattered his forces, till you had taken possession of his inheritance." This mighty conquest was achieved by the battles of Jalula and Nehavend.   After the loss of the former, Yezdegerd fled from Holwan, and concealed his shame and despair in the mountains of Farsistan, from whence Cyrus had descended with his equal and valiant companions.   The courage of the nation survived that of the monarch ; among the hills to the south of Ecbatana or Hamadan, 150,000 Persians made a third and final stand for their religion and country ; and the decisive battle of Nehavend was styled by the Arabs the victory of victories. If it be true that the flying general of the Persians was stopt and overtaken in a crowd of mules and camels laden with honey, the incident, however slight or singular, will denote the luxurious impediments of an Oriental army.

The geography of Persia is darkly delineated by the Greeks and Latins ; but the most illustrious of her cities appear to be more ancient than the invasion of the Arabs. By the reduction (A.D. 637— 651) of Hamadan and Ispahan, of Caswin, Tauris, and Rei, they gradually approached the shores of the Caspian Sea ; and the orators of Mecca might applaud the success and spirit of the faithful, who had already lost sight of the northern bear, and had almost transcended the bounds of the habitable world. Again turning towards the West and the Roman empire, they repassed the Tigris over the bridge of Mosul, and, in the captive provinces of Armenia and Mesopotamia, embraced their victorious brethren of the Syrian army. From the palace of Madayn their Eastern progress was not less rapid or extensive. They advanced along the Tigris and the Gulf; penetrated through the passes of the mountains into the valley of Estachar or Persepolis ; and profaned the last sanctuary of the Magian empire. The grandson of Chosroes was nearly surprised among the falling columns and mutilated figures ; a sad emblem of the past and present fortune of Persia : he fled with accelerated haste over the desert of Kirman, implored the aid of the warlike Segastans, and sought an humble refuge on the verge of the Turkish and Chinese power. But a victorious army is insensible of fatigue : the Arabs divided their forces in the pursuit of a timorous enemy ; and the caliph Othman promised the government of Chorasan to the first general who should enter that large and populous country, the kingdom of the ancient Bactrians. The condition was accepted ; the prize was deserved ; the standard of Mahomet was planted on the walls of Herat, Merou, and Balch ; and the successful leader neither halted nor reposed till his foaming cavalry had tasted the waters of the Oxus. In the public anarchy, the independent governors of the cities and castles obtained their separate capitulations : the terms were granted or imposed by the esteem, the prudence, or the compassion, of the victors ; and a simple profession of faith established the distinction between a brother and a slave. After a noble defence, Harmozan, the prince or satrap of Ahwaz and Susa, was compelled to surrender his person and his state to the discretion of the caliph ; and their interview exhibits a portrait of the Arabian manners. In the presence, and by the command, of Omar, the gay Barbarian was despoiled of his silken robes embroidered with gold, and of his tiara bedecked with rubies and emeralds : "Are you now sensible," said the conqueror to his naked captive ; " are you now sensible of the judgment of God, and of the different rewards of infidelity and obedience ?" " Alas !" replied Harmozan, " I feel them too deeply. In the days of our common ignorance, we fought with the weapons of the flesh, and my nation was superior. God was then neuter : since he has espoused your quarrel, you have sub- verted our kingdom and religion." Oppressed with this painful dia- logue, the Persian complained of intolerable thirst, but discovered some apprehensions lest he should be killed whilst he was drinking a cup of water. "Be of good courage," said the caliph, "your life is safe till you have drank this water :" the crafty satrap accepted the assurance, and instantly dashed the vase against the ground. Omar would have avenged the deceit ; but his companions represented the sanctity of an oath : and the speedy conversion of Harmozan entitled him not only to a free pardon, but even to a stipend of 2000 pieces of gold. The administration of Persia was regulated by an actual survey of the people, the cattle, and the fruits of the earth ; and this monu- ment, which attests the vigilance of the caliphs, might have instructed the philosophers of every age.

The flight of Yezdegered had carried him (A.D. 651) beyond the Oxus, and as far as the Jaxartes, two rivers of ancient and modern renown, which descend from the mountains of India towards the Cas- pian Sea. He was hospitably entertained by Tarkhan, prince of Fargana, a fertile province on the Jaxartes ; the king of Samarcand, with the Turkish tribes of Sogdiana and Scythia, were moved by the lamentation and promises of the fallen monarch ; and he solicited by a suppliant embassy, the more solid and powerful friendship of the emperor of China. The virtuous Taitsong, the first of the dynasty of the Tang, may be justly compared with the Antonines of Rome : his people enjoyed the blessings of prosperity and peace ; and his do- minion was acknowledged by forty-four hordes of the Barbarians of Tartary. His last garrisons of Cashgar and Khoten maintained a frequent intercourse with their neighbours of the Jaxartes and Oxus ; a recent colony of Persians had introduced into China the astronomy of the Magi ; and Taitsong might be alarmed by the rapid progress and dangerous vicinity of the Arabs. The influence, and perhaps the supplies, of China, revived the hopes of Yezdegard and the zeal of the worshippers of fire ; and he returned with an army of Turks to con- quer the inheritance of his fathers. The fortunate Moslems, without unsheathing their swords, were the spectators of his ruin and death. The grandson of Chosroes was betrayed by his servant, insulted by the seditious inhabitants of Merou, and oppressed, defeated, and pur- sued, by his Barbarian allies. He reached the banks of a river, and offered his rings and bracelets for an instant passage in a miller's boat. Ignorant or insensible of royal distress, the rustic replied, that four drams of silver were the daily profit of his mill, and that he would not suspend his work unless the loss were repaid. In this moment of hesitation and delay, the last of the Sassanian kings was overtaken and slaughtered by the Turkish cavalry, in the nineteenth year of his

unhappy reign. His son Firuz, an humble client of the Chinese emperor, accepted the station of captain of his guards ; and the Magian
worship was long preserved by a colony of loyal exiles in the province of Bucharia. His grandson inherited the regal name ; but after
a faint and fruitless enterprise, he returned to China, and ended his
days in the palace of Sigan. The male line of the Sassanides was extinct ; but the female captives, the daughters of Persia, were given to
the conquerors in servitude, or marriage ; and the race of the caliphs
and imaums was ennobled by the blood of their royal mothers.

After the fall of the Persian kingdom, the river Oxus divided the
territories of the Saracens and of the Turks. This narrow boundary
was soon (A.D. 710) overleaped by the spirit of the Arabs : the governors of Chorasan extended their successive inroads, and one of their
triumphs was adorned with the buskin of a Turkish queen, which she
dropt in her precipitate flight beyond the hills of Bochara. But the
final conquest of Transoxiana, as well as of Spain, was reserved for
the glorious reign of the inactive Walid ; and the name of Catibah,
the camel-driver, declares the origin and merit of his successful lieutenant. While one of his colleagues displayed the first Mahometan
banner on the banks of the Indus, the spacious regions between the
Oxus, the Jaxartes, and the Caspian Sea, were reduced by the arms of
Catibah to the obedience of the prophet and of the caliph. A tribute
of two millions of pieces of gold was imposed on the infidels : their
idols were burnt or broken ; the Mussulman chief pronounced a sermon in the new mosque of Carizme ; after several battles the Turkish
hordes were driven back to the desert ; and the emperors of China
solicited the friendship of the victorious Arabs. To their industry,
the prosperity of the province, the Sogdiana of the Ancients, may in a
great measure be ascribed ; but the advantages of the soil and climate had been understood and cultivated since the reign of the Macedonian kings. Before the invasion of the Saracens, Carizme, Bochara,
and Samarcand, were rich and populous under the yoke of the shepherds of the north. These cities were surrounded with a double wall :
and the exterior fortification, of a larger circumference, inclosed the
fields and gardens of the adjacent district. The mutual wants of
India and Europe were supplied by the diligence of the Sogdian
merchants ; and the inestimable art of transforming linen into paper,
has been diffused from Samarcand over the western world.

II. No sooner had Abubeker restored (A.D. 632) the unity of faith
and government, than he dispatched a circular letter to the Arabian
tribes. " In the name of the most merciful God, to the rest of the true
believers. Health and happiness, and the mercy and blessing of
God be upon you. I praise the most high God, and I pray for his
prophet Mahomet. This is to acquaint you, that I intend to send
the true believers into Syria to take it out of the hands of the infidels. And I would have you know, that the fighting for religion is

5

an act of obedience to God." His messengers returned with the tidings of pious and martial ardour which they had kindled in every province; and the camp of Medina was successively filled with the intrepid bands of the Saracens who panted for action, complained of the heat of the season and the scarcity of provisions, and accused with impatient murmurs the delays of the caliph. As soon as their numbers were complete, Abubeker ascended the hill, reviewed the men, the horses, and the arms, and poured forth a fervent prayer for the success of their undertaking. In person and on foot, he accompánied the first day's march; and when the blushing leaders attempted to dismount, the caliph removed their scruples by a declaration, that those who rode and those who walked, in the service of religion, were equally meritorious. His instructions to the chiefs of the Syrian army, were inspired by the warlike fanaticism which advances to seize, and affects to despise, the objects of earthly ambition. " Remember," said the successor of the prophet, " that you are always in the presence of God, on the verge of death, in the assurance of judgment, and the hope of paradise. Avoid injustice and oppression; consult with your brethren, and study to preserve the love and confidence of your troops. When you fight the battles of the Lord, acquit yourselves like men, without turning your backs; but let not your victory be stained with the blood of women or children. Destroy no palm-trees, nor burn any fields of corn. Cut down no fruit-trees, nor do any mischief to cattle, only such as you kill to eat. When you make any covenant or article, stand to it, and be as good as your word. As you go on, you will find some religious persons who live retired in monasteries, and propose to themselves to serve God that way : let them alone, and neither kill them nor destroy their monasteries : And you will find another sort of people that belong to the synagogue of Satan, who have shaven crowns; be sure you cleave their skulls, and give them no quarter till they either turn Mahometans or pay tribute." All profane or frivolous conversation, all dangerous recollection of ancient quarrels, was severely prohibited among the Arabs : in the tumult of a camp, the exercises of religion were assiduously practised; and the intervals of action were employed in prayer, meditation, and the study of the Koran. The abuse, or even the use, of wine was chastised by fourscore strokes on the soles of the feet, and in the fervour of their primitive zeal many secret sinners revealed their fault, and solicited their punishment. After some hesitation the command of the Syrian army was delegated to Abu Obeidah, one of the fugitives of Mecca and companions of Mahomet; whose zeal and devotion were assuaged, without being abated, by the singular mildness and benevolence of his temper. But in all the emergencies of war, the soldiers demanded the superior genius of Caled; and whoever might be the choice of the prince, *the sword of God* was both in fact and fame the foremost leader of the Saracens.

He obeyed without reluctance ; he was consulted without jealousy ; and such was the spirit of the man, or rather of the times, that Caled professed his readiness to serve under the banner of the faith, though it were in the hands of a child or an enemy. Glory, and riches, and dominion, were indeed promised to the victorious Mussulman ; but he was carefully instructed, that if the goods of this life were his only incitement, *they* likewise would be his only reward.

One of the fifteen provinces of Syria, the cultivated lands to the eastward of the Jordan, had been decorated by Roman vanity with the name of *Arabia;* and the first arms of the Saracens were justified by the semblance of a national right. The country was enriched by the various benefits of trade ; by the vigilance of the emperors it was covered with a line of forts : and the populous cities of Gerasa, Philadelphia, and Bosra, were secure, at least from a surprise, by the solid structure of their walls. The last of these cities was the eighteenth station from Medina : the road was familiar to the caravans of Hejaz and Irak, who annually visited this plenteous market of the province and the desert : the perpetual jealousy of the Arabs had trained the inhabitants to arms ; and 12,000 horse could sally from the gates of Bosra, an appellation which signifies, in the Syriac language, a strong tower of defence. Encouraged by their first success against the open towns and flying parties of the borders, a detachment of 4000 Moslems presumed to summon and attack the fortress of Bosra. They were oppressed by the numbers of the Syrians ; they were saved by the presence of Caled, with 1500 horse ; he blamed the enterprise, restored the battle, and rescued his friend, the venerable Serjabil, who had vainly invoked the unity of God and the promises of the apostle. After a short pause, the Moslems performed their ablutions with sand instead of water ; and the morning prayer was recited by Caled before they mounted on horseback. Confident in their strength, the people of Bosra threw open their gates, drew their forces into the plain, and swore to die in the defence of their religion. But a religion of peace was incapable of withstanding the fanatic cry of "Fight, fight ! Paradise, paradise !" that re-echoed in the ranks of the Saracens ; and the uproar of the town, the ringing of bells, and the exclamations of the priests and monks, increased the dismay and disorder of the Christians. With the loss of two hundred and thirty men, the Arabs remained masters of the field ; and the ramparts of Bosra, in expectation of human or divine aid, were crowded with holy crosses and consecrated banners. The governor Romanus had recommended an early submission : despised by the people, and degraded from his office, he still retained the desire and opportunity of revenge. In a nocturnal interview, he informed the enemy of a subterraneous passage from his house under the wall of the city : the son of the caliph, with an hundred volunteers, were committed to the faith of this new ally, and their successful intrepidity gave an easy entrance to their companions. After Caled had imposed the terms of servitude and tribute, the apostate or convert avowed in the assembly of the people his meritorious treason. " I renounce your society," said Romanus, " both in this world, and the world to come. And I deny him that was crucified, and whosoever worships him. And I chuse God for my Lord, Islam for my faith, Mecca for my temple, the Moslems for my brethren, and Mahomet for my prophet ; who was sent to lead us in the right way, and to exalt the true religion in spite of those who join partners with God."

The conquest of Bosra, four days' journey from Damascus, encouraged the Arabs to besiege (A.D. 633) the ancient capital of Syria. At some distance from the walls, they encamped among the groves and fountains of that delicious territory, and the usual option of the Mahometan faith, of tribute, or of war, was proposed to the resolute citizens, who had been lately strengthened by a reinforcement of 5000 Greeks. In the decline as in the infancy of military art, an hostile defiance was frequently offered and accepted by the generals themselves : many a lance was shivered in the plain of Damascus, and the personal prowess of Caled was signalized in the first sally of the besieged. After an obstinate combat, he had overthrown and made prisoner one of the Christian leaders, a stout and worthy antagonist. He instantly mounted a fresh horse, the gift of the governor of Palmyra, and pushed forwards to the front of the battle. " Repose yourself for a moment," said his friend Derar, "and permit me to supply your place : you are fatigued with fighting with this dog." " O Derar !" replied the indefatigable Saracen, "we shall rest in the world to come. He that labours to-day, shall rest to-morrow." With the same unabated ardour, Caled answered, encountered and vanquished a second champion ; and the heads of his two captives who refused to abandon their religion were indignantly hurled into the midst of the city. The event of some general and partial actions reduced the Damascenes to a closer defence : but a messenger whom they dropt from the walls, returned with the promise of speedy and powerful succour, and their tumultuous joy conveyed the intelligence to the camp of the Arabs. After some debate it was resolved by the generals to raise or rather to suspend the siege of Damascus, till they had given battle to the forces of the emperor. In the retreat, Caled would have chosen the more perilous station of the rear-guard ; he modestly yielded to the wishes of Abu Obeidah. But in the hour of danger he flew to the rescue of his companion, who was rudely pressed by a sally of 6000 horse and 10,000 foot, and few among the Christians could relate at Damascus the circumstances of their defeat. The importance of the contest required the junction of the Saracens who were dispersed on the frontiers of Syria and Palestine ; and I shall transcribe one of the circular mandates which was addressed to Amrou the future conqueror of Egypt. " In the name of the most merciful God : from Caled to Amrou, health and happiness. Know that thy brethren the Moslems design to march to Aiznadin, where there is an army of 70,000 Greeks, who purpose to come against us, *that they may extinguish the light of God with their mouths; but God preserveth his light in spite of the infidels.* As soon therefore as this letter of mine shall be delivered to thy hands, come with those that are with thee to Aiznadin, where thou shalt find us if it please the most high God." The summons was cheerfully obeyed, and the 45,000 Moslems who met on the same day, on the same spot, ascribed to the blessing of providence the effects of their zeal.

About four years after the triumphs of the Persian war, the repose of Heraclius and the empire was again disturbed by a new enemy, the power of whose religion was more strongly felt than it was clearly understood by the Christians of the East. In his palace of Constantinople or Antioch, he was awakened by the invasion of Syria, the loss of Bosra, and the danger of Damascus. An army of 70,000 veterans, or new levies, was assembled at Hems or Emesa, under the command of his general Werdan ; and these troops, consisting chiefly of cavalry, might be indifferently styled either Syrians, or Greeks, or Romans : *Syrians*, from the place of their birth or warfare ; *Greeks*, from the religion and language of their sovereign ; and *Romans*, from the proud appellation which was still profaned by the successors of Constantine. On the plain of Aiznadin, as Werdan rode on a white mule decorated with gold chains, and surrounded with ensigns and standards, he was surprised by the near approach of a fierce and naked warrior, who had undertaken to view the state of the enemy. The adventurous valour of Derar was inspired, and has perhaps been adorned, by the enthusiasm of his age and country. The hatred of the Christians, the love of spoil, and the contempt of danger were the ruling passions of the audacious Saracen ; and the prospect of instant death could never shake his religious confidence, or ruffle the calmness of his resolution, or even suspend the frank and martial pleasantry of his humour. In the most hopeless enterprises, he was bold, and prudent, and fortunate : after innumerable hazards, after being thrice a prisoner in the hands of the infidels, he still survived to relate the achievements, and to enjoy the rewards, of the Syrian conquest. On this occasion, his single lance maintained a flying fight against thirty Romans, who were detached by Werdan ; and after killing or unhorsing seventeen of their number, Derar returned in safety to his applauding brethren. When his rashness was mildly censured by the general, he excused himself with the simplicity of a soldier. " Nay," said Derar, " I did not begin first : but they came out to take me, and I was afraid that God should see me turn my back : and indeed I fought in good earnest, and without doubt God assisted me against them ; and had I not been apprehensive of disobeying your orders, I should not have come away as I did ; and I perceive already that they will fall into our hands." In the presence of both armies, a venerable Greek advanced from the ranks with a liberal offer of peace ; and the departure of the Saracens would have been purchased by a gift to each soldier, of a turban, a robe, and a piece of gold ; ten robes and an hundred pieces to their leader ; one hundred robes and a thousand pieces to the caliph. A smile of indignation expressed the refusal of Caled. " Ye Christian dogs, you know your option ; the Koran, the tribute, or the sword. We are a people whose delight is in war, rather than in peace ; and we despise your pitiful alms, since we shall be speedily masters of your wealth, your families, and your persons." Notwithstanding this apparent disdain, he was deeply conscious of the public danger : those who had been in Persia, and had seen the armies of Chosroes, confessed that they never beheld a more formidable array. From the superiority of the enemy, the artful Saracen derived a fresh incentive of courage : " You see before you," said he, " the united force of the Romans, you cannot hope to escape, but you may conquer Syria in a single day. The event depends on your discipline and patience. Reserve yourselves (A.D. 633. July 13) till the evening. It was in the evening that the prophet was accustomed to vanquish." During two successive engagements, his temperate firmness sustained the darts of the enemy and the murmurs of his troops. At length, when the spirits and quivers of the adverse line were almost exhausted, Caled gave the signal of onset and victory. The remains of the Imperial army fled to Antioch, or Cæsarea, or Damascus ; and the death of 470 Moslems was compensated by the opinion that they had sent to hell above 50,000 of the infidels. The spoil was inestimable ; many banners and crosses of gold and silver, precious stones, silver and gold chains, and innumerable suits of the richest armour and apparel. The general distribution was postponed till Damascus should be taken ; but the seasonable supply of arms became the instrument of new victories. The glorious intelligence was transmitted to the throne of the caliph, and the Arabian tribes, the coldest or most hostile to the prophet's mission, were eager to share the harvest of Syria.

The sad tidings were carried to Damascus by the speed of grief and terror ; and the inhabitants beheld from their walls the return of the heroes of Aiznadin. Amrou led the van at the head of 9000 horse : the bands of the Saracens succeeded each other in formidable review ; and the rear was closed by Caled in person, with the standard of the black eagle. To the activity of Derar he entrusted the commission of patrolling round the city with 2000 horse, of scouring the plain, and of intercepting all succour or intelligence. The rest of the Arabian chiefs were fixed in their respective stations before the seven gates of Damascus ; and the siege was renewed with fresh vigour and confidence. The art, the labour, the military engines, of the Greeks and Romans are seldom to be found in the simple, though successful, operations of the Saracens : it was sufficient for them to invest the city with arms,

rather than with trenches; to repel the sallies of the besieged ; - to attempt a stratagem or an assault ; or to expect the progress of famine
and discontent. Damascus would have acquiesced in the trial of Aiznadin, as a final and peremptory sentence between the emperor and
the caliph : her courage was rekindled by the example and authority
of Thomas, a noble Greek, illustrious in a private condition by the
alliance of Heraclius. The tumult and illumination of the night proclaimed the design of the morning sally ; and the Christian hero, who
affected to despise the enthusiasm of the Arabs, employed the resource
of a similar superstition. At the principal gate, in the sight of both
armies, a lofty crucifix was erected; the bishop, with his clergy,
accompanied the march, and laid the volume of the New Testament
before the image of Jesus; and the contending parties were scandalized
or edified by a prayer, that the Son of God would defend his servants and
vindicate his truth. The battle raged with incessant fury ; and the dexterity of Thomas, an incomparable archer, was fatal to the boldest Saracens, till their death was revenged by a female heroine. The wife of Aban,
who had followed him to the holy war, embraced her expiring husband.
" Happy," said she, " happy art thou, my dear ; thou art gone to thy
Lord who first joined us together, and then parted us asunder. I
will revenge thy death, and endeavour to the utmost of my power to
come to the place where thou art, because I love thee. Henceforth
shall no man ever touch me more, for I have dedicated myself to the
service of God." Without a groan, without a tear, she washed the
corpse of her husband, and buried him with the usual rites. Then grasping the manly weapons, which in her native land she was accustomed
to wield, the intrepid widow of Aban sought the place where his murderer fought in the thickest of the battle. Her first arrow pierced the
hand of his standard-bearer ; her second wounded Thomas in the eye ;
and the fainting Christians no longer beheld their ensign or their
leader. Yet the generous champion of Damascus refused to withdraw
to his palace : his wound was dressed on the rampart ; the fight was
continued to the evening ; and the Syrians rested on their arms. In
the silence of the night, the signal was given by a stroke on the great
bell ; the gates were thrown open, and each gate discharged an im-
petuous column on the sleeping camp of the Saracens. Caled was the
first in arms ; at the head of 400 horse he flew to the post of danger
and the tears trickled down his iron cheeks, as he uttered a fervent
ejaculation ; " O God, who never sleepest, look upon thy servants, and
do not deliver them into the hands of their enemies." The valour
and victory of Thomas were arrested by the presence of the *sword of
God;* with the knowledge of the peril, the Moslems recovered their
ranks, and charged their assailants in the flank and rear. After the loss
of thousands, the Christian general retreated with a sigh of despair,
and the pursuit of the Saracens was checked by the military engines of
the rampart.

After a siege of seventy days (A.D. 634), the patience, and perhaps the provisions, of the Damascenes were exhausted ; and the bravest of their chiefs submitted to the hard dictates of necessity. In the occurrences of peace and war, they had been taught to dread the fierceness of Caled, and to revere the mild virtues of Abu Obeidah. At the hour of midnight, one hundred chosen deputies of the clergy and people were introduced to the tent of that venerable commander. He received and dismissed them with courtesy. They returned with a written agreement, on the faith of a companion of Mahomet, that all hostilities should cease ; that the voluntary emigrants might depart in safety with as much as they could carry away of their effects ; and that the tributary subjects of the caliph should enjoy their lands and houses, with the use and possession of seven churches. On these terms, the most respectable hostages, and the gate nearest to his camp, were delivered into his hands : his soldiers imitated the moderation of their chief ; and he enjoyed the submissive gratitude of a people whom he had rescued from destruction. But the success of the treaty had relaxed their vigilance, and in the same moment the opposite quarter of the city was betrayed and taken by assault. A party of an hundred Arabs had opened the eastern gate to a more inexorable foe. " No quarter," cried the rapacious and sanguinary Caled, " no quarter to the enemies of the Lord :" his trumpets sounded, and a torrent of Christian blood was poured down the streets of Damascus. When he reached the church of St. Mary, he was astonished and provoked by the peaceful aspect of his companions : their swords were in the scabbard, and they were surrounded by a multitude of priests and monks. Abu Obeidah saluted the general : " God," said he, " has delivered the city into my hands by way of surrender, and has saved the believers the trouble of fighting." " And am *I* not," replied the indignant Caled, " am *I* not the lieutenant of the commander of the faithful ? Have I not taken the city by storm ? The unbelievers shall perish by the sword. Fall on." The hungry and cruel Arabs would have obeyed the welcome command : and Damascus was lost, if the benevolence of Abu Obeidah had not been supported by a decent and dignified firmness. Throwing himself between the trembling citizens and the most eager of the Barbarians, he adjured them by the holy name of God, to respect his promise, to suspend their fury, and to wait the determination of their chiefs. The chiefs retired into the church of St. Mary ; and after a vehement debate, Caled submitted in some measure to the reason and authority of his colleague ; who urged the sanctity of a covenant, the advantage as well as the honour which the Moslems would derive from the punctual performance of their word, and the obstinate resistance which they must encounter from the distrust and despair of the rest of the Syrian cities. It was agreed that the sword should be sheathed, that the part of Damascus which had surrendered to Abu Obeidah, should be immediately entitled to the

benefit of his capitulation, and that the final decision should be referred
to the justice and wisdom of the caliph.*   A large majority of the people
accepted the terms of toleration and tribute ; and Damascus is still
peopled by 20,000 Christians.   But the valiant Thomas, and the free-
born patriots who had fought under his banner, embraced the alternative of poverty and exile.   In the adjacent meadow, a numerous
encampment was formed of priests and laymen, of soldiers and citizens,
of women and children : they collected, with haste and terror, their
most precious movables ; and abandoned, with loud lamentations or
silent anguish, their native homes, and the pleasant banks of the Phar-
phar.   The inflexible soul of Caled was not touched by the spectacle
of their distress : he disputed with the Damascenes the property of a
magazine of corn ; endeavoured to exclude the garrison from the benefit
of the treaty ; consented, with reluctance, that each of the fugitives
should arm himself with a sword, or a lance, or a bow ; and sternly
declared, that, after a respite of three days, they might be pursued and
treated as the enemies of the Moslems.

  The passion of a Syrian youth completed the ruin of the exiles of
Damascus.   A nobleman of the city, of the name of Jonas, was be-
trothed to a wealthy maiden ; but her parents delayed the nuptials,
and their daughter was persuaded to escape with the man whom she
had chosen.   They corrupted the nightly watchmen of the gate Keisan : the lover, who led the way, was encompassed by a squadron of
Arabs : but his exclamation in the Greek tongue, " the bird is taken,"
admonished his mistress to hasten her return.   In the presence of
Caled, and of death, the unfortunate Jonas professed his belief in one
God, and his apostle Mahomet ; and continued, till the season of his
martyrdom, to discharge the duties of a brave and sincere Mussulman.
When the city was taken, he flew to the monastery where Eudocia
had taken refuge ; but the lover was forgotten ; the apostate was
scorned ; she preferred her religion to her country : and the justice of
Caled, though deaf to mercy, refused to detain by force a male or female
inhabitant of Damascus.   Four days was the general confined to the
city by the obligation of the treaty, and the urgent cares of his new
conquest.   His appetite for blood and rapine would have been extinguished by the hopeless computation of time and distance : but he
listened to the importunities of Jonas, who assured him that the weary
fugitives might yet be overtaken.   At the head of 4000 horse, in the
disguise of Christian Arabs, Caled undertook the pursuit.   They halted
only for the moments of prayer ; and their guide had a perfect knowledge of the country.   For a long way the footsteps of the Damascenes
were plain and conspicuous : they vanished on a sudden ; but the Saracens were comforted by the assurance that the caravan had turned

* It appears from Abulfeda (p. 125) and Elmacin (p. 32), that this distinction of the two
parts of Damascus was long remembered, though not always respected, by the Mahometan
sovereigns. Eutych. (Annal. ii. 379, 383.)

aside into the mountains, and must speedily fall into their hands. In traversing the ridges of the Libanus, they endured intolerable hardships, and the sinking spirits of the veteran fanatics were supported and cheered by the unconquerable ardour of a lover. From a peasant of the country, they were informed that the emperor had sent orders to the colony of exiles, to pursue without delay the road of the sea-coast, and of Constantinople ; apprehensive, perhaps, that the soldiers and people of Antioch might be discouraged by the sight and the story of their sufferings. The Saracens were conducted through the territories of Gabala and Laodicea, at a cautious distance from the walls of the cities ; the rain was incessant, the night was dark, a single mountain separated them from the Roman army ; and Caled, ever anxious for the safety of his brethren, whispered an ominous dream in the ear of his companion. With the dawn of day, the prospect again cleared, and they saw before them, in a pleasant valley, the tents of Damascus. After a short interval of repose and prayer, Caled divided his cavalry into four squadrons, committing the first to his faithful Derar, and reserving the last for himself. They successively rushed on the pro- miscuous multitude, insufficiently provided with arms, and already vanquished by sorrow and fatigue. Except a captive who was pardoned and dismissed, the Arabs enjoyed the satisfaction of believing that not a Christian of either sex escaped the edge of their scymetars. The gold and silver of Damascus was scattered over the camp, and a royal wardrobe of 300 load of silk might clothe an army of naked Barbarians. In the tumult of the battle, Jonas sought and found the object of his pursuit ; but her resentment was inflamed by the last act of his perfidy ; and as Eudocia struggled in his hateful embraces, she struck a dagger to her heart. Another female, the widow of Thomas, and the real or supposed daughter of Heraclius, was spared and released without a ransom ; but the generosity of Caled was the effect of his contempt ; and the haughty Saracen insulted, by a message of defiance, the throne of the Cæsars. Caled had penetrated above 150 miles into the heart of the Roman province : he returned to Damascus with the same secrecy and speed. On the accession of Omar, the *sword of God* was removed from the command : but the caliph, who blamed the rashness, was compelled to applaud the vigour and conduct of the enterprise.

Another expedition of the conquerors of Damascus will equally dis- play their avidity and their contempt for the riches of the present world. They were informed that the produce and manufactures of the country were annually collected in the fair of Abyla, about 30 miles from the city ; that the cell of a devout hermit was visited at the same time by a multitude of pilgrims ; and that the festival of trade and superstition would be ennobled by the nuptials of the daughter of the governor of Tripoli. Abdallah, the son of Jaafa, a glorious and holy martyr, undertook, with a banner of 500 horse, the pious and profitable commission of despoiling the infidels. As he approached the fair of

Abyla, he was astonished by the report of the mighty concourse of Jews and Christians, Greeks and Armenians, of natives of Syria and of strangers of Egypt, to the number of 10,000, besides a guard of 5000 horse that attended the person of the bride. The Saracens paused : " For my own part," said Abdallah, " I *dare not* go back : our foes are many, our danger is great, but our reward is splendid and secure, either in this life or in the life to come. Let every man, according to his inclination, advance or retire." Not a Mussulman deserted his standard. " Lead the way," said Abdallah to his Christian guide, " and you shall see what the companions of the prophet can perform." They charged in five squadrons : but after the first advantage of the surprise they were encompassed and almost overwhelmed by the multitude of their enemies ; and their valiant band is fancifully compared to a white spot in the skin of a black camel. About the hour of sunset, when their weapons dropped from their hands, when they panted on the verge of eternity, they discovered an approaching cloud of dust, they heard the welcome sound of the *tecbir*,* and they soon perceived the standard of Caled, who flew to their relief with the utmost speed of his cavalry. The Christians were broken by his attack, and slaughtered in their flight as far as the river of Tripoli. They left behind them the various riches of the fair : the merchandises that were exposed for sale, the money that was brought for purchase, the gay decorations of the nuptials, and the governor's daughter, with forty of her female attendants. The fruits, provisions, and furniture, the money, plate, and jewels, were diligently laden on the backs of horses, asses, and mules ; and the holy robbers returned in triumph to Damascus. The hermit, after a short and angry controversy with Caled, declined the crown of martyrdom, and was left alive in the solitary scene of blood and devastation.

Syria, one of the countries that have been improved by the most early cultivation, is not unworthy of the preference. The heat of the climate is tempered by the vicinity of the sea and mountains, by the plenty of wood and water ; and the produce of a fertile soil affords the subsistence, and encourages the propagation, of men and animals. From the age of David to that of Heraclius, the country was overspread with ancient and flourishing cities : the inhabitants were numerous and wealthy ; and, after the slow ravage of despotism and superstition, after the recent calamities of the Persian war, Syria could still attract and reward the rapacious tribes of the desert. A plain, of ten days' journey, from Damascus to Aleppo and Antioch, is watered, on the western side, by the winding course of the Orontes. The hills of Libanus and Anti-Libanus are planted from north to south, between the Orontes and the Mediterranean, and the epithet of *hollow* (Cœlesyria) was applied to a long and fruitful valley, which is confined in

---

* This word, so formidable in their holy wars, signifies saying *Alla Acbar*, God is most mighty !

the same direction by the two ridges of snowy mountains. Among the cities, which are enumerated by Greek and Oriental names in the geography and conquest of Syria, we may distinguish Emesa or Hems, Heliopolis or Baalbec, the former as the metropolis of the plain, the latter as the capital of the valley. Under the last of the Cæsars, they were strong and populous : the turrets glittered from afar : an ample space was covered with public and private buildings ; and the citizens were illustrious by their spirit, or at least by their pride ; by their riches, or at least by their luxury. In the days of paganism, both Emesa and Heliopolis were addicted to the worship of Baal, or the sun ; but the decline of their superstition and splendour has been marked by a singular variety of fortune. Not a vestige remains of the temple of Emesa, which was equalled in poetic style to the summits of mount Libanus, while the ruins of Baalbec, invisible to the writers of antiquity, excite the curiosity and wonder of the European traveller. The measure of the temple is 200 feet in length, and 100 in breadth : the front is adorned with a double portico of eight columns ; fourteen may be counted on either side ; and each column, 45 feet in height, is composed of three massy blocks of stone or marble. The proportions and ornaments of the Corinthian order express the architecture of the Greeks ; but as Baalbec has never been the seat of a monarch, we are at a loss to conceive how the expence of these magnificent structures could be supplied by private or municipal liberality. From the conquest of Damascus the Saracens proceeded (A.D. 635) to Heliopolis and Emesa : but I shall decline the repetition of the sallies and combats which have been already shown on a larger scale. In the prosecution of the war, their policy was not less effectual than their sword. By short and separate truces they dissolved the union of the enemy ; accustomed the Syrians to compare their friendship with their enmity ; familiarized the idea of their language, religion, and manners ; and exhausted, by clandestine purchase, the magazines and arsenals of the cities which they returned to besiege. They aggravated the ransom of the more wealthy, or the more obstinate ; and Chalcis alone was taxed at 5000 ounces of gold, 5000 ounces of silver, 2000 robes of silk, and as many figs and olives as would load 5000 asses. But the terms of truce or capitulation were faithfully observed ; and the lieutenant of the caliph, who had promised not to enter the walls of the captive Baalbec, remained tranquil and immovable in his tent till the jarring faction solicited the interposition of a foreign master. The conquest of the plain and valley of Syria was achieved in less than two years. Yet the commander of the faithful reproved the slowness of their progress, and the Saracens, bewailing their fault with tears of rage and repentance, called aloud on their chiefs to lead them forth to fight the battles of the Lord. In a recent action, under the walls of Emesa, an Arabian youth, the cousin of Caled, was heard aloud to exclaim, " Methinks I see the black-eyed girls looking upon me ; one of whom, should she appear in this world, all mankind would die for love of her. And I see in the hand of one of them, an handkerchief of green silk, and a cap of precious stones, and she beckons me, and calls out, come hither quickly, for I love thee." With these words, charging the Christians, he made havoc wherever he went, till, observed at length by the governor of Hems, he was struck through with a javelin.

It was incumbent on the Saracens to exert the full powers of their valour and enthusiasm against the forces of the emperor, who was taught by repeated losses, that the rovers of the desert had undertaken, and would speedily achieve, a regular and permanent conquest. From the provinces of Europe and Asia, 80,000 soldiers were transported by sea. and land to Antioch and Cæsarea : the light troops of the army consisted of 60,000 Christian Arabs of the tribe of Gassan. Under the banner of Jabalah, the last of their princes, they marched in the van ; and it was a maxim of the Greeks, that, for the purpose of cutting diamond, a diamond was the most effectual. Heraclius withheld his person from the dangers of the field ; but his presumption, or perhaps his despondency, suggested a peremptory order, that the fate of the province and the war should be decided by a single battle. The Syrians were attached to the standard of Rome and of the cross ; but the noble, the citizen, the peasant, were exasperated by the injustice and cruelty of a licentious host, who oppressed them as subjects, and despised them as strangers and aliens. A report of these mighty preparations was conveyed to the Saracens in their camp of Emesa ; and the chiefs, though resolved to fight, assembled a council : the faith of Abu Obeidah would have expected on the same spot the glory of martyrdom ; the wisdom of Caled advised an honourable retreat to the skirts of Palestine and Arabia, where they might await the succours of their friends, and the attack of the unbelievers. A speedy messenger soon returned from the throne of Medina, with the blessings of Omar and Ali, the prayers of the widows of the prophet, and a reinforcement of 8000 Moslems. In their way they overturned a detachment of Greeks, and when they joined at Yermuk the camp of their brethren, they found the pleasing intelligence, that Caled had already defeated and scattered the Christian Arabs of the tribe of Gassan. In the neighbourhood of Bosra, the springs of mount Hermon descend in a torrent to the plain of Decapolis, or ten cities ; and the Hieromax, a name which has been corrupted to Bermuk, is lost after a short course in the lake of Tiberias. The banks of this obscure stream were illustrated by a long and bloody encounter. On this momentous occasion, the public voice, and the modesty of Abu Obeidah, restored (A.D. 636. Nov.) the command to the most deserving of the Moslems. Caled assumed his station in the front, his colleague was posted in the rear, that the disorder of the fugitives might be checked by his venerable aspect and the sight of the yellow banner which Mahomet had displayed before the walls of Chaibar. The last line was occupied by the sister of Derar, with the Arabian women who had enlisted in this holy war, who were accustomed to wield the bow and the lance, and who in a moment of captivity had defended their chastity and religion. The exhortation of the generals was brief and forcible : " Paradise is before you, the devil and hell-fire in your rear." Yet such was the weight of the Roman cavalry, that the right wing of the Arabs was broken and separated from the main body. Thrice did they retreat in disorder, and thrice were they driven back to the charge by the reproaches and blows of the women. In the intervals of action, Abu Obeidah visited the tents of his brethren, prolonged their repose, by repeating at once the prayers of two different hours ; bound up their wounds with his own hands, and administered the comfortable reflection, that the infidels partook of their sufferings without partaking of their reward. Four thousand and thirty of the Moslems were buried in the field of battle ; and the skill of the Armenian archers enabled 700 to boast that they had lost an eye in that meritorious service. The veterans of the Syrian war acknowledged that it was the hardest and most doubtful of the days which they had seen. But it was likewise the most decisive : many thousands of the Greeks and Syrians fell by the swords of the Arabs ; many were slaughtered, after the defeat, in the woods and mountains ; many, by mistaking the ford, were drowned in the waters of the Yermuk ; and however the loss may be magnified, the Christian writers confess and bewail the bloody punishment of their sins. Manuel, the Roman general, was either killed at Damascus, or took refuge in the monastery of mount Sinai. An exile in the Byzantine court, Jabalah lamented the manners of Arabia, and his unlucky preference of the Christian cause. He had once inclined to the profession of Islam ; but in the pilgrimage of Mecca, Jabalah was provoked to strike one of his brethren, and fled with amazement from the stern and equal justice of the caliph. The victorious Saracens enjoyed at Damascus a month of pleasure and repose : the spoil was divided by Abu Obeidah : an equal share was allotted to a soldier and to his horse, and a double portion was reserved for the noble coursers of the Arabian breed.

After the battle of Yermuk, the Roman army no longer appeared in the field ; and the Saracens might securely choose among the fortified towns of Syria the first object of their attack. They consulted the caliph whether they should march to Cæsarea or Jerusalem ; and the advice of Ali determined the immediate siege of the latter. To a profane eye, Jerusalem was the first or second capital of Palestine ; but after Mecca and Medina, it was revered and visited by the devout Moslems, as the temple of the Holy Land which had been sanctified by the revelation of Moses, of Jesus, and of Mahomet himself. The son of Abu Sophian was sent with 5000 Arabs to try the first experiment of surprise or treaty : but (A.D. 637) on the eleventh day, the town was invested by the whole force of Abu Obeidah. He addressed the

customary summons to the chief commanders and people of *Ælia.*
" Health and happiness to every one that follows the right way ! We
require of you to testify that there is but one God, and that Mahomet
is his apostle. If you refuse this, consent to pay tribute, and be
under us forthwith. Otherwise I shall bring men against you who
love death better than you do the drinking of wine or eating hog's
flesh. Nor will I ever stir from you, if it please God, till I
have destroyed those that fight for you, and made slaves of your children." But the city was defended on every side by deep valleys and
steep ascents ; since the invasion of Syria, the walls and towers had
been anxiously restored ; the bravest of the fugitives of Yermuk had
stopped in the nearest place of refuge ; and in the defence of the
sepulchre of Christ, the natives and strangers might feel some sparks
of the enthusiasm which so fiercely glowed in the bosoms of the Saracens. The siege of Jerusalem lasted four months ; not a day was
lost without some action of sally or assault ; the military engines incessantly played from the ramparts ; and the inclemency of the winter
was still more painful and destructive to the Arabs. The Christians
yielded at length to the perseverance of the besiegers. The patriarch
Sophronius appeared on the walls, and by the voice of an interpreter
demanded a conference. After a vain attempt to dissuade the lieutenant of the caliph from his impious enterprise, he proposed, in the
name of the people, a fair capitulation, with this extraordinary clause,
that the articles of security should be ratified by the authority and
presence of Omar himself. The question was debated in the council
of Medina ; the sanctity of the place, and the advice of Ali, persuaded the caliph to gratify the wishes of his soldiers and enemies,
and the simplicity of his journey is more illustrious than the royal
pageants of vanity and oppression. The conqueror of Persia and
Syria was mounted on a red camel, which carried, besides his person,
a bag of corn, a bag of dates, a wooden dish, and a leathern bottle of
water. Wherever he halted, the company, without distinction, was
invited to partake of his homely fare, and the repast was consecrated
by the prayer and exhortation of the commander of the faithful.
But in this expedition or pilgrimage, his power was exercised in the
administration of justice ; he reformed the licentious polygamy of the
Arabs, relieved the tributaries from extortion and cruelty, and chastised the luxury of the Saracens, by despoiling them of their rich
silks, and dragging them on their faces in the dirt. When he came
within sight of Jerusalem, the caliph cried with a loud voice, " God is
victorious. O Lord, give us an easy conquest ;" and pitching his
tent of coarse hair, calmly seated himself on the ground. After
signing the capitulation, he entered the city without fear or precaution ; and courteously discoursed with the patriarch concerning its
religious antiquities. Sophronius bowed before his new master, and
secretly muttered, in the words of Daniel, " The abomination of deso-

lation is in the holy place." At the hour of prayer, they stood together in the church of the Resurrection ; but the caliph refused to perform his devotions, and contented himself with praying on the steps of the church of Constantine. To the patriarch he disclosed his prudent and honourable motive. " Had I yielded," said Omar, " to your request, the Moslems of a future age would have infringed the treaty under colour of imitating my example." By his command, the ground of the temple of Solomon was prepared for the foundation of a mosque ; and, during a residence of ten days, he regulated the present and future state of his Syrian conquests. Medina might be jealous, lest the caliph should be detained by the sanctity of Jerusalem or the beauty of Damascus ; her apprehensions were dispelled by his prompt and voluntary return to the tomb of the apostle.

To achieve what yet remained of the Syrian war, the caliph had (A.D. 638) formed two separate armies ; a chosen detachment, under Amrou and Yezid, was left in the camp of Palestine : while the larger division, under the standard of Abu Obeidah and Caled, marched away to the north against Antioch and Aleppo. The latter of these, the Beræa of the Greeks, was not yet illustrious as the capital of a province or a kingdom ; and the inhabitants, by anticipating their submission and pleading their poverty, obtained a moderate composition for their lives and religion. But the castle of Aleppo, distinct from the city, stood erect on a lofty artificial mound : the sides were sharpened to a precipice, and faced with freestone ; and the breadth of the ditch might be filled with water from the neighbouring springs. After the loss of 3000 men, the garrison was still equal to the defence ; and Youkinna, their valiant and hereditary chief, had murdered his brother, an holy monk, for daring to pronounce the name of peace. In a siege of four or five months, the hardest of the Syrian war, great numbers of the Saracens were killed and wounded : their removal to the distance of a mile could not seduce the vigilance of Youkinna ; nor could the Christians be terrified by the execution of 300 captives, whom they beheaded before the castle wall. The silence, and at length the complaints, of Abu Obeidah informed the caliph that their hope and patience were consumed at the foot of this impregnable fortress. " I am variously affected," replied Omar, " by the diffe-rence of your success ; but I charge you by no means to raise the siege of the castle. Your retreat would diminish the reputation of our arms, and encourage the infidels to fall upon you on all sides. Re-main before Aleppo till God shall determine the event, and forage with your horse round the adjacent country." The exhortation of the commander of the faithful was fortified by a supply of volunteers from all the tribes of Arabia, who arrived in the camp on horses or camels. Among these was Dames, of a servile birth, but of gigantic size and intrepid resolution. The forty-seventh day of his service he proposed, with only thirty men, to make an attempt on the castle.

The experience and testimony of Caled recommended his offer, and Abu Obeidah admonished his brethren not to despise the baser origin of Dames, since he himself, could he relinquish the public care, would cheerfully serve under the banner of the slave. His design was covered by the appearance of a retreat, and the camp of the Saracens was pitched about a league from Aleppo. The thirty adventurers lay in ambush at the foot of the hill ; and Dames at length succeeded in his inquiries, though he was provoked by the ignorance of his Greek captives. " God curse these dogs," said the illiterate Arabs, "what a strange barbarous language they speak !" At the darkest hour of the night, he scaled the most accessible height which he had diligently surveyed, a place where the stones were less entire, or the slope less perpendicular, or the guard less vigilant. Seven of the stoutest Saracens mounted on each other's shoulders, and the weight of the column was sustained by the broad and sinewy back of the gigantic slave. The foremost in this painful ascent could grasp and climb the lowest part of the battlements ; they silently stabbed and cast down the sentinels ; and the thirty brethren, repeating a pious ejaculation, " O apostle of God, help and deliver us !" were successively drawn up by the long folds of their turbans. With bold and cautious footsteps, Dames explored the palace of the governor, who celebrated, in riotous merriment, the festival of his deliverance. From thence, returning to his companions, he assaulted on the inside the entrance of the castle. They overpowered the guard, unbolted the gate, let down the drawbridge, and defended the narrow pass, till the arrival of Caled, with the dawn of day, relieved their danger and assured their conquest. Youkinna, a formidable foe, became an active and useful proselyte ; and the general of the Saracens expressed his regard for the most humble merit, by detaining the army at Aleppo till Dames was cured of his honourable wounds. The capital of Syria was still covered by the castle of Aazaz and the iron bridge of the Orontes. After the loss of those important posts, and the defeat of the last of the Roman armies, the luxury of Antioch trembled and obeyed. Her safety was ransomed with 300,000 pieces of gold : but the throne of the successors of Alexander, the seat of the Roman government in the East, which had been decorated by Cæsar with the titles of free, and holy, and inviolate, was degraded under the yoke of the caliphs to the secondary rank of a provincial town.

In the life of Heraclius, the glories of the Persian war are clouded on either hand by the disgrace and weakness of his more early and his later days. When the successors of Mahomet unsheathed the sword of war and religion, he was astonished at the boundless prospect of toil and danger ; his nature was indolent, nor could the infirm and frigid age of the emperor be kindled to a second effort. The sense of shame, and the importunities of the Syrians, prevented his hasty departure from the scene of action ; but the hero was no more, and the

6

loss of Damascus and Jerusalem, the bloody fields of Aiznadin and Yermuk, may be imputed in some degree to the absence or misconduct of the sovereign. Instead of defending the sepulchre of Christ, he involved the church and state in a metaphysical controversy for the unity of his will ; and while Heraclius crowned the offspring of his second nuptials, he was tamely stripped of the most valuable part of their inheritance. In the cathedral of Antioch, in the presence of the bishops, at the foot of the crucifix, he bewailed the sins of the prince and people ; but his confession instructed the world, that it was vain, and perhaps impious, to resist the judgment of God. The Saracens were invincible in fact, since they were invincible in opinion ; and the desertion of Youkinna, his false repentance and repeated perfidy, might justify the suspicion of the emperor, that he was encompassed by traitors and apostates, who conspired to betray his person and their country to the enemies of Christ. In the hour of adversity, his superstition was agitated by the omens and dreams of a falling crown : and after bidding an eternal farewell to Syria, he (A.D. 638) secretly embarked with a few attendants, and absolved the faith of his subjects. Constantine, his eldest son, had been stationed with 40,000 men at Cæsarea, the civil metropolis of the three provinces of Palestine. But his private interest recalled him to the Byzantine court ; and after the flight of his father, he felt himself an unequal champion to the united force of the caliph. His vanguard was boldly attacked by 300 Arabs and 1000 black slaves, who, in the depth of winter, had climbed the snowy mountains of Libanus, and who were speedily followed by the victorious squadrons of Caled himself. From the north and south the troops of Antioch and Jerusalem advanced along the sea-shore, till their banners were joined under the walls of the Phœnician cities : Tripoli and Tyre were betrayed ; and a fleet of fifty transports, which entered without distrust the captive harbours, brought a seasonable supply of arms and provisions to the camp of the Saracens. Their labours were terminated by the unexpected surrender of Cæsarea : the Roman prince had embarked in the night ; and the defenceless citizens solicited their pardon with an offering of 200,000 pieces of gold. The remainder of the province, Ramlah, Ptolemais or Acre, Sichem or Neapolis, Gaza, Ascalon, Berytus, Sidon, Gabala, Laodicea, Apamea, Hierapolis, no longer presumed to dispute the will of the conqueror ; and Syria bowed under the sceptre of the caliphs 700 years after Pompey had despoiled the last of the Macedonian kings.

The sieges and battles of six campaigns (A.D. 633—639) had consumed many thousands of the Moslems. They died with the reputation and the cheerfulness of martyrs ; and the simplicity of their faith may be expressed in the words of an Arabian youth, when he embraced, for the last time, his sister and mother : " It is not," said he, " the delicacies of Syria, or the fading delights of this world, that have prompted me to devote my life in the cause of religion. But I seek the favour of God and his apostle; and I have heard, from one of the companions of the prophet, that the spirits of the martyrs will be lodged in the crops of green birds, who shall taste the fruits, and drink of the rivers, of paradise. Farewell, we shall meet again among the groves and fountains which God has provided for his elect." The faithful captives might exercise a passive and more arduous resolution; and a cousin of Mahomet is celebrated for refusing, after an abstinence of three days, the wine and pork, the only nourishment that was allowed by the malice of the infidels. The frailty of some weaker brethren exasperated the implacable spirit of fanaticism; and the father of Amer deplored, in pathetic strains, the apostacy and damnation of a son, who had renounced the promises of God, and the intercession of the prophet, to occupy, with the priests and deacons, the lowest mansions of hell. The more fortunate Arabs, who survived the war and persevered in the faith, were restrained by their abstemious leader from the abuse of prosperity. After a refreshment of three days, Abu Obeidah withdrew his troops from the pernicious contagion of the luxury of Antioch, and assured the caliph that their religion and virtue could only be preserved by the hard discipline of poverty and labour. But the virtue of Omar, however rigorous to himself, was kind and liberal to his brethren. After a just tribute of praise and thanksgiving, he dropt a tear of compassion: and sitting down on the ground, wrote an answer, in which he mildly censured the severity of his lieutenant: " God," said the successor of the prophet, " has not forbidden the use of the good things of this world to faithful men, and such as have performed good works. Therefore you ought to have given them leave to rest themselves, and partake freely of those good things which the country affordeth. If any of the Saracens has no family in Arabia, they may marry in Syria; and whosoever of them wants any female slaves, he may purchase as many as he hath occasion for." The conquerors prepared to use, or to abuse, this gracious permission; but the year of their triumph was marked by a mortality of men and cattle; and 25,000 Saracens were snatched away from the possession of Syria. The death of Abu Obeidah might be lamented by the Christians; but his brethren recollected that he was one of the ten elect whom the prophet had named as the heirs of paradise. Caled survived his brethren about three years: and the tomb of the sword of God is shown in the neighbourhood of Emesa. His valour, which founded in Arabia and Syria the empire of the caliphs, was fortified by the opinion of a special providence; and as long as he wore a cap, which had been blessed by Mahomet, he deemed himself invulnerable amidst the darts of the infidels.

The place of the first conquerors was supplied by a new generation of their children and countrymen; Syria became (A.D. 639—655) the seat and support of the house of Ommiyah; and the revenue, the soldiers, the ships of that powerful kingdom, were consecrated to enlarge on every side the empire of the caliphs. But the Saracens despise a superfluity of fame ; and their historians scarcely condescend to mention the subordinate conquests which are lost in the splendour and rapidity of their victorious career.   To the *north* of Syria, they passed Mount Taurus, and reduced to their obedience the province of Cilicia, with its capital Tarsus, the ancient monument of the Assyrian kings.   Beyond a second ridge of the same mountains, they spread the flame of war, rather than the light of religion, as far as the shores of the Euxine and the neighbourhood of Constantinople.   To the *east* they advanced to the banks and sources of the Euphrates and Tigris : the long-disputed barrier of Rome and Persia was for ever confounded ; the walls of Edessa and Amida, of Dara and Nisibis, which had resisted the arms and engines of Sapor and Nushirvan, were levelled in the dust ; and the holy city of Abgarus might vainly produce the epistle of the image of Christ to an unbelieving conqueror.   To the *west*, the Syrian kingdom is bounded by the sea ; and the ruin of Aradus, a small island or peninsula on the coast, was postponed during ten years.   But the hills of Libanus abounded in timber, the trade of Phœnicia was populous in mariners ; and a fleet of 1700 barks was equipped and manned by the natives of the desert.   The imperial navy of the Romans fled before them from the Pamphylian rocks to the Hellespont ; but the spirit of the emperor, a grandson of Heraclius, had been subdued before the combat by a dream and a pun.   The Saracens rode masters of the sea ; and the islands of Cyprus, Rhodes, and the Cyclades were successively exposed to their rapacious visits. Three hundred years before the Christian æra, the memorable though fruitless siege of Rhodes by Demetrius, had furnished that maritime republic with the materials and the subject of a trophy.   A gigantic statue of Apollo, or the sun, 70 cubits in height, was erected at the entrance of the harbour, a monument of the freedom and the arts of Greece.   After standing 56 years, the colossus of Rhodes was overthrown by an earthquake : but the massy trunk and huge fragments lay scattered eight centuries on the ground, and are often described as one of the wonders of the ancient world.   They were collected by the diligence of the Saracens, and sold to a Jewish merchant of Edessa, who is said to have laden 900 camels with the weight of the brass metal : an enormous weight, though we should include the hundred colossal figures and the 3000 statues which adorned the prosperity of the city of the sun.

   II. The conquest of Egypt may be explained by the character of the victorious Saracen, one of the first of his nation, in an age when the meanest of his brethren was exalted above his nature by the spirit of enthusiasm.   The birth of Amrou was at once base and illustrious. The youth of Amrou was impelled by the passions and prejudices of his kindred ; his poetic genius was exercised in satirical verses against the person and doctrine of Mahomet ; his dexterity was employed by

the reigning faction to pursue the religious exiles who had taken refuge
in the court of the Æthiopian king. Yet he returned from this embassy, a secret proselyte ; his reason or his interest determined him to
renounce the worship of idols ; he escaped from Mecca with his friend
Caled, and the prophet of Medina enjoyed at the same moment the
satisfaction of embracing the two firmest champions of his cause. The
impatience of Amrou to lead the armies of the faithful, was checked
by the reproof of Omar, who advised him not to seek power and
dominion, since he who is a subject to-day, may be a prince to-morrow.
Yet his merit was not overlooked by the two first successors of
Mahomet ; they were indebted to his arms for the conquest of Palestine, and in all the battles and sieges of Syria, he united with the temper
of a chief, the valour of an adventurous soldier. In a visit to Medina,
the caliph expressed a wish to survey the sword which had cut down
so many Christian warriors : the son of Aasi unsheathed a short and
ordinary scymetar : and as he perceived the surprise of Omar, " Alas,"
said the modest Saracen, " the sword itself, without the arm of its
master, is neither sharper nor more weighty than the sword of Phar-
ezdak the poet." After the conquest of Egypt he was recalled by the
jealousy of the caliph Othman ; but in the subsequent troubles, the
ambition of a soldier, a statesman, and an orator, emerged from a
private station. His powerful support, both in council and in the field,
established the throne of the Ommiades ; the administration and
revenue of Egypt were restored by the gratitude of Moawiyah to a
faithful friend who had raised himself above the rank of a subject ;
and Amrou ended his days in the palace and city which he had founded
on the banks of the Nile. His dying speech to his children is celebrated by the Arabians as a model of eloquence and wisdom : he
deplored the errors of his youth ; but if the penitent was still infected
by the vanity of a poet, he might exaggerate the venom and mischief
of his impious compositions.

From his camp in Palestine, Amrou had surprised or anticipated
the caliph's leave for the invasion of Egypt. The magnanimous
Omar trusted in his God and his sword, which had shaken the thrones
of Chosroes and Cæsar ; but when he compared the slender force of
the Moslems with the greatness of the enterprise, he condemned his
own rashness, and listened to his timid companions. The pride and
the greatness of Pharoah were familiar to the readers of the Koran ;
and a tenfold repetition of prodigies had been scarcely sufficient to
effect, not the victory, but the flight, of 600,000 of the children of
Israel ; the cities of Egypt were many and populous ; their architecture
was strong and solid ; the Nile, with its numerous branches, was alone
an insuperable barrier ; and the granary of the Imperial city would be
obstinately defended by the Roman powers. In this perplexity, the
commander of the faithful resigned himself to the decision of chance,
or, in his opinion, of providence. At the head of only 4000 Arabs, the

intrepid Amrou had (A.D. 638. June) marched away from his station of Gaza, when he was overtaken by the messenger of Omar. "If you are still in Syria," said the ambiguous mandate, "retreat without delay; but if, at the receipt of this epistle, you have already reached the frontiers of Egypt, advance with confidence, and depend on the succour of God and of your brethren." The experience, perhaps the secret intelligence, of Amrou had taught him to suspect the mutability of courts; and he continued his march till his tents were unquestionably pitched on Egyptian ground. He there assembled his officers, broke the seal, perused the epistle, gravely inquired the name and situation of the place, and declared his ready obedience to the commands of the caliph. After a siege of thirty days, he took possession of Farmah or Pelusium, and that key of Egypt, as it has been justly named, unlocked the entrance of the country, as far as the ruins of Heliopolis and the neighbourhood of the modern Cairo.

On the western side of the Nile, at a small distance to the east of the Pyramids, at a small distance to the south of the Delta, Memphis, 150 furlongs in circumference, displayed the magnificence of ancient kings. Under the reign of the Ptolemies and Cæsars, the seat of government was removed to the sea-coast; the ancient capital was eclipsed by the arts and opulence of Alexandria; the palaces, and at length the temples, were reduced to a desolate and ruinous condition: yet in the age of Augustus, and even in that of Constantine, Memphis was still numbered among the greatest and most populous of the provincial cities. The banks of the Nile, in this place of the breadth of 3000 feet, were united by two bridges of sixty and of thirty boats, connected in the middle stream by the small island of Rouda, which was covered with gardens and habitations. The eastern extremity of the bridge was terminated by the town of Babylon and the camp of a Roman legion, which protected the passage of the river and the second capital of Egypt. This important fortress, which might fairly be described as a part of Memphis or *Misrah*, was invested by the arms of the lieutenant of Omar: a reinforcement of 4000 Saracens soon arrived in his camp: and the military engines which battered the walls may be imputed to the art and labour of his Syrian allies. Yet the siege was protracted to seven months; and the rash invaders were encompassed and threatened by the inundation of the Nile. Their last assault was bold and successful: they passed the ditch, which had been fortified with iron spikes, applied their scaling-ladders, entered the fortress with the shout of "God is victorious!" and drove the remnant of the Greeks to their boats and the isle of Rouda. The spot was afterwards recommended to the conqueror by the easy communication with the gulf and the peninsula of Arabia: the remains of Memphis were deserted; the tents of the Arabs were converted into permanent habitations: and the first mosque was blessed by the presence of fourscore companions of Mahomet. A new city arose in their camp on the eastward bank of the Nile; and the contiguous quarters of Babylon and Fostat are confounded in their present decay by the appellation of old Misrah or Cairo, of which town they form an extensive suburb. But the name of Cairo, the town of victory, more strictly belongs to the modern capital, which was founded in the tenth century by the Fatimite caliphs. It has gradually receded from the river, but the continuity of buildings may be traced by an attentive eye from the monuments of Sesostris to those of Saladin.

Yet the Arabs, after a glorious and profitable enterprise, must have retreated to the desert, had they not found a powerful alliance in the heart of the country. The rapid conquest of Alexander was assisted by the superstition and revolt of the natives: they abhorred their Persian oppressors, the disciples of the Magi, who had burnt the temples of Egypt, and feasted with sacrilegious appetite on the flesh of the god Apis. After a period of ten centuries the same revolution was renewed (A.D. 638) by a similar cause; and in the support of an incomprehensible creed, the zeal of the Coptic Christians was equally ardent. The persecution of the emperors, which converted a sect into a nation, alienated Egypt from their religion and government. The Saracens were received as the deliverers of the Jacobite church; and a secret and effectual treaty was opened during the siege of Memphis between a victorious army and a people of slaves. A rich and noble Egyptian, of the name of Mokawkas, had dissembled his faith to obtain the administration of his province: in the disorders of the Persian war he aspired to independence: the embassy of Mahomet ranked him among princes; but he declined, with rich gifts and ambiguous compliments, the proposal of a new religion. The abuse of his trust exposed him to the resentment of Heraclius; his submission was delayed by arrogance and fear; and his conscience was prompted by interest to throw himself on the favour of the nation and the support of the Saracens. In his first conference with Amrou, he heard without indignation the usual option of the Koran, the tribute, or the sword. "The Greeks," replied Mokawkas, "are determined to abide the determination of the sword; but with the Greeks I desire no communion, either in this world or in the next, and I abjure for ever the Byzantine tyrant, his synod of Chalcedon, and his Melchite slaves. For myself and my brethren, we are resolved to live and die in the profession of the gospel and unity of Christ. It is impossible for us to embrace the revelations of your prophet; but we are desirous of peace, and cheerfully submit to pay tribute and obedience to his temporal successors." The tribute was ascertained at two pieces of gold for the head of every Christian; but old men, monks, women, and children, of both sexes, under sixteen years of age, were exempted from this personal assessment: the Copts above and below Memphis swore allegiance to the caliph, and promised an hospitable entertainment of three days to every Mussulman who should travel through their country. By this charter of security, the ecclesiastical and civil tyranny of the Melchites was destroyed : the anathemas of St. Cyril were thundered from every pulpit ; and the sacred edifices, with the patrimony of the church, were restored to the national communion of the Jacobites, who enjoyed without moderation the moment of triumph and revenge. At the pressing summons of Amrou, their patriarch Benjamin emerged from his desert ; and after the first interview, the courteous Arab affected to declare, that he had never conversed with a Christian priest of more innocent manners and a more venerable aspect. In the march from Memphis to Alexandria the lieutenant of Omar entrusted his safety to the zeal and gratitude of the Egyptians : the roads and bridges were diligently repaired ; and in every step of his progress, he could depend on a constant supply of provisions and intelligence. The Greeks of Egypt, whose numbers could scarcely equal a tenth of the natives, were overwhelmed by the universal defection ; they had ever been hated, they were no longer feared : the magistrate fled from his tribunal, the bishop from his altar ; and the distant garrisons were surprised or starved by the surrounding multitudes. Had not the Nile afforded a safe and ready conveyance to the sea, not an individual could have escaped, who by birth, or language, or office, or religion, was connected with their odious name.

By the retreat of the Greeks from the provinces of Upper Egypt, a considerable force was collected in the island of Delta : the natural and artificial channels of the Nile afforded a succession of strong and defensible posts ; and the road to Alexandria was laboriously cleared by the victory of the Saracens in two and twenty days of general or partial combat. In their annals of conquest, the siege of Alexandria is perhaps the most arduous and important enterprise. The first trading city in the world was abundantly replenished with the means of subsistence and defence. Her numerous inhabitants fought for the dearest of human rights, religion and property ; and the enmity of the natives seemed to exclude them from the common benefit of peace and toleration. The sea was continually open ; and if Heraclius had been awake to the public distress, fresh armies of Romans and Barbarians might have been poured into the harbour to save the second capital of the empire. A circumference of ten miles would have scattered the forces of the Greeks, and favoured the stratagems of an active enemy ; but the two sides of an oblong square were covered by the sea and the lake Maræotis, and each of the narrow ends exposed a front of no more than ten furlongs. The efforts of the Arabs were not inadequate to the difficulty of the attempt and the value of the prize. From the throne of Medina, the eyes of Omar were fixed on the camp and city : his voice excited to arms the Arabian tribes and the veterans of Syria ; and the merit of an holy war was recommended by the peculiar fame and fertility of Egypt. Anxious for the ruin or expulsion of their tyrants, the faithful natives devoted their labours to the service of Amrou ; some sparks of martial spirit were ·perhaps rekindled by the example of their allies ; and the sanguine hopes of Mokawkas had fixed his sepulchre in the church of St. John of Alexandria. Eutychius the patriarch observes, that the Saracens fought with the courage of lions ; they repulsed the frequent and almost daily sallies of the besieged, and soon assaulted in their turn the walls and towers of the city. In every attack, the sword, the banner of Amrou, glittered in the van of the Moslems. On a memorable day he was betrayed by his imprudent valour : his followers who had entered the citadel were driven back ; and the general, with a friend and a slave, remained a prisoner in the hands of the Christians. When Amrou was conducted before the præfect, he remembered his dignity and forgot his situation ; a lofty demeanour, and resolute language, revealed the lieutenant of the caliph, and the battle-axe of a soldier was already raised to strike off the head of the audacious captive. His life was saved by the readiness of his slave, who instantly gave his master a blow on the face, and commanded him, with an angry tone, to be silent in the presence of his superiors. The credulous Greek was deceived ; he listened to the offer of a treaty, and his prisoners were dismissed in the hope of a more respectable embassy, till the joyful acclamations of the camp announced the return of their general, and insulted the folly of the infidels. At length, after a siege of fourteen months, and the loss of 23,000 men, the Saracens prevailed : the Greeks embarked their dispirited and diminished numbers, and the standard of Mahomet was planted on the walls of the capital of Egypt. " I have taken," said Amrou to the caliph, " the great city of the West. It is impossible for me to enumerate the variety of its riches and beauty; and I shall content myself with observing, that it contains 4000 palaces, 4000 baths, 400 theatres or places of amusement, 12,000 shops for the sale of vegetable food, and 40,000 tributary Jews. The town has been subdued by force of arms, without treaty or capitulation, and the Moslems are impatient to seize the fruits of their victory." The commander of the faithful rejected with firmness the idea of pillage, and directed his lieutenant to reserve the wealth and revenue of Alexandria for the public service and the propagation of the faith : the inhabitants were numbered ; a tribute was imposed ; the zeal and resentment of the Jacobites were curbed, and the Melchites who submitted to the Arabian yoke, were indulged in the obscure but tranquil exercise of their worship. The intelligence of this disgraceful and calamitous event afflicted the declining health of the emperor ; and Heraclius died of a dropsy about seven weeks after the loss of Alexandria. Under the minority of his grandson, the clamours of a people, deprived of their daily sustenance, compelled the Byzantine court to undertake the recovery of the capital of Egypt. In the space of four years, the harbour and fortifications of Alexandria were twice occupied by a fleet and army of Romans. They were twice expelled by the valour of Amrou, who was recalled by the domestic peril from the distant wars of Tripoli and Nubia. But the facility of the attempt, the repetition of the insult, and the obstinacy of the resistance provoked him to swear, that if a third time he drove the infidels into the sea, he would render Alexandria as accessible on all sides as the house of a prostitute. Faithful to his promise, he dismantled several parts of the walls and towers, but the people was spared in the chastisement of the city, and the mosque of *Mercy* was erected on the spot where the victorious general had stopped the fury of his troops.

I should deceive the expectation of the reader, if I passed in silence the fate of the Alexandrian library, as it is described by the learned Abulpharagius. The spirit of Amrou was more curious and liberal than that of his brethren, and in his leisure hours, the Arabian chief was pleased with the conversation of John, the last disciple of Ammonius, and who derived the surname of *Philoponus*, from his laborious studies of grammar and philosophy. Emboldened by this familiar intercourse, Philoponus presumed to solicit a gift, inestimable in *his* opinion, contemptible in that of the Barbarians ; the royal library, which alone, among the spoils of Alexandria, had not been appropriated by the visit and the seal of the conqueror. Amrou was inclined to gratify the wish of the grammarian, but his rigid integrity refused to alienate the minutest object without the consent of the caliph ; and the well-known answer of Omar was inspired by the ignorance of a fanatic. " If these writings of the Greeks agree with the book of God, they are useless and need not be preserved : if they disagree, they are pernicious and ought to be destroyed." The sentence was executed with blind obedience : the volumes of paper or parchment were distributed to the 4000 baths of the city ; and such was their incredible multitude, that six months were barely sufficient for the consumption of this precious fuel. Since the Dynasties of Abulpharagius have been given to the world in a Latin version, the tale has been repeatedly transcribed ; and every scholar, with pious indignation has deplored the irreparable shipwreck of the learning, the arts, and the genius, of antiquity. For my own part, I am strongly tempted to deny both the fact and the consequences. The fact is indeed marvellous ; " Read and wonder !" says the historian himself : and the solitary report of a stranger who wrote at the end of six hundred years on the confines of Media, is overbalanced by the silence of two annalists of a more early date, both Christians, both natives of Egypt, and the most ancient of whom, the patriarch Eutychius, has amply described the conquest of Alexandria. The rigid sentence of Omar is repugnant to the sound and orthodox precept of the Mahometan casuists : they expressly declare, that the religious books of the Jews and Christians, which are acquired by the right of war, should never be committed to the flames ; and that the works of profane

science, historians or poets, physicians or philosophers, may be lawfully applied to the use of the faithful. A more destructive zeal may
perhaps be attributed to the first successors of Mahomet ; yet in this
instance, the conflagration would have speedily expired in the deficiency of materials. I shall not recapitulate the disasters of the Alexandrian library, the involuntary flame that was kindled by Cæsar in
his own defence, or the mischievous bigotry of the Christians, who
studied to destroy the monuments of idolatry. But if we gradually
descend from the age of the Antonines to that of Theodosius, we shall
learn from a chain of contemporary witnesses, that the royal palace
and the temple of Serapis no longer contained the four, or the seven
hundred thousand volumes, which had been assembled by the curiosity
and magnificence of the Ptolemies. Perhaps the church and seat of
the patriarchs might be enriched with a repository of books ; but if
the ponderous mass of Arian and Monophysite controversy were indeed consumed in the public baths, a philosopher may allow, with a
smile, that it was ultimately devoted to the benefit of mankind. I
sincerely regret the more valuable libraries which have been involved
in the ruin of the Roman empire ; but when I seriously compute the
lapse of ages, the waste of ignorance, and the calamities of war, our
treasures, rather than our losses, are the object of my surprise. Many
curious and interesting facts are buried in oblivion ; the three great
historians of Rome have been transmitted to our hands in a mutilated
state, and we are deprived of many pleasing compositions of the lyric,
iambic, and dramatic poetry of the Greeks. Yet we should gratefully
remember, that the mischances of time and accident have spared the
classic works to which the suffrage of antiquity had adjudged the
first place of genius and glory : the teachers of ancient knowledge,
who are still extant, had perused and compared the writings of their
predecessors ; nor can it fairly be presumed that any important
truth, any useful discovery in art or nature, has been snatched away
from the curiosity of modern ages.

In the administration of Egypt, Amrou balanced the demands of
justice and policy ; the interest of the people of the law, who were defended by God ; and of the people of the alliance, who were protected
by man. In the recent tumult of conquest and deliverance, the tongue
of the Copts and the sword of the Arabs were most adverse to the
tranquillity of the province. To the former, Amrou declared, that faction and falsehood would be doubly chastised, by the punishment of
the accusers, whom he should detest as his personal enemies, and by
the promotion of their innocent brethren, whom their envy had
laboured to injure and supplant. He excited the latter by the motives
of religion and honour to sustain the dignity of their character, to
endear themselves by a modest and temperate conduct to God and the
caliph, to spare and protect a people who had trusted to their faith,
and to content themselves with the legitimate and splendid rewards

of their victory. In the management of the revenue he disapproved the simple but oppressive mode of a capitation, and preferred with reason a proportion of taxes, deducted on every branch from the clear profits of agriculture and commerce. A third part of the tribute was appropriated to the annual repairs of the dykes and canals, so essential to the public welfare. Under his administration the fertility of Egypt supplied the dearth of Arabia ; and a string of camels, laden with corn and provisions, covered almost without an interval the long road from Memphis to Medina. But the genius of Amrou soon renewed the maritime communication which had been attempted or achieved by the Pharaohs, the Ptolemies, or the Cæsars ; and a canal, at least eighty miles in length, was opened from the Nile to the Red Sea. This inland navigation, which would have joined the Mediterranean and the Indian ocean, was soon discontinued as useless and dangerous : the throne was removed from Medina to Damascus ; and through it the Grecian fleets might have explored a passage to the holy cities of Arabia.

Of his new conquest, the caliph Omar had an imperfect knowledge from the voice of fame and the legends of the Koran. He requested that his lieutenant would place before his eyes the realm of Pharaoh and the Amalekites ; and the answer of Amrou exhibits a lively and not unfaithful picture of that singular country. " O commander of the faithful, Egypt is a compound of black earth and green plants, between a pulverized mountain and a red sand. The distance from Syene to the sea is a month's journey for an horseman. Along the valley descends a river, on which the blessing of the Most High reposes both in the evening and morning, and which rises and falls with the revolutions of the sun and moon. When the annual dispensation of providence unlocks the springs and fountains that nourish the earth, the Nile rolls his swelling and sounding waters through the realm of Egypt : the fields are overspread by the salutary flood ; and the villages communicate with each other in their painted barks. The retreat of the inundation deposits a fertilizing mud for the reception of the various seeds : the crowds of husbandmen who blacken the land may be compared to a swarm of industrious ants ; and their native indolence is quickened by the lash of the task-master, and the promise of the flowers and fruits of a plentiful increase. Their hope is seldom deceived ; but the riches which they extract from the wheat, the barley, and the rice, the legumes, the fruit-trees, and the cattle, are unequally shared between those who labour and those who possess. According to the vicissitudes of the seasons, the face of the country is adorned with a *silver* wave, a verdant *emerald*, and the deep yellow of a *golden* harvest." Yet this beneficial order is sometimes interrupted ; and the long delay and sudden swell of the river in the first year of the conquest might afford some colour to an edifying fable. It is said, that the annual sacrifice of a virgin had been interdicted by the piety of Omar ; and that the Nile lay sullen and inactive in his shallow bed, till the mandate of the caliph was cast into the obedient stream, which rose in a single night to the height of sixteen cubits. The admiration of the Arabs for their new conquest encouraged the license of their romantic spirit. We may read, in the gravest authors, that Egypt was crowded with 20,000 cities or villages : *that*, exclusive of the Greeks and Arabs, the Copts alone were found, on the assessment, six millions of tributary subjects, or twenty millions of either sex, and of every age : *that* three hundred millions of gold or silver were annually paid to the treasury of the caliph. Our reason must be startled by these extravagant assertions ; and they will become more palpable, if we assume the compass and measure the extent of habitable ground ; a valley from the tropic to Memphis, seldom broader than 12 miles, and the triangle of the Delta, a flat surface of 2100 square leagues, compose a twelfth part of the magnitude of France. A more accurate research will justify a more reasonable estimate. The three hundred millions, created by the error of a scribe, are reduced to the decent revenue of four millions three hundred thousand pieces of gold, of which nine hundred thousand were consumed by the pay of the soldiers. Two authentic lists, of the present and of the twelfth century, are circumscribed within the respectable number of 2700 villages and towns. After a long residence at Cairo, a French consul has ventured to assign about four millions of Mahometans, Christians, and Jews, for the ample, though not incredible, scope, of the population of Egypt.

IV. The conquest of Africa, from the Nile to the Atlantic ocean, was first (A.D. 647) attempted by the arms of the caliph Othman. The pious design was approved by the companions of Mahomet and the chiefs of the tribes ; and 20,000 Arabs marched from Medina, with the gifts and the blessing of the commander of the faithful. They were joined in the camp of Memphis by 20,000 of their countrymen ; and the conduct of the war was entrusted to Abdallah, the son of Said and the foster-brother of the caliph, who had lately supplanted the conqueror and lieutenant of Egypt. Yet the favour of the prince, and the merit of his favourite, could not obliterate the guilt of his apostasy. The early conversion of Abdallah, and his skilful pen, had recommended nim to the important office of transcribing the sheets of the Koran ; he betrayed his trust, corrupted the text, derided the errors which he had made, and fled to Mecca to escape the justice, and expose the ignorance, of the apostle. After the conquest of Mecca, he fell prostrate at the feet of Mahomet : his tears, and the entreaties of Othman, extorted a reluctant pardon ; but the prophet declared that he had so long hesitated, to allow time for some zealous disciple to avenge his injury in the blood of the apostate. With apparent fidelity and effective merit, he served the religion which it was no longer his interest to desert : his birth and talents gave him an honourable rank among the

Koreish; and, in a nation of cavalry, Abdallah was renowned as the boldest and most dexterous horseman of Arabia. At the head of 40,000 Moslems, he advanced from Egypt into the unknown countries of the West. The sands of Barca might be impervious to a Roman legion; but the Arabs were attended by their faithful camels; and the natives of the desert beheld without terror the familiar aspect of the soil and climate. After a painful march, they pitched their tents before the walls of Tripoli, a maritime city, in which the *name*, the wealth, and the inhabitants, of the province had gradually centered, and which now maintains the third rank among the states of Barbary. A reinforcement of Greeks was surprised and cut in pieces on the sea-shore; but the fortifications of Tripoli resisted the first assaults; and the Saracens were tempted by the approach of the præfect Gregory to relinquish the labours of the siege for the perils and the hopes of a decisive action. If his standard was followed by 120,000 men, the regular bands of the empire must have been lost in the naked and disorderly crowd of Africans and Moors, who formed the strength, or rather the numbers, of his host. He rejected with indignation the option of the Koran or the tribute; and during several days, the two armies were fiercely engaged from the dawn of light to the hour of noon, when their fatigue and the excessive heat compelled them to seek shelter and refreshment in their respective camps. The daughter of Gregory, a maid of incomparable beauty and spirit, is said to have fought by his side: from her earliest youth she was trained to mount on horseback, to draw the bow, and to wield the scymetar; and the richness of her arms and apparel was conspicuous in the foremost ranks of the battle. Her hand, with 100,000 pieces of gold, was offered for the head of the Arabian general, and the youths of Africa were excited by the prospect of the glorious prize. At the pressing solicitation of his brethren, Abdallah withdrew his person from the field; but the Saracens were discouraged by the retreat of their leader, and the repetition of these equal or unsuccessful conflicts.

A noble Arabian, who afterwards became the adversary of Ali and the father of a caliph, had signalized his valour in Egypt, and Zobeir was the first who planted a scaling-ladder against the walls of Babylon. In the African war he was detached from the standard of Abdallah. On the news of the battle, Zobeir, with twelve companions, cut his way through the camp of the Greeks, and pressed forwards, without tasting either food or repose, to partake of the dangers of his brethren. He cast his eyes round the field: "Where," said he, "is our general?" "In his tent." "Is the tent a station for the general of the Moslems?" Abdallah represented with a blush the importance of his own life, and the temptation that was held forth by the Roman præfect. "Retort," said Zobeir, "on the infidels their ungenerous attempt. Proclaim through the ranks, that the head of Gregory shall be repaid with his captive daughter, and the equal sum of 100,000 pieces of gold." To

the courage and discretion of Zobeir the lieutenant of the caliph entrusted the execution of his own stratagem, which inclined the long
disputed balance in favour of the Saracens.   Supplying by activity
and artifice the deficiency of numbers, a part of their forces lay concealed in their tents, while the remainder prolonged an irregular skirmish with the enemy, till the sun was high in the heavens.   On both
sides they retired with fainting steps : their horses were unbridled,
their armour was laid aside, and the hostile nations prepared, or
seemed to prepare, for the refreshment of the evening, and the
encounter of the ensuing day.   On a sudden, the charge was sounded ;
the Arabian camp poured forth a swarm of fresh and intrepid warriors :
and the long line of the Greeks and Africans was surprised, assaulted,
overturned, by new squadrons of the faithful, who, to the eye of fanaticism, might appear as a band of angels descending from the sky.
The præfect himself was slain by the hand of Zobeir : his daughter,
who sought revenge and death, was surrounded and made prisoner ;
and the fugitives involved in their disaster the town of Sufetula, to
which they escaped from the sabres and lances of the Arabs.   Sufetula
was built 150 miles to the south of Carthage : a gentle declivity is
watered by a running stream, and shaded by a grove of Juniper trees ;
and, in the ruins of a triumphal arch, a portico, and three temples of
the Corinthian order, curiosity may yet admire the magnificence of the
Romans.   After the fall of this opulent city, the provincials and Barbarians implored on all sides the mercy of the conqueror.   His vanity
or his zeal might be flattered by offers of tribute or professions of faith :
but his losses, his fatigues, and the progress of an epidemical disease,
prevented a solid establishment ; and the Saracens, after a campaign
of fifteen months, retreated to the confines of Egypt, with the captives
and the wealth of their African expedition.   The caliph's fifth was
granted to a favourite, on the nominal payment of 500,000 pieces of
gold ; but the state was doubly injured by this fallacious transaction,
if each foot-soldier had shared 1000, and each horseman 3000 pieces,
in the real division of the plunder.   The author of the death of Gregory
was expected to have claimed the most precious reward of the victory :
from his silence it might be presumed that he had fallen in the battle,
till the tears and exclamations of the præfect's daughter at the sight of
Zobeir revealed the valour and modesty of that gallant soldier.   The
unfortune virgin was offered, and almost rejected as a slave, by her
father's murderer, who coolly declared that his sword was consecrated
to the service of religion ; and that he laboured for a recompense far
above the charms of mortal beauty, or the riches of this transitory life.
A reward congenial to his temper, was the honourable commission of
announcing to the caliph Othman the success of his arms.   The companions, the chiefs, and the people, were assembled in the mosque of
Medina, to hear the interesting narrative of Zobeir ; and, as the orator
forgot nothing except the merit of his own counsels and actions, the

name of Abdallah was joined by the Arabians with the heroic names of Caled and Amrou.

The western conquests of the Saracens were suspended near twenty years, till their dissensions (A.D. 665—689) were composed by the establishment of the house of Ommiyah : and the caliph Moawiyah was invited by the cries of the Africans themselves. The successors of Heraclius had been informed of the tribute which they had been compelled to stipulate with the Arabs ; but instead of being moved to pity and relieve their distress, they imposed, as an equivalent or a fine, a second tribute of a similar amount. The ears of the Byzantine ministers were shut against the complaints of their poverty and ruin : their despair was reduced to prefer the dominion of a single master ; and the extortions of the patriarch of Carthage, who was invested with civil and military power, provoked the sectaries, and even the Catholics, of the Roman province to abjure the religion as well as the authority of their tyrants. The first lieutenant of Moawiyah acquired a just renown, subdued an important city, defeated an army of 30,000 Greeks, swept away 80,000 captives, and enriched with their spoils the bold adventurers of Syria and Egypt. But the title of conqueror of Africa is more justly due to his successor Akbah. He marched from Damascus at the head of 10,000 of the bravest Arabs ; and the genuine force of the Moslems was enlarged by the doubtful aid and conversion of many thousand Barbarians. It would be difficult, nor is it necessary, to trace the accurate line of the progress of Akbah. The interior regions have been peopled by the Orientals with fictitious armies and imaginary citadels. In the warlike province of Zab or Numidia, 80,000 of the natives might assemble in arms : but the number of 360 towns is incompatible with the ignorance or decay of husbandry ; and a circumference of three leagues will be justified by the ruins of Erbe or Lambesa, the ancient metropolis of that inland country. As we approach the sea-coast, the well-known cities of Bugia and Tangier define the more certain limits of the Saracen victories. A remnant of trade still adheres to the commodious harbour of Bugia, which in a more prosperous age, is said to have contained about 20,000 houses; and the plenty of iron which is dug from the adjacent mountains might have supplied a braver people with the instruments of defence. The remote position and venerable antiquity of Tangi, or Tangier, have been decorated by the Greek and Arabian fables ; but the figurative expressions of the latter, that the walls were constructed of brass, and that the roofs were covered with gold and silver, may be interpreted as the emblems of strength and opulence. The province of Mauritania Tingitana, which assumed the name of the capital, had been imperfectly discovered and settled by the Romans ; that five colonies were confined to a narrow pale, and the more southern parts were seldom explored except by the agents of luxury, who searched the forests for ivory and the citron wood, and the shores of the ocean for the purple shell-fish.

The fearless Akbah plunged into the heart of the country, traversed the wilderness in which his successors erected the splendid capitals of Fez and Morocco, and at length penetrated to the verge of the Atlantic and the great desert. The river Sus descends from the western sides of Mount Atlas, fertilizes, like the Nile, the adjacent soil, and falls into the sea at a moderate distance from the Canary, or Fortunate, islands. Its banks were inhabited by the last of the Moors, a race of savages, without laws or discipline, or religion : they were astonished by the strange and irresistible terrors of the Oriental arms : and as they possessed neither gold nor silver, the richest spoil was the beauty of the female captives, some of whom were afterwards sold for 1000 pieces of gold. The career, though not the zeal, of Akbah was checked by the prospect of a boundless ocean. He spurred his horse into the waves, and raising his eyes to heaven, exclaimed with the tone of a fanatic : " Great God ! if my course were not stopped by this sea, I would still go on to the unknown kingdoms of the West, preaching the unity of thy holy name, and putting to the sword the rebellious nations who worship any other Gods than thee." Yet this Mahometan Alexander, who sighed for new worlds, was unable to preserve his recent conquests. By the universal defection of the Greeks and Africans, he was recalled from the shores of the Atlantic, and the surrounding multitudes left him only the resource of an honourable death. The last scene was dignified by an example of national virtue. An ambitious chief, who had disputed the command and failed in the attempt, was led about as a prisoner in the camp of the Arabian general. The insurgents had trusted to his discontent and revenge ; he disdained their offers and revealed their designs. In the hour of danger, the grateful Akbah unlocked his fetters, and advised him to retire ; he chose to die under the banner of his rival. Embracing as friends and martyrs, they unsheathed their scymetars, broke their scabbards, and maintained an obstinate combat, till they fell by each other's side on the last of their slaughtered countrymen. The third general or governor of Africa, Zuheir, avenged and encountered the fate of his predecessor. He vanquished the natives in many battles ; he was overthrown by a powerful army, which Constantinople had sent to the relief of Carthage.

It had been the frequent practice of the Moorish tribes to join the invaders, to share the plunder, to profess the faith, and to revolt to their savage state of independence and idolatry, on the first retreat or misfortune of the Moslems. The prudence of Akbah had proposed to found an Arabian colony in the heart of Africa ; a citadel that might curb the levity of the barbarians, a place of refuge to secure against the accidents of war, the wealth and the families of the Saracens. With this view, and under the modest title of the station of a caravan, he planted this colony in the fiftieth year (A.D. 670—698) of the Hegira. In its present decay, Cairoan still holds the second rank in the kingdom of Tunis, from which it is distant about 50 miles to the south ; its inland situation, 12 miles westward of the sea, has protected the city from the Greek and Silician fleets.   When the wild beasts and serpents were extirpated, when the forest, or rather wilderness, was cleared, the vestiges of a Roman town were discovered in a sandy plain ; the vegetable food of Cairoan is brought from afar ; and the scarcity of springs constrains the inhabitants to collect in cisterns and reservoirs a precarious supply of rain-water.   These obstacles were subdued by the industry of Akbah ; he traced a circumference of 3600 paces, which he encompassed with a brick wall ; in the space of five years, the governor's palace was surrounded with a sufficient number of private habitations ; a spacious mosque was supported by 500 columns of granite, porphyry, and Numidian marble ; and Cairoan became the seat of learning as well as of empire.   But these were the glories of a later age ; the new colony was shaken by the successive defeats of Akbah and Zuheir, and the western expeditions were again interrupted by the civil discord of the Arabian monarchy.   The son of the valiant Zobeir maintained a war of twelve years, a siege of seven months, against the house of Ommiyah.   Abdallah was said to unite the fierceness of the lion with the subtlety of the fox ; but if he inherited the courage, he was devoid of the generosity of his father.

The return of domestic peace allowed the caliph Abdalmalek to resume the conquest of Africa ; the standard was delivered to Hassan, governor of Egypt, and the revenue of that kingdom, with an army of 40,000 men, was consecrated to the important service.   In the vicissitudes of war, the interior provinces had been alternately won and lost by the Saracens.   But the sea-coast still remained in the hands of the Greeks ; the predecessors of Hassan had respected the name and fortifications of Carthage ; and the number of its defenders was recruited by the fugitives of Cabes and Tripoli.   The arms of Hassan were bolder (A.D. 692—698) and more fortunate : he reduced and pillaged the metropolis of Africa ; and the mention of scaling-ladders may justify the suspicion that he anticipated, by a sudden assault, the more tedious operations of a regular siege.   But the joy of the conquerors was soon disturbed by the appearance of the Christian succours.   The præfect and patrician John, a general of experience and renown, embarked at Constantinople the forces of the Eastern empire ; they were joined by the ships and soldiers of Sicily, and a powerful reinforcement of Goths was obtained from the fears and religion of the Spanish monarch.   The weight of the confederate navy broke the chain that guarded the entrance of the harbour ; the Arabs retired to Cairoan, or Tripoli ; the Christians landed ; the citizens hailed the ensign of the cross, and the winter was idly wasted in the dream of victory or deliverance.   But Africa was irrecoverably lost : the zeal and resentment of the commander of the faithful prepared in the ensuing spring a more numerous armament by sea and land ; and the patrician in his turn was compelled to evacuate the post and fortifications of Carthage. A second battle was fought in the neighbourhood of Utica : the Greeks and Goths were again defeated ; and their timid embarkation saved them from the sword of Hassan, who had invested the slight and insufficient rampart of their camp. Whatever yet remained of Carthage, was delivered to the flames, and the colony of Dido and Cæsar lay desolate above two hundred years, till a part, perhaps a twentieth, of the old circumference was repeopled by the first of the Fatimite caliphs. In the beginning of the sixteenth century, the second capital of the West was represented by a mosque, a college without students, twenty-five or thirty shops, and the huts of five hundred peasants, who, in their abject poverty, displayed the arrogance of the Punic senators. Even that paltry village was swept away by the Spaniards whom Charles the fifth had stationed in the fortress of the Goletta. The ruins of Carthage have perished ; and the place might be unknown if some broken arches of an aqueduct did not guide the footsteps of the inquisitive traveller.

The Greeks were expelled, but the Arabians were not yet masters of the country. In the interior provinces the Moors or *Berbers*, so feeble under the first Cæsars, so formidable to the Byzantine princes, maintained a disorderly resistance to the religion and power of the successors of Mahomet. Under the standard of their queen Cahina, the independent tribes acquired some degree of union and discipline ; and as the Moors respected in their females the character of a prophetess, they attacked the invaders, with an enthusiasm similar to their own. The veteran bands of Hassan were inadequate to the defence of Africa ; the conquests of an age were lost in a single day ; and the Arabian chief, overwhelmed by the torrent, retired to the confines of Egypt, and expected, five years, the promised succours of the caliph. After the retreat of the Saracens, the victorious prophetess assembled the Moorish chiefs, and recommended a measure of strange and savage policy. " Our cities," said she, " and the gold and silver which they contain, perpetually attract the arms of the Arabs. These vile metals are not the objects of *our* ambition ; we content ourselves with the simple productions of the earth. Let us destroy these cities ; let us bury in their ruins those pernicious treasures ; and when the avarice of our foes shall be destitute of temptation, perhaps they will cease to disturb the tranquillity of a warlike people." The proposal was accepted with unanimous applause. From Tangier to Tripoli the buildings, or at least the fortifications, were demolished, the fruit-trees were cut down, the means of subsistence were extirpated, a fertile and popu-lous garden was changed into a desert, and the historians of a more recent period could discern the frequent traces of the prosperity and devastation of their ancestors. Such is the tale of the modern Arabians. Yet I strongly suspect that their ignorance of antiquity, the love of the marvellous, and the fashion of extolling the philosophy of barbarians, has induced them to describe as one voluntary act, the calamities of three hundred years since the first fury of the Donatists and Vandals. In the progress of the revolt Cahina had most probably contributed her share of destruction ; and the alarm of universal ruin might terrify and alienate the cities that had reluctantly yielded to her unworthy yoke. They no longer hoped, perhaps they no longer wished, the return of their Byzantine sovereigns : their present servitude was not alleviated by the benefits of order and justice ; and the most zealous Catholic must prefer the imperfect truths of the Koran to the blind and rude idolatry of the Moors. The general of the Saracens was again received as the saviour of the province : the friends of civil society conspired against the savages of the land ; and the royal prophetess was slain in the first battle which overturned the baseless fabric of her superstition and empire. The same spirit revived under the successor of Hassan ; it was finally quelled by the activity of Musa and his two sons ; but the number of the rebels may be presumed from that of 300,000 captives, 60,000 of whom, the caliph's fifth, were sold for the profit of the public treasury, Thirty thousand of the Barbarian youth were enlisted in the troops ; and the pious labours of Musa to inculcate the knowledge and practice of the Koran, accustomed the Africans to obey the apostle of God and the commander of the faithful. In their climate and government, their diet and habitation, the wandering Moors resembled the Bedouins of the desert. With the religion, they were proud to adopt the language, name, and origin of Arabs : the blood of the strangers and natives was insensibly mingled : and from the Euphrates to the Atlantic the same nation might seem to be diffused over the sandy plains of Asia and Africa. Yet I will not deny that 50,000 tents of pure Arabians might be transported over the Nile, and scattered through the Libyan desert ; and I am not ignorant that five of the Moorish tribes still retain their *barbarous* idiom, with the appellation and character of *white* Africans.

V. In the progress of conquest from the north and south, the Goths and the Saracens encountered each other on the confines of Europe and Africa. In the opinion of the latter, the difference of religion is a reasonable ground of enmity and warfare. As early as the time of Othman their piratical squadrons had ravaged the coast of Andalusia ;* nor had they forgotten the relief of Carthage by the Gothic succours. In that age, as well as in the present, the kings of Spain were possessed of the fortress of Ceuta ; one of the columns of Hercules, which is divided by a narrow strait from the opposite pillar or point of Europe. A small portion of Mauritania was still wanting to the African conquest ; but Musa, in the pride of victory, was repulsed from the walls

---

* The name of Andalusia is applied by the Arabs not only to the modern province, but to the whole peninsula of Spain. The etymology has been most improbably deduced from Vandalusia, country of the Vandals. But the Handalusia of Casiri, which signifies in Arabic the region of the evening, of the West, in a word, the Hesperia of the Greeks, is perfectly apposite.

of Ceuta, by the vigilance and courage of Count Julian, the general of the Goths. From his disappointment and perplexity, Musa was relieved (A.D. 709) by an unexpected message of the Christian chief, who offered his place, his person, and his sword, to the successors of Mahomet, and solicited the disgraceful honour of introducing their arms into the heart of Spain. If we inquire into the cause of his treachery, the Spaniards will repeat the popular story of his daughter Cava ; of a virgin who was seduced, or ravished, by her sovereign ; of a father who sacrificed his religion and country to the thirst of revenge. The passions of princes have often been licentious and destructive ; but this well-known tale, romantic in itself, is indifferently supported by external evidence ; and the history of Spain will suggest some motives of interest and policy more congenial to the breast of a veteran statesman. After the decease or deposition of Witiza, his two sons were supplanted by the ambition of Roderic, a noble Goth, whose father, the duke or governor of a province, had fallen a victim to the preceding tyranny. The monarchy was still elective ; but the sons of Witiza, educated on the steps of the throne, were impatient of a private station. Their resentment was the more dangerous, as it was varnished with the dissimulation of courts : their followers were excited by the remembrance of favours and the promise of a revolution ; and their uncle Oppas, archbishop of Toledo and Seville, was the first person in the church, and the second in the state. It is probable that Julian was involved in the disgrace of the unsuccessful faction, that he had little to hope and much to fear from the new reign ; and that the imprudent king could not forget or forgive the injuries which Roderic and his family had sustained. The merit and influence of the count rendered him a useful or formidable subject : his estates were ample, his followers bold and numerous, and it was too fatally shown that, by his Andalusian and Mauritanian commands, he held in his hands the keys of the Spanish monarchy. Too feeble, however, to meet his sovereign in arms, he sought the aid of a foreign power ; and his rash invitation of the Moors and Arabs produced the calamities of eight hundred years. In his epistles, or in a personal interview, he revealed the wealth and nakedness of his country ; the weakness of an unpopular prince ; the degeneracy of an effeminate people. The Goths were no longer the victorious Barbarians, who had humbled the pride of Rome, despoiled the queen of nations, and penetrated from the Danube to the Atlantic ocean. Secluded from the world by the Pyrenæan mountains, the successors of Alaric had slumbered in a long peace : the walls of the cities were mouldered into dust : the youth had abandoned the exercise of arms ; and the presumption of their ancient renown would expose them in a field of battle to the first assault of the invaders. The ambitious Saracen was fired by the ease and importance of the attempt ; but the execution was delayed till he had consulted the commander of the faithful ; and his messenger returned with the permission of Walid to annex the unknown kingdoms of the West to the religion and throne of the caliphs. In his residence of Tangier, Musa, with secresy and caution, continued his correspondence and hastened his preparations. But the remorse of the conspirators was soothed by the fallacious assurance that he should content himself with the glory and spoil, without aspiring to establish the Moslems beyond the sea that separates Africa from Europe.

Before Musa would trust an army of the faithful to the traitors and infidels of a foreign land, he made a less dangerous trial of their strength and veracity. One hundred Arabs, and four hundred Africans, passed over (A.D. 710. July), in four vessels, from Tangier or Ceuta ; the place of their descent on the opposite shore of the strait, is marked by the name of Tarif their chief; and the date of this memorable event is fixed to the month of Ramadan, of the ninety-first year of the Hegira, to the month of July, 748 years from the Spanish æra of Cæsar, 710 after the birth of Christ. From their first station, they marched 18 miles through an hilly country to the castle and town of Julian ; on which (it is still called Algezire) they bestowed the name of the Green Island, from a verdant cape that advances into the sea. Their hospitable entertainment, the Christians who joined their standard, their inroad into a fertile and unguarded province, the richness of their spoil, and the safety of their return, announced to their brethren the most favourable omens of victory. In the ensuing spring (A.D. 711. April), 5000 veterans and volunteers were embarked under the command of Tarik, a dauntless and skilful soldier, who surpassed the expectation of his chief ; and the necessary transports were provided by the industry of their too faithful ally. The Saracens landed at the pillar or point of Europe ; the corrupt and familiar appellation of Gibraltar *(Gebel al Tarik)* describes the mountain of Tarik ; and the intrenchments of his camp were the first outline of those fortifications, which, in the hands of our countrymen, have resisted the art and power of the house of Bourbon. The adjacent governors informed the court of Toledo of the descent and progress of the Arabs ; and the defeat of his lieutenant Edeco, who had been commanded to seize and bind the presumptuous strangers, admonished Roderic of the magnitude of the danger. At the royal summons, the dukes and counts, the bishops and nobles of the Gothic monarchy, assembled at the head of their followers ; and the title of king of the Romans, which is employed by an Arabic historian, may be excused by the close affinity of language, religion, and manners, between the nations of Spain. His army consisted of 90,000 or 100,000 men ; a formidable power, if their fidelity and discipline had been adequate to their numbers. The troops of Tarik had been augmented to 12,000 Saracens ; but the Christian mal-contents were attracted by the influence of Julian, and a crowd of Africans most greedily tasted the temporal blessings of the Koran. In the neighbourhood of Cadiz, the town of Xeres has been illustrated

by the encounter (July 19—26) which determined the fate of the kingdom; the stream of the Guadalete, which falls into the bay, divided
the two camps, and marked the advancing and retreating skirmishes
of three successive and bloody days.   On the fourth day, the two
armies joined a more serious and decisive issue; but Alaric would
have blushed at the sight of his unworthy successor, sustaining on his
head a diadem of pearls, encumbered with a flowing robe of gold and
silken embroidery, and reclining on a litter, or car of ivory, drawn by
two white mules.   Notwithstanding the valour of the Saracens, they
fainted under the weight of multitudes, and the plain of Xeres was
overspread with 16,000 of their dead bodies.   "My brethren," said
Tarik to his surviving companions, "the enemy is before you, the sea
is behind; whither would ye fly? Follow your general: I am resolved either to lose my life, or to trample on the prostrate king of
the Romans."   Besides the resource of despair, he confided in the
secret correspondence and nocturnal interviews of count Julian, with
the sons and the brother of Witiza.   The two princes and the archbishop of Toledo occupied the most important post : their well-timed
defection broke the ranks of the Christians; each warrior was
prompted by fear or suspicion to consult his personal safety ; and the
remains of the Gothic army were scattered or destroyed in the flight
and pursuit of the three following days.   Amidst the general disorder,
Roderic started from his car, and mounted Orelia, the fleetest of
his horses; but he escaped from a soldier's death to perish more
ignobly in the waters of the Bœtis or Guadalquivir.   His diadem, his
robes, and his courser, were found on the bank ; but as the body of
the Gothic prince was lost in the waves, the pride and ignorance of
the caliph must have been gratified with some meaner head, which
was exposed in triumph before the palace of Damascus.   "And such,"
continues a valiant historian of the Arabs, "is the fate of those kings
who withdraw themselves from a field of battle."

Count Julian had plunged so deep into guilt and infamy, that his
only hope was in the ruin of his country.   After the battle of Xeres he
recommended the most effectual measures to the victorious Saracen.
" The king of the Goths is slain ; their princes are fled before you, the
army is routed, the nation is astonished.   Secure with sufficient
detachments the cities of Bœtica ; but in person, and without delay,
march to the royal city of Toledo, and allow not the distracted
Christians either time or tranquillity for the election of a new
monarch.   Tarik (A.D. 711) listened to his advice.   A Roman captive and proselyte, who had been enfranchised ·by the caliph himself, assaulted Cordova with 700 horse : he swam the river, surprised
the town, and drove the Christians into the great church, where they
defended themselves above three months.   Another detachment reduced the sea-coast of Bœtica, which in the last period of the Moorish
power has comprised in a narrow space the populous kingdom of

Grenada. The march of Tarik from the Bœtis to the Tagus, was directed through the Sierra Morena, that separates Andalusia and Castille, till he appearèd in arms under the walls of Toledo. The most zealous of the Catholics had escaped with the relics of their saints ; and if the gates were shut, it was only till the victor had sub-scribed a fair and reasonable capitulation. The voluntary exiles were allowed to depart with their effects ; seven churches were appropriated to the Christian worship ; the archbishop and his clergy were at liberty to exercise their functions, the monks to practise or neglect their penance ; and the Goths and Romans were left in all civil and criminal cases to the subordinate jurisdiction of their own laws and magistrates. But if the justice of Tarik protected the Christians, his gratitude and policy rewarded the Jews, to whose secret or open aid he was indebted for his most important acquisitions. Persecuted by the kings and synods of Spain, who had often pressed the alternative of banishment or baptism, that outcast nation embraced the moment of revenge : the comparison of their past and present state was the pledge of their fidelity ; and the alliance between the disciples of Moses and of Mahomet, was maintained till the final æra of their common expulsion. From the royal seat of Toledo, the Arabian leader spread his conquests to the north, over the modern realms of Castille and Leon ; but it is needless to enumerate the cities that yielded on his approach, or again to describe the table of emerald, transported from the East by the Romans, acquired by the Goths among the spoils of Rome, and pre-sented by the Arabs to the throne of Damascus. Beyond the Asturian mountains, the maritime town of Gijon was the term of the lieutenant of Musa, who had performed, with the speed of a traveller, his vic-torious march, of 700 miles, from the rock of Gibraltar to the bay of Biscay. The failure of land compelled him to retreat ; and he was recalled to Toledo, to excuse his presumption of subduing a kingdom in the absence of his general. Spain, which, in a more savage and disorderly state, had resisted, two hundred years, the arms of the Romans, was overrun in a few months by those of the Saracens ; and such was the eagerness of submission and treaty, that the governor of Cordova is recorded as the only chief who fell, without conditions, a prisoner into their hands. The cause of the Goths had been irre-vocably judged in the field of Xeres ; and, in the national dismay, each part of the monarchy declined a contest with the antagonist who had vanquished the united strength of the whole. That strength had been wasted by two successive seasons of famine and pestilence ; and the governors, who were impatient to surrender, might exaggerate the difficulty of collecting the provisions of a siege. To disarm the Christians, superstition likewise contributed her terrors : and the subtle Arab encouraged the report of dreams, omens, and prophecies, and of the portraits of the destined conquerors of Spain, that were discovered on the breaking open an apartment of the royal palace. Yet a spark of the vital flame was still alive : some invincible fugitives preferred a life of poverty and freedom in the Asturian valleys ; the hardy mountaineers repulsed the slaves of the caliph ; and the sword of Pelagius has been transformed into the sceptre of the catholic kings.

On the intelligence of this rapid success, the applause of Musa degenerated into envy ; and he began, not to complain, but to fear that Tarik would leave him nothing to subdue. At the head of 10,000 Arabs and 8000 Africans, he (A.D. 712, 713) passed over in person from Mauritania to Spain : the first of his companions were the noblest of the Koreish : his eldest son was left in the command of Africa ; the three younger brethren were of an age and spirit to second the boldest enterprise of their father. At his landing in Algezire, he was respectfully entertained by count Julian, who stifled his inward remorse, and testified, both in words and actions, that the victory of the Arabs had not impaired his attachment to their cause. Some enemies yet remained for the sword of Musa. The tardy repentance of the Goths had compared their own numbers and those of the invaders ; the cities from which the march of Tarik had declined, considered themselves as impregnable ; and the bravest patriots defended the fortifications of Seville and Merida. They were successively besieged and reduced by the labour of Musa, who transported his camp from the Bœtis to the Anas, from the Guadalquivir to the Guadiana. When he beheld the works of Roman magnificence, the bridge, the aqueducts, the triumphal arches, and the theatre, of the ancient metropolis of Lusitania, " I should imagine," said he to his four companions, " that the human race must have united their art and power in the foundation of this city ; happy is the man who shall become its master !" He aspired to that happiness, but the *Emeritans* sustained on this occasion the honour of their descent from the veteran legionaries of Augustus. Disdaining the confinement of their walls, they gave battle to the Arabs on the plain ; but an ambuscade rising from the shelter of a quarry, or a ruin, chastised their indiscretion and intercepted their return. The wooden turrets of assault were rolled forwards to the foot of the rampart ; but the defence of Merida was obstinate and long ; and the *castle of the martyrs* was a perpetual testimony of the losses of the Moslems. The constancy of the besieged was at length subdued by famine and despair ; and the prudent victor disguised his impatience under the names of clemency and esteem. The alternative of exile or tribute was allowed ; and the churches were divided between the two religions ; and the wealth of those who had fallen in the siege, or retired to Gallicia, was confiscated as the reward of the faithful. In the midway between Merida and Toledo, the lieutenant of Musa saluted the vicegerent of the caliph, and conducted him to the palace of the Gothic kings. The first interview was cold and formal : a rigid account was exacted of the treasures of Spain : the character of Tarik was exposed to suspicion and obloquy ;

and the hero was imprisoned, reviled, and ignominiously scourged by the hand, or the command, of Musa. Yet so strict was the discipline, so pure the zeal, or so tame the spirit, of the primitive Moslems, that, after this public indignity, Tarik could serve and be trusted in the reduction of the Tarragonese province. A mosque was erected at Saragossa, by the liberality of the Koreish : the port of Barcelona was opened to the vessels of Syria ; and the Goths were pursued beyond the Pyrenean mountains into their Gallic province of Septimania or Languedoc. In the church of St. Mary at Carcassonne, Musa found, but it is improbable that he left, seven equestrian statues of massy silver ; and from his *term* or column of Narbonne, he returned on his footsteps to the Gallician and Lusitanian shores of the ocean. During the absence of the father, his son Abdelaziz chastised the insurgents of Seville, and reduced, from Malaga to Valentia, the sea-coast of the Mediterranean : his original treaty with the discreet and valiant Theodemir will represent the manners and policy of the times. "*The conditions of peace agreed and sworn between Abdelaziz, the son of Musa, the son of Nassir, and Theodemir, prince of the Goths.* In the name of the most merciful God, Abdelaziz makes peace on these conditions : *that* Theodemir shall not be disturbed in his principality ; nor any injury be offered to the life or property, the wives and children, the religion and temples, of the Christians : *that* Theodemir shall freely deliver his seven cities, Orihuela, Valentola, Alicant, Mola, Vacasora, Bigerra (now Bejar), Ora (or Opta), and Lorca : *that* he shall not assist or entertain the enemies of the caliph, but shall faithfully communicate his knowledge of their hostile designs : *that* himself, and each of the Gothic nobles, shall annually pay one piece of gold, four measures of wheat, as many of barley, with a certain proportion of honey, oil, and vinegar ; and that each of their vassals shall be taxed at one moiety of the said imposition. Given the fourth of Regeb, in the year of the Hegira ninety-four, and subscribed with the names of four Mussulman witnesses." Theodemir and his subjects were treated with uncommon lenity ; but the rate of tribute appears to have fluctuated from a tenth to a fifth, according to the submission or obstinacy of the Christians. In this revolution, many partial calamities were inflicted by the carnal or religious passions of the enthusiasts : some churches were profaned by the new worship : some relics or images were confounded with idols : the rebels were put to the sword ; and one town (an obscure place between Cordova and Seville) was razed to its foundations. Yet if we compare the invasion of Spain by the Goths, or its recovery by the kings of Castile and Arragon, we must applaud the moderation and discipline of the Arabian conquerors.

The exploits of Musa were performed in the evening of life, though he affected to disguise his age by colouring with a red powder the whiteness of his beard. But in the love of action and glory, his breast was still fired with the ardour of youth ; and the possession of Spain was considered only as the first step to the monarchy of Europe. With a powerful armament by sea and land, he was preparing to repass the Pyrenees, to extinguish in Gaul and Italy the declining kingdoms ot the Franks and Lombards, and to preach the unity of God on the altar of the Vatican. From thence subduing the Barbarians of Germany, he proposed to follow the course of the Danube from its source to the Euxine sea, to overthrow the Greek or Roman empire of Constantinople, and returning from Europe to Asia, to unite his new acquisitions with Antioch and the provinces of Syria. But his vast enterprise, perhaps of easy execution, must have seemed extravagant to vulgar minds ; and the visionary conqueror was soon reminded of his dependence and servitude. The friends of Tarik had effectually stated his services and wrongs : at the court of Damascus, the proceedings of Musa were blamed, his intentions were suspected, and his delay in complying with the first invitation was chastised by an harsher and more peremptory summons. An intrepid messenger of the caliph (A.D. 714) entered his camp at Lugo in Gallicia, and in the presence of the Saracens and Christians arrested the bridle of his horse. His own loyalty, or that of his troops, inculcated the duty of obedience : and his disgrace was alleviated by the recall of his rival, and the permission of investing with his two governments his two sons, Abdallah and Abdelaziz. His long triumph from Ceuta to Damascus displayed the spoils of Afric and the treasures of Spain ; 400 Gothic nobles, with gold coronets and girdles, were distinguished in his train : and the number of male and female captives, selected for their birth or beauty, was computed at 18,000, or even at 30,000 persons. As soon as he reached Tiberias in Palestine, he was apprised of the sickness and danger of the caliph, by a private message from Soliman, his brother and presumptive heir ; who wished to reserve for his own reign, the spectacle of victory. Had Walid recovered, the delay of Musa would have been criminal : he pursued his march, and found an enemy on the throne. In his trial before a partial judge, against a popular antagonist, he was convicted of vanity and falsehood ; and a fine of 200,000 pieces of gold either exhausted his poverty or proved his rapaciousness. The unworthy treatment of Tarik was revenged by a similar indignity ; and the veteran commander, after a public whipping, stood a whole day in the sun before the palace gate, till he obtained a decent exile, under the pious name of a pilgrimage to Mecca. The resentment of the caliph might have been satiated with the ruin of Musa ; but his fears demanded the extirpation of a potent and injured family. A sentence of death was intimated with secrecy and speed to the trusty servants of the throne both in Africa and Spain : and the forms, if not the substance, of justice were superseded in this bloody execution. In the mosque or palace of Cordova, Abdelaziz was slain by the swords of the conspirators ; they accused their governor of claiming the honours of royalty ; and his scandalous marriage with Egilona, the widow of Roderic, offended the prejudices both of the Christians and Moslems. By a refinement of cruelty, the head of the son was presented to the father with an insulting question, whether he acknowledged the features of the rebel? " I know his features," he exclaimed with indignation : " I assert his innocence ; and I imprecate the same, a juster, fate, against the authors of his death." The age and despair of Musa raised him above the power of kings ; and he expired at Mecca of the anguish of a broken heart. His rival was more favourably treated : his services were forgiven ; and Tarik was permitted to mingle with the crowd of slaves. I am ignorant whether count Julian was rewarded with the death which he deserved indeed, though not from the hands of the Saracens ; but the tale of their ingratitude to the sons of Witiza is disproved by the most unquestionable evidence. The two royal youths were reinstated in the private patrimony of their father ; but on the decease of Eba the elder, his daughter was unjustly despoiled of her portion by the violence of her uncle Sigebut. The Gothic maid pleaded her cause before the caliph Hasheim, and obtained the restitution of her inheritance ; but she was given in marriage to a noble Arabian, and their two sons, Isaac and Ibrahim, were received in Spain with the consideration that was due to their origin and riches.

A province is assimilated to the victorious state by the introduction of strangers and the imitative spirit of the natives ; and Spain, which had been successively tinctured with Punic, and Roman, and Gothic blood, imbibed, in a few generations, the name and manners of the Arabs. The first conquerors, and the twenty successful lieutenants of the caliphs, were attended by a numerous train of civil and military followers, who preferred a distant fortune to a narrow home : the private and public interest was promoted by the establishment of faithful colonies ; and the cities of Spain were proud to commemorate the tribe or country of their Eastern progenitors. The victorious though motley bands of Tarik and Musa asserted, by the name of *Spaniards*, their original claim of conquest ; yet they allowed their brethren of Egypt to share their establishments of Murcia and Lisbon. The royal legion of Damascus was planted at Cordova : that of Emesa at Seville ; that of Kinnisrin or Chalcis at Jaen ; that of Palestine at Algezire and Medina Sidonia. The natives of Yemen and Persia were scattered round Toledo and the inland country ; and the fertile seats of Grenada were bestowed on 10,000 horsemen of Syria and Irak, the children of the purest and most noble of the Arabian tribes. A spirit of emulation, sometimes beneficial, more frequently dangerous, was nourished by these hereditary factions. Ten years after the conquest, a map of the province was presented to the caliph : the seas, the rivers, and the harbours, the inhabitants and cities, the climate, the soil, and the mineral productions of the earth. In the space of two centuries, the gifts of nature were improved by the agriculture, the manufactures, and the commerce of an industrious people ; and the effects of their diligence have been magnified by the idleness of their fancy. The first of the Ommiades who reigned in Spain solicited the support of the Christians ; and, in his edict of peace and protection, he contents himself with a modest imposition of 10,000 ounces of gold, 10,000 pounds of silver, 10,000 horses, as many mules, 1000 cuirasses, with an equal number of helmets and lances. The most powerful of his successors derived from the same kingdom the annual tribute of 12,045,000 dinars or pieces of gold, about £6,000,000 ; a sum which, in the tenth century, most probably surpassed the united revenues of the Christian monarchs. His royal seat of Cordova contained 600 mosques, 900 baths, and 200,000 houses : he gave laws to 80 cities of the first, to 300 of the second and third order ; and the fertile banks of the Guadalquivir were adorned with 12,000 villages and hamlets. The Arabs might exaggerate the truth, but they created and they describe the most prosperous æra of the riches, the cultivation, and the populousness of Spain.

The wars of the Moslems were sanctified by the prophet ; but, among the various precepts and examples of his life, the caliphs selected the lessons of toleration that might tend to disarm the resistance of the unbelievers. Arabia was the temple and patrimony of the God of Mahomet ; but he beheld with less jealousy and affection the nations of the earth. The polytheists and idolaters who were ignorant of his name, might be lawfully extirpated by his votaries ; but a wise policy supplied the obligation of justice : and after some acts of intolerant zeal, the Mahometan conquerors of Hindostan have spared the pagodas of that devout and populous country. The disciples of Abraham, of Moses, and of Jesus, were solemnly invited to accept the more *perfect* revelation of Mahomet ; but if they preferred the payment of a moderate tribute, they were entitled to the freedom of conscience and religious worship. In a field of battle, the forfeit lives of the prisoners were redeemed by the profession of *Islam ;* the females were bound to embrace the religion of their masters, and a race of sincere proselytes was gradually multiplied by the education of the infant captives. But the millions of African and Asiatic converts, who swelled the native band of the faithful Arabs, must have been allured, rather than constrained, to declare their belief in one God and the apostle of God. By the repetition of a sentence and the loss of a foreskin, the subject or the slave, the captive or the criminal, arose in a moment the free and equal companion of the victorious Moslems. Every sin was expiated, every engagement was dissolved : the vow of celibacy was superseded ; the active spirits who slept in the cloister were awakened by the trumpet of the Saracens ; and in the convulsion of the world, every member of a new society ascended to the natural level of his capacity and courage. The minds of the multitude were tempted by the invisible as well as temporal blessings of the Arabian prophet ;´ and charity will hope that many of his proselytes entertained a serious conviction of the truth and sanctity of his revelation. In the eyes of an inquisitive polytheist, it must appear worthy of the human and the divine nature. More pure than the system of Zoroaster, more liberal than the law of Moses, the religion of Mahomet might seem less inconsistent with reason, than the creed of superstition, which, in the seventh century, disgraced the simplicity of the gospel.

In the extensive provinces of Persia and Africa, the national religion has been eradicated by the Mahometan faith. The ambiguous theology of the Magi stood alone among the sects of the East : but the profane writings of Zoroaster might, under the reverend name of Abraham, be dexterously connected with the chain of divine revelation. Their evil principle, the dæmon Ahriman, might be represented as the rival or as the creature of the God of light. The temples of Persia were devoid of images ; but the worship of the sun and of fire might be stigmatized as a gross and criminal idolatry. The milder sentiment was consecrated by the practice of Mah met and the prudence of the caliphs ; the Magians or Ghebers were ranked with the Jews and Christians among the people of the written law ; and as late as the third century of the Hegira, the city of Herat will afford a lively contrast of private zeal and public toleration. Under the payment of an annual tribute, the Mahometan law secured to the Ghebers of Herat their civil and religious liberties : but the recent and humble mosque was overshadowed by the antique splendour of the adjoining temple of fire. A fanatic Imaum deplored, in his sermons, the scandalous neighbourhood, and accused the weakness or indifference of the faithful. Excited by his voice, the people assembled in tumult ; the two houses of prayer were consumed by the flames, but the vacant ground was immediately occupied by the foundations of a new mosque. The injured Magi appealed to the sovereign of Chorasan ; he promised justice and relief ; when, behold ! four thousand citizens of Herat, of a grave character and a mature age, unanimously swore that the idolatrous fane had *never* existed ; the inquisition was silenced, and their conscience was satisfied (says the historian Mirchond) with this holy and meritorious perjury. But the greatest part of the temples of Persia were ruined by the insensible and general desertion of their votaries. It was *insensible*, since it is not accompanied with any memorial of time or place, of persecution or resistance. It was *general*, since the whole realm, from Shiraz to Samarcand, imbibed the faith of the Koran ; and the preservation of the native tongue reveals the descent of the Mahometans of Persia. In the mountains and deserts, an obstinate race of unbelievers adhered to the superstition of their fathers ; and a faint tradition of the Magian theology is kept alive in the province of Kirman, along the banks of the Indus, among the exiles of

Surat, and in the colony, which, in the last century, was planted by Shaw Abbas at the gates of Ispahan. The chief pontiff has retired to mount Elbourz, eighteen leagues from the city of Yezd : the perpetual fire (if it continue to burn) is inaccessible to the profane ; but his residence is the school, the oracle, and the pilgrimage, of the Ghebers, whose hard and uniform features attest the unmingled purity of their blood. Under the jurisdiction of their elder, 80,000 families maintain an innocent and industrious life ; their subsistence is derived from some curious manufactures and mechanic trades ; and they cultivate the earth with the fervour of a religious duty. Their ignorance withstood the despotism of Shaw Abbas, who demanded with threats and tortures the prophetic books of Zoroaster ; and this obscure remnant of the Magians is spared by the moderation or contempt of their present sovereigns.

The northern coast of Africa is the only land in which the light of the Gospel, after a long and perfect establishment, has been totally extinguished. The arts, which had been taught by Carthage and Rome, were involved in a cloud of ignorance ; the doctrine of Cyprian and Augustin was no longer studied. Five hundred episcopal churches were overturned by the hostile fury of the Donatists, the Vandals, and the Moors. The zeal and numbers of the clergy declined ; and the people, without discipline, or knowledge, or hope, submissively sunk under the yoke of the Arabian prophet. Within fifty years, (A.D. 749) after the expulsion of the Greeks, a lieutenant of Africa informed the caliph that the tribute of the infidels was abolished by their conversion ; and, though he sought to disguise his fraud and rebellion, his specious pretence was drawn from the rapid and extensive progress of the Mahometan faith. In the next age (A.D. 837), an extraordinary mission of five bishops was detached from Alexandria to Cairoan. They were ordained by the Jacobite patriarch to cherish and revive the dying embers of Christianity : but the interposition of a foreign prelate, a stranger to the Latins, an enemy to the Catholics, supposes the decay and dissolution of the African hierarchy. It was no longer the time when the successor of St. Cyprian, at the head of a numerous synod, could maintain an equal contest with the ambition of the Roman pontiff. In the eleventh century (A.D. 1053—1076), the unfortunate priest who was seated on the ruins of Carthage, implored the arms and the protection of the Vatican ; and he bitterly complains that his naked body had been scourged by the Saracens, and that his authority was disputed by the four suffragans, the tottering pillars of his throne. Two epistles of Gregory the seventh are destined to soothe the distress of the Catholics and the pride of a Moorish prince. The pope assures the sultan that they both worship the same God, and may hope to meet in the bosom of Abraham ; but the complaint, that three bishops could no longer be found to consecrate a brother, announces the speedy and inevitable ruin of the episcopal order. The

Christians of Africa and Spain had long since (A.D. 1149, &c.) sub·
mitted to the practice of circumcision and the legal abstinence from
wine and pork; and the name of *Mozarabes* (adoptive Arabs) was applied to their civil or religious conformity. About the middle of the
twelfth century the worship of Christ and the succession of pastors
were abolished along the coast of Barbary, and in the kingdoms of
Cordova and Seville, of Valencia and Grenada. The throne of the
Almohades, or Unitarians, was founded on the blindest fanaticism,
and their extraordinary rigour might be provoked or justified by the
recent victories and intolerant zeal of the princes of Sicily and Castille,
of Arragon and Portugal. The faith of the Mozarabes was occasion-
ally revived by the Papal missionaries; and, on the landing (A.D. 1535)
of Charles the fifth, some families of Latin Christians were encouraged
to rear their heads at Tunis and Algiers. But the seed of the gospel
was quickly eradicated, and the long province from Tripoli to the
Atlantic has lost all memory of the language and religion of Rome.

After the revolution of eleven centuries, the Jews and Christians of
the Turkish empire enjoy the liberty of conscience which was granted
by the Arabian caliphs. During the first age of the conquest, they
suspected the loyalty of the Catholics, whose name of Melchites betrayed their secret attachment to the Greek emperor while the Nestorians and Jacobites, his inveterate enemies, approved themselves
the sincere and voluntary friends of the Mahometan government.
Yet this partial jealousy was healed by time and submission; the
churches of Egypt were shared by the Catholics; and all the Oriental
sects were included in the common benefits of toleration. The rank,
the immunities, the domestic jurisdiction, of the patriarchs, the
bishops, and the clergy, were protected by the civil magistrate: the
learning of individuals recommended them to the employments of secretaries and physicians; they were enriched by the lucrative collection
of the revenue; and their merit was sometimes raised to the command
of cities and provinces. A caliph of the house of Abbas was heard to
declare that the Christians were most worthy of trust in the administration of Persia. "The Moslems," said he, "will abuse their present
fortune; the Magians regret their fallen greatness; and the Jews are
impatient for their approaching deliverance." But the slaves of despotism are exposed to the alternatives of favour and disgrace. The
captive churches of the East have been afflicted in every age by the
avarice or bigotry of their rulers; and the ordinary and legal restraints
must be offensive to the pride or the zeal of the Christians. About two
hundred years after Mahomet, they were separated from their fellow-
subjects by a turban or girdle of a less honourable colour; instead of
horses or mules, they were condemned to ride on asses, in the attitude
of women. Their public and private buildings were measured by a
diminutive standard; in the streets or the baths it is their duty to give
way or bow down before the meanest of the people; and their testi-

mony is rejected, if it may tend to the prejudice of a true believer. The pomp of processions, the sound of bells or of psalmody, is interdicted to their worship : a decent reverence for the national faith is imposed on their sermons and conversations ; and the sacrilegious attempt to enter a mosque or to seduce a Mussulman, will not be suffered to escape with impunity. In a time however of tranquillity and justice the Christians have never been compelled to renounce the Gospel or to embrace the Koran ; but the punishment of death is inflicted upon the apostates who have professed and deserted the law of Mahomet. The martyrs of Cordova provoked the sentence of the cadi, by the public confession of their inconstancy, or their passionate invectives against the person and religion of the prophet.

At the end (A.D. 718) of the first century of the Hegira, the caliphs were the most potent and absolute monarchs of the globe. Their prerogative was not circumscribed, either in right or in fact, by the power of the nobles, the freedom of the commons, the privileges of the church, the votes of a senate, or the memory of a free constitution. The authority of the companions of Mahomet expired with their lives ; and the chiefs or emirs of the Arabian tribes left behind, in the desert, the spirit of equality and independence. The regal and sacerdotal characters were united in the successors of Mahomet ; and if the Koran was the rule of their actions, they were the supreme judges and interpreters of that divine book. They reigned by the right of conquest over the nations of the East, to whom the name of liberty was unknown, and who were accustomed to applaud in their tyrants the acts of violence and severity that were exercised at their own expence. Under the last of the Ommiades, the Arabian empire extended two hundred days' journey from east to west, from the confines of Tartary and India to the shores of the Atlantic ocean. And if we retrench the sleeve of the robe, as it is styled by their writers, the long and narrow province of Africa, the solid and compact dominion from Fargana to Aden, from Tarsus to Surat, will spread on every side to the measure of four or five months of the march of a caravan. We should vainly seek the indissoluble union and easy obedience that pervaded the government of Augustus and the Antonines ; but the progress of the Mahometan religion diffused over this ample space a general resemblance of manners and opinions. The language and laws of the Koran were studied with equal devotion at Samarcand and Seville : the Moor and the Indian embraced as countrymen and brothers in the pilgrimage of Mecca ; and the Arabian language was adopted as the popular idiom in all the provinces to the westward of the Tigris.

When the Arabs first issued from the desert, they must have been surprised at the ease and rapidity of their own success. But when they advanced in the career of victory to the banks of the Indus and the summit of the Pyrenees ; when they had repeatedly tried the edge of their scymetars and the energy of their faith, they might be equally astonished that any nation could resist their invincible arms, that any boundary should confine the dominion of the successor of the prophet. The confidence of soldiers and fanatics may indeed be excused, since the calm historian of the present hour, who strives to follow the rapid course of the Saracens, must study to explain by what means the church and state were saved from this impending, and, as it should seem, from this inevitable danger. The deserts of Scythia and Sarmatia might be guarded by their extent, their climate, their poverty, and the courage of the northern shepherds ; China was remote and inaccessible ; but the greatest part of the temperate zone was subject to the Mahometan conquerors, the Greeks were exhausted by the calamities of war and the loss of their fairest provinces, and the Barbarians of Europe might justly tremble at the precipitate fall of the Gothic monarchy. In this inquiry I shall unfold the events that rescued our ancestors of Britain, and our neighbours of Gaul, from the civil and religious yoke of the Koran ; that protected the majesty of Rome, and delayed the servitude of Constantinople ; that invigorated the defence of the Christians, and scattered among their enemies the seeds of division and decay.

Forty-six years after the flight of Mahomet from Mecca, his disciples appeared (A.D. 668—675) in arms under the walls of Constantinople. They were animated by a genuine or fictitious saying of the prophet, that, to the first army which besieged the city of the Cæsars, their sins were forgiven. No sooner had the caliph Moawiyah suppressed his rivals and established his throne, ʌhan he aspired to expiate the guilt of civil blood, by the success and glory of his holy expedition ; his preparations by sea and land were adequate to the importance of the object ; his standard was entrusted to Sophian, a veteran warrior, but the troops were encouraged by the example and presence of Yezid, the son and presumptive heir of the commander of the faithful. Without delay or opposition, the naval forces of the Saracens passed through the unguarded channel of the Hellespont, which even now, under the feeble and disorderly government of the Turks, is maintained as the natural bulwark of the capital. The Arabian fleet cast anchor, and the troops were disembarked near the palace of Hebdomon, seven miles from the city. During many days, from the dawn of light to the evening, the line of assault was extended from the golden gate to the eastern promontory, and the foremost warriors were impelled by the weight and effort of the succeeding columns. But the besiegers had formed an insufficient estimate of the strength and resources of Constantinople. The solid and lofty walls were guarded by numbers and discipline : the spirit of the Romans was rekindled by the last danger of their religion and empire : the fugitives from the conquered provinces more successfully renewed the defence of Damascus and Alexandria ; and the Saracens were dismayed by the strange and pro-

digious effects of artificial fire. This firm and effectual resistance diverted their arms to the more easy attempts of plundering the European and Asiatic coasts of the Propontis ; and, after keeping the sea
from the month of April to that of September, on the approach of
winter they retreated 80 miles from the capital, to the isle of Cyzicus,
in which they had established their magazine of spoil and provisions.
So patient was their perseverance, or so languid were their operations,
that they repeated in the six following summers the same attack and
retreat, with a gradual abatement of hope and vigour, till the mischances of shipwreck and disease, of the sword and of fire, compelled
them to relinquish the fruitless enterprise. They might bewail the loss
or commemorate the martyrdom of 30,000 Moslems, who fell in the
siege of Constantinople ; and the solemn funeral of Abu Ayub, or Job,
excited the curiosity of the Christians themselves. That venerable
Arab, one of the last of the companions of Mahomet, was numbered
among the *ansars*, or auxiliaries, of Medina, who sheltered the head of
the flying prophet. In his youth he fought, at Beder and Ohud, under·
the holy standard : in his mature age he was the friend and follower
of Ali ; and the last remnant of his strength and life was consumed in
a distant and dangerous war against the enemies of the Koran. His
memory was revered ; but the place of his burial was neglected and
unknown, during a period of 780 years, till the conquest of Constantinople by Mahomet the second. A seasonable vision (for such are
the manufacture of every religion) revealed the holy spot at the foot
of the walls and the bottom of the harbour ; and the mosque of Ayub
has been deservedly chosen for the simple and martial inauguration of
the Turkish sultans.

The event of the siege revived, both in the East and West, the
reputation of the Roman arms, and cast a momentary shade over the
glories of the Saracens. The Greek ambassador was (A.D. 677) favourably received at Damascus, in a general council of the emirs of
Koreish : a peace, or truce, of thirty years was ratified between the
two empires ; and the stipulation of an annual tribute, fifty horses of a
noble breed, fifty slaves, and 3000 pieces of gold, degraded the majesty
of the commander of the faithful. After the revolt of Arabia and
Persia, the house of Ommiyah was reduced to the kingdoms of Syria
and Egypt : but as soon as the empire was again united by the arms
and policy of Abdalmalek, he disclaimed a badge of servitude not less
injurious to his conscience than to his pride : he discontinued the payment of the tribute. Till the reign of Abdalmalek, the Saracens had
been content with the free possession of the Persian and Roman treasures, in the coin of Chosroes and Cæsar. By the command of that
caliph, a national mint was established, both for silver and gold, and
the inscription of the Dinar, though it might be censured by some
timorous casuists, proclaimed the unity of the God of Mahomet.
Under the reign of the caliph Waled, the Greek language and charac-

ters were excluded from the accounts of the public revenue. If this change was productive of the invention or familiar use of our present numerals, the Arabic or Indian cyphers, as they are commonly styled, a regulation of office has promoted the most important discoveries of arithmetic, algebra, and the mathematical sciences.

Whilst the caliph Waled sat idle on the throne of Damascus, while his lieutenants achieved the conquest of Transoxiana and Spain, a third army of Saracens overspread (A.D 716—718) the provinces of Asia Minor, and approached the borders of the Byzantine capital. But the attempt and disgrace of the second siege was reserved for his brother Soliman, whose ambition appears to have been quickened by a more active and martial spirit. The most formidable of the Saracens, Moslemah, the brother of the caliph, advanced at the head of 120,000 Arabs and Persians, the greater part mounted on horses or camels; and the successful sieges of Tyana, Amorium, and Pergamus, were of sufficient duration to exercise their skill and to elevate their hopes. At the well-known passage of Abydos, on the Hellespont, the Mahometan arms were transported, for the first time, from Asia to Europe. From thence, wheeling round the Thracian cities of the Propontis, Moslemah invested Constantinople on the land side, surrounded his camp with a ditch and rampart, prepared and planted his engines of assault, and declared, by words and actions, a patient resolution of expecting the return of seed-time and harvest, should the obstinacy of the besieged prove equal to his own. The Greeks would gladly have ransomed their religion and empire, by a fine or assessment of a piece of gold on the head of each inhabitant of the city; but the liberal offer was rejected with disdain, and the presumption of Moslemah was exalted by the speedy approach and invincible force of the navies of Egypt and Syria. They are said to have amounted to 1800 ships : the number betrays their inconsiderable size; and of the twenty stout and capacious vessels, whose magnitude impeded their progress, each was manned with no more than 100 heavy-armed soldiers. This huge armada proceeded on a smooth sea and with a gentle gale towards the mouth of the Bosphorus; the surface of the strait was overshadowed, in the language of the Greeks, with a moving forest, and the same fatal night had been fixed by the Saracen chief for a general assault by sea and land. To allure the confidence of the enemy, the emperor had thrown aside the chain that usually guarded the entrance of the harbour; but while they hesitated whether they should seize the opportunity or apprehend the snare, the ministers of destruction were at hand. The fireships of the Greeks were launched against them, the Arabs, their arms, and vessels, were involved in the same flames, the disorderly fugitives were dashed against each other or overwhelmed in the waves; and I no longer find a vestige of the fleet, that had threatened to extirpate the Roman name. A still more fatal and irreparable loss was that of the caliph Soliman, who died of an indigestion in his camp near Kinnisrin or Chalcis in

Syria, as he was preparing to lead against Constantinople the remaining forces of the East. The brother of Moslemah was succeeded by a kinsman and an enemy; and the throne of an active and able prince was degraded by the useless and pernicious virtues of a bigot. While he started and satisfied the scruples of a blind conscience, the siege was continued through the winter by the neglect rather than by the resolution of the caliph Omar. The winter proved uncommonly rigorous: above an hundred days the ground was covered with deep snow, and the natives of the sultry climes of Egypt and Arabia lay torpid and almost lifeless in their frozen camp. They revived on the return of spring; a second effort had been made in their favour; and their distress was relieved by the arrival of two numerous fleets, laden with corn, and arms, and soldiers; the first from Alexandria, of 400 transports and galleys; the second of 360 vessels from the ports of Africa. But the Greek fires were again kindled, and if the destruction was less complete, it was owing to the experience which had taught the Moslems to remain at a safe distance, or to the perfidy of the Egyptian mariners, who deserted with their ships to the emperor of the Christians. But the calamities of famine and disease were soon felt by the troops of Moslemah, and as the former was miserably assuaged, so the latter was dreadfully propagated by the pernicious nutriment which hunger compelled them to extract from the most unclean or unnatural food. The spirit of conquest, and even of enthusiasm, was extinct: the Saracens could no longer straggle beyond their lines, either single or in small parties, without exposing themselves to the merciless retaliation of the Thracian peasants. At length, after a siege of thirteen months, the hopeless Moslemah received from the caliph the welcome permission of retreat. The march of the Arabian cavalry over the Hellespont and through the provinces of Asia, was executed without delay or molestation; but an army of their brethren had been cut in pieces on the side of Bithynia, and the remains of the fleet was so repeatedly damaged by tempest and fire, that only five galleys entered the port of Alexandria to relate the tale of their various and almost incredible disasters.

Constantinople and the Greek fire might exclude the Arabs from the eastern entrance of Europe; but in the West, on the side of the Pyrenees, the provinces of Gaul were threatened and invaded (A.D. 721, &c.) by the conquerors of Spain. The decline of the French monarchy invited the attack of these insatiate fanatics. Under Eudes, duke of Aquitain, who usurped the authority and even the title of king, the Goths, the Gascons, and the Franks, were assembled, and he repelled the first invasion of the Saracens; and Zama, lieutenant of the caliph, lost his army and his life under the walls of Tholouse. The ambition of his successors was stimulated by revenge; they repassed the Pyrenees with the means and the resolution of conquest. The advantageous situation which had recommended Narbonne as the first

Roman colony, was again chosen by the Moslems; they claimed the province of Septemania or Languedoc as a just dependence of the Spanish monarchy: the vineyards of Gascony and the city of Bourdeaux were possessed by the sovereign of Damascus and Samarcand; and the south of France, from the mouth of the Garonne to that of the Rhône, assumed the manners and religion of Arabia.

But these narrow limits were scorned by the spirit of Abdalrahman, or Abderame, who had been restored by the caliph Hashem to the wishes of the soldiers and people of Spain. That veteran and daring commander adjudged to the obedience of the prophet whatever yet remained of France or Europe; and prepared (A.D. 731) to execute the sentence, at the head of a formidable host, in the full confidence of surmounting all opposition, either of nature or of man. His first care was to suppress a domestic rebel, who commanded the most important passes of the Pyrenees: Munuza, a Moorish chief, had accepted the alliance of the duke of Aquitain; and Eudes, from a motive of private or public interest, devoted his beauteous daughter to the embraces of the African misbeliever. But the strongest fortresses of Cerdagne were invested by a superior force; the rebel was overtaken and slain in the mountains; and his widow was sent a captive to Damascus, to gratify the vanity of the commander of the faithful. From the Pyrenees, Abderame proceeded without delay to the passage of the Rhône and the siege of Arles. An army of Christians attempted the relief of the city: the tombs of their leaders were yet visible in the thirteenth century; and many thousands of their dead bodies were carried down the rapid stream into the Mediterranean sea. The arms of Abderame were not less successful on the side of the ocean. He passed without opposition the Garonne and Dordogne, which unite their waters in the gulf of Bourdeaux; but he found, beyond those rivers, the camp of the intrepid Eudes, who had formed a second army, and sustained a second defeat, so fatal to the Christians, that, according to their sad confession, God alone could reckon the number of the slain. The victorious Saracen overran the provinces of Aquitain, whose Gallic names are disguised, rather than lost, in the modern appelations of Perigord, Santoigne, and Poitou: his standards were planted on the walls, or at least before the gates, of Tours and of Sens; and his detachments overspread the kingdom of Burgundy as far as the well-known cities of Lyons and Besançon. The memory of these devastations, for Abderame did not spare the country or the people, was long preserved by tradition; and the invasion of France by the Moors or Mahometans, affords the ground-work of those fables, which have been so wildly disfigured in the romances of chivalry, and so elegantly adorned by the Italian muse. In the decline of society and art, the deserted cities could supply a slender booty to the Saracens; their richest spoil was found in the churches and monasteries, which they stripped of their ornaments and delivered to the flames: and the tutelar saints, both Hilary of Poitiers and Martin of Tours, forgot their miraculous powers in the defence of their own sepulchres. A victorious line of march had been prolonged above 1000 miles from the rock of Gibraltar to the banks of the Loire ; the repetition of an equal space would have carried the Saracens to the confines of Poland and the Highlands of Scotland : the Rhine is not more impassable than the Nile or Euphrates, and the Arabian fleet might have sailed without a naval combat into the mouth of the Thames. Perhaps the interpretation of the Koran would now be taught in the schools of Oxford, and her pulpits might demonstrate to a circumcised people the sanctity and truth of the revelation of Mahomet.

From such calamities was Christendom delivered by the genius and fortune of one man. Charles, the illegitimate son of the elder Pepin, was content with the titles of mayor or duke of the Franks, but he deserved to become the father of a line of kings. In a laborious administration of twenty-four years, he restored and supported the dignity of the throne, and the rebels of Germany and Gaul were successively crushed by the activity of a warrior, who, in the same campaign, could display his banner on the Elbe, the Rhône, and the shores of the ocean. In the public danger, he was summoned by the voice of his country ; and his rival, the duke of Aquitain, was reduced to appear among the fugitives and suppliants. "Alas !" exclaimed the Franks, " what a misfortune ! what an indignity ! We have long heard of the name and conquests of the Arabs : we were apprehensive of their attack from the East ; they have now conquered Spain, and invade our country on the side of the West. Yet their numbers, and (since they have no buckler) their arms, are inferior to our own." "If you follow my advice," replied the prudent mayor of the palace, " you will not interrupt their march, nor precipitate your attack. They are like a torrent, which it is dangerous to stem in its career. The thirst of riches, and the consciousness of success, redouble their valour, and valour is of more avail than arms and numbers. Be patient till they have loaded themselves with the incumbrance of wealth. The possession of wealth will divide their counsels and assure your victory." This subtle policy is perhaps a refinement of the Arabian writers ; and the situation of Charles will suggest a more narrow and selfish motive of procrastination ; the secret desire of humbling the pride, and wasting the provinces, of the rebel duke of Aquitain. It is yet more probable, that the delays of Charles were inevitable and reluctant. A standing army was unknown under the first and second race : more than half the kingdom was now in the hands of the Saracens : according to their respective situation, the Franks of Neustria and Austrasia were too conscious or too careless of the impending danger ; and the voluntary aids of the Gepidæ and Germans were separated by a long interval from the standard of the Christian general. No sooner had he collected his forces, than he sought and found the enemy in the centre of France, between Tours and Poitiers. His well-conducted march was covered by a range of hills, and Ab-derame appears to have been surprised by his unexpected presence. The nations of Asia, Africa, and Europe, advanced with equal ardour to an encounter which would change the history of the world. In the six first days of desultory combat, the horsemen and archers of the East maintained their advantage : but in the closer onset of the seventh day, the Orientals were oppressed by the strength and stature of the Germans, who, with stout hearts and *iron* hands, asserted the civil and religious liberty of their posterity. The epithet of *Martel*, the *Hammer*, which has been added to the name of Charles, is ex-pressive of his weighty and irresistible strokes : the valour of Eudes was excited by resentment and emulation ; and their companions, in the eye of history, are the true Peers and Paladins of French chivalry. After a bloody field (A.D. 732), in which Abderame was slain, the Sara-cens, in the close of the evening, retired to their camp. In the disorder and despair of the night, the various tribes of Yemen and Damascus, of Africa and Spain, were provoked to turn their arms against each other : the remains of their host was suddenly dissolved, and each *emir* consulted his safety by an hasty and separate retreat. At the dawn of day, the stillness of an hostile camp was suspected by the victorious Christians : on the report of their spies, they ventured to ex-plore the riches of the vacant tents ; but, if we except some celebrated relics, a small portion of the spoil was restored to the innocent and lawful owners. The joyful tidings were soon diffused over the Catho-lic world, and the monks of Italy could affirm and believe that 350,000 or 375,000 of the Mahometans had been crushed by the hammer of Charles ; while no more than 1500 Christians were slain in the field of Tours. But this incredible tale is sufficiently disproved by the cau-tion of the French general, who apprehended the snares and accidents of a pursuit, and dismissed his German allies to their native forests. The inactivity of a conqueror betrays the loss of strength and blood, and the most cruel execution is inflicted, not in the ranks of battle, but on the backs of a flying enemy. Yet the victory of the Franks was complete and final ; Aquitain was recovered by the arms of Eudes; the Arabs never resumed the conquest of Gaul, and they were soon driven beyond the Pyrenees by Charles Martel and his valiant race.

The loss of an army, or a province, in the western world, was less painful to the court of Damascus, than the rise and progress (A.D. 749, 750) of a domestic competitor. Except among the Syrians, the caliphs of the house of Ommiyah had never been the objects of the public favour. The Life of Mahomet recorded their perseverance in idolatry and rebellion : their conversion had been reluctant, their elevation irregular and factious, and their throne was cemented with the most holy and noble blood of Arabia. The best of their race, the pious Omar, was dissatisfied with his own title : their personal virtues were insufficient to justify a departure from the order of succession ; and the eyes and wishes of the faithful were turned towards the line of Hashem and the kindred of the apostle of God. Of these the Fatimites were either rash or pusillanimous ; but the descendants of Abbas cherished, with courage and discretion, the hopes of their rising fortunes. From an obscure residence in Syria, they secretly dispatched their agents and missionaries, who preached in the Eastern provinces their hereditary indefeasible right ; and Mohammed, the son of Ali, the son of Abdallah, the son of Abbas, the uncle of the prophet, gave audience to the deputies of Chorasan, and accepted their free gift of 400,000 pieces of gold. After the death of Mohammed, the oath of allegiance was administered in the name of his son Ibrahim to a numerous band of votaries, who expected only a signal and a leader ; and the governor of Chorasan continued to deplore his fruitless admonitions and the deadly slumber of the caliphs of Damascus, till he himself with all his adherents was driven from the city and palace of Meru, by the rebellious arms of Abu Moslem. That maker of kings, the author, as he is named, of the *call* of the Abbassides, was at length rewarded for his presumption of merit with the usual gratitude of courts. A mean, perhaps a foreign, extraction, could not repress the aspiring energy of Abu Moslem. Jealous of his wives, liberal of his wealth, prodigal of his own blood and of that of others, he could boast with pleasure, and possibly with truth, that he had destroyed 600,000 of his enemies : and such was the intrepid gravity of his mind and countenance, that he was never seen to smile except on a day of battle. In the visible separation of parties the *green* was consecrated to the Fatimites ; the Ommiades were distinguished by the *white;* and the *black*, as the most adverse, was naturally adopted by the Abbassides. Their turbans and garments were stained with that gloomy colour : two black standards on pike-staves nine cubits long, were borne aloft in the van of Abu Moslem : and their allegorical names of the *night* and the *shadow* obscurely represented the indissoluble union and perpetual succession of the line of Hashem. From the Indus to the Euphrates the East was convulsed by the quarrel of the white and the black factions : the Abbassides were most frequently victorious ; but their public success was clouded by the personal misfortune of their chief. The court of Damascus, awakening from a long slumber, resolved to prevent the pilgrimage of Mecca, which Ibrahim had undertaken with a splendid retinue, to recommend himself at once to the favour of the prophet and of the people. A detachment of cavalry intercepted his march and arrested his person ; and the unhappy Ibrahim, snatched away from the promise of untasted royalty, expired in iron fetters in the dungeons of Haran. His two younger brothers, Saffah and Almansor, eluded the search of the tyrant, and lay concealed at Cufa, till the zeal of the people and the approach of his eastern friends allowed them to expose their persons to the impatient public. On Friday, in the dress of a caliph, in the colours of the sect, Saffah proceeded with religious and military pomp to the mosque : ascending the pulpit, he prayed and preached as the lawful successor of Mahomet ; and, after his departure, his kinsmen bound a willing people by an oath of fidelity. But it was on the banks of the Zab, and not in the mosque of Cufa, that this important controversy was determined. Every advantage appeared to be on the side of the white faction : the authority of established government ; an army of 120,000 soldiers, against a sixth part of that number ; and the presence and merit of the caliph Mervan, the fourteenth and last of the house of Ommiyah. Before his accession to the throne, he had deserved, by his Georgian warfare, the honourable epithet of the ass of Mesopotamia ; and he might have been ranked among the greatest princes, had not, says Abulfeda, the eternal order decreed that moment for the ruin of his family ; a decree against which all human prudence and fortitude must struggle in vain. The orders of Mervan were mistaken or disobeyed : the return of his horse, from which he had dismounted on a necessary occasion, impressed the belief of his death ; and the enthusiasm of the black squadrons was ably conducted by Abdallah, the uncle of his competitor. After an irretrievable defeat, the caliph escaped to Mosul ; but the colours of the Abbassides were displayed from the rampart ; he suddenly repassed the Tigris, cast a melancholy look on his palace of Haran, crossed the Euphrates, abandoned the fortifications of Damascus, and, without halting in Palestine, pitched his last and fatal camp at Busir on the banks of the Nile. His speed was urged by the incessant diligence of Abdallah, who in every step of the pursuit acquired strength and reputation : the remains of the white faction were finally vanquished in Egypt ; and the lance, which terminated (A.D. 750. Feb. 10) the life and anxiety of Mervan, was not less welcome perhaps to the unfortunate than to the victorious chief. The merciless inquisition of the conqueror eradicated the most distant branches of the hostile race : their bones were scattered, their memory was accursed, and the martyrdom of Hossein was abundantly revenged on the posterity of his tyrants. Fourscore of the Ommiades, who had yielded to the faith or clemency of their foes, were invited to a banquet at Damascus. The laws of hospitality were violated by a promiscuous massacre : the board was spread over their fallen bodies ; and the festivity of the guests was enlivened by the music of their dying groans. By the event of the civil war the dynasty of the Abbassides was firmly established ; but the Christians only could triumph in the mutual hatred and common loss of the disciples of Mahomet.

Yet the thousands who were swept away by the sword of war might have been speedily retrieved in the succeeding generation, if the consequences of the revolution had not tended to dissolve the power and unity of the empire of the Saracens. In the proscription of the Ommiades, a royal youth of the name of Abdalrahman alone escaped the

rage of his enemies, who hunted the wandering exile from the bank
of the Euphrates to the valleys of mount Atlas. His presence in the
neighbourhood of Spain revived the zeal of the white faction. The
name and cause of the Abbassides had been first vindicated by the
Persians : the West had been pure from civil arms ; and the servants
of the abdicated family still held, by a precarious tenure, the inheritance of their lands and the offices of government. Strongly prompted
by gratitude, indignation, and fear, they (A.D. 755) invited the grandson of the caliph Hashem to ascend the throne of his ancestors : and
in his desperate condition, the extremes of rashness and prudence
were almost the same. The acclamations of the people saluted his
landing on the coast of Andalusia ; and, after a successful struggle,
Abdalrahman established the throne of Cordova, and was the father
of the Ommiades of Spain, who reigned above 250 years from the Atlantic to the Pyrenees. He slew in battle a lieutenant of the Abbassides, who had invaded his dominions with a fleet and army : the head
of Ala, in salt and camphire, was suspended by a daring messenger
before the palace of Mecca ; and the caliph Almansor rejoiced in his
safety, that he was removed by seas and lands from such a formidable adversary. Their mutual designs or declarations of offensive
war evaporated without effect ; but instead of opening a door to the
conquest of Europe, Spain was dissevered from the trunk of the
monarchy, engaged in perpetual hostility with the East, and inclined
to peace and friendship with the Christian sovereigns of Constantinople and France. The example of the Ommiades was imitated by
the real or fictitious progeny of Ali, the Edrissites of Mauritania, and
the more powerful Fatimites of Africa and Egypt. In the tenth century, the chair of Mahomet was disputed by three caliphs or commanders of the faithful, who reigned at Bagdad, Cairoan, and Cordova, excommunicated each other, and agreed only in a principle of
discord, that a sectary is more odious and criminal than an unbeliever.

Mecca was the patrimony of the line (A.D. 750—960) of Hashem,
yet the Abbassides were never tempted to reside either in the birth-
place or the city of the prophet. Damascus was disgraced by the
choice, and polluted with the blood, of the Ommiades ; and after
some hesitation, Almansor, the brother and successor of Saffah, laid
the foundations of Bagdad, the Imperial seat of his posterity during
a reign of 500 years. The chosen spot is on the eastern bank of the
Tigris about fifteen miles above the ruins of Modain : the double wall
was of a circular form ; and such was the rapid increase of a capital,
now dwindled to a provincial town, that the funeral of a popular saint
might be attended by 800,000 men and 60,000 women of Bagdad and
the adjacent villages. In this *city of peace*, amidst the riches of the
East, the Abbassides soon disdained the abstinence and frugality of
the first caliphs, and aspired to emulate the magnificence of the Persian kings. After his wars and buildings, Almansor left behind him

in gold and silver about thirty millions sterling; and this treasure was exhausted in a few years by the vices or virtues of his children. His son, Mahadi, in a single pilgrimage to Mecca, expended six millions of dinars of gold. A pious and charitable motive may sanctify the foundation of cisterns and caravanseras which he distributed along a measured road of 700 miles; but his train of camels, laden with snow, could serve only to astonish the natives of Arabia, and to refresh the fruits and liquors of the royal banquet. The courtiers would surely praise the liberality of his grandson Almamon, who gave away four-fifths of the income of a province, a sum of two millions four hundred thousand gold dinars, before he drew his foot from the stirrup. At the nuptials of the same prince, a thousand pearls of the largest size were showered on the head of the bride, and a lottery of lands and houses displayed the capricious bounty of fortune. The glories of the court were brightened rather than impaired in the decline of the empire; and a Greek ambassador might admire or pity the magnificence of the feeble Moctader. "The caliph's whole army," says the historian Abulfeda, "both horse and foot, was under arms, which together made a body of 160,000 men. His state officers, the favourite slaves, stood near him in splendid apparel, their belts glittering with gold and gems. Near them were 7000 eunuchs, 4000 of them white, the remainder black. The porters or doorkeepers were in number seven hundred. Barges and boats, with the most superb decorations, were seen swimming upon the Tigris. Nor was the place itself less splendid, in which were hung up 38,000 pieces of tapestry, 12,500 of which were of silk embroidered with gold. The carpets on the floor were twenty-two thousand. An hundred lions were brought out, with a keeper to each lion. Among the other spectacles of rare and stupendous luxury, was a tree of gold and silver spreading into eighteen large branches, on which, and on the lesser boughs, sat a variety of birds made of the same precious metals, as well as the leaves of the tree. While the machinery affected spontaneous motions, the several birds warbled their natural harmony. Through this scene of magnificence, the Greek ambassador was led by the visir to the foot of the caliph's throne." In the West, the Ommiades of Spain supported, with equal pomp, the title of commander of the faithful. Three miles from Cordova, in honour of his favourite sultana, the third and greatest of the Abdalrahmans constructed the city, palace, and gardens of Zehra. Twenty-five years, and above three millions sterling, were employed by the founder: his liberal taste invited the artists of Constantinople, the most skilful sculptors and architects of the age; and the buildings were sustained or adorned by twelve hundred columns of Spanish and African, of Greek and Italian marble. The hall of audience was encrusted with gold and pearls, and a great bason in the centre, was surrounded with the curious and costly figures of birds and quadrupeds. In a lofty

pavilion of the gardens, one of these basons and fountains, so delightful in a sultry climate, was replenished not with water, but with the
purest quicksilver. The seraglio of Abdalrahman, his wives, concubines, and black eunuchs, amounted to 6300 persons ; and he was attended to the field by a guard of 12,000 horse, whose belts and scymetars were studded with gold.

In a private condition, our desires are perpetually repressed by
poverty and subordination ; but the lives and labours of millions are
devoted to the service of a despotic prince, whose laws are blindly
obeyed, and whose wishes are instantly gratified. Our imagination
is dazzled by the splendid picture ; and whatever may be the cool dictates of reason, there are few among us who would obstinately refuse
a trial of the comforts and the cares of royalty. It may therefore be
of some use to borrow the experience of the same Abdalrahman,
whose magnificence has perhaps excited our admiration and envy, and
to transcribe an authentic memorial which was found in the closet of
the deceased caliph. " I have now reigned about fifty years in victory or peace ; beloved by my subjects, dreaded by my enemies, and
respected by my allies. Riches and honours, power and pleasure,
have waited on my call, nor does any earthly blessing appear to have
been wanting to my felicity. In this situation, I have diligently numbered the days of pure and genuine happiness which have fallen to
my lot : they amount to FOURTEEN :—O man ! place not thy confidence in this present world." The luxury of the caliphs, so useless to their private happiness, relaxed the nerves, and terminated the
progress, of the Arabian empire. Temporal and spiritual conquest
had been the sole occupation of the first successors of Mahomet ; and
after supplying themselves with the necessaries of life, the whole
revenue was scrupulously devoted to that salutary work. The Abbassides were impoverished by the multitude of their wants and their
contempt of economy. Instead of pursuing the great object of ambition, their leisure, their affections, the powers of their mind, were
diverted by pomp and pleasure : the rewards of valour were em-
bezzled by women and eunuchs, and the royal camp was encumbered
by the luxury of the palace. A similar temper was diffused among
the subjects of the caliph. Their stern enthusiasm was softened by
time and prosperity : they sought riches in the occupations of industry, fame in the pursuits of literature, and happiness in the tranquillity
of domestic life. War was no longer the passion of the Saracens ;
and the increase of pay was insufficient to allure the posterity of those
voluntary champions who had crowded to the standard of Abubeker
and Omar for the hopes of spoil and of paradise.

Under the reign of the Ommiades, the studies of the Moslems were
confined to the interpretation of the Koran, and the eloquence and
poetry of their native tongue. A people continually exposed to the
dangers of the field, must esteem the healing powers of medicine or

rather of surgery : but the starving physicians of Arabia murmured a complaint, that exercise and temperance deprived them of the greatest part of their practice.   After their civil and domestic wars, the sub-jects of the Abbassides, awakening (A.D. 754, &c. 813, &c.) from this mental lethargy, found leisure and felt curiosity for the acquisition of profane science.   This spirit was first encouraged by the caliph Al-mansor, who besides his knowledge of the Mahometan law, had ap-plied himself with success to the study of astronomy.   But when the sceptre devolved to Almamon, the seventh of the Abbassides, he com-pleted the designs of his grandfather, and invited the muses from their ancient seats.   His ambassadors at Constantinople, his agents in Armenia, Syria, and Egypt, collected the volumes of Grecian science : at his command they were translated by the most skilful interpreters into the Arabic language : his subjects were exhorted assiduously to peruse these instructive writings ; and the successor of Mahomet as-sisted with pleasure and modesty at the assemblies and disputations of the learned.   " He was not ignorant," says Abulpharagius, " that *they* are the elect of God, his best and most useful servants, whose lives are devoted to the improvement of their rational faculties.   The mean ambition of the Chinese or the Turks may glory in the industry of their hands or the indulgence of their brutal appetites.   Yet these dexterous artists must view, with hopeless emulation, the hexagons and pyramids of the cells of a bee-hive : these fortitudinous heroes are awed by the superior fierceness of the lions and tigers.   The teachers of wisdom are the true luminaries and legislators of a world, which, without their aid, would again sink in ignorance and bar-barism."   The zeal and curiosity of Almamon were imitated by succeeding princes of the line of Abbas : their rivals, the Fatimites of Africa and the Ommiades of Spain, were the patrons of the learned, as well as the commanders of the faithful : the same royal prerogative was claimed by their independent emirs of the provinces ; and their emulation diffused the taste and the rewards of science from Samarcand and Bochara to Fez and Cordova.   The visir of a sultan consecrated a sum of 200,000 pieces of gold to the foundation of a college at Bag-dad, which he endowed with an annual revenue of 15,000 dinars.   The fruits of instruction were communicated, perhaps at different times, to 6000 disciples of every degree, from the son of the noble to that of the mechanic : a sufficient allowance was provided for the indigent scholars ; and the merit or industry of the professors was repaid with adequate stipends.   In every city the productions of Arabic literature were copied and collected by the curiosity of the studious and the vanity of the rich.   A private doctor refused the invitation of the sultan of Bochara, because the carriage of his books would have required 400 camels.   The royal library of the Fatimites consisted of 100,000 manu-scripts, elegantly transcribed and splendidly bound, which were lent, without jealousy or avarice, to the students of Cairo.   Yet this collection must appear moderate, if we can believe that the Ommiades of Spain had formed a library of 600,000 volumes, forty-four of which were employed in the mere catalogue. Their capital, Cordova, with the adjacent towns of Malaga, Almeria, and Murcia, had given birth to more than 300 writers, and above 70 public libraries were opened in the cities of the Andalusian kingdom. The age of Arabian learning continued about 500 years, till the great eruption of the Moguls, and was coeval with the darkest and most slothful period of European annals ; but since the sun of science has arisen in the West, it should seem that the Oriental studies have languished and declined.

In the libraries of the Arabians, as in those of Europe, the far greater part of the innumerable volumes were possessed only of local value or imaginary merit. The shelves were crowded with orators and poets, whose style was adapted to the taste and manners of their countrymen ; with general and partial histories, which each revolving generation supplied with a new harvest of persons and events ; with codes and commentaries of jurisprudence, which derived their authority from the law of the prophet ; with the interpreters of the Koran, and orthodox tradition ; and with the whole theological tribe, polemics, mystics, scholastics, and moralists, the first or the last of writers, according to the different estimate of sceptics or believers. The works of speculation or science may be reduced to the four classes of philosophy, mathematics, astronomy, and physic. The sages of Greece were translated and illustrated in the Arabic language, and some treatises, now lost in the original, have been recovered in the versions of the East, which possessed and studied the writings of Aristotle and Plato, of Euclid and Apollonius, of Ptolemy, Hippocrates, and Galen. Among the ideal systems, which have varied with the fashion of the times, the Arabians adopted the philosophy of the Stagirite, alike intelligible or alike obscure for the readers of every age. Plato wrote for the Athenians, and his allegorical genius is too closely blended with the language and religion of Greece. After the fall of that religion, the peripatetics, emerging from their obscurity, prevailed in the controversies of the Oriental sects, and their founder was long afterwards restored by the Mahometans of Spain to the Latin schools. The physics, both of the Academy and the Lycæum, as they are built, not on observation, but on argument, have retarded the progress of real knowledge. The metaphysics of infinite, or finite, spirit, have too often been enlisted in the service of superstition. But the human faculties are fortified by the art and practice of dialectics ; the ten predicaments of Aristotle collect and methodize our ideas, and his syllogism is the keenest weapon of dispute. It was dexterously wielded in the schools of the Saracens, but as it is more effectual for the detection of error than for the investigation of truth, it is not surprising that new generations of masters and disciples should still revolve in the same circle of logical argument. The mathematics are distinguished by a peculiar privilege, that, in the course of ages, they may always advance, and can never recede. But the ancient geometry, if I am not misinformed, was resumed in the same state by the Italians of the fifteenth century : and whatever may be the origin of the name, the science of algebra is ascribed to the Grecian Diophantus by the modest testimony of the Arabs themselves. They cultivated with more success the sublime science of astronomy, which elevates the mind of man to disdain his diminutive planet and momentary existence. The costly instruments of observation were supplied by the caliph Almamon, and the land of the Chaldæans still afforded the same spacious level, the same unclouded horizon. In the plains of Shinar, and a second time in those of Cufa, his mathematicians accurately measured a degree of the great circle of the earth, and determined at 24,000 miles the entire circumference of our globe. From the reign of the Abbassides to that of the grandchildren of Tamerlane, the stars, without the aid of glasses, were diligently observed ; and the astronomical tables of Bagdad, Spain, and Samarcand, correct some minute errors, without daring to renounce the hypothesis of Ptolemy, without advancing a step towards the discovery of the solar system. In the eastern courts, the truth of science could be recommended only by ignorance and folly, and the astronomer would have been disregarded, had he not debased his wisdom or honesty by the vain predictions of astrology. But in the science of medicine, the Arabians have been deservedly applauded. The names of Mesua and Geber, of Razis and Avicenna, are ranked with the Grecian masters ; in the city of Bagdad, 860 physicians were licensed to exercise their lucrative profession : in Spain, the life of the Catholic princes was entrusted to the skill of the Saracens, and the school of Salerno, their legitimate offspring, revived in Italy and Europe the precepts of the healing art. The success of each professor must have been influenced by personal and accidental causes but we may form a less fanciful estimate of their general knowledge of anatomy, botany, and chemistry, the threefold basis of their theory and practice. A superstitious reverence for the dead confined both the Greeks and Arabians to the dissection of apes and quadrupeds the more solid and visible parts were known in the time of Galen, and the finer scrutiny of the human frame was reserved for the microscope, and the injections of modern artists. Botany is an active science, and the discoveries of the torrid zone might enrich the herbal of Dioscorides with two thousand plants. Some traditionary knowledge might be secreted in the temples and monasteries of Egypt ; much useful experience had been acquired in the practice of arts and manufactures but the *science* of chemistry owes its origin and improvement to the industry of the Saracens. They first invented and named the alembic for the purposes of distillation, analyzed the substances of the three kingdoms of nature, tried the distinction and affinities of alkalis and acids, and converted the poisonous minerals into soft and salutary medicines. But the most eager search of Arabian chemistry was the transmutation of metals, and the elixir of immortal health : the reason and the fortunes of thousands were evaporated in the crucibles of alchemy, and the consummation of the great work was promoted by the worthy aid of mystery, fable, and superstition.

But the Moslems deprived themselves of the principal benefits of a familiar intercourse with Greece and Rome, the knowledge of antiquity, the purity of taste, and the freedom of thought. Confident in the riches of their native tongue, the Arabians disdained the study of any foreign idiom. The Greek interpreters were chosen among their Christian subjects ; they formed their translations, sometimes on the original text, more frequently perhaps on a Syriac version : and in the crowd of astronomers and physicians, there is no example of a poet, an orator, or even an historian, being taught to speak the language of the Saracens. 'The mythology of Homer would have provoked the abhorrence of those stern fanatics : they possessed in lazy ignorance the colonies of the Macedonians, and the provinces of Carthage and Rome : the heroes of Plutarch and Livy were buried in oblivion ; and the history of the world before Mahomet was reduced to a short legend of the patriarchs, the prophets, and the Persian kings. Our education in the Greek and Latin schools may have fixed in our minds a standard of exclusive taste ; and I am not forward to condemn the literature and judgment of nations, of whose language I am ignorant. Yet I *know* that the classics have much to teach, and I *believe* that the Orientals have much to learn : the temperate dignity of style, the graceful proportions of art, the forms of visible and intellectual beauty, the just delineation of character and passion, the rhetoric of narrative and argument, the regular fabric of epic and dramatic poetry. The influence of truth and reason is of a less ambiguous complexion. The philosophers of Athens and Rome enjoyed the blessings, and asserted the rights, of civil and religious freedom. Their moral and political writings might have gradually unlocked the fetters of Eastern despotism, diffused a liberal spirit of inquiry and toleration, and encouraged the Arabian sages to suspect that their caliph was a tyrant and their prophet an impostor. The instinct of superstition was alarmed by the introduction even of the abstract sciences : and the more rigid doctors of the law condemned the rash and pernicious curiosity of Almamon. To the thirst of martyrdom, the vision of paradise, and the belief of predestination, we must ascribe the invincible enthusiasm of the prince and people. And the sword of the Saracens became less formidable, when their youth was drawn away from the camp to the college, when the armies of the faithful presumed to read and to reflect. Yet the foolish vanity of the Greeks was jealous of their studies, and reluctantly imparted the sacred fire to the Barbarians of the East.

In the bloody conflict of the Ommiades and Abbassides, the Greeks

9

had stolen the opportunity of avenging their wrongs and enlarging their limits. But a severe retribution was exacted by Mohadi, the third caliph of the new dynasty, who seized (A.D. 781—805) in his turn the favourable opportunity, while a woman and a child, Irene and Constantine, were seated on the Byzantine throne. An army of 95,000 Persians and Arabs was sent from the Tigris to the Thracian Bosphorus, under the command of Harun, or Aaron, the second son of the commander of the faithful. His encampment, on the opposite heights of Chrysopolis or Scutari, informed Irene, in her palace of Constantinople, of the loss of her troops and provinces. With the consent or connivance of their sovereign her ministers subscribed an ignominious peace : and the exchange of some royal gifts could not disguise the annual tribute of 70,000 dinars of gold, which was imposed on the Roman empire. The Saracens had too rashly advanced into the midst of a distant and hostile land : their retreat was solicited by the promise of faithful guides and plentiful markets ; and not a Greek had courage to whisper, that their weary forces might be surrounded and destroyed in their necessary passage between a slippery mountain and the river Sangarius. Five years after this expedition, Harun ascended the throne of his father and his elder brother ; the most powerful and vigorous monarch of his race, illustrious in the West, as the ally of Charlemagne, and familiar to the most childish readers, as the perpetual hero of the Arabian tales. His title to the name of *Al Rashid* (the *Just*) is sullied by the extirpation of the generous, perhaps the innocent, Barmecides ; yet he could listen to the complaint of a poor widow who had been pillaged by his troops, and who dared, in a passage of the Koran, to threaten the inattentive despot with the judgment of God and posterity. His court was adorned with luxury and science ; but, in a reign of three-and-twenty years, Harun repeatedly visited his provinces from Chorasan to Egypt ; nine times he performed the pilgrimage of Mecca ; eight times he invaded the territories of the Romans ; and as often as they declined the payment of the tribute, they were taught to feel that a month of depredation was more costly than a year of submission. But when the unnatural mother of Constantine was deposed and banished, her successor Nicephorus resolved to obliterate this badge of servitude and disgrace. The epistle of the emperor to the caliph was pointed with an allusion to the game of chess, which had already spread from Persia to Greece. "The queen (he spoke of Irene) considered you as a rook and herself as a pawn. That pusillanimous female submitted to pay a tribute, the double of which she ought to have exacted from the Barbarians. Restore therefore the fruits of your injustice, or abide the determination of the sword." At these words the ambassadors cast a bundle of swords before the foot of the throne. The caliph smiled at the menace, and drawing his scymetar, *samsamah*, a weapon of historic or fabulous renown, he cut asunder the feeble arms of the Greeks, without turning the edge, or endangering the temper, of his blade. He then dictated an epistle of tremendous brevity : " In the name of the most merciful God, Harun al Rashid, commander of the faithful, to Nicephorus, the Roman dog. I have read thy letter, O thou son of an unbelieving mother. Thou shalt not hear, thou shalt behold my reply." It was written in characters of blood and fire on the plains of Phrygia ; and the warlike celerity of the Arabs could only be checked by the arts of deceit and the show of repentance. The triumphant caliph retired, after the fatigues of the campaign, to his favourite palace of Racca on the Euphrates ; but the distance of 500 miles, and the inclemency of the season, encouraged his adversary to violate the peace. Nicephorus was astonished by the bold and rapid march of the commander of the faithful, who repassed, in the depth of winter, the snows of Mount Taurus : his stratagems of policy and war were exhausted : and the perfidious Greek escaped with three wounds from a field of battle over-spread with 40,000 of his subjects. Yet the emperor was ashamed of submission, and the caliph was resolved on victory. One hundred and thirty-five thousand regular soldiers received pay, and were inscribed in the military roll ; and above 300,000 persons of every denomination marched under the black standard of the Abbassides. They swept the surface of Asia Minor far beyond Tyana and Ancyra, and invested the Pontic Heraclea, once a flourishing state, now a paltry town ; at that time capable of sustaining in her antique walls a month's siege against the forces of the East. The ruin was complete, the spoil was ample ; but if Harun had been conversant with Grecian story, he would have regretted the statue of Hercules, whose attributes, the club, the bow, the quiver, and the lion's hide, were sculptured in massy gold. The progress of desolation by sea and land, from the Euxine to the isle of Cyprus, compelled the emperor Nicephorus to retract his haughty defiance. In the new treaty, the ruins of Heraclea were left for ever as a lesson and a trophy ; and the coin of the tribute was marked with the image and superscription of Harun and his three sons. Yet this plurality of lords might contribute to remove the dishonour of the Roman name. After the death of their father, the heirs of the caliph were involved in civil discord, and the conqueror, the liberal Almamon, was sufficiently engaged in the restoration of domestic peace and the introduction of foreign science.

Under the reign of Almamon at Bagdad, of Michael the Stammerer at Constantinople, the islands of Crete and Sicily were subdued (A.D. 823) by the Arabs. The former of these conquests is disdained by their own writers, who were ignorant of the fame of Jupiter and Minos, but it has not been overlooked by the Byzantine historians, who now begin to cast a clearer light on the affairs of their own times. A band of Andalusian volunteers, discontented with the climate or government of Spain, explored the adventures of the sea : but as they sailed in no more than ten or twenty galleys, their warfare must be branded with the name of piracy. As the subjects and sectaries of the *white* party, they might lawfully invade the dominions of the *black* caliphs. A rebellious faction introduced them into Alexandria ; they cut in pieces both friends and foes, pillaged the churches and the mosques, sold above 6000 Christian captives, and maintained their station in the capital of Egypt, till they were oppressed by the forces and the presence of Almamon himself. From the mouth of the Nile to the Hellespont, the islands and sea-coasts both of the Greeks and Moslems were exposed to their depredations ; they saw, they envied, they tasted, the fertility of Crete, and soon returned with forty galleys to a more serious attack. The Andalusians wandered over the land fearless and unmolested ; but when they descended with their plunder to the sea-shore, their vessels were in flames, and their chief, Abu Caab, confessed himself the author of the mischief. Their clamours accused his madness or treachery. " Of what do you complain ?" replied the crafty emir. " I have brought you to a land flowing with milk and honey. Here is your true country ; repose from your toils, and forget the barren place of your nativity." "And our wives and children ?" " Your beauteous captives will supply the place of your wives, and in their embraces you will soon become the fathers of a new progeny." The first habitation was their camp, with a ditch and rampart, in the bay of Suda ; but an apostate monk led them to a more desirable position in the eastern parts ; and the name of Candax; their fortress and colony, has been extended to the whole island, under the corrupt and modern appellation of *Candia.* The hundred cities of the age of Minos were diminished to thirty ; and of these, only one, most probably Cydonia, had courage to retain the substance of freedom and the profession of Christianity. The Saracens of Crete soon repaired the loss of their navy ; and the timbers of mount Ida were launched into the main. During an hostile period of 138 years, the princes of Constantinople attacked these licentious corsairs with fruitless curses and ineffectual arms.

The loss of Sicily (A.D. 827—878) was occasioned by an act of superstitious rigour. An amorous youth who had stolen a nun from her cloister, was sentenced by the emperor to the amputation of his tongue. Euphemius appealed to the reason and policy of the Saracens of Africa, and soon returned with the Imperial purple, a fleet of 100 ships, and an army of 700 horse and 10,000 foot. They landed at Mazara near the ruins of the ancient Selinus ; but after some partial victories, Syracuse was delivered by the Greeks, the apostate was slain before her walls, and his African friends were reduced to the necessity of feeding on the flesh of their own horses. In their turn they were relieved by a powerful reinforcement of their brethren of Andalusia ; the largest and western part of the island was gradually reduced, and the commodious harbour of Palermo was chosen for the seat of the naval and military power of the Saracens. Syracuse preserved about fifty years the faith which she had sworn to Christ and to Cæsar. In the last and fatal siege, her citizens displayed some remnant of the spirit which had formerly resisted the powers of Athens and Carthage. They stood above twenty days against the battering-rams and *catapultæ*, the mines and tortoises of the besiegers : and the place might have been relieved, if the mariners of the Imperial fleet had not been detained at Constantinople in building a church to the Virgin Mary. The deacon Theodosius, with the bishop and clergy, was dragged in chains from the altar to Palermo, cast into a subterraneous dungeon, and exposed to the hourly peril of death or apostasy. His pathetic, and not inelegant complaint, may be read as the epitaph of his country. From the Roman conquest to this final calamity, Syracuse, now dwindled to the primitive isle of Ortygea, had insensibly declined. Yet the relics were still precious ; the plate of the cathedral weighed 5000 pounds of silver ; the entire spoil was computed at 1,000,000 of pieces of gold (about £400,000 sterling), and the captives must outnumber the 17,000 Christians who were transported from the sack of Tauromenium into African servitude. In Sicily, the religion and language of the Greeks were eradicated ; and such was the docility of the rising generation, that 15,000 boys were circumcised and clothed on the same day with the son of the Fatimite caliph. The Arabian squadrons issued from the harbours of Palermo, Biserta, and Tunis ; 150 towns of Calabria and Campania were attacked and pillaged ; nor could the suburbs of Rome be defended by the name of the Cæsars and Apostles. Had the Mahometans been united, Italy must have fallen an easy and glorious accession to the empire of the prophet. But the caliphs of Bagdad had lost their authority in the West : the Aglabites and Fatimites usurped the provinces of Africa ; their emirs of Sicily aspired to independence ; and the design of conquest and dominion was degraded to a repetition of predatory inroads.

In the sufferings of prostrate Italy, the name of Rome awakens a solemn and mournful recollection. A fleet of Saracens from the African coast presumed to enter (A.D. 846) the mouth of the Tyber, and to approach a city which even yet, in her fallen state, was revered as the metropolis of the Christian world. The gates and ramparts were guarded by a trembling people ; but the tombs and temples of St. Peter and St. Paul were left exposed in the suburbs of the Vatican and of the Ostian way. Their invisible sanctity had protected them against the Goths, the Vandals, and the Lombards ; but the Arabs disdained both the gospel and the legend ; and their rapacious spirit was approved and animated by the precepts of the Koran. The Christian *idols* were stripped of their costly offerings ; a silver altar was torn away from the shrine of St. Peter ; and if the bodies or the buildings were left entire, their deliverance must be imputed to the haste, rather than the scruples, of the Saracens. In their course along the Appian way, they pillaged Fundi and besieged Gaeta ; but they had turned aside from the walls of Rome, and by their divisions, the Capitol was saved from the yoke of the prophet of Mecca. The same danger still impended on the heads of the Roman people ; and their domestic force was unequal to the assault of an African emir. They claimed the protection of their Latin sovereign ; but the Carlovingian standard was overthrown by a detachment of the Barbarians : they meditated the restoration of the Greek emperors ; but the attempt was treasonable, and the succour remote and precarious. Their distress appeared to receive some aggravation from the death of their spiritual and temporal chief ; but the pressing emergency superseded the forms and intrigues of an election ; and the unanimous choice of Pope Leo the Fourth was the safety of the church and city. This pontiff was born a Roman ; the courage of the first ages of the republic glowed in his breast ; and, amidst the ruins of his country, he stood erect, like one of the firm and lofty columns that rear their heads above the fragments of the Roman forum. The first days of his reign were consecrated to the purification and removal of relics, to prayers and processions, and to all the solemn offices of religion, which served at least to heat the imagination, and restore the hopes, of the multitude. The public defence had been long neglected, not from the presumption of peace, but from the distress and poverty of the times. As far as the scantiness of his means and the shortness of his leisure would allow, the ancient walls were repaired by the command of Leo ; fifteen towers, in the most accessible stations, were built or renewed ; two of these commanded on either side the Tyber ; and an iron chain was drawn across the stream to impede the ascent of an hostile navy. The Romans were assured of a short respite by the welcome news, that the siege of Gaeta had been raised, and that a part of the enemy, with their sacrilegious plunder, had perished in the waves.

But the storm, which had been delayed, soon burst upon them with redoubled violence. The Aglabite, who reigned in Africa, and inherited from his father a treasure and an army : a fleet of Arabs and Moors, after a short refreshment in the harbours of Sardinia, cast anchor before the mouth of the Tyber, sixteen miles from the city ; and their discipline and number appeared to threaten, not a transient inroad, but a serious design of conquest and dominion. But the vigilance of Leo had (A.D. 849) formed an alliance with the vassals of the Greek empire, the free and maritime states of Gaeta, Naples, and Amalfi ; and in the hour of danger, their galleys appeared in the port of Ostia under the command of Cæsarius, the son of the Neapolitan duke, a noble and valiant youth, who had already vanquished the fleets of the Saracens. With his principal companions, Cæsarius was invited to the Lateran palace, and the dexterous pontiff affected to enquire their errand, and to accept with joy and surprise their providential succour. The city bands, in arms, attended their father to Ostia, where he reviewed and blessed his generous deliverers. They kissed his feet, received the communion with martial devotion, and listened to the prayer of Leo, that the same God who had supported St. Peter and St. Paul on the waves of the sea, would strengthen the hands of his champions against the adversaries of his holy name. After a similar prayer, and with equal resolution, the Moslems advanced to the attack of the Christian galleys, which preserved their advantageous station along the coast. The victory inclined to the side of the allies, when it was less gloriously decided in their favour by a sudden tempest, which confounded the skill and courage of the stoutest mariners. The Christians were sheltered in a friendly harbour, while the Africans were scattered and dashed in pieces among the rocks and islands of an hostile shore. Those who escaped from shipwreck and hunger, neither found nor deserved mercy at the hands of their implacable pursuers. The sword and the gibbet reduced the dangerous multitude of captives ; and the remainder was more usefully employed, to restore the sacred edifices which they had attempted to subvert. The pontiff, at the head of the citizens and allies, paid his grateful devotion at the shrines of the apostles ; and, among the spoils of this naval victory, thirteen Arabian bows of pure and massy silver were suspended round the altar of the fisherman of Galilee. By his liberality a colony of Corsicans, with their wives and children, was planted in the station of Porto at the mouth of the Tiber ; the falling city was restored for their use, the fields and vineyards were divided among the new settlers : their first efforts were assisted by a gift of horses and cattle ; and the hardy exiles, who breathed revenge against the Saracens, swore to live and die under the standard of St. Peter.

The emperor Theophilus, son of Michael the Stammerer, was one of the most active and high-spirited princes who reigned at Constantinople during the middle age. In offensive or defensive war, he marched in person five times against the Saracens, formidable in his attack, esteemed by the enemy in his losses and defeats. In the last of these expeditions he penetrated into Syria, and besieged the obscure town of Sozopetra ; the casual birth-place of the caliph Motassem, whose father Harun was attended in peace or war by the most favourite of his wives and concubines. The revolt of a Persian impostor employed at that moment the arms of the Saracen, and he could only intercede in favour of a place for which he felt and acknowledged some degree of filial affection. These solicitations determined the emperor to wound his pride in so sensible a part. Sozopetra was levelled with the ground, the Syrian prisoners were marked or mutilated with ignominious cruelty, and a thousand female captives were forced away from the adjacent territory. Among these a matron of the house of Abbas invoked, in an agony of despair, the name of Motassem ; and the insults of the Greeks engaged the honour of her kinsman to avenge his indignity, and to answer her appeal. Under the reign of the two elder brothers, the inheritance of the youngest had been confined to

Anatolia, Armenia, Georgia, and Circassia ; this frontier station had exercised his military talents ; and among his accidental claims to the name of *Octonary*, the most meritorious are the *eight* battles which he gained or fought against the enemies of the Koran. In this personal quarrel, the troops of Irak, Syria, and Egypt, were recruited from the tribes of Arabia and the Turkish hordes : his cavalry might be numerous, though we should deduct some myriads from the 130,000 horses of the royal stables ; and the expence of the armament was computed at £4,000,000, or 100,000 pounds of gold. From Tarsus, the place of assembly, the Saracens advanced (A.D. 838) in three divisions along the high road of Constantinople : Motassem himself commanded the centre, and the vanguard was given to his son Abbas, who, in the trial of the first adventures, might succeed with the more glory, or fail with the least reproach. In the revenge of his injury, the caliph prepared to retaliate a similar affront. The father of Theophilus was a native of Amorium in Phrygia : the original seat of the Imperial house had been adorned with privileges and monuments ; and whatever might be the indifference of the people, Constantinople itself was scarcely of more value in the eyes of the sovereign and his court. The name of AMORIUM was inscribed on the shields of the Saracens ; and their three armies were again united under the walls of the devoted city. It had been proposed by the wisest counsellors, to evacuate Amorium, to remove the inhabitants, and to abandon the empty structures to the vain resentment of the Barbarians. The emperor embraced the more generous resolution of defending, in a siege and battle, the country of his ancestors. When the armies drew near, the front of the Mahometan line appeared to a Roman eye more closely planted with spears and javelins ; but the event of the action was not glorious on either side to the national troops. The Arabs were broken, but it was by the swords of 30,000 Persians, who had obtained service and settlement in the Byzantine empire. The Greeks were repulsed and vanquished, but it was by the arrows of the Turkish cavalry ; and had not their bow-strings been damped and relaxed by the evening rain, very few of the Christians could have escaped with the emperor from the field of battle. They breathed at Dorylæum, at the distance of three days ; and Theophilus, reviewing his trembling squadrons, forgave the common flight both of the prince and people. After this discovery of his weakness, he vainly hoped to deprecate the fate of Amorium : the inexorable caliph rejected with contempt his prayers and promises ; and detained the Roman ambassadors to be the witnesses of his great revenge. They had nearly been the witnesses of his shame. The vigorous assaults of fifty-five days were encountered by a faithful governor, a veteran garrison, and a desperate people ; and the Saracens must have raised the siege, if a domestic traitor had not pointed to the weakest part of the wall, a place which was decorated with the statues of a lion and a bull. The vow of Motassem was accomplished with unrelenting rigour : tired, rather than satiated, with destruction, he returned to his new palace of Samara, in the neighbourhood of Bagdad, while the *unfortunate* Theophilus implored the tardy and doubtful aid of his Western rival the emperor of the Franks. Yet in the siege of Amorium above 70,000 Moslems had perished : their loss had been revenged by the slaughter of 30,000 Christians, and the sufferings of an equal number of captives, who were treated as the most atrocious criminals. Mutual necessity could sometimes extort the exchange or ransom of prisoners : but in the national and religious conflict of the two empires, peace was without confidence, and war without mercy. Quarter was seldom given in the field ; those who escaped the edge of the sword were condemned to hopeless servitude, or exquisite torture ; and a Catholic emperor relates, with visible satisfaction, the execution of the Saracens of Crete, who were flayed alive, or plunged into caldrons of boiling oil. To a point of honour Motassem had sacrificed a flourishing city, two hundred thousand lives, and the property of millions. The same caliph descended from his horse and dirtied his robe to relieve the distress of a decrepit old man, who, with his laden ass, had tumbled into a ditch. On which of these actions did he reflect with the most pleasure, when he was summoned by the angel of death ?

With Motassem, the eighth of the Abbassides, the glory of his family and nation expired. When the Arabian conquerors had spread themselves over the East, and were mingled with the servile crowds of Persia, Syria, and Egypt, they insensibly lost the freeborn and martial virtues of the desert. The courage of the South is the artificial fruit of discipline and prejudice ; the active power of enthusiasm had decayed, and the mercenary forces of the caliphs were recruited in those climates of the North, of which valour is the hardy and spontaneous production. Of the Turks who dwelt beyond the Oxus and Jaxartes, the robust youths, either taken in war, or purchased in trade, were educated in the exercises of the field, and the profession of the Mahometan faith. The Turkish guards stood in arms round the throne of their benefactor, and their chiefs usurped the dominion of the palace and the provinces. Motassem, the first author of this dangerous example, introduced into the capital above 50,000 Turks : their licentious conduct provoked the public indignation, and the quarrels of the soldiers and people induced the caliph to retire from Bagdad, and establish his own residence and the camp of his Barbarian favourites at Samara on the Tigris, about twelve leagues above the city of Peace. His son Motawakkel was a jealous and cruel tyrant : odious to his subjects, he cast himself on the fidelity of the strangers, and these strangers, ambitious and apprehensive, were tempted by the rich promise of a revolution. At the instigation, or at least in the cause of his son, they burst into his apartment at the hour of supper, and the caliph was cut into seven pieces by the same swords which he had recently distri-

buted among the guards of his life and throne. To this throne, yet
streaming with a father's blood, Montaffer was triumphantly led; but
in a reign of six months, he found only the pangs of a guilty conscience.
If he wept at the sight of an old tapestry which represented the crime
and punishment of the son of Chosroes; if his days were abridged by
grief and remorse, we may allow some pity to a parricide, who exclaimed in the bitterness of death, that he had lost both this world and
the world to come. After this act of treason, the ensigns of royalty,
the garment and walking-staff of Mahomet, were given and torn away
by the foreign mercenaries, who in four years created, deposed, and
murdered three commanders of the faithful. As often as the Turks
were inflamed by fear, or rage, or avarice, these caliphs were dragged
by the feet, exposed naked to the scorching sun, beaten with iron clubs,
and compelled to purchase, by the abdication of their dignity, a short
reprieve of inevitable fate. At length, however, the fury of the tempest
(A.D. 841—870) was spent or diverted: the Abbassides returned to the
less turbulent residence of Bagdad; the insolence of the Turks was
curbed with a firmer and more skilful hand, and their numbers were
divided and destroyed in foreign warfare. But the nations of the East
had been taught to trample on the successors of the prophet; and the
blessings of domestic peace were obtained by the relaxation of strength
and discipline. So uniform are the mischiefs of military despotism,
that I seem to repeat the story of the prætorians of Rome.

While the flame of enthusiasm was damped by the business, the
pleasure, and the knowledge, of the age, it burnt with concentrated
heat in the breasts of the chosen few, the congenial spirits, who were
ambitious of reigning either in this world or in the next. How carefully soever the book of prophecy had been sealed by the apostle of
Mecca, the wishes, and (if we may profane the word) even the reason,
of fanaticism, might believe that, after the successive missions of
Adam, Noah, Abraham, Moses, Jesus, and Mahomet, the same God,
in the fulness of time, would reveal a still more perfect and permanent
law. In the year 277 of the Hegira, and in the neighbourhood of
Cufa, an Arabian preacher, of the name of Carmath, assumed the
lofty and incomprehensible style of the Guide, the Director, the Demonstration, the Word, the Holy Ghost, the Camel, the Herald of the
Messiah, who had conversed with him in a human shape, and the representative of Mohammed the son of Ali, of St. John the Baptist,
and of the angel Gabriel. In his mystic volume, the precepts of the
Koran were refined to a more spiritual sense; he relaxed the duties
of ablution, fasting, and pilgrimage; allowed the indiscriminate use
of wine and forbidden food; and nourished the fervour of his disciples
by the daily repetition of fifty prayers. The idleness and ferment of
the rustic crowd awakened the attention of the magistrates of Cufa;
a timid persecution assisted the progress of the new sect; and the
name of the prophet became more revered after his person had been

withdrawn from the world. His twelve apostles dispersed themselves among the Bedouins, " a race of men," says Abulfeda, " equally devoid of reason and of religion ;" and the success of their preaching seemed to threaten Arabia with a new revolution. The Carmathians were ripe for rebellion (A.D. 890—951) since they disclaimed the title of the house of Abbas, and abhorred the worldly pomp of the caliphs of Bagdad. They were susceptible of discipline, since they vowed a blind and absolute submission to their Imaum, who was called to the prophetic office by the voice of God and the people. Instead of the legal tithes, he claimed the fifth of their substance and spoil ; the most flagitious sins were no more than the type of disobedience ; and the brethren were united and concealed by an oath of secrecy. After a bloody conflict, they prevailed (A.D. 900, &c.) in the province of Bah-rein, along the Persian Gulf : far and wide, the tribes of the desert were subject to the sceptre, or rather to the sword, of Abu Said and his son Abu Taher ; and these rebellious imaums could muster in the field 107,000 fanatics. The mercenaries of the caliph were dismayed at the approach of an enemy who neither asked nor accepted quarter ; and the difference between them in fortitude and patience, is express-ive of the change which three centuries of prosperity had effected in the character of the Arabians. Such troops were discomfited in every action ; the cities of Racca and Baalbec, of Cufa and Bassora, were taken and pillaged ; Bagdad was filled with consternation ; and the caliph trembled behind the veils of his palace. In a daring in-road beyond the Tigris, Abu Taher advanced to the gates of the capital with no more than 500 horse. By the special order of Moc-tader, the bridges had been broken down, and the person or head of the rebel was expected every hour by the commander of the faithful. His lieutenant, from a motive of fear or pity, apprised Abu Taher of his danger, and recommended a speedy escape. " Your master," said the intrepid Carmathian to the messenger, " is at the head of 30,000 soldiers : three such men as these are wanting in his host :" at the same instant, turning to three of his companions, he commanded the first to plunge a dagger into his breast, the second to leap into the Tigris, and the third to cast himself headlong down a precipice. They obeyed without a murmur. " Relate," continued the imaum, " what you have seen ; before the evening your general shall be chained among my dogs." Before the evening, the camp was surprised and the menace was executed. The rapine of the Carmathians was sanc-tified by their aversion to the worship of Mecca : they robbed a cara-van of pilgrims, and 20,000 devout Moslems were abandoned on the burning sands to a death of hunger and thirst. Another year they suffered the pilgrims to proceed without interruption ; but, in the festival of devotion, Abu Taher stormed (A.D. 929) the holy city, and trampled on the most venerable relics of the Mahometan faith. Thirty thousand citizens and strangers were put to the sword ; the sacred precincts were polluted by the burial of 3000 dead bodies ; the well of Zemzem overflowed with blood ; the golden spout was forced from its place ; the veil of the Caaba was divided among these impious sectaries ; and the black stone, the first monument of the nation, was borne away in triumph to their capital. After this deed of sacrilege and cruelty, they continued to infest the confines of Irak, Syria, and Egypt ; but the vital principle of enthusiasm had withered at the root. Their scruples or their avarice again opened the pilgrimage of Mecca, and restored the black stone of the Caaba ; and it is needless to inquire into what factions they were broken, or by whose swords they were finally extirpated. The sect of the Carmathians may be considered as the second visible cause of the decline and fall of the empire of the caliphs.

The third and most obvious cause was the weight and magnitude of the empire itself. The caliph Almamon might proudly assert, that it was easier for him to rule the East and the West, than to manage a chess-board of two feet square ; yet I suspect, that in both those games, he was guilty of many fatal mistakes ; and I perceive, that in the distant provinces, the authority of the first and most powerful of the Abbassides was already impaired. The analogy of despotism invests the representative with the full majesty of the prince ; the division and balance of powers might relax the habits of obedience, might encourage the passive subject to inquire into the origin and administration of civil government. He who is born in the purple is seldom worthy to reign ; but the elevation of a private man, of a peasant perhaps, or a slave, affords a strong presumption of his courage and capacity. The viceroy of a remote kingdom aspires to secure the property and inheritance of his precarious trust ; the nations must rejoice in the presence of their sovereign ; and the command of armies and treasures are at once the object and the instrument of his ambition. A change was scarcely visible as long as the lieutenants of the caliph were content with their vicarious title ; while they solicited for themselves or their sons a renewal of the Imperial grant, and still maintained on the coin, and in the public prayers, the name and prerogative of the commander of the faithful. But in the long and hereditary exercise of power, they assumed the pride and attributes of royalty ; the alternative of peace or war, of reward or punishment, depended solely on their will ; and the revenues of their government were reserved for local services or private magnificence. Instead of a regular supply of men and money, the successors of the prophet were flattered with the ostentatious gift of an elephant, or a cast of hawks, a suit of silk hangings, or some pounds of musk and amber.

After the revolt of Spain, from the temporal and spiritual supremacy of the Abbassides, the first symptoms of disobedience broke forth in the province of Africa. Ibrahim, the son of Aglab, the lieutenant of the vigilant and rigid Harun, bequeathed to the dynasty of *Agla-*

bites (A.D. 800—941) the inheritance of his name and power. The indolence or policy of the caliphs dissembled the injury and loss, and pursued only with poison the founder of the *Edrisites* (A.D. 829—907), who erected the kingdom and city of Fez on the shores of the Western ocean. In the East, the first dynasty was that of the *Taherites* (A.D. 813—872); the posterity of the valiant Taher, who, in the civil wars of the sons of Harun, had served with too much zeal and success the cause of Almamon the younger brother. He was sent into honourable exile, to command on the banks of the Oxus; and the independence of his successors, who reigned in Chorasan till the fourth generation, was palliated by their modest and respectful demeanour, the happiness of their subjects, and the security of their frontier. They were supplanted by one of those adventurers so frequent in the annals of the East, who left his trade of a brazier (from whence the name of *Soffarides*, A.D. 872—902), for the profession of a robber. In a nocturnal visit to the treasure of the prince of Sistan, Jacob, the son of Leith, stumbled over a lump of salt, which he unwarily tasted with his tongue. Salt, among the Orientals, is the symbol of hospitality, and the pious robber immediately retired without spoil or damage. The discovery of this honourable behaviour recommended Jacob to pardon and trust; he led an army at first for his benefactor, at last for himself, subdued Persia, and threatened the residence of the Abbassides. On his march towards Bagdad, the conqueror was arrested by a fever. He gave audience in bed to the ambassador of the caliph; and beside him on a table were exposed a naked scymetar, a crust of brown bread, and a bunch of onions. "If I die," said he, "your master is delivered from his fears. If I live, *this* must determine between us. If I am vanquished, I can return without reluctance to the homely fare of my youth." From the height where he stood, the descent would not have been so soft or harmless: a timely death secured his own repose and that of the caliph, who paid with the most lavish concessions the retreat of his brother Amrou to the palaces of Shiraz and Ispahan. The Abbassides were too feeble to contend, too proud to forgive: they invited the powerful dynasty of the *Samanides* (A.D. 874—999), who passed the Oxus with 10,000 horse, so poor, that their stirrups were of wood; so brave, that they vanquished the Soffarian army, eight times more numerous than their own. The captive Amrou was sent in chains, a grateful offering to the court of Bagdad; and as the victor was content with the inheritance of Transoxiana and Chorasan, the realms of Persia returned for a while to the allegiance of the caliphs. The provinces of Syria and Egypt were twice dismembered by their Turkish slaves, of the race of *Toulun* (A.D. 868—905) and *Ikshid* (A.D. 934—968). These Barbarians, in religion and manners the countrymen of Mahomet, emerged from the bloody factions of the palace to a provincial command and an independent throne: their names became famous and formidable in their time ; but the founders of these two potent dynasties confessed, either in words or actions, the vanity of ambition. The first on his death-bed implored the mercy of God to a sinner, ignorant of the limits of his own power : the second, in the midst of 400,000 soldiers and 8000 slaves, concealed from every human eye the chamber where he at-tempted to sleep. Their sons were educated in the vices of kings ; and both Egypt and Syria were recovered and possessed by the Ab-bassides during an interval of thirty years. In the decline of their empire, Mesopotamia, with the important cities of Mosul and Aleppo, was occupied (A.D. 892—1001) by the Arabian princes of the tribe of *Hamadan.* The poets of their court could repeat without a blush, that nature had formed their countenances for beauty, their tongues for eloquence, and their hands for liberality and valour : but the genuine tale of the elevation and reign of the *Hamadanites*, exhibits a scene of treachery, murder, and parricide. At the same fatal period, the Persian kingdom was again usurped by the dynasty of the *Bowides* (A.D. 933—1005), by the sword of three brothers, who, under various names, were styled the support and columns of the state, and who, from the Caspian sea to the ocean, would suffer no tyrants but themselves. Under their reign, the language and genius of Persia revived, and the Arabs, 304 years after the death of Mahomet, were deprived of the sceptre of the East.

Radhi, the twentieth of the Abbassides, and the thirty-ninth of the successors of Mahomet, was the last who deserved the title of (A.D. 936, &c.) commander of the faithful : the last (says Abulfeda) who spoke to the people, or conversed with the learned : the last who, in the expence of his household, represented the wealth and magnificence of the ancient caliphs. After him, the lords of the Eastern world were reduced to the most abject misery, and exposed to the blows and insults of a servile condition. The revolt of the provinces circumscribed their dominions within the walls of Bagdad ; but that capital still con-tained an innumerable multitude, vain of their past fortune, discon-tented with their present state, and oppressed by the demands of a treasury which had formerly been replenished by the spoil and tribute of nations. Their idleness was exercised by faction and controversy. Under the mask of piety, the rigid followers of Hanbal invaded the pleasures of domestic life, burst into the houses of plebeians and princes, spilt the wine, broke the instruments, and beat the musicians. In each profession, which allowed room for two persons, the one was a votary, the other an antagonist, of Ali ; and the Abbassides were awakened by the clamorous grief of the sectaries, who denied their title and cursed their progenitors. A turbulent people could only be repressed by a military force ; but who could satisfy the avarice or assert the discipline of the mercenaries themselves ? The African and the Turkish guards drew their swords against each other, and the chief commanders, the emirs al Omra, imprisoned or deposed their sovereigns, and violated the sanctuary of the mosque and harem. If the caliphs escaped to the camp or court of any neighbouring prince, their deliverance was a change of servitude, till they were prompted by despair to invite the Bowides, the sultans of Persia, who silenced the factions of Bagdad by their irresistible arms. The civil and military powers were assumed by Moezaldowlat, the second of the three brothers, and a stipend of £60,000 was assigned by his generosity for the private expense of the commander of the faithful. But on the fortieth day, at the audience of the ambassadors of Chorasan, and in the presence of a trembling multitude, the caliph was dragged from his throne to a dungeon, by the command of the stranger, and the rude hands of his Dilemites. His palace was pillaged, his eyes were put out, and the mean ambition of the Abbassides aspired to the vacant station of danger and disgrace. In the school of adversity, the luxurious caliphs resumed the grave and abstemious virtues of the primitive times. Despoiled of their armour and silken robes, they fasted, they prayed, they studied the Koran and the tradition of the Sonnites ; they performed with zeal and knowledge, the functions of their ecclesiastical character. The respect of nations still waited on the successors of the apostle, the oracles of the law and conscience of the faithful ; and the weakness or division of their tyrants sometimes restored the Abbassides to the sovereignty of Bagdad. But their misfortunes had been embittered by the triumph of the Fatimites, the real or spurious progeny of Ali. Arising from the extremity of Africa, these successful rivals extinguished, in Egypt and Syria, both the spiritual and temporal authority of the Abbassides ; and the monarch of the Nile insulted the humble pontiff on the banks of the Tigris.

In the declining age of the caliphs, in the century which elapsed after the war of Theophilus and Motassem, the hostile transactions of the two nations were confined to some inroads by sea and land, the fruits of their close vicinity and indelible hatred. But when the Eastern world was convulsed and broken, the Greeks were roused (A.D. 960) from their lethargy by the hopes of conquest and revenge. The Byzantine empire, since the accession of the Basilian race, had reposed in peace and dignity ; and they might encounter with their entire strength the front of some petty emir, whose rear was assaulted and threatened by his national foes of the Mahometan faith. The lofty titles of the morning star, and the death of the Saracens, were applied in the public acclamations to Nicephorus Phocas, a prince as renowned in the camp as he was unpopular in the city. In the subordinate station of great domestic, or general of the East, he reduced the island of Crete, and extirpated the nest of pirates who had so long defied, with impunity, the majesty of the empire. His military genius was displayed in the conduct and success of the enterprise, which had so often failed with loss and dishonour. The Saracens were confounded by the landing of his troops on safe and level bridges,

which he cast from the vessels to the shore. Seven months were consumed in the siege of Candia ; the despair of the native Cretans was
stimulated by the frequent aid of their brethren of Africa and Spain ;
and, after the massy wall and double ditch had been stormed by the
Greeks, an hopeless conflict was still maintained in the streets and
houses of the city. The whole island was subdued in the capital, and
a submissive people accepted, without resistance, the baptism of the
conqueror. Constantinople applauded the long-forgotten pomp of a
triumph ; but the imperial diadem was the sole reward that could
repay the services, or satisfy the ambition, of Nicephorus.

After the death of the younger Romanus, the fourth in lineal descent
of the Basilian race, his widow Theophania successively married
Nicephorus Phocas and his assassin John Zimisces, the two heroes
(A.D. 963—975) of the age. They reigned as the guardians and
colleagues of her infant sons ; and the twelve years of their military
command form the most splendid period of the Byzantine annals.
The subjects and confederates, whom they led to war, appeared, at
least in the eyes of an enemy, 200,000 strong ; and of these about
30,000 were armed with cuirasses : a train of 4000 mules attended
their march ; and their evening camp was regularly fortified with an
enclosure of iron spikes. A series of bloody and undecisive combats
is nothing more than an anticipation of what would have been effected
in a few years by the course of nature ; but I shall briefly prosecute
the conquests of the two emperors from the hills of Cappadocia to the
desert of Bagdad. The sieges of Mopsuestia and Tarsus in Cilicia
first exercised the skill and perseverance of their troops, on whom, at
this moment, I shall not hesitate to bestow the name of Romans. In
the double city of Mopsuestia, which is divided by the river Sarus,
200,000 Moslems were predestined to death or slavery, a surprising
degree of population, which must at least include the inhabitants of
the dependent districts. They were surrounded and taken by assault ;
but Tarsus was reduced by the slow progress of famine ; and no sooner
had the Saracens yielded on honourable terms than they were mortified
by the distant and unprofitable view of the naval succours of Egypt.
They were dismissed with a safe conduct to the confines of Syria ; a
part of the old Christians had quietly lived under their dominion ; and
the vacant habitations were replenished by a new colony. But the
mosque was converted into a stable ; the pulpit was delivered to the
flames ; many rich crosses of gold and gems, the spoils of Asiatic
churches, were made a grateful offering to the piety or avarice of the
emperor ; and he transported the gates of Mopsuestia and Tarsus,
which were fixed in the wall of Constantinople, an eternal monument
of his victory. After they had forced and secured the narrow passes
of mount Amanus, the two Roman princes repeatedly carried their
arms into the heart of Syria. Yet, instead of assaulting the walls of
Antioch, the humanity or superstition of Nicephorus appeared to

respect the ancient metropolis of the East : he contented himself with drawing round the city a line of circumvallation ; left a stationary army ; and instructed his lieutenant to expect, without impatience, the return of spring. But in the depth of winter, in a dark and rainy night, an adventurous subaltern, with 300 soldiers, approached the rampart, applied his scaling-ladders, occupied two adjacent towers, stood firm against the pressure of multitudes, and bravely maintained his post till he was relieved by the tardy, though effectual, support of his reluctant chief. The first tumult of slaughter and rapine subsided ; the reign of Cæsar and of Christ was restored ; and the efforts of 100,000 Saracens, of the armies of Syria and the fleets of Afric, were consumed without effect before the walls of Antioch. The royal city of Aleppo was subject to Seifeddowlat, of the dynasty of Hamadan, who clouded his past glory by the precipitate retreat which abandoned his kingdom and capital to the Roman invaders. In his stately palace that stood without the walls of Aleppo, they joyfully seized a well-furnished magazine of arms, a stable of 1400 mules, and 300 bags of silver and gold. But the walls of the city withstood the strokes of their battering-rams ; and the besiegers pitched their tents on the neighbouring mountain of Jaushan. Their retreat exasperated the quarrel of the townsmen and mercenaries ; the guard of the gates and ramparts was deserted ; and, while they furiously charged each other in the market-place, they were surprised and destroyed by the sword of a common enemy. The male sex was exterminated by the sword ; 10,000 youths were led into captivity ; the weight of the precious spoil exceeded the strength and number of the beasts of burthen ; the superfluous remainder was burnt ; and, after a licentious possession of ten days, the Romans marched away from the naked and bleeding city. In their Syrian inroads they commanded the husbandmen to cultivate their lands, that they themselves, in the ensuing season, might reap the benefit : more than an hundred cities were reduced to obedience ; and eighteen pulpits of the principal mosques were committed to the flames to expiate the sacrilege of the disciples of Mahomet. The classic names of Hierapolis, Apamea, and Emesa, revive for a moment in the list of conquest : the emperor Zimisces encamped in the Paradise of Damascus, and accepted the ransom of a submissive people ; and the torrent was only stopped by the impregnable fortress of Tripoli, on the sea-coast of Phœnicia. Since the days of Heraclius, the Euphrates, below the passage of Mount Taurus, had been impervious, and almost invisible, to the Greeks. The river yielded a free passage to the victorious Zimisces ; and the historian may imitate the speed with which he overran the once famous cities of Samosata, Edessa, Martyropolis, Amida, and Nisibis, the ancient limit of the empire in the neighbourhood of the Tigris. His ardour was quickened by the desire of grasping the virgin treasures of Ecbatana, a well-known name, under which the Byzantine writer has concealed the capital of the Abbassides. The consternation of the fugitives had already diffused the terror of his name; but the fancied riches of Bagdad had already been dissipated by the avarice and prodigality of domestic tyrants. The prayers of the people, and the stern demands of the lieutenant of the Bowides, required the caliph to provide for the defence of the city. The helpless Mothi replied that his arms, his revenues, and his provinces, had been torn from his hands, and that he was ready to abdicate a dignity which he was unable to support. The emir was inexorable; the furniture of the palace was sold; and the paltry price of 40,000 pieces of gold was instantly consumed in private luxury. But the apprehensions of Bagdad were relieved by the retreat of the Greeks: thirst and hunger guarded the desert of Mesopotamia; and the emperor, satiated with glory, and laden with Oriental spoils, returned to Constantinople, and displayed, in his triumph, the silk, the aromatics, and three hundred myriads of gold and silver. Yet the powers of the East had been bent, not broken, by this transient hurricane. After the departure of the Greeks, the fugitive princes returned to their capitals; the subjects disclaimed their involuntary oaths of allegiance; the Moslems again purified their temples, and overturned the idols of the saints and martyrs; the Nestorians and Jacobites preferred a Saracen to an orthodox master; and the numbers and spirit of the Melchites were inadequate to the support of the church and state. Of these extensive conquests, Antioch, with the cities of Cilicia and the isle of Cyprus, was alone restored, a permanent and useful accession to the Roman empire.

THE

HISTORY OF THE SARACENS.

CONTAINING

The LIVES of the CALIPHS ABUBEKER, OMAR, OTHMAN,
ALI, HASAN, MOAWIYAH I., YEZID I., MOAWIYAH II.,
ABDOLLAH, MERWAN I., and ABDOLMELICK, the
Immediate Successors of MAHOMET.

GIVING AN ACCOUNT OF

THEIR MOST REMARKABLE BATTLES, SIEGES, &c.

ILLUSTRATING

THE RELIGION, RITES, CUSTOMS, AND MANNER OF LIVING OF THAT
WARLIKE PEOPLE.

COLLECTED FROM THE MOST AUTHENTIC ARABIC AUTHORS, ESPECIALLY MSS.

BY

SIMON OCKLEY, B.D.,

PROFESSOR OF ARABICK IN THE UNIVERSITY OF CAMBRIDGE.

The Narrative of SIMON OCKLEY, which Edward Gibbon has characterised as instructive, and his translations of Arabic MSS., as 'learned and spirited,' make his History of the Saracens a fitting sequel to what has been offered in this volume from Gibbon's great work.

SIMON OCKLEY was born at Exeter in 1678; sent in 1693, to Queen's College, Cambridge, where he took the degrees in Arts, and became a Bachelor in Divinity. Having taken orders he was presented to the Vicarage of Swavesey, near Cambridge; and, in 1711, he was chosen Arabic Professor of the University of Cambridge.

OCKLEY had early devoted his talents to the culture of Oriental languages, having published various works about them, but the book which has given him reputation was his History of the Saracens, which he was at vast pains in collecting materials for, residing long at Oxford, that he might consult the Arabic MSS., which are preserved in the Bodleian library.

SIMON OCKLEY married early, was soon burthened with a family, he knew little of economy, and suffered all the pains of poverty; dying August 9, 1720.

THE PREFACE.

THE Arabians, a people as little taken notice of by the Greek and Roman authors, as could be well supposed, considering their nearness, and the extent of their country, have, since the time of Mahomet, rendered themselves so very considerable, both by their arms and learning, that the understanding their affairs seems no less, if not more necessary than the being acquainted with the history of any people whatsoever, who have flourished since the declension of the Roman empire : Not only because they have had as great men, and performed as considerable actions, as any other nation under heaven; but, what is of more concern to us Christians, because they were the first ruin of the eastern church.

It might reasonably have been expected, that the Greeks, who bore the greatest share of that grievous calamity, and whose vices and divisions, it is to be feared, brought it upon the Christian world, should have taken particular care to have given a just account of it. Whereas, on the contrary, they have been as jejune and sparing in this particular, as any tolerable historian could have been supposed, relating matters at a much greater distance. Not to enumerate a catalogue of their defects, I shall content myself with producing the words of an* ingenious author, who was very well aware of the imperfections of the Greeks with relation to this history, and fully express the true sense of that matter in these words : This (says he) in substance is the account of those wars, and the beginning of the Saracenical Empire, left us by the Grecian writers of that age, who are justly to be accused for their succinctness and obscurity, in a subject that deserved to be more copiously handled ; for undoubtedly it must needs have been various as well as surprising in its circumstances, containing no less than the subduing whole nations, altering antient governments, and introducing a new face of affairs in the world. There is nothing more just than this observation, and what lame accounts must we then expect from those who compile histories of the Saracens out of the Byzantine historians?

I was no sooner convinced of this, but, having, by the study of their language, fitted myself in some measure for the reading their authors, I had a great desire to attempt the communicating some part of this hitherto unknown history to the world ; being equally affected with wonder and concern, that, considering the multitude of learned men which the last age produced, it should have been so long neglected. But I conceive the reason of that to have been, because those very few who were masters of the Arabick learning have been otherwise employed, and spent their time in paving the way for posterity, by pub-

* Continuation of *Eachard's* Roman History, vol. 2, p. 304, A.D. 637.

lishing such books as were absolutely necessary in order to the attaining a competent skill in that difficult language: Others, who have not been sufficiently acquainted with that nation, have entertained too mean an opinion of them, looking upon them as mere barbarians, which mistaken notion of theirs, has hindered all further enquiry.

As for those great men who first restored that learned, copious and elegant language in this last age to us Europeans ; I mean Erpenius, Giggeius, Golius, Sionita, and our incomparable Dr. Pocock ; it is not to be expressed how much we are indebted to them for their learned labours, without which the Arabick tongue would still have been inaccessible to us.   But since there are other persons of a quite different taste, who, for want of due information, have conceived a wrong opinion of the Arabians ; it will not be amiss, before we give a particular account of our present undertaking, to speak something concerning that people.

Before Mahomet's time they were idolaters.   They were always a warlike people, seldom being at peace either with one another or their neighbours.   They were divided into two sorts : some of them living in towns and villages, others having no fixed, settled habitations, lived in tents, and removed from one part of the country to another, according as their necessities compelled, or conveniences invited them. Their chief excellency consisted in breeding and managing horses, and the use of bows, swords, and lances : Their learning lay wholly in their poetry, to which their genius did chiefly incline them.   Mahomet and his successors soon rooted out idolatry, and united those jarring tribes in the profession of that new superstition, which he pretended to have received by inspiration from God, delivered to him immediately by the angel Gabriel.

For about two hundred years, little else was minded but war, except what concerned the interpretation of the Alcoran, and the sects and divisions among themselves upon that account, which daily multiplied and increased upon them : But there was, as yet, no curiosity of inquiring into foreign learning, nor desire of being acquainted with the arts and sciences.   At last, in Almamôun's reign, who was the twenty-seventh after Mahomet, and was inaugurated Caliph in the 108 year of the Hegirah (A.D. 813), learning began to be cultivated to a very great degree, mathematicks especially, and astronomy : And in order to promote it, that noble Caliph spared no cost, either to procure such Greek books as were serviceable to that purpose, or to encourage learned men to the study of them   Nor did the sagacity and application of that ingenious penetrating people in the least disappoint the designs of their munificent benefactor ; their progress in learning, after they had once entered upon it, seeming no less wonderful than that of their conquests ; for in a few years time they had plenty of translations out of Greek, not only mathematicians and astronomers, but philosophers, botanists and physicians.   Which love of learning was not confined to the Eastern parts, but diffused throughout the whole dominions of the Saracens, being first carried into Africa, (where they erected a great many universities) and from thence into Spain : so that when learning was quite lost in these western parts, it was restored by the Moors, to whom what philosophy was understood by the Christians was owing. Greek not being understood in this part of the world till the taking of Constantinople by the Turks, which was in the year 1453. At which time several learned Greeks escaping with their libraries, and coming westward, that language was restored: Our former philosophers and schoolmen having contented themselves with Latin translations, not only of Averroes, Alpharabius and Algazâli, and other Mahometan authors, but also of Aristotle and other philosophers, which translations of Greek authors were not made out of the original Greek, but out of the Arabick versions which were immediately translated from the Greek.

Had they, after having taken the pains to learn the Greek tongue, with equal care applied themselves to the historians, as they did to the philosophers; and studied Herodotus, Thucydides, Xenophon, and such other masters of correct writing as that language could have afforded them; we might have expected from them a succession of historians worthy to write those great actions which have been performed among them. But they never turned their thoughts that way, studying Greek only for the sake of the sciences, and not valuing either that or any other language in respect of their own. Which, though it must be granted, is extremely fine and copious, so as to afford words sufficient to treat handsomely upon any subject whatsoever, is not sufficient of itself, any more than any other language to make a man an author.

The great esteem which I have for the Eastern learning, makes me heartily wish that we had not too much cause to complain of our arabick historians, they not having regard to the due qualifications of an historian, but telling things after a careless manner, and stuffing their works with a great many trifling materials, at other times jingling upon words, and to show the copiousness of their language, and variety of expression, spinning out a slender matter of fact into a long story. So that it is a work of difficulty to follow or compile these authors, which nevertheless deserves very well to be undertaken, and will abundantly recompense the pains, at least of the reader.

For in these authors is contained an account of all the most remarkable actions done in the East and other parts for above one thousand years. During which space of time Asia and Africa have been the scene of as great performances as ever they were in the time of the Roman Empire, to which that of the Saracens was, in many respects, equal. And certainly it is a great deal of pity, that we have not these things more enquired into, especially since they may be so easily come at.

It were most heartily to be wished, that we had a complete history of the affairs of the East, especially the Fall of the Saracenical Empire. It would be very well worth observing, how learning first came in, grew and increased among the Saracens; and what great men they have had among them; all which would be very well comprehended in a history of the Caliphs or successors of Mahomet, of which I here present the reader with a specimen.

I ought indeed to have begun with the life of Mahomet, but that is already written by the reverend and learned Dr. Prideaux, now Dean of Norwich; in which life, besides what does immediately concern Mahomet's person, there are interspersed other things necessary to be known (by any person that is desirous to be acquainted with the history of the East), which I have not repeated in my book, but supposed to be already known to the reader : proceeding to write the lives of the three immediate successors of Mahomet, in which the reader will plainly see by what steps, and from how small beginnings, that once contemptible people rose to such a formidable greatness.

In order to prosecute my design, after I had made such a draught out of Elmakîn, Abu'lpharagius and Eutychius, as the scantness of my materials would afford, I was obliged to go to the Bodleian Library, which is, without question, the best furnished with oriental manuscripts of any in Europe. For besides a great number of the best authors purchased by the University of Oxford, out of the studies of Dr. Hyde, Dr. Huntington, and Dr. Pocock, not to mention Mr. Samuel Clark's, Gravius's, or Selden's ; there is an invaluable collection given by Archbishop Laud, but his princely munificence having been at prodigious expence to restore oriental learning in those Northern climates, both by purchasing such an excellent collection of authors in that kind, and encouraging men of abilities to apply themselves that way, cannot, without the greatest ingratitude, be passed by in silence, by any one that has any due regard to oriental learning. It was among the manuscripts of that reverend prelate that I found the best copy (MSS. Laud, Num. A. 118) of that author, which I have here endeavoured to make speak English, and of whom I am now going to give an account.

His name is Abu Abdo'llah Mohammed Ebn Omar Alwâkidi. At what time he lived I have not yet found any information, nor could I, by the diligent reading of him, make any observation by which I could give a probable guess. Perhaps the publishing an author without giving an account of his age, may seem to some readers to require an apology ; but I would desire such to consider, that the case is not the same in these studies as it is in Greek and Latin : In which there is such plenty of excellent editions of most authors easy to be come at ; and such numbers of critics, dictionaries, chronologers, and copious Indexes ; that a man (though no great scholar) that does but know how to make use of a book when he has it, may be almost sure of finding what he looks for. But, alas ! the case is vastly different here ; we have but just as it were learned the alphabet, and if we will know almost anything further than the rudiments of the language, we must look for it in dusty manuscripts, without translation, without index ; destitute altogether of those helps which facilitate other studies.

However, though I cannot precisely fix his age, it is most certain that he lived above 200 years after the matter of fact which he relates. For page 313, he mentions Almotásem the Caliph, whose reign began in 833, and if so, 'tis the same thing as if he had lived 600 years after. For that author that lives 1000 years after any matter of fact, is as much a witness of it, as he that lives but at 200 years distance. They are both of them obliged to take upon trust, and if there be no loss of good authors during that interval, he that writes latest is as credible an historian as the first.

Besides, the particulars relating to the first rise of kingdoms and empires are generally obscure. The reason of which is, because arms take place first, and a government must be well established, before learning can get room to breathe in it. Wherefore in these cases, it is allowed by all, that those accounts which have been handed down from time to time, and received by the best judges, ought to be looked upon as authentick; nor was there ever any person yet that enquired after the age of Livy, in order to know how far he might be accounted a competent relator of what was done in the reigns of Romulus and Numa Pompilius.

In these cases it is, as that excellent author very well observes, *famæ rerum standum est, ubi certam derogat vetustas fidem :* When a long interval of time has set things at too great a distance, we must be content with the current report, and rest satisfied with the best account we can get. However, that Author consults his own reputation, and his readers' satisfaction most, who does not without distinction set down every thing he meets with, but uses as much caution as the circumstances of the matter will admit. Our author Alwákidi has not been wanting in this particular. Sometimes he ushers in a story after this manner, ' I have been informed by a credible person.' In another place he says, ' We are informed by Moses Ebn Asem, who had it from Jonas Ebn Abdo'llah, who had it from his grandfather Abdo'rrahmân Ebn Aslam Arràbii, who was in the wars of Syria.' (Page 214). In that place where he gives an account of Derar and some others, who were put into chests at Arreân, he says, ' I was informed by Ahmed Almatîn Aljorhami, who had it from Raphâa Ebn Kais Alàmiri, who had it from Saiph Ebn Jabalah Alchátgami, who had it from Thabet Ebn Alkamah, who said he was present at the action.' These expressions (not to insinuate that they may afford a hint to guess at the age of the author), are most evident proofs that he was as careful as he could, neither to be imposed upon himself, nor to deceive his reader. And though there are a great many such like expressions dispersed throughout his whole work, yet I have not thought fit to intermix them in the history, because it is such a different way from what we are used to. However, I thought it necessary to give a taste of it here for the vindication of my author. And certain it is, that such things as these, nay of less consideration, were thought a good defence of Herodotus against Plutarch's objections, by no less a person than the learned Harry Stephens.

Alwákidi's design was not to write the life of any particular Caliph, but to give an account of the conquest of Syria. I should have been very glad if he had given me an opportunity of comparing him with some noble Greek or Latin historian, but his manner of writing will not allow it. He is chiefly valuable for this, that we find materials in him which we have no where else, and he is not so sparing of them, but there is liberty enough to pick and chuse. How I have succeeded in this performance I must submit to the judgment of the learned reader ; only taking the liberty to say, that though I have not transcribed my author in every particular, yet I have done him no injury in any thing that I have related ; nor have I taken a liberty of writing carelessly, in hopes of being secure from discovery (the language not being generally understood), but have used the same diligence as I would have done, were I sure that every one of my readers would instantly have collated my book with the manuscripts.

The Archbishop's copy which I chiefly used is 250 years old ; being written in the year of the Hegirah 863, A.D. 1458. There is another copy of it among Dr. Pocock's MSS. D'Herbelot says there is one in the King of France his library, which are all that I know of in Europe.

I have, as occasion served, made such use of other authors that were for my purpose, as the shortness of the time I could allow my self at Oxford would permit. Alwákidi writ also a history of the Conquest of Ægypt, which I have not met with ; otherwise my account of that matter might have been more compleat. All that I can say is, that I have done what I could ; and if this small beginning shall be a means to excite any person of greater abilities and more opportunity, to bring to light any part of the Eastern History, I shall have reason to think my time very well spent.

SIMON OCKLEY.

FOR the greater illustration of the Mahometan creed and practice, I thought fit to insert their famous doctor Algazàli's interpretation of their two articles of their faith, viz. There is no God but God ; and Mahomet is the Apostle of God.

PRAISE be to God the creator and restorer of all things : who does whatsoever he pleases, who is master of the glorious throne and mighty force, and directs his sincere servants into the right way and the straight path : who favoureth them, after their having borne testimony to the unity, with the preservation of their confessions from the dark-nesses of doubt and hesitation : who directs them to follow his chosen apostle, upon whom be the blessing and peace of God ; and to go after his most honourable companions to whom he hath vouchsafed his assist-ance and direction which is revealed to them in his essence and opera-tions by the excellencies of his attributes, to the knowledge whereof no man attains but he that hath been taught by hearing. Who maketh known to them that as touching his essence, he is one, who hath no partner : singular, without any thing like him. Uniform, having no contrary : separate, having no equal. That he is ancient, having no first : eternal, having no beginning ; remaining for ever, having no end ; continuing to eternity, without any termination. Who persists, without ceasing to be ; who remains without failing, who never did cease nor ever shall cease ; to be described by glorious attributes, nor is subject to any decree so as to be determined by any precise limits or set times, but is the first and the last, and is within and without.

* What is not] And that HE, (glorified be his name) is not a Body endued with form, nor a substance circumscribed with limits or deter-mined by measure ; neither doth he resemble bodies as they are cap-able of being measured or divided. Neither is he a substance, neither do substances exist in him, neither is he an accident, nor do accidents exist in him ; but that neither is he like to any of those things that do exist, neither is anything like to him ; nor is he terminated by quantity nor comprehended in bounds, nor circumscribed by the differences of situation nor contained in the heavens : but that he sits upon the throne, after that manner which he himself hath described, and in that same sense which He himself means, which is a sitting that is far removed from any notion of contact, or resting upon, or local situation ; but both the throne itself, and whatsoever is upon it are sustained by the goodness of his power, and are subject to the grasp of his hand. But he is above the throne and above all things even to the utmost ends of the earth ; but so above as at the same time not to be a whit nearer the throne and the heaven ; since he is exalted by [infinite] degrees above the throne no less than he is exalted above the earth, and at the same time is near to everything that hath a being ; nay, nearer to men than their jugular veins, and is witness to everything *(Alcoran):* though his nearness is not like the nearness of bodies, as neither is His essence like the essence of bodies. Neither doth he exist in anything, neither doth anything exist in him, but that he is too high to be contained in any place, and too holy to be determined by time ; for He was before time and place were created, and is after the same manner as he always was. And that he is distinct from the creatures by his attributes, neither is there anything besides himself in his essence, nor is his essence in any other besides him. And that he is too holy to be subject to change, or any local motion, neither do any accidents dwell in him nor any contingencies befall him, but he abides through all generations with his glorious attributes, free from all danger of dissolution. And that as to the attributes of his perfection, he wants no addition of perfection. And that as to his being, he is known to exist by the apprehension of the understanding ; and seen as he is by ocular intuition out of his mercy and grace to the holy in the eternal mansion, compleating their joy by the vision of his glorious presence.

*   His power.]   And that HE, praised be his name, is living, powerful, mighty, omnipotent, not liable to any defect or impotence ; who neither slumbers nor sleeps, nor is obnoxious to decay nor death. To whom belongs the kingdom, and the power, and the might. His is the dominion, and the excellency ; and the creation, and the command thereof. And the heavens are folded up in his right hand, and all the creatures are couched within his grasp. And that his excellency consists in his creating and producing ; and his unity in communicating existence and original. He created men and their works, and measured out their maintenance and their determined times. Nothing can escape his grasp that is possible, nor the vicissitudes of things get out of the reach of his power. The effects of his power are innumerable, and the objects of his knowledge infinite.

*   His knowledge.]   And that HE, praised be his name, knows all things that can be understood, and comprehends whatsoever passes ; from the extremities of the earth to the highest heavens ; so that the weight of a pismire should not escape him either in earth or heaven ; but he would know the creeping of the black pismire in the dark night upon the hard stone, and apprehend the motion of an atom in the open

air; and knows what is secret and conceals it; and views the concep-
tions of the minds, and the motions of the thoughts and the inmost re-
cesses of secrets by a knowledge ancient, eternal, that never ceased to
be his attribute from eternal eternity. Not by a new knowledge, super-
added to his essence, either inhering or adventitious.

  * His will.] And that HE, praised be his name, doth will those
things to be that are, and disposeth of all accidents, and that there
passes nothing in the empire, nor the kingdom, neither little nor much,
nor small nor great, nor good nor evil, nor profitable nor hurtful, nor
faith nor infidelity, nor knowledge nor ignorance, nor prosperity nor
adversity, nor increase nor decrease, nor obedience nor rebellion, but
by his determinate counsel and decree, and his definitive sentence,
and will. Nor doth the wink of him that seeth, nor the stricture of him
that thinketh exceed the bounds of his will; but that it is he who gave
all things their beginning, he is the creator and restorer, the sole ope-
rator of what he pleases, there is no reversing his decree nor delaying
what he hath determined, nor is there any refuge to man from his rebellion against him, but only his help and mercy; nor hath any man any
power to perform any duty towards him, but through his love and will:
though geniuses, angels and devils should conspire together either to
put one single atom in motion or cause it to cease its motion without his
will and approbation, they would not be able to do it: and that his will
subsists in his essence amongst the rest of his attributes, and was from
eternity one of his eternal attributes; by which he willed from eternity
the existence of those things that he had decreed, which were produced
in their proper seasons according to his eternal will; without any before or after, but as they were agreeable to his knowledge and will.
Not by methodizing of thoughts, nor waiting for a proper time; for
which reason one thing doth not hinder him from another.

  * His hearing and sight.] And that HE, praised be his name, is
hearing and seeing, and heareth and seeth; no audible object, how still
soever, escapeth his hearing; nor is anything visible so small as to
escape his sight. For distance is no hindrance to his hearing, nor
darkness to his sight: he sees without apple of the eye or eye-lids;
and hears without any passage or ear; as he knoweth without a heart,
and performs his actions without the assistance of any corporeal limb;
and creates without any instrument; for his attributes are not like
those of men any more than his essence is like theirs.

  * His word.] Furthermore, that HE doth speak, command, forbid,
promise and threaten by an eternal ancient word subsisting in his
essence: neither is it like to the word of the creatures, nor doth it con-
sist in a voice arising from the commotion of the air and the collision
of bodies, nor letters which are separated by the joyning together of
the lips or the motion of the tongue. And that the Alcoran, the law,
the gospel and the psalter, are books sent down by him to his
apostles; and that the Alcoran indeed is read with tongues, written in
books, and kept in hearts; subsisting·in the essence of God, neither
doth it become liable to separation and division whilst it is transferred
into the hearts and the papers. Also that Moses did hear the word of
God without voice or letter, even as the saints behold the essence of
God without substance or accident. And that since these are his

attributes, he liveth and knoweth, is powerful and willeth and ope-
rateth, and seeth and speaketh, by life and knowledge, and will and
hearing, and sight and word, not by his simple essence.

* His works.] And that HE, praised be his name, exists after such
a manner that nothing besides him hath any being but what is produced by his work, and floweth from his justice after the best, most
excellent, most perfect and most just manner, and that he is wise in
his works, and just in his decrees : nor is his justice to be compared
with the justice of men, because a man may be suspected of acting
unjustly by invading the possession of another; but no injustice can be
conceived of God, who can find nothing belonging to any other besides
himself, so as if any injury could be imputed to him as concerning
himself with things not appertaining to him ; but all things, He only
excepted, geniuses, men, the devil, angels, heaven, earth, animals,
plants, substance, accident, intelligible, sensible, were all created anew ;
and that he created them by his power after meer privation, and
brought them into light when they were nothing at all, but he alone
existed from eternity, neither was there any other with him.   Now he
produced the creatures anew for the manifestation of his power, and
his precedent will, and the confirmation of his word which was true
from all eternity, not that he stood in need of them, nor wanted them :
and that he manifestly declared his glory in creating, and producing,
and commanding, without being under any obligation, not out of necessity ; since loving-kindness, and shewing favour and grace and bene-
ficence, belong to him ; whereas it is in his power to pour forth upon
men variety of torments, and afflict them with various kinds of sor-
rows and diseases, which if he should do, it would be justice in him,
not reproachful nor injustice.   And that he rewards those that worship
him for their obedience upon the account of his promise and benefi-
cence not of merit nor necessity, since there is nothing which he can
be tied to perform, nor can any injustice be feigned in him, nor can he
be under any obligation to any person whatsoever.   But that the creatures are obliged to serve him ariseth from his having declared by the
tongues of the prophets that it was due to him from them : not by the
simple dictate of the understanding, but that he sent them messengers
whose veracity he had proved by manifest miracles, who brought down
from him to men commands and promises and threats, whereby men
are therefore obliged to give credit to them in those things that they
relate.

The signification of the second article.] That is the testimony concerning the apostle.   And that HE, Most High, sent Mahomet the illiterate prophet of the family of the Koreish to deliver his message to
all the Arabians and Barbarians, and genii and men ; and abrogated
by his religion all other religions except those things which he confirmed : and gave him the preference over all the rest of the prophets,
and made him lord over all mortal men.   Neither would he have the
faith be compleated by the testimony of the unity, that is the saying
there is but one God, without the addition of the testimony of the
apostle, by saying Mohammed is the apostle of God.   And he hath
made it necessary to men to give credit to him in those things which
he hath related both with regard to this present world and the life to

come. For a man's faith is not accepted till he is fully persuaded of those things which he hath affirmed shall be after death. The first of which is the examination of Munkir and Nakir, who are two persons of a most terrible and horrible aspect that shall set man upright in his grave, consisting both of soul and body, and ask him concerning the unity and the mission, saying, who is thy lord ? And what is thy religion ? And who is thy prophet ? And that these are the searchers of the grave, and their examination the first tryal after death : and that he believe the torment of the sepulchre, and that it is due, and right and just both upon the body and the soul according to his will.

He shall also believe in the balance with two scales and a beam that shall equal the extent of the heavens and the earth : wherein the works of men shall be weighed by the power of God ; at which time weights not heavier than atoms or mustard-seeds shall be brought out that things may be balanced with the utmost exactness, and perfect justice administered. Then the books of the good works, beautiful to behold, shall be cast into the balance of light, by which the balance shall be depressed according to their degrees with God, out of the favour of God. But the books of evil deeds, nasty to look upon, shall be cast into the balance of darkness, with which the scale shall lightly ascend by the justice of the most high God.

He must also believe that there is a real way, which is a body extended over the middle of hell, sharper than a sword, and finer than an hair, upon which the feet of the infidels shall slip by the decree of God, so as they shall fall into hell-fire, whilst the feet of the faithful shall remain firm, and they shall be conducted into the eternal habitation.

He shall also believe the pond where they go down to be watered, that is the pond of Mahomet, upon whom be the blessing and peace of God, out of which the faithful drink before they enter into paradise after they have passed over that way, and out of which whosoever drinketh once shall thrist no more for ever. Its breadth is a month's journey, it is whiter than milk, and sweeter than honey. Round about it stand cups as innumerable as the stars, and it hath two canals whereby the water of the river Cauthar is derived into it.

He shall also believe the last account, in which men shall be divided into those that shall be reckoned withal with the utmost strictness, and those that shall be dealt withal more favourably, and those that shall be admitted into paradise without any manner of examination at all, namely those whom God shall cause to approach near to himself. And that God will ask any of his apostles, whomsoever he shall please, concerning their mission, and whomsoever he shall please of the unbelievers what was the reason why they accused those that were sent to them of lying : he will also examine the hereticks concerning tradition, and the faithful concerning their good works.

He shall also believe that they that confess one God shall at length go out of the fire after they have underwent the punishment due to their sins, so that by the favourable mercy of God no person shall remain in hell who acknowledged the unity of the Godhead.

Also the intercession of the prophets, next of the doctors, then of the martyrs, and finally of the rest of the faithful, every one according to his excellency and degree, and that whosoever remain of the faithful besides these, and have no intercessor, shall go out by the grace of God ; neither shall any one of the faithful remain for ever in hell, but shall go out from thence though he had but so much faith in his heart as the weight of an atom.

It is also necessary that he acknowledge the excellency of the companions of Mahomet and their degrees ; and that the most excellent of men next to Mahomet is Abubeker, then Omar, then Othman, and then Ali, and that he entertain a good opinion of all the companions, and celebrate their memories, according as God and his apostle hath celebrated them all. And all these things are received by tradition, and evinced by evident tokens, and he that confesseth all these things, and surely believeth them, is to be reckoned amongst the number of those that embrace truth, and of the congregation of those that walk in the received way, separated from the congregation of those that err, and the company of hereticks.

These are the things that every one is obliged to believe and confess that would be accounted worthy of the name of a Musleman, and that according to the literal meaning of the words, not as they may be made capable of any sounder sense. According to the same author of this exposition, who says that, some pretending to go deeper, have put an interpretation upon those things that are delivered concerning the world to come, as the balance and the way and some other things besides, but it is heresy.

MONSIEUR D'HERBELOT,

To whose works I am much indebted, was a learned Frenchman. One of the greatest Orientalists that ever Europe bred. He, with incredible application, read over not only all the Arabic, Persian and Turkish books in the French king's library, and that of Florence, but several others that he had purchased for his own use. He made a compleat Turkish and Persian dictionary in three large volumes in folio, never yet published. His famous Bibliotheque Orientale, containing a prodigious treasure of whatsoever is curious or valuable in the eastern authors, was published after his decease in the year one thousand six hundred and ninety-seven. It is common in the hands of the learned, and therefore I forbear saying any more concerning it.

S. O.

OCKLEY'S HISTORY

OF THE

SARACENS' CONQUEST

OF

SYRIA, PERSIA, AND ÆGYPT.

ABUBEKER, FIRST CALIPH AFTER MAHOMET.

MAHOMET, founder of the Saracenical Empire, died at Medinah, (*Elmakîn, chap.* i.), June 6th, 632. After he was dead, the next care to be taken was for a successor ; and it was indeed very necessary, their government and religion being yet very tender, and many of Mahomet's followers being no great bigots, as not having yet forgotten their ancient rites and customs, but rather forced to leave them for fear, than upon conviction ; affairs could by no means admit of an Interregnum. The day that he expired, the Muslemans met for the election of a Caliph or successor. In which assembly there had like to have been such a fray, as might, had not Omar and Abubeker interposed, have greatly endangered, if not proved the utter ruin of this new religion and polity. For Mahomet left no directions concerning a successor, or at least, they not being known to any but his wives, who might conceal them out of their partiality in favour of Omar, a hot dispute arose between the inhabitants of Meccah and Medinah : those of Meccah claiming most right in the prophet, as being his countrymen and relations, and having embraced his religion first ; and having accompanied him in his flight for religion from Meccah to Medinah, when he, being persecuted at Meccah, was forced to make his escape. They urged that none could pretend to have so great a right of naming a successor as themselves. The inhabitants of Medinah urged that the prophet and their religion were as much obliged to them as to the others, because they had received him in his flight, and by their help and assistance put him in capacity of making head against his enemies, and upon that score insisted upon the right of electing a Caliph. In short, they were just upon falling from words to blows, when one of the (Helpers) Ansars, or inhabitants of Medinah, fearing

11

TS–K

the consequences of this disturbance, called out in the midst of the company, that they would have two Caliphs, that is, each party one. But Abubeker and the rest of the Mohagerins or inhabitants of Meccah, were desirous that the government should remain in the hands of their own party. Then Abubeker stepped forth and told them, that he would name two persons, and they should chuse which of them both parties could agree upon. The one was Omar, the other Abu Obeid, upon which motion the company was again divided, and the contention renewed afresh. At last, Omar being wearied out, and seeing no likelihood of deciding the matter, was willing to give over, and bad Abubeker give him his hand; which he had no sooner done than Omar promised him fealty. The rest followed his example, and by the consent of both parties Abubeker was saluted Caliph, and acknowledged the rightful successor of their prophet Mahomet, and was now absolute judge of all causes both sacred and civil. It was a very great oversight in Mahomet not to name a successor positively and publicly all the time of his sickness; which if he had done would have prevented that disturbance, by which the religion which he had been planting with so much difficulty and hazard, had like to have been endangered seriously.

One author tells us, that Mahomet, when he was sick, commanded some that were about him to bid Abubeker to say prayers publickly in the congregation : which desire of his to have Abubeker officiate in his place, looks very much as if he designed he should succeed him ; and was so understood by his wives Ayesha and Haphsah, who were both present when Mahomet gave this order, and endeavoured what they could to have it revoked. For as soon as Mahomet had spoken, Ayesha told him, that if Abubeker went into his place (meaning the pulpit from which he used to speak to the people) the congregation would not be able to hear him for weeping, and desired him to order Omar to go up ; which he refusing, Ayesha spoke to Haphsah to second her. The importunity of them both put the prophet into such a violent passion, that he told them they were as bad as Joseph's mistress, and commanded them again to send Abubeker. To which Haphsah answered, O Apostle of God, now thou art sick, and hast preferred Abubeker. He answered, 'Tis not I that have given him the preference, but God.

The contest which happened makes it evident, that these words of his had no influence in the election of Abubeker, but that it was chiefly owing to Omar's resignation. Who notwithstanding that he was the first that proposed Abubeker to the assembly, and owned him as Caliph, did not so well approve afterwards of that choice, which necessity put him upon, as appears by what he said : ' That he prayed to God to ' avert the ill consequences, which it was to be feared would follow ' upon such an indiscreet choice. That if ever any one should do such

' a thing again, he would deserve death ; and if any one should ever
' swear fealty to another without the consent of the rest of the Musle-
' mans, both he that took the Government upon him, and he that swore
' to him, ought to be put to death.' (*Abu'lpharagius.*) These were
signs of his dislike ; but it being done and past, there was no other
remedy, but to sit down at quiet, and rest himself contented.

Now though the government was actually settled upon Abubeker,
yet all parties were not equally satisfied : for a great many were
of opinion, that the right of succession did belong to Ali, the son of
Abu Taleb. Upon which account the Mahometans were ever since
that time divided ; some maintaining that Abubeker, and those other
two, Omar and Othman, that came after him, were the rightful and
lawful successors ; and others disclaiming their title altogether as
usurpers, and constantly asserting the right of Ali. Of the former
opinion are the Turks at this day ; of the latter, the Persians. Which
makes such a difference between those two nations, that notwithstanding their agreement in other points of their superstition, they do upon
this account treat one another as most damnable hereticks. Ali had
this to recommend him, that he was Mahomet's cousin german, and
was the (*Elmakîn*) first that embraced his religion, except his wife
Cadijah, and his slave Zeid, and besides was Mahomet's son-in-law,
having married his daughter Phatemah. Abubeker was Mahomet's father-
in-law, and was very much respected by him, so that he gave him the
surname of Assidîck, which signifies in Arabick, one that is a great speaker
of truth (*Elmakîn*,) because he resolutely asserted the truth of that story
which Mahomet told of his* going one night to heaven. And oftentimes he used to express a great deal of kindness for him.† Once as
he saw him coming towards him, he said to those that were about
him : if any one takes delight in looking upon a man that has escaped
from the fire of hell, let him look upon Abubeker. God, whose name
be blessed, hath given man his choice of this world or that which is
with him, and this servant (meaning Abubeker) hath chosen that
which is with God. Such marks of esteem as these must needs procure him a great respect from those who looked upon Mahomet as a
person inspired, and the apostle of God ; and did facilitate his promotion to the dignity of Caliph.

Ali was not present at this election, and when he heard the news,
was not well pleased, as hoping that he should have been the man.
Abubeker sent Omar to Phatemah's house, where Ali and some of his
friends were, with orders to compel them to come in by force, if they
would not do it by fair means. Omar was just a going to fire the
house, and Phatemah asked him, what he meant ? He told her that
he would certainly burn the house down, unless they would be content

---

* Alcoran, chap. XVII. 1.
† Ibrahim Ebn Mohammed Ebn Dokmâk, M.S. Arab. Laud. Num. 806. 11.

to do as the rest of the people had done. Upon which Ali came forth and went to Abubeker and acknowledged his sovereignty (*Abu'lpharagius*), though he did not forget to tell him, that he wondered that he would take such a thing without his notice. To which Abubeker answered, that the exigency of the matter was such as would by no means admit of deliberation, because if it had not been done on a sudden, it was to be feared that the government would have been wrung out of their hands by the opposite party. And, to make things slide the more easily, seemed to be desirous of quitting his charge and resigning the government : and so goes up into the pulpit, and there openly before them all desired that they would give him leave to resign and confer that charge upon some more worthy person ; but Ali, fearing the ill will of the people, (*Elmakin, chap. ii.*), whose minds he perceived were estranged from him, for having already stood out so long, and being loath to make any new disturbance, utterly refused to hear of it, and told him, that they would neither depose him themselves, nor desire that he should resign. And thus things were pretty well accommodated, and those of Medinah, as well as those of Meccah, consented to own Abubeker, as the true and rightful successor of their prophet Mahomet ; only Ali, though he made no stir, looked upon himself as injured (*Abu'lpheda*), and there is a story told by tradition, which is reported to have been delivered by Ayesha, that Ali did not come in till after the decease of his wife Phatemah, who lived six months after the death of Mahomet, her father. (*Abu'lpharagius.*) The Caliph Abubeker being thus fixed in his new government, had work enough to secure it ; for the Mahometan religion had not as yet taken such deep root in the hearts of men, but that they would very willingly have shaken it off again, if they had known how. The Arabians therefore, being a people of an unquiet restless disposition, would not omit this opportunity of rebelling, which they thought was fairly offered them by the death of Mahomet, but immediately take arms, and refuse to pay the usual tribute, tithes and alms, and begin to neglect those rites and customs, which had been imposed upon them by Mahomet. Abubeker, and those about him at Medinah, took the alarm, and fearing a general revolt, began to consider how they might best provide for the security of themselves and their families. They disposed of their women and children, and such as were not able to bear arms, in the clefts and cavities of the rocks and mountains, and put themselves in a posture of defence. In the mean time Abubeker sends Caled Ebn Waled, with an army of 4,500, to suppress the rebels, who having routed them in a set battle, brought off a great deal of plunder, and made slaves of their children.

The chief amongst those who refused to pay the Zacât (*Abu'lpheda*) which is that part of a man's substance, which is consecrated to God, as tithes, alms, and the like, and is strictly enjoyn'd by the Mahometan law, was Malec Ebn Noweirah, a man that made considerable figure in those days, being the chief of an eminent family among the Arabs, and celebrated for his skill in poetry, as well as manhood and horsemanship. Abubeker sent Caled to him, to talk with him about it; Malec told him, that he could say his prayers without paying that. Caled asked him, if he did not know that prayers and alms must go together, and that the one would not be accepted without the other? What! does your master say so? says Malec. Then don't you own him for your master? said Caled; and swore that he had a good mind to strike his head off. They disputed the matter a while; and at last, Caled told him he should die. Did your master say so? says Malec. What! again? says Caled, and resolved upon his death, tho' Abdo'llah Ebn Amer and Kobâdah interceded for him in vain. When Malec saw there was no way for him to escape, he turned him about, and looked upon his wife, who was a woman of admirable beauty, and said, this woman has killed me. Nay, says Caled, God has killed thee, because of thy apostacy from the true religion. I profess the true religion, says Malec, meaning the Mahometan. The word was no sooner out of his mouth, but Caled ordered Derar Ben Alazwar, a person we shall see more of hereafter, to strike his head off. At which Abubeker was very much concerned, and would have put Caled to death, if Omar had not interceded for him; and indeed he did out of his great zeal exceed the limits of his commission; for Mahomet himself would have pardoned an apostate, provided he had been very well assur'd of his repentance.

Having this opportunity of mentioning this great man Caled, we must not pass him by, without taking some notice of his character. He was the best general of the age he liv'd in, and it was to his courage and conduct that the Saracens chiefly owe the subduing of the rebels, the conquest of Syria, and the establishment of their religion and polity. 'Tis to be questioned whether his love and tenderness towards his own soldiers, or his hatred and aversion to the enemies of the Mahometan religion, was greatest; for upon all occasions he used to give very signal instances of both. He was a most irreconcileable and implacable enemy to those who had once embrac'd the Mahometan religion, and then apostatized; nor would he spare them, though shewing the greatest signs of unfeigned repentance. His valour was so surprising, that the Arabs call'd him the sword of God; which surname of his was known also to his enemies, and is mentioned* by Greek as well as by Arab authors. If it did at any time (which was not often) carry him beyond the bounds of his conduct, it always brought him off safe again. He never, in the greatest danger lost his wonted presence of mind, but could as well extricate himself and his men from present difficulties, as prevent future ones.

* Ἐξῆλδεν δὲ εἰς Ἀμερᾶ ὁ Χάλεδος ὃν λέγνσι μάχαιραν τὃ Θεὃ. Theophanes, p. 278. Edit. Paris.

By him the rebels being suppressed, the Mahometans were in some measure eas'd of the fear they stood in before, but there were still more difficulties behind ; for about this time several, perceiving the success and prosperity of Mahomet and his followers, set up for prophets too, in hopes of the like good fortune, and making themselves eminent in the world : such were Osud Alabbasi and Tuleihah Ebn Choweieed, with several others, which quickly came to nothing. But the most considerable of these was Moselam, who had emulated Mahomet in his life-time, and trumpt up a book in imitation of the Alcoran. He had formerly been (*Abu'lpheda*) with Mahomet, and professed himself of his religion, and might have been partner with him in his imposture ; but looking upon that to be beneath him, he utterly renounced all further familiarity and correspondence with him, and was resolved to set up for himself, which he did the year before Mahomet died. He had now gathered together a very considerable body of men in Yemamah, a province of Arabia, and began to be so formidable, that the Muslemans were under some apprehensions of his growing greatness, and did not think it any way consistent with prudence to neglect him any longer, knowing very well, that as soon as he should be strong enough, they and their religion would quickly come to nothing. They therefore thought it most advisable to set upon him first, and rather hazard the event of a battle at the beginning, than by suffering him to go on too long, and gather more strength, frustrate all manner of hopes of a victory. Upon this they move Abubeker to send sufficient forces, under the conduct of some experienced commander, in order to destroy him. Abubeker forthwith despatches Akramah, and Sergíl, with an army and order to march directly towards Yemamah. After them he sends Caled, the scourge of rebels, apostates and false prophets, who having joined forces with them, they had an army of 40,000 Muslemans. Moseilam was not idle, knowing that his life and reputation were now at stake prepared to give them battle. The Muslemans encamped at a place called Akreba ; and Moseilam with his army, was just Ópposite to them. They drew near as fast as they could, and Moseilam charged them with such fury, that they were not able to make good their ground against him, but were forced to retire with the loss of 1,200 men. The Muslemans, rather provoked than discouraged by this defeat, not long after renewed the fight, and then began a most bloody battle, Moseilam all the while behaving himself courageously, was at last thrust through with a javelin, (the same with which Hamza, Mahomet's uncle, was killed) by a slave, a black. He being dead, the victory easily enclined to the Muslemans ; who having killed the false prophet, and 10,000 of his men, and obliged those who were left to turn Mahometans, returned to Medinah, the seat of the Caliph, richly laden with the spoil of their enemies.

This year being the first of Abubeker's reign, Al Ola was sent with a considerable army to reduce the rebels in Baerein, which he did without any great difficulty, killing a great many of them, and seizing their effects, so that a great many of them chose rather to return to the Mahometan superstition, which upon the death of Mahomet they had forsaken, than expose themselves, by obstinately standing it out, to all the miseries of War.

'Tis strange and surprising, to consider from how mean and contemptible beginnings the greatest things have, by the providence of God, been raised in a short time, of which the Saracenical empire is a very considerable instance ; for if we look back about eleven years, we shall find how Mahomet, unable to support his cause, routed and oppressed by the powerful party of the Korashites at Meccah, attended by a very small number of his despairing followers, fled to Medinah, no less for the preservation of his life than his imposture ; and now, within so short a time after, we find the undertakings of his successor prosper so much beyond expectation, as to become a terror to all his neighbours ; and the Saracens in a capacity, not only of keeping in their own hands their Peninsula of Arabia, but of extending their arms over larger territories, than ever were subject to the Romans themselves. Whilst they were employed in Arabia, they were little regarded by the Grecian Emperor, who now too late felt them pouring in upon him like a torrent, and driving all before them. The proud Persian too, who so very lately had been domineering in Syria, and sacked Jerusalem and Damascus, must be forced to part with his own dominions, and submit his neck to the Saracenic yoke. It may be supposed that, had the empire been in the same flourishing condition as it had been formerly, they might have been checked at least, if not extinguished . but besides that the western empire had been torn away by the barbarous Goths, the eastern part of it had received so many shocks from the Hunns on the one side, and the Persians on the other, that it was not in a capacity to stop the violence of such a powerful invasion. In the Emperor Mauricius his time, the empire paid tribute to the Chagân or King of the Hanns. And after Phocas had murdered his master, such lamentable havoc there was among the soldiers, that when Heraclius came (not much above seven years after) to muster the army, there were only two soldiers left alive, of all those who bore arms when Phocas first usurped the empire. And though Heraclius was a prince of admirable courage and conduct, and had done what possibly could be done to restore the discipline of the army, and had had great success against the Persians, so as to drive them not only out of his dominions, but even out of their own ; yet still the vitals of the empire seemed to be mortally wounded ; that there could no time have happened more fatal to the empire, nor more favourable to the enterprises of the Saracens, who seem to have been raised up on purpose by God to be a scourge to the Christian church, for not living answerably to that most holy religion which they had received.

Abubeker had now set affairs at home in pretty good order. The apostates, who upon the death of Mahomet had revolted to the idolatry in which they were born and bred up, were reduced. The forces of Moseilamah, the false prophet, were broken, and himself killed ; so that there was little or nothing left to be done in Arabia. For though there were a great many christian Arabs, as particularly the tribe of Gaffân, yet they were generally employed in the Grecian Emperor's service. So that the next business the Caliph had to do, was pursuant to the tenor of his religion, to make war upon his neighbours for the propagation of the truth, (for so they call their superstition) and compel them either to become Mahometans (*Alcoran, chap. ix.*, 29), or tributaries (see the *Alcoran, chap. viii.*, 40). For their Prophet Mahomet had given them a commission of a very large, nay unlimited extent, which was, to fight till all people were of their religion. And those wars which are undertaken upon this account, they call holy wars, with no less absurdity than we call that so which was once undertaken against them by the Europeans. Abubeker therefore sends Caled with some forces into Irâk or Babylonia ; but his greatest longing was after Syria, which being a delicate, pleasant, fruitful country, and near to Arabia, seemed to lie very conveniently for him. After he had fully resolved to invade it, he called his friends about him, and made a speech, in which he set before them the great success they had been prospered with already, and told them that the prophet (Mahomet) had assured him before his decease, that their religion should make a great progress, and their territories be vastly enlarged, and that he had thoughts himself of invading Syria ; but since it had pleased God to prevent the prophet's designs by taking him away, and he was left successor, he desired their advice. They answered unanimously, that they were all at his service, and ready to obey to the utmost of their power whatever he should be pleased to command them. Upon this he sends circular letters to the petty princes of Arabia Fælix, and other Mahometan officers and præfects, and to the inhabitants of Meccah in particular, to command them to raise the utmost of their forces, and with all possible speed repair to him at Medinah. The contents of the letter were as follows :

'In the name of the most merciful God,—Abdollah Athik Ebn Abi Kohâpha (these were Abubeker's Sirnames), to the rest of the true believers. Health and happiness, and the mercy and blessing of God be upon you. I praise the most high God, I pray for his prophet Mahomet. This is to acquaint you, that I intend to send the true believers into Syria, to take it out of the hands of the infidels. And I would have you know, that the fighting for religion is an act of obedience to God.'

He had sent the letter out but a few days, ere the messenger that carried it returned, and brought him word, that he had not delivered his letter to any one person but what had received it with great expressions of satisfaction, and a readiness to comply with his commands. And accordingly in a short time after, a very considerable army, raised out of the several provinces of Arabia, came to wait upon him at Medinah, and pitched their tents round about the city. They waited some time, without receiving any orders from the Caliph. But the weather was so extremely hot, and the country so barren, that they were very hard put to it for provision both for themselves and their horses. Which made them complain to their officers, and desired them to speak to Abubeker about it. Upon which one of them made bold to tell him, ' You were pleased to send for us, and we obeyed your commands with all possible speed ; and now we are come here we are kept in such a barren place, that we have nothing to subsist our army. Therefore if your mind be altered, and you have no further occasion for us, be pleased to dismiss us.' The rest of the heads of the tribes seconded him. Abubeker told them that he was far from designing them any injury in detaining them so long, but only he was willing to have his army as compleat as he could. To which they answered that they had not left a man behind them that was fit for service. Then Abubeker went with some of his friends to the top of a hill, to take a view of the army, and prayed to God to endue them with courage, and assist them, and not deliver them into the hands of their enemies. Afterwards he walked on foot with them a little way, and the generals rode. At last they told him that they were ashamed to ride whilst he was on foot. To which he answered, ' I shall find my account with God for these steps, and you ride for the service of God ;' meaning that there was no difference in that matter, so long as they were all concerned in the propagating their religion. Then he took his leave of them, and directed his speech to Yezid Ebn Abi Sophyan, whom he had appointed general of these forces, after this manner : ' Yezid, be sure you do not oppress your own people, nor make them uneasy, but advise with them in all your affairs, and take care to do that which is right and just, for those that do otherwise shall not prosper. When you meet with your enemies quit yourselves like men, and don't turn your backs ; and if you get the victory kill no little children, nor old people, nor women. Destroy no palm-trees, nor burn any fields of corn. Cut down no fruit trees, nor do any mischief to cattle, only such as you kill to eat. When you make any covenant or article, stand to it, and be as good as your word. As you go on, you will find some religious persons, that live retired in monasteries, who propose to themselves to serve God that way, let them alone, and neither kill them, nor destroy their monasteries ; and you will find another sort of people that belong to the synagogues of Satan, who have shaven crowns ; be sure you cleave their skulls, and give them no quarter, till they either turn Mahometans or pay tribute.' When he had given them this charge he went back to Medinah, and the army marched towards Syria.

The news of this preparation quickly came to the ears of the emperor Heraclius, who called a council forthwith, and inveighed against the wickedness and insincerity of his subjects, and told them that these judgments were come upon them because they had not lived answerably to the rules of the gospel. He represented to them, that whereas in former times, powerful princes, as the Turk and Persian, had not been able to overcome them, they were now insulted by the Arabs, a pitiful, contemptible people. Then he sent some forces with all possible speed, but with ill success, for their general with 1200 of his men was killed upon the spot, and the rest routed, the Arabs in that battle losing only 120 men. There were afterwards a great many skirmishes, in which the Christians came off by the worst. The Arabs enriched with spoil, concluded to make the Caliph a present of all they had gotten, as the first fruits of their expedition ; arms and ammunition only excepted. As soon as Abubeker had received the spoil, he sent a letter to the inhabitants of Meccah, and the adjacent territories, in which he acquainted them with the good success of his forces, and called upon them not to be behind hand in fighting for the cause of God. The good success of their brethren gave them such encouragement, that they obeyed the motion with as much cheerfulness, as if their being called to war had been nothing else but being invited to partake of the spoil. Whereupon they quickly raised an army, and waited upon Abubeker at Medinah, who forthwith ordered them to join those forces which he had before sent into Syria. He had made Saëd Ebn Caled general of this army ; but when Omar expressed his dislike of it, the Caliph was in a streight, being loth to take away Saëd's commission as soon as he had given it him ; and on the other hand, not willing to disoblige Omar. In this difficulty he applies himself to Ayesha (Mahomet's widow), for whom they had a great respect upon the account of her near relation to their prophet Mahomet, and used frequently to consult her after his decease, supposing that she, being his best beloved wife, might be better acquainted with his thoughts both of persons and things than any other. When he came to her, she told him, that for Omar's part he meant for the best when he gave that advice, and that she was sure he did not speak it out of any hatred or ill will. Upon this Abubeker sends a messenger to Saëd, to remand the standard, which he very patiently resigned, and said, he cared not who had the standard ; let whosoever will have it, he was resolved to fight under it for the propagation of religion. So vehement and earnest were those men whom God had raised up to be a scourge to the church, that no affront whatsoever could disoblige them so far as to make them lay aside their resolutions.

Whilst the Caliph was in doubt how to dispose of this commission, Amrou Ebno'l Aa's, a very good soldier, who afterwards conquered Ægypt, went to Omar, and desired him to make use of his interest with the Caliph, that it might be conferred upon him. But Omar, whether out of any antipathy to his person, or because he thought no man worthy of a charge that sought after it, utterly refused to meddle in it. And when Amrou persisted, and was very instant with him, Omar bade him not seek for the superiority and dominion of this world; and told him, that if he was not a prince to-day, he would be one to-morrow; meaning in a future State. And now Amrou was out of all hopes of having any command; when presently the Caliph, of his own accord, made him general of his army, and bade him, ' Take care to live religiously, and let the enjoying the presence of ' God and a future state, be the end and aim of all his undertakings, ' and look upon himself as a dying man, and always have regard to ' the end of things; and remember that we must in a short time all ' die, and rise again, and be called to an account. He ordered him ' not to go where the other Muslemans had been before him, but ' march into Palestine. And that he should take care to inform him- ' self of Abu Obeidah's circumstances, and assist him what he could. ' That he should not be inquisitive about men's private concerns; but ' take care that his men were diligent in reading the Alcoran, and not ' suffer them to talk about those things which were done in the times ' of ignorance (so they call all the time before Mahomet) because that ' would be the occasion of dissension among them.'

After he had dismissed Amrou, he sent Abu Obeidah into Syria, to command all the forces there, and told him, that there was no need of saying anything new to him, since he had heard the charge he had given to Amrou. One of the Grecian emperor's generals had the good fortune to beat the Muslemans in Syria; and Abu Obeidah, appre- hensive of the emperor's power, durst not act offensively. Which as soon as the Caliph understood, he judged him unworthy of that post, and recalled Caled from Irak to take his place. Caled had performed great things, considering the short time he had been gone. He had taken Hirah (afterwards the imperial seat of Alseffâh), and several other places, not able to endure a siege, had submitted to him, and paid tribute. Elmakin says, that this was the first tribute that was ever brought to Medinah. He had fought several battles in which he never failed of success, and would without doubt have pushed on his conquest if he had not been recalled. When he came into Syria, he took different measures from those which had been used before; and the soldiers found a great difference between a pious and a warlike general. Abu Obeidah was patient, meek and religious; Caled coura- geous and enterprising. At that time when he came to the army, Abu Obeidah had sent Serjabil with 4000 horse towards Bostra, a city

of Syria Damascena, and very populous, in which there were at that
time 12,000 horse.   It was a great trading town, which the Arabs used
to frequent much.   The governor's name was Romanus, who, as soon
as he heard that the Saracens were upon their march, went to meet
them, and asked Serjabil the reason of his coming, and several other
questions relating to Mahomet and his successor.   Serjabil told him
that the reason of their coming was to give them their choice of becoming Mahometans or tributaries ; and added, that they had taken
Aracah, Sachnah, Tadmor, and Hawrân, and would not be long before
they came to Bostra.   The governor, hearing this melancholy story,
went back, and would have persuaded the people to have paid tribute.
They utterly refused it, and prepared themselves for a vigorous defence.   Serjabil continued his march till he came before Bostra ; the
besieged sallied out, and gave him battle.   The prayer which he used
was this : ' O thou eternal being ! O thou creator of heaven and earth !
O thou who art great and munificent ! who hast promised us victory
by the tongue of thy prophet Mahomet, and the conquest of Syria,
Irak, and Persia ! O God, confirm our hopes, and help those who
assert thy unity against those that deny thee.   O God, assist us as
thou didst thy prophet Mahomet.   O Lord, endue us with patience,
and (*Alcoran*, III., 141) keep our feet sure, and help us against the
infidels.'   The Christians had the advantage by much in the battle,
and the Saracens were like to have been beaten off, if Caled had not
come seasonably to their relief: but his arrival turned the fortune of
the day, and the besieged were forced to retire into the city.   Then
Caled asked Serjabil, what he meant by attacking such a place as
Bostra, which was as it were the market-place of Syria, Irâk, and
Hejàz, and where there was always such a great resort of all sorts of
persons, and a great many officers and soldiers, with such an handful
of men ?   Serjabil told him, that he did not go of his own accord, but
by Abu Obeidah's command.   Abu Obeidah, said Caled, is a very
honest man, but understands nothing of military affairs.   Then Caled
took care and refreshed his men, and ordered them to rest, for they
were all extremely fatigued, as well those that had marched that day
with him, as those that had fought under Serjabil ; only he took a
fresh horse himself, and rode about all night, sometimes going round
the city, and sometimes round the camp, for fear the besieged should
make any excursions, especially at such a time as his men were tired,
and out of order.   In the morning, about break of day, he came into
the camp, and the Muslemans arose, and, according to their custom,
some of them purified themselves with water ; and others, who could
not conveniently furnish themselves with water, rubbed themselves
with sand (for that is allowed in case of necessity, and is frequently
used, especially by such Mahometans as travel in those desert countries, where there is great scarcity of water), and their general Caled

said the morning prayer among them, and then they took horse immediately, for the besieged had set open the gates of the city, and drawn out their men into the plain, and taken an oath to be true to one another, and fight it out to the last man ; which when Caled saw, he said, 'these villains come out now, because they know we are weary: come, let us go on, and the blessing of God go along with us.' Both armies were set in battle array, and now Romanus the governor, who thought it the best way to secure himself and his wealth, though at the expense of honour, soul, and conscience, took an opportunity to let Caled know, that he had more friends than he was aware of. He rides before the rest of the army, and with a loud voice challenges the Saracen general, who quickly came forth to him ; he tells him, that he had for a long time entertained a favourable opinion of the Mahometan religion, and seemed to be very willing to renounce his own, upon condition, that Caled would secure him, and what belonged to him ; which he readily promised. Romanus added, that he had, upon Serjabil's first coming to besiege the town, advised the inhabitants to submit to the Muslemans, and pay tribute ; but that instead of being heard, he had only purchased the ill-will of the citizens by his good counsel. In short, he said whatever he could think on that might ingratiate himself with the Saracen, and proffered his service to go back again, and persuade the besieged to surrender. Caled told him, that it would not be safe for him to go back again, without having first fought with him, because then it would appear plainly how well they were agreed, which might occasion some danger to him from his own people : so they agreed to make a show of fighting, to colour the matter the better ; and after a while Romanus, as being beaten, was to run away. The armies on both sides saw them together, but nobody knew what they said. Immediately this mock combat began, and Caled laid on so furiously, that Romanus was in danger of his life, and asked Caled, whether that was his way of fighting in jest, and if he designed to kill him ? Caled smiled, and told him, no, but that it was necessary for them to show something of a fight, to prevent their being suspected. Romanus made his escape ; and indeed it was high time, for the Saracen had handled him so roughly, that whosoever had seen him after the combat, would have had little reason to have thought he had fought in jest, for he was bruised and wounded in several places. As soon as he came back, the citizens asked him, what news ? He told them what a brave soldier Caled was, and extolled the valour and hardiness of the Saracens, and desired them to be ruled and advised in time, before it was too late ; concluding that it would be altogether in vain to make any opposition. But this enraged the besieged, and they asked him, if he could not be content to be a coward himself, but he must needs make them so too ? They would certainly have killed him, if it had not been for fear of the emperor. However they confined him to his house, and charged him at his peril not to meddle nor interpose in their affairs, and told him, that if he would not fight, they would. Romanus, upon this, went home divested of all power and authority, but he still comforted himself with the hopes of being secured and exempted from the common calamity, if the Saracens should take the town, as he expected they would. The besieged having deprived him, substituted in his room the general of those forces which the emperor had sent to their assistance, and desired him to challenge Caled, which he did; and when Caled was preparing himself to go, Abdo'rrahamân, the Caliph's son, a very young man, but of extraordinary hopes, begged of him to let him answer the challenge. Having obtained leave, he mounted his horse, and took his lance, which he handled with admirable dexterity, and when he came near the governor, he said, 'come, thou Christian dog, come on.' Then the combat began; and after a while, the governor finding himself worsted, having a better horse than the Saracen, ran away, and made his escape to the army. Abdo'rrahmân, heartily vexed that his enemy had escaped, fell upon the rest, sometimes charging upon the right hand, sometimes upon the left, making way where he went. Caled and the rest of the officers followed him, and the battle grew hot between the Saracens and the miserable inhabitants of Bostra, who were at their last struggle for their fortunes, their liberty, their religion, and whatsoever was dear to them, and had now seen the last day dawn, in which they were ever to call anything their own, without renouncing their baptism. The Saracens fought like lions, and Caled their general still cried out, *alhámlah, alhámlah, aljannáh, aljannáh;* that is, *fight, fight, paradise, paradise.* The town was all in an uproar, the bells rung, and the priests and monks ran about the streets, making exclamations, and calling upon God, but all too late; for his afflicting Providence had determined to deliver them into the hands of their enemies. Caled and Serjabil (for the Saracens could pray as well as fight, and England as well as Arabia has had some that could do so too) said, 'O God! these vile wretches pray with idolatrous expressions, and take to themselves another God besides thee; but we acknowledge thy unity, and affirm, that there is no other God but thee alone; help us, we beseech thee, for the sake of thy prophet Mahomet, against these idolaters.' The battle continued for some time; at last the poor Christians were forced to give way, and leave the field to the victorious Saracens, who lost only 230 men. The besieged retired as fast as they could, and shut up the gates, and set up their banners and standards, with the sign of the cross upon the walls, intending to write speedily to the Grecian emperor for more assistance.

And now we must leave the poor inhabitants of Bostra in their melancholy circumstances, and come to the deposed governor Romanus, who was extremely well satisfied with the success of the Saracens, and

was now going to act a master-piece of villany. The Saracens kept
watch in their camp all night; and as they went their rounds, they
saw a man come out from the city, with a camlet-coat on, wrought
with gold. Abdo'rrahmân, who happened to be that night upon the
watch, was the first that met him, and set his lance to his breast.
'Hold,' said he, 'I am Romanus, the governor of Bostra; bring me
before Caled the general.' Upon this Abdo'rrahmân went with him to
the general's tent. As soon as Caled saw him he knew him, and asked
him, how he did? 'Sir,' said he, 'my people have been disobedient,
and mutinied, and deposed me, and confined me to my house, and
threatened me with death if I intermeddled with any of their affairs.
Wherefore, that I may chastise them according to their deserts, I have
ordered my sons and servants to dig a hole in the wall (for his house
stood upon the wall of the town) and if you please to send such
persons as you can trust, I will take care to deliver the town into your
hands.' Upon this Caled immediately dispatched Abdo'rrahmân with
100 men, and ordered him, so soon as he had taken possession, to fall
upon the Christians, and open the gates. Romanus conducted them
to the wall, and took them into his house; and after he had given
them a treat, he brought every one of them a suit of such clothes as
the Christian • soldiers used to wear, and disguised them. Then
Abdo'rrahmân divided them into four parts, 25 in a company, and
ordered them to go into different streets of the city, and commanded
them, that as soon as they heard him, and those that were with him
cry out, Alláh Acbar (God is most mighty), they should do so too.
Then Abdo'rrahmân asked Romanus, where the governor was which
fought with him, and ran away from him? Romanus proffered his
service to show him, and away they marched together to the castle,
attended with 25 Muslemans. When they came there, the governor
asked Romanus, 'what he came for?' Who answered, 'that he had no
business of his own, but only came to wait upon a friend of his, that
had a great desire to see him.' 'Friend of mine!' says the governor;
'what friend?' 'Only your friend Abdo'rrahmân,' said Romanus, 'is come
to send you to hell.' The unhappy governor finding himself betrayed,
endeavoured to make his escape. 'Nay, hold,' says Abdo'rrahmân,
'though you ran away from me once in the day-time, you must not serve
'me so again;' and struck him with his sword, and killed him. As he
fell, Abdo'rrahmân cried out Alláh Acbar. The Saracens which were
below hearing it, did so too; so did those which were dispersed about
the streets, that there was nothing but Alláh Acbar heard round about
the city. Then those Saracens which were disguised killed the guards,
opened the gates, and let in Caled with his whole army. The town
being now entirely lost, the conquering Saracens fell upon the inhabitants, and killed and made prisoners all they met with; till at
last the chief men of the city came out of their houses and churches,

and cried Quarter, Quarter. The general, Caled, immediately commanded them to kill no more ; for, said he, 'the apostle of God used to
say, if any one be killed after he has cried out, Quarter, 'tis none of my
fault.'

Thus was the condition of Bostra altered on a sudden, and they
which had been before a wealthy and flourishing people, were now
brought under the Saracenical yoke, and could enjoy their Christian
profession upon no other terms than paying tribute. Some of the
inhabitants asked Caled the next morning, who it was that betrayed
the city to him. To which he making no answer, as being unwilling
to expose the person who had done him such signal service ; Romanus,
the traitor, with most unparalleled impudence, started up himself, and
said, ' O you enemies of God, and enemies of his apostle, I did it,
desiring to please God.' To whom they answered, ' Are not you one of
us ?' ' No,' said he, ' I have nothing to do with you, either in this world
or that which is to come. And I deny him that was crucified, and
whosoever worships him. And I choose God for my Lord, Mahometanism for my religion, the temple of Meccah for the place* of my
worship, the Muslemans for my brethren, and Mahomet for my
prophet and apostle. And I witness that there is but one God, and
that he has no partner, and that Mahomet is his servant and apostle,
whom he sent with direction into the right way and the true religion,
that he might exalt it above every religion, in spite of those who join
partners with God.' After he had given such an ample testimony, and
made so full a confession of his faith, Caled appointed some men to
take care of his effects, for he durst not venture himself any longer in
Bostra, after having been guilty of such unexampled villany.

Then Caled wrote to Abu Obeidah, to acquaint him with his success,
and withal to command him, to bring those forces which he had with
him, that they might all march together to the siege of Damascus.
Then he put a garrison of 400 horse into Bostra, and sent Abubeker
the news of his victory, and his intention to besiege Damascus. There
were at that time 7000 Saracens with AmrouEbnòl Aâs in Palestine ; and
with Abu Obeidah 37,000, which had been raised at several times out
of Hejaz Yemen, Hadramut, the sea-coasts of Ammàn, and the territories of Meccah and Thayef. Caled had with him only 1500 horse
which he brought with him out of Irâk. Heraclius, the Grecian
emperor, was now at Antioch, and being informed what havoc the
Saracens had made in his dominions, thought it time to look about

---

* Arabic, *Keblah*, which signifies the place towards which they turn themselves when they
say their prayers. For as the Jews, though in captivity, used to turn their faces towards the
temple of Jerusalem when they prayed ; so do the Mahometans towards the temple at Meccah. And there are books in Arabic (one of which I have seen in the Bodleian library)
teaching how to find out the zenith, or vertical point of the Keblah, or temple of Meccah,
mathematically : that let a Musleman be where he will, he may know which way to set his
face when he said his prayers.

him. He could not endure to think of losing Damascus, but sends a general, which our Arabick author (not exact at all in the names of the Christians) calls Calous, and with him 5,000 men, to defend it. Calous came first to Hems formerly called Emessa, being the chief city of the adjacent territory which is called by the same name. It lies between Aleppo and Damascus, distant five days' journey from each of them ; a place of a most healthful and pleasant air, compassed about with beautiful gardens and fruitful orchards, which are plentifully watered by a rivulet drawn from the river Orontes, called by the Arabian geographers, Alâsi, which passes by the city at the distance of about half a mile. When he came there, he found the place very well provided both with soldiers, arms, and ammunition. For the conquests of the Saracens had struck such a terror into all the country, that every place had fortified itself as well as possible. He stayed a day and a night at Hems, and passed from thence to Baalbec. He no sooner came near that place, but there came out to meet him a mixed multitude of men and women, with their hair about their ears, weeping and ringing their hands, and making most pitiful lamentation. Calous asked them what was the matter. 'Matter?' said they, 'why the Arabs have overrun all the country, and taken Aracah, and Sachnah and Tadmor, and Hawrân, and Bostra, and are now set down before Damascus.' He asked them what was their general's name, and how many men he had? They told him that his name was Caled, and that he had but 1,500 horse. Calous despised so inconsiderable a number of men, and bad the people be of good cheer, and swore that when he came back again he would bring Caled's head along with him upon the point of his spear.

As soon as he came to Damascus, he produced the Emperor's letter, and told the people, that he expected to have the whole command of the town himself : and would have had Israîl, the former governor, sent out of town : but the Damascens did by no means approve of that, for they liked their old governor very well, and would not hear of parting with him in such a time of extremity, when they had as great occasion for men of courage, as ever they had since they were a people. Upon this they were divided into factions and parties, and continued wrangling and quarrelling one with another, at that very time when there was the greatest need of unity and a right understanding ; for now the Saracens were expected every moment. It was not long before they came ! the Christians went forth to meet them, and both armies were drawn up in order of battle.

When both were ready to fight, Caled called out to Derar Ebno'l Azwar, and said, ' Now Derar quit thyself like a man, and follow the steps of thy father, and others of thy countrymen, who have fought for the cause of God. Help forward religion, and God will help thee.' Derar was mounted upon a fine mare, and Caled had no sooner spoken,

12

but he immediately charged the horse, and killed four troopers, and then wheeled off, and fell upon the foot, and killed six of them, and never left charging them till he had broken their ranks, and put them into disorder. At last they threw stones at him, and pressed upon him so hard, that he was forced to retire among his own men, where he received due thanks. Then Caled called out to Abdo'rrahmàn, the Caliph's son, whom we have mentioned before, who did the like. Caled himself insulted the Christians, and gave them reproachful language, and challenged any of them to fight with him. Izraîl upon this called to Calous, and told him, that it would be very proper for him, who was the protector of his country, and whom the Emperor had sent on purpose to fight, to answer the challenge; however Calous would rather have stayed behind, if he had not been in a manner compelled to go by the importunity of the people. At last, with much ado, he arms himself, and goes forwards; and because he had a mind to discourse with his adversary, he takes an interpreter along with him. As they went on together, Calous began to shake in his harness for fear of the Saracen, and would fain have persuaded the interpreter, with large promises, to have taken his part, if the Saracen should fall upon him. The interpreter begged his pardon, and told him that as far as words would go, he was at his service, but he did not care for blows; and therefore, says he, look to yourself, Sir: 'for my part I will not be concerned: for if I should meddle, and be knocked on the head for my pains, I pray what good would all your fair promises do me?' When they came to Caled, the interpreter began after this manner; 'Sir' said he, ' I'll tell you a story: There was a man had a flock of sheep, and he put them to a negligent shepherd, and the wild beasts devoured them. Which when the owner perceived, he turned away the shepherd, and got another, that was a man of application and courage; then when the wild beasts came again, the shepherd killed him. Have a care that this does not prove to be your case: you Arabians were a contemptible, vile people and went about with hungry bellies, naked and barefoot, and lived upon barley-bread, and what you could squeeze out of dates. Now since you are come into our country, and have fared better, you begin to rebel. But now the Emperor has taken care to send a man that is a soldier indeed, and therefore it concerns you to look to yourselves. And he has brought me along with him to talk with you, out of compassion towards you.' 'Prithee,' says Caled, 'don't tell me thy stories; as for what thou sayest of our country, 'tis true enough. But you shall find that times are well amended with us, and that instead of our barley-bread and coarse fare, you twit us withal, we shall be masters of all your wealth and good things, nay your persons and wives, and children too. And as for this same great man thou speakest of; what dost tell me of a great man for, who have taken Tadmor, Hawràn, and Bostra? Let him be as great as he will ; if he be the support of your kingdom, so am I of our religion. Calous did not. like the mien and behaviour of his adversary at all, and bad the interpreter ask him to defer the combat until the next day ; intending, if he had once made his escape, never to have come so near him any more. But the Saracen did not design to part with him so, but said, that he would not be fooled, and immediately got between him and the Christian army, to prevent his running away, and began to lay about him with his spear most vehemently. They both fought bravely for a while ; in the mean time the interpreter perceiving them engaged, moved off, and escaped to the Christian camp. At last Calous grew weary and began to stand altogether upon the defensive part. The Saracen perceiving that he stood upon his guard, left off pushing him, and came up close to him, and dexterously shifting his spear from his right hand to his left, laid hold on him, and drew him to him, and flung him from his saddle to the ground. The Saracens immediately shouted out, 'Allah Acbar,' which made the whole camp echo, and the poor Christians tremble. Caled took care of his prisoner, and changed his horse, and took a fresh one, which the governor of Tadmor had presented him with, and went into the field again. Derar desired him to stay behind, 'for,' says he, 'you have tired yourself with fighting with this dog, therefore rest yourself a little, and let me go.' To which Caled answered, ' O Derar, we shall rest in the world to come ; he that labours to-day, shall rest to-morrow,' and rode forwards. He was but just gone when Romanus, the treacherous Governor of Bostra, called him back, and told him, that Calous would speak with him ; who, even in those calamitous circumstances, had not laid aside his resentment. When he came back, Calous gave him some account of the difference which had been between him and Izraîl the governor of Damascus, and told him, that if he should overcome him, it would be of great moment, in order to the taking the city ; he advised him therefore to challenge him, and get him out to single combat, and kill him if he could. Caled told him that he might be sure he would not spare any infidel or idolater.

Calous being now a prisoner, his 5,000 men, which he had brought to the relief of Damascus, were very urgent with Izraîl to go out, and answer Caled's challenge ; which he declined at first ; but afterwards, when they threatened him with death, if he persisted in his refusal, he told them, that the reason why he refused at first, was not because he was afraid, but because he had a mind to let their master Calous try his valour first. Then he armed himself, and mounted upon a good horse, rode up to the Saracen ; who, amongst other discourse, asked him his name? He answered 'my name is Izraîl,' (which is the name of the angel, whom the Mahometans suppose to take care of the souls of persons deceased). Caled laughed, and said, ' well your names-sake Israîl is just ready at your service, to convey your soul to hell.' Izraîl asked him what he had done with his prisoner Calous ; He told him that he had him bound. ' Why did you not kill him ?' said Izraîl. ' Because,' said the Saracen, ' I intend to kill you both together.' Then the combat began, and was managed on both sides with great dexterity and vigour. Izraîl behaved himself so well, that Caled admired him. At last the victory inclined to Caled ; and Izraîl finding himself over-matched, and having the better horse of the two, turned his back, and rode away. Caled pursued him as fast as he could, but could not overtake him. When Izraîl perceived that his adversary did not come up, imagining that this slackness of his proceeded from an unwilling-ness to fight, he resumed his courage, and faced about, in hopes to have taken him prisoner ; which Caled perceiving, alighted from his horse, and chose rather to fight on foot ; and as Izraîl rushed upon him, he struck at the legs of his horse, and brought him down to the ground, and took him prisoner. Having now in his possession both the general and the governor, he asked them, if they were willing to renounce their Christianity, and turn Mahometans ? Which they both constantly refusing, were instantly beheaded. Caled having ordered the heads to be brought to him, took them, and threw them over the walls into the town.

There were several battles fought before Damascus, in which the Christians for the most part were beaten. At last, when they saw that by sallying out they had many men killed and taken prisoners, they determined to save the remainder for the defence of the walls, and expose themselves no more to the hazard of a field-fight. Thus they shut up themselves within the town, and Caled pitched his tents over against the east gate, and Abu Obeidah set down before the gate which they call Aljábiyab. The city being thus straightly beseiged, and the inhabitants not daring to depend altogether upon those forces which they had at present, they resolved to despatch a mes-senger speedily to the Grecian emperor Heraclius, then at Antioch : so they wrote a letter to him, in which they acquainted him with what had passed, and the death of Calous and Izraîl, and what con-quests the Saracens had made on that side of the country. When they had closed the letter, they delivered it into the hands of a fit person, and let him down on the outside of the wall in the night. The messenger managed his business so well, that he escaped the Saracens, who were a people not very negligent in their watch. When he came to Antioch, and delivered his letter, the Emperor was extremely con-cerned and sent Werdàn with 100,000 men to relieve Damascus.

Our author tells us, that Werdàn refused to accept of this com-mission at first, as thinking himself slighted, because the Emperor had not employed him at the beginning of the war. But I never give much credit to authors that speak of things done in foreign courts, and out of their knowledge, however worthy of credit they may be, when they write of things done by their own countrymen, and give an account of such transactions, as they may reasonably be supposed to have sufficient opportunities of informing themselves about. For this reason I would as little heed an Arabick author, writing about the affairs of the Christians, as I would a Greek or Latin one giving an account of the Arabians ; because in this case, both must needs take a great deal upon trust, by hearsay, and uncertain reports, and consequently be imposed on themselves, and deceive their readers. Wherefore I have rather chosen to take this history out of their own authors, than depend upon the Christian writers, who were very little acquainted with the affairs of the Saracens.

Werdàn, however, undertook the command of that army ; and after the emperor and some of the nobility had gone part of the way with him, and taken their leave, he marched with all possible speed towards Damascus, the Emperor having given him particular charge, to take care to cut off all supplies from the Saracen army, which was with Caled and Abu Obeidah.

Within a short time after, the Saracens heard that the Emperor's army was upon their march, near Ajnadîn. Caled immediately goes to Abu Obeidah, to advise with him what was proper to be done in this case. Caled was for having the siege raised, and the Saracens go in a full body against the Grecian army ; and then, if they got the victory, return to the siege again : but Abu Obeidah told him, that he was by no means of that opinion, because the inhabitants of Damascus were already in a very great straight, and their going away would only give them an opportunity of getting fresh supplies, both of arms and provision, into the town, and thereby enable them to prolong the siege.

Werdàn's army was very slow upon their march, and the poor besieged Christians were now in great distress. Finding no assistance from the Emperor, they proposed terms to the general, and would have given him 1,000 ounces of gold, and 200 suits of silk, upon condition that he would raise the siege. To which he answered, that he would not raise the siege unless they would either become tributaries or Mahometans : if neither of these conditions pleased them, they must be content to fight it out. About six weeks after this, the Saracens heard an unusual noise in the city, great exclamations and expressions of joy. They could not imagine what should be the meaning of it, but in a very short time they were satisfied, for their scouts brought them word, that the Emperor's army was at hand. Caled again would very willingly have gone to meet them ; but Abu Obeidah would by no means consent that the siege should be raised. At last they agreed to choose some very good soldier, and send him with part of their forces, to give the Emperor's army diversion, that they might not come and disturb the siege. The man that Caled pitched upon to have the management of this expedition, was Derar Ebn'ol Azwàr, an excellent soldier, and most mortal enemy of the Christians, (as indeed all of them were, Abu Obeidah only excepted) who accepted of this post very cheerfully, and cared not how many or how few men he had with him, provided he might be employed in some glorious action against the Christians. But Caled told him, that though they were obliged to fight for their religion, yet God had commanded no man to throw himself away, and therefore bad him be content to accept of such assistance as he should think fit to send along with him ; and ordered him, in case of great danger, to retire to the army. Derar immediately prepared to go ; and as they were upon their march, the Emperor's vast army drew near. When the Saracens saw such a multitude, they were afraid, and would willingly have retired ; but Derar swore, that he would not stir a step back without fighting. And Raphi Ebn Omeirah told them, that it was a common thing for the Muslemans to rout a great army with an handful of men. The armies drew near, and notwithstanding the vast disproportion of their numbers, Derar advanced, without showing the least token of fear or concern ; and when he came up he always fought most where Werdàn the general was. And first of all he killed his right-hand man, and then the standard-bearer. The standard had in it the sign of the cross, and was richly adorned with precious stones. As soon as Derar saw it fall, he commanded his Saracens to alight and take it up whilst he defended them. Immediately they obeyed, and he in the mean time laid about him so furiously, that none durst come within his reach to save the standard. Werdàn, the Emperor's general, had a son that was his father's lieutenant in Hems, who marched with 10,000 men when he heard that his father was going against the Muslemans ; and had the fortune to join him whilst the armies were engaged. He observing Derar's activity, and what execution he did among the Greeks, watched his opportunity, and wounded him in the left arm with a javelin. Derar turned himself about, and struck him with a lance so violently, that when he drew it back again, he left the point of it sticking in the bones. Notwithstanding which he made as vigorous a defence as could be expected from a man disarmed ; but the Greeks pressed hard upon him, and with much ado took him prisoner. When the Saracens saw their captain taken prisoner, they fought as long as they could, in hopes of recovering him but all in vain : which discouraged them so much, that they had like to have run away. Which Raphi Ebn Omeirah perceiving, called out to them with a loud voice, and said, 'What ! don't you know, that whosoever turns his back upon his enemies, offends God and his prophet ? And that the prophet said that the gates of paradise should be open to none but such as fought for religion ? Come on ! I'll go before you. If your captain be dead or taken prisoner, yet your God is alive, and sees what you do.' With these words he restored the battle. In the mean time news came to Caled, that Derar was taken. Upon which he immediately applies himself to Abu Obeidah, to know what was best to be done. Abu Obeidah sent him word, that he should leave somebody in his place and go himself to rescue Derar. Upon this he leaves Meisarah Ebn Mesrouk in his place with 1000 horse, and taking a considerable force along with him, went with all possible speed to relieve the Saracens. When those that were engaged saw the recruit come up, they fell on like lions ; and Caled charged in the thickest part of them, where there was most banners and standards, in hopes of finding Derar prisoner there, but all in vain. At last there revolted a party of them that came with Werdàn's son from Hems, and begged of Caled protection and security for themselves and their families. Caled told them, that he would consider that when he came to Hems, and not in this place. Then he asked them if he knew what was become of Derar. They told him that as soon as he was taken prisoner, Werdàn, the general, had sent him with a guard of 100 horse prisoner to Hems, in order to make a present of him to Heraclius the Emperor. Caled was glad to hear it, and immediately dispatched Raphi Ebn Omeirah with 100 horse to retake Derar. They made all possible haste and took the direct road to Hems ; at last they overtook them, and killed and routed them, and recovered their friend Derar, and hastened back to join Caled, who by this time had entirely defeated the Grecian army. They pursued them as far as Wadi'l Hâyat, and brought off what plunder, and horses, and arms, they could, and returned to the siege of Damascus, which had now but little hopes of holding out long.

The emperor Heraclius not willing to part with Syria thus, sent to Werdàn again, and gave him the command of 70,000 men at Ajnadîn; and commanded him to go and give the Saracens battle, and raise, if possible, the siege of Damascus. When the news of this preparation came to Caled's ears, he went to Abu Obeidah, to consult what was proper to be done ; who told him, that he knew that most of their great* men were absent ; and it would be his best way to send for them as soon as he could, that having joined their forces, they might in a full body give the emperor's army battle. Yezid Ebn Abi Sophyan was then in Balka, a territory upon the confines of Syria ; Serjabil Ebn Hasanah in Palestine ; Meâd in Harrân ; Nomân Ebno'l Mundir at Tadmor ; and Amrou Ebno'l Aâs in Irâk. Upon this Caled wrote the following letter.

'In the name of the most merciful God.

'From Caled Ebno'l Waled to Amrou Ebno'l Aâs, health and hap-
'piness. Know that thy brethren the Muslemans design to march to

---

* Arab. *Kobarao Ashhab Resoul Allah*, i.e. The great men of the companions of the apostle of God.

' Ajnadîn, where there is an army consisting of 70,000 Greeks, who
' purpose to come against us,* that they may extinguish the light of
' God with their mouths ; but God preserveth his light in spite of the
' infidels. As soon therefore as this letter of mine shall come to thy
' hands, come with those that are with thee to Ajnadin, where thou
' shalt find us, if it pleases the most high God.'

The like he sent to the rest of the generals, and immediately gave
orders for the whole army to march with bag and baggage. Caled
himself went in the front, and Abu Obeidah brought up the rear. The
Damascens perceiving the siege raised, and their enemies upon their
march, took courage, and ventured out upon them with an army of
6,000 horse, and 10,000 foot ; the horse under the command of Paul :
the foot, of Peter. As soon as Paul came up, he fell upon Abu Obeidah, and kept him employed whilst Peter went to seize the spoil ; for
all their baggage, and wealth, and women, and children were in the
rear. Peter brought off a good part of it, and some of the women ;
and taking a guard bcth of horse and foot, returned towards Damascus, leaving his brother Paul with the rest of the army to engage the
Muslemans. Paul behaved himself so well, that he beat Abu Obeidah,
and those that were in the rear, who now wished at his heart that he
had taken Caled's advice, when he would have persuaded him at first
to have marched in the front, and would have brought up the rear himself. The women and children made grievous lamentation, and all
things went ill on that side. Upon this Said Ebn Sabahh, being well
mounted, rode as hard as he could to the front of the army, where
Caled was, and gave him an account how matters went ; and desired
him with all possible speed to succour Abu Obeidah. 'Well,' said Caled,
'God's will be done ; I would have been in the rear at first, but he would
not let me ; and now you see what is come on it.' Immediately he
dispatches Raphi with 2,000 horse, to relieve the Saracens in the rear,
and after him Kais Ebn Hobeirah with 2,000 more ; then Abdo'rrahman with 2,000 more ; then Derar Ebno'l Azwar with 2,000 more ; the
rest of the army he brought up himself. When Raphi, Derar, and
Abdo'rrahmân came up, the state of the matter was quite altered ; and
the Christians which had the better of it before, were beaten down on
every side, and their standards and colours turned upside down. Derar
pursued Paul the general, who durst not encounter him ; for he had
seen how he behaved himself at the siege of Damascus, and heard how
he had fought against Werdàn. Derar turned himself about, and said
to Abu Obeidah, 'did not I tell you that this* devil would not stand
me ;' and followed up closely. Paul being pursued hard, flung himself
off from his horse, and endeavoured to get away on foot. Derar

---

* These words are a text of the *Alcoran*. See *Alcoran*, chap. ix., 32, and lxi., 8.
† Arab. *Shaithân*, which is the same with the Hebrew word *Satan*.

alighted too, and had just overtaken him, and was a-going to chine him ; but he cried out, hold ! for in saving me, you save your wives and children which we have taken. Derar upon this forbore, and took him prisoner. The Christians were all routed ; so that of those 6,000 which came out of Damascus, there escaped only 100 ; as they were afterwards informed when the city was taken.

Among those other captives which Peter had taken, it fortuned that Caulah, Derar's sister, a brave virago, and a very beautiful woman, was one. Derar was extremely concerned in the loss of his sister, and made his complaint to Caled : who bade him be of good cheer ; for, says he, we have taken their general, and some other prisoners, which we shall exchange for our own ; and there is no question but we shall find them all at Damascus. However, they resolved to go and see if they could recover them before they got thither. Caled, Raphi, Mei-sarah, and Derar, went in search of the captives ; and ordered Abu Obeidah to march on slowly with the army. There were among the women which were taken prisoners, some of the Hamyarites (a tribe so-called amongst the Arabs) which the Arabians suppose to be de-scended from the ancient Amalekites. These women are used to ride on horseback, and fight as the Amazons did of old. Peter, when he had got his prisoners and plunder at some convenient distance, did not make haste to convey them to Damascus, but stayed by the way, being desirous, if possible, to hear of his brother Paul's success before he went home. Whilst they rested, they took an account of the wo-men, and what else they had gotten ; and Peter chose Caulah, Derar's sister, for himself, and told his men that she, and no other, should be his, and nobody's else. The rest chose each of them one as long as they lasted. The Greeks went into their tents to refresh themselves, and in the meantime the women got altogether, and Caulah said to them : 'What ! will you suffer yourselves to be abused by these Bar-barians, and become handmaids and slaves to these idolaters ? where's your courage ? For my part, I'll sooner die than any of these idolatrous slaves shall touch me.' Opheirah, who was one of them, told her that their patience was not the effect of cowardice, but necessity. 'For,' says she, 'we are defenceless ; we have neither sword nor spear, nor bow, nor anything else.' 'But cannot we,' says Caulah, 'take each of us a tent-pole, and stand upon our guard ? Who knows but that it may please God to give us the victory, or deliver us by some means or other ? If not, we shall die, and be at rest, and preserve the honour of our country.' Opheirah swore she was much in the right of it. They in-stantly resolved upon it, and provided themselves with staves, and Caulah commanded in chief. 'Come,' says she, 'stand round in a circle, and be sure you leave no space between you for any of them to come in and do us a mischief. Strike their spears with your staves, and break their swords and their skulls.' As she spoke, she stepped forwards one step, and struck a fellow that stood within her reach, and shattered his skull. Immediately there was a great uproar, and the Greeks came running out of their tents to see what was the matter. When they came out, there stood the women all up in arms. Peter called out to Caulah, whom he had chosen for his mistress, 'What's the meaning of this, my dear?' 'Woe be to thee,' said she, 'and to all of you, thou (Arab. *Ya kelbo'nnasraniyah*) Christian dog. The meaning of it is, that we design to preserve our honour, and to beat your brains out with these staves: come, why don't you come to your sweetheart now, for which you reserved yourself? It may be you may receive something at her hands, which may prove worth your while.' Peter only laughed at her, and ordered his men to compass them round, and not do them any harm, but only take them prisoners, and gave them an especial charge to be careful of his mistress. They endeavoured to obey his commands, but with very ill success; for when any horse-man came near the women, they let drive at the horse's legs, and if they brought him down, his rider was sure to rise no more. When Peter perceived that they were in earnest, he grew very angry, and alighted from his horse, and bid his men do so too, and fall upon them with their cymiters. The women stood close together, and said one to another, 'Come, let us die honourably, rather than live scandalously.' Peter looked with a great deal of concern upon his mistress, and when he viewed her beauty and comely proportion and stature, loath to part with her, he came near, and gave her good words, and would fain have persuaded her to desist from her enterprise. He told her, that he was rich and honourable, that he had a great many fine seats, and the like, which should all be at her service, and desired her to take pity of her-self, and not to be accessary to her own death. To which she answered, 'Thou infidel, scoundrel, vile rascal, why dost not come a little nearer, that I may beat thy brains out?' This nettled him to purpose; so he drew his sword, and bid his men fall upon them; and told them that it would be a very scandalous thing to them in all the neighbourhood of Syria and Arabia, if they should be beaten by the women. The women were just now at their last prayers, but they held up bravely; and it happened fortunately, that whilst they were thus engaged, Caled and his party came up. They wondered what was the matter when they saw the dust fly, and the swords glitter. Caled sent Raphi to enquire into the business; who rode in great haste, and came back quickly, and gave him an account how things stood. Caled said he did not at all wonder at it, for the women of those tribes were used to it. As soon as Derar heard the news, he put forward his horse in all haste to go and help the women. 'Softly, Derar, softly,' said Caled; 'not so fast, a man that goes leisurely about his business, shall sooner gain his point, than he that goes to work rashly.' Derar answered, 'I havn't patience, I must go and help my sister.' Then Caled set his

men in order, and commanded them, as soon as they came up, to en-
compass their enemies. As soon as Caulah saw the Saracens appear,
she cried out, 'Look ye, my girls, God has sent us help now.' When the
Greeks saw the Saracens draw near, they were in a pitiful condition,
and began to look upon one another very sorrowfully. Peter was now
willing to contrive some way for his own safety, and called out to the
women, 'Hark ye,' said he, 'I pity your condition, for we have sisters
and mothers, and wives of our own ; therefore I let you go freely for
Christ's sake : wherefore, when your people come up, let them know
how civil I have been to you.' Having said thus, he turned towards
the Saracens, and saw two horsemen coming apace before the rest.
One of them (Caled) was completely armed, the other (Derar) naked,
with a lance in his hand, upon a horse without a saddle. As soon as
Caulah saw her brother, she called out, ' Come hither, brother, though
God is sufficient without thy help.' Then Peter called out to her, and
said, 'Get thee, thy brother, I give thee to him,' and turned away to get
off as fast as he could. She called after him, and said, 'This fickleness
of yours is not like the manner of us Arabians ; sometimes you are
wonderfully fond of me, and express a great deal of love, and then
again you are as cold and indifferent as may be.' 'Away with thee,' says
he, 'I am not so fond of thee now as I was before.' 'Well,' says she, ' I
am fond of you, and must have you by all means.' Then she ran up
to him, and Caled and Derar were just at hand. As soon as Peter saw
Derar, he called out to him, and said, 'There's your sister, take her, and
much good may she do you ; I make a present of her to you.' Derar
answered, 'I thank you, sir, I accept of your kind present ; but I have
nothing to return you in lieu of it, but only the point of this spear,
therefore be pleased to accept of it.' At the same time, Caulah struck
the legs of his horse, and brought him down. Derar took him as he
fell, and struck him through and through, and cut off his head, and
put it upon his lance. Then all the Saracens fell on, and fought till
they had killed 3000 men. The rest ran away, and the Saracens pursued them to the gates of Damascus, and returned enriched with
plunder, horses, and armour. Caled now thought it high time to return to Abu Obeidah, fearing that Werdân should have fallen upon
him. They marched forthwith, and as soon as the army saw Caled
and his company, they shouted out an 'Allah Acbar,' and Caled answered them. When they came up to the army, they gave them a
particular account of their whole adventure, especially the battle of
the women, with which they made themselves very merry. Then Caled
called for Paul, who was taken prisoner before, and bid him turn Mahometan, or else he would serve him as he had done his brother.
'What's that?' said Paul. 'Why,' says Caled, 'I have killed him, and here
is his head.' When he saw the head he wept, and said, that he did
not desire to survive him : upon which Caled commanded him to be
beheaded.

The above-mentioned Saracen captains, whom Caled wrote to, to meet him at Ajnadìn, prepared to come as soon as they had received the letter ; and that which was most remarkable was, though they were at places of a different distance, yet they all happened to meet there the same day, Friday, 13th July, 633, which they all interpreted as a singular providence. The armies came within sight of one another, and the Saracens were something at a stand when they saw the Emperor's army, consisting of no less than 70,000. Those who had been in Persia, and seen the vast armies of Cosroes, confessed that they had never seen any thing beyond this, either in respect of their number, or military preparation. They sat down in sight of one another that night, and early the next morning prepared for battle. Caled rode about amongst the ranks of his men, and told them, 'that they now saw the biggest army of the Greeks, that ever they were like to see ; that if they came off conquerors, all was their own, and nothing would be able to stand against them for the time to come.' ' Therefore,' adds he, ' fight in good earnest, and take religion's part, and (*Alcoran*, chap. viii., v. 15, 16.) be sure that you do not turn your backs, and so be damned for your pains. Stand close together, and don't make any assault, till you hear the word of command ; and see that you mind your business, and have your wits and your hearts about you.' Nor was Werdân, on the other side, negligent in encouraging his men to do their best. He called his officers together and said, ' You know that the Emperor has a great concern upon him for you, and if you should shrink now you come to face your enemies, and lose the field, 'twould be such a blow, as could never be recovered, and these Arabs will take possession of all, and kill your men, and make slaves of your wives and children. All is now at stake, therefore stand to it stoutly, and don't flinch, but fight unanimously and courageously. Besides we have three to their one for your comfort, and call upon Christ, and he will help you.' Caled was very apprehensive of that great army, and therefore was willing to go to work as warily as he could. He asked his men, which of them would go and take a view of the army, and bring him account of their order and number ? Derar, who was never backward in anything that belonged to a soldier, proffered his service. ' Well then,' says Caled, ' thou shalt go, and God go along with thee ; but I charge thee, Derar, that thou do not assault them, nor strike a stroke without my order, and so be accessary to thy own destruction.' Away he goes, and views their order, their arms and standards, and banners displayed, and colours flying. Werdân cast his eye upon him, and imagining him to be a scout, sent a party of 30 horse to seize him, and bring him into the army. When they advanced Derar ran away, and they after him, till he had drawn them a good way from the army, and then he faced about, and fell upon them like a lion. First he pushed one through with his lance, and then another ; and terrified them, and beat them grievously until of 30 he had unhorsed 17. The rest fled before him until they came pretty near the Grecian camp, and then he turned off, and came back to Caled. ' Did not I warn you not to fight without order?' said Caled. 'Nay,' said Derar, 'I did not begin first, but they came out to take me, and I was afraid that God should see me turn my back; and indeed I fought with good earnest, and without doubt God assisted me against them; and if it had not been for disobeying your order, I should not have come away as I did; and I perceive already that they will fall into our hands.'

Then Caled set his army in good order. Meâd Ebn Jabel, and Nomân Ebno'lmokarren led the right wing; and Said Ebn Amer, and Serjabil Ebn Hasanah the left. Yezid Ebn Abi Sophyan with 4,000 horse guarded the baggage, women, and children. Caulah and Opheirah, and several other women in the highest rank and chief families of the Arabian tribes, with a great many more of inferior note, prepared themselves for the battle. Caled turned about to them and said, ' Noble girls assure yourselves that what you do is very acceptable to God and his apostle, and the Muslemans; you will hereby purchase a lasting memory, and the gates of paradise will be opened to you. And assure yourselves, that I repose a great deal of confidence in you. If any party of the Greeks fall upon you, fight for yourselves; and if you see any of the Muslemans turn his back, stay him, and ask him whether he runs from his family and children; for by this means you will encourage the Muslemans to fight.' Opheirah told him, that they were all ready to fight till they died.

Then he rode about, and encouraged his men, and bid them fight for the sake of their wives and children, and religion, and stand close to it; for if they were beaten, they had no place to escape to, nor any thing left to trust to. After this he went into the main body of the army, and stood there with Amrou Ebno'l Aâs, Abdo'rrahmân the Caliph's son, Kais Ebn Hobéirah, Raphi Ebn Omeirah, and several other Saracens of note. The two armies covered all the plains: the Christians made a great noise, and the Saracens repeated as fast as they could, 'La I'laba illa Allâh, Mahammed Resoul Allâh:' that is, 'there is but one God; Mahomet is the apostle of God.' Our author tells us, that just before the battle began, there came out a grave old man from the Christian army, and went towards the Saracens, and enquired for the general. Caled came forth to him, and the old man asked him if he was the general? 'They look upon me as such' (said Caled) 'so long as I continue in my duty towards God, and the observance of what he has left us by his prophet Mahomet of blessed memory; otherwise I have no command or authority over them. The old man told him that they were come to invade a land which had been attempted oftentimes before, but with very ill success. That those who had undertook the conquest of it had found their sepultures in that very place where they designed to erect their empire. That, though they had lately obtained a victory over the Christians, yet they must not expect that the advantage would long continue on their side : that the emperor had sent a very numerous army : that the general, how-ever, had sent him to acquaint him that if they would depart without any acts of hostility, he would present every Saracen in the army with a suit of clothes, a turbant, and a piece of money, and the general him-self with 10 suits, and 100 pieces. And to their master, Abubeker, the Caliph, 100 suits, and 1000 pieces. 'No,' said the Saracen, 'no peace, but either become tributaries forthwith, or else Mahometans ; otherwise the sword must determine the controversy betwixt us. And as for your great army you speak of ; we are promised the victory by our prophet Mahomet, in the book which was sent down to him. And then for your proffer of giving us vests, turbants, and money, we shall in a short time be masters of all your clothes, and all the good things you have about you.' Meâd encouraged the Saracens with the hopes of paradise, and the enjoyment of everlasting life, if they fought for the cause of God and religion. 'Softly,' said Caled, ' let me get them all into good order before you set them upon fighting.' When he had done setting them in order, he said, ' Look to it, for your enemies are two to your one, and there is no breaking them, but by out-winding them. Hold out until the evening, for that is the time in which the prophet obtained the victory. Have a care you don't turn your backs, for God sees you.' The armies were now come very near, and the Armenian archers shot at the Saracens, and killed and wounded a great many ; but Caled would not let a man stir. Derar, at last, impatient of delay, said, 'What do we stand still for ? The enemy will think we are afraid of him ; prithee give us the word of command, and let us go.' Caled gave him leave, and he began the battle ; and in a little time a great part of both the armies were engaged, and a great many fell on both sides, but more Christians than Saracens. Werdàn perceiving the great disadvantage his men laboured under, was in great perplexity, and advised with his officers what was best to be done. For no art of a general, nor any terms he could propose, were sufficient to encourage the Christians to fight so desperately as the Saracens, who cared not for their lives, being all of them fully persuaded, that whosoever was killed in fighting for the propagation of their religion should certainly receive a crown of martyrdom. And it is most true, that nothing will make men expose themselves unconcernedly to the greatest dangers, like a spirit of enthusiasm. It was agreed that the best thing they could do would be to circumvent the general of the Saracens by some stratagem, which would extremely discourage the rest, and facilitate the victory. This was attempted after this manner : a messenger was to be sent to Caled, to desire him to sound a retreat, and let the battle cease for that day, and meet Werdàn the next morning at a certain place within view of both the armies, where they, the two generals alone, might treat, in order to find out some expedient for the preventing the effusion of so much blood, as must of necessity be lost on both sides, if the war continued. There was to be an ambuscade of 10 men conveniently placed, to seize the Saracen. The message was delivered to one David, who was privy to the secret. When he had received his errand, he went and enquired for Caled, who rode to him, and with a stern look presented his lance. 'Sir,' said David, 'I am no soldier, but have only a message to deliver to you ; therefore pray turn your lance away whilst I am talking with you.' Upon which Caled laid his lance across upon the pummel of his saddle, and said, 'Speak to the purpose then, and tell no lies.' 'So I will,' says David, 'if you will promise me security for myself and my family.' Which Caled had no sooner done, but he acquainted him thoroughly with the whole business. 'Well,' said Caled, 'go and tell him it shall be so.' Presently after Abu Obeidah met Caled, and observing an unusual briskness and gaiety in his countenance, asked him what was the matter? Caled told him the contrivance, and added, 'I durst venture to go alone, and engage to bring thee all their heads along with me.' Abu Obeidah told him that he was a person likely enough to do such a thing ; but since the prophet had no where commanded them to expose themselves to unnecessary danger, he would have him take 10 men to answer them. Derar thought it not the best way to defer it till the morning, but was for going that evening to surprise that ambuscade. Having obtained leave, he went, after it was dark, towards the place whither Werdàn had sent his ambuscade before. When he came near, he ordered his men to stand still, whilst he went to observe their posture. Then he put off his clothes (for he was as often used to go without as with) and took his sword, and went creeping along, till he came so near as to hear them snore, for they were all drunk and asleep, and their arms lay under their heads. Having so fair an opportunity, he had much ado to forbear killing them himself ; but considering that one of them might possibly awaken the other, he came back, and brought his companions along with him, who took each of them his man, and dispatched the ambuscade with all imaginable silence and secrecy. The next thing to be done was to strip these men, and put on their clothes, for fear any of the Greeks should chance to come by the place, and seeing them in their Arabian habit, make a discovery. Derar told them that it was a good omen, and that he did not at all question but that God would fulfil his promise to them.

About break of day, Caled said the morning prayer in the camp, and drew up his army in order of battle : then he put on a yellow silk vest and green turbant. As soon as the Christians saw the Saracens in order, Werdàn sent up an horseman, who rode to the front of the Saracen army, and cried out, 'Hark ye, you Arabians ; is this fair play ?

'Have you forgot the agreement you made with us yesterday ?' 'How !' said Caled ; 'what ! charge us with breach of promise ?' 'The general,' answered the messenger, 'expects you should be as good as your word, and meet him, in order to treat of peace.' ' Go and tell him,' says Caled, 'that I am just a coming.' Quickly after, Caled saw Werdàn go out upon a mule, very richly dressed and adorned with gold chains and precious stones.' 'Hah !' says he, 'this will be all ours by-and-by, if it please God.' Then he went after him, and when he was almost at him they both alighted. When Werdàn had drawn him pretty near the place where the ambush lay, they sat down opposite to one another to discourse, but Werdàn still kept his hand upon the hilt of his sword, for fear the Saracen should chance to fall upon him on a sudden. 'Come,' says Caled, 'now let us hear what you have to say ; but be sure you deal fairly, and like a man, and tell no lies ; for it does not at all become men in eminent stations to deal deceitfully, and use tricks.' 'What I desire of you,' said Werdàn, 'is, that you would let us know what you would have, and come to some reasonable terms, that we may have peace, and live at quiet on both sides ; and whatsoever you desire of us, we will give you freely, for we know that you are a poor sort of people, and live in a barren country, and in great scantiness and scarcity ; therefore if a small matter will content you, we will give it you willingly.' 'Alas ! for thee, thou Christian dog,' said Caled, ' we bless God that he has provided a great deal better for us than to live upon your charity, and what you please to spare ; for he has given all that you have freely to us, nay, even your wives and your children to be divided amongst us, unless you can say, ' LA ILAHA, &c.   There is but one God, Mahomet is the apostle of God :' or if you do not like that, pay tribute.   If that will not do, then let the sword determine between us, and God give the victory to which side he pleases.   There are no other terms to be had of us.   And for your talking of peace to us, we for our parts take more delight in war ; and for your saying that we are such a contemptible people, I would have you know that we reckon you no better than dogs. You see I don't talk like a man that is much inclined to peace ; and if the meaning of your calling me hither was, that you might have me alone ; here we are in a place by ourselves, far enough both from my army and yours : come and fight with me if you dare.'   Immediately upon this, Werdàn rode up, but trusting to his ambuscade, made no haste to draw his sword.   Caled seized him forthwith, and shook him, and turned him about every way.   Then he cried, ' Come out, come hither, this Arab has seized me.'   As soon as they heard his voice, they came forth, and Werdàn, at first sight, took them to be his own men ; but when they came nearer, and he saw Derar before them, with nothing on but a pair of breeches, and shaking his sword at him, he began to be extremely uneasy, and said to Caled, ' I beg of you not to deliver me into the hands of that devil (Arab. *Shaithân*); I hate the sight of him, it was he that killed my son. Caled swore by God, that when he came up, he would kill him too. By this time Derar was come up, and said, 'Now thou cursed wretch, what is become of thy deceit, with which thou wouldst have ensnared the companions of the apostle of God?' And was just going to kill him. 'Hold,' said Caled, 'let him alone till I give you the word.' When he saw himself in the midst of his enemies, he fell upon the ground, and began to cry quarter : but Caled answered, 'Là Amân illà Beimán ; no quarter (or security) where there is no faith kept. You pretended to peace, and at the same time designed to murder me treacherously.' The word was no sooner out of his mouth, but Derar struck his head off. They then stripped him, and put his head upon the point of Caled's lance, and marched towards the army. As soon as the Christians espied them, they thought they had been their own men, and that Werdàn had brought the Saracen's head along with him. The Saracens thought so too, and were under great concern for Caled. As soon as ever they came near, they charged the Christians, and Abu Obeidah (who commanded the army in Caled's absence) knew them, and told his men. Then they fell on, and engaged in all parts with all the vigour imaginable. The fight, or rather the slaughter, continued till evening. The Christian army was entirely routed and defeated. The Saracens killed that day 50,000 men. Those that escaped fled, some of them to Cæsarea, others to Damascus, and some to Antioch. The Saracens took plunder of inestimable value, and a great many banners, and crosses made of gold and silver, precious stones, silver and gold chains, rich clothes, and arms without number ; which Caled said he would not divide till Damascus was taken. Upon this Caled sends a messenger with the following letter, to Abubeker, the Caliph :—

'In the name of the most merciful God. From the servant of God,
'Caled Ebn Walled, to the successor of the apostle of God, upon
'whom be the blessing of God. I praise God, who is the only God,
'and there is none other besides him ; and I pray for his prophet
'Mahomet, upon whom be the blessing of God ; and I praise him, and
'give thanks to him still more, for his delivering the true believers, and
'destroying the idolaters, and extinguishing the light of those that err.
'I acquaint thee, O Emperor of the faithful, that we met with the
'Grecian army at Ajnadîn, with Werdàn the Prefect of Hems ; and
'they swore by (Arab. *Bidinihim*, i. e. by their religion) Christ, that
'they would not run away, nor turn their backs, though they were
'killed to the last man ; so we fell upon them, calling upon God, and
'trusting upon him, and God supported us, and gave us the victory,
'and our enemies were decreed to be overcome, and we killed them on
'all sides to the number of 50,000 men ; and we lost of the Muslemans
'in two battles, 474 men ; and this letter is written on the fifth day of
'the week, being the thirtieth of the first Jomadah ; and we are now

13

'returning to Damascus, if it please God. Pray for our success and
'prosperity. Farewell. The peace and blessing of God be upon thee
'and all the Muslemans.'

As soon as the messenger told the Caliph the news, he fell down and
worshipped God. Then he opened the letter and read it over, first to
himself, and then to those that were about him. The news immediately flew through all the country, and the hungry Arabians came
thronging to Medinah, to beg leave of the Caliph to go into Syria, all
of them expecting great places and large possessions, and were very
willing to exchange the uncultivated deserts of Arabia Petræa, for the
delicacies of Damascus. Omar did by no means approve of their
motion, but said to Abubeker, 'You know what sort of fellows these
'were to us, when time was: when they were able to oppose us, and we
'were but few in number, they endeavoured to the utmost of their
'power, to ruin our religion, and put out the light of God ; and when
'they did turn, it was only to save themselves ; and now they see God
'has been pleased to bless our forces with success, they are willing to
'share in the spoil, and they will go and make a disturbance among
'those who have got it with their swords. Therefore I pray let none of
'them go ; but let those who have won it, wear it.' Abubeker was of
his mind. As soon as the inhabitants of Meccah heard it, they were
greatly concerned, and thought themselves very much affronted. Some
of the Coreistæ (a noble tribe among the Arabs and which had violently opposed Mahomet at his first setting out, and made him flee
from Meccah to Medinah) came in a body to make their complaint to
Abubeker the Caliph, whom they found sitting with some Muslemans,
Ali on the right hand and Omar on his left. When they had paid due
reverence to the Caliph, Abu·Sophyan accosted Omar after this
manner : 'It is true, in the times of ignorance,* there used to be clash-
ing and difference amongst us, and we did what we could against you,
and you the like to us. But now since it has pleased God to direct us
both into the true religion, that ought to destroy all hatred and animos·
ities between us. For the faith destroys hatred and variance, as well
as idolatry ; and yet you continue your hatred still, notwithstanding we
are your brethren in religion, and your near relations besides. What
is the meaning of this spite both formerly and now ? Is it not time to
purify your hearts from envy ? That you did come into the profession
of the true religion before us we confess, and are willing, upon that
score, to pay you all the respect which is due.' Having said thus he
held his peace, and Arak commended and seconded him. Then Abu
Sophyan desired the Caliph and all the Muslemans to bear witness
that he took upon himself freely to fight for the cause of God; the
like did all the chief of Meccah which were present. This satisfied
the Caliph, and made him be content to let them go. Upon which

* So they all call the time before Mahomet.

he prayed to God to confirm them in their good resolutions, and bless them with answerable success. Then he wrote a letter to Caled, in which he acquainted him that he had received his with great satisfac- tion ; and that he had sent to him some of the chief of Meccah and the adjacent country, particularly Amrou Ebn Maadi, and Malek Alashtar ; and ordered him, after he had conquered Damascus, to go on to Hems, Mearrah, and Antioch ; and bid him be kind to the Muslemans, and think upon mortality, and so concluded. When he had done, he sealed it with Mahomet's seal, and delivered it to Abdo'rrah· man, the same that brought him the letter from Caled.

When Caled sent the letter to Abubeker he was on his march from Ajnadin to Damascus. The poor inhabitants had heard the lamen- table news of the loss of the Emperor's general and army. In the mean- time, whilst the Saracens were absent, a great many of the inhabitants of the neighbouring villages to secure themselves got into Damascus. The return of the Saracens was daily expected, and all manner of war- like preparation was made for the enduring a siege. Their engines were planted upon the walls, and banners displayed. In a little time their hearts ached, when they saw the Saracens appear with a formidable army, flushed with success, and enriched with the spoils of their coun- trymen and neighbours. Amrou Ebno'l Aas led the front, consisting of above 9,000 horse. After him came Abu Sophyan with 2,000, then Serjabil Ebn Hasanah (who was one of Mahomet's secretaries when he wrote the Alcoran), and after him Omar Ebn Rebiyah. Caled marched in the rear, and brought up the rest of the army under the standard of the black eagle. When they were within a mile of the city, Caled called all the generals together, and gave them their respective charges, and said to Abu Obeidah ' You know very well the villainy and deceit ' of these people, and how they came and fell upon our rear, as we ' were in our march to Ajnadin. Have a care of them therefore, and ' don't be so favourable, nor agree to give them security, for they will ' certainly play some trick with you. Go and sit down before the gate ' Jabiyah, at a good distance, and assault them frequently, and don't let ' the length of time make you uneasy, for victory is the reward of ' patience.' Abu Obeidah went according to order, and pitched his tent, which was made of hair, for he would by no means suffer them to set up one of those rich tents which he had taken from the Greeks at Ajnadin. Which my author says, ' proceeded from his great humi- ' lity to God, and the shortness of his hope (Arab. *Kesra'lami*), and ' that he might not please himself with the gay things of this world, ' and the possessions of it. For they did not fight for dominion, but in ' hopes of receiving a reward from God, and having their portion in a ' future state. And they used to set those tents and spoil which they ' had taken at a great distance from them ; and if at any time they found ' any victuals of the Christians, they would not eat it, because the name

13—2

' of God was not mentioned over it when it was killed.'   Abu Sophyan was placed over against the little gate ; Serjabil Ebn Hasanah at St. Thomas's gate, with 2,000 horse ; Amrou Ebn'ol Aas at Paradise gate ; Kais Ebn Hobeirah sat down before the gate Kaisan.   There was another which was called St. Mark's gate, where there never was any fighting (whether because of the incommodiousness of the place, or for what other reason I know not), which upon that account was called Bao'bassalmah, the gate of peace.   After he had given orders he went himself and sat down before the East gate.   Then he called Derar to him, and gave him the command of 2,000 horse, and ordered him to keep riding round about the camp, and never stand still long in any place, for fear any succours should come from the Emperor and surprise the camp ; 'and,' says he, 'if they be too hard for thee, send to me and I will help thee.'   'I suppose then,' said Derar, 'that I am to stand still the meanwhile.'   'No, no,' said Caled, 'I don't mean so neither.'   There were none of the Saracens on horse-back, but those which were with Derar, whose business it was to ride round the camp, and guard it ; for the Saracens, if they engaged horse, used their horses, if otherwise, they for the most part fought on foot.   Caled having thus formed his siege, the next morning early the besieged sallied out, and the fight continued till the evening.   That same day Caled received Abubeker's letter, and after the fight was over sent it to the generals, who were posted at the several gates.

The poor inhabitants perceiving themselves now besieged in good earnest, began to think of coming to terms, and rather submit to pay tribute, and to secure their lives and fortunes, than by standing it out, expose themselves to inevitable death.   The chief of them met, and a considerable part of them were very much inclined to surrender. Thomas, the Emperor's son-in-law, lived then in Damascus, but as a private man, not in any commission ; for though the Emperor had offered him honourable posts, he refused to accept of any employment ; but was nevertheless a person of great courage, and an excellent soldier.   Out of respect to his quality and abilities, the citizens thought it advisable to do nothing rashly, without having first consulted him. When they came to his palace, he seemed to wonder, that these vile Arabs, poor wretches, naked and barefoot, and far from completely armed, should be able to put them in such a consternation.   He told them that the Arabs were masters of no courage, but what was wholly owing to their fear : that there was a great deal of difference, both in respect of number, arms, and every thing else that made an army considerable, between them and the Damascens.   Adding, that they had no reason to despair of the victory.   The citizens told him, with submission, that he was under a great mistake : for the late victories of the Arabs had furnished them very well with arms.   'Besides' (said they) 'they all fight like mad men ; for they encounter us naked, or any way, though under never so great disadvantages; for they steadfastly believe that every one of their own men that is killed passes immediately to paradise, and every one of ours to hell; and this makes them desperate.' To which Thomas answered, that it was plain from thence that they had no true courage who were forced to make use of such an artifice to encourage themselves to fight. 'Well, sir,' said they, 'if you will be pleased to help us, and put us in a way to make a defence, we shall be at your service, otherwise we must surrender.' Thomas was afraid they should be in earnest; and, after a little pause, he promised to go out with them the next morning.

They kept watch all the night, and supplied the absence of the sun with numberless lights placed in the turrets. The Saracens were encouraging one another to do their utmost against the enemies of God, as they used to call all but themselves. In the morning early they prepared for battle; and the Saracens were ready to make a general assault. All the generals said their prayers among their men, and Caled bad them hold out, for they should rest after death; adding, that is the best rest which shall never be succeeded by any labour. Thomas was ready in the morning, and just as he was going out, they set up a crucifix at the gate, and the bishop, attended with some other of the clergy, brought the New Testament, and placed it at a little distance from the crucifix. As Thomas went out at the gate, he laid his hand upon the cover of the Testament, and said, 'O God! if our religion be true, help us, and deliver us not into the hand of our enemies; but overthrow the oppressor, for thou knowest him. O God, help those which profess the truth, and are in the right way.' Serjabil heard him say something, but could not tell what; and when Romanus (who was the treacherous governor of Bostra, and used to be their interpreter) had explained it to him, he was very angry, and cried out, 'Thou liest, thou enemy of God; for Jesus is of no more account with God than Adam. He created him out of the dust, and made him a living man, walking upon the earth, and afterwards raised him to heaven. The battle was joined forthwith, and Thomas fought admirably well; he was an incomparable archer, and shot a great many of the Saracens. Among the rest, he wounded Abân Ebn Said with a poisoned arrow. Abân drew out the arrow, and, unfolding his turban, bound up the wound. But he quickly felt the effect of the poison in his body, and not being able to hold up any longer, was carried into the camp, where his friends would by all means unbind the wound, to dress it; but he told them if they did, he should die instantly. Which accordingly happened, for they had no sooner opened it, but he immediately languished; and when he could speak no longer, continued testifying, by signs, the steadfastness of his belief in God and Mahomet. He was newly married; no longer ago than when the Saracens were at Ajnadîn, to a brave virago, one of the fighting sort, who could use a bow and arrows very well. As soon as she heard the news of his death, she came running in great haste ; and when she saw him, she bore it with admirable patience, and said, ' Happy art thou, my dear, thou art gone to thy Lord, who first joined us together, and then parted us asunder : I will revenge thy death, and endeavour to the utmost of my power to come to the place where thou art, because I love thee. Henceforth shall no man ever touch me more, for I have dedicated myself to the service of God.' Then they washed him (as is their custom) and buried him forthwith, with the usual solemnities. She never wept nor wailed, but with a courage above what could be expected from the weakness of her sex, armed herself with his weapons, and went into the battle without Caled's notice. When she came into the field, she asked whereabouts it was that Abân was killed. They told her, over against St. Thomas's Gate, and that Thomas, the Emperor's son-in-law, was the man that did it. Away she went towards the place, and with the first arrow shot the standard-bearer in the hand. The standard fell down, and the Saracens instantly snatched it up, and carried it off. Thomas was grievously concerned at the loss of the standard, and laid about him furiously, and ordered his men to look about them narrowly, to see if they could find it any where, and retake it, if possible. When the Saracens that had it saw themselves hard beset, they shifted it from one to another, till it came to Serjabil's hands. The Damascens followed Thomas with a great deal of courage and vigour, and there began a most bloody battle ; and all the while the engines played from the walls upon the Saracens, and threw stones and arrows as thick as hail. They plied them so well from the walls, that the Saracens were forced to retreat, and fight out of the reach of the engines. Thomas at last spied the standard in Serjabil's hand, and made up to him, and fell upon him like a lion. Upon which Serjabil threw the standard away, and engaged his adversary. Whilst they were fighting, and every one admired Thomas's valour, Abân's wife saw him, and asked who it was : they told her, it was the same man that killed her husband. As soon as she heard that, she levelled an arrow at him, and shot him in the eye ; so that he was forced to retire into the city. The Saracens followed him close, and killed 300 in the pursuit, and would have gone fter him further, but they durst not for the engines.

Thomas had his eye dressed, but would by no means be persuaded to go to his house, though the inhabitants of the town entreated him very much, and told him that there was no good to be done with these Arabs, but that the best way would be to surrender the town. But he, being a man of undaunted courage and resolution, said, ' They should not come off so ; that they should not take his standard, and put his eye out unrevenged.' He considered what a reflection it would be upon his honour, and how the Emperor would look upon it,

if he should suffer himself to be disheartened and daunted by the
Arabs. The battle continued till night parted them ; Thomas
all the while continued in the gate, meditating revenge. When
it was dark, he sent for the chief men of the city, and not at all
daunted, said to them, ' Look ye, you have to do with a people who
have neither good manners, nor religion, nor any faith or honesty
belonging to them (for which words my author is very angry with him,
and gives him an hearty curse*) and if they should make any agreement with you, and give you security, they'll never stand to their word,
but lay the country waste : and how can you bear to see what is
dearest to you invaded, and your poor children made slaves, and yourselves turned out of house and harbour, and deprived of all the conveniences of life ?' They told him they were ready at his service,
either to fight upon the walls, or to sally. Then he ordered them
every man to make ready with all possible speed and all the silence
imaginable, that they might not give the least alarm to the Saracens.
All the armed men were drawn up at the several gates, and upon a
signal given by one single stroke upon a bell, the gates were all opened
at the same instant ; the Christians (some few only excepted, who
were left to secure the gates and the walls) sallied out all together, and
poured in upon the Saracen camp like a torrent, in hopes of finding them
wounded and tired, and altogether unprovided to receive so vigorous
an attack. The whole camp was immediately alarmed ; and as soon
as Caled knew it, he said, ' O God, who never sleepest, look upon thy
servants, and do not deliver them into the hands of their enemies.'
Then he ordered Pheljân Ebn Zeyad to supply his place, and rode
with 400 men as fast as he could, and the tears lay upon his cheeks for
the concern he had upon him for his dear Saracens. The care of
Serjabil and Abu Obeidah made him very anxious, being well aware of
Thomas's valour. When he came near the gate, he found how things
stood ; Thomas had fallen violently upon the Saracens, and before he
came out, commanded his men to give quarter to none but the general.
The Jews, which were in Damascus, plaid the engines upon the Saracens. Thomas was again engaged with his former adversary, Serjabil.
Aban's wife was among Serjabil's men, and did great execution with
her bow and arrows, till she had spent them all but one, which she
kept to make signs with as she saw occasion. Presently one of the
Christians advanced up towards her, she shot him in the throat, and
killed him, and was then taken prisoner. Serjabil at last struck a
violent stroke, which Thomas receiving upon his buckler, Serjabil's
sword broke. Thomas thought himself sure of him, and had certainly
either killed him or taken him prisoner, but Abdo'rrahmán and Aban
(Othman's son, who was afterwards Caliph) came up at that instant

---

* Arab. *Kádaba'llain Achzàho'lláh ;* that is, the accursed (meaning Thomas) lyed, God
confound him.

with a regiment of fresh horse, and rescued both him and Aban's wife. Thomas perceiving the Saracens came in so fast upon him, retired into the city. We said before that Abu Obeidah was posted at the Gate Jabiyah ; he was in his tent when the Christians first sallied out, and went to prayers. Afterwards, whilst his men were engaged, he took a party, and got between the Christians and the city : so that they were surrounded, and charged on both sides. They made a quick dispatch for them, for never a man that went out at that gate, returned again : and though those that sallied at the other gates escaped something better, yet the Christians had no reason to boast of any advantage, having lost that night several thousand men.

The Christians now quite disheartened, came about Thomas, with repeated intreaties to surrender ; they told him, they had lost above half their men, and what were left were not sufficient for the defence of the town : they told him at last, in plain terms, that as to what concerned himself, he might manage as he pleased, but for their parts they were resolved to get as good terms for themselves as they could. Thomas, however, endeavoured to persuade them to stay till he should write to the Grecian emperor, and accordingly did write. The Saracens continued fighting hard, and reduced the besieged to very great straights, who now every day made a worse defence than other. They desired Caled to leave off the assault, that they might have a little time to consider: but he turned a deaf ear to them, for he had rather take them by force, put them to the sword, and let his Saracens have the plunder, than that they should surrender, and have security for themselves and their fortunes. But Abu Obeidah was of a quite different disposition, a well meaning, merciful man, who had rather at all times that they should surrender, and become tributaries, than be exposed to any extremity ; and this the besieged knew very well: wherefore, one night they sent a messenger that understood Arabick, out at that gate where Abu Obeidah was posted, who called out to the centinels, and desired safe conduct for some of the inhabitants of Damascus to come to their master Abu Obeidah, in order to talk of an agreement. As soon as Abu Obeidah was acquainted with the news, he was very glad to hear it, and sent Abu Hobeirah to the Damascens, to let them know that they should have free liberty to go where they pleased. They asked him whether or no he was one of Mahomet's companions, that they might depend upon him? He told them that he was, but that made no difference ; for if the meanest slave among them had given them security, it would have been all one, for they should have performed it, because God had said, in the book which he sent to their prophet Mahomet, ' Perform your covenant, for that shall be called to an account' (*Alcoran*, chap. xvii. 36). Upon this, about an hundred of the chief of the citizens and clergy went out, and when they came near the camp, some of the Saracens met them, and took off their circingles, and conducted them to Abu Obeidah's tent ; who used them very civilly, and bid them sit down, and told them that their prophet Mahomet had commanded them to pay respect to persons of rank and quality.   They were very glad to find him so courteous, and when they came to talk of terms, they first desired that their churches might be secured to them, and not any way alienated.   He granted them seven churches, and gave them a writing, but did not set his own name to it, nor any witnesses, because he was not general.   Then he went, attended with about 100 men, to take possession: when he came to the gates, he demanded hostages ; which being delivered, he entered into the city.

Caled was altogether ignorant of this transaction, and was, at the very same time when this business was concluded, making a sharp assault at the east gate, being especially provoked at the loss of Caled Ebn Said (Amrou Ebno'l Aas his brother, by the mother's side) whom one of the besieged had shot with a poisoned arrow.   In the meantime, there came to Caled from the town one Josias a priest, who told him, that having been long conversant with ancient writings and prophecies, and especially the prophet Daniel, he was abundantly satisfied of the future greatness of the Saracen empire ; and proffered his service to introduce him and his army into the town, upon condition that Caled would grant him security for him and his.   Whether any conviction that he had met with in reading that prophet, or the desire he had to preserve himself, was the prevailing motive with him, I shall not determine.   Neither did Caled much trouble himself about that, but gave him his hand to perform the condition, and sent with him 100 men, most of them Homerites, (a warlike tribe of the Arabs) and bid them as soon as they were entered to cry out as loud as they could 'Allah Acbar,' and make themselves masters of the gates, and break the bolts, and remove the chains, that he with the rest of the army might march into the city without any difficulty.   This was accordingly performed.   The poor Christians, as soon as ever they heard the Tecbir (so the Arabs call the crying out Allah Acbar), were sensible that the city was lost ; and were seized with such an astonishment, that they let their weapons fall out of their hands.   Caled entering at the east gate with the Saracens, put all to the sword, and Christian blood streamed down the streets of Damascus.   They went on thus murdering all they found, till they came to St. Mary's church, where they met with Abu Obeidah and his company.   When Caled saw Abu Obeidah, and his men in their march, and the priests and monks before them, and all the Saracens with their swords by their sides, not so much as one drawn, he wondered what was the matter.   Abu Obeidah perceived in him tokens of dislike, and said, ' God has delivered the city into my hands by way of surrender, and saved the believers the trouble of fighting.' At which Caled was very angry, and said, ' that he had taken it by the sword, and they should have no security.' Abu Obeidah told him, 'that he had given them an article in writing, which he had here to show.' 'And how,' said Caled, 'came you to agree with them, without acquainting me first? Did not you know me? Did not you know that I am your general, and (Arab. *Sáhhibo Ryecha*) master of your counsels? And therefore I'll put them every one to the sword.' 'I did not think,' said Abu Obeidah, 'that when I had made an agreement, or (Arab. *Raáito Ráyan*) designed to do anything, you would ever have contradicted me, or have gone about to make it void. But you shall not make it void, for I have given all these people my protection, and that in the name of God and his prophet ; and all the Muslemans that were with me liked it, and approved it, and we don't use to be worse than our word.'

There was a great noise made on both sides, and Caled would not abate an ace. The hungry Arabs that were with him were eager to fall on, and thirsted after blood and plunder. The poor inhabitants were now in a very calamitous condition, for every man of them had been murdered or made a slave, if Abu Obeidah had not stood their friend ; who seeing the Arabs fall on, killing some and taking others prisoners, was extremely concerned, and called out in a passion: ** 'By God, my word is looked upon as nothing, the covenant which I make is broken.' Then he turned his horse, and rode about among the soldiers, and said, 'I adjure you by the apostle of God, that you meddle with none of them, till you see how Caled and I can adjust this matter.' With much ado he made them forbear ; then the chief officers came to them, and they all went together into the church, to debate this affair. Several of them enclined to the more merciful side, for which they gave this very substantial reason, viz.—' That there were a great many cities still to be taken, and if it should once be reported about the country that the Saracens had broke their promise, after they had given security, they must never expect to have any other place surrender, but make the most obstinate defence imaginable.' At last, some advised that Caled should have the disposal of that part of the town which he had taken by the sword, and Abu Obeidah of that which he had taken upon articles ; at least till such time as they could appeal to the Caliph, and be determined by his sentence. This was so reasonable a proposal, that Caled could not refuse it ; so at last he consented that the people should have their protection, but would give no quarter to Thomas and Herbis, nor any of their soldiers. Abu'Obeidah told him that they were all included, and begged of him not to make any further disturbance about it.

And now we have seen Damascus, the most noble and ancient city

---

* Arab. *Wallah*, an oath frequently used by the Arabs, who do not account it any profanation of the Divine Name, to swear by it ; but rather an acknowledgment of his omnipotence and omnipresence ; and therefore we find it used by the most religious among them.

of Syria, taken by the Saracens ; we must leave the conquerors in possession, and the miserable inhabitants in their deplorable circumstances,
and take a view of affairs at Medinah. Abubeker the Caliph died
(*Alwákidi*) the same day that Damascus was taken (*Elmakin*), which
was on Friday, 23rd August, 634, and of the Hegirah the thirteenth.*
There are various reports concerning his death : some say that he was
poisoned by the Jews, eating rice with Hareth Ebn Caldah, and that
they both died of it within a twelvemonth after.† But Ayesha says,
'that he bathed himself upon a cold day, which threw him into a
fever, of which he died within fifteen days, all which time Omar said
prayers publicly in his place.

When he perceived himself near his departure, he called his secretary, and gave him directions to write as follows :—

' In the name of the most merciful God.

'This is the testament of Abubeker Ebn Abi Kohapha, which he
' made at that time when he was just a-going out of this world, and
' entering into the other. ‡A time in which the infidel shall believe,
' and the wicked person shall be assured, and the liar shall speak
' truth. I appoint Omar Ebno'l Chitab my successor over you ; there-
' fore hearken to him, and obey him. If he does that which is right
' and just, 'tis what I think and know of him. If he does otherwise,
' every man must be rewarded according to his works. I intend to do
' for the best, but I don't know hidden things : But those who do evil
' shall find the consequences of it. Fare ye well, and the mercy and
' blessing of God be upon you.'

When he designed to make Omar his successor, Omar desired to be
excused, and said, he had no need of that place. To which Abubeker
answered, that the place had need of him, and so appointed him
Caliph against his will. Then he gave him such instructions as he
thought proper ; and when Omar was gone out of his presence, he
lifted up his hand, and said, ' O God ! I intend nothing by this but
the people's good, and I fear lest there should be any difference among
them ; and I have set over them the best man amongst them. They
are thy servants ; unite them with thy hand, and make their affairs
prosperous, and make him a good governour ; and spread abroad the
doctrine of the Prophet of mercy, and make his followers good men.'

Elmakin says, that he was the first that gathered together the
scattered chapters of the Alcoran, and digested it into one volume.
For in Mahomet's time they were only in loose writings. But when in
the war which they had with Moseilamah, a great many of those who

---

* *Abu'lpheda.*

† *Ahmod Ebn Mohammed Ebn Abdi Rabbihi and Abu'lpheda.*

‡ That is, the infidel and wicked shall then be assured of the reality of those things relating
to a future state which they disbelieved and ridiculed in their lifetime.

could read and repeat the Alcoran were killed ; Abubeker was afraid lest any part of it should be lost ; and gathered together what was extant in writing, or what any of the Muslemans could repeat, and making one volume of it, called it Mus-haph ; which in the Arabick tongue signifies a book (*Abu'lpheda*). This book was committed to the custody of Hapsah, Omar's daughter, and one of Mahomet's wives. But Joannes Andreas, who was himself a Moor by birth, and Alfaqui or chief doctor of the Muslemans in Sciatinia, in the kingdom of Valencia in Spain, and afterwards converted to the Christian religion in 1487, says, that this was not done till the time of Othman, the third Caliph after Mahomet. Eutychius in his annals says the same. I believe them both to be mistaken, because I find in* Abu'lpheda, that when Othman came to be Caliph, he observing the variety of different readings which were spread abroad, copied this book which had been delivered to Haphsah, and abolish'd and destroyed all other copies, which had different readings from this ; obliging all the Mahometans to receive this copy as the only authentick Alcoran. Which action of his, I am fully persuaded, gave occasion to some to report, that Othman was the first that gathered the chapters of it into one volume ; a work of that importance that it can scarcely be believed to have escaped the zeal and diligence of Abubeker and Omar.

As to the character of this Caliph ; (*Elmakîn*) he was a tall, lean man, of a ruddy complexion, and a thin beard, which he used to tinge with such colours as are frequently used in the eastern countries, to make it look more graceful. He never saved any money in the public treasury ; but every Friday night, distributed what there was among persons of merit ; to the soldiers first. His chastity, temperance, and neglect of the things of this life, were exemplary. He desired Ayesha to take an account of all that he had gotten since he was Caliph, and distribute it among the Muslemans ; being resolved not to be enriched by his preferment ; only he took three Drachmæ (a piece of gold in use among the Arabs at that time ; the true value of which is now unknown) out of the public treasury, as a reward of his service. His whole inventory amounted to no more than five of those Drachmæ ; which when Omar heard, he said, that Abubeker had left his successor a hard pattern.

'Tis usual with some authors, when they give characters of great men, to mention some of their wise sayings. The Arabs have not been deficient in this particular. Nisaburiensis, (called so from Nisabour, the metropolis of Chorasan ; as it is most common for Arabick authors to be distinguished by the place of their birth as much as by their names) has collected in a little book the grave and witty sayings of Mahomet and his successors, and some of the kings of Persia. Among some others which he has recorded of Abubeker,

---

* *Kitâb Almoctaser phi Abbârí'l bashar.*

there are these two very remarkable ones ; * 'Good actions are a guard against the blows of adversity.' And this ; 'Death is the easiest (or least considerable) of all things after it, and the hardest of all things before it.'

He was sixty-three years old when he died ; having reigned two (Lunar) years, three months and nine days.

OMAR EBNO'L CHITAB,

THE SECOND CALIPH AFTER MAHOMET.

ABUBEKER having taken care of his succession, all disturbance was prevented. I do not find that Ali or his party made any opposition ; but the same day that Abubeker died, Omar was invested with the regal and pontifical dignity, and saluted by universal consent (*Elma-kîn*), 'The Caliph of the Caliph of the apostle of God ;' that is the successor of the successor of Mahomet. But when they considered that this title was something too long ; and that at the coming on of every new Caliph, it would grow longer still, they invented another, which should serve for all the Caliphs to come, and that was, Amiro'l Mumenina ; Imperator Credentium, Emperor of the Believers. Which afterwards was used to the succeeding Caliphs ; Omar being the first that was ever called by that title.

Being thus confirmed in his new dignity, he goes into the pulpit, to make a speech to the people. He did not say much ; but the substance of it was ; 'That he should not have taken such a troublesome ' charge upon himself, had it not been for the good opinion that he ' had of them, and the great hopes which he had conceived of their ' perseverance in their duty, and doing that which was commendable ' and praise-worthy.' Thus the ceremony being over, which in the infancy of that government, whilst they had not yet attained that grandeur which their successors afterwards arrived at, was not very great ; every man went home very well satisfied.

Omar having taken upon him the government, was desirous of nothing more than to make some conquests in Irak ; and in order to this, sends Abu Obeid with an army, joining to him Almothanna, Amrou, and Salit, who marched with their forces till they came to Thaalabyah, where they pitched their tents just by the river. Salit, considering all things well ; and justly fearing that the forces of the Persians were too great for them to encounter withal, did what he

could to persuade Abu Obeid not to cross the river ; telling him, that
since the Persians were apparently too strong for them, it would be
more adviseable to reserve themselves for a fairer opportunity, and
retire into the deserts, and there secure themselves as well as they
could, till they had sent to the Caliph for fresh supplies. But Abu
Obeid was so far from being persuaded by what he said, that he called
him coward. Mothanna took him up, and told him, that what Salit
had said was not the effect of cowardice, but that he had told him
what he thought would be the best way ; adding, that he was also of
the same opinion himself, and bad him have a care how he passed
over to the enemies, for fear he should bring himself and those
that were with him, into such danger as he could not bring them out
of again. But Abu Obeid, deaf to all good counsel, and impatient of
delay, forthwith commands a bridge to be made, and marches over his
army. Salit and Mothanna, though they did not at all approve of his
conduct, yet having spoke, what they thought to no purpose, went
over after him. The soldiers followed him with an heavy heart,
grieved at the rashness of their general, which they had just reason to
fear would prove fatal to them.

As soon as they were got over the bridge, Abu Obeid put his men
in battle-array, as well as the shortness of the time would permit ;
for the Persian archers lay very hard at him, and wounded the
Muslemans grievously. However Abu Obeid having got some part of
his army in tolerable order, charged the Persians so furiously, that
they could no longer keep their ground, but ran away. Abu Obeid
pursued, as being now assured of the victory ; but the Persians rallying
again, and renewing their charge, killed Abu Obeid, and routed the
Muslemans. Those that remained of them made up to the bridge ;
Mothanna all the while behaving himself like an experienced captain,
fought in the rear, and brought them off with as little loss as could be
expected. At last they got over the bridge, and Mothanna after them ;
who was no sooner over, but he ordered the bridge to be cut down, to
prevent the pursuit of the Persians.

Mothanna having now secured himself, sent the Caliph an account
of the whole matter ; and having acquainted him with Abu Obeid's
rashness in passing the river with so small a number, contrary to the
judgment of all the officers, together with the success which had
followed so unadvised an undertaking, staid expecting further orders.
The Caliph commanded him to secure himself in his camp as well as
he could, and not stir till he should receive the supplies which he
would take care to raise for him with all possible expedition. Mothanna obeys the order ; in the mean time the Caliph sends special
messengers to the tribes of the Arabs, to raise men for the service,
which they speedily performed. The new-raised soldiers were mustered
at Medinah, and Jarîr Ebn Abd'ollah was appointed their general,

and was sent with orders to join Mothanna, and, as opportunity should
serve, give battle to the Persians. Jarîr being come to Thaalabiyah,
where the rest of the army was, they marched to Dir Hind, where
·they encamped, and made frequent excursions, plundering and
destroying that part of Irak, which lies next the Euphrates. Arzemidocht, queen of the Persians, perceiving the great damage which she
every day received from the Arabian army, thought it high time to
look about her, and out of all the cavalry, chose 12,000, and appointing
Mahran general of them, sent them to repress the insolences of the
Arabs. They marched till they came to Hirah; where the
Arabians, having called back those troops which were gone
to forage, met them. Both armies were immediately joined. Mothanna fought amongst the thickest of the Persians, and was gotten
into the midst of their army, but bravely recovered himself, and
returned to his own men. The Persians behaved themselves so well,
that some of the Arabs gave ground. Mothanna perceiving his Arabs
flinch, tore his beard; labouring as much as in him lay to stay the
flight of his men and restore the battle, which he did in a great
measure: and then began a most furious engagement, which lasted
from noon till sunset, neither party giving way. It is hard to guess
which side would have prevailed, had not the death of Mahran
determined it; for Mothanna meeting him in the battle, they fought
hand to hand. Mahran struck at Mothanna, but his sword did not
pierce his armour: then immediately Mothanna gave him such a blow
upon his shoulder, that he fell down dead. The Persians having lost
their general, were quite disheartened, quitted the field, and fled
to Madayen. The Arabs contented with their victory, did not pursue
them far, but returned to bury their dead.

The Persian nobility perceiving the Saracens every way too hard for
them, and that they had now made themselves masters of the borders
of their country, and were very likely to get more, began to be very
uneasy, and laid all the blame upon their Queen, Arzemidocht.
'Tis very common in those eastern countries to measure things
by the success; and if things go ill, neither the Grand Signior
himself, nor the Sultan of Persia, nor the Emperor of the Moguls,
can be secured from the murmurs, and often-times mutinies of
their subjects; who, though things be managed with all the care
and circumspection that human capacity can be master of, yet
if the success does not answer their expectation, never fail to complain of male-administration, and represent their princes as persons
unfit for government, either for want of abilities, or else because
they look upon them to be unlucky and unfortunate, in which matter
the eastern nations are extremely superstitious. This the Queen experienced; for after this battle was lost, and things went ill on all sides
the next thing they said, was, 'This we get by suffering a woman to

rule over us ;' as if all their misfortunes had been owing to her mismanagement ; or, as if they might not have met with the same ill
success, under the government of the wisest prince in the world.
However they considered nothing of this, but resolved to depose the
poor Queen : which they did, and placed Yazdejerd upon the throne
in her stead, who was a young man of the royal family, descended
from Cosroes the son of Hormisdas.   But they did not much mend
the matter, for the government of this new king of theirs was more
inauspicious than that of the Queen could be ; for in her reign, the
confines of the empire were only invaded, but in his, all was entirely
lost, and the whole kingdom and country of the Persians fell into the
hands of the Muslemans.

Yazdejerd being king, forthwith raised an army out of the several
provinces of his kingdom, and made Rustam their general, who was
descended of a noble family, and had years and experience sufficient
to recommend him.   Yazdejerd gave him orders to march to Hirah,
where the Arabs lay ; and at the same time sent another great army,
under the command of Alharzaman, a Persian nobleman, to Ehwàs,
where Abu Musa Alashari, another of Omar's captains, lay foraging'
and spoiling the country.   But all to no purpose : the Persians, as if
the period of their empire was at hand, could have no success, but
were forced to submit to the rising greatness of the Saracenical
empire.   Both these Persian generals were killed, and both the armies
entirely routed.

Abu'lpharagius, from whom I have taken this account of the transactions relating to Persia, is mistaken two years, as to the time in
which they were done ; for he places them at the beginning of Omar's
reign, which, as we have shewn before, was in the year 634.   Now it
is very well known that the Persian Æra (which they use to this day)
bears date from the beginning of that year, in which Yazdejerd, the
last of the Persian kings, came to the crown ; which was, as is confessed on all hands, June 16, 632.   However, since Abu'lpharagius has
placed these actions in Omar's life, I have contented myself with
giving the reader this hint, and followed that author in this ; because I
could not find any place so proper for the interrupting the history of
Syria, as the taking of Damascus, and the death of Abubeker ; both
which happening at the same time (according to Alwakidi the historian) made a sort of a period, and gave me a fair opportunity of
inserting whatever was done by the Saracens in any other country
within that compass of time.

And now the series of our history requires us to return to the
Damascens, whom we left just at that time when Abu Obeidah had
with great intreaty scarcely prevailed with Caled to ratify the articles
which he had made with the besieged.   Having obtained it at last
with much ado, he told them that they were at their liberty to go

where they pleased ; but when they were out of the bounds of that part of the country, which was taken by the Muslemans, they were also out of their protection, and free from any article of agreement whatsoever. The Christians, not content with this, desired their protection for the space of three days, which way soever they went, and that none of the Saracens should pursue them during that time ; after which they must be content to take their fortune. To which Caled consented, but told them withal, that they should carry nothing with them out of the city, but provision ; which provoked Abu Obeidah afresh, who answered, ' That to use them so would still be a breach of promise, he having engaged to give them leave to go out with bag and baggage.' ' Then ' (said Caled) ' if they have that, they shall have no arms.' To which Herbîs answered, ' That they must have arms, it being impossible for them to travel safely without.' Abu Obeidah said, ' Then let every one of them have something ; he that has a lance shall have no sword, and he that takes a bow shall have no lance ;' with which they were pretty well contented. Thomas and Herbîs were the captains of this unhappy caravan, who had now lost all but what they could carry away ; and instead of lofty and stately palaces, pleasant gardens and delicious fare, must be glad to shift about where they can, and expose themselves to all the difficulties and hazards of a tedious journey, without any regard had to age, sex, or degree. The tender and delicate lady that once scarce knew how to set her foot upon the ground, must now be forced to go through inhospitable deserts and craggy mountains, deprived not only of her superfluities, but of all the conveniences, and even the very necessaries of life. Thomas pitched a tent on the outside of the city, and ordered his men to bring the best of the things, the plate, jewels, silk, and the like, into it, in order to pack them up, and carry them away. The Emperor Heraclius had then in Damascus a wardrobe, in which there were above 300 loads of dyed silks and cloath of gold, which were all pack'd up. The poor miserable wretches took every one what they could any way carry, of the best things they had, and made all possible haste to be gone. Damascus, once their joy and delight, could now no more be thought on without regret. The Emperor Heraclius's daughter went out among the rest, which followed Thomas and Herbîs. Derar (who was vexed at the heart because Abu Obeidah had let them come off so well) stood by as they went out, and gnashed his teeth for spite and indignation. The princess thought that the reason of his anger was because of the spoil, and said to him as she passed by, ' What's the reason, Derar, that you mutter thus ? Don't you know that (Arab. *Ind'allah*) with God there are more and better things than these are ?' Derar swore, ' That it was not the plunder that he valued ; but what vexed him was the people's escaping, and not being all murdered ;' adding, that Abu Obeidah had done a great injury to the Muslemans,

14

in giving them quarter. Athi Ebn Ammar hearing him say so, answered, 'That Abu Obeidah had done for the best, in preventing the effusion of the blood of the Muslemans (the most sacred thing under the sun) and giving them rest from their labours. Besides, God has made the hearts of the true believers the seat of mercy, and those of the infidels the seat of cruelty : and God has said in some of the inspired books, that he was most merciful ; and that he would not shew mercy, but only to the merciful.' Then he quoted a passage in the Alcoran, to prove to him that agreement was better. Derar told him, that he talked like an honest man, but he swore that for his part ' he would never have mercy upon any that said that God had a Son, and joined a partner with God.' Thomas and Herbîs paid Abu Obeidah what they had bargained with him for, as the redemption of their lives and liberties ; and then those of them who chose to stay behind, and be tributaries, staid ; the rest, which were by far the greater number, went away.

Caled, O bloody and insatiable Saracen ! saw these poor wretches carry away the small remainder of their plentiful fortunes, with a great deal of regret : so mortally did he hate the Christians, that to see any of them alive was death to him. What does he do ? Why! he orders his men to keep themselves and their horses well ; and told them, that after the three days had expired (for they had security for that time) he designed to pursue them ; and said, ' That his mind gave him that they should still overtake them, and have all the plunder :' ' For,' says he, ' they have left nothing valuable behind them, but have taken all the best of their cloaths, and plate, and jewels, and whatever is worth carrying along with them.' Having thus prepared for his journey, there happened another controversy between him and the townsmen that staid behind, concerning a great quantity of wheat and barley. The townsmen which had surrendered to Abu Obeidah said that it belonged to them ; Caled said that it was his (and indeed so was every thing else of the Christians that he could lay his hands upon). Abu Obeidah, who was always more courteous to the Christians than could have been expected from a Saracen, took the citizens' part. The contention grew so high, that they had like once more to have fallen together by the ears, till at last they determined to write to Abubeker about it, not having yet received the news of his death. This disturbance detained Caled from pursuing the poor Damascens ; for there were now four days and as many nights passed since they went away, and there were but little hopes of overtaking them ; for he was well assured that as soon as possibly they could they would secure themselves in some walled town ; so that he had quite laid aside the thoughts of following them, had it not been for a very unfortunate circumstance, which was thus.

The reader may be pleased to remember that Derar Ben Alazwar, during the siege, had 2000 men given him to ride round about, and survey the camp, lest they should be surprised by succours from the emperor, or sallies from the town. It chanced one night, as some of these men were upon duty, they heard a horse neigh, which came out of the gate Keisan. They stood still, and let him alone till he came up close to them, and took his rider prisoner. Immediately after, there came another horseman out of the same gate; who called the man that was taken prisoner by his name. The Saracens bade him answer him, that he might come up, and they might take him too. But instead of that, he spoke out aloud in Greek, 'The bird is taken.' The person he spoke to understood his meaning very well, and returned back into the city. The Saracens could not tell what he said; only they knew that they had lost another prisoner by his means: upon which they had like to have killed him, but upon better consideration they re-solved to carry him to the general Caled, that he might dispose of him as he pleased. Caled asked him what he was? 'I am,' said he, 'a nobleman, and I married a young lady, which I loved as my life; and when I sent for her home, her parents gave a slight answer, and said that they had something else to do. Wherefore I took a convenient opportunity of speaking with her, and we agreed to come out in the evening, and give a good round sum of money to him that was upon the guard that night. I coming out first, was surprised by your men, and to prevent her falling into your hands, I called out, "the bird is taken." She apprehending my meaning, went back with the two ser-vants that were with her; and who can blame me?' 'Well,' said Caled, 'and what have you to say to the Mahometan religion? If you like that, when we take the city, you shall have your wife: if not, you are a dead man.' The poor wretch being surprised, and not having faith enough to die a martyr, renounced his Christianity, and made confession of his Mahometanism in these words: 'I testify, that there is but one God; he has no partner; and Mahomet is the apostle of God.' Then he was entirely theirs, and used to fight among them valiantly. When the city was surrendered, he went with all speed to find his beloved. Upon enquiry, he received information that she had shut herself up in a nunnery; which was true enough. For she never expected to see him more, after he was once fallen into the hands of the Saracens; and since all her joy and delight in this world was gone, she resolved to spend the rest of her days in the contemplation of a better. He goes to the church where she was, expecting to be received with abundance of joy; in which he was very much deceived: for when he had asked her the reason why she turned nun, and she had told him, he no sooner made himself known, and acquainted her with the change of his religion, but she treated him with the utmost con-tempt and aversion, worthily thinking that he ought himself to be re-nounced by her, who had first renounced his Christianity; nor would

14—2

the remembrance of former love, nor the consideration of that extremity who had obliged him to it, move her, nor beget in her one
charitable thought towards him ; but she still continued firm in her
resolution to bid adieu to all the enjoyments of this present life, and
never converse with him any more.   Wherefore, when Thomas and
Herbîs, attended with the rest of the miserable Damascens, went away,
she went along with them. Her departure wounded her husband
(Jonas) to the heart : he was very instant with Caled to detain her by
force ; who answered, 'that since they had surrendered themselves, it
could not be done ; but they must all of them have free liberty to go
where they pleased.' Here then is the main spring of this action. As
soon as Jonas understood that Caled had a design of pursuing the
Damascens, he was very forward, and teazed him to go, and proffered
his service to be their guide. But Caled, who was willing to pursue
them after three days were expired, being obliged to stay longer upon
the account of the controversy concerning the corn, thought four days
too much advantage on their side, and had infallibly laid aside the
thoughts of it, if it had not been for the incessant importunity of this
damned apostate, who was resolved to gratify his own humour, though
it were by betraying into the hands of merciless and unrelenting Saracens, thousands of his innocent countrymen, women, and children,
who had already laboured under the calamities and distresses of a consuming war. However nothing would satisfy him but this woman ;
and when Caled told him they were too far gone, he never ceased
spurring him forwards, telling him, 'That he knew all the country,
and how to follow them the nearest way ;' and whatever else he could
think on to encourage the undertaking. Caled, who was not backwards of himself to go about anything that afforded the least prospect
of success, yielded to his importunity.

Caled chose out 4000 of the best horse, which Jonas ordered to be
clothed in the habit of Christian Arabs ; that, being to travel in the
enemies' country, they might pass unsuspected. Then, committing the
care of the town and army to Abu Obeidah, they departed. It was no
hard matter to follow such a great multitude of people as went out of
Damascus ; for besides that the footsteps of their mules were visible
enough, they scattered things enough in their hasty flight, to direct
those who came after which way to pursue. The Saracens kept riding
night and day, and never stood still, but only in prayer-time. For a
long time together they could trace them very plainly ; but at last there
appeared no footsteps at all, nor any signs by which they might make
any guess which way they were gone. 'What's the news now?' said
Caled to Jonas. 'Oh,' says he, 'they are turned out of the great road,
for fear of being pursued ; you are in a manner as sure of them, as if
you had already taken them.' So he turns them out of the high road,
and leads them among the mountains, where it was very bad travelling.

The way was so extremely rough and uneven, that they could not ride without the greatest hazard. The horses struck fire at every step, they beat off their shoes, and battered their hoofs to pieces, that it was almost impossible for them to travel. They were forced to alight from their horses, and then they could scarce get forwards on foot, and those who had strong boots on, well soaled with iron, had the soals torn off from the upper leathers. The Saracens who had been used to a great many hardships, began to be extremely uneasy, and wished themselves again in the right road. In short, every man was heartily tired, but the indefatigable lover. Caled himself could not tell what to think on't ; but complained to Jonas, and told him that it was all his doing. At last they perceived a great many footsteps, which made them imagine that the people were gone before them. The guide told Caled, that he was sure they could not be far before, because the dung of their horses was not yet dry. Upon this Caled called to his men to mend their pace ; but they told him they were quite tired and worn out, and must of necessity stay and bait a while before they went any further. When they had refreshed their horses, they kept going on ; and wherever they passed, the country people mistook them for Christian Arabs. The guide brought them to Jabalah and Laodicea ; but they durst not pass through those towns, for fear of being discovered. Jonas at last enquired of a countryman ; who told them that the emperor hearing that the Damascens were upon their march towards Antioch, was fearful lest by their coming, and giving a terrible account of the sharpness of the siege, and the courage of the Saracens, those about him should be disheartened ; and had therefore sent an express to forbid their coming any nearer to Antioch, and commanded them to go to Constantinople. He told him also, that the emperor was raising forces to send to Yermouk (Sept. 1, 634). When Jonas had received this intelligence, he was at a loss, and could not tell what to do. Caled enquired of him what news ? and he told him how it was, and that there was no hope of overtaking them ; and besides, that there was but one mountain between them and the place where the emperor's officers were raising forces to send against them. As soon as Caled heard him mention the forces, he turned as pale as ashes. Derar, who had never observed in him any signs of fear before in all his lifetime, asked him, 'what was the matter?' 'Alas,' says he, ''tis not that I fear death, or anything that may befall myself, but because I am afraid lest the emperor's forces should get to Damascus, and do our people some mischief in my absence ; especially remembering a dream which I had not long since, and I cannot tell the meaning of it.' One of the men asked him what it was ? When he had told him, Abdo'rrahman, soldier-like, interpreted it all in favour of the Saracens. So they continued their march, and there fell abundance of rain that night, which put them to a great deal of inconvenience, but the poor

Damascens to much more. In the morning, after a tedious march, the Damascens found a pleasant meadow, and the sun shined comfortably upon them. Glad of this opportunity, they sat down to rest their weary limbs, and spread out their wet cloaths to dry them. A great many of them, quite tired and fatigued, lay down to sleep.

In this posture the Saracens found them. As soon as Caled understood the matter, he divided his 4,000 men into four regiments. The first was commanded by Derar Ebn Alazwar ; the second by Raphi Ebn Omeirah ; the third by Abdo'rrahman, Abubeker's son. Caled himself brought up the fourth, having first charged the officers, that they should not make their appearance all at once, but leave a little space one between the other, which was a very proper way to strike terror into the Damascens, and was frequently used by the Saracens, both in their field fights, and when they came to invest any town. He bade them not begin till they saw him fall on first, and not touch any of the plunder till the fight was over. The sight of the meadow was so pleasant and diverting, especially after they had been so harrassed with that dismal journey through the rocks and mountains, that they had like to have forgot what they came about. There they saw the purling streams, the fine flowers, and unspeakable variety of rich silks and all sorts of colours, curiously wrought, spread all over the meadow ; all which together afforded them a very entertaining prospect, extremely delightful and refreshing. After a little pause Caled began the attack, more like a lion or a tiger than a man, and bade his men fall upon the enemies of God. The Christians quickly knew who they were, but seeing but a few of them at first, despised the smallness of their number, and prepared to fight. Thomas and Herbîs encouraged their men, and put them in as good order as the time would permit. Thomas engaged Caled with 5,000 men, and after a sharp dispute was killed, and his men routed. As soon as Abdo'rrahman saw Thomas fall from his horse, he alighted, and cut off his head, and put it upon the point of the standard of the cross, and said, 'Alas for you, you Grecian dogs, here's your master's head.'

Whilst they were thus engaged, it is no hard matter to guess what was become of Jonas ; he was engaged too, but after a different manner, being among the women, in search of his lady. Raphi Ebn Omeirah came up that way, and saw him and his lady fighting ; and at last he threw her violently against the ground, and took her prisoner. Whilst Raphi was making up to them, the women stood upon their defence and pelted him with stones. At last a young lady happened to hit his horse in the forehead, and killed him. Raphi ran after with his sword drawn, and was just about striking her head off, but she cried 'quarter,' so he took her prisoner. She was a person of no less dignity than the Emperor's daughter, and Thomas's wife ; a princess of incomparable features, richly dressed, and had a great many jewels about her head. When Raphi had disposed of this rich prisoner, he came to the place where Jonas was, and found him bathed in tears, and his lady weltering in blood. Raphi enquiring what was the matter, Jonas wrung his hands, and said, 'Alas for me, the most miserable man in the world ! I came to this woman, whom I loved above all things in this life, and would fain have persuaded her to return with me ; but she continuing obstinate because I had changed my religion, and vowing she would go to Constantinople, and there end her days in a Nunnery, I resolved if I could not persuade her by fair means to make myself master of her by force ; so I threw her down, and took her prisoner. When she saw that she was in my power, she sat quietly awhile, and secretly drawing out a knife, stabbed herself in the breast before I was aware, and fell down dead immediately.' Raphi hearing this lamentable story wept too, and said, ' God did not design that you should live with her, and therefore has provided better for you.' 'What's that ?' said Jonas. ' I'll show you,' answered Raphi, ' a prisoner I have taken, a person of admirable beauty, and richly dressed, which I will present to you to recompense your loss.' When they came together, Jonas and the Princess talked together in Greek, and Raphi freely gave her to him.

In the meantime Caled was employed in the search of Herbîs. At last he saw a huge tall man richly dressed, which he imagined at first to have been the same, and beat him down to the ground with his lance, saying, ' Alas for thee, Herbîs, didst thou think to escape me ?' The man could speak Arabic well, and told him that he was not Herbîs, but another ; and if he would spare him, he would give him more than he was aware of. ' No quarter,' says Caled, ' unless you direct me to Herbîs, that I may kill him ; and if so, I shall let you go your way without any ransom.' ' Well,' says the man, ' I'll tell you ; but make first a firm agreement with me, that if I show you where he is, you will let me go.' ' Yes,' says Caled, ' if he falls into my hands.' ' This is one of your tricks,' said the Christian, ' so you gave us security and protection, and then afterwards followed us to this place, when we never expected any one should have pursued us ; and now you tell me, that if Herbîs falls into your hands, you will let me go. I can tell you where he is, but how can I promise that ?' At this Caled was angry, and said, ' Thou Christian dog ! dost thou accuse us of breach of promise, who are the companions of the apostle of God ? When we promise anything we are as good as our word. We did not come out after you till the fourth day was expired.' The Christian desired him to get off from him, that he might show him where Herbis was ; for Caled, when he had beaten him down, sat upon him all the while. Then he looked about, and showed him a party of horse at a distance, and told him that Herbis was among them. Caled, upon this, called a Saracen to him, and bade him take care of the Christian ; and if Herbis was among that company, he should let him go, but if he was caught in a lie, he should strike his head off. When Caled came thither, he alighted, and betook himself to his sword and target ; and whilst he was fighting among the thickest of the Christians, Herbîs came behind him, and gave him such a blow, that he cleaved his helmet through to his turbant, and with the violence of the stroke, his sword fell out of his hand. About this time, Caled's men came in timely to his assistance, and fell upon the Christians, and cut them all to pieces. When they had now entirely ruined and de-stroyed those miserable creatures, which had escaped at the taking of Damascus, Caled called for the man that had shewn him the way to Herbîs, and told him, 'that since he had performed what he promised to them, they would do the same to him ;' only they were obliged to exhort and admonish him first : wherefore he asked him 'whether he could find it in his heart to become one of the fasting and praying people, the followers of Mahomet ?' Upon his refusing to change his religion, they dismissed him, and he took the road towards Constantinople, being the only person that the Saracens knew of, that escaped the being killed or taken prisoner, of all that numerous train that followed Thomas and Herbîs out of the gates of Damascus.

Caled, when he came back, asked Jonas 'What was become of his wife ?' who gave him an account of that dismal story, which we have already related. Hearing that the princess was taken prisoner, he commanded her to be brought into his presence ; and when he beheld her excellent beauty, comely proportion and agreeable mein, he turned away his head, and said, ' Glory be to thee, O God ! we praise thee, who createst what thou pleasest.' Then he told Jonas, 'that if the Emperor did not redeem her, he should have her.' Jonas accepted his present very thankfully, and withal told him, that they were in a streight nar-row place, and that it was high time to be marching ; for they may be sure that what they had done was noised about the country, and it would not be long before they should be pursued. Before they got back to Damascus they saw a great dust behind them. Upon which Caled dispatches a scout, to enquire what was the matter ? Who quickly dis-covered the crosses in the colours, and brought him word ; but contrary to the expectation of the Saracens, there was no hostility intended ; only there came an old man from among the Christians, who being at his request conducted to the general, begged of him, in the Emperor's name, to dismiss the Princess his daughter. Caled having advised with Jonas about it, consented to let her go ; and said to the old man, ' Tell your master, the Emperor, that there will never be any peace between him and me, till I have gotten every foot of land he has ; and though I have sent him his daughter now, I hope to have him instead of her one of these days.'

It was not long before they came to Damascus, where they were so much the more welcome, because their long absence had made their friends there despair of their return. Old Abu Obeidah was surprised at Caled's valour. Caled, reserving a fifth part of the spoils to be sent to the Caliph, and put into the public treasury, according to their precept in the Alcoran, distributed the rest among the soldiers. He gave Jonas a good round sum to buy him a wife withal ; but Jonas answered him in a very melancholy tone, ' that he would never entertain any such thoughts again in this world, but his next wife should be one of those black-eyed women mentioned in the Alcoran.' He continued among the Saracens, and was serviceable to them, till at last, at the battle of Yermouk, he was shot in the breast. Thus fell the apostate. However my author, for the encouragement of new proselytes (for more sorts of people than one will lye for religion) tells us that after he was dead, he was seen in a vision by Raphi Ebn Omeirah, very richly clothed, and with gold shoes upon his feet, walking in a most beautiful verdant meadow ; and when Raphi asked him ' what God had done for him ?' Jonas answered, ' that he had given him seventy young women, so bright and beautiful, that if any one of them should appear in this world, the sun and moon could not be seen for the resplendency of her beauty.' When Caled heard of this vision, he said, 'This it is to be a martyr, happy is he that attains to it.'

Caled, not having yet receiv'd advice of Abubeker's death, wrote a letter to him, to acquaint him with the taking of Damascus, the controversy between him and Abu Obeidah, and the recovery of the spoil which the Damascens had carried away. The messenger being come to Medinah, wondered to find Omar in Abubeker's stead ; and Omar finding the letter directed to Abubeker, wonder'd the Saracens in Syria should be still ignorant of the alteration in the government, and told the messenger that he had written to Abu Obeidah about it, and given him the chief command over the Muslemans in Syria, and deposed Caled, tho' he thought that Abu Obeidah was not fond of that employ. The truth of it is, Abu Obeidah had received the letter, but kept it private : for being a very modest man, and one that had not the least spark of ambition in him, he was very unwilling to take the commission out of Caled's hands : wherefore he took no notice of it to him, nor said any thing to hinder his writing to the Caliph, after his return from the pursuit of the Damascens. Omar liked Abu Obeidah for his piety, but had no opinion at all of Caled. One day as he was speaking to the people from the pulpit (as it was usual for the Caliphs then to talk about what concern'd the publick, in a very familiar manner) he mention'd the taking away Caled's commission, and conferring that charge upon Abu Obeidah. A young man that was present, took the freedom of telling him, that he wonder'd he would deprive such a person as he had been the instrument of so good success to the Muslemans ; and that when Abubeker was moved by some about him to depose him, his answer was, ' That he would not lay

aside, nor sheath that sword, which God had drawn for the assistance of the true religion :' and withal told Omar that if he did, he
must answer it to God. Omar made but very little answer, but came
down from the pulpit, and consider'd of it that night. The next day
he came again, and told them that since the care and charge of the
Muslemans was committed to him, he thought himself oblig'd to take
the best care of them he could, as one that must give an account ; and
for that reason was resolv'd to dispose of places of trust to such as
deserv'd them, and not to such as did not : that he would give the command of the army to Abu Obeidah, whom he knew to be a man of a
tender and gentle disposition, and one that would be kind to the
Muslemans : that he did not approve of Caled, because he was
prodigal and extravagant ; adding, ' I would not have your enemies
think that it is ever the better for them, because I have depos'd a
fierce man, and put a mild one in his place ; for God will be with him,
and assist and strengthen him.' Then he came down from the pulpit,
and took a sheet of parchment, and wrote to Abu Obeidah a large
letter, full of good advice. He told him that he had given him the
chief command of the army, and bad him not to be too modest ; and
that he should take care not to expose the Muslemans to danger, in
hopes of getting plunder. By which last words he very plainly grated
upon Caled's following the Damascens into the enemies country. He
charged him not to be deceived with this present world, and by
that means to perish, as a great many had done before him, and bad
him look upon those who had gone before, and assure himself that he
must follow them. Then he adds, ' As for the wheat and barley, it
belongs to the Muslemans, and so does the gold and silver, but there
must be a fifth taken out of it (*Alcoran, chap. viii.* 15.) As for the
controversy between you and Caled concerning the city's being surrendered or taken by the sword ; it was surrendered. You must have
it your way : you are commander in chief, and have the power of
determining that matter. 'If the townsmen did surrender, upon
condition that they should have the wheat and barley, let them have
it. As for Caled's pursuing the Damascens, it was a rash undertaking ;
and if God had not been the more merciful, you had not come off so
well. Then the taking the Emperor's daughter, and letting her go
unransomed, was prodigally done. You might have had a large sum
of money from her, which would have done a kindness among the poor
Muslemans. Farewell,' &c.

Having seal'd it up, he call'd Shaddâd Ebn Aus, and ordered him,
that as soon as he came to the army, he should, after the letter was
read, cause the Muslemans to proclaim him Caliph in Damascus, and
bad him be his representative. Shaddâd Ben Aus and Amrou Ben
Abi Wakkâs made what haste they could to Damascus, and came to
Caled's tent, and paid their respects, and told him how the government

was dispos'd of, and that they had a letter from the Caliph, which was
to be read in the hearing of the Muslemans.   Caled did not like that
very well, for he knew that Omar was not well affected towards him.
They all wept when they heard of Abubeker's death.   Caled swore,
' That tho' there was nothing upon the earth dearer to him than
Abubeker ; nor that he had a greater aversion to than to Omar.   But
since Abubeker was dead, and had appointed Omar his successor, he
was very willing to submit to God and to Omar.'   Then the letter was
read, and the same day being October 1, 634, Shaddâd was proclaim'd
Caliph at Damascus in Omar's stead.   Upon this Caled resigns his
commission, and Abu Obeidah takes the whole charge of the army,
and all the affairs of the Muslemans in Syria upon himself.   Abu
Obeidah was afraid that Caled would have taken disgust at his
removal ; and (which is generally the effect of want of encouragement)
have been remiss in his business ; but he made the contrary appear
sufficiently, in that great action perform'd at Dair Abi'l Kodos ; or, the
monastery of the holy father.

  Dair Abi'l Kodos lies between Tripoli and Harran.   There lived in
that place a priest eminent for his singular learning, piety and austerity
of life, to such a degree, that all sorts of persons, young and old, rich
and poor, used to frequent his house, to ask his blessing, and receive
his instructions.   There was no person of what rank or quality soever,
but thought themselves happy if they had his prayers ; and whenever
any young couple amongst the nobility and persons of the highest rank
were married, they were carried to him to receive his blessing.   Every
Easter there used to be a great fair kept at his house, where they sold
rich silks and satins, plate and jewels, and costly furniture of all sorts.
Abu Obeidah, now possessed of Damascus, was in doubt whither to
go next.   One while he had thoughts of turning to Jerusalem; another,
to Antioch.   Whilst he was thus deliberating, a Christian that was
under the Saracens protection, informed him of this great fair, which
was about 30 miles distant from Damascus.   When he understood that
there never used to be any guards at the fair, the hopes of an easy
conquest, and large spoil, encouraged him to undertake it.   He looked
round about upon the Muslemans, and asked which of them would
undertake to command the forces he should send upon this expedition ;
and at the same time cast his eye upon Caled, but was ashamed to
command him, that had been his general so lately.   Caled understood
his meaning ; but his being laid aside stuck a little in his stomach, so
that he would not proffer his service.   At last Abdo'llah Ebn Jaafar
(whose mother was, after his father Jaafar was killed in the wars,
married to Abubeker) offered himself.   Abu Obeidah accepted him
cheerfully, and gave him a standard and 500 horse.   There was never
a man among them but had been in several battles.   The Christian
who had first informed them of this fair, was their guide.   And when

they staid to rest themselves in their march, he went before to take a view of the fair. When he came back, he brought a very discouraging account; for there had never been such a fair seen before. He told them that there was a most prodigious number of people, abundance of clergy, officers, courtiers and soldiers. The occasion of which was, that the prefect of Tripoli had married his daughter to a great man, and they had brought the young lady to this reverend priest, to receive the communion at his hands. He added, that taking them altogether, Greeks, Armenians, Cophties, Jews, and Christians, there could be no fewer than 10,000 people, besides 5,000 horse, which were the lady's guard. Abdo'llah asked his friends what they thought of it? They told him that it was the best way to go back again, and not to be accessary to their own destruction. To which he answered, 'That he was afraid, if he should do so, God would be angry with him, and reckon him amongst the number of those who are backward in his service; and so he should be miserable.' 'I am not,' said he, 'willing to go back before I fight; and if anyone will help me, God reward him: if not, I shall not be angry with him.' The rest of the Saracens hearing that, were ashamed to flinch from him; and told him he might do as he pleased, they were ready at his command. 'Now,' says Abdo'llah to the guide, 'come along with us, and you shall see what the companions of the apostle of God are able to perform. 'Not I,' answered the guide, 'go yourselves; I have nothing to say to you.' Abdo'llah persuaded him, with a great many good words, to bear them company till they came within sight of the fair. Having conducted them as far as he thought fit, he bade them stay there, and he close till morning. In the morning they consulted which way to attack them to the best advantage. Omar Ebn Rebiyah thought it most advisable to stay till the people had opened their wares, and the fair was begun, and then fall upon them when they were all employed. This advice of his was approved of by all. Abdo'llah divided his men into five troops, and ordered them to charge in five different places, and not regard the spoil, nor taking prisoners, but put all to the sword. When they came near the monastery, the Christians stood as thick as possible. The reverend father had begun his sermon, and they thronged on all sides to hear him with a great deal of attention. The young lady was in the house and her guard stood round about it, with a great many of the nobility and officers richly clothed. When Abdo'llah saw this number of people, he was not in the least discouraged, but turned himself about to the Saracens, and said, 'The apostle of God has said, that paradise is under the shadow of swords; either we shall succeed, and then we shall have all the plunder; or else die, and so the next way to paradise.' The words were no sooner out of his mouth, but he fell upon them, and made a bloody slaughter. When the Christians heard the Saracens make such a noise, and cry out,

'Allah Acbar,' they were amazed and confounded, imagining that the whole Saracen army had come from Damascus, and fallen upon them; which put them at first into a most terrible consternation. But when they had taken time to consider and look about themselves a little, and saw that there was but an handful of men, they took courage, and hemmed them in round on every side; so that Abdo'llah and his party were *like a little island in the midst of the ocean. As soon as Abdo'llah Ebn Anis (the reader is desired to observe the distinction of names, for a great many of them are very much alike) perceived that Abdo'llah Ebn Jaafar was in so much danger, he immediately turned his horse, and rather flew than rode to Abu Obeidah, who asked him what news ? Ebn Anis told him that ' Abdo'llah, and all the Muslemans with him, were in apparent hazard of being lost ; and if they were not succoured instantly, would infallibly be cut all to pieces.' And now it was high time to look out for Caled (none like him and Derar in a case of extremity) ; so Abu Obeidah turned to him, and said, 'I beg of thee, for God's sake, not to fail in this exigency, but go and help thy brethren the Muslemans.' Caled swore, that if Omar had given the command of the army to a child, he would have obeyed him ; adding, 'That he would not contradict him, but respected him as one that came into the profession of the Mahometan religion before himself.' All that were present were wonderfully pleased with Caled's modest answer ; which does indeed deserve to be particularly taken notice of, especially considering how lately he had been turned out of his commission. Abu Obeidah hastened him and he immediately put on his armour. His coat of mail was that which he took from Moseilamah, the false prophet. Then he put on his helmet, and over that a cap, which he called the blessed cap ; it having received Mahomet's benediction. Upon which he valued it more than all his armour besides, and used frequently to attribute his security and success to it. His men were instantly ready, and away they flew with all possible speed : and if we consider the circumstances, they had need make as much haste as they did ; for that small number of Saracens which had made the first attack, was quite drowned and overwhelmed in that great multitude of Christians, and there was scarce any of them but what had more wounds than one. In short, they were at their last gasp, and had nothing left to comfort them but paradise. Fighting in this desperate condition, about sunset they saw the dust fly and horsemen coming full speed, which did rather abate than add to their courage ; they imagining at first that they might be Christians. At last Caled appeared, fierce as a lion, with his colours flying in his hand, and made up to Abdo'llah, who, with much ado, had borne up his

* *Arab.* Were like a white spot in a black camel's skin. A camel being a creature very frequent and very serviceable in the eastern countries, they often mention and allude to it in their proverbs.

standard all this while, and was now quite spent.   But as soon as they heard Caled's voice, and saw the Mahometan banner, the sinking, drooping Saracens, who were scarce able to hold their swords, as if they had had new blood and spirits infused into them, took fresh courage, and all together rent the skies with Allah Acbar.   Then Abdo'llah charged the guard, which was round the monastery, on the one side ; and Derar Ebno'l Azwar on the other.   The prefect of Tripoli himself was engaged with Derar, and was too hard for him, got him down, and lay upon him ; at which time Derar secretly drew a knife, which he used to carry about him against such occasions, and stabbed him.   Then he mounted the prefect's horse, and cried out, 'Allah Acbar.'   Whilst Derar was engaged with the prefect, Abdo'llah Ebn Jaafar had taken possession of the house, but meddled with nothing in it, till Caled came back, who was gone in pursuit of those Christians he had beaten, and followed them to a river which was between them and Tripoli.   The Greeks, as soon as they came to the river, took the water.   Caled pursued them no further ; but when he came back, found the Saracens in the monastery.   They seized all the spoil, silks, cloaths, household stuff, fruits and provision, that were in the fair ; and all the hangings, money and plate in the house ; and took the young lady, the governor's daughter, and forty maids that waited upon her.   So they loaded all their jewels, wealth and furniture upon horses, mules, and asses, and returned to Damascus, having left nothing behind them in the house but the old religious.

While the Saracens were driving away the spoil, Caled called out to the old priest in the house, who would not vouchsafe him an answer. When he called a second time ; 'What would you have ?' (said the priest) 'get you gone about your business ; and assure yourself that God's vengeance will light upon your head, for spilling the blood of so many Christians.'   'How can that be' (said Caled) 'when God has commanded us to fight with you, and kill you? (*Alcoran, chap. viii.* 40). And if the apostle of God (of blessed memory) had not commanded us to let such men as you are alone, you should not have escaped any more than the rest, but I would have put you to a most cruel death.' The poor religious held his peace at this, and answered him never a word.

Abu Obeidah was all the while waiting with great impatience to hear what news.   When they returned, he received them with all the imaginable expressions of kindness and affection, taking most particular notice of Caled and Abdo'llah.   Having taken out a fifth, he distributed the rest of the spoil among the soldiers.   He gave to Derar Ebno'l Azwâr the prefect of Tripoli's horse and saddle, who made a present of them to his sister Caulah.   She, as soon as she had them, picked out all the precious stones and jewels, of which there was a great number in the trappings and saddle, and divided them among

the women of her acquaintance. Then they presented the prisoners to
Abu Obeidah, among which was the prefect's daughter. Abdo'llah
asked that he might have her ; but Abu Obeidah desired him to stay
till he could write to the Caliph about it, and have his leave. Omar
ordered him to let him have her, and he kept her till Yezid's reign
(which began in the year 679), who begged her of him, and had her.
There were a great many rich cloaths curiously wrought, upon one of
which was our blessed Saviour, which was carried with the rest into
Arabia Fælix, and sold for ten times its weight in gold. Whether the
esteem they had for the person it represented, or the fineness of the
work, raised it to such a price, my author does not determine ; but I
believe it was both. Then Abu Obeidah sent a letter to the Caliph, in
which he gave him a particular account of this last victory, and praised
Caled extremely ; telling him how modestly and obediently he behaved
himself, and how well he performed ; and desired that he would be so
kind as to write to him, and encourage him, and keep up his spirits :
but I never yet have met with any answer to that particular ; for the
old gentleman always turned a deaf ear to every thing that was said in
praise of Caled ; whatever the reason was, 'tis most certain he did not
like him. Among other particulars which Abu Obeidah wrote of to the
Caliph, he desired that he might either go and besiege Antioch (then
the seat of the Grecian Emperor, who, upon the taking of Damascus,
had removed from Hems thither), or else Jerusalem, which he pleased.
He acquainted him also that the Muslemans had learned to drink
wine in Syria. The messenger went with the letter to Medinah, and
found Omar with his friends in the Mosque. When Omar had read
the letter, and came to that last particular, he shewed it to Ali (afterwards Caliph) and asked him what he thought on't ? Ali gravely
answered, 'That whoever drank wine should have fourscore stripes
upon the soles of their feet.' Omar sent word to Abu Obeidah to deal
with them accordingly, and swore, 'That nothing would suit with those
fellows but poverty and hardship ; whereas it would better become
them to direct their intentions aright, and observe the commands
of their most mighty Lord, and serve him, and believe in him, and
give him thanks.' Abu Obeidah having received the letter, published
the offenders according to order ; and desired his men, that if any of
them were conscious to themselves of having been guilty of this fault,
they would, as a testimony of the sincerity of their repentance, offer
themselves to undergo this penance of their own accord. Upon which
a great many came in, and submitted to the punishment voluntarily,
having no accuser but their own conscience. Then he told them that
his design was to march to Antioch, against the Grecian dog (for that
was the best compliment they could afford the Emperor). The Saracens, according to their wonted custom, encouraged him to fight
against the enemies of God, and told him they were ready at his

service. He told them that he would go to Aleppo first, and then to
Antioch.   When they were ready to march, he called Caled, and
ordered him to go in the front, and the flag which Abubeker had given
him at first, viz., the black eagle.   With him went Derar, Raphi Ebn
Omeirah, and several others of note, with a considerable number of
men.   Abu Obeidah having placed in Damascus a garrison of 500
horse, under the command of Sefwàn Ebn Amîr, marched after them.
When he overtook them, he ordered Caled to ravage the country all
about Hems and Kennisrîn, while he himself should go to Baalbec
(formerly called Heliopolis).   As he was upon his march towards
Baalbec, when he came near Jushiyah, the governour of Jushiyah
came to meet him with a present, and made a truce with him for one
whole year ; telling him that if they conquered Baalbec, Hems, and
Labwah, he should not stand in opposition to him.   Abu Obeidah consented, upon condition, that he should pay him down 4000 pieces of
gold, and 50 silk vests. This done, he goes forward in his march : as he
was going, there came one upon a camel, riding towards him full speed.
When he drew near, Abu Obeidah knew him to be Asâmah Ebn Zeid,
who, making his camel kneel, alighted ; and, having paid his respects,
delivered him the following letter :—

'In the name of the most merciful God.

'From the servant of God, Omar Ebn Alchitâb, to his lieutenant,
' greeting.   I praise the only God, besides whom there is no other ;
' and I pray for his prophet Mahomet, upon whom be the blessing of
' God.   There is no turning back the decree and determination of
' God ; and he that is written an INFIDEL in the secret book,* shall
' have no faith.   My speaking thus is occasioned by Jabalah Ebno'l
' Ayham, of the tribe of Gassân, who came to us with his relations,
' and the chief men of his tribe, whom I received and entertained
' kindly.   They made profession of the true religion before me ; and I
' was glad that God has strengthened the true religion, and the
' professors of it, by their coming in, and knowing what was in†
' secret.   We went together on pilgrimage to Meccah, and Jabalah
' went round the temple ‡ seven times : as he was going round, it
' chanced that a man of the tribe of Fezàrah trod upon his vest, so
' that it fell from his shoulders.   Jabalah turned himself about, and
' said, "Woe be to thee !   Thou hast uncovered my back in the
' sacred temple of God."   The man swore that he did not design it :
' but Jabalah boxed him, broke his nose, and beat out four of his fore-
' teeth.   The poor man hastened to me and made his complaint,

---

* The Mahometans believe that there is kept in heaven a register of all persons and things,
which they call *Allâuh ho'hnehphoud*, the table which is kept secret.   In this book all the
decrees of God, and whatsoever shall come to pass, are supposed to be written.

† Arab. *Algaib*, which signifies whatsoever is secret and unknown to us, as things
spiritual, invisible and future.   It is frequently in Arab. Authors opposed to what falls within
the compass of our senses and understanding.

‡ This is a religious ceremony used by all that go on pilgrimage to Meccah.

' desiring my assistance.   I commanded Jabalah to be brought before
' me, and asked him what moved him to beat his brother Musleman
' after this fashion, and knock his teeth out, and break his nose.   He
' told me that the man had trod upon his vest, and uncovered his
' back, adding, " That if it had not been for the reverence he bore to
' the holy temple, he would have killed him."   I told him he had made
' a fair confession against himself ; and if the injured person would
' not forgive him, I must proceed with him by way of retaliation.*
' He answered, " That he was king, and the other a peasant."   I told
' him no matter for that, they were both Muslemans, and in that
' respect equal.   Upon which he desired that his punishment might be
' deferred till the next day.   I asked the injured person whether he was
' willing to stay so long?   To which he gave his consent.   In the
' night, Jabalah and his friends made their escape, and he is gone to
' the Grecian dog ; but I hope in God that he will give thee the
' victory over him.   Sit down before Hems, and keep close to it ; and
' send thy spies towards Antioch, for fear of the Christian Arabs.
' Health and happiness, and the blessing of God be upon thee, and all
' the Muslemans.'

What might not be expected from a government, in which there
flourished such impartial administration of justice ?   Abu Obeidah
having read over the letter, first to himself, and then to the Muslemans, went on towards Hems, (whither Caled was gone before with a
third part of the army) and sat down before it in Nov. 635.   The
governor of the town chanced to die that same day that Caled came
before it.   The inhabitants expected that the Saracens would have
taken Baalbec in their way, before they should have had their company at Hems ; and therefore were not so well provided to endure a
siege.   Upon which consideration, in hopes of gaining opportunity to
augment their stores, they conclude to make application to Abu
Obeidah, to make a truce with him, telling him, that if the Saracens
conquered Haleb (Aleppo) Albâdir, and Kinnasrîn, and beat the
Emperor's forces, they should willingly submit.   Abu Obeidah consented to make a truce with them for the space of one whole year, and
no longer, which was to commence on the first day of Dulhagjah of

---

* Retaliation, or *Lex Talionis*, whereby the offending person is obliged to suffer the same
hurt which he doth to another, was commanded the Jews (*Exod. xxi.* 24) ; Eye for eye,
tooth for tooth, hand for hand, foot for foot : and is expressly enjoined by Mahomet
(*Alcoran ii.* 173), who inserted a great many things which he had from the Jews.   The
modern Rabbins interpret this command of the Mosaical law, as if it were only a pecuniary
mulct.   Don Isaac Abarbanel has a great many arguments to prove that it ought not to
be understood in a literal sense.   To instance in one or two : he asks, 'Whether if the
offending person should have but one eye or one hand, he ought to be deprived of either,
because he had struck out an eye or cut off another man's hand that had two ?'   Again,
' How would it be possible for a judge to inflict a punishment, which should be exactly
the same with the injury, since that stroke might prove mortal to one man, which was so
to another ; and so a man might pay for a wound which was not mortal, with the loss of
his life ?'   Thus far Abarbanel.   But the practice of the Mahometans is contrary.   Only
the injured person may, if he pleases, accept of any other satisfaction ; but if he comes to
a judge and demands retaliation, he is obliged to let him have it.

15

the present year, and expire on the last day of the month Sjewal, in the following year, being the fifteenth of the Hegirah ; upon condition that they should pay him down 10,000 pieces of gold, and 200 silk vests. The cessation of arms was no sooner concluded upon, than the Hemessens opened their gates, and came out and kept a market in the Saracen camp. The Arabians, now enriched with the spoils of the country, gave them what they asked, and never stood for a price ; so that the citizens turned the penny well. In the mean time the Arabian horse foraged all about the country, both far and near. Among the rest Mesab Ebn Mohárib brought in abundance of spoil, sheep and oxen, with a great many horses and camels loaded with furniture, and 400 captives, making most piteous lamentation for the calamity which had fallen upon them. Abu Obeidah, moved with compassion, asked them, why they did not come into the profession of the Mahometan religion ? and by that means secure their lives and fortunes, wives and children. They told him that they were altogether surprised, not expecting any hostilities from the Saracens, at the distance they lived. Abu Obeidah, having asked advice of the Muslemans, and they referring it wholly to himself, set four pieces of gold upon every head, as Omar had ordered him to do in such cases, and laying tribute upon them, and obliging them, every one in his respective capacity, to assist the Muslemans as opportunity should serve, gave them all their cattle, furniture, wives and children back again, having first entered their names, and the places of their habitation, in a book kept for that purpose. The poor people were overjoyed to find themselves in such a happy condition, after having been plunged into the depth of despair, and acquainted their neighbours with what an unexpected favour they had received at the hands of the Saracens. This conduct did greatly facilitate the conquest of the Arabians ; for whereas an unrelenting cruelty would have made every one desperate, and have fought it out to the last drop of blood ; when they saw that there was a possibility of enjoying their religion, and a competency, by submitting themselves to those who would otherwise have taken all that they had by force, and either have murdered them every one, or at best made them slaves ; a great many chose rather to embrace the former condition while it might be had, than run the hazard of falling into the latter. By this means the Saracens were strengthened, for they made use of these people on all occasions. They served them for interpreters, for guides when they marched, and several other purposes ; and from them they received advice of all the motions of the Christians, and intelligence of whatever was debated or taken in hand to their disadvantage. Quickly after, the news of Abu Obeidah's gentle behaviour flew about the country, a great many of the Greeks came in upon the same terms, whom he booked and dismissed peaceably. The inhabitants of Alhadir and

Kinnisrîn hearing this, entertained some thoughts of following their example ; but privately, and without the notice of Luke their governor, who was a warlike man, and resolved to make a vigorous resistance. This Luke had an antipathy against the governor of Aleppo ; insomuch that when Heraclius sent for them both to consult which way was best to manage the war, and both of them had assured him, they would do their best ; they would not nevertheless join their forces together, but looked each man to the defence of his own province. As soon as Luke understood that his people were disposed to submit themselves to the Saracens, he was very much displeased ; but dissembling his anger, in hopes of preventing their design by stratagem, he calls a council, and asked their advice. They told him that they understood the Arabs were a people that received into their protection such as came to them, and used to stand to their word : that since they had come into Syria, their constant practice had been, to kill and make slaves of all that opposed them : at the same time protecting those in the peaceable enjoyment of their possessions who submitted to them. For which reason they thought it most adviseable to follow the example of their neighbours. He answered, that they were in the right, and therefore he designed to make a truce with them, till the emperor's succours should come up, and then oppress them when they least suspected it. Upon this he dispatches Astachar, a priest, a very learned man, master of the Arabick tongue, and thoroughly versed in the Jewish and Christian theology, with a letter to the Saracen general ; in which he magnified the greatness of the emperor, and the strength of the place ; adding that all attempts upon it would be in vain, not only upon the account of its being well fortified and furnished with plenty of military stores, but because the emperor was now raising a vast army in Europe, which were shortly to be transported over the Bosphorus, and mustered at Tyre, for the relief of Syria : that notwithstanding all these advantages, they were nevertheless desirous to live at quiet, and were willing to have a year's truce, and the general should set a mark at their bounds ; that when any of the Saracen horse that foraged, came that way and saw the sign, they should go no further to do any mischief in their country. That this agreement of a truce was a secret, and must not be known to Heraclius the emperor, for fear of his displeasure. With these instructions Astachar goes to Hems, where he found the Mahometans at prayers. Prayers done, Abu Obeidah admits him, and when he offered to bow down to the ground, would not suffer him. When Caled had heard the contents of the letter, he did not like it, but shaked his head, and said, 'That this did not look like the style of a man that desired peace in earnest ;' and would fain have perswaded Abu Obeidah not to hearken to him. 'But (said he) let us go to the place, and by Mahomet* I'll make that city a prey to the Muslemans, if it please God, and a terror to the rest.' ' Softly ! (said Abu Obeidah) no man knows the hearts of men, but God only.' ' Well then,' answered Caled, ' make no agreement with them, unless it be for good-and-all ; and if they will accept of this, well and good ; if not let them alone. I hope, by the help of God, I shall be a match for them.' Astachar was surprised at Caled's roughness, and said, 'that the character which he had heard of the Arabs was not true ; for the Christians had been informed that they were very gentle and courteous to all such persons as came to seek their protection : but now (adds he) I find the contrary, for I come to you to propose terms of peace, and you are not willing to accept them.'

To which Caled answered, ' That they were not willing to be imposed upon, but had great reason to suspect the sincerity of these overtures ; and if there should come any assistance from the Emperor, and they saw any advantage on their side, they would be the first that would take up arms against the Saracens, notwithstanding their present pretended desire of peace. However a cessation of arms should be granted for a twelvemonth, upon condition, that if any forces were sent by the Grecian Emperor, the inhabitants of the city should keep themselves within their own walls, and not stir out to their assistance.' This done, Astachar asked for a copy of the agreement, which Abu Obeidah having given him, he desired that there might be some sign set up at the limits of their territories, that when the soldiers saw it they might not forage in their country. Abu Obeidah said, ' he would take care to have it done ;' but Astachar told him, ' He need not trouble any of his own men, for they intended, with his leave, to do it themselves.' Accordingly the Greeks erected a pillar,† upon the top of which they carved the Grecian Emperor sitting on his throne. All things being thus made easy for a while, between the Saracens and the Governor of Kinnisrîn, there happened an unlucky accident, which had like to have occasioned a misunderstanding between them. Some of the Saracen horse passing that way, and observing the curious workmanship of the pillar, admired it. They spent some time in viewing it, riding past it backward and forward, and exercising themselves round about it. At last, as one of them past by in a full career, with his javelin in his hand ; the iron which was fastened in the lower end of the javelin, accidentally struck out one of the eyes of the carved emperor. This taking air was misconstrued by the Greeks as a most vile indignity offered to the Emperor in effigie, and a manifest breach of the truce. Upon this messengers are dispatched to Abu Obeidah, who expostulate with him upon the injury with a great deal of clamour,

---

* Arab. *Wahákki diui Resoul Allah.* By the Veracity or Truth of the Religion of the apostle of God. Sometimes *Wahákki Resoul Allah.* As it may be in this place.

† This same story is in *Eutychius'* Annals.

and insist upon satisfaction. He declares, 'that his intent was to keep his word inviolably, and that he was well assured, that whoever did it, had no design to show any disrespect to the Emperor ; and that the sincerity of his intentions might appear, proffered any reasonable satis-faction.' Nothing would satisfy them but retaliation, and the affront offered to the Emperor must be returned upon the Caliph. In which demand, when he that spoke, expressed himself unwarily, and talked of putting out one of Omar's eyes ; the rude Saracens thinking he meant literally as he spoke, were so inflamed, that had not Abu Obei-dah restrained them, by telling them 'that these people wanted sense and must be borne with,' they had rushed upon them instantly, and killed them upon the spot. Abu Obeidah told them, 'that they might set up his statue if they would, and do what they pleased with it ; but nothing would serve but the statue of the Caliph. To which at last, wearied with importunity, he consented. They having made a statue to represent Omar, and put two glass eyes in the head of it, ordered one of their men to strike out one of them with a lance. And thus, having received sufficient reparation for the injury received, they were pacified.

Abu Obeidah continued at Hems, sending out his horse to forage, and expecting with impatience the expiration of the truce, which had tied up his hands from offering any hostility within the territories of Hems, Alhâdir, and Kinnisrîn. Omar in the meantime wondered at Abu Obeidah's silence, and not having heard of any considerable action a long time, grew very angry. At last he wrote a short snapping sort of a letter to Abu Obeidah, as follows :

'In the name of the most merciful God,

'From Omar Ebno'l Chitâb, to Abu Obeidah Ebno'l Jerahh, his lieu-
'tenant in Syria, greeting. I praise God, besides whom there is no
'other ; and I pray for his prophet Mahomet, upon whom be the bless-
'ing of God. I command thee to put thy trust in God ; and I bid
'thee take heed that thou be not one of those, concerning whom God*
'says : "Say,† if your parents, or children, or friends, or wives, or fam-
'"ilies, or the riches you have gained, or the merchandise which you
'"are afraid you should not sell, or the houses which you delight in be
'"dearer to you than God and his apostle, and the fighting for his
'"service ; stay still God shall accomplish what he has decreed. God
'"does not direct those that do wickedly." '

The Muslemans had no sooner heard the letter, then they perfectly understood that Omar designed by it to rebuke them for their negli-

---

* So they quote the Alcoran, but when they mention any of Mahomet's sayings, they set down his name.
† This is the 24th verse, 9th chap. of the *Alcoran*. In which (as also in a multitude of other places), Mahomet introduces God speaking to him thus, SAY (to the people), if your parents, &c.

gence. Abu Obeidah repented himself heartily that he had granted the truce to the inhabitants of Alhâdir and Kinnisrîn, and all the Muslemans wept for sorrow, because they had been so remiss in their duty ; and asked Abu Obeidah, 'why he sat still, and did not lead them forth to fight the (Arab. *Jehad, Bellum Sacrum*) battles of the Lord ?' desiring of him at the same time to leave Kinnisrîn, and march either to Aleppo or Antioch, before either of which were taken, the truce would be expired. Upon this he had thoughts of going to Aleppo ; and having left Salmah with a party of horse at Hems, the first place he came at was Arrestân ; from thence he marched to Hamah (afterwards the seat of the famous Abu'lpheda), and from thence to Shaizar ; with all which places he made truce upon conditions. At Shaizar, he received information, that the Governor of Kinnisrîn (contrary to the articles of truce) had wrote to the Emperor for fresh supplies ; who had sent Jabalah Ebno'l Ayham to his assistance. Upon which Abu Obeidah defers his intended march to Aleppo, designing to fall upon Kinnisrîn, as soon as the truce should be expired, which did not now want quite a month. The Governor of Kinnisrîn going out to meet Jabalah, and the prefect of Ammouriyah coming to his assistance, was unfortunately intercepted by Caled ; who having ventured upon that undertaking with an inconsiderable number of men, escaped the greatest danger, being on every side surrounded with the Christians. After he had killed the prefect of Kinnisrîn, Raphi Ebn Omeirah said to him, ' Our time is come ' (*Jaa Ajalona*). To which he answered, ' That he believed so, because he had forgot his cap, which used to do him such singular service ; and which he should not have left behind him, if it had not been so decreed ; but speedy relief coming from Abu Obeidah they were delivered beyond all expectation.

Abu Obeidah fully resolving now to besiege Kinnisrîn, sent a party of horse before, who foraged and wasted all the country round about. The prisoners which they took were sent to the Caliph, and he took care to put the boys to the writing-school, according to the command of their prophet Mahomet ; who though he could neither write nor read himself, was very well sensible of the use of it. The inhabitants of Kinnisrîn having lost their Governor, and being altogether out of hopes of escaping, sued for protection, and submitted to pay tribute, being first polled, according to Omar's order, at the rate of four ducats an head. Kinnisrîn being taken, Abu Obeidah called his Muslemans together, and said, ' Tell me (God bless you) your advice ; for God has said in the mighty book (the *Alcoran*), to his prophet Mahomet ; ASK THEIR ADVICE IN A MATTER, AND TRUST UPON GOD ; and the apostle of God has said, HE THAT TAKES ADVICE IS SECURE ; shall we go to Aleppo, or Antioch ?' They told him, ' that the time of the truce which he had made with the neighbouring places was almost expired, and therefore they were of opinion, that it would be most advisable to take them in their way, before they moved any further into the country ; especially they chose to go to Baalbec, where they had reason to expect a vigorous opposition. Abu Obeidah hereupon, leaving Caled to besiege Hems, marched himself to Baalbec ; where when the Saracens came, they found themselves not at all disappointed in their expectation, for the place was very well fortified, and stored with warlike provision. The Saracens intercepted a caravan, with 400 loads of silks and sugars, upon their journey to Baalbec. Abu Obeidah put none to death as (not bearing arms), but gave them leave to ransom themselves. Some of them going to Baalbec, acquainted the inhabitants with the loss of the caravan ; who under the conduct of Herbis their Governor, went out in hopes of recovering it, to the number of 6,000 horse, attended with a rabble of the undisciplined multitude ; who imagining that the main body of the Saracen army had still continued at Hems, and that the caravan had been spoiled only by a party of foragers ; encountering with Abu Obeidah under so great a disadvantage, were overthrown and routed, Herbis, their general receiving no less than seven wounds, and with great difficulty and hazard retiring to the city. When Abu Obeidah came before it, the Saracens resolved to besiege it streightly.   Meâd Ebn Jabel told Abu Obeidah, that he knew the people of the town were ready to tread one upon another, and he thought it could scarce contain them all ; adding, 'If we hold out against it, we hope that God will deliver it into the hands of the Muslemans ; for God will not cease to give the earth for an inheritance to his servants the saints, because he has said, "we have written in the psalms, that my servants the saints shall inherit the earth."' (*Alcoran*, chap. XXI, 105).   The next day Abu Obeidah wrote a letter to the besieged, in which he put them in mind of the victories which God had already granted to the faithful, over those which opposed them, and offered to receive them, paying tribute as others had done before them. This letter he gave to a country-man that was under their protection, and a reward of twenty pieces of silver, saying, ' That he was none of those that would make use of any man's service, and not pay him for it.'   The messenger coming to the wall, they let down a rope, which he having tied about his middle, they drew him up.   The letter being read (for Abu Obeidah, when he wrote to the Greeks, made use of a Greek secretary), the besieged were divided in their opinions, and a great many of them inclined to surrender ; which Herbîs, the governor, was so averse to, that he tore the letter in pieces, and threw it to the messenger, commanding him to be forthwith sent back again, which was all the answer he vouchsafed to give to it.

The Saracens, upon this, besieging the city, were bravely repulsed by the besieged, who did them a great deal of damage with their engines planted upon the walls.   The valour of the citizens, together with the extreme coldness of the weather, made the Saracens glad to lay by their assault. The next morning, after prayers were over, a crier went round the camp, commanding in the general's name, that never a man of them should stir, or do anything else, before he got himself ready some hot victuals. The order was no sooner heard than obeyed, and every man went to work for himself. Whilst they were in the midst of their cookery, the besieged sallied. The Saracens were immediately alarmed. Among the rest, Ahmed Ebn Ased was just a-going to put his hand to his mouth, when Abu Obeidah struck him a good blow with a truncheon, and gave him an hearty curse into the bargain. The poor man started up on a sudden, and like one scared out of his wits, snatched up a tent-pole, and ran and charged the enemy, scarce knowing where he was, till he was got in the midst of them. The Saracens surprised in this disorder, did with much ado beat back the besieged, who nevertheless carried off with them some prisoners and plunder. In the evening the chief of the Saracens met at Abu Obeidah's tent, and said, 'You see the courage of these people, what do you think to do in this case?' To which he answered, 'That the damage sustained by the Saracens was decreed by God, who was pleased to honour those persons that were killed with the degree of martyrdom.' Then he commanded them to remove their tents to a greater distance from the city, that they might have a larger space for their horses to course in. He gave to Said Ebn Zeid the command of 500 horse, and 300 foot, with orders to go into the valley, and keep the Greeks in play at that gate, which was opposite to the mountains, that their forces might be divided, and they obliged to fight in parcels. Derar was placed at the gate which looks towards Damascus, with 300 horse and 200 foot. The next morning, about break of day, Herbis the governor, with a strong body of men, sallied out at the gate where Abu Obeidah himself was posted; encouraging his men, and telling them that the Saracens were afraid of them, and bidding them remember that they fought for their religion, wives, children, and fortunes; in a word, whatsoever was dear to them. They answered him cheerfully, that though they were afraid of the Arabs at first, yet they were not so now, being a little better acquainted with their manner of fighting: besides, the Arabs were half naked; some of them fighting without armour, others with scarce clothes enough to cover them; whereas, said they, we have good helmets, breast-plates, and coats of mail. Abu Obeidah, on the other side, was not wanting to tell the Saracens that they must have patience: 'for God had promised good success to those that held out to the last.' The Greeks, encouraged with yesterday's victory, charged the Saracens home, and the battle was maintained with great obstinacy on both sides, yet so as the Greeks had apparently the advantage. At that time Sohail Ebn Sabah received a wound in his right arm, which disabled him so, that he could not hold up his sword: upon which he alighted from his horse, and having told his friends that he was no longer able to defend himself, retired out of the battle to a neighbouring hill : which having clambered up, not without some pain and difficulty, he had a clear prospect of both armies. The Greeks, as we said, having sallied out upon Abu Obeidah's quarters, there was nothing to do at those gates where Derar and Said Ebn Zeid were posted. Sohail observing this, and that Abu Obeidah was forced to give ground, without any order from the general, or any person's knowing it, kindled a fire, and with some green sticks, made a great smoke upon the top of the hill. As soon as Said and Derar perceived it, they imagined it to have been a signal from the general for them to come up, that being the most usual signal among the Saracens by day, as fire was by night, when they had a mind to call those together, who were posted at any distance. Upon this Derar and Said rode with their men full speed, and came season-ably to the relief of their brethren ; for the Greeks by this time thought themselves secure of the victory ; but finding themselves surrounded, the case was quite altered with them ; and they who so few minutes ago expected to have won the field, now despaired of getting back to their own city : however, they joining close together, and fighting bravely, made an impenetrable phalanx ; which, maugre all opposition, gained the top of an hill, on which there stood an old deserted monas-tery, whither Herbîs and his men retired, and stood upon their own defence. Abu Obeidah, who as yet knew nothing of Said and Derar's being come from the places where he had posted them, perceiving with what undaunted courage these men fought, imagined their retreat feigned, only with a design to draw the Saracens out of order, and therefore would not let his men pursue them. But Said Ebn Zeid hearing nothing of the general's order, followed them to the top of the hill. There leaving one in his room with orders not to suffer a man to stir out of the house, he with 20 of his men went to acquaint Abu Obeidah with the news. Who seeing him come with so few, was sur-prised, and asked him what was become of the rest. Said told him they were all safe and sound, and had besieged the enemies of God (a compliment they are very liberal of to the Christians) in an old house, acquainting him with all the circumstances of the story. Then Abu Obeidah enquired of him and Derar what made them stir from their posts ? Said swore that he did nothing contrary to order, for he never stirred till he saw the smoke. Abu Obeidah confessed that it was well they came, for he was afraid the Greeks would have seized their camp, and wished for them, or for somebody to make a smoke. Said again positively affirming that there was a smoke, Abu Obeidah was astonished, and made proclamation throughout the camp, ' Whoever be he that kindled the fire and smoke upon the hill, let him speak ;' and this with an adjuration. Upon this Sohail came forth and con-fessed it, and told the reason why he did it. Abu Obeidah was very glad it happened so well, but charged them all strictly, that none of them should ever dare to attempt any such thing again, without the permission of their general.

Whilst Abu Obeidah was talking to Sohail, a Saracen came with all speed from the mountain, and alarmed the whole camp. Herbîs perceiving by how small a number he was besieged in the house, being now fewer than 500, took courage, and sallied, in hopes of recovering the city. They fought bravely, and handled the Saracens at such a rate, that Mesab Ebn Adi, who was present in most of the battles fought in Syria, said, that of all he ever beheld, he never saw any men behave themselves better, nor stand closer to it, than those Greeks, which were then with the governor. It was he that rode and gave notice to Abu Obeidah, who had no sooner heard it, than he dispatched Said with 100 archers, and commanded Derar to assist him. When they came to the hill, they found their friends in a pitiful condition, for there were no less than 70 Saracens upon the ground, wounded or killed, and the Greeks laid about them very eagerly. But overpowered with fresh numbers of their enemies, they were forced once more to retire to their monastery, where they were watched with such a vigilant eye, that one of them could not so much as offer to peep out but the Saracens let fly an arrow at him.

Abu Obeidah leaving Said Ebu Zeid to take care of the governour, drew up his men, and ordered them to pitch their tents about the city ; ' For ' (says he) ' God has circumvented your enemy, and performed that promise which he made to us, to help us ; and this is because God is a protector of those who put their trust in him ; but as for the infidels, they have no protector.' Herbîs, the governour, finding himself streightened, began to repent himself that ever he came into that old house. He considered with great concern, that in a very short time he and his men must needs be reduced for want of provision. Nor could any about him, supposing they could have found a possibility of sending, think of any person capable of assisting them in these deplorable circumstances. The Saracens having taken so many places already, had spread such a terror around the country, that those which remained were under too great a concern for their own preservation, to be at leisure to lend an helping hand to their distressed neighbours. A great many others had by agreement to a truce, rendered themselves incapable of bearing arms at that time against the Saracens. In this miserable state, no other prospect offering itself, compelled by necessity, they were forced to surrender themselves into the hands of their conquerors. Herbîs calls out aloud, and asks if there were any person that understood him. Being asked by an interpreter what he would have, he desired that he might be secured from danger of the archers, and that Said would come near and talk with him. Said answered that he owed him no such respect ; but if he had any thing to say, he might come to him. Loath to venture himself, he, by means of the interpreter, got leave to send a messenger, who, coming before Said, offered to fall down upon his face by way of respect. Said made a sign to him to forbear, and the Saracens came about him, and held him from doing it : of which he having asked the reason, Said said to the interpreter, 'Because both he and I are servants of God, and it is not lawful to use adoration and worship to any but God, who is the proper object of worship.' Being examined about his errand, he said that he came to desire protection for Herbîs and his men ; which was accordingly granted, upon condition, that they should lay down their arms, and surrender themselves. The messenger asked whether that security was only from himself, or from the general too ? Said told him, from all the Saracens. When Herbîs heard this, he came out, and, my author tells us, that he has learnt from persons worthy of credit, that Herbîs, when he came out to surrender himself, put off all his silks, and exchanging with some of his men, put on woollen apparel, suiting his habit to the meanness of his present condition. Said seeing him come along in this humble mein, fell down and worshipped God, saying, 'Praised be God, who hath humbled their great ones before us, and given us dominion over their rulers.' Then he went to meet him, and bad him come nearer, and sit down by him ; and asked him whether that which he had on was his proper habit ; to which he answered 'That he never had any woollen on before in his life, nor knew what it was to wear anything but silk.' He demanding of Said whether he had power, or was willing to grant security, as well for those in the city as those present with him ? Said told him, 'That as for those which were with him, he would grant them security, upon two conditions : either that they should turn Mahometans, and so have one common interest with them : or, if they chose rather to continue in the profession of their own religion, they should never more bear arms against the Muslemans. But as for those in the city, they were at the general's disposal ; to whom, if he was willing to go, he proffered his service to conduct him ; and if they could agree upon any terms, well and good : if not, he should, if he desired it, have free leave, with as many of his men as were willing to go back with him, to return to his monastery again ; there to be besieged till God should determine the matter between them.'

Being brought into the presence of Abu Obeidah, and taking a view of the Saracens about him, considering at the same time what a condition they had brought him and his men into, he shaked his head, and bit his fingers' ends for indignation. Being asked what was the reason of that behaviour ? he answered, 'That he thought their number had been much greater than he found it was, now he was come among them. Abu Obeidah bad his interpreter tell him, 'That the number of the true believers seemed greater in the eyes of the idolaters than it really was, because the angels helped them, as they did at the battle of Beder, which is the grace of God towards us ; and by this means God gives us the victory over your country, and makes your armies flee before us.' That the angels helped Mahomet in battle, he has expressly told them in the *Alcoran, chap. ix.* 26, 40 ; and they believed and depended upon the same assistance, and oftentimes attributed their success to it ; not that any of them pretended ever to have seen these auxiliary troops of militant angels ; it being sufficient for their purpose to be seen by their enemies. Herbîs offered for the whole city of Baalbec 1,000 ounces of gold, 2,000 of silver, and 1,000 silk vests. Abu Obeidah told him, ' If they would have peace, they must double the sum, and add to it 1,000 swords, and all the arms belonging to those men that were shut up in the monastery, and pay tax and tribute the next year, and never bear arms for the time to come, nor write to the Emperor, nor attempt either directly, or indirectly, any thing against the Saracens, nor build any churches or monasteries.' Herbîs complaining of the severity of the articles, as being all in favour of the Saracens, desired that the besieged might at least have this one article on their side, viz., ' That whosoever shall be appointed lieutenant over Baalbec, should not come into the city, nor any of his men ; but pitching his tents on the outside of the walls, should there receive the tribute imposed upon the inhabitants.' This being granted, all was agreed upon, only there wanted the townsmen's consent ; who, having heard the articles, did not approve of them, and said they would never surrender the strongest city in Syria into the hands of the Saracens upon such terms : but when Herbîs had remonstrated to them the danger to which he and his men must be exposed, if there were not some agreement made, and the provision he had made for their repose and quiet, in excluding all the Saracens from once entering into the town ; adding withal, ' That he would lay down a fourth part of what was imposed upon them himself,' they at last consented. Herbîs alone going into the city to raise the promised sum, Abu Obeidah detained all the rest of his men as hostages, till it should be paid. In twelve days time he brought it ; upon which Abu Obeidah dismissed the men, and calling for Raphi Ebn Abdo'llah, left him to take care of Baalbec with 500 Saracens, giving him a most strict charge to do nothing but what was right and just, telling him that he had heard the prophet say, ' That God had commanded Moses and David the same thing.' He bad him prevent all manner of disturbance between his men and the inhabitants of the city, and have an eye to the sea shore, and pillage all those places in the neighbourhood, which had not entered into articles. Having left him with this charge, he moved towards Hems ; and before he came thither, the prefect of Jushiyah met him with a present, which he accepting, renewed the truce with him.

Raphi very punctually executed his charge, and both he and his men behaved themselves so inoffensively that the citizens and the Saracens grew very well acquainted. The Saracens, according to their custom, plundering all the neighbourhood, sold what they got to the citizens, who began to be in a fair way of growing rich with the spoils of their countrymen and fellow-Christians. Herbîs, formerly their governour, perceiving this, began to consider which way he might bring himself in for a share of the gains: wherefore, calling them together, he represented what hazard he had exposed himself to for their preservation, whilst it was in his power, and what pains he had taken to procure them those articles of peace, of which they now reaped the benefit; besides the paying down, at his own proper expence, the fourth part of what was imposed upon them all; adding, ' That he thought it nothing but reasonable, that since they were in a capacity, he should be reimbursed.' This was consented to without any opposition; but he told them that he did not desire to deprive any of them of any part of their substance, but only they should agree to pay him the tenth of what they saved in their trading with the Arabs. They were at first very unwilling to come to this; but after debate, considering his quality, as having been once their governour, though now reduced to the same condition with themselves, and that when necessity required it, he had not spared his own private substance for the publick good, they at last agreed to it. This done, he appoints a tythe-man to gather it, and in a few days it amounted to a very considerable sum. The sweetness of this gain, instead of extinguishing, encreased his thrift; whereupon in a second meeting he told them that it would be a long time before what he had laid out would be repaid at this rate, and proposed, that either they should admit him one of their company, or else instead of a tenth, pay him a fourth part of all their gains. The people, vexed to the heart at this squeezing, insatiable temper, cryed out, ' Away with him, and all such unreasonable wretches, we had better be governed by the Saracens than such; for they are better, and more just;' and, with a great noise and shout, rushed upon him, and killed him. The Saracens without heard the noise, but did not know what was the matter; neither would Raphi go into the city contrary to the agreement, but said, ' If there was any difference between them, and they came out to him, he would endeavour to make them friends.' Presently after they came thronging out to him, and acquainted him with what they had done; how civil they were to their prefect, in answering his first demand, and how unreasonable he had been in coveting more, desiring Raphi to come into the city, and govern it himself; which he refused, till he had wrote to Abu Obeidah; who sent him word, ' That since the people were willing, he ought not to scruple it.' Upon which he and his men went into Baalbec, on Jan. 20, A.D. 636.

Leaving Baalbec, we must now march to Hems; before which Abu

Obeidah having brought his army, before any attempt made upon it, sent to the governour the following letter :—

'In the name of the most merciful God.

'From Abu Obeidah Ebn Aljerâhh, lieutenant in Syria to the 'Emperor of the faithful Omar, Ebn Alchitâb (whom God bless) and 'general of his forces. The most mighty God hath conquered several 'places by our hands; wherefore do not let the greatness of your city, 'nor the strength of your buildings, nor the plenty of your stores, nor 'the bigness of your bodies, deceive you : for your city is no more in 'our hands, when we come to war against it, than if we should set a 'pot upon a stone in the midst of our camp, and all the army should 'come round about it, to take every one of them a mouthful. In the 'first place, therefore, I invite you to our religion, and that law which 'our prophet Mahomet, of blessed memory, brought us. Which, if 'you shall receive, then shall you partake with us in all our fortunes, 'good and bad ; and we will send you men to instruct you in your 'religion, as God has commanded us. If you refuse the Mahometan 'religion, we shall continue you in your possessions, paying tribute. 'If neither of these conditions please you, come out and fight us, till 'God, who is the best judge, shall determine between us.'

This being no sooner received than rejected with the utmost scorn, both sides prepared themselves, the Saracens for an assault, the besieged for their defence. The besieged sallying, made so good a days work of it, that the Saracens had little reason to boast of their victory. There was present a great man among the Arabs, a person of extraordinary sagacity and penetration, and had himself many times commanded an army with good conduct and success : he, considering well the strength of the place, and the courage and resolution of the inhabitants, told Abu Obeidah privately, that he might sooner expect to conquer Hems by stratagem than by force of arms, and proposed to him to raise the siege, if he could induce the besieged to let him have five days provision for his men and horses, upon that condition : by which means their stock of provision would be very much diminished, and he might take a fit opportunity of surprising them. This advice being approved, Abu Obeidah acquainted the besieged with his design of intermitting the siege of Hems, and trying his fortune at other places, of which there still remained unconquered a great number in Syria very well fortified, upon the condition aforementioned. The people willing at any rate to get rid of such troublesome neighbours, considering with all those many accidents that might prevent them ever returning thither, or at least defer it a long time, easily assented. The governour himself being as willing as any to compound with the Saracens upon these terms, told his people, that the Arabs were like wild beasts, greedy of prey ; wherefore he thought it the best way to give them something to fill their bellies, and send them packing. Upon this he sends some of the chief clergy to Abu Obeidah, to make the agreement, and take a copy of the articles : which being done, the citizens brought out their provision, according to the agreement. Abu Obeidah told them, that since their intended march was likely to be tedious, he should be very glad to buy the remainder of their provision. The people were willing to sell, and the Mahometans bought as long as they had any thing left to buy withal, or exchange for.

Some spies belonging to the emperor, being at that time in the Saracen Camp, and perceiving the Emessens set open their gates, and bring out their provisions, without taking time to inform themselves thoroughly of the cause of it, went and spread a report about the country, that Hems was surrendered, to the great surprize and discouragement of the rest, who had their hearts daily filled with the increasing terror of the Saracens. Abu Obeidah from Hems went to Arrestân, a strong place, well watered, and full of soldiers ; where his summons being rejected, he desired the favour of the governour of the castle to leave some old lumber, which would be troublesome and cumbersome to them in their speedy march. This was without much scruple granted, all being desirous of their absence upon any terms. Upon this he takes 20 chests, and enclosing in them 20 chosen men ; to prevent all suspicion put locks upon the outsides of them, the bottoms of the chests being so contrived, as to slip backwards and forwards as he within pleased. These received into the castle, the Saracens marched, only Caled was left with some forces, by way of ambuscade, to assist those in the chests. The Saracens gone the Christians went to church to give thanks for the departure of their enemies, and were heard singing psalms by Derar, Abdo'rrahmân, and Abdo'llah in the chests, who taking this opportunity, came forth, and having seized the governour's lady, demanded the keys of the gates. From thence they went to the church, where they, without difficulty, surprized the unarmed multitude. Then Abdo'llah Ebn Jaasar, who commanded them, sent five of them with the keys to open the gates, and cry out Allâh Acbar; which done, Caled, who was within hearing, came up, and Arrestân was taken without opposition.

This made the conditions much more easy to the inhabitants, the Saracens not expecting such an unbloody conquest. Wherefore, they resigning themselves without any more to do, had their liberty granted to go where they pleased. Some of them changed their religion, though the greater number still retained their Christianity and went to Hems.

Two thousand men being left in garrison at Arrestân, Abu Obeidah moves with his army to Shaizar. He had no sooner sent his summons, than there arose a great dispute about surrendering the place : the conquest of Arrestân, Baalbec, Damascus, Bostra, and as they supposed of Hems, gave them just reason to fear, that they should not be able to defend Shaizar, not superior to those places, either in strength of its situation, or number of its soldiers. The governour held out obstinately, and gave them a great deal of reproachful language, swearing and cursing them, and commanded his servants to strike some of them. The chief men provoked at this tyrannical usage, drew their swords, and fell upon him and his party. Having made a quick dispatch of them, they opened the gates, and surrendered to Abu Obeidah, who received them very gladly, and gave them hearty thanks for saving him the trouble of fighting : adding 'that since they had behaved themselves so well, and expressed such a desire of living under the government of the Saracens, he would not dismiss them without some distinguishing mark of his favour.' Upon which he told them, ' That he would not force any of them to change their religion against their will, nor put them to any extremities ; but if any of them would come in of their own accord, they should pay no tax or custom, as other Mahometans did, for two years. If they chose to continue in their own religion, they should pay no tribute for the space of one year.'

Shaizar was now taken into possession, and Abu Obeidah reminded his Muslemans, that they were no longer under any obligation to the people of Hems, having punctually performed whatever they had promised them. The governour of Hems was not so well satisfied, for as soon as the Saracen army came to appear before the city, he sent a messenger to expostulate with Abu Obeidah concerning his perfidy and breach of promise : who gave him no other answer, than that he desired those clergy who had made the agreement with him first should come to him again, and let themselves be judges whether or no he had fulfill'd his promise to a tittle. Upon their coming, he asked them, ' Did not I make an agreement with you, to leave Hems, till I had conquered some other city of Syria ? And was it not left to my liberty after that, either to go to any other place, or to return to you? When this could not be denied, ' Well then,' answered he, ' since we have conquered Arrestân and Shaizar, we are under no further obligation to you, and there remains nothing but that you surrender.'

There being no remedy left, nor any one whom they might justly blame but themselves, for not having taken better care at first, they prepared to fight. The inhabitants though not a little disheartened when they reflected upon their scarcity of provision, to which their unseasonable credulity had exposed them ; encouraged by their governour, resolved to try their fortune in the field. That evening they went to prayers, to implore the divine assistance, the governour himself receiving the communion at St. George's Church, (since turned into a Mosque). When he came back, he eat for his supper a whole roasted kid, and sat up drinking wine all night. Thus prepared for battle, having put on very rich cloaths, he sallied out in the morning at the head of 5000 horse, compleatly armed, all men of approv'd courage, and resolv'd to die for the defence of their country. And though the Saracens came out against them with a much greater number, yet they nevertheless stood their ground, without the least expression of fear or concern. The Christian archers galled the Saracens terribly with poisoned arrows, and charged them with such courage, that they were forced to give way. Whilst Caled was labouring to restore the battle, he made a very narrow escape; for, engaging with one of the Greeks, his sword broke in his hand: Upon which closing with his adversary, he squeezed him so close to him, that he broke his ribs, and threw him down dead off from his horse. About noon, Mirkal and Mcisarah made an impression upon the right wing of the Christians, and Kais Ebn Hobeirah upon the left. But among all the Saracens, none signalized himself so much that day as I'krimah, Caled's cousin: he, thirsting after the imaginary joys of Mahomet's fools paradise, cried out aloud, ' Methinks I see the black-eyed girls looking upon me, one of which, if she should appear in this world, all mankind would die for the love of her. And I see in the hand of one of them a handkerchief of green silk, and a cup made of precious stones, and she beckons me, and calls out, come hither quickly, for I love thee.' With these words charging the Christians, he made havoc where he went, till observed at last by the governour of Hems, he was stuck through with a javelin. When night parted them, the Saracens returned to their camp, having had the worst of it all that day. Caled, assuring himself that this success would easily induce the Greeks to believe the Saracens afraid of them, persuaded Abu Obeidah to fly before them the next morning, to draw them into disorder. Nor did this advice fail of the desired success; for the Greeks had beaten them too well the day before, to entertain the least suspicion that their flight was feigned. Thereupon, pursuing them unwarily, and out of order, they were about noon surrounded by the returning Saracens; who, to use my author's own expression, 'fell upon them like eagles upon a carcase.' Some of the Greeks had ventured to plunder the Saracens' tents; but whilst they were differently employed, some in the pursuit, others in the spoil, the far greater part of them were intercepted by the Saracens; nor had any of them escaped, unless relieved by some of the besieged sallying from the city. The governour fell among the rest, easily distinguished by his red face, large size, and rich apparel, perfumed with musk. This defeat determined the besieged to surrender; but the Saracens, who having heard so often of the Emperor's preparation against them, expected a bloody battle daily, had no leisure to stay and take possession, nor any man to spare by way of garrison: wherefore they took the Christians at their word, and never a man of them went into the city,

16

till after the great battle of Yermouk, which determined the fate of
Syria, and put the Saracens out of all fear of ever meeting from the
emperor the like opposition. The Saracens departed from Hems,
having lost that day 235 men. The Christians burying their dead
found them above 1600.

Heraclius, wearied with a constant and uninterrupted succession of
messengers of ill news ; which like those of Job, came every day treading one upon the heels of another ; grieved at the heart to see the
Roman empire, once the mistress of the world, now become the scorn
and triumph of Barbarian insolence ; resolved, if possible, to put an
end to the outrages of the Saracens once for all ; and, in order to it,
raised such an army out of all parts of his dominions, as since the first
invasion of the Saracens, had never appeared in Syria before. Not
much unlike one engaged in single combat, who, distrustful of his own
abilities, and fearing the worst, summons together his whole strength,
in hopes of ending the dispute with one determining stroke. Forces were
sent to all defensible places, which this inundation of the Saracens had
as yet left untouched ; particularly to Cæsarea, and all the sea-coast of
Syria, as Tyre and Sidon, Accah, Joppa, Tripolis, Beirout, and Tiberias, besides another army to defend Jerusalem. But the main body
of all, which was designed to give battle to the whole forces of the
Saracens, was commanded by one Mahân, an Armenian, whom I take
to be the very same that the Greek historians call Manuel. When the
Emperor had given the generals his best advice, and charged them to
behave themselves like men, and especially to take care that there was
no differences nor dissensions among themselves ; he asked them ' What
should be the reason of this surprising success of the Arabs, inferior to
the Greeks both in number, strength, arms, and discipline?' After a short
silence, a grave man stood up and told him that the reason was, ' Because
the Greeks had walked unworthy of their christian profession, and
changed their religion from what it was when Jesus Christ first delivered
it to them, injuring and oppressing one another, taking usury, committing fornication, and fomenting strife and variance among themselves.' And indeed the vices of these Christians were at that time so
flagrant, as to make them stink in the nostrils of the very Infidels,* confessed by the Greek writers themselves, and aggravated by the Arabick
ones. The Emperor answered ' That he was too sensible of it ;' adding,
' that he had thoughts of continuing with them no longer ; but leaving
his army to their management, would withdraw himself to Constantinople.' In answer to which, they represented to him, how much his
departure would reflect upon his honour, what a lessening it would be

---

* 'Ουτῶ δε καὶ τῆς ἐκκλησίας τότε ὑπὸ τε τῶν βασιλέων καὶ τῶν δυσσεβῶν
'Ιερέων ταρατρομένης, ἀνέστη ἐρήμικος· 'Αμαλὴκ τύπτων ἡμᾶς τον λαὸν τῦ
Χριστῦ, καὶ γίνεται πρῶτη φόρα πτώσις τῶ ρωμαϊκῦ Στρατῦ, ἡ κατὰ τὸ
Γαβιθὰν λέγω καὶ 'Ιερμῦχὰν καὶ τὴν ἄθεσμον αἱματοχυσίαν. *Theop. p.* 276.

to him in the eyes of his own subjects, and what occasion of triumph it would afford to his enemies the Saracens. Upon this they took their leave, and prepared for their march ; Mahân, besides a vast army of Asiatics and Europeans, having joined to him Jabalah Ebno'l Ayham, King of the Christian Arabs, who had under him 60,000 men. These Mahân commanded to march always in the front, saying, 'There is nothing like diamond to cut diamond.' This great army raised for the defence of the Christian people, was little less insupportable than the Saracens themselves, committing all manner of disorder and outrage as they passed along, especially when they came to any of those places which had made an agreement with the Saracens, or surrendered to them, they swore and cursed, and reviled the inhabitants with reproachful language and compelled them by force to bear them company. The poor people excused their submission to the Saracens, by their inability to defend themselves, and told the soldiers, that if they did not approve of what they had done, they ought themselves to have come sooner to their relief.

The news of this great army having reached the Saracens ears, whilst they were at Hems, filled them full of apprehensions, and put them to a very great streight which way to manage in this critical juncture. Some of them would very willingly have shrunk back, and returned to Arabia ; in which they proposed to themselves a double advantage ; speedy assistance from their friends, and the great scarcity to which the numerous army of the enemy must needs be reduced in that barren country ; but Abu Obeidah fearing lest such a retreat might by the Caliph be interpreted cowardice in him, durst not approve of this advice. Others rather chose to die in the defence of those stately buildings, fruitful fields, and pleasant meadows they had won by the sword, than retire volunteers to their former starving condition ; and proposed to stay there where they were, and expect the approach of the enemy. Caled was not for staying there, it being too near Cæsarea, where Constantine, the Emperor's son, lay with 40,000 men ; but proposed to march to Yermouk, where they might expect assistance from the Caliph. As soon as Constantine heard of their departure, he sent a chiding letter to Mahân, and bad him mend his pace. Mahân advanced, but made no haste to give the Saracens battle, having received orders from the Emperor to make overtures of peace, which were no sooner proposed than rejected by Abu Obeidah. There passed several messages between them. The Saracens endeavouring to bring their countryman Jabalah Ebno'l Ayham, with his Christian Arabs, to a neutrality, were answered, that they were obliged to serve the Emperor, and resolved to fight. Upon this, Caled, contrary to the advice of all, prepared to give him battle first, before Mahân should come up, with a very inconsiderable number of men, picked out of the whole army ; urging that the Christians being the army of the Devil, had no advantage by their numbers against the Saracens, the army of God. It was observed that Caled in choosing his men, called out more Ansers* than Mohagarens,† which occasioned some grumbling among them, being in doubt whether it was because he respected them most, or because he had a mind to expose them to the greatest danger, that he might favour the others ; a very impertinent scruple, in my opinion, since he was to go with them himself. Caled told them, 'That he had chosen them without any such regard, only because they were persons he could depend upon, whose valour he had proved, and who had the faith rooted in their hearts. One Cathib happening to be called after his brother Sahal, looking upon himself to be the better man, resented it as an high affront, and abused Caled, who gave him very gentle modest answers, to the great satisfaction of all, especially Abu Obeidah, who, after a short contention, made them shake hands. Caled indeed was admirable for this, he knew no less how to govern his passions, than command an army, the latter of which proves to most great generals the easier task of the two. His success in this very hazardous undertaking was beyond all expectation, for he put Jabalah's Arabs into disorder, and killed a great many, losing very few of his own upon the spot, and five prisoners, three of which were Yezid Ebn Abi Sophyan, Raphi Ebn Omeirah, and Derar Ebno'l Azwàr, all men of great note, and frequently mentioned before. Abu Omeirah sent Abdo'llah Ebn Kort with an express to Omar, acquainting him with their whole circumstances, begging his prayers, and some fresh recruits of UNITA-RIANS (Arab. *Mowahhidîna*) a title they glory in, reckoning themselves the only asserters of the unity of the deity. Omar and the whole court were extremely surprised, but comforted themselves with the promises made to them in the Alcoran, which seemed now to be all they had left to trust to. To encourage the people he went into the pulpit, and showed them the excellency of fighting for the cause of God, and returned an answer to Abu Obeidah, full of such spiritual consolation as the Alcoran could afford. Omar commanded Abdo'llah, that as soon as ever he came near the camp, before he delivered the letter, he should cry out, ' Good news,' to comfort the Muslemans, and ease them in some measure of those perplexing apprehensions they laboured under. He having received his letter and message, together with Omar's blessing, set forwards on his journey towards the army ; but recollecting himself, he remembered that he had forgot to pay his respects at Mahomet's tomb, which whether or no he should ever see again was very uncertain ; upon which he hastens to Ayesha's house (the place where Mahomet was buried), and finds her sitting by the

---

* Those of Medinah, are called by that name, because they helped Mahomet their prophet, in his flight from Meccah.

† Those that fled with him are called Mohagerins : and by these names the inhabitants of Meccah and Medinah are often known.

tomb, with Ali and Abbas, and Hasan and Hosein (Ali's sons), one upon Ali's lap, the other upon Abbas's. Ali was reading the chapter of beast's, being the sixth of the Alcoran ; and Abbas the chapter of Hud, which is the eleventh. Abdo'llah having paid his respects to Mahomet, Ali asked him, ' Whether he did not think of going ?' He answered, ' Yes ; but he feared he should not get to the army before the battle, which he willingly would do, if possible.' ' If you desired a speedy journey,' answered Ali, ' why did you not ask Omar to pray for you ? Don't you know that the prayers of Omar will not be turned back ? Because the apostle of God said to him, " If there were to be a " prophet to be expected after me, it would be Omar, whose judg- " ment agrees with the book of God." The prophet said of him besides, " If an (universal) calamity were to descend from heaven upon man- " kind Omar would escape from it." Wherefore if Omar prayed for thee, thou shalt not stay long for an answer from God.' Abdo'llah told him, ' That he had not spoken one word in praise of Omar, but what he was very sensible of before, only he desired to have his prayers and those of the rest of the Muslemans added to, especially being at the tomb of the prophet.' All that were present lifting up their hands to heaven, Ali said, ' O God ! I beseech thee, for the sake of this chosen apostle (in whose name Adam prayed, and thou answeredst his petition, and forgavest his sins) that thou wouldest grant to Abdo'llah Ebn Kort a safe and speedy return, and assist the followers of thy prophet with help, O thou who alone art great and munificent !' Immediately he set forth, and returned to the camp with such incredible speed, that the Saracens there were surprised. But their admiration ceased, when he informed them of the blessing of Omar their caliph, and of Ali's prayers at Mahomet's tomb.

Recruits were instantly raised to send out of Arabia to the army. Said Ebn Amir commanded them, having received a flag of red silk at the hands of Omar, who told him that he gave him that commission in hopes of his behaving himself well in it ; advising him, among other things, not to follow his appetites ; not forgetting to put him in hopes of further encouragement, if he should deserve it. Said thanked him for his advice ; adding, that if he followed it, he should be saved. ' And now,' says Said, ' as you have advised me, so let me advise you.' ' Speak on,' says Omar. ' I bid you then,' added the other, ' Fear God more than men, and not the contrary ; and love all the Muslemans as yourself and your family, as well those at a distance, as those near you. And command that which is praiseworthy, and forbid that which is otherwise.' Omar, all the while he spoke, stood looking steadfastly upon the ground, leaning his forehead upon his staff. Then he lift up his head, and the tears ran down his cheeks, and he said, ' Who is able to do this without the Divine assistance ?' Ali bade Said make good use of the Caliph's advice, and dismissed him. Said marching towards the army lost his way, unfortunately for the Christians; for by that means he happened upon the prefect of Amman with 5,000 men. Said cut all the foot to pieces; the prefect flying with the horse, was intercepted by a party sent out from the Saracen camp to forage. Said at first thought they had fallen together by the ears among themselves, but when he came up, and heard the Tecbir, he was well satisfied. Zobeir thrust the prefect through with a lance; of the rest never a man escaped. The Saracens cut off all their heads, then flayed them, and so carried them upon the points of their lances, presenting a most horrible spectacle to all that part of the country, till they came to the army, which received new courage, by the accession of this recruit sent from the Caliph, consisting of 8,000 men.

However their satisfaction was very much allayed by the loss of those five prisoners, which Jabalah Ebno'l Ayham had taken. It fortuned that Mahan desired Abu Obeidah to send somebody to him to discourse with; which being granted, Caled proffered his service, and by Abu Obeidah's advice took along with him 100 chosen men, of the best soldiers in the army. Being met by the out-guards, the chief of which was Jabalah Ebno'l Ayham, and examined, they were ordered to stay there till the general's pleasure should be known. Mahan would have had Caled come to him alone, and leave his men behind him: which he refusing, they were commanded, when they came near, to alight from their horses, and deliver their swords; to which when they would not submit, they were at last permitted to enter as they pleased. They found Mahan sitting upon a throne, and there were seats prepared for them. But they refused to sit on them, and removing them, sat down upon the ground. Mahan asked them the reason of their doing so, and taxed them with want of breeding. To which Caled answered, 'That that was the best breeding which was from God, and what God has prepared for us to sit down upon, is purer than your tapestries;' defending their practice from a sentence of their prophet Mahomet, backed with this text of the *Alcoran*, 'Out of it (meaning the earth), we have created you, and to it we shall return you, and out of it we shall bring you another time' (chap. xx., 57). Mahan began then to expostulate with Caled, concerning their coming into Syria, and all those hostilities which they had committed there. Mahan seemed satisfied with Caled's way of talking, and said, that he had before that time entertained a quite different opinion of the Arabs, having been informed that they were a foolish ignorant people. Caled confessed that that was the condition of most of them, till God sent their prophet Mahomet to lead them into the right way, and teach them to distinguish good from evil, and truth from error. Sometimes they argued very coolly, and then again flew into a violent passion, till at last Caled told Mahan, that he should one day see him led with a rope around his neck to Omar, to be beheaded. Mahan told him that the received law of all nations secured ambassadors from violence, which he supposed had encouraged him to take that indecent freedom; however he was resolved to chastise his insolence in the persons of his friends the five prisoners, who should instantly be beheaded. Caled bid him attend, and swore by God, by Mahomet, and the holy Temple of Meccah, that if he killed them, he should die by his hands, and every Saracen present should kill his man, let the consequences be what they would; and immediately rose from his place, and drew his sword. The like did all the rest of the Saracens. But when Mahan told him that he would not meddle with him for the aforesaid reasons, they sheathed their swords, and talked calmly again; after which Mahan made Caled a present of the prisoners, and desired him to give him his scarlet tent, which Caled had brought with him, and pitched hard by. Caled freely gave it him, and refused to take anything (though Mahan gave him his choice of whatever he liked best), thinking his kindness abundantly recompensed in the restoring the prisoners.

Both sides now prepared for that fight which was to determine the fate of Syria. Abu Obeidah resigned the whole command of the army to Caled, standing himself in the rear, under the yellow flag, which Abubeker had given him at his first setting forth into Syria; being the same which Mahomet himself had fought under at the battle of Chaibar. That was judged by Caled the properest place for him, not only because he was no extraordinary soldier, but that the reverence of him might prevent the flight of the Saracens, who were now like to be as hard put to it, as at any time since they first bore arms. For the same reason the women were placed in the rear. The Greeks charged so courageously, and with such vast numbers, that the right wing of the Saracen horse was quite borne down, and broken off from the main body of the army. But no sooner did they turn their backs, but they were so warmly received by the women, who used them so ill, and loaded them with such plenty of reproaches, that they were glad to return every man to his post, and chose rather to face the enemy, than endure the storm. However they had much ado to bear up, and were pressed so hard by the Greeks, that they were sometimes obliged to forget what their generals had said a little before the fight, who told them, 'That paradise was before them, and the devil and hell fire behind them.' Abu Sophyan, who had used that very expression himself, was forced to retreat, and received from one of the women an hearty blow over the face with a tent-pole for his pains. Night at last parted them, about such time as the victory began to incline to the Saracens, who had been thrice beaten back, and as often restored by the women. Then Abu Obeidah said at once those prayers which belonged to two several hours; I suppose because his men should have the more time to rest, which he was very tender of; walking about the camp, looking after the wounded men, and oftentimes binding up their wounds with

his own hands ; telling them, ' That their enemies suffered the same
pain which they did, but had not that reward to expect from God which
the Muslemans had.'

Among other single combats, of which there were several fought
between the two armies ; it chanced that Serjabil Ebn Shahhnah was
engaged with an officer of the Christians, who was much too strong
for him.   The reason our author assigns, is because Serjabil was
wholly given up to watching and fasting.   Derar thought he ought not
to stand still and see the prophet's secretary killed ; and took his
dagger, whilst the combatants were over head and ears in dust, and
coming behind the Christian, stabbed him to the heart.   The Saracens
gave Derar thanks for his service ; but he said that he would receive
no thanks but from God.   Upon this there arose a difference between
Serjabil and Derar concerning the spoil of this officer. Derar claimed
it, as being the person that killed him.   Serjabil, as having engaged
him, and tired him out first.   The matter being referred to Abu
Obeidah, he proposed the case of the Caliph, concealing the names of
the persons concerned; who sent him word that the spoil of any enemy
was due to him that killed him : upon which Abu Obeidah took it from
Serjabil, and adjudged it to Derar.

Another day, the Christian archers did such execution, that besides
those Saracens which were killed and wounded in other parts, there
were 700 which lost each of them one or both of their eyes ; upon
which account, the day in which the battle was fought is called
Yaumo'ttéwîr, the day of blinding : and if any of those that lost their
eyes that day, were afterwards asked by what mischance he was
blinded ? he answered, ' That it was not a mischance, but a token of
favour from God ;' for they gloried as much in those wounds they
received in the defence of their superstition, as our enthusiasts do in
what they call persecution, and with much the same reason. Abdo'llah
Ebn Kort, who was present in all the wars in Syria, says, ' That he
never saw so hard a battle as that which was fought on that day at
Yermouk ; and though the generals fought most desperately, yet after
all they had been beaten, if the battle had not again been restored by
the women.'   Caulah, Derar's sister, was wounded and fell down.
Opherah revenged her quarrel, and struck off the man's head that did
it ; and after asking her how she did, she answered, ' Very well with
God, but a dying woman.'   However, she proved to be mistaken, for
in the evening she was walking about as if she had ailed nothing, and
looking after the wounded men.

The Greeks in the night had another calamity added to their
misfortune of losing the victory, drawn upon them by their own
inhuman barbarity.   There was at Yermouk a gentleman of a very
plentiful fortune, who had removed from Hems thither for the sweet·
ness of the air.   When Mahân's army came thither, this gentleman

used to entertain the officers, and treat them nobly. To requite him for his courtesy, whilst they were revelling at his house, they bad him bring out his wife to them; which he refusing, they took her by force, and abused her all night; and, to add to his affliction, they took a little son of his, and cut his head off. The poor lady took her child's head, and carried it to Mahân; and having given him an account of the outrages committed by his officers, demanded satisfaction. He took but little notice of it, and put her off with a slight answer. Upon which her husband resolved to take the first opportunity of being revenged, went privately over to the Saracens, and acquainted them with his design.   Returning back to the Greeks, he told them it was now in his power to do them singular service : he takes a great number of them, and brings them to a great water, very deep, and fordable only at one place : 500 Saracen horse, instructed by him, come over where the water was shallow, and attack the Greeks, but in a very little time return orderly the same way they came. The injured gentleman calls out, and encourages the Greeks to pursue,* who plunging into the water confusedly, and not at all acquainted with the place, perished in great numbers. In those battles fought afterwards at Yermouk (which were all in Nov., 636), the Christians had the worst, till at last Mahân's vast army being broken, and shattered to pieces, he was forced to fly, and leave the Saracens masters of the field, now quite delivered from those terrible apprehensions, which the news of this great preparation had filled them with at first.

A short time after Abu Obeidah wrote to the Caliph the following letter :—

' In the name of the most merciful God, &c.

' This is to acquaint thee, that I encamped at Yermouk, and Mahân
' was near us, with such an army as the Muslemans never beheld a
' greater ; but God overthrew this multitude, and gave us the victory
' over them, out of his abundant grace and goodness.   We killed of
' them about 150,000, and took 40,000 prisoners.   Of the Muslemans
' were killed 4,030, to whom God has decreed the honour of martyr-
' dom.   I found some heads cut off, not knowing whether they
' belonged to the Muslemans or Christians, and I prayed over them
' and buried them.   Mahân was afterwards killed at Damascus by
' Nomân Ebn Alkamah.   There was one Abu Joaîd, that belonged to
' them before the battle, that came from Hems, he drowned of them a
' great number, unknown to any but God.   As for those that fled into
' the deserts and mountains, we have destroyed them all, and stopped
' all the roads and passages, and God has made us masters of their
' country, and wealth, and children.   Written after the victory from
' Damascus, where I stay expecting the orders concerning the division

* Καὶ ἑαυτοὺς Βάλλοντες εἰς τὰς στενόδους τοῦ Ἱερμύχθη ποταμοῦ ἐχεῖ ἀπώ-
λοντο ἄρδην. *Theoph. p.* 2δ9.

' of the spoil. Fare thee well, and the mercy and blessing of God be
' upon thee, and all the Muslemans.'

Omar, in a short letter, expressed his satisfaction, and gave the
Saracens thanks for their perseverance and diligence ; commanding
Abu Obeidah to continue where he was till further orders, but mentioned nothing concerning the spoil : upon which Abu Obeidah looking upon it as left to his own discretion, divided it, without staying for
further orders.   To an horseman he gave thrice as much as to a foot-
man, and made a further difference between those horses which were
of the right Arabian breed (which they looked upon to be far the best)
and those that were not, allowing twice as much to the former as to
the latter ; with which division, they not being satisfied, Abu Obeidah
told them that the prophet did the same after the battle of Chaibar ;
which, upon appeal made to Omar, was by him confirmed. Zobeir had
at the battle of Yermouk two horses, which he used to ride by turns :
he received five lots, three for himself, and two for his horses. If any
slaves had run away from their masters before the battle, and were
afterwards retaken, they were restored to their proper masters, who
nevertheless received an equal share of the spoil with the rest.

The Saracens having rested a month at Damascus, and refreshed
themselves, Abu Obeidah sent to Omar to know whether he should go
to Cæsarea or Jerusalem.   Ali being present when Omar was
deliberating, said, ' To Jerusalem first ;' adding that he had heard the
prophet say as much.   This city they had a great longing after, as
being the seat and burying-place of a great many of the ancient
prophets, in whom they reckoned none to be so much interested as
themselves.   Abu Obeidah having received orders to besiege it, sent
Yezid Ebn Abi Sofyan thither first, with 5,000 men ; and for five days
together sent after him considerable numbers of men, under such
officers as he thought fit to appoint.   The Ieresolymites expressed no
signs of fear, nor would they vouchsafe so much as to send out a
messenger to parley, but made preparation for a vigorous defence, and
planted their engines upon the walls. Yezid at last went near the
walls, with an interpreter, to know their minds, and propose the usual
terms ; which being rejected, the Saracens would willingly have assaulted
the besieged, had not Yezid told them that the general had not commanded them to make any assault, but only to sit down before the
city ; and thereupon sent to Abu Obeidah, who forthwith gave them
order to fight.   The next morning the generals said the morning
prayer, each at the head of his men ; and, as it were with one consent,
it seems every one of them quoted this versicle out of the *Alcoran*, as
being very apposite and pertinent to their present purpose, ' O people !
enter ye into the holy land which God hath decreed for you ;' being
verse 24 of chap. 50 of the *Alcoran*, where the impostor introduces
Moses speaking to the children of Israel : which words the Saracens

dexterously interpreted to belong no less to themselves than to their
predecessors, the Israelites.   Nor have these parts of the world been
altogether destitute of such able expositors, who, whatever they find in
Scripture graciously expressed in favour of the people of God, apply
to themselves, without limitation or exception : whatever is said of the
wicked and ungodly, and all the terrors and judgments denounced,
with a liberal hand they bestow upon their neighbours.   After their
prayers were over, they began their assault.   The Ieresolymites never
flinched, but sent them showers of arrows from the walls, and maintained the fight with undaunted courage, till the evening.   Thus they
continued fighting ten days, and on the eleventh, Abu Obeidah came
up with the remainder of the army ; he had not been there long before
he sent the besieged the following letter :—

'In the name of the most merciful God.

' From Abu Obeidah Ebn Aljerahh, to the chief commanders of the
' people of Ælia, and the inhabitants thereof,* health and happiness to
' every one that follows the right way, and believes in God and the
' apostle.   We require of you to testify, that there is but one God, and
' Mahomet is his apostle, and that there shall be a day of judgment,
' when God shall raise the dead out of their sepulchres ; and when you
' have born witness to this, it is unlawful for us either to shed your
' blood, or meddle with your substance or children.   If you refuse
' this, consent to pay tribute, and be under us forthwith ; otherwise I
'ᶜ shall bring men against you, who love death better than you do the
' drinking of wine, or eating hog's flesh : nor will I ever stir from you,
' if it please God, till I have destroyed those that fight for you, and
' made slaves of your children.'

The eating swine's flesh,† and drinking wine,‡ are both forbidden in
the Alcoran, which occasioned that reflection of Abu Obeidah upon
the practice of the Christians.   The former prohibition is borrowed
from the Jewish law ; and as for the latter, the reader may see more
in Prideaux's life of Mahomet.   The besieged, never a whit daunted,
held out four months entire ; in all which space there did not one day
pass without fighting ; and it being winter time, the Saracens suffered
a great deal of hardship through the extremity of the weather.   At last,
when the besieged had well considered the obstinacy of the Saracens ;
who, they had good reason to believe, would never raise the siege till
they had taken the city, whatever time it took up, or cost them pains ;
Sophronius, the patriarch went to the wall, and by an interpreter discoursed with Abu Obeidah, telling him that Jerusalem was the holy
city, and whoever came into the holy land with any hostile intent,
would render himself obnoxious to the divine displeasure.   To which

---

* *Alcoran, chap. xx.* 49.   They use it almost always when they write to Christians ; and
so the king of Fez writes to our princes of Great Britain.

† *Alcoran, chap. ii.* 168.   ‡ *Alcoran, chap. v.* 92, 93.

Abu Obeidah answered, ' We know that it is a noble city, and that our prophet Mahomet went from it in one night to heaven (*chap. xvii.* 1, *and liii.* 10), and approached within two bows shot of his Lord, or nearer; and that it is the mine of the prophets, and their sepulchres are in it, and we are more worthy to have it in possession than you are ; neither will we leave besieging it till God delivers it up to us, as he hath done other places, before it.' I shall not here transcribe the story of Mahomet's journey to heaven ; the reader may find a sufficient account of it in Dr. Prideaux's life of Mahomet. At last the patriarch consented that the city should be surrendered, upon condition that the inhabitants should receive the articles of their security and protection from the Caliph's own hands, and not by proxy. And their insisting upon this, I take to have been the principal motive of Omar's coming, rather than believe a blind story fabled by some Arab authors, of an old prophecy kept in Jerusalem concerning Omar; in which his name and religion were specified, and his person described, and that he was the only man that could take Jerusalem : which, however strange it may seem, is nevertheless not so absurd and ridiculous as what they tell of Sophronius's giving an account of all this to Abu Obeidah, who thereupon sent for Omar. I should rather believe that this idle story of the prophecy may be better explained by Theophanes, who tells us, that when the city was taken, the patriarch said,* ' This is of a truth the abomination of desolation spoken of by Daniel the prophet standing in the holy place.' The Saracens hearing afterwards that the patriarch had confessed them to have been prophesied of, made the foregoing story out of it.† Jelalo'ddin Affoyúti a celebrated Arabick author, who, among other works, has written an history of Jerusalem, confesses, that there is great variety and difference in the accounts of the taking it : however, all agree in this, that Omar was there. The same Jelalo'ddin agrees with Alwákidi, where he tells us, that upon Abu Obeidah's writing to Omar to come, he advised with his friends. Othman, who afterwards succeeded him in the government, disswaded him from going, that the Ieresolymites might see themselves despised, and thought beneath his notice ; but Ali was of a quite different opinion, urging that the Muslemans had endured great hardship in so long a siege, and suffered much from the extremity of the cold ; that the presence of the Caliph would be a great refreshment and encouragement to them ; adding, that the great respect which the Christians had for Jerusalem, as being the place to which they went on pilgrimage, ought to be considered ; that it ought not to be supposed that they would easily part with it, but soon be reinforced

* Τᾶτον ἰδὼν Σωφόνιος ἔφη, τᾶτ' ἐστιν ἐπ' ἀληθείας τὸ βδέλυγμα τῆς ἐρημόσεως τὸ ῥηθὲν διὰ Δανιὴλ τοῦ προφήτᾶ, ἐστὼς ἐν τόπῳ ἁγίῳ· Πολλοῖστε δάκρυσι τὸ χριστιανὸν φύλον ἀπεδύο ρετ τῆς εὐσιβίας ὁ ϖρόμαχος,   *Theop.*
p. 281. Edit. Par.
† MSS. Arab. Huntington. numb. 510.

with fresh supplies. This advice of Ali being preferred to Othman's, the Caliph resolved upon his journey; which, according to his frugal management, required no great expense or equipage. When he had said his prayers in the Mosque, and paid his respects at Mahomet's tomb, he substituted Ali in his place, and set forwards with some attendance; the greatest part of which, having kept him company a little way, returned back to Medinah. He rode upon a red camel, with a couple of sacks; in one of which he carried that sort of provision, which the Arabs called Sawîk, which is either barley, rice, or wheat, sodden and unhusken; the other was full of fruits. Before him he carried a very great leather bottle (very necessary in those desert countries to put water in), behind him a large wooden platter. Thus furnished and equipped, the Caliph travelled, and when he came to any place where he was to rest all night, he never went from it till he had said the morning prayer. After which, turning himself about to those that were with him, he said, 'Praise be to God, who has strengthened us with the true religion, and given us his prophet, and led us out of error, and united us (who were at variance) in the confession of the truth, and given us the victory over our enemy, and the possession of his country. O ye servants of God! Praise him for these abundant favours; for God gives increase to those that ask for it, and are desirous of those things which are with him; and fulfils his grace upon those that are thankful.' Then filling his platter with the Sawîk, he very liberally entertained his fellow-travellers, who did, without distinction, eat with him all out of the same dish.

Whilst he was upon his journey, there came, at one of his stages, a complaint before him of a man that had marryed two wives, that were sisters both by father and mother; a thing which the old Arabians so long as they continued in their idolatry, made no scruple of, as appears from that passage in the Alcoran, where it is forbidden for the time to come, and expressed after such a manner, as makes it evident to have been no uncommon practice among them. Omar was very angry, and cited him and his two wives to make their appearance before him forthwith. After the fellow had confessed that they were both his wives, and so nearly related, Omar asked him what religion he might be of, or whether he was a Musleman? 'Yes,' said the fellow. 'And did you not know then,' said Omar, 'that it was unlawful for you to have them when God has said,' 'neither marry two sisters any more,' (chap. iv. 27). The fellow swore, that he did not know that it was unlawful, neither was it unlawful. Omar swore, he lyed, and that he would make him part with one of them, or else strike his head off. The fellow began to grumble, and said, 'that he wished he had never been of that religion, for he could have done as well without it, and had never been a whit the better for it since he had first professed it.' Upon which Omar called him a little nearer, and gave him two blows upon the crown with his stick, to teach him better manners, and learn him to speak more reverently of Mahometanism ; saying, ' O thou enemy of God, and of thy self, dost thou revile Islâm ;* which is the religion that God and his angels, and apostles, and the best of the creation have chosen ?' And threatened him severely if he did not make a quick dispatch, and take which of them he loved best. The fellow was so fond of them both that he could not tell which he'd rather part with : upon which some of Omar's attendants cast lots for the two women. The lot falling upon one of them three times, the man took her, and was forced to dismiss the other. Omar called to him, and said, ' Pray mind what I say to you ; if any man makes profession of our religion, and then leaves it, we kill him ; therefore see you do not renounce Islâm. And take heed to your self, for if ever I hear that you lie with your wife's sister, which you have put away, you shall be stoned.'

Passing on a little further, he happened to see some poor tributaries, whom their hard masters, the Saracens, were punishing for non-payment, by setting them in the sun ; which in that torrid zone is very grievous. When Omar understood the cause of it, he asked the poor people what they had to say for themselves ? Who answered that they were not able. Upon which he said, ' Let them alone, and don't compel them to more than they are able to bear ; for I heard the apostle of God say, DO NOT afflict men ; for those who afflict men in this world, God shall punish them in hell-fire at the day of judgment.' And immediately commanded them to let them go.

Before he got to his journey's end, he was informed of an old man that suffered a young one to go partner with him in his wife ; so that one of them was to have her four and twenty hours, and then the other, and so successively. Omar having sent for them, and upon examination found them to be Muslemans, wondered at it, and asked the old man, if he did not know that it was forbidden by the law of God ? They both swore that they knew no such thing. Omar asked the old man, what made him consent to such a beastly thing? Who answered, that he was in years, and his strength failed him, and he had never a son to look after his business, and this young man was very serviceable to him in watering and feeding his camels, and he had recompensed him that way ; but since it was unlawful, he promised that it should be so no more. Omar bid him take his wife by the hand, and told him, ' That no body had anything to do with her but himself : and for your part, young man (says he) if ever I hear that you come near her again, off goes your head.'

Omar, having all the way he went, set things aright that were amiss, and distributed justice impartially, for which he was singularly eminent

---

* That is the word by which they express what we call the Mahometan religion ; and sig-nifies *delivering a man's self to God*.

among the Saracens, came at last into the confines of Syria, and when he drew near Jerusalem he was met by Abu Obeidah, and conducted to the Saracen camp with abundance of joy. He did not reach it the same day Abu Obeidah met him. In the morning he said the usual prayers, and if we may take my author's word for it, preached a good sermon. In which, as he quoted this text out of the Alcoran ; ' He whom God shall direct is led in the right way ; but thou shalt not find a friend to direct him aright whom God shall lead into error,' (chap. xviii. 16) ; a Christian priest that sat before him, stood up, and said, ' God leads no man into error ;' and repeated it. Omar said nothing to him, but bid those that stood by strike his head off if he should say so again. The old man understood what he said, and held his peace whilst Omar proceeded in his sermon.

Omar met with some of the Saracens richly dressed in silks that they had taken by way of plunder after the battle of Yermouk. He spoiled all their pride, for he caused them to be dragged along in the dirt with their faces downwards, and their cloaths to be rent all to pieces. As soon as he came within sight of the city, he cry'd out, ' Allàh Acbar : O God give us an easy conquest.' Pitching his tent, which was made of hair, he sat down in it upon the ground. The Christians hearing that Omar was come, from whose hands they were to receive their articles, were desirous of seeing him. Upon which the Muslemans would have perswaded him not to expose his person, for fear of some treacherous design. But Omar resolutely answered, in the words of the Alcoran ; ' SAY, there shall nothing befall us but what God hath decreed for us ; he is our Lord, and in God let all the believers put their trust.' (Chap. ix. 51). Afterwards upon parley, the besieged resigned, and because those articles of agreement made by Omar with the Ieresolymites, are as it were, the pattern which the Mahometan princes have chiefly imitated, I shall not think it improper to give the sense of them in this place, as I find it in the author of the history of Jerusalem (M.S. Arab Pocock, Num. 362).

The articles were these ; ' That the Christians should build no new ' churches, either in the city, or the adjacent territory : neither should ' they refuse the Muslemans entrance into their churches, either by ' night or day. That they should set open the doors of them to ' all passengers and travellers. If any Musleman should be upon ' a journey, they should be obliged to entertain him gratis the space ' of three days. That they should not teach their children the Al- ' coran, nor talk openly of their religion, nor perswade any one to be ' of it ; neither should they hinder any of their relations from becoming ' Mahometans, if they had an inclination to it. They should pay ' respect to the Muslemans, and rise up to them if they have a mind ' to sit down, that they should not go like the Muslemans in their dress ; ' nor wear such caps, shoes, nor turbants, nor part their hair as they

' do, nor speak after the same manner, nor be called by the same
' (*Kinaon*, *Cognomina*) names used by the Muslemans. Neither
' should they ride upon saddles. nor bear any sort of arms, nor use the
' Arabick tongue in the inscriptions of their seals : nor sell any wine.
' That they should be obliged to keep to the same sort of habit where-
' soever they went, and always wear girdles upon their wastes. That
' they should set no crosses upon their churches, nor show their
' crosses nor their books openly in the streets of the Muslemans.
' That they should not ring, but only toll their bells. Nor take any
' servant that had once belonged to the Muslemans. Neither should
' they overlook them in their houses. Some say, that Omar com-
' manded the inhabitants of Jerusalem to have the fore parts of their
' heads shaven, and obliged them to ride upon their pannels sideways,
' and not like the Muslemans.'

Upon these terms the Christians had liberty of conscience, paying
such tribute as their masters thought fit to impose upon them ; and
Jerusalem, once the glory of the East, was forced to submit to a heavier
yoke than ever it had borne before. For though the number of the
slain, and the calamities of the besieged were greater when it was taken
by the Romans, yet the servitude of those that survived was nothing
comparable to this, either in respect of the circumstances or duration.
For however it might seem to be utterly ruined and destroyed by Titus,
yet was it very much recovered before Adrian's time. Now, it fell as
it were, once for all, into the hands of the most mortal enemies of the
Christian religion, in which it has continued ever since; excepting only
that interval of near ninety years, in which it was possessed by the
Christians in the holy war.

The Christians having submitted to the terms, Omar gave them the
following writing under his hand :—

' In the name of the most merciful God,

' From Omar Ebno'l Alchitâb to the inhabitants of Ælia. They
' shall be protected and secured both in their lives and fortunes, and
' their churches shall neither be pulled down, nor made use of by any
' but themselves.'

Immediately upon this (A.D. 637) the gates were opened, and the
Caliph and those that were with him went in. The patriarch kept
them company, and the Caliph talked with him familiarly, and asked
him questions concerning the antiquities of the place. Among other
places which they visited, they went into the temple of the resurrection,
and Omar sat down in the midst of it. When the time of prayers was
come (the Mahometans have five set times of prayer in a day), Omar
told the patriarch that he had a mind to pray, and desired him to show
him a place where he might perform his devotion. The patriarch bade
him pray where he was ; but he altogether refused it. Then he brought

him out from thence, and went with him into Constantine's church, and laid a mat for him; but he would not pray there. At last he went alone to the steps which were at the east gate of St. Constantine's church, and kneeled by himself upon one of them. Having ended his prayers, he sat down, and asked the patriarch if he knew why he had refused to pray in the church; the patriarch confessed that he could not tell what should be the reason of it. 'Why then,' says Omar, 'I will tell you. You know I promised you that none of your churches should be taken away from you, but that you should possess them quietly yourselves. Now if I had prayed in any one of these churches, I should no sooner have been gone from hence, but the Muslemans would infallibly have taken it away from you. And notwithstanding all you could have alleged, they would have said, "this is the place where Omar prayed, and we will pray here too." And so you would have been turned out of your church, contrary both to my intention and your expectation. But because my praying so much as upon the steps may perhaps give some occasion to the Muslemans to give you some disturbance, I shall take what care I can to prevent that.' So he called for pen, ink, and paper, and wrote expressly, 'that none of the Muslemans should pray upon the steps in any multitudes, but one by one. That they should never meet there to go to prayers. And that the muezzin, or crier, that calls the people to prayers (for the Mahometans never use bells) should not stand there.' This paper he gave to the patriarch for security, lest his praying upon the steps of the church should have set such an example to the Muslemans as might occasion any inconvenience to the Christians. A noble instance of singular fidelity and religious observation of promise. This Caliph did not think it enough to perform what he engaged himself, but used all possible diligence to oblige others to do so too. And when the unwary patriarch had desired him to pray in the church, not well considering what might be the consequence, the Caliph well knowing how apt men are to be superstitious in the imitation of their princes and great men, especially such as they look upon to be successors of a prophet, made the best provision he could, that nothing which might be pretended to be done in imitation of him, might any way infringe the security he had already given.

There goes a story, that the Caliph desired the patriarch to assign him a place where he might build a mosque for the celebration of the Mahometan service, and that the patriarch showed him the place where Jacob's stone lay, which he slept upon when he saw the vision (*Genesis* 28). It seems the stone was quite covered with dirt, and the Caliph took up as much as he could of it in his vest, and removed it. The Muslemans perceiving what the Caliph did, very readily assisted him; some filling their bucklers, some their vests, others baskets, that in a short time they had removed all the rubbish and dirt, and cleared

17

the stone.* Omar leaving the churches to the Christians, built a new temple in the place where Solomon's formerly stood, and consecrated it to the Mahometan superstition. From thence he went to Bethlehem, and going into the church, prayed there ; and when he had done he gave the patriarch, under his hand, the same security for the church, as he had done before at Jerusalem, strictly forbidding any of the Mahometans to pray there, unless one single person at a time ; and that no muezzin should ever call the people to prayers there. But notwithstanding all the Caliph's precaution, the Saracens afterwards seized the church for their own use ; and so they did St. Constantine's church at Jerusalem ; for they took half the porch where those steps were which Omar had prayed upon, and built a mosque there, in which they included those steps : and had Omar said his prayers in the body of the church, they would without all question have taken that too.

This same year in which Jerusalem was taken, Saed Ebn Abi Wakkas, one of Omar's captains, was making havock in the territories of Persia. He went to Madayen, formerly the treasury and magazine of Cosroes, King of Persia ; where they found money and rich furniture of all sorts, inestimable. Elmakin says that they took there no less than 3000 million of ducats, besides Cosroe's crown and wardrobe, which was exceeding rich, his clothes being all adorned with gold and jewels of great value. Then they opened the roof of Cosroe's his porch, where they found another very considerable sum. They plundered his armoury, well stored with all sorts of weapons. Among other things they brought to Omar a piece of silk hangings, sixty cubits square, all curiously wrought with needlework. That it was of great value, appears from the price which Ali had for that part of it which fell to his share when Omar divided it ; which, though it was none of the best of it, yielded him 20,000 pieces of silver. After this, in the same year, the Persians were defeated by the Saracens in a great battle near Jaloulah. Yazdejerd perceiving things grow every day worse and worse, retired to Ferganah, a city of Persia.

We must now proceed with the conquest of Syria. Omar having taken Jerusalem continued there about ten days, to put things in order. Here my author tells us a story of one Caab, a Jew, who came to him to be proselyted, and told, that his father, who was thoroughly skilled in the law of Moses, had told him concerning Mahomet being the seal of the prophets, and that after him all inspiration was to cease. Among other things, Caab asked him what was said concerning the Mahometan religion in the Alcoran.' Omar quoted such texts out of it as were

---

* *Theoph.* p. 281. His words are these : Εἰσελθὼν δὲ Οὔμαρος εἰς τὴν ἁγίαν πόλιν τριχίνοις ἐκ καμήλων ἐνδύμασιν ἠμφιεσμένος ἐρρυπωμένοις, ὑπόκρισίν τε σατανικὴν ἐνδεικνύμενος, τὸν ναὸν ἐζήτησεν τοῦν Ἰουδαίων ἰδεῖν, ὃν ᾠκοδόμησε Σολομὼν, προσκυντήριον αὐτὸν ποιῆσαι τῆς αὐτοῦ βλασφημίας.

suited to his palate, as having been brought up a Jew; namely,
' Abraham commanded his sons concerning it, and so did Jacob
(*chap. ii.*, 126), saying, O children! God has made choice of a religion for you; (*chap. iii.*, 96) wherefore do not die before you be Muslemans.' Again (*chap. iii.*, 60), 'Abraham was neither a Jew nor a
Christian, but a religious Musleman, and was not of the number of
those who join partners with God.' And then (*chap. iii.*, 78), ' He that
shall desire any other religion but Islama, it shall not be accepted of
him.' Again (*chap. iii.*, 77), ' Will they desire any other than God's
religion, to whom everything in heaven and earth (*Aslama*) submits
itself?' And then (*chap. xxii.*, 77), ' The religion of Abraham your
father; he gave you the name of Muslemans.' The Rabbi convinced
with so many pregnant texts, that the Mahometan religion was no
other than that of Abraham and the patriarchs, repeated instantly, 'La
Ilaha, &c. There is but one God, and Mahomet is his apostle.' Omar
was very well pleased with his new proselyte, and invited him to go
along with him to Medinah, to visit the Prophet's tomb, to which he
consented. I have inserted this story in the place where I found it in
my author, because I would not willingly omit anything that might
any way contribute to the illustrating the manners or religion of that
people concerning whom I write; notwithstanding which, I have a strong
suspicion that this is the very same Caab who was proselyted in Mahomet's
time, above ten years before Omar took Jerusalem, and concerning
whom the reader may see a larger account in the Life of Mahomet.
For our authors are not always so very accurate; especially those who
write the histories of the beginnings of the Saracenical Empire.

Now Omar thought of returning to Medinah, having first disposed
his affairs after the following manner. Syria he divided into two parts;
and committed all that lies between Hauran and Aleppo to Abu Obeidah, with orders to make war upon it till he conquered it. Yezid Ebn
Abi Sofyan took the charge of all Palestine and the sea shore. Amrou
Ebno'l Aas was sent to invade Ægypt, no inconsiderable part of the
Emperor's dominions, which now mouldered away continually. The
Saracens at Medinah had almost given Omar over; and began to conclude that he would never stir from Jerusalem, considering the richness of the country, and the sweetness of the air; but especially it
being the country of the prophets, and the Holy Land, and the place
where we must all be summoned together at the resurrection. At last
he came, so much the more welcome, by how much he was the less
expected. Abu Obeidah in the mean time received Kinnisrin and
Alhadir; the inhabitants paying down 5000 ounces of gold, and as
many of silver, 2000 suits of cloaths of several sorts of silk, and 500
asses' loads of figs and olives. Yezid marched against Cæsarea in
vain, that place being too well fortified to be taken by his little army,
especially since it had been reinforced by the Emperor, who had sent

store of all sorts of provision by sea, and a recruit of 2000 men. The inhabitants of Aleppo were much concerned at the loss of Kinnisrin and Alhadir, knowing very well that it would not be long before it would come to their turn, to experience themselves what they had known till then only by report.   They had two governors, brothers, who dwelt in the castle (the strongest in all Syria) which was not then encompassed by the town, but stood out at a little distance by itself. The name of one of these brethren, if my author mistakes not, was Youkinna, the other John. Their father held of the Emperor Heraclius all the territory between Aleppo and Euphrates, after whose decease his son Youkinna managed the affairs ; John not troubling himself with secular employments, did not meddle with the government, but led a monkish life ; spending his time in retirement, reading, and deeds of charity.   He would have persuaded his brother to have secured himself, by compounding with the Arabs for a good round sum of money ; who told him, 'that he talked like a monk, and did not understand what belonged to a soldier.   That he had wealth and warlike preparation enough, and was resolved to make the best opposition he could.' Accordingly the next day he called his men together, among which there were several Christian Arabs, and having armed them, and for their encouragement distributed some money among them, told them, ' that he was fully purposed to act offensively, and give the Saracens battle, if possible, before they should come too near to Aleppo.   That the Saracen army was weakened by their division, some of them being gone to Cæsarea, others to Damascus, and some into Ægypt.   Thus encouraging his men, he marched forwards with 12,000. Abu Obeidah had sent before him Caab Ebn Damarah with 1000 men, but with express orders not to fight till he had received information of the strength of the enemy.   Youkinna's spies found Caab and his men resting themselves, and watering their horses, secure, and free from apprehensions of danger : upon which he lays an ambuscade, and falls upon them with the rest of his men.   There was a sharp engagement in which the Saracens had the better of it at first ; but the ambuscade breaking in upon them, they were in great danger of being overpowered by the multitude ; 170 of them were killed upon the spot, and most of the rest grievously wounded, and they were upon the very brink of despair, and cried out, ' Ya Mahommed ! Ya Mahommed !' O Mahomet ! O Mahomet !   With much ado they made shift to hold up till night parted them, earnestly expecting the coming of Abu Obeidah.

In the meantime, whilst Youkinna was gone out with his forces to engage the Saracens, the wealthy and trading people of Aleppo, knowing very well how hard it would go with them if they should stand it out obstinately to the last, and be taken by storm, upon debate, resolved to go and article with Abu Obeidah, that, let Youkinna's success be what it would, they might be secure.   Thirty of the chief of them

went to him, being then at Kinnisrîn, and just upon his march ; and
as soon as they came near, cried out, ' Legoun, Legoun :' Abu Obeidah understood that it meant quarter, and had formerly written to the
captains in Syria, that if any of them heard any man use that word,
they should not be hasty to kill him, otherwise they must answer it at
the. day of judgement, and the Caliph would be clear. They were
brought before Abu Obeidah, and perceiving that there were fires in
the camp, and some were saying their prayers, others reading the
Alcoran, and all very easy and secure, one of them said, ' They have
most certainly gotten the victory.' An interpreter that stood by told
Abu Obeidah, who till then knew nothing of the battle. Upon examination, they told him that they were merchants, and the chief traders
of Aleppo, and were come to make articles for themselves ; that Youkinna was a tyrant ; that he marched out against the Saracens yesterday. Abu Obeidah hearing this, gave Caab Ebn Damarah over for
lost, which made him at first the more unwilling to article with the
Aleppians ; but upon their earnest and repeated intreaty, and being
always naturally inclined to compassion, and withal considering that
these persons (for there were several belonging to the neighbouring
villages that had joined themselves with them) might be serviceable in
helping the army to provision and provender, he cried out, ' God loves
those that are inclined to do good' (*Alcoran, chap. ii.* 190, *iii.* 129, 141,
v. 16) ; and turning himself to the Saracens, he represented the advantages which might accrue to them by receiving these people into
their protection : but one that was present told him that the town was
very near the castle, and he did not believe they were in earnest, or
ought to be trusted ; for, says he, ' they come to impose upon us, and
no question but they have trapanned Caab.' To whom Abu Obeidah
answered, ' Entertain, man, a better opinion of God, who will not deceive us, nor give them the dominion over us. Then he proposed to
them the same conditions which they of Kinnisrîn and Hader had
agreed to ; but they desired to be excused, alledging, that through the
oppression and tyranny of Youkinna, their city of Aleppo was nothing
near so well peopled, nor half so rich as Kinnisrîn ; but if he pleased
to accept of half so much, they would endeavour to raise it : which
was accepted, upon condition that they should take care to furnish the
camp with all things necessary, and give all possible intelligence that
might be any use to the Muslemans, and also hinder Youkinna from
returning to the castle. They undertook all but the last article, which
they said was altogether out of their power. Then he swore them every
one (such an oath as they had been used to), and bade them take care
how they broke it, for if they did, there would be no quarter. When
they were going away, he proffered them a guard to see them safe
home ; but they told him they would, if he pleased, save him that
trouble, since they could go home the same way they came, without
any fear of Youkinna.

As they were going back, they chanced to meet with one of You-kinna's officers, who, enquiring what news? They gave him an account of the whole transaction. Upon this he goes with all possible speed to his master; who was with impatience expecting the morning, that he might dispatch Caab and his men, whom the coming of the night had preserved: but hearing this news, he began to fear lest there should be any attempt made upon the castle, and thought it safest to make the best of his way homeward. In the morning the Saracens were surprised to see no enemy, and wondered what was the matter with them. Caab would have pursued them, but none of his men had any inclination to go with him; so they rested themselves, and in a little time Caled and Abu Obeidah came up with the rest of the army. Then they went about burying their martyrs, as they call them, and put them into the ground all bloody as they were, with their clothes, arms, and all together. Abu Obeidah said that he had heard the apostle of God say that, ' The martyrs and those who are killed in the service of God, shall be raised at the day of judgement with their blood upon their throats, which shall have the colour of blood, and the smell of musk, and they shall be led directly into paradise, without their being called to an account.'

As soon as they were buried, Abu Obeidah reminded Caled of the obligation they were under to protect the Aleppians, now their confederates, who were likely to be exposed to the utmost outrage and cruelty of Youkinna, who, in all probability, would severely resent their desertion. They marched as fast as they could, and when they drew near Aleppo, found that they were not at all deceived in what they feared. Youkinna had drawn up his soldiers with a design to fall upon the townsmen, and threatened them with present death, unless they would break their covenant with the Arabs, and go out with him to fight them, and bring out to him the person that was the first contriver and proposer of it. At last he fell upon them in good earnest, and killed about 300 of them. His brother John, who was in the castle, hearing a piteous outcry and lamentation, came down from the castle, and intreated his brother to spare the people, representing to him that Jesus Christ had commanded us not to contend with our enemies, much less with those of our own religion. Youkinna told him that they had agreed with the Arabs, and assisted them. Which John excused, telling him, ' That what they did was only for their own security, because they were no fighting men. In short, he took their part so long, till he provoked his brother to that degree, that he charged him with being the chief contriver and manager of the whole business; and at last, in a great passion, cut his head off: but our author says, that he first made profession of the Mahometan religion, and went forthwith to paradise. But very likely the reason of his saying so is, because he was a sober man, and of a good character, and he grudged that any such should die a Christian, and therefore made a Mahometan of him, envying the Christians the credit of having a good man among them. Whilst he was murdering the unhappy Aleppians, Caled (better late than never) came to their relief. Which Youkínna perceiving, retired with a considerable number of soldiers into the castle. The Saracens killed that day 3000 of his men: however he prepared for a siege, and planted engines upon the castle walls. The Aleppians brought out forty prisoners, and delivered them to Abu Obeidah, who bade his interpreter ask them, why they had made prisoners of them? They answered, 'Because they belonged to Youkínna, and having fled to them, they durst not conceal them, not being included in the articles.' Abu Obeidah commended their fidelity, and told them, 'They should find the benefit of it;' and for their further encouragement, added, 'That what plunder soever they got from any of the Christians should be their own, as a reward of their good service.' Seven of these prisoners turned Mahometans; the rest were beheaded.

Abu Obeidah next, in a council of war, deliberated what measures were most proper to be taken. Some were of opinion, that it would be the best way to besiege the castle with some part of the army, and let the rest be sent out to forage. Caled would not hear of it, but was for having the castle attacked by the whole force at once; that if possible, it might be taken before fresh supplies should come from the Grecian emperor. This concluded upon, they made a most vigorous assault, and had as hard a battle as any in all the wars of Syria. The besieged made a noble defence, and threw stones from the walls in such plenty, that a great many of the Saracens were killed, and a great many more maimed. Youkínna, encouraged with his success, designed to act offensively, and take all advantages. The Saracens looked upon all the country as their own, and knowing that there was no army of the enemy near them, nor fearing anything from the besieged, kept guard negligently. Youkínna, in the dead of the night, sent out a party, who, as soon as the fires were out in the camp, fell upon the Saracens, and having killed about sixty, carried off fifty prisoners. Caled pursued and cut off about 100 of them; the rest escaped to the castle with the prisoners, who by the command of Youkínna, were the next day beheaded in the sight of the Saracen army. Youkínna upon this ventured once more to send out another party, having received information from one of his spies (most of which were Christian Arabs) that some of the Muslemans were gone out to forage. They fell upon the Muslemans, killed 150 of them, and seized all their camels, mules and horses, which having killed or ham-stringed, they retired into the mountains, in hopes of lying hid that day, and returning to the castle in the silence of the night. In the mean time, some that had escaped brought the news to Abu Obeidah, who sends Caled and Derar to pursue them. Coming to the place where the fight had been, they found their men and camels dead, and the country people making great lamentation, for they were afraid lest the Saracens should suspect them of treachery, and revenge the loss of their men upon them. Whereupon they fell down before Caled, and told him they were altogether innocent, and had not any way, either directly or indirectly, been instrumental in it ; but that it was done by a party of horse that sallied from the castle. Caled having sworn them that they did not know any thing more, and taking some of them for guides, beset the only passage by which the besieged could return to the castle. When about a fourth part of the night was past, they perceiving them coming, and falling upon them took 300 prisoners, and killed the rest. The prisoners would have redeemed themselves, but they were all beheaded next morning before the castle.

The Saracens laid a close siege, but perceiving that they got no advantage, Abu Obeidah removed the camp about a mile's distance from the castle ; hoping by this means to tempt the besieged to security and negligence in their watch, which might at some time afford him an opportunity of taking the castle by surprize. But all would not do ; for Youkínna kept a very strict watch, and suffered not a man to stir out. Abu Obeidah thought there might be some Christian spies in the army ; whereupon he and Caled walked about the camp, to see if they could pick up any suspicious persons. Caled at last observed a man sitting with a vest before him, which he turned first on the one side, and then on the other. Caled stept to him, and asked him what tribe he was of ? The fellow designed to have named another tribe, if he had not been surprised ; but having the question put to him on a sudden, the word slipt out of his mouth, and he answered, ' of Gussân.' ' Sayest thou so ?' answered Caled ; ' thou enemy of God, thou art a Christian Arab, and a spy,' and seized him. The fellow said that he was not, but a Musleman. Caled carried him to Abu Obeidah, who bad him examine him in the Alcoran, and make him say his prayers. But the poor fellow had not one word to say for himself, being altogether ignorant of those things : upon which without much arguing, he confessed himself a spy, and that he was not alone, but there were three of them in all, two of which were returned to the castle. Abu Obeidah bad him take his choice, either of Mahometanism or death, and he embraced the former.

The siege continued four months, and some say, five. In the mean time Omar was very much concerned, having heard nothing from the camp in Syria. He writes to Abu Obeidah, to let him know how tender he was over the Muslemans, and what a great grief it was to him to hear no news of them in so long a time. Abu Obeidah answered, that Kinnisrîn, Hader and Aleppo were surrendered to him, only the castle of Aleppo held out, and that they had lost a considerable number of men before it. That he had some thoughts of raising the siege, and passing forward into that part of the country which lies between Aleppo and Antioch ; but only he stayed for his answer. About the time that Abu Obeidah's messengers got to Medinah, there came out of the several tribes of the Arabs a considerable number of men, who proffered their service to the Caliph. Omar ordered 70 camels to help their foot, and dispatched them into Syria, with a letter to Abu Obeidah ; in which he acquainted him, ' that he was variously affected according to the different success they had had ; but charged them by no means to raise the siege of the castle, for that would make them look little, and encourage their enemies to fall upon them on all sides.   Wherefore,' adds Omar, ' continue besieging it, till God shall determine the event, and forage with your horse round about the country.'

Among those fresh supplies which Omar sent last to the Saracen camp, there was a very remarkable man, whose name was Dames, of a gigantick size, and an admirable soldier. When he had been in the camp forty-seven days, and all the force and cunning of the Saracens could do nothing to the castle, he desired Abu Obeidah to let him have the command of 30 men, and he would try his best. Caled had heard much of the man, and told Abu Obeidah a long story of a wonderful performance of this Dames in Arabia ; that he was looked upon as a very proper person for such an undertaking. Abu Obeidah bad those who were to go with him not despise their commander, because of the meanness of his condition, he being a slave ; and swore that if the care of the whole army did not lye upon him, he would be the first man that should go under him upon such an enter- prize. To which they answered with entire submission and profound respect. Dames, who lay hid at no great distance, went out several times, and brought in with him five or six Greeks, but never a man of them understood one word of Arabick, which made him angry, and say, ' God curse these dogs ! What a strange barbarous language they use.'

At last he went again, and there fell a man down from the wall , him he took, and by the help of a Christian Arab, which he took afterwards, examined him ; who gave him an account, that immedi- ately upon the departure of the Saracens, Youkínna began to abuse the townsmen that had agreed with the Arabs, and exact large sums of money of them ; that he was one of them, and had endeavoured to make his escape from the oppression and tyranny of Youkínna, by leaping down from the wall. They let him go, as being under their protection by virtue of the articles made between Abu Obeidah and the Aleppians ; but beheaded all the rest.

Dames then takes out of a knapsack a goat's skin ; with this he covers his back and shoulders, and takes a dry crust in his hand, creep-

ing upon all fours as near to the castle as he could ; and if he heard
any noise, or suspected any person being near, to prevent being discovered, he makes such a noise with his crust, as a dog makes that is
gnawing a bone. • The rest of the company came after, sometimes
sculking and creeping along, at other times walking.   He had sent two
of his men to Abu Obeidah, to send him some horse about sunrise.
When they came to the castle, they found it in a manner inaccessible.
However Dames was resolved to leave nothing unattempted.   Having
found a place where he thought it might be easiest getting up, he sits
down upon the ground, and orders another to sit upon his shoulders,
and so till seven of them were gotten up, and sat one upon the others
shoulders, all of them leaning against the wall with all their strength.
Then he that was uppermost of all stood upright upon the shoulders of
the second.   The second arose next, and so on all in order, till at last
Dames himself stood up, who bore the weight of all the rest upon his
shoulders, unless they could relieve him, by bearing any part of their
weight against the wall.   By this time he that was uppermost could
make shift to reach the top of the wall.   They all said, ' O apostle of
God help us and deliver us !'   When he was got up, he found a watch-
man drunk and asleep.   He seized him hand and foot, and threw him
down among the Saracens, who immediately cut him to pieces.   Two
other watchmen, whom he found in the same condition, he stabbed
with his dagger, and threw down from the wall.   Then he let down his
turbant, and drew up the second ; they two the third, till at last they
drew up Dames too, who enjoined them silence, till he should bring
them further information.   He went and peeped in, where he found
Youkinna richly dressed, sitting upon a tapestry of scarlet silk flowered
with gold, and a large company with him eating and drinking, and very
merry.   He came and told his men, that he did not think it advisable
to fall upon them then, because of the great inequality of their numbers, but had rather take the advantage of them about break of day ;
at which time there was no fear but that there would come some help
from the army.   In the meantime he went alone, and privately stab-
bing the porters, and setting open the gates, came back to his men,
and bad them hasten to take possession of the gates.   This was not
done so secretly, but they were at last taken notice of, and the castle
alarmed.   There was no hopes of escaping, but everyone of them
expected to perish.   It was now towards morning ; Dames behaved
himself bravely, but overpowered with multitude, they were not able to
hold up, when Caled came to their relief.   As soon as the besieged
perceived the Saracens rushing in upon them, they threw down their
arms, and cried ' quarter !'   Abu Obeidah was not far behind with the
rest of the army.   Having taken the castle, and proposed Mahometanism to the Christians, the first that embraced it was Youkinna, and
some of the chief men with him, who immediately had their wives and

children, and all their wealth restored to them. Abu Obeidah set the old and impotent people at liberty, and having taken out a fifth part of the spoil of the castle (which was of great value), divided the rest among the Muslemans. Dames was talked of, and admired by all, and Abu Obeidah paid him the respect of making the army continue in that place, till he and his men were cured of their wounds.

Having taken the castle of Aleppo, he had thoughts of marching next to Antioch, then the seat of the Grecian Emperor. But Youkinna, the late Governor of the castle of Aleppo, with the changing of his religion, being become an utter enemy to the Christian interest, persuaded him to defer his march to Antioch, till they had first taken the castle of Aazaz, held by Theodorus his cousin-german ; a place of importance, and which, if not taken, would prove a great nuisance to the Saracens on that side of the country ; and proffered his service. The way that he proposed was to take with him 100 Saracens, dressed in Grecian habit, and with him to ride to Aazaz. These 100 were to be pursued at a little interval by 1,000 other Saracens in their proper habit. He said, ' That he did not at all question a kind reception at the hands of his kinsman Theodorus. Whom he was to tell that he had only feigned himself a Mahometan, till he could find an opportunity of escaping ; that he was pursued by the Saracens, &c. If they were received, of which there was no doubt, they would in the night fall upon the inhabitants ; and those other who pretended to pursue them, and should be ordered to stay at a village called Morah, not far 'distant from Aazaz, should come to their assistance.' Abu Obeidah asked Caled what he thought of it, who approved of the stratagem, provided they could be well assured of Youkinna's sincerity in the execution of it. Youkinna used a great many very earnest expressions to satisfy them of his integrity ; and after Abu Obeidah had, in a long discourse, set before him the danger of being treacherous on the one hand ; and on the other, the benefits that would accrue to him by faithfully serving the Saracens ; they resolved to venture him, and chose ten a piece out of ten several tribes of the Arabs ; each ten being commanded by a decurion, and all of them committed to Youkinna. When they were gone about a league, Abu Obeidah sent after them 1,000 men, under Malec Alashtari, with order to lie still by way of ambush, when they came near to Aazaz, till night. They found the village void of inhabitants, which the terror of the Saracens had scared further up into the country. Whilst Malec was at that village he intercepted a Christian Arab, who upon examination told him, ' That he and his men must look to themselves, for all their design was discovered : that there was a spy in the camp, who had heard all Youkinna's contrivance, and given the Governor of Aazaz secret intelligence of it, by a letter tied under the wing of a tame pigeon (a practice not uncommon in these parts). Upon which he (meaning himself) had been sent to Lucas, Governor of Arrawendan, to desire his assistance. That he was coming, and could not be far off with 500 horse. Youkinna in the meantime coming to Aazaz, found the town and castle in a posture of defence, and his cousin Theodorus, the Governor, at the head of 3,000 Greeks, and 10,000 Christian Arabs, besides others that came out of the villages. Theodorus made up to Youkinna, and alighting from his horse, made profound reverence, as if he would have kissed Youkinna's stirrup. In the meantime, he slily cut his girth, and with one push threw him flat on his face upon the ground. Then he and all his men were immediately taken prisoners. Theodorus spit in his face, and reproached him with his apostatizing from the Christian religion ; threatening death to all his Arabs, and to send him to answer for himself before his master the Grecian Emperor. All this while Theodorus knew nothing of Malec's being so near ; his spy having only informed him of Youkinna's intended treachery, and not one word of Malec's feigned pursuit. The prefect of Arrawendan came in the night, according as he had promised Theodorus, with his 500 men, and were all intercepted by Malec, who had two to their one. Having made prisoners of them, they disguised themselves in their cloaths, and took the Christian colours in their hands. Then Malec asked the spy to turn Mahometan, which he did. He had been one before at the same time when Jabalah Ebno'l Ayham made profession of that superstition ; but Jabalah thinking himself affronted by Omar, and revolting, those Christian Arabs that depended upon him, went off along with him ; among which number, this spy taken by Malec at Morah, was one. He told Malec, that he had heard that Mahomet had said, ' That whosoever changed his religion should be killed.' Malec said, ' It was true, but God had said, 'Illa man taba Waamana ; except he that repents and believes ;' adding, ' That the prophet himself had accepted of Wahshy's repentance, notwithstanding he had killed his uncle Hamzah.' Tharik Algassani (that was the spy's name) hearing this, repeated the ' La Ilaha, &c.,' and Malec said, ' May God accept thy repentance, and strengthen thy faith.' This done, he bad him go and tell the governor of Aazaz, that the Governor of Arrawendan was coming to his assistance ; which he undertook, and attended only by one companion, went till he came near the walls, where they heard a very great noise of shouting and trumpets, which was occasioned after this manner.

Theodorus, Governor of Aazaz, had a son, whose name was Leon ; whom he used to send, now and then for a month or two, to be with his uncle Youkinna at Aleppo castle. There he fell in love with his uncle's daughter, a very beautiful lady. Returning back, he acquaints his mother with his passion ; who, very tenderly, was willing to contribute anything that might be a means of procuring the proper remedy. His father Theodorus had put these prisoners, Youkinna and his 100 dignified Saracens into Leon's apartment. He, glad of this opportunity of ingratiating himself with his uncle, came and told him that he had a mind to release him and his friends. Youkínna told him that if he had any inclination to turn Mahometan, he ought not to do it upon any prospect of worldly advantage. To which the young villain, fired with lust, and resolved upon the match, answered, 'That his family and relations were dear to him ; but the faith was dearer.' In short, he set them all at liberty, gave them their arms, and bade them go in the name of God, whilst he went and killed his father, whom he was sure to find drunk and asleep. Immediately the Saracens, now enlarged, fell upon the Greeks, who made a stout resistance. During which time the spies went back to Malec, to acquaint him how things stood, who rode on a-pace, and came time enough to relieve their friends, and take the castle. They gave great thanks to Youkínna, who bade them 'thank God, and this young man ;' meaning his kinsman Leon, and told them all the story : to which Malec answered, 'When God will have a thing done, he prepares the causes of it.' Then he asked who killed Theodorus ? Leon answered, 'My elder brother Luke.' Malec wondered, and asked him how that came about, since such a thing was scarce ever heard of among the Greeks, that a child should murder his own father. Luke, it seems, told them, 'That it was out of love to them, their prophet and religion. That they had a priest who used to bring them up, who had told him long since of Mahomet ; and that the Saracens should most certainly conquer the country, and that they had several prophecies relating to it ;' and much to that purpose : 'Wherefore he was glad of this opportunity of becoming one of them ; and had designed to have set his uncle You-kinna and the prisoners at liberty, if his brother Leon had not prevented him.' Hopeful youths! who had prevented each other in a masterly piece of villany : the one in murdering his father; the other, in setting at liberty his most mortal enemies, and betraying all his friends! Malec gave him his blessing, and having set Said Ebn Amer over the Castle, with that 100 men that came along with Youkínna, marched with the spoils to Aleppo. There were in the castle of Aazaz, when the Muslemans took it, 1000 young men, Greeks, 245 old men and monks, 1000 young women and girls, and 180 old women.

Just as Malec was upon his march, the Saracens upon the castle wall gave such a shout, as alarmed all the rest, and gave them notice, that they saw a great dust not far off. When they came near, it appeared that they were only 1,000 Saracens, which Abu Obeidah had sent under the command of Alphadl Bno'l Abbás, to plunder round about Menbigz (formerly Heirapolis) and the adjacent villages, which they had done, and brought off the spoil. Malec and Alphadl marched together ; but Youkínna having had such bad success, could not be perswaded to go along with them, being resolved not to appear at the camp, nor show himself to the army, till he had by some signal service made amends for his miscarriage, and retrieved his credit; but chose rather to go to Antioch. And though Alphadl endeavoured to convince him that he was in no fault, neither ought to be concerned for it, and proved it by a text of the Alcoran ; yet he could not be satisfied nor reconciled to himself. Among Alphadl's men there were 200 Renegados, who had, as well as their master Youkínna, renounced their Christianity, and entered into the service of the Saracens, and had their families and effects in the castle of Aleppo : these seemed to him to be the most proper instruments to work withal. With these he marches towards Antioch. After the first watch of the night was past, he took four of his relations, and commanded the rest to keep the direct high road to Antioch, used by the caravans, and to pretend that they fled from before the Saracens ; telling them, 'That they should see him at Antioch, if it pleased God.' He, with his friends, going another way, was examined by some of the Emperor's men, who no sooner understood that he was the late governour of Aleppo, but they sent him with a guard of horse to Antioch. Heraclius wept at the sight of him, and told him, 'That he was informed he had changed his religion.' To which he answered, ' That what he had done was only in order to reserve himself for his majesty's further service : that he had taken this opportunity of flying to him from Aazâz : that the vigorous defence he had made at Aleppo, was a sufficient testimony of his zeal for his religion and his fidelity to his majesty.' The Emperor received the apostate with great tenderness and respect, and the greatest part of the court were inclined to entertain a charitable opinion of him. Nay, so favourably did the Emperor judge of him, that he not only made him commander over those 200 which belonged to him, when they came to Antioch ; but when his youngest daughter, who was then in another place, had sent to her father, the Emperor, for a guard to conduct her safe to Antioch, Youkínna was entrusted with this charge, and had under him for this purpose 2,200 men. Whilst they were upon this expedition, as he was in his return, about midnight, the Greek horses pricked up their ears, and began to neigh, and some of his advanced guards brought him intelligence of a party of Saracens in a very negligent posture, most of them being asleep, and their horses feeding. Youkínna seemingly encouraged his men ; but, that he might do the Saracens what secret service he could, commanded them not to kill, but to take them prisoners, that they might afterwards serve to exchange for the Christians. When they came a little nearer, they found themselves mistaken ; for those which they took to be Mahometans, proved to be 1,000 Christian Arabs, under the command of Haim, son of Jabalah Ebno'l Ayham, who had surprised Derar, and taken him prisoner, and with him 200 Saracens, sent out by Abu Obeidah, to forage in the northern parts of Syria. Upon which Youkínna alights from his horse, and pays his respects to Haim, hypocritically congratulating his good success. Abu Obeidah now resolved, pursuant to the Caliph's command, to march without delay to Antioch. The Emperor in the mean time was acquainted with the approach of his daughter, and Haim's good success, which caused great rejoicing in Antioch. The prisoners were brought into the Emperor's presence, and being commanded to fall down in a posture of adoration, they took no notice of those that spoke to them, nor looking that way, nor made any answer. At last, being urged to it, Derar answered, 'That they did not think adoration was due to any creature; besides our prophet has forbidden us to pay it.' The Emperor asked several questions concerning their prophet, and they beckoned to Kais Ebn Amer, an old man, and thoroughly acquainted with those matters, to answer him. Among other questions, the Emperor asked him, after what manner inspiration used to come upon their prophet, at his first setting forth? Kais told him that Mahomet himself having been formerly asked that question by an inhabitant of Meccah. answered, 'That sometimes it used to be like the sound of a bell, but stronger and sharper; sometimes an angel appeared to me in human shape, and discoursed with me, and I committed to memory what he said. Ayesha said, that once the spirit of prophecy descended upon him on a very cold day, and when it was gone off from him, his forehead ran down with sweat. The first message he received was in a dream; and whenever he saw a vision, it appeared to him like the breaking forth of the morning brightness. Then he shut himself up in a close place alone, where he continued till the TRUTH came to him. An angel came to him, being thus shut up, and said, " Read." To which he answered, " I cannot read." Then the angel repeated it, and having instructed him in things to come, sent him forth, and said to him, " Read in the name of the Lord who created,"* &c. With which the apostle of God (Mahomet) returned to his place, with his flesh trembling. Then he went into the house to Chadijah, and said, " Zammilouni, Zammilouni, wrap me up, wrap me up."' Upon which they wrapped him up in blankets, till he came to himself, and his fear was gone off: after which he gave an account of the whole matter to Chadijah, after this manner.

'As I was walking' (said he), 'I heard a voice from heaven; and lifting up my eyes, I saw the same angel which came to me before, sitting upon a throne between heaven and earth. Being afraid of him, I went home, and said, " Zammilouni, Datthirouhi, wrap me up in blankets and matts." And at that time God sent down to me that chapter which begins with these words, " O thou that art wrapped in blankets :"† and part of that which begins with these words, " O thou that art wrapped in matts," to these words, " And flee from the punishment ;"‡ which is the fifth verse of that chapter.'

---

* *Alcoran, chap. xcvi. ver.* 1. According to the order of the copies now in use; though the Mahometans take it for the first chapter of the whole *Alcoran.*
  † *LXIII. of the Alcoran.*   ‡ *Chap. lxxiv.*

The Byzantine historians, and those other writers who have followed them blindfold in their account of Mahomet, will needs have it, that Mahomet was troubled with the falling sickness : and Hottinger (*Historia Orientalis, lib. i. cap. ii. p.* 10, 11) takes his being wrapped up in matts and blankets for an undeniable proof of it.   As for the Byzantines, their authority in this matter is of no great weight, especially considering they always make it their business to represent Mahomet as full of all manner of imperfections, both of body and mind as possible ; as if the Christian religion was best served by perverting of history.   As to his being wrapped up in blankets, there might be many occasions of that besides the falling sickness ; and his being troubled with that disease having no foundation in any Arabick historian, it ought, till it be better made appear, to be rejected among the rest of those idle stories which have been so frequently told of Mahomet by the Christians.

To return to our history.   The Emperor afterwards asked him what he had seen of Mahomet's miracles.   Kais told him, that being once upon a journey with him, there came an Arabian up to them, whom Mahomet asked if he would testify that there was but one God, and that he was his prophet.   The Arabian asked him what witness he had that what he said was true?   To which Mahomet answered, 'This tree :' and calling the tree to him, it came upright, plowing the ground up with its roots.   Mahomet bad it bear witness : which it did; saying three times, 'Thou art the apostle of God.'   After which it returned, and stood in its place as before.   Heraclius said he had heard that it was a part of their religion to believe that if any of them did any good, it should be returned to them ten-fold : if evil, only once.   Kais told him that it was true, and quoted this text out of the *Alcoran* (*chap. vi.* 161 ; *xl.* 43) ; 'He that does good shall receive ten times so much ; but he that does evil, shall receive only so much.'   The Emperor asked him if their prophet was not called the witness.   To which Kais answered 'That he was the witness in this world, and the witness against men in the world to come,' because God says, 'O prophet ! we have sent thee a witness, and a preacher of good news, and a warner.'*   The Emperor asked him concerning Mahomet's night's journey to heaven, and his discoursing there with the most High : which Kais affirmed to be true, and proved it from the first verse of the seventeenth chapter of the *Alcoran.*   Then the Emperor asked him concerning their fasting in the month Ramadan ; in which Mahomet affirmed that the *Alcoran* came down from heaven ; which Kais acknowledged.   A bishop who was present at this conference, speaking something to the disparagement of Mahomet, provoked Derar Ebnol Azwâr (one of the prisoners) to such a degree, that he gave him the lye, and reviled him in a most reproachful language, affirming that Mahomet was a prophet,

* *Chap. xlviii.* 8, *and xxxiii.* 44.

but the veil of infidelity hindered them from the knowledge of him. Upon which some of the Christians drew their swords, to chastize his insolence : but it seems he had a most wonderful deliverance ; for though they struck at him fourteen times, he escaped safe. However, if Youkínna had not interceded for a reprieve till the next day, he would certainly have been executed by the Emperor's command.

In the meantime Abu Obeidah proceeded in his march, receiving by surrender those places which remained, till he came to that bridge which they called the iron bridge, very near Antioch. The emperor commits the gate of the army, and the city to Youkínna, and delivered to him a crucifix out of the church, which was never shown publicly, but upon extraordinary occasions. Then he called for the prisoners. But Youkinna told him that it would be the best way to spare them, because if any of the Christians should be taken, they might be exchanged : upon this suggestion their execution was deferred, and by the advice of the bishops, they were carried into the great church, to see if any of them would embrace the Christian religion, and be baptised. Amer, the son of Rephâa, turned ; but our author will needs have it, that it was the dress and beauty of the Grecian ladies influenced the young man more than any conviction of conscience. When his father Rephâa heard of it, he broke out into this passionate exclamation : ' What ! turn infidel after having embraced the faith ! Alas for thee ! Thou art driven from the gate of the most merciful. Alas for thee ! thou hast denied the king, the judge. Alas for thee, thou reprobate ! How hast thou denied the Lord of might and perfect power ? I swear by God, that I weep not for thee, because I must part with thee in this world, but because I must part with thee in the next ; when thou must go one way, and I another. When thou shalt go to the habitation of devils, and be placed with those priests and deacons in the (Arab. *Sadisati*, i.e., The Sixth) lowest mansion of hell, I shall go with the followers of Mahomet (upon whom be the blessing of God), to meet those spirits which converse with him. O son ! choose not the delights of this present world before that to come. Oh ! how shall I be astonished and confounded for this that thou hast done, when thou comest to stand in the presence of the Lord of all power and might, the king of this world and that to come ? And how shall I be ashamed before Mahomet, the elect prophet of God ? O son ! from whom wilt thou seek intercession another day.'* The young man was baptised, and received with great courtesy both by the emperor and the bishops. The emperor gave him a horse, and a young woman, and listed him into Jabalah Ebno'l Ayham's army, consisting of Christian Arabs. The patriarch asked the rest, what hindered them from turning Christians too. To which they answered, ' The truth of our

* Arab. *Gadan*, i.e., to-morrow. It is used to express future time ; and signifies in this place the day of judgment.

18

religion.' The patriarch represented to them the danger they incurred by displeasing Jesus Christ. To which Rephâa replied, ' That it would one day be determined which party was rejected, and which in the favour of God.' Heraclius told them that he had been informed that their Caliph used to wear very mean apparel ; adding, that he had gotten enough from the Christians to afford himself a better dress, and asked what should hinder him from going like other princes. Rephâa told him, ' That the consideration of the other world, and the fear of God hindered him.' To the other questions proposed by the emperor, they answered in a cant so very much like what our ears have for some late years been used to, that were it not for the difference of the language, we might justly have suspected them to have been nearer neighbours. The emperor asked them, ' what sort of a palace their Caliph had ?' They said it was made of mud. ' And who,' said the emperor, ' are his attendants ?' ' The beggars and poor people.' ' What tapestry does he sit upon ?' ' Justice and uprightness.' ' And what is his throne ?' ' Abstinence and certain knowledge.' ' And what is his treasure ?' ' Trust in God.' ' And who are his guard ?' ' The stoutest of the UNITARIANS.' They added, ' Dost thou not know, O king ! that several have said unto him, O Omar ! Lo, thou possessest the treasures of the Cæsars; and kings and great men are subdued unto thee; now therefore why puttest thou not on rich garments ?' He said unto them, ' Ye seek the outward world, but I seek the favour of him that is Lord both of this world, and that to come.'

The emperor having discoursed with them as long as he thought fit, remanded them to prison, and went to take a view of his army, which he found drawn up without the city in very good order. At the head of every regiment there was a little church made of wood, for the soldiers to go to prayers in. On a sudden, he was informed that the Arabs were masters of the iron bridge. He was very much surprised to hear that they had taken two towers, in which there were no fewer than 300 officers, in so short a time ; but it seems they were betrayed : which was occasioned thus ; a great officer at court used to go every day to see that these towers were well guarded, and not neglected. One day he found those whose business it was to take care of these towers, drinking and revelling, and nobody upon duty. Provoked with this intolerable negligence, he ordered them fifty lashes a-piece. This severe discipline made them study revenge ; and accordingly, when Abu Obeidah and his army drew near, they made articles for themselves, and delivered the towers into the hands of the Saracens.

The emperor having now no hopes left, assembled the bishops and great men together in the great church, and there bewailed the unhappy fate of Syria. Jabalah told him that if the Caliph was killed, the affairs of the Saracens would be embroiled, and it would be of great moment towards the recovery of what he had lost. Having obtained leave, he sent one of his Christian Arabs, whose name was Wathek Ebn Mosápher, a resolute young man, with orders to take a convenient opportunity of killing the Caliph. Omar, after prayers, went out of the city to take a walk, according to his custom. Wathek went before him, and got upon a tree, where he sat privately, till at last he observed Omar lie down to sleep very near him. Having this fair opportunity, he drew his dagger, and was just coming down, when, casting his eyes about, he saw a lion walking round about Omar, and licking his feet; who guarded him till he awoke, and then went away. Surprised at this, and struck with a profound reverence for the Caliph, whom he now looked upon as the peculiar care of Heaven, he came down and kissed his hand, and having told him his errand, made profession of the Mahometan religion immediately, being strangely affected with this wonderful deliverance.

In the meantime the armies before Antioch drew near to battle, and the Christian general's name was Nestorius. He went out first and challenged any Saracen to single combat. Dames answered him; but in the engagement, his horse stumbling, he was seized before he could recover himself, and being taken prisoner, was conveyed to Nestorius his tent, and there bound. Nestorius returning to the army, and offering himself a second time, was answered by one Dehâc. The combatants behaved themselves bravely, and the victory was doubtful, which made all the soldiers desirous of being spectators. The justling and thronging both of horse and foot to see this engagement, threw down Nestorius his tent and chair of state. He had three servants left in the tent, who fearing they should be beaten when their master came back, and having nobody else to help them, told Dames, that if he would lend them an hand to set up the tent, and put things in order, they would unbind him, upon condition that he should voluntarily return to his bonds again, till their master came home, at which time they promised to speak a good word for him. He readily accepted the terms; but as soon as he was at liberty, he immediately seized two of them, one in his right hand, the other in his left, and dashed their two heads so violently against the third man's, that they all three fell down dead upon the place. Then he opened a chest, and took out a good suit of clothes, and mounting a good horse of Nestorius's, he wrapped up his face as well as he could, and made towards the Christian Arabs, where Jabalah, with the chief of his tribe, stood on the left hand of Heraclius. In the meantime, Dehâc and Nestorius, being equally matched, continued fighting, till both their horses were quite tired out, and they were obliged to part by consent, to rest themselves. Nestorius returning to his tent, and finding things in such a posture, easily guessed that it must be Dames his doing. The news flew instantly through all the army, and every one was surprised at the strangeness of the action. Dames, in the meantime, had gotten among the Christian Arabs, and striking off at one blow a man's head that stood next him, made a speedy escape to the Saracen army.

All this while Youkínna was contriving which way to do the Saracens service; and when Derar and his companions had been prisoners eight months, and were just about being beheaded, he interceded with the Emperor to spare them; assuring him that if he put them to death, the Saracens would never more give quarter to any Christian, when ever any of them should fall into their hands. The Emperor, not suspecting any treachery, committed them to his care; who, watching a convenient opportunity, set them at liberty, and gave them their arms, assuring them that there were a great many persons of the highest quality in the Emperor's service who were fully resolved to go over to the Saracens. The Emperor, disheartened with a constant course of ill-success, and terrified with a dream which he had of one thrusting him out of his throne, and his crown falling from his head, took some of his domesticks, and escaping privately to the sea shore, embarked for Constantinople.

Our author tells us a strange story of the Emperor's turning Mahometan, which was occasioned by a great pain in his head, for which he could get no help, till he applied himself to Omar, who sent him a cap, which, so long as he wore, he was well; but when he took it off, it returned again. The Emperor wondering at this strange effect, would have the cap ripped open; but found nothing in it but a little piece of paper, with Bismillah, Arrahmani 'rrahhími, ' In the name of the most merciful God,' written upon it. This cap, it seems, was possessed by the Christians till the reign of Almotàsem (which began in the year of our Lord 833), who, besieging Ammoytriyah, was grievously afflicted with the head-ach; upon which the governour of the town promised him the cap, upon condition that he should raise the siege. The Caliph, Almotásem, undertook it, provided the cap produced the desired effect, which it did incontinently, and the siege was accordingly raised. The same curiosity which moved the Emperor Heraclius to have the cap opened, made this Caliph do so too; but he found nothing in it but the above-mentioned scrip of paper, whose virtue was not in the least impaired or diminished in the space of two hundred years; which period of time would, in all probability, have made some alteration in an ordinary medicine. But the case is quite different here, for we have been told by other hands that the relicks of holy men are never the worse for wearing. What is it that men will not believe and write when once bigoted to superstition !

To return to the army. Antioch was not lost without a set battle; but through the treachery of Youkínna, and several other persons of note, together with the assistance of Derar and his company, who were mixt with Youkínna's men, the Christians were beaten entirely. The people of the town perceiving the battle lost, made agreement, and surrendered, paying down 300,000 ducats. Upon which Abu Obeidah entered into Antioch on Tuesday, being the 21st of August, A.D. 638.

Thus fell that ancient and famous city, the seat of so many kings and princes, into the hands of the infidels. The sweetness of the situation, and abundance of all things contributing to delight and luxury, was so great, that Abu Obeidah, fearing lest the Saracens, effeminated with the delicacies of that place, should remit any thing of their wonted vigour and bravery, durst not let them continue there long ; but after three days refreshment, withdrew them from thence.

Then he wrote a letter to the Caliph, in which he gave him an account of his great success in taking the metropolis of Syria, and Heraclius his flight to Constantinople ; telling him withal, what was the reason why he staid no longer there. He added, ' That the Saracens were desirous of marrying the Grecian women, which he had forbidden. That he was afraid lest the love of the things of this world should take possession of their hearts, and draw them off from their obedience to God. That he staid expecting further orders,' &c.

Having written this letter, he asked who would carry it. Zeid Ebn Waheb, who was Omar Ebn Auf's slave, proffered his service. Abu Obeidah told him, that since he was a slave, he could not in any case dispose of his service, but must first ask his master's leave. Zeid hereupon went to his master, and bowed himself down to the ground, to touch it with his forehead, according to the manner of prostration in the Eastern countries : but his master forbad him, being a man altogether abstracted from the love of the things of this world, and not desiring any such respect, being wholly intent and fixed upon the other world. He was abstinent to such a degree, that his whole inventory consisted in these few necessaries ; a sword, a launce, a horse, a camel, a knapsack, a platter, and an Alcoran. When any part of the spoil fell to his share, he never laid up any thing for himself, but always divided it amongst his friends ; and if there was any thing left, he sent it to the Caliph, to be distributed among the poor. Zeid having asked his leave to carry the letter, he was so well pleased to see such a good inclination in his slave, to be a messenger of good news to the Caliph, that he immediately gave him his freedom. When Zeid came near to Medinah, he was surprised with an unusual noise ; but upon enquiry, he was informed that the Caliph was going on pilgrimage to Meccah, and the prophet's wives along with him. Omar, having heard the news, fell down and worshipped, saying, ' O God ! praise and thanks be to thee, for thine abundant grace.' Having read the letter, he wept, and said that Abu Obeidah had not been kind to the Muslemans. Then sitting down upon the ground, he wrote an answer to Abu Obeidah, in which, after having expressed with what satisfaction he received the news of his good success ; he blamed him for not having been more indulgent to the Muslemans ; adding, ' That God did not forbid the use of the good things of this life to faithful men, and such as performed good works : wherefore he ought to have given them leave to rest themselves, and partake freely of those good things which the country afforded. That if any of the Saracens had no family in Arabia, they might marry in Syria ; and whosoever of them wanted any female slaves might purchase as many as he had occasion for.' He ordered him to pursue the enemy, and enter into the mountainous part of the country ; and then concluded.

Zeid returning to the army with the Caliph's letter, found the Saracens full of joy ; occasioned by Caled's good success, who had gone through the country as far as the Euphrates, and taken Menbigz, and some other neighbouring towns, as Berâa and Báles, upon surrender ; the inhabitants paying down 100,000 ducats for their present security, and submitting to tribute for the time to come. This was done in January, A.D. 638.

Abu Obeidah having received the Caliph's letter, asked the Muslemans which of them would undertake to make an attempt upon the mountainous part of the country. Whether the difficulty of the service, or what other reason discouraged them, is uncertain ; but no body answered him the two first times. At last Méisarah Ebn Mesroùk proffered his service, and received at the hands of the general a black flag, with his inscription upon it in white letters, ' THERE IS BUT ONE GOD : MAHOMET IS THE APOSTLE OF GOD.' He took along with him 300 chosen Arabs, besides 1,000 slaves, blacks, commanded by Dames. They found it a very uneasy undertaking ; for though the summer came on a-pace, they were forced to make use of all the cloaths they had, and knew very well what to have done with more ; for they met with nothing but frost and snow amongst the mountains ; which was extreamly disagreeable to their bodies, who had been brought up under the Torrid Zone. Marching a long way, they came to a village ; but finding nobody in it (for the country fled before them) they took what there was, and moved forwards. At last they took a prisoner, who informed them that there were forces of the Emperor, to the number of 30,000, sent to guard that part of the country, not above 3 leagues distant. They asked him whether it was most advisable to advance towards them, or stand their ground. To which he answered, ' That it were better for them to stay where they were, than to hazard themselves by going any further among the mountains.' The Saracens having examined him as long as they thought fit, offered him the Mahometan religion ; which he refusing, was beheaded. In a short time after, the Greeks came within sight, and the battle was joined. Méisarah, overpowered with multitudes, was soon surrounded. However, he sent a messenger to Abu Obeidah, who made such haste, that as soon as he came into his presence, he was not able to speak a word, but fell down in a swoon. Abu Obeidah having caused some water to be sprinkled on his face, and refreshed him with meat and drink, he came to himself, and delivered his errand.   Upon which Abu Obeidah sent Caled to Méisarah's assistance with 3,000 horse ; and after him Ayâd Ebn Ganam with 2,000 more. But before they came up, Abdollâh Ebn Hodâpha, a Saracen of note, and much beloved by the Caliph, was taken prisoner, and sent towards Constantinople.   The Greeks perceiving there were fresh supplies come to the Saracens, durst not run the hazard of another battle the next day, but withdrew in the night, and left their tents to the Saracens.   They not thinking it a prudent part to pursue the enemy any further in that mountainous country, returned to Abu Obeidah, who, writing an account of the whole business to Medinah, the Caliph was extremely concerned at the loss of Abdollah Ebn Hodapha, which occasioned his writing the following letter to the Emperor Heraclius :—

     ' In the name of the most merciful God.

    ' Praise be to God, (*Alcoran, chap. i.* 1.) Lord of this and the other
' world (*chap. lxxii.* 3.) : who has neither (*Arab. Sahhibah*) female-
' consort, nor son.   And the blessing of God be upon Mahomet,
' his prophet and apostle (*Arab. Almowayad*) divinely assisted.   From
' the servant of God, Omar Ebn Alchitab to Heraclius king of Greece.
' As soon as this letter of mine shall come to thy hands, send to me the
' prisoner that is with thee ; whose name is Abhollâh Ebn Hodapha :
' Which if thou shalt do, I shall hope that God will direct thee into
' the right way.*   But if thou refusest, I shall send thee men, (*Chap.*
' *xxiv.* 37, *lxiii.* 9,) whom trade and merchandize shall not divert from
' the remembrance of God.   (*Chap. xx.* 49.)   Health and happiness
' be upon every one that follows the right way.'

    I do not question but the reader will think this letter writ in a very particular style ; but it is no other than what might be expected from those most inveterate and mortal enemies of Christianity, who made it always their business to treat the professors of it with the utmost contempt and aversion.   This prisoner, Abdollah Ebn Hodapha was Mahomet's cousin-german.   Our author tells us, that the Emperor made him very large proffers, if he would have renounced his Mahometanism ; but all in vain.   Nor were his threats more influencing than his promises.   It seems he proffered him his liberty, if he would but have made one single adoration before a crucifix.   The Emperor would have perswaded him to have drunk wine, and eat hogs flesh ; which he refusing, was shut up into a room where he had nothing else. Upon the fourth day they visited him, and found all untouched.   The Emperor asked him what hindered him from eating and drinking? to which he answered, ' The fear of God and his apostle : notwithstanding (added he) I might lawfully have eat it after three days abstinence, yet I abstained, because I would not be reproached by

---

* That is, into the profession of the Mahometan religion.

the Muslemans.' Heraclius having received Omar's letter, not only dismissed the prisoner, but gave both him and the messenger that brought the letter, several presents, and rich cloaths, and allowed them a sufficient guard to conduct them safe through his territories. Besides all this, he made a present of a costly jewel to Omar, who offered it to the jewellers of Medinah ; but they were ignorant of the worth of it. The Muslemans would have perswaded him to have kept it for his own use ; but he said, he could not answer that to the publick. Wherefore it was afterwards sold, and the price of it put into the public treasury ; of which the Caliph was in these days only the steward or manager : for though it was all at his disposal, yet he very seldom applyed any of it to his own private use, much less to extravagance and luxury ; but took care to lay it out so as it might do most service to the publick.

We have before acquainted the reader, that after Omar had taken Jerusalem, he divided the army, and sent one part of it under Abu Obeidah, towards Aleppo ; the other under Amrou Edno'l Aás to Ægypt. Amrou did not march directly to Ægypt, but continued a while in Palestine, to take some places there which as yet held out. As he was marching towards Cæsarea, the Saracens found the weather extreamly cold. Sobeih Ebn Hamzah, eating some grapes at that time was so chilled that he was scarcely able to endure it. An old Christian that was present, told him, that if he found himself cold with eating the grapes, the best remedy would be to drink some of the juice of them, and withal produced a large vessel of wine. Sobeih and some of his friends took the old man's advice, and drank so freely of his liquor, that they went staggering to the army. Amrou understanding their condition, wrote to Abu Obeidah ; by whose order they all received a sufficient number of stripes upon soles of their feet. The refreshment they received by drinking the wine, was so far, in their opinion, from counter-balancing the severity of the punishment, that Sobeih swore he would kill the fellow that helped him to it ; and had been as good as his word, if one that was present had not told him, that the man was under protection of the Saracens.

Constantine, the Emperor Heraclius his son, guarded that part of the country where Amrou lay, with a considerable army ; and frequently sent spies (Christian Arabs) into his camp. One of them went one time, and sat down amongst some Arabs of Ayáman, or Arabia Fælix, that had made them a fire. Having conversed with them as long as was for his purpose, without being suspected ; as he was rising to go away, he trod upon his vest and stumbled ; upon which he swore, by Christ, unawares. The oath was no sooner out of his mouth, but they immediately knew him to be a Christian spy, and cut him to pieces in an instant. Amrou was angry when he heard it, because he would have had the examining him first. Besides, he told them, ' That it oftentimes happened, that a spy, when put to it, came over to them, and embraced the Mahometan religion.' Upon which he gave a strict order throughout the camp, that if ever they met with a stranger or spy, they should convey them to him.

The armies drawing near, there came a Christian priest to the Saracens, who desired that an Emîr, or principal officer, might be sent to Constantine, to discourse with him. There was a huge, monstrous fellow, a black, whose name was Belâl Ebn Rébah, who proffered his service. But Amrou told him that it would be better to send an Arabian, who could talk more politely than an Æthiopian. Belâl, resolving, if possible, to take no denial, adjured him by God to let him go. To which Amrou answered, ' That since he had adjured him by the most mighty, it should be so.' This Belâl had formerly been Mahomet's crier ; that is, the person that calls the people together to prayers. And never exercised that office (as the author of the history of Jerusalem says) (*MS. Arab. Pococ. Num.* 362) after Mahomet's death, but only once, when Omar commanded him to perform that service at the taking of Jerusalem : otherwise, I suppose it would have been beneath him to have served any other person, who had been employed after that manner by the prophet ; but the taking of Jerusalem, which had been the seat of the ancient prophets, and was a place very much reverenced by the Mahometans, was an extraordinary occasion. (*Alwâkídi.*) When he came to the priest, he disdained to have an Æthiopian sent, and bad him go back again, telling him, that his master Constantine had not sent for a slave, but an officer. Belâl, who valued himself very much upon his office, and expected every one should do so too, thought himself affronted ; and let him know, that he had been no less a person than the Muézzin of the apostle of God, and that he was able to give his master an answer. But this not being received, he was forced to go back again ; and at last Amrou resolved to go himself. It will not be amiss to insert a short account of their conference, as delivered by our author, that the reader may see what sort of a notion the Mahometans have of ancient history.

When Amrou came into Constantine's presence, he offered him a seat, but according to the practice of the Saracens, he refused to make use of it, choosing rather to sit cross-legged upon the ground, with his sword upon his thigh, and his lance laid across before him. Constantine told him, 'that the Arabs and Greeks were near kindred, and that it was a pity they should make war one upon the other.' Amrou answered, ' That their religion was different ; upon which score it was lawful for brothers to quarrel. However,' he said, ' he desired to know which way the Koreishæ* came to be so near akin to the Greeks ?' Constantine answered (according to our author) ' Was not our first father Adam,

---

* A noble tribe among the Arabs, of which Mahomet was.

then Noah, then Abraham, then Esau, then Isaac, which were both
sons of Abraham (the blessing of God be upon them all).* Now one
brother ought not to do injustice to another, and quarrel about that division which was made for them by their forefathers.' 'Thus far you
say true,' answered Amrou, 'That †Esau begot Isaac, and Ishmael is
Esau's uncle ; and so are we the sons of one father, and Noah was our
Father. Now Noah divided the land into parts when he was angry
with his son Ham ; with which division they were not pleased, but
quarrelled about it ; and this land in which you are, is not yours properly, but belongs to the Amalekites, who had it before you. For Noah
divided it among his three sons, Sem, Ham, and Japhet ; and gave
his son Sem, Syria, and what lies round it, from Arabia Fælix and
Hadramut to Amman ; and all the Arabs are the offspring of Sem
and Kahtan, and Tesm, and Jodais, and Amalek, who is the father of the
Amalekites. To his son Ham he gave the west and sea-shore ; and he
left Japhet between the east and west ;‡ for the earth is the Lord's,
he gives it an inheritance to which of his servants he pleases, and the
latter end is to the faithful. We therefore,' adds Amrou, 'desire to
have this ancient division restored, and make things equal after this
manner. We will take what is in your hands, and you shall take the
stones and thorns, and barren grounds which we possess, in lieu of
these pleasant rivers, rich pastures, and stately buildings.' Constantine told him, 'That the division was already made, and that it would
be great injustice in them not to be content with what had fallen to
their share.' To which Amrou answered, 'That they liked the provision and manner of living in Syria, so much better than their own
coarse fare at home, that they could never think of leaving the country till they had conquered it, and could sit down at quiet under those
shady trees.' A little while after, he told those that were present,
'That it would be no hard matter for them to continue in the possession of what they had ; for it was only changing their religion, and the
business was done.' But both that and payment of tribute being refused, Amrou told them, 'That there was nothing now left, but to determine it by the sword. God knows,' said he, 'that I have called you to
the means by which you might save yourselves, but you are rebellious,
just as your father Esau§ was disobedient to his mother ; you reckon
yourselves akin to us, but we desire to have nothing to do with your
affinity, so long as you continue infidels. You besides, are the offspring

---

* This is an expression used by the Arab writers, whenever they mention any of the
ancient prophets.
† He makes strange work of this genealogy ; but the Arabick may be read, Esau Walado
Ishàc ; i. e. Esau is the son of Isaac ; not wàlada, begot Isaac. But if, to help him out, we
should read it so, we contradict him, for just before he reckons Esau before Isaac.
‡ Chap. vii., 125.
§ This the Mahometans have from the Jews, who believe most Europeans to be the offspring of Esau. Abarbanel takes a great deal of pains to prove it, and those Jews I have
conversed with are of the same opinion.

of Esau, we of Ishmael ;* and God chose our prophet Mahomet from Adam, to the time that he came out of the loins of his father ; and made him the best of the sons of Ishmael (and his father Ishmael was the first that spoke Arabick), and he made the tribe of Kenanah the best of the Arabs ; and the family of Korcishæ the best of Kenanah ; and the offspring of Hashem, the best of the Koreishæ ; and the best of the sons of Hashem, Abdo'lmutaleb the prophet's grandfather ; and sent the angel Gabriel down to him (Mahomet) with inspiration.'

The conference ending without any hopes of accommodation, Amrou returned to his army, and both sides prepared for battle, as soon as a convenient opportunity should offer itself. One day there came forth out of Constantine's army, an officer very richly dressed, which made several of the Saracens desirous of fighting with him in hopes of carrying off his spoil. Amrou used to say, ' That he would have no man go to fight out of greediness ; for the reward which was to be expected from God, was much better than the spoil of the enemy.' He added, ' That whosoever was killed in battle, lost his life either for the sake of God or else for some other end which he proposed to himself. If the former, then God would be his reward, but if he proposed any temporal thing, he was to expect nothing else, and that he had heard the prophet speak to the same purpose.' There came forth to this officer a beardless stripling, whose forward zeal had prompted him on to leave Arabia Fælix, and venture himself in the wars. His mother and sister had hitherto bore him company in his travels. This youth used to say, ' That it was not the delights of Syria, that moved him to go thither (because the delights of this world were fading, but those of the other durable). But that his desire was to fight for the service of God, seeking the favour of God and his apostle. Because he had heard one say, " That the martyrs shall be maintained with their Lord." ' ' How can that be,' answered his sister, ' how can they be maintained when dead?' He answered, ' That he had heard one that was acquainted with the apostle of God, say, " That the spirits of the martyrs shall be put into the crops of green birds that live in Paradise, which birds shall eat the fruits of Paradise, and drink the rivers ; this is the maintenance which God has provided for them.' He went out to fight with the Christian, after he had taken his last leave of his mother and sister, and told them, ' that they should meet again at that (*Hbaud*) large water which belongs to the apostle of God in Paradise.' The Christian officer not only killed this youth, but two or three more. At last Serjabil Ebn Hasanah came forth to him ; but he was so emaciated with watching

---

* Amongst other blind stories which some of the Christian writers have told of the Saracens, that is one, viz., that they called themselves Saracens, because they would have the world believe that they were descended from Sarah, Abraham's lawful wife ; being ashamed of Hagar his slave. But the contrary is most evident, for they are neither ashamed of Ishmael nor Hagar ; as for Ishmael we have an instance in this very place ; and for Hagar, the reader may consult the Jaubarian (a famous Arab Lexicographer), who in the word Agara, says Hagar is the mother of Ishmael, upon whom be peace.

and fasting, that he was unable to stand before him.   The Christian at last got him down, sat upon him, and was just going to cut his throat ; when on a sudden there came a horseman out of the Grecian army, who immediately kicked the Christian off, and taking him at advantage, struck his head off.   Serjabil, surprised at this unexpected deliverance, asked him who he was, and from whence he came ?   'I am,' said he, 'the unhappy Tuléiha Ebn Cowailed, who pretended to prophecy like the apostle of God ; and lyed against God saying, " That inspiration came down to me from heaven." '   Serjabil answered, 'O brother ! God's mercy is infinite ; and he that repents, and forsakes, and turns himself to God ; he accepts of his repentance, and forgives him what he has done ; for the prophet says, " Repentance takes away what was done before it."   And dost thou not know, O Ebn Cowailed, that God said to our prophet, " My mercy is extended to every creature that desires it ?" '   adding moreover whatever he could to comfort him.   Notwithstanding which, conscious to himself of the grossness of his crime, he could not find in his heart to return to the Saracens ; but being very much pressed to it by Serjabil, he at last told him in plain terms, that he was afraid of Caled (the scourge of false prophets, who broke them to pieces at first, and killed Moseilamah, the chief of them).   Serjabil assured him, that Caled was not present, but staid at Aleppo with Abu Obeidah.   At last, with much ado, he perswaded him to go with him to the army.   This Tuléiha, after Moseilamah was killed, withdrew himself out of Arabia, which would then have been soon too hot for him, and went and lived privately with a Mahometan in Syria, who maintained him for a while ; till at last they became very familiar, and thoroughly acquainted, Tuléiha made himself known, and gave him an account of his whole story.   His landlord, as soon as he understood his character, treated him with the utmost aversion, and would entertain him no longer, but turned him out of doors.   Reduced to this extremity, he was almost at his wits end, and had some thoughts of taking ship, and retiring into some island ; but Constantine's army coming into those parts before he could put his design into execution, he chose rather to list himself under him, in hopes of finding an opportunity of ingratiating himself with the Muslemans.

Being at last prevailed upon to go back to the Saracens, he was very courteously received by Amrou ; who not only gave him thanks for his singular service, but upon his expressing his apprehensions of Caled, promised to secure him, and wrote a recommendatory letter to Omar, acquainted him with the signal proof which Tuléiha had given of his sincere and unfeigned repentance.   Tuléiha found the Caliph at Meccah: delivering the letter, and withal telling him that he repented, Omar asked who he was ? and had no sooner heard his name mentioned, but he made off as fast as he could, saying, ' Alas for thee ! If I forgive thee, how shall I give an account to God of the murder of

Ocasah?' Tuléiha answered, ' Ocasah, indeed, suffered martyrdom by my hands, which I am very sorry for, and I hope that God will forgive me what I have done.' Omar desired to know what proof he could give of his sincerity ; but having perused Amrou's letter, he was abundantly satisfied, and kept him with him till he returned to Medinah, after which he employed him in his wars against the Persians.

To return to Constantine's army. The weather was very cold, and the Christians were quite disheartened, having been frequently beaten and discouraged daily with the encreasing power of the Saracens ; so that a great many grew weary of the service, and withdrew themselves from the army. Constantine, having no hopes of the victory, and fearing lest the Saracens should seize Cæsarea, took an opportunity in a tempestuous night to move off ; and left his camp to the Saracens. Amrou acquainting Abu Obeidah with all that had happened, received express orders to march directly to Cæsarea, where he promised to join them speedily, in order to go against Tripoli, Accah and Tyre. In a little time after Tripoli was surprised by the treachery of Youkínna, who having gotten it on a sudden, and without any noise, there came thither a little while after, about fifty ships with provision and arms for Cyprus and Crete, which were to go to Constantine. The officers not knowing that Tripoli was fallen into the hands of new masters, made no scruple of landing there, where they were courteously received by Youkínna, who proffered the utmost of his service, and promised to go along with them. But immediately seized both them and their ships, and delivered the town into the hands of Caled, who was just come.

With these ships the traitor Youkínna goes to Tyre, where he tells the inhabitants that he had brought arms and provision for Constantine's army. Upon which he was kindly received, and he with 900 of his men landed, and were entertained. But being betrayed by one of his own men, he and his crew were seized and bound ; receiving all the while such treatment from the soldiers, as their villainous practices best deserved. In the meantime Yezid Ebn Abi Sophyan, being sent by Abu Obeidah from the siege of Cæsarea, came within sight of Tyre. The governor perceiving this, caused Youkínna and his men to be conveyed to the castle, and there secured. Having done this, he prepares for the defence of the town ; and perceiving that Yezid had but a small number (his army not exceeding 2000), he resolved to make a salley. In the meantime, the rest of the inhabitants ran up to the walls, to see the engagement. Whilst they were fighting, Youkínna and his men were set at liberty by one Basil, of whom they give the following account : viz., ' That this Basil going one day to pay a visit to Bohei- ' rah the monk, the caravan of the Koreishæ came by, with which ' were Cadijah's camels, which were looked after by Mahomet. He ' looked towards the caravan, in the middle of which was Mahomet, ' and there was a cloud upon him to keep him from the sun. Then

' the caravan alighted, and Mahomet, leaning against an old withered
' tree, it immediately brought forth leaves. Boheirah perceiving this,
' made an entertainment for the caravan, and invited them into the
' monastery; Mahomet staying behind with the camels. Boheirah
' missing him, asked if there were all of them? Yes, they said, all
' but a little boy they had left to look after their things, and feed the
' camels. "What is his name?" says Boheirah. They told him Ma-
' hommed Ebn Abdo'llah. Boheirah asked if his father and mother
' were not dead, and if he was not brought up by his grandfather and
' his uncle. Being satisfied that it was so, he said, "O Koreish! set
' a great value upon him, for he is your lord, and by him will your
' power be great both in this world, and that to come; for he is your
' ornament and glory." They asked him how he knew that? "Be-
' cause," answered Boheirah, "as you were coming, there was never a
' tree, nor stone, nor clod, but bowed itself and worshipped God."
' Boheirah besides told this Basil, that a great many prophets had
' leaned against this tree, and sat under it, but it never bore any leaves
' before, since it was withered. "And I heard him say," says this same
' Basil, "this is the prophet, concerning whom Isa (Jesus) spake,
' happy is he that believes in him, and follows him, and gives credit to
' his mission."' This Basil, after the visit to Boheirah, had gone to
Constantinople, and other parts of the Greek emperor's territories, and
upon information of the great success of the followers of this prophet,
was abundantly convinced of the truth of his mission. This inclined
him, having so fair an opportunity offered, to release Youkínna and his
men; who, sending word to the ships, the rest of their forces landed
and joined them. In the meantime, a messenger in disguise was sent
to acquaint Yezid with what was done. As soon as he returned, Youkínna was for falling upon the townsmen upon the wall; but Basil said,
' Perhaps God might lead some of them into the right way;' and persuaded him rather to place the men so, as their coming down from the
wall might be prevented. This done, they cry out, 'La Ilaha,' &c.
The people perceiving themselves betrayed, and the prisoners at liberty,
were in the utmost confusion; none of them being able to stir a step
or lift up an hand. Those in the camp hearing the noise in the city,
knew what was the occasion of it, and Youkínna opened the gates and
let them in. Those that were in the city, fled; some one way, and
some another; and were pursued by the Saracens, and put to the
sword. Those upon the wall cried, 'quarter;' Zeid told them, 'That
since they had not surrendered, but the city was taken by force, they
were all slaves.' 'However,' said he, 'we of our own accord set you
free, upon condition you pay tribute; and if any of you has a mind to
change his religion, he shall fare as well as we do.' The greatest part
of them turned Mahometans. When Constantine heard of the loss of
Tripoli and Tyre, his heart failed him, and, taking shipping with his

family and wealth, he departed for Constantinople. All this while Amrou Ebno'l Aâs lay before Cæsarea. In the morning, when the people came to enquire after Constantine, and could hear no tidings of him nor his family, they advised together, and with one consent surrendered the city to Amrou, paying down for their security 2000 pieces of silver, and delivering into his hands whatsoever belonged to Constantine, that he had not carried away with him. Thus was Cæsarea lost, A.D. 639, and the 5th of Omar's reign, or the 29th year of the reign of the emperor Heraclius. Upon which, those other places in Syria, which as yet held out—namely, Ramlah, Accah, Joppe, Ascalon, Gaza, Sichem (or Nabolos), and Tiberias surrendered ; and in a little time after, the people of Beirout, Zidon, Jabalah, and Laodicea, followed their example ; so that there remained nothing more to be done in Syria, but all was entirely subdued to the Saracens, who had not spent above six years (from the time of their first expedition in Abubeker's reign) in subduing that large, wealthy, and populous country.

THUS have I given the reader the best account I was able, of the Saracens' conquest of Syria ; following all along, as to matter of fact, my author Alwákidi, who has written the most particular relation of that part of the history that I have yet met with ; or that is extant, to the best of my knowledge. As for that little which remains, in order to the compleating the lives of this and the succeeding Caliph, since the short time of my continuance at Oxford would not permit me to search for, or excerp any more manuscripts, I must be content to depend upon those authors which have been already published ; as Eutychius, Elmakîn, and Abu'lpharagius ; in which, though not so large and particular an account as in the former part of our history ; yet the reader will find something which shall still contribute to the better knowledge of that people, and increase his admiration, at the wonderful success of the Saracen arms, by which they arrived at that stupendous greatness.

Syria, being conquered, remained not long in the possession of those persons who had the chief hand in subduing it ; for in the eighteenth year of the Hegirah, A.D. 639, there was such terrible mortality both of men and beasts, in Syria, particularly at Emáus, and the adjacent territory, that the Arabs called that year ' The year of destruction,' by way of distinction *(Amo'l remádah).* The Saracens lost by that plague 25,000 men ; among which were Abu Obeidah (who was then 58 years old) Serjabil Ebn Hasanah, formerly Mahomet's secretary, and Yezid Ebn Abi Sophyan, with several other Saracens of note. Caled* survived them about three years, and then died ; but the place of his burial (consequently of his death, for they did not use in those days to carry them far) is uncertain ; some say at Hems ; others at Medinah.

* Author of the History of Jerusalem, above cited.

Amrou Ebno'l Aâs, having stayed as long in Syria as was necessary, pursuant to the Caliph's command, prepared for his expedition into Ægypt. Whilst he was upon his march, whether it proceeded from envy, which always attends great men, or whether Othman Ebn Affâni did not think him so proper a person for such a service; certain it is, that Omar was perswaded by some that were about him, to recall him. That Omar himself entertained a good opinion of him, and that he wrote to him rather to gratify the importunate humour of his friends, than out of any dislike, seems plain from the contents of the letter. For whereas he could have commanded him positively to have returned, he writes only thus : ' If this letter comes to you before you get into Ægypt, return. But if you be entered into Ægypt, when the messenger comes to you, go on with the blessing of God, and assure yourself, that if you want any supplies, I will take care to send them.' The messenger overtook Amrou before he was out of Syria ; who either suspecting, or having received secret information of the business, ordered him to wait upon him, till he should be at leisure to read the letter. In the mean time he hastens his march, fully resolved not to open it till he came into the confines of Ægypt. When he came to a place called Arish, having assembled the officers in his tent, he called for the messenger, and opened the letter with the same gravity and formality as if he had been altogether ignorant of the contents of it. Having read it, he told the company what was in it, and enquired of them, whether the place they then were, belonged to Syria or Ægypt. They answered to Ægypt. Then said Amrou, we will go on. From thence he went to Phârmah ; which he took after a month's siege. From thence to Misrah, (formerly Memphis) now Cairo, situate on the western bank of the river Nilus, and which had been the seat of the ancient Ægyptian kings. This place the Greeks had fortified, as being the most considerable (except Alexandria) in all that kingdom. There was an ancient castle there, of great strength. The Greeks made a large moat or trench round about it, into which they threw great quantities of nails, and iron spikes, to make it more difficult for the Muslemans to pass. Amrou with 4000 men laid hard siege to it ; but when he had been there about seven months, and could do nothing, he was forced to send to the Caliph for fresh supplies ; who, as soon as might be, recruited him with 4000 more. The Præfect or lieutenant of Misrâh, that held it for the Emperor Heraclius, was one Mokaukas, of the sect of the Jacobites, and a mortal enemy to the Greeks. He had no design at all to serve the Emperor, but to provide for himself ; having behaved himself so ill, that he durst not come into the Emperor's presence. For when Cosroës, the Persian, had besieged Constantinople, Mokaukas perceiving the Emperor in distress, and daily expecting his ruin, thought he had a fair opportunity offered of making his fortune, and took all the tribute of Ægypt into his own hand, without giving account to the Emperor of one penny. From that time, being conscious to himself of his deserts, he used all the means he could to prejudice and hinder the Emperor; so natural is it for men to hate those whom they have injured. I shall not interrupt the smooth course of history with examining how far this account agrees with the Greek historians; but only say, that my author, Eutychius, was himself patriarch of Alexandria: Mokaukas his chief care was not to defend the castle in good earnest, but to surrender it so as to procure good terms for himself, and secure that vast treasure which he had so ill gotten, whatever became of all the Greeks and the orthodox Christians, whom he mortally hated. There was in the river, between the besieged castle and opposite bank, a little island; Mokaukas perswades the Greeks to go with him out of the castle into that island; telling them, 'That since Amrou had fresh supplies sent him, it would be impossible for them to defend the castle much longer; and that if they went into that island, the river would be a much better security for them, than the castle.' This he did on purpose to leave the castle naked, that the Saracens might take it more easily, and upon that account grant him the better terms. At last he prevailed, and they went out of the south-gate, and going aboard some little vessels which they had there, they quickly landed in the island, having left only a few Greeks to defend the castle, for all the Cophties went out with Mokaukas. The Nile then began to overflow. Then Mokaukas sent messengers to Amrou with orders to this effect; 'You Arabians have invaded our 'country, and given us a great deal of trouble and disturbance, without 'any provocation on our side: and now assure yourselves, that the 'Nile will quickly surround your camp, and you will all fall into our 'hands. However, send some body to treat with us, and let us 'know your business, and what you demand; perhaps when we come 'to talk about the matter, things may be so settled, as both parties 'may be made easy, and a peace concluded.' Mokaukas his messengers had no sooner delivered their errand, but Amrou despatched Abadah Ebno'l Samet, a black, with orders to go to Mokaukas with the messengers, and tell him his mind. Abadah coming into Mokaukas his presence, he bad him sit down, and asked him what they (meaning the Arabs) meant, and what they would have. Abadah gave him the same answer as the Saracens always used to do to all that asked them that question; telling him, 'that he had three things to propose to him by the command of Amrou, who had received the same order from his master Omar the Caliph; viz., that they should either change their religion, and become Mahometans, and so have a right and title to all privileges in common with them; or else pay perpetual tribute yearly, and so come under their protection; or else they must fight it out till the sword decided the controversy between them.' These, as we have observed before, were the conditions which they proposed to all people where they came : the propagating their religion being to them a just occasion of making war upon any nation whatsoever. To these hard terms Mokaukas made answer, 'that as to the first of them they would never submit ; but he and his friends the Cophties would willingly pay tribute.' The Greeks obstinately refused to become tributaries, and were resolved to fight it out to the last : but Mokaukas cared not what became of them, so he might save himself and his money. Abadah having finished his business, returned from the castle to the camp ; and when he had acquainted Amrou with all that had passed, and that there were only a few Greeks in the castle, the Saracens renewed their assault, and Zobair scaled the walls, and cried out, 'Allàh Acbar.' The Greeks perceiving that the castle was lost, went into their boats as fast as they could, and escaped to the island. The Saracens possessed of the castle, killed and took prisoners those few that remained. The Greeks now plainly under-standing Mokaukas his fraud, durst trust themselves now no longer so near him, but going aboard their ships, got to shore, and marched to to Keram'l Shoraik, a place between Cairo and Alexandria, and put themselves into as good a posture of defence as they could. In the mean time Mokaukas discoursed with Amrou about the conditions of peace ; which were, 'that all the Cophties which lived both above and below Cairo shall pay yearly two ducats, without any difference or distinction to be made between rich or poor ; only boys under 16 years of age, decrepit old men, and all women, were exempted from paying anything.' The number of the Cophties which were then polled, was six millions ; according to which account, the yearly tribute of Cair, and the neighbouring territory, amounted to twelve millions of ducats. Mokaukas begged of Amrou, that he might be always reckoned among the Cophties, and taxed as they were ; declaring, that he desired to have nothing in common with the Greeks, for he was none of them, nor of their religion ; but had only for a while dissembled the matter, for fear of his life ; and intreated him never to make peace with the Greeks, but persecute them to death ; and for his part, he desired that when he died, he might be buried in St. John's church in Alexandria. All this Amrou promised to per-form, upon condition that the Cophties should be obliged to entertain any Musleman whatsoever, who had occasion to pass through the country three days gratis, and repair two bridges which were broken, and prepare places for the entertainment of himself and his army, and take care that the country people should bring in pro-vision to be sold in the camp, and clear the way from Cairo to Alexandria, (which he was then going to besiege) building such bridges as were necessary for the army to march. These terms were readily accepted by the Cophties, who assisted them with every thing they wanted.   Amrou marched till he came to Keramo'l Shoraik, where the Greeks that fled from Cairo were.   They fought three days continually, but at last the Greeks were forced to give way.   They had some other battles before they came to Alexandria, in which the Saracens were always superior.   Those Greeks which escaped, retired to Alexandria, where they made the best preparation they could for a siege.

Amrou was not long after them, but quickly came up, and laid siege to the city.   However, the Greeks made a stout resistance, and sallied out frequently, so that there was a great many killed on both sides. The Saracens at last made a vigorous attack upon one of the towers, and entered it ; the Greeks all the while defending it to their utmost. They fought a considerable time in the tower, till the Saracens at last were pressed upon so hard, that they were forced to retire.   In this attempt, Amrou the general, Muslemah Ebno'l Mochalled, and Werdan, Amrou's slave, were taken prisoners.   Being brought before the governor, he asked them what they meant by running about the country after this manner, and disturbing their neighbours ?   Amrou answered according to the usual form, and told him that they designed to make them either Muslemans or tributaries before they had done.   But this resolute answer of his had like to cost him his life, for, the governor having taken notice of his behaviour, concluded that he was no ordinary person, and spoke to some that stood near him to cut off his head.   Werdan, his slave, understood Greek ; and as soon as he heard what the governor said, took his master Amrou by the collar, and gave him a box on the ear ; telling him, 'That he was always putting himself forward, and prating, when 'twould better become him to hold his tongue : that he was a mean, contemptible fellow, and that he would advise him to learn more manners, and let his betters speak before him.'   By this time, Muslemah Ebno'l Mochalled had bethought himself, and told the governor, ' That their general had thoughts of raising the siege : that Omar the Caliph had wrote to him touching that matter, and designed to send an honourable embassy, consisting of several worthy persons, and men of note, to treat with him about matters, and if he pleased to let them go, they would acquaint their general how courteously they had been used, and employ the utmost of their endeavours to promote an accommodation.'   He added, ' That he did not in the least question, but when the Caliph's ambassadors had treated with him, things would be made very easy on both sides, and the siege speedily raised.'   Our historian tells us, that this impolitic governor observing how Werdan treated his master, concluded him to have been as mean as Werdan represented him, and believed the story that Muslemah had told him, concerning Omar's sending some of the chief Arabs to treat with him.   Wherefore, considering that it would be of greater consequence to kill six or ten considerable men, than three or four of the vulgar, he dismissed these, in hopes of catching the other. They were no sooner out of danger, but they shouted out as loud as they could, 'Allàh Acbar.' And when the Greeks upon the wall perceived those great tokens of joy, which were shown in the camp upon their return, they knew very well that they were not such persons as the governor had taken them for, and too late repented their letting them go. Quickly after, the Saracens renewed their assault, and so straightened the Alexandrians, that they were not able to hold out any longer. At last the city was taken, and the Greeks which were in it, were dispersed; some considerable parties of them going up further into the country, others getting off to sea; so that the Saracens entered, and took possession (A.D. 640), after they had besieged it fourteen months, and lost 23,000 men before it.

Amrou, to make all things secure, and prevent any alarm or disturbance which might follow, thought it proper to secure those Greeks, which, escaping from the siege of Alexandria, had gone further up into the country; reasonably concluding, that so long as there was any body of them in arms, the Saracens could not enjoy their new possessions in peace and security. He therefore marches out of Alexandria upon this design, leaving but a few of his Saracens behind him in the town, as apprehending no danger on that side. During his absence, the Greeks who had gone aboard their ships at the taking the town, and whose return was not in the least feared or suspected; came on a sudden, and surprised the town, and killed all the Saracens that were in it. This quickly came to Amrou's ear, upon which he returned to Alexandria with the greatest speed; where he found the remnant of the Greeks which came back from sea, already possessed of the castle. They gave him a warm reception, and fought bravely: at last, being overpowered, as many of them as could get fairly off, were obliged to retire to their ships, and try their fortune at sea once more, leaving Amrou and his Saracens in full and quiet possession. This done, Amrou acquaints the Caliph with his success; letting him know withal, that the Muslemans were desirous of plundering the city. Omar having received his letter, gave him thanks for his service; but blamed him for so much as once mentioning the plundering of so rich a city; and charged him strictly, that he should by no means suffer the soldiers to make any waste, or spoil anything in it; but that he should carefully treasure up what was valuable, to help him to defray charges in the time of war: and that the tribute which was raised in that part of the country should be laid up at Alexandria, to supply the necessities of the Muslemans.

Then they polled the inhabitants of Alexandria; which, being taken, all Ægypt followed the fortune of its metropolis, and the inhabitants compounded for their lives, fortunes, and free liberty of living in the profession of their own religion, at the expense of two ducats a year, without any distinction; except any man held any land, farm, or vineyard. For, in such cases, everyone paid proportionably to the yearly value of what he held. So that there arose a most prodigious revenue to the Caliph. After the Saracens were once arrived to this pitch, it is no wonder if they went further; for what would not such a revenue do in such hands? They knew very well how to husband their money, being sumptuous at that time in nothing but their places of public worship. Their diet was plain and simple: no wine, nor any of those dainties, the products of modern luxury, which spoil the stomach, and destroy men's constitutions, appeared upon their tables. Their chief drink was water; their food consisted in a great measure in milk, rice, and the fruits of the earth.

The Arabians had as yet applied themselves to no manner of learning, nor the study of anything but poetry in their own language, which they understood very well, after their way, and valued themselves upon long before Mahomet's time, being altogether ignorant of the sciences, and every language but their own. Amrou, however, though no scholar, was a man of quick parts, and a good capacity, and one that, when his affairs would give him leave, was more delighted with the conversation of learned men, and rational and philosophical discourses, than men of his education commonly used to be. There was at that time in Alexandria, one John, sirnamed, The Grammarian; a man eminent for learning, with whose conversation Amrou was very well pleased, and would oftentimes take delight in hearing him discourse in several sciences, and ask him questions. The man perceiving the great respect shown him by Amrou, ventured one day to petition him for the books in the Alexandrian library; telling him, 'That he perceived he had taken an account of all things which he thought valuable in the city, and sealed up all the repositories and treasuries, but had taken no notice of the books. That, if they would have been any way useful to him, he would not have been so bold as to ask for them; but since they were not, he desired he might have them.' Amrou told him, 'That he had desired a thing which was altogether out of his power to grant; and that he could by no means dispose of the books, without having first asked leave of the Caliph. However,' he said, 'he'd write, and see what might be done in it.' This he accordingly performed, and having given a due character of the abilities of this learned man, and acquainted him with his petition; the Caliph returned this answer, 'What is contained in these books you mention, is either agreeable to what is written in the book of God (meaning the *Alcoran*) or it is not: if it be, then the *Alcoran* is sufficient without them; if otherwise, 'tis fit they should be destroyed.' Amrou, in obedience to the Caliph's command, distributed the books throughout all the city, amongst those that kept warm baths (of which there was at that time in Alexandria no fewer than 4000), to heat the baths with. And notwithstanding the great havoc that must needs be made of them at this rate, the number of books which the diligence of former princes had collected was so great, that it was six months before they were consumed. A loss never to be made up to the learned world. This John, The Grammarian, was an Alexandrian by birth, of the sect of the Jacobites: afterwards he denied the Trinity. Being admonished by the bishops of Ægypt to renounce his erroneous opinions, he was, upon his refusal, excommunicated.

Amrou being now possessed of Ægypt, began to look a little further towards the western part of Africa ; and in a short time made himself master of all that country which lies between Barcah and Zeweilah ; the inhabitants of Barcah bringing in the tribute imposed upon them punctually at the time prefixed, without any collectors going among them to gather it. While these things were doing in Ægypt, there was a dearth in Arabia ; so that the inhabitants of Medinah and the neighbouring country, were reduced to a starving condition. Upon which Omar wrote to Amrou, and acquainting him with their extremity, ordered him to supply the Arabs with corn out of Ægypt. Which Amrou did in such plenty, that the train of camels which were loaden with it, reached in a continued line from Ægypt to Medinah ; so that when the foremost of them were got to Medinah, the latter part of the gang were still in the bounds of Ægypt. But this way of conveying their provision being too tedious and chargeable, the Caliph commanded Amrou to dig a passage from the Nile to the Red Sea, for the more speedy and easy conveyance of their provision to the Arabian shore. Shortly after Amrou took Tripoli : and if we should consider the greatness of his success, it might seem wonderful, though there had been nothing done in any other part. But their victorious arms made no less progress eastward, and the Mahometan crescent began now to shed its malignant influence upon as large and considerable dominions as had ever been flown over by the Roman Eagle. About this time, Aderbijàn, Ainwerdah, Harràn, Roha, Rakkah, Nisibin, Ehwàz, Siwàs, and Choràsan, were all brought under subjection to the Saracens ; in which conquests there were, without doubt, a great many noble actions performed, and well worth the relating ; but the particular history of that part of their conquests not being yet come into my hands, the reader is desired to excuse me.

About two years after, Omar the Caliph was killed. The account we have of it is this : there was one Phirouz, a Persian, of the sect of the Magi or Persees, who having, as being of a different religion from the Muslemans, a tribute of two pieces of silver imposed upon him daily by his master, made his complaint to Omar, to have some part of it remitted. Omar told him he did not think it at all unreasonable, considering he might well afford it out of what he earned. Phirouz was so provoked with this answer, that he did as good as threaten the Caliph to his face ; but he took little notice of it. Not long after he waited his opportunity, and whilst Omar was saying the morning prayer in the mosque, he stabbed him thrice in the belly with a dagger. The Saracens in the mosque immediately rushing upon him, he made a desperate defence, and stabbed thirteen of them, of whom seven died. At last, one that stood by threw his vest over him and seized him—he, perceiving himself caught, stabbed himself. Omar lived three days after it and then died, in the month Du'lhagjah, in the 23rd year of the Hegirah, A.D. 643, after he had reigned 10 years 6 months and 8 days, and was sixty-three years old, which is the same age at which, according to some authors, Mahomet, Abubeker, and Ayesha, Mahomet's wife, died.

He was of a dark complexion, very tall, and had a bald head. As to his behaviour in the government, the Arabick authors give him an extraordinary character. His abstinence from the things of this life, piety, and gravity of behaviour, procured him more reverence than his successors could command by their grandeur. 'His walking-stick,' says Alwákidi, 'struck more terror into those that were present than another man's sword. His diet was barley-bread; his sauce, salt; and oftentimes, by way of abstinence and mortification, he eat his bread without salt; his drink was water. He was a constant observer of religious duties, and in those 10 years he reigned went 9 times on pilgrimage to Medinah. His administration of justice was very impartial, his ears being always open to the complaints of the meanest; nor could the greatness of any offender exempt him from punishment.' In his decisions he always kept punctually to the sense of the Alcoran and the traditions of Mahomet, in whose time he gave a signal proof of the sense he had of the duty of inferiors to their governours, which was occasioned thus :—

An obstinate Musleman had a suit at law with a Jew, before Mahomet. The Jew being in the right, Mahomet pronounced sentence against the Musleman, who said, 'That he would not be so satisfyed, unless Omar, who was then only a private man, had the rehearing and examining the cause. The plaintiff and defendant went both together to Omar, whom they found at his own door, and opening their case and acquainting him with the decision of it, desired him to examine it again. Omar, going into his own house, bade them stay a moment, and told them he would despatch their business in a trice. Coming back, he brings his cymiter along with him, and at one single stroke cuts off the Musleman's head that refused to be determined by Mahomet's decision, saying with a loud voice, 'See what they deserve who will not acquiesce in the determination of their judges.' It was upon this occasion that Mahomet, informed of the fact, gave him the title or sirname of Farouk—intimating that Omar knew as well how to distinguish truth from falsehood, and justice from injustice, as he did to separate the head of that knave from his body.

The conquests gained by the Saracens in his reign were so considerable, that though they had never been extended any further, the countries they had subdued would have made a very formidable empire. He drove all the Jews and Christians out of Arabia; subdued Syria, Ægypt, and other territories in Africa, besides the greatest part of Persia. And yet all this greatness, which would have been too weighty for an ordinary man to have borne—especially if we consider that it did not descend to them as an hereditary possession, for the ruling of which they had been prepared by a suitable education, but was gotten all on a sudden by men that had been acquainted with nothing great before—had no effect on the Caliph, but he still retained his old way of living, nor did the increase of his riches ever appear by his retinue or expences. He built a wall about Cusa, and repaired, or rebuilt rather, the temples of Jerusalem and Medinah. He was the first of the Saracens that made rolls to enter the names of all that were in military service, or all that received any stipend from the publick. He first made use of the date of the Hegirah, concerning which the reader may see more in Prideaux's 'Life of Mahomet,' which I shall not here transcribe. He was the first of them that forbad any woman who had ever born a child, should be sold for a slave. The author of the 'History of Jerusalem,' above-mentioned, adds, 'That if he had nothing else to recommend him but the taking of Jerusalem and purging it from idolatry, even that had been sufficient.'

He never used to save any money in the treasury, but divided it every Friday, at night, amongst his men, according to their several necessities; in which particular, his practice was preferable to Abubeker's, for Abubeker used to proportion his dividends to the merit of the persons that were to receive it; but Omar had regard only to their necessities, saying, 'That the things of this world were given us by God for the relief of our necessities and not for the reward of virtue, because the proper reward of that belonged to another world.'

OTHMAN EBN AFFAN,

(*Hegirah 23, Nov. 18, 643.*)

THIRD CALIPH AFTER MAHOMET.

IN the space of those three days which Omar lived, after he had received his mortal wound, his friends came about him, soliciting him to make his will and name a successor. To which he answered, 'That if Salem were alive, he should approve of none so well as him.' Then they named several to him, but he still found some fault or other with all they proposed. Some recommended Ali, upon the account of his near relation to Mahomet, besides his valour and other qualifications ; but Omar did not think him serious enough for such a weighty charge. Then Othman Ebn Affan being named, Omar rejected him as a person too much inclined to favour his own friends and relations. When they perceived that it was impossible for them to pitch upon any person against whom he would not make an exception, they had good reason to think that this proceeded from a desire that his son should succeed him. But his son being mentioned to him, he answered, ' That it was enough for one in a family to have an account to give of so weighty a charge as the governing the Muslemans was.' At last, when they could not perswade him to name a successor, he appointed six persons, to whom he allowed three days time to consult about the matter after his decease. He ordered his son to be present whilst they debated, but gave him no liberty of voting. The six commissioners were Othman, Ali, Telhha, Azzobeir, Abdo'rrahman Ebn Auf, and Saed Ebn Abi Wakkas, all of which had been the familiar acquaintance and companions of Mahomet. Omar being dead, they met to consult ; and Abdo'rrahman said, ' That for his part he would willingly lay aside all pretensions to it, provided they would agree to chuse one of those that were present.' All of them consented to it but Ali, who thought himself injured, because he was not the immediate successor of Mahomet. At last he consented too, after Abdo'rrahman had sworn to him that he would neither vote for nor favour any man whatsoever that should offer himself. Abdo'rrahman, upon this, advises with the rest, who inclining to Othman Ebn Affan, he was chosen Caliph, and inaugurated three days after Omar's death. Abu'lpharagius says that Abu Obeidah (whom he puts in the room of Abdo'rrahman) came to Ali and asked him, ' If he would take the government upon him, upon condition that he should be obliged to administer according to what was contained in the book of God, the tradition of his prophet, and the determination of two seniors.' Ali answered, ' That as for the book of God and the tradition of his prophet, he was contented ; but he would not be obliged to be determined by the constitutions of the seniors.' The same terms being offered to Othman, he embraced them without exception, and was immediately chosen Caliph.

Being established in the government, he followed the example of his predecessors, and sends his forces abroad, to enlarge his dominions. In a short time Maho'l Bosarah, and what remained of the borders of Isphahan and Raya were taken ; so that the poor Persian king was now eaten up on all sides, and had very little left him. The same year that Othman was made Caliph, Birah and Hamden were taken, and Moawiyah, who was then prefect of Syria, and afterwards Caliph, invaded the territories of the Grecian Emperor, took a great many towns, and wasted the country.

We have observed before that Othman was taken notice of for being too much inclined to favour his friends ; upon which account Omar judged him unworthy to succeed him : which inclination now appeared plainly, when he had got the government into his hands, and was in a capacity of obliging them. For notwithstanding Amrou Ebno'l Aas had done the Saracens such singular service, and added Ægypt to their empire, yet Othman deposed him, A.D. 645, and took away his præfecture, or lieutenancy of Ægypt, from him, without any just reason at all that ever I could learn ; but only because he had a mind to prefer Abdo'llah Ebn Said, his foster-brother, to a place of such dignity and profit : than which, there could scarce be a greater im- prudence ; for Amrou, having been a considerable time in Ægypt, had made both the persons and the customs of the Ægyptians familiar to him, and was very well beloved by them : upon which account, and his admirable skill in military affairs, he was, without doubt the fittest man for such a charge that the Saracens had. However, the order of the Caliph must be obeyed ; but it was not attended with very good success. For Constantine, the Grecian Emperor, sent for Manuel, an eunuch, with an army, to retake Alexandria ; which was accordingly performed by the assistance of the Greeks in the city ; who, keeping secret correspondence with the Emperor's army, then at sea, received them at their landing ; and Alexandria, which Amrou had taken four years before, was now once more in the hands of the Grecian Emperor. And now it was evidently seen of what use Amrou was in Ægypt. He was immediately restored to his former dignity ; for the Ægyptians, conscious to themselves of dealing treacherously with the Emperor, fearing, lest falling into the hands of the Grecians, they should be punished according to their deserts, humbly petitioned the Caliph, that they might have their old general Amrou restored, both upon the account of his being well acquainted with the state of that kingdom, and his experience in war. This was no sooner asked than granted ; the exigency of affairs indispensably requiring it. Amrou being now in full power, goes against Alexandria with his army, in which were a great many Cophties, and among them the traitor Mokaukas, whose business it was to provide things necessary for the army in their march. Amrou being come before Alexandria, found the Greeks in a good posture of defence. They gave him battle several days together, and held out bravely. The obstinacy of their defence provoked him so, that he swore, 'If God gave him the victory, he would pull down the walls of the town, and make it as easy of access as a bawdy- house.' He was as good as his word ; for when he had taken the town, which was not long after, he demolished all the walls and forti- fications, and entirely dismantled it. However, he dealt very merci- fully with the inhabitants, and saved as many of their lives as he could. And built a Mosque in that very place, where he stayed the fury of the Saracens, who were killing all they met ; which Mosque was upon that account called (*Jámi'orráhhmati*), the Mosque of mercy. Manuel, the Grecian Emperor's general, being quite routed, retired, with so many of his men as he could carry off, to the sea shore : where weighing anchor with all possible speed, they hoisted sail, and returned to Constantinople. From that time that most flourishing city, once the metropolis of Ægypt, dwindled away and declined a-pace ; so that there is little belonging to it that is worth taking notice of, only a good haven, and some merchants store-houses.

About this time, A.D. 647, Moawiyah invaded Cyprus, and agreed with the inhabitants upon this condition, that he should share the revenues of that island with the Grecian Emperor. So that the Cyprians were obliged to pay 7,200 ducats every year to Moawiyah, and the like sum to the Emperor. The Mahometans enjoyed this tribute near two years, and were then dispossessed by the Christians.

The same year that Moawiyah agreed with the Cyprians, Othman sent Abdo'llah Ebn Amir and Said Ebno'l Aas to invade Chorasan ; and to encourage their diligence, told them, ' That which of them soever got thither first should have the prefecture of that territory.' They took a great many strong places, and so streightened Yazdejerd, the Persian king, that he was now so far from being able to meet the Saracens in open field, that he was forced to shift about every way to save himself. And lest any misfortune should be wanting to compleat his ruin, he was at last betrayed by a treacherous servant ; an unhappiness which frequently happens to princes in distress : for those who have any private pique against them take the opportunity offered by their misfortunes of being revenged : others, hoping to ingratiate themselves with the conquering party, stick to do nothing that will oblige them, though to the utter ruin of their former masters.

For Yazdejerd, distressed on every side, called in Tarchan, the Turk, to his assistance, who came accordingly with an army. But their stay was short, for Yazdejerd, upon a frivolous account, affronted Tarchan, and sent him back again : imprudently done in those desperate circumstances. He had acted a much wiser part, in putting up a great many little affronts, rather than sending away those allies, which he could not subsist without. Mahwa, a person of note, who had a spite against his master, Yazdejerd, takes the advantage of the Turk's indignation, who highly resented the affront, and sends to Tarchan; telling him, ' That if he would come back and revenge the affront, he would not be wanting to his assistance.' Upon this Tarchan returns ; Yazdejerd meets him with the best preparation he could make ; but was beaten. In his flight, the traitor Mahwa sets upon him, and quite destroys and disperses the shattered remains of his army which had escaped. Yazdejerd got off himself, and coming to a mill, proffered the miller his belt, his bracelets, and his ring : but this churlish brute, not considering the worth of the things which were offered him, much less the compassion which humanity obliges us to show to all in distress, especially our princes, told him, ' That he earned four pieces of silver with his mill every day, and if he would give him so much money, he would let it stand still upon his account : if not, he would not.' Whilst they were debating this matter, a party of horse, which were in search of him, happened to come to this place, where they found him, and killed him. He was the last king of the Persians; and at the beginning of his reign, the Persian Æra, or date, which they use to this day, begins ; which is from him called Yazdejerdica. Thus the Persian government was entirely destroyed, and all the territories belonging to it fell into the hands of the Caliphs in the year 31 of the Hegirah, which began on August 20, A.D. 651.

OTHMAN, though a religious man in his way, and of a good disposition, was nevertheless very unfit for government ; for he did a great many very impolitick things, which alienated the minds of his subjects from him, and gave occasion to his enemies both to open their mouths and take up arms against him. The first that we hear of who began to make a stir, and talk publickly against the Caliph, was one Abúdar Alacádi, who openly railed at him, and made it his business to defame him. Othman took no other notice of it, than only to forbid him coming into his presence. Upon this, Abúdar goes into Syria, where he continued detracting from the Caliph, and aggravating every thing that might be objected against him. Moawiyah, at that time lieutenant of Syria, wrote to Othman : who thereupon sent for Abúdar to Medinah, and put him into prison ; in which he continued till his death, which was but the year after.

But this was only the beginning of troubles to the Caliph ; for the Saracens grew every day worse than other. Factious and uneasy spirits, when once they begin to disturb any government, never rest till they be either entirely crushed themselves, or else obtain their ends. The murmuring increased daily, and almost every province in the empire had something or other to complain of, peculiar to itself, besides those grievances which were common to them all ; so that all things were in a flame (*Hegirah* 35, *July* 10, 665). Every man's mouth was full of grievous accusations against the Caliph, and complaints of his mal-administration. Those things which they principally laid to his charge, were : ' That he had recalled Hhakem Ebno'l Aâs to Medinah, ' who had been banished by the prophet, and had not been recalled by ' either of his predecessors, Abubeker or Omar. That he removed ' Said Ebn Abi Wakkâs, one of those six to whom Omar had com- ' mitted the election of a Caliph from his prefecture, and put in ' another man of scandalous conversation, a drinker of wine, and ' notorious for other debaucheries. That he had been too lavish of ' the publick treasure to his friends, and had given Abdo'llah 400,000

' ducats, and Hhakem 100,000. That he had removed Amrou Ebno'l
' Aâs from the lieutenancy of Ægypt, and put Said Abi Shárehh into
' his place.' This Said had been one of those that had helped to
write the *Alcoran*, and afterwards apostatized and left the profession of
Mahometanism : whereupon Mahomet resolved to kill him when he
took Meccah, which was in the eighth year of the Hegirah ; but at
Othman's intreaty, spared his life, and was content, to banish him.
' That when he was first made Caliph, he presumed to sit upon the
' uppermost part of the Suggestum or pulpit, where Mahomet himself
' used to sit ; whereas Abubeker always sat one step lower, and Omar
' two.' These and a great many other things made the people murmur
at him.   At last, in a publick assembly, he told them from the pulpit,
' That the money which was in the treasury was sacred, and belonged
' to God ; and that he [as being the successor of the prophet] would
' dispose of it to whomsoever he thought fit, in spight of them ; and
' threatened and cursed whosoever should show any dislike of
' what he had said.' Ammâr Ebn Yaser declared that he disliked it.
Upon which Othman commanded him to be beaten, and immediately
some that stood by fell upon him, and beat him till he swooned.   This
sort of treatment so incensed the Arabs, that they gathered together,
took arms, and encamped within a league of Medinah.   From their
camp they sent an insolent message to the Caliph, demanding of him
either to do that which was right and just (i.e., what they thought so),
or else resign the government.   The poor Caliph would now have done
any thing with all his heart to have been at quiet.   But this is observable, that the risings of seditious subjects are not to be laid by complying with their demands, for the more is granted by the prince in such
circumstances, the more they crave.   He goes into the pulpit which
was in the Mosque at Medinah, and there solemnly before the whole
congregation, calls God to witness, that he was heartily sorry for what
was, past, and that he repented.   But all to no purpose ; for by this
time all the provinces were in an uproar, and the strength of the rebels
encreased daily.   There were few provinces but what sent some considerable men, who met together at Medinah, to depose Othman :
Malec Alashtar brought 200 men with him from Cusa ; there came 150
from Basora ; 600 from Ægypt, all upon this occasion.   The Caliph
being now in great perplexity, sent Mogeirah Ebn Shahah, and Amrou
Ebno'l Aâs, to treat with' the malcontents, and endeavour to perswade
them to be determined by the *Alcoran* and the *Sunnèt* ; that is, the
traditions of Mahomet ; but that they had very little thanks for their
pains, for the rebels used them scurvily.   Then he sent Ali to them
(who ever since the death of Mahomet had expected to be Caliph, and
had a very considerable party) him they received with more reverence,
and he bound himself to see that all that Othman promised them
should be performed ; and to make them the more easy, Othman and

Ali set both their hands to a paper, in which they promised to remove the causes of their grievances. Then the Ægyptians demanded to have Abdo'llah Ebn Said removed from the lieutenancy of Ægypt, and Mahommed, the son of Abubeker, put in his room : which Othman readily complied with, and signed his commission. This condescension of the Caliph, seemingly satisfied them pretty well ; so that the parties were dissolved, and every man returned to his own country. The storm seemed to be blown over, and any man would have thought that the Caliph had no reason to doubt of going to the grave in peace. But what will not treachery do ? There was nothing omitted by the Caliph's enemies, which might foment these prejudices in the people, that they had already conceived against him. Ayesha, Mahomet's widow, was his mortal enemy. Certainly it would much better have become one that pretended to have been the wife of an inspired prophet, to have spent the days of her widowhood in devotion and good works, rather than in doing mischief, and embroiling the state. But she was so prejudiced in favour of Telha, the son of Zobeir, whom she would fain have raised to the dignity of Caliph, that no consideration of goodness or decency could hinder her from designing the death of Othman. Another of his greatest enemies was Mahomet, Abubeker's son, the same whom the Ægyptians had desired for their prefect. But none did him more harm than Merwân Ebno'l Hhakem, his secretary, who may justly be looked upon as the principal cause of his ruin, which was occasioned thus.

As the Ægyptians which were gathered together to depose Othman were upon their journey homewards from Medinah, with Mahomet, the son of Abubeker, their new lieutenant, they met with a messenger carrying letters from the Caliph to Abdo'llah Ebn Said, at that time lieutenant of Ægypt. Him, upon examination, they detained, and opened his letters, in which they found orders given to Abdo'llah to this effect : 'As soon as Mahomet, the son of Abubeker, and N. and N. &c., shall arrive in Ægypt, cut off their hands and feet, and impale them.' This letter had Othman's seal and superscription, the whole business being managed by the villany of the secretary, Merwan, who contrived this letter himself (as he had done many others to the Caliph's great disadvantage), and ordered it so as it might fall into the hands of the Ægyptians, on purpose to re-inflame the difference which had, by the care of Ali and the condescension of the Caliph, been in a great measure composed. It is no hard matter to guess how Mahomet, Abubeker's son, and the Ægyptians that were with him, were affected with this letter. They were stark mad ; and no ill language, no revenge, was thought sufficient for him that designed such cruelty to them. They immediately hasten back to Medinah, making large speeches all the way of the treachery and perfidiousness of the Caliph, and how narrowly and accidentally they had escaped so imminent a

danger. Such stories as this seldom lose anything in the telling, especially considering that the wound was but just skinned over and not
healed—there being, besides the faction at court, a great many disaffected persons, who spared not to say the worst of the Caliph. The
news of the Ægyptians returning flies immediately all over the country,
and how, if they had not accidentally intercepted Othman's letter to
Abdo'llah, they must have suffered the utmost cruelty. Upon this, all
people unanimously detested the person of the Caliph; and those who
had come before from Cufa and Basora, and had returned upon the
accommodation that was made, were scarce got home before, alarmed
with this news, they came back again to assist the Ægyptians in the
deposing Othman. This letter, they thought, excused whatsoever they
did, and those who did not believe that the Caliph wrote it, could make
use of that pretence to vilify him, in order to gain their end. At last,
they besieged him in his own house; he, in the meantime, proffering
all manner of satisfaction that could reasonably be demanded, and
declaring his repentance for what he had done amiss. But all in vain
—they were resolved to be revenged on him, who, indeed, had never
intended them any injury. When he perceived himself streightened,
he sent to his cousin Ali, and asked him, ' If he had a desire to see his
cousin murthered, and his own kingdom rent in pieces?' Ali answered,
' By no means.' And upon this sent his two sons, Hasan and Hosein,
to defend him and keep the gate, that he might not suffer any violence.
I am verily perswaded that Ali did not mean any harm to the Caliph,
but whether it was because he had a prospect of succeeding him, and
upon that account was loath to disoblige the Muslemans, who he perceived were altogether set against Othman, or for what other reason, it
is plain that he did not assist him with that vigour and earnestness
which might otherwise have been expected. 'Tis true, he sent Hasan
and Hosein, but they, when the besiegers had streightened the Caliph
for want of water, left him to their mercy. Then Mahomet, Abubeker's
son, and Ammar Ebn Yaser with several others, entered the house,
where they found the Caliph with the Alcoran in his lap. They immediately fell upon him, and one of them wounded him in the throat with
a dart; a second stabbed him with his sword. As soon as he fell,
another sat upon his breast, and wounded him in nine places. Thus
died Othman, the third after Mahomet, when he was 82 years old, of
which he had reigned near twelve. Authors differ concerning the time
of his being besieged in his house, but it seems to have been about six
weeks. He lay unburied for three days; at last he was removed (by
whose order I find not), bloody as he was, and buryed in the same
cloaths he was killed in, without so much as being washed, or the least
funeral solemnity—a remarkable instance of the vanity of human greatness, and the uncertainty of all worldly felicity.

As to his person, he was very tall, of a good countenance, dark com-

plexion, and a large beard. His way of living was commendable enough
for a Saracen. He was very constant and diligent in performing religious
exercises, frequent in reading and meditating the Alcoran, and fasted
very often. His charity was very extensive, his riches very great.
Though he was very hardly used, yet it must not be denied that he had
given some occasions for the people to think ill of him, which a politick
governour would have avoided : for he was so much inclined to prefer
his own family and friends, that he scarce ever considered their merit;
from whence this inconvenience must necessarily follow—that a great
many men would at this rate be put into places of the greatest trust,
which were no way qualified for the discharge of their duty ; and if
they did anything amiss, the Caliph who preferred them was sure to
bear a great share in the reflections which were made. Besides,
through the treachery of that villain Merwan, his secretary, a great
many ill things were laid to his charge which he had no hand in. For
it was a common thing with him to set Othman's seal to letters which
oftentimes contained very scandalous commands to governours of provinces, by which means the people were kept in an aversion to him ;
and these disturbances being constantly fomented by his enemies, they
never ceased, till at last they deprived him both of government and life.

ALI ELECTED CALIPH,

An. Heg. 35. July 10, A.D. 655.

FOURTH FROM MAHOMET.

IT is very well worth observing in the beginning of this history, that
the seeming agreement of the Arabians in the possession of the same
religion had not sufficient influence upon them to extinguish old grudges
and family quarrels. Telha and Azzobêir, two leading men amongst them,
and Ayesha, Mahomet's youngest and best beloved wife, were Ali's irre-
concilable and implacable enemies. However, Ali having married Phatemah, Mahomet's daughter, the Arabians, there being no male issue remaining of their prophet, favoured his interest, desirous of being governed by
a succession of Caliphs descended from the loyns of Mahomet. Telha
and Azzobéir were so well apprized of this, that they thought it prudence to dissemble their hatred so far, that the very same day on
which Othman was murdered, they took the oath of allegiance to Ali,
with a stedfast resolution of breaking it, as soon as a favourable opportunity should offer itself. The case was that the inhabitants of several
provinces, who had come together from all quarters of the empire—
from Syria, Ægypt, Mesopotamia, Persia, and Arabia—upon the account
of the complaints made against Othman, were resolved not to be kept

in suspense, but to know whom they were to depend upon for their emperor, and threatened all the candidates with death if they did not speedily fix upon some one or other. Some of the Bassorians favoured Telha ; the Cusians, Egyptians, and the greatest part of the Arabians, were for Ali. Zobéir had a party of the Bassorians in his interest, who threatened him with death if he did not either take the government upon himself, or take care to see it conferred upon some other person.

In this confusion several of them came to Ali, and desired him to accept of the government ; to which he answered, ' That he had no need of it himself, but had much rather give his consent to the choice of any person they should agree upon.' They still insisted that there was none so well qualified as he, whether he were considered with regard to his personal accomplishments or his near relation to the prophet. He replied, ' That he had much rather serve any person they should think fit to chuse, in the capacity of a Vizier, than take the government upon himself. Upon his obstinate refusal, a great many of them of the several provinces, who were all well enough satisfyed with the murder of Othman, but could not so well agree in the choice of a successor, perceiving also that all those of the family of Ommiyah, of which more hereafter, that had an opportunity, had withdrawn themselves, came in a tumultuous manner to the chief inhabitants of Medinah, and told them that they were the proper persons to determine this controversy ; adding, that they would allow them one day to consider of it, in which time, if it was not concluded, Telha, Zobéir, Ali, and several others, should be put to the sword. Upon this they came to Ali in the evening, earnestly intreating him to consider the condition of their religion, who still declining it, and desiring them to think of some other person, they said, ' We adjure thee by God ! Dost not thou consider in what condition we are ?—dost thou not consider the religion (Arab. *Alislam*) ?— dost not thou consider the distraction of the people ?—dost thou not fear God ?' Overcome at last with these pathetical expostulations, he answered, ' If I comply with you in this, I shall deal with you according to the best of my knowledge ; and, if you excuse me, there will be no other difference between you and me but this : that I shall be one of the most submissive and obedient to whomsoever you shall set over me.' He resolved not to accept of their allegiance in private, for they proffered to give him their hands—the customary ceremony then in use among them upon such occasions—at his own house, but would have it performed publickly at the mosque, that all parties might be satisfied, and have no justifiable cause of complaint ; knowing very well that Ayesha, Telha, Azzobeir (or Zobeir), and the whole house of Ommiyah —of which Moawiyah, then Othman's lieutenant in Syria, was chief— would never omit the least opportunity of giving him the utmost disturbance that lay in their power. Wherefore, in the morning he went to the mosque, dressed in a thin cotton gown, tied about him with a

20

girdle, a coarse turbant upon his head, his slippers in one hand and a bow in the other, instead of a walking-staff. Telha and Zobeir, not being present, they were sent for, and came and offered him their hands as a mark or token of their approbation. Ali bad them, if they did do it, be in good earnest, otherwise he would give his own hand to either of them that would accept of the government, which they both refused, and gave him theirs. The eastern nations are generally addicted to superstition, and great observers of omens. When Telha offered Ali his hand, which had been very much damaged and broken by some wounds which he had received in the wars, one that was present said, 'That it was a bad sign, and that it was like to be but a lame sort of business that was begun with a lame hand.'

Soon after this was over, Telha and Zobeir, with some others of their party, came to Ali, and complained to him of the murder of Othman; insinuating, that it ought by all means to be revenged, and proffering their service. Their secret design was to take the first opportunity of making a disturbance among the people, which they did not in the least question would end infallibly in the destruction of Ali and his party. Ali told them, ' That he very well understood their meaning ;
' representing to them at the same time, how impracticable an under-
' taking it would be to pretend to do any thing to such a number, and
' of such considerable force ; desiring them to inform him, if it were
' in their power, what proper method they could propose to answer their
' end. They told him, they knew of none. He swore, nor he either,
' unless it were the uniting of all parties together, if it should so please
' God ; adding, that these dissentions had their foundation laid in the
' times of ignorance ; (meaning, that they were ancient family quarrels
' before Mahomet's pretence to inspiration) that these discontented
' people would still increase ; for the Devil never left the place he had
' taken possession of, after once he had made a beginning. In such an
' affair as this, says he, one party will approve of what you propose, a
' second will be of a different opinion, and the third will dissent from
' both the former. Wherefore consult among yourselves.'

Ali in the mean time was very instant with the Coreish (the most noble tribe of the Arabians) walking about from one to the other, and taking all possible opportunities of caressing them. He did not fail to express the sense he entertained of their excellency, and the depend-ance of the welfare of the people upon their authority; for he was extremely concerned at the heats and divisions which he observed among the people, and especially at the sudden departure of the Om-miyan family. When nothing could be concluded upon, Telha and Zobeir begged of Ali, one of them the government of Cufah, the other Basorah (both places of very great importance, the one situate upon the eastern bank of the river Euphrates, the other two miles westward of the Tigris) upon pretence that if any thing extraordinary should happen, they would take horse at a minute's warning. He told them that he would consider of that matter. Though other historians say, that he put them off with a compliment, telling them that he had no body about him of equal capacity with themselves, or so proper to consult withal in such emergencies, as such a new established government was likely to be exposed to ; which answer of his touched them to the quick ; and they knowing that Ayesha was at Meccah, having gone thither on pilgrimage whilst Othman was besieged, begged leave of him to go thither, which was granted.

As soon as Ali was acknowledged Caliph, he resolved to take away the governments and lieutenancies from all those persons who had been put in by Othman his predecessor. Almogeirah the son of Said advised him to forbear a little, at least till he should find himself more firmly established in his government, which Ali did not approve of. The day after Almogeirah made him another visit, and told him that he had changed his opinion, at the same time advising him to follow his own way, and proceed according to what he had at first proposed himself. In the midst of this conference between Ali and Almogeirah Abdollah the son of Abbas (who was at Meccah when Othman was killed, but upon the election of Ali was newly returned to Medinah) chanced to come in, and finding Ali and Almogeirah together, took occasion to enquire of Ali what had been the subject of their discourse. Ali told him that Almogeirah had advised him to continue Moawiyah and the rest of Othman's lieutenants in their places till they should come in of their own accord, and he was fixed in his government ; which I, added he, not approving, he came and told me to day that he had altered his opinion, and that I was in the right. The son of Abbas told him, ' That Almogeirah had given him good advice the first time, but the last was treachery.' He told him, ' That he was afraid that all Syria, over which Moawiyah was lieutenant would fall off from him ; that there was no confidence to be reposed in Telha and Zobeir ; that there was reason rather to suspect that they would both be in arms against him. Wherefore,' says he, ' I advise you to continue Moawiyah in his place till he submits to your government ; and when he has once done that, leave it to me to pull him out of his house by the ears for you whensoever you desire it.' Ali swore by God, ' That nothing should be Moawiyah's fortune but the sword.' Upon which the other told him, ' That he was indeed a man of courage, but wanted conduct.' Ali told him, ' That it was his business to obey.' Almogeirah replied, ' That he did not find himself under any such obligation.' Thus the conference broke up, and in a short time Almogeirah retired to Meccah.

The greatest part of the helpers came in, except a few that had been Othman's almoners and other officers. Hence it seems came the title of the Motazeli, which in English signifies Separatiss, because when Ali was proclaimed, they were of the opposite party.

Ali, deaf to all representations to the contrary, resolved to make a thorough reformation of all the lieutenancies ; and in the beginning of the next year, sent out his new officers to their respective provinces. Othman the son of Haniph was ordered to Basorah. Ammarah the son of Sahal to Cufah (he was one of the flyers). Abdollah the son of Abbas to Arabia Fælix (he was one of the helpers). And Sahel the son of Haniph, another of the helpers, to Syria.

When Sahel came to Tabuk he met with a party of horse ; who demanded of him, ' To give an account of himself.' He answered, ' That he was governor of Syria ;' they told him, ' That if anyone besides Othman had sent him, he might go back again about his business.' He asked them, ' If they had not been informed of the fate of Othman ?' They told him, ' Yes.' Perceiving that there was no room for him there, he returned back to Ali. Kais went into Ægypt, where he was opposed by a party of the Othmanians, who refused to submit to Ali's government till justice was done upon the murtherers of Othman. Othman the son of Haniph went to Basorah, where he found the people divided. And receiving information that the Cufians were resolved not to change their governor, returned to Ali, with the news of their resolution. Abu Muṣa Alashari was then the governor of Cufah, put in by Othman. Abidollah went to Arabia Fælix, where Yali governed by Othman's commission. Yali resigned to him ; but plundered the treasury first ; and making the best of his way to Meccah, delivered the money to Ayesha, Telha and Zobeir.

The Separatists in the mean time, least they should be wanting in any thing that might possibly give any disturbance to Ali's government, carried Othman's bloody shirt, in which he was murthered, into Syria; where they made a very good use of it. Sometimes it was spread upon the pulpit ; and sometimes carried about in the army. To inflame the matter, his wife's fingers, that were cut off at the time when he was murthered, were pinned upon the shirt. This sight daily exposed to open view, put the Syrian army, who were very much indebted to Othman's munificence, into a rage ; nothing would serve but the revenging his death. And they indeed were in good earnest ; but the whole secret of this affair lyes here. Ayesha, Telha, and Zobeir were always enemies to Othman, and the contrivers of his death and destruction. But when they saw Ali elected, whom they equally hated, they made use of Othman's real and sincere friends as instruments of their malice against him. So that upon different accounts they all unanimously joined in demanding satisfaction for the murther of Othman.

As soon as Sahel returned with his answer from Syria, which was before Telha and Zobeir had taken their leave, he sent for them both, and told them ' what he had cautioned them against before, was now come to pass ; that things were carried to too great an height already to be made up without such an expedient, as should make all parties easy ; that sedition was like fire, the more it burnt, the stronger it grew and the brighter it shined.' They then asked him, ' To give them leave to go out of Medinah, and if the disturbance increased, they would be answerable for it.' What answer he gave them I cannot so well tell, because I am not sure of the true reading in my obscure manuscript. Here give me leave once to say, that if I were not destitute of Arabick types, I would never be ashamed to confess my ignorance of any passage that I did not perfectly understand, but print it in the original in the margin ; that I might have an opportunity of being informed by the learned ; and they might collate it with other copies. But to guess once at his sense ; the first that I should chuse should be this : ' I will contain as long as it is possible ; if nothing will do, I must apply caustics.' He wrote forthwith to Moawiyah in Syria, and Abu Musa at Cufah. Abu Musa satisfied him that all the Cufians were entirely at his service ; but sent him at the same time a catalogue of those who came in of their own accord at first ; and those that afterwards of course followed the majority. Moawiyah did not vouchsafe to give him one word of answer to all his messages ; till about three months after Othman's death, he called a messenger and delivered him a letter sealed up with this subscription : ' From Moawiyah to Ali.' Then giving him private instructions, he sent him away to Medinah, and Ali's messenger along with him, whom he had detained all this while. He went into Medinah, according to his directions, in the evening (when he was like to be seen by most people ; for in those hot countries the streets are most frequented in the cool of the day) and carried the packet aloft upon a staff. The people who were well enough appraised of Moawiyah's disaffection to Ali, thronged after him with listening ears, earnestly expecting the contents of his message. When Ali opened the letter it was a meer blank, not so much as one word written in it, which he rightly understood as a token of the utmost contempt and defiance. Then asking the messenger, ' What news,' he answered, 'That there were no less than 60,000 men in arms under Othman's shirt, which was set up as a standard upon the pulpit of Damascus.' Ali asked, ' Whether or no they required the blood of Othman at his hands ? Calling God to witness that he was not guilty of it and begging his assistance.' Then turning to Ziyad who sat by him, he told him ' That there must of necessity be a war in Syria :' which Ziyad soon communicated to the people. Ali did all that in him lay to encourage them, and wrote circular letters round about to all the provinces to demand their assistance.

Whilst he was making this preparation, he was informed of the revolt of Telha, Zobeir, and Ayesha, who had formed a terrible conspiracy against him at Meccah. For all the mal-contents, particularly those of the house of Ommiyah, which was Othman's family, joined to

the cashiered governors ; and having their prophet's widow at the head
of them, who declared herself openly against Ali, gathered together
considerable forces, and resolved upon a war. Telha and Zobeir had
acquainted them at Meccah, in what an unsettled condition Ali's affairs
were at Medinah, which induced Ayesha to perswade them to go
thither, and strike at the very root. Others were of opinion that it was
best to join the Syrians : but upon consideration that Moawiyah alone
was sufficient to secure that part of the country, and besides that Telha
had a good interest at Basorah, they resolved upon that expedition ;
and accordingly caused this proclamation to be made about the streets
of Meccah : ' The mother of the faithful, and Telha, and Zobeir are
going in person to Basorah. Whosoever therefore is desirous of
strengthening the religion, and fighting voluntarily to revenge the death
of Othman, if he hath no convenience of riding let him come.' They
mounted 600 volunteers upon the like number of camels. They went
out of Meccah about 1000 strong ; and the people joined them in their
march till they were about 3000. Menbah had presented Ayesha with
a camel, whose name was Alascar, which in the Arabick language signifies the army. It cost him 100 pieces. There is no certainty as to
the value of the Arabick coins. As near as I can guess, I should take
one of those pieces of gold to be worth almost half a guinea of our
money ; according to which computation, Ayesha's camel cost about
50 pounds. Mounted upon this camel in a litter she headed the forces
in their march from Meccah towards Basorah. As they were on the
road they came to a rivulet called Jowab, on the side of which there
was a village of the same name. All the dogs of the village came running out in a body, and fell a barking at Ayesha; who thereupon immediately asked what was the name of the place in a great surprize. Being
informed that it was called Jowab, she quoted that versicle of the
Alcoran, which is frequently made use of in cases of imminent danger,
' We are resigned to God, and to him we have recourse' (*chap. xi.* 151),
declaring, ' That she would not stir a step further ; that she had heard
the prophet say when he was travelling with his wives, " I wish I had
known it, and they should have lodged within the barking of the dogs
of Jowab." Besides that he had told her formerly " That one of his
wives should at some time or other be barked at by the dogs of this
place ; that she ought to take care of it, because she would find herself
in a bad condition, and in very great danger." ' Hereupon she struck
her camel upon the leg to make him kneel, in order to alight, and resolved to stay there all night. Telha and Azzobeir could not tell what
to make of this whimsy ; and knowing of what importance it was for
them to precipitate their march ; as having very good reason to think
that Ali would not be long after them, told her, and suborned 50 witnesses to swear it, that it was a mistake of the guide, and that the place
had never been called by any such name. But all to no purpose, she

would not stir ; at last one of them cried out, ' Quick, quick, yonder comes Ali !' upon which they all immediately scampered, and made the best of their way to Basorah.

The historians say, that this was the first solemn and publick lye that was ever told since the beginning of Mahometism ; whether it be so or not, is not so very material ; this is most certain that they who made it, found their account in it, for it conveyed them with incredible speed to Basorah.

Othman, who was Ali's governor in that place, was able to make but a weak resistance. After a skirmish in which he lost forty of his men, he was taken prisoner. They tore his beard and eye-brows out by the roots, and after a short confinement dismissed him.

One of our authors is a little more particular. He says that Ayesha wrote to Othman at Basorah, and to the rest of the provinces, exciting them to revenge the death of Othman ; magnifying his good qualities ; and applauding (as she always had done since his death) the sincerity of his repentance, and the barbarity of the murder : inveighing against his enemies, as if they had broke through and trampled upon every thing that was sacred. Othman sent two messengers to her. She gave them a hearing, answered them in such like terms. When they returned and made their report, the Basorians were in confusion. Othman, a helpless timorous man, disswaded them from enterprising anything till the arrival of the emperor of the faithful, and having substituted Ammar in his room, withdrew to his own house. Ammar called the men to arms, and went to the mosque to hold a consultation. One of them stood up and said, ' If these people come hither out of fear, they are come out of a country where a bird may be safe. If they make enquiry after the blood of Othman, we did not kill Othman : wherefore take my advice, and send them back to the place from whence they came.' Then another rose up and said, ' Either they suspect us guilty of the murther of Othman ; or they come to ask our assistance against those that did murther him, whether belonging to us or not.' This orator had no sooner spoke, but some of the company threw dust in his face ; by which Ammar perceived that they had a faction in the Basorah which much discouraged him. In the mean time, Ayesha advancing nearer, the Basorians went out to meet her ; and they that were so inclined went over to her. They had a debate : Telha began first, and harangued the people in the praise of Othman ; he was seconded by Zobéir, who was succeeded by Ayesha. When she had uttered what she had to say with her loud shrill voice, the company was divided, some said she had spoken right, the opposite party gave them the lie ; till at last they came to throwing the gravel and pebbles in one another's faces. Which when Ayesha perceived she alighted ; and one of the Arabs made up to her and said ; ' O mother of the faithful ! The murthering of Othman was a thing of less moment, than thy coming out from thy house upon this cursed camel. Thou hadst a veil and a protection from God; but thou hast rent the veil, and set at nought the protection. The same persons that are now witnesses of thy quarrelling here will also be witnesses of thy death. If thou camest to us of thy own accord return back to thy own house; if thou camest hither by force, call for assistance.' At the same time a young man came up to Telha and Zobeir, and told them he perceived they had brought their mother along with them, and asked them whether or no they had not brought their wives too? All this was to reproach Ayesha for her impudence, in engaging herself in this expedition. At last they drew their swords, and fought till night parted them. The next day they fought again; in which skirmish most were killed on Othman's side, and a great many wounded on both sides. When they grew weary of fighting they began to parley: and agreed upon this article: that a messenger should be sent to Medinah to enquire whether Telha and Zobeir came into the inauguration of Ali voluntarily or by compulsion. For there lay the whole difficulty. If they came in voluntarily, all the Muslemans would have treated them as rebels; if by compulsion, their party thought they could justify their standing by them. When the messenger arrived at Medinah, and delivered his errand, they were all silent for a while. At last Asamah stood up and said that they were compelled. His saying so had like to have cost him his life; if a friend of his, a man of authority among them, had not taken him by the hand and led him home. To whom Asamah said, he did not think it to be a matter of such importance as now he perceived it was. As soon as Ali heard this news, he wrote to Othman, and taxed the weakness of his conduct; telling him that Ayesha, Telha and Zobeir had not rejected or set themselves in opposition to a party, but to the whole body of the people. That if nothing less' than the deposing him would satisfy them, they were altogether without excuse: but if they had any other proposals to make, they might be considered on both sides. While these matters were transacting at Medinah, Ayesha's party sent to Othman to come out. Who answered that their demand was not conformable to the agreement, which was to stay for an answer from Medinah. Notwithstanding which, Telha and Zobeir, resolved to omit no favourable opportunity, took the advantage of a tempestuous night, and got into the Mosque; where after a skirmish, in which about forty of Othman's men were killed, he was himself seized, and word sent to Ayesha to know which way she would please to dispose of him. The first sentence she pronounced was death; but upon one of her women saying to her, 'I adjure thee by God and the companions of the apostle do not kill him;' that sentence was changed into forty stripes, and imprisonment.

We now leave Ayesha, Telha and Zobeir in the possession of Ba-sorah, taking the suffrages of the people for themselves, and look back to Medinah. Where Ali made a speech to the people, having first (as is always their custom) given due praise and thanks to God; in which he said, ' the latter end of this affair will not be rectified by any other means than those by which it was begun; wherefore help God, and he will help you, and direct your affairs.' But this is the case always when there is a strong competition; most people love to stand neuter, and act the part of spectators, till they see on which side the scale will turn, rather than expose themselves to apparent danger. Though Ali was exceedingly well beloved, and they knew very well that he was fairly elected; yet all his eloquence, though he was allowed to be the best orator in that age, was not sufficient to move his audience to stir in good earnest. Which Ziyad perceiving, he stept to Ali of his own accord, and said, ' Let whosoever will hold back, we ' will hold forward.' Then stood up two of the religious, helpers, doctors of the law, and pronounced this sentence. Alhucm, that is, the decision is this. THE IMAN OTHMAN MASTER OF THE TWO TESTIMONIES DID NOT DYE BY THE MASTER OF THE TWO TESTI-MONIES. That is in short, Ali is not guilty of the death of Othman. By the two testimonies they mean the two articles of their faith, ' There is but one God, Mahomet is the apostle of God.' Which sen-tence formally pronounced in favour of Ali was a mighty inducement to them to engage in his quarrel. One of the Ansars said to Ali, ' The apostle of God, upon whom be peace, put me on this sword : which I have sheathed a long while; but now it is high time to draw it against these wicked men who are always deceiving the people.' The mother of Salnah said, ' O emperor of the faithful ! If it would not be a sin against God, and that thou wouldest not accept of me, I would go with thee myself; but here is my cousin german, who, by God is dearer to me than my own life, let him go with thee and partake of thy fortunes.' Him Ali accepted, and afterwards made governor of Beh-brin. There marched with him about 900 out of Medinah, and at first he conceived some hopes of overtaking Ayesha and her company before their arrival at Basorah; but being informed at a place called Arrabdah that it was in vain : he rested here to take farther consider-ation.

Thither came his son Hasan to him, and told him that he had given him his advice in three particulars, and that now as the consequence of his refusing it, he might expect to be murdered to-morrow without anybody to help him. Upon Ali's demanding what those particulars might be; Hasan answered, ' In the first place, I advised you when Othman was besieged, to go out of the city, that you might not be in it when he should be killed. Then secondly, I advised you not to be inaugurated till the ambassadors of the tribes of the Arabs should come to you; and all the provinces were come in. Last of all, I advised you when this woman and those men went out, to sit still at home till they should be reconciled: so that if there were any mischief done, the blame might rather be laid upon some other person than yourself.' To which Ali answered: 'As to your first, if I had gone out of the city when Othman was besieged; that had been the way for me to have been surrounded myself. Then, as to your saying that I ought not to have been inaugurated till all the tribes came in; you ought to know that the disposal of the government is a privilege peculiar to the Medinians or Helpers; and we were not willing to lose it. As for your last advice, that I should have sat still at home after Ayesha and Zobeir were gone forth; how could I do that in these circumstances, or who would? Would you have me lurk in a hole like a wild beast till she is digged out? If I do not myself look after what concerns me in this affair, and provide for my necessary defence, who will look after it? Therefore, son, hold you your tongue.'

During his stay at Arrabdah, he sent Mahomet the son of Abubeker, and Mahomet the son of Jaafa, to his friends at Cufah with a letter, in which he did not so much press them to fight for him, as to come and arbitrate between him and those that had made a separation from him. He told them, 'How much he preferred them to all the rest of 'the provinces, and what confidence he reposed in them in the time 'of his extremity. That they should help the religion of God, and 'repair to him in order to make use of such means as might be proper 'for the reconciling this divided people, and making them brethren 'again.' He did not neglect in the meantime sending to Medinah, from whence he was plentifully supplied with horses, arms, and all necessaries. In his public harangues he represented to the people, 'the great blessing which God had indulged them in giving them the 'religion, whereby those tribes were united that formerly used to re- 'duce one another to a despicable condition. That this peace con- 'tinued, till this man (meaning Othman) fell into the hands of this 'people, whom the devil had set on work to make a disturbance. 'However that it was NECESSARY that this people should be divided 'as other nations had been before it; and that we must call to God to 'avert the present evil.' Then turning to his son, he said, 'Whatso- 'ever IS, is of NECESSITY. And the time will come when this people 'shall be divided into seventy-three sects; the worst of which will be 'that that shall set me at nought and will not follow my example. 'You have known this and seen it; wherefore keep close to your 'religion, and be directed in the right way, for it is the direction of 'your prophet. Let what is too hard for you alone, till you bring it to 'the test of the *Alcoran*, and what the *Alcoran* approveth stand to, 'and what it disapproveth reject. Delight in God for your Lord; and 'in ISLAM for your religion; in Mahomet for your prophet, and in the '*Alcoran* for your guide and director.'

When they were about decamping from Arrabdah for Basorah, the son of Rephaa stood up and asked him, ' O emperor of the faithful ! What is it thou wouldest have, and whither wouldest thou carry us ?' Ali answered, 'What I would have and intend is peace, if they will accept of it at our hands, if not, we will leave them alone to their rashness, and do what is just on our part and bear with patience.' ' But how,' replied Rephaa, 'if that will not satisfy them ?' ' Why then,' says Ali, ' we will let them alone so long as they let us alone ; if not, the last remedy is to defend ourselves.' Upon this, one of the Ansars stood up, and told him that he liked his discourse better than his management ; but subjoined immediately with an oath, ' That they would help God since he had called them HELPERS.'

Soon after there came a party of the tribe of Tai, to proffer their service to him. Their chief, whose name was Said, the son of Obeid, thus addressed him : ' O emperor of the faithful ! There are some men whose tongues are not according to their hearts, but I do not find it so with me. I always have a respect for thee both secretly and openly, and will fight thy enemies wheresoever I meet them. For I look upon thee as a person of the greatest merit, and the most ex· cellent qualifications of any in the age thou livest in.' Ali gave him his blessing (God have mercy upon you) and told him that he was satisfied with his sincerity. He then removed from Arrabdah, and the tribe of Ased and some more of Tai proffered their service, but he said to them, ' They might go home, for he had mohagerins (*refugees*) enough for his purpose.'

In the meanwhile, Ali was full of expectation of news from his two messengers that he had sent to Cufah. Abu Musa, who, as we have before observed, had sent him word at first, that all was well on that side of the country, and acquainted him with the particulars of all that concerned him there ; perceiving how the face of things was altered on a sudden, and apprehensive of the success of Ayesha, Telha and Zobeir at Basorah, began to find himself in some sort of suspence. So that when Mahomet, the son of Abubeker, and Mahomet the son of Jaafar, came to Cufah with Ali's letter, and stood up among the people according to his command, there was a perfect silence. It is worth observing here, that upon all such occasions, the way was, for all the congregation to run to the mosque, where everything was published in the hearing of all that were present ; and everyone (slaves excepted) had the liberty of assenting or dissenting, according as he was influenced by his prejudice or judgment. At last, in the evening, there came some of the Hagis, or pilgrims (they having been once on pil-grimage at Meccah, entitles them to that name, and procures them reverence as long as they live), and asked Abu Musa, what he thought of going out ? meaning to assist Ali. To which he gravely answered, ' My opinion to-day is different from what it was yesterday. What you despised in time past, hath drawn upon you what you see now ; the going out, and sitting still at home, are two things. Sitting still at home is the heavenly way. The going out, is the way of the world. Therefore, take your choice.' None of the people took any notice of what he said, nor returned him any answer. But both the Mahometans were in a rage, and gave him reproachful language. To which he answered, with an oath, 'That the inauguration of Othman hung still both over his own neck and their master's (meaning Ali), and they were resolved not to engage themselves, unless compelled by absolute necessity, till they had got their hands clear of the murderers of Othman, wheresoever they were. Wherefore,' adds he, ' you may both get you back to Ali and tell him so.'

Ali was then advanced as far as Dulkhar, where his governor Othman came to wait upon him, and told him that he had sent him to Basorah with a beard, but he was come back without one. ' Thy sufferings,' says Ali, ' are meritorious. All mankind were satisfied in the choice of two of my predecessors, who managed agreeably both to the written law and the traditional. Then a third presided over them, to whom they submitted. At last they chose me ; and Telha and Zobeir came unto the election, but did not stand to their word. What I wonder at is their voluntary submission to Abubeker, Omar and Othman, and their opposition to me ! But by God, they shall both know that I am not one jot inferior to any of my predecessors.'

As soon as Ali had received Abu Musa's answer ; he dispatched Alashtar (a man of resolution, and fit to be made use of in cases of difficulty) together with Ebn Abbas to Cufa, with instructions at large to make use of their own discretion in rectifying whatsoever they should find amiss. When they had delivered their errand, and desired the assistance of the Cufians, Abu Musa made this speech to them :— ' Friends, the companions of the apostle of God, upon whom be ' peace, know more of God and his apostle than those who have not ' conversed with him. And you have a right over us. I give you ' this advice. It is my opinion that you should not assume to your- ' selves the authority of God, nor make war against God. Let those ' that are come along with you from Medinah, return thither again, till ' they be all agreed ; they know best who is fit to be trusted.' For this disturbance is such a one (it is a sentence of Mahomet's) as he that sleepeth in it is better than he that is awake ; and he that is awake better than he that sitteth ; and he that sitteth better than he that standeth ; and he that standeth better than he that walketh on foot ; and he that walketh on foot better than he that rideth. ' Sheath ' your swords and take the heads off your lances ; cut your bow ' strings, and receive him that is injured into your houses till this ' business is made up, and the disturbance ceased.'

Ebn Abbas and Alashtar returning to Ali with this news, he last of

all sent his eldest son Hasan, and Ammar along with him : Abu Musa
received Hasan with respect ; but when they came into the Mosque to
debate the matter, he opposed it with the same vigour that he had
done all along before, repeating that saying of Mahomet's (which he
affirmed to have had from his own mouth), 'That there should
be a sedition, in which he that sat should be ' better than him
that stood,' &c. Ammar took him up briskly, and told him,
that the apostle directed that speech to him, who was better
sitting than standing at any time. Still Abu Musa persisted in exert-
ing his utmost to hinder them from complying with Ali's proposals.
When the people began to be in a tumult, Zeid, the son of Sauchan,
stood up and pulled out a letter from Ayesha, commanding him either
to stay at home, or else come to her assistance : together with another
to the Cufians to the same effect. Having read them both to the
people, he said, ' SHE was commanded to stay at home in her house,
and WE to fight till there should be no sedition. Now she has commanded us to do her part, and hath taken ours upon herself.' This
provoked the opposite party, who reproached him for reflecting upon
the Mother of the Faithful. The debate grew very warm on both
sides, till at last Hasan, the son of Ali, rose up and said, ' Hearken to
the request of your Emperor, and help us in this calamity which is
fallen both upon you and us. Thus saith the Emperor of the faithful,
either I do injury myself, or else I suffer injury. If I suffer injury
God will help me ; if I do injury he will take vengeance upon me.
By God, Telha and Zobeir were the first that inaugurated me,
and the first that prevaricated. Have I discovered any covetous inclination, or perverted justice ? Wherefore come on, and
command that which is good, and forbid that which is evil.'*
This moved the audience, and the heads of the tribes spoke
one after another, telling the people that since they had given their
allegiance to this man, and he had done them the honour to send
several messages to them before, and afterwards his son, to make them
judges and arbitrators in an affair of such importance ; that it was
highly requisite for them to comply with such a reasonable demand,
and go to his assistance. Hasan told them that he was going back to
his father, and they that thought fit might go along with him, and the
rest follow by water. There came over to him near 9,000 in all 6,2,00
by land, and 2,400 by water. Some say that Ali had sent Ashtar and
Ammar along with him after his son Hasan to Cufah, and whilst they
were debating it in the Mosque, and every one intent upon the issue,
Ashtar took a party of men and seized the castle by surprise ; then
having ordered some of Abu Musa's men, whom he found there, to be
severely banged, he sent them back with this lamentable news to their
master, Abu Musa, who was speeching it with great vehemency

* A text that frequently occurs in the *Alcoran.*

against the supply. This management of Alashtar made Abu Musa appear so ridiculous and contemptible, that if Alashtar had not interposed and prevented it, his goods would immediately have been plundered by the mob.

Ali was very easy upon the accession of these new recruits, and went forwards to meet them and make them welcome. When they came up to him, and said, 'You Cufians were always men of distinguished valour; you conquered the kings of Persia, and dispersed their forces till you took possession of their inheritance. You have both protected the weak ones among yourselves, and afforded your assistance to your neighbours. I have called you hither to be witnesses between us and our brethren of Basorah : if they return, it is what we desire : if they shall persist we will heal them with gentle usage, till they fall upon us injuriously. We on our part will omit nothing that may by any means contribute to an accommodation, which we must prefer to the desolation of war.'

Ayesha and her party, upon this news, began to be in some perplexity at Basorah. They had very frequent consultations, and seemed now to be in a despairing condition. Messages passed backwards and forwards in order to compromise the matter ; and it came so far that Ali, Telha, and Zobeir had several interviews, walking about together in the sight of both the armies, so that every one expected that there would have been a peace concluded. Ali's army consisted of 30,000 men all experienced soldiers, and if that of his enemies exceeded his in number, yet it was composed of such as they could get ; besides that, they had never a general to command them that was any ways comparable to Ali. In one of their conferences he reproached their infidelity, and put them in mind of the judgments of God, who would infallibly take vengeance upon their perfidiousness. He asked Zobeir if he did not remember how Mahomet had asked him once if he did not love his dear son Ali ; and he having answered yes, that Mahomet replyed, 'Notwithstanding this, there will come a day when you shall rise up against him, and be the occasion of a great many miseries both to him and all the Muslemans.'

Zobeir told him that he remembered it perfectly well, and that if he had recollected it before, he would never have carried things to that extremity. It is said that upon this hint he declined fighting with Ali ; but that having acquainted Ayesha with the circumstances, that woman was so envenomed against him, that she would not upon any terms give the least ear to an accommodation. Others say that his son Abdollah gave him a turn, by asking him whether or no he was afraid of Ali's colours? Zobeir answering no, but that he was sworn to the contrary. Abdollah bad him expiate his oath, which he did, by giving a slave his liberty, and forthwith put himself in a condition of fighting against Ali.

The two armies lay in order of battle on their arms opposite to one another. There happened some disturbance in the night, the author of which is uncertain. When Telha and Zobeir heard it, upon enquiry into the cause of it, they were answered that the Cufians had fallen upon them in the night. They said they knew very well that Ali would never put up the matter without bloodshed : and Ali, upon his first hearing it, said the same of them. Thus they were of necessity drawn to a battle. Ayesha, to give life and courage to her friends, mounted upon her great camel, was carried up and down in the battle, riding in a litter of the shape of a cage.

Upon which occasion, the day whereon this bloody battle was fought, is called, the 'Day of the camel ;' and the men that were engaged on that side, the 'People of the camel.' In the heat of the battle, when the victory began to incline towards Ali, Merwan said to him, ''Tis but a little while ago since Telha was amongst the murderers of Othman, and now he is so attached to worldly grandeur, that he appears amongst those that seek to revenge his blood ;' and with those words let fly an arrow, and wounded him in the leg. His horse threw him. He called for help, and said, ' O God ! take vengeance upon me for Othman, according to thy will !' Perceiving his boot full of blood, he ordered his man to take him up behind him, who conveyed him into a house in Basorah, where he died. But just before he saw one of Ali's men, and asked him if he belonged to the Emperor of the faithful. Being informed that he did ; ' Give me, then,' said he, ' your hand, that I may put mine in it ; and by this action renew the oath of fidelity which I have already made to Ali.' The words were no sooner out of his mouth but he expired immediately. When Ali heard it, he said, ' God would not call him to heaven till he had blotted out his first breach of his word by this last protestation of fidelity.'

Mircond writes, that Zobeir being informed that Ammar Jasser was in Ali's camp ; and knowing that Mahomet had formerly said that he was a person that was always for justice and what was right, withdrew himself out of the battle, and took the road towards Meccah. Being come as far as a valley which is crossed by a rivulet called Sabaa, he met with Hanaph Ben Kais, who was encamped there with all his men, and attending to the success of the battle, in order to join himself with the conqueror.

Hanaph knew who he was at a distance, and said to his men, ' Is there no body can bring me any tidings of Zobeir ? One of them, whose name was Amrou Ben Jarmuz, went off immediately, and came up to him. Zobeir bad him keep his distance. But after some discourse, growing into greater confidence of him, he crying out ' Salat,' that is, ' To prayers ' (the hour of prayer being then come) Salat said, ' Amrou ;' and as Zobeir was prostrating himself, took his opportunity, and struck his head off at one blow with his sabre ; and carried it to

Ali. When Ali saw the head, he let fall some tears, and said, ' Go wretched villain and carry this good news to Ben Safiah in hell.' Amrou was so moved with these words, that laying aside all respect, he said to him, ' You are the ill destiny of all the Muslemans ; if one delivers you from any of your enemies, you immediately denounce hell to him : and if a man kills any one of yours, he becomes instantly a companion of the devil.' His passion increasing into rage and despair, he drew his sword and ran himself through.

So long as Ayesha's camel stood upon his legs, the hottest of the battle was about him. Tahari says that there were 70 mens hands cut off that held his bridle. Ayesha's litter was stuck so full of arrows and javelins that it looked like a porcupine. At last the camel was hamstringed, and Ayesha was forced to lye there till all was over. Ali having got an entire victory, came to her and asked her how she did. Some historians say that there was some reproachful language exchanged between them. However, he treated her civilly, and dismissed her handsomely with a very good equipage, and commanded his two sons, Hasan and Hosein, to wait upon her a day's journey. He confined her to her house at Medinah, and laid a restraint upon her not to intermeddle any more with affairs of state. She went to Meccah, and staid out the time of the pilgrimage there, after which she returned to Medinah. As for the spoils, Ali was for dividing them among the heirs of his men that were killed, which did not exceed a thousand. Then constituting Abdollah Ben Abbas his lieutenant over Basorah, went to Cufah, where he established the seat of his government or Caliphate.

This compleat victory rendered Ali exceeding powerful. He is now master of Irack, Ægypt, Arabia, Persia, and Chorasan. So that there was none left that could give him the least disturbance but Moawiyah and the Syrians under his command. Ali seemed not to be apprehensive of any molestation from them after such great success, and sent a messenger to him to come in. Moawiyah put off the messenger without giving him any satisfactory answer, till Amrou, the son of Ali, who was then in Palestine could come to him. Amrou, to his great satisfaction, found the Syrians very eager to revenge the blood of Othman, and did what in him lay to spur them on. Upon this, Amrou and Moawiyah resolved to stand it out to the last against Ali, Amrou having first stipulated for himself, that in case of success, he should have the lieutenancy of Ægypt, which he had conquered in the reign of Omar. This agreed to, Amrou, in the presence of all the army, took the oath of allegiance to Moawiyah, acknowledging him to be lawful Caliph and prince of the Muslemans. This action which had been concerted between them two, was followed by the acclamations of the people, who unanimously took the same oath.

As soon as Ali was apprised of these commotions in Syria, he made use of all manner of gentle means to reduce the rebels to a sense of their duty. But perceiving that the people of that large province had unanimously declared against him, he began to fear that it would be to no purpose, to set on foot any further negotiation ; and marched with an army of 90,000 men towards that part of the country. Just upon his entrance into the confines of Syria he was obliged to encamp in a place where he wanted water.

Not far from his camp there was an hermitage under ground, the hermit whereof, who was a Christian, came and offered himself to him. Ali enquired of him if there was never a spring within the neighbour-hood ; the hermit told him that there was nothing but a cistern, which had hardly three buckets of water in it. Ali answered, ' I know, how-ever, that some ancient prophets of the people of Israel have made their abode here, and that they digged a pit here.' The hermit said he had been informed by some ancient men that there was one indeed that was shut up, and nobody knew where it was digged ; but that the tradition of the country was, that no body could find it, and open it, but a prophet, or one sent by a prophet. Ali was not long a finding it, and ordering them to dig in a place, which he pointed out, found a stone of a vast bigness that lay over it, which he instantly removed, with the greatest ease imaginable.

The hermit, surprized at his sight, embraced Ali's knees, and would never leave him after. Besides, he presented him with an old parch-ment, which he said was written by the hand of Simeon, the son of Safa (that is Simon Cephas), one of the greatest apostles of Jesus Christ, wherein there was an account given of the coming of the last prophet, the arrival of his lawful heir and successor, and the miracu-lous discovery of this well.

Ali, after having given thanks to God, and taken water sufficient for his army, continued his march towards Seffein, a place between Irak and Syria, where the enemies army was posted, consisting of 80,000 men. At last, both the armies advancing, they came in sight of one another, in the last month of the 36th year of the flight of Mahomet.

The first month of the next year was spent without doing anything but sending messengers backwards and forwards, in order to an accom-modation between them, to no purpose. But upon the entrance of the next month they began to fight in parties, without running the hazard of a general engagement. It is reported that in the space of 110 days, there were no less than 90 skirmishes between them ; that the number of the slain on Moawiyah's side was 45,000, and that on Ali's 25,000— 26 of which had been present at the battel of Beder, and were honoured with the title of Sahabah—that is, the companions of the prophet. Ali had commanded his men never to begin the battel first, but stay till they gave the onset, nor kill any man that had turned his back, nor take any of their plunder, nor use any indecent behaviour towards the

21

women. Nor were Moawiyah and Amrou wanting on their side in expressing their concern for the effusion of the blood of the Muslemans,
especially when Ammar Ben Jassar, Ali's general of the horse, was
killed. He was about 90 years of age, and had been in three several
engagements with Mahomet himself. He lived reverenced, and died
lamented by all. ' Do you see,' said Moawiyah, ' at what a rate the
people expose their lives on our account?' ' See !' says Amrou,
' would to God I had died twenty years ago.'   Upon the death of
Ammar, Ali took 12,000 chosen men, and made such an impression
upon Moawiyah's army, that all the ranks of it were broken. Then
Ali called out to Moawiyah, ' How long shall the people lose their lives
between us ? Come hither. I challenge you to appeal to the decision
of God ; and which soever of us two kills his man, has all entire to
himself.' Whereupon Amrou said to Moawiyah, ' Your cousin has
made you a fair proffer.' Moawiyah said it was not fair, because that
Ali knew that no man ever came out against him, but he killed him.
Amrou told him that his refusal would look dishonourably. Moawiyah
answered, ' You have a mind to enjoy the government yourself, after I
am gone.'

The last battel they fought at Seffein continued all night, to the great
disadvantage of the Syrians.   Alashtar pushed them back to their
camp, and Ali supported him.   It was very near a compleat victory,
when Amrou bethought himself of this stratagem : he sends for Moawiyah in great haste, and advises him to hoist up the Alcorans upon
the points of their lances, and cry out, ' This is the book that ought to
decide all our differences—this is the book of God between us and
you.'   This stratagem did not fail of the desired success ; for as soon
as the Irakians, in whom the chief strength of Ali's army consisted,
saw this, they threw down their arms, and said to Ali, ' Will you not
answer to the book of God ?'   To which Ali answered, ' As you are
men of truth and honour, go on and fight your enemy, for Amrou and
Moawiyah have no relation to religion nor the Alcoran. Alas for you !
I know them better than you do : by God, they have not put up these
Alcorans, but with a design to trick us.'   They answered that should
not hinder them from being determined by the book of God. ' That
is it,' said Ali, ' which I have been fighting to bring them to ; but they
have rebelled against God and his commandment.'   In short, they
threatened not only to desert him, but to deliver him into the hands of
his enemies, if he did not sound a retreat ; and some of the sectaries
(Charegites)—an enthusiastick people, that refuse obedience to their
superiors, both in things sacred and civil—declared to him, that they
would serve him as they did the son of Affan—that is, Othman—whom
they murdered.   So that Ali was forced to call off Alashtar, who came
back with great reluctancy, and not under three or four messengers—

grieved at the heart to see such a glorious victory wrested out of his hands by such a stratagem.

As soon as the battle was over, Moawiyah being asked what was the meaning of that action, answered, ' That the difference might be put to the arbitration of two persons, who should determine it according to the true sense of the Alcoran and the tradition (sunnet) of the apostle. Ashaath, the son of Kais, one of those that had the greatest credit among the soldiers of Irak, and who was suspected to have been corrupted by Moawiyah, asked Ali how he approved of this expedient. Ali answered him coldly, ' He that is not at liberty, cannot give his advice. It belongs to you to manage this affair according as you shall think fit among yourselves.' The person that they nominated for Ali was Abu Musa Alashari, a good, honest, well-meaning man, but exceedingly simple. Ali did not approve of him, because he had formerly been drawn aside, and forsaken his interest. He had rather have had Ben Abbas, but was answered that he was his cousingerman, and they would have none but such as should deal impartially between him and Moawiyah. He next nominated Alashtar, but they were resolved he should accept of Abu Musa. Moawiyah, on his part, nominated Amrou, the son of Aasi, deservedly reputed the quickest-witted man of his age. These two referees took a security, signed by Ali and Moawiyah, and both the armies, for themselves and their families, to ratify and confirm what they should agree upon, which was to be determined the next Ramadan. This agreed upon, Ali retired to Cufah and Moawiyah to Damascus, leaving each of them the command of their several armies to one of their generals, and the authority of things relating to religion in the hands of a particular Imâm. But as soon as Ali came to Cufah, 12,000 of those that could read the Alcoran reproached him with his base submission to this accommodation, as having out of fear of temporal calamity submitted to the determination of men, when the Alcoran expressly says that judgment belongeth to God alone.

Eight months after the battel of Seffein, the two arbitrators met in a place (Arab. *Dumat-al-jondel*) which lieth between Meccah, Cufah, and Syria. There came along with them several of the Sahabah, or companions of the prophet. Ebn Abbas bad Abu Musa remember this, whatsoever else he forgot : that Ali had no blemish to render him incapable of the government, nor Moawiyah any virtue to qualify him for it. Amrou, who knew very well the genius of his partner, treated him with the utmost civility and respect, till at last he had insinuated himself so far into him as to make him believe that it would be altogether impracticable ever to bring things to an accommodation, without deposing both these competitors, and leaving the choice of a third to the people. This important article once fixed, they erected a tribunal between both the armies, from which each of the umpires was publickly to declare his opinion. Abu Musa would have had Amrou gone up first, but he alledged so many reasons why he ought to give him the preference, that at last he over-perswaded him.

Then Abu Musa, going up first, pronounced these words with a loud voice, ' I depose Ali and Moawiyah from the caliphate (or government) to which they pretend, after the same manner as I take this ring from my finger.' Having made this declaration, he immediately came down. Then Amrou went up and said, ' You have heard how Abu Musa has, for his part, deposed Ali ; as, for my part, I depose him, too ; and I give the caliphate to Moawiyah, and invest him with it after the same manner as I put this ring upon my finger ; and this I do with so much the more justice, because he is Othman's heir and avenger, and the worthiest of all men to succeed him.'

After this publication, Ali's party, ashamed and confounded at this unexpected success, began to complain grievously of Abu Musa. He, for his own part, accused Amrou of not having performed the agreement made between them. From complaints they came to ill language —and, in short, Abu Musa, ashamed of his arbitration, and justly fearing Ali's displeasure, besides not thinking himself safe in the army, took his flight, and retired to Meccah. This Abu Musa was celebrated for the most harmonious voice that ever was heard—it is said that his common discourse was perfect melody.

The Syrians went back to Moawiyah, and wished him joy ; and from that time Ali's interest began to decline, and Moawiyah's increased daily. The two opposite parties not only cursed one another, but carried the matter so far as to come to a mutual solemn excommunication, which was always pronounced when they made any harangue to the people in the mosque, and continued a long time between the house of Ali and that of Ommiyah, of which were Othman and Moawiyah.

Before we proceed any further, we must here observe, that when the treaty of peace that followed the suspension of arms between Ali and Moawiyah was a writing, the Secretary began with these words. ' Ali, chief and commander, general of the Muslemans, agrees to a peace with Moawiyah upon these following terms.' Moawiyah having read these first words, said, ' Certainly I should be a very wicked man indeed, if I should make war upon him, whom I acknowledge to be the chief, and commander general of the Faithful.'

Upon this, Amrou Ebno'l Asi said, ' That it was absolutely necessary to blot out that title of chief, or emperor of the faithful.' Ahnaf the son of Kais, addressing himself to Ali said, ' That he ought by no means to suffer himself to be deprived of that title.' Ali told him, ' That when he was formerly secretary to his father-in-law Mahomet, he had himself drawn up articles of peace between him and Sohail, who had revolted against him. That upon his having intituled Mahomet, apostle and messenger of God ; Sohail said to him, if I had acknowledged your father-in-law for the apostle and messenger of God, I should never have had any peace to sign with him, for I would never have made any war. I acquainted Mahomet with this difficulty, who answered me, Make no scruple of blotting out that title ; that doth not depend upon this treaty, time will discover the truth of that ; and remember, that there will come a day when you shall find yourself in the same case.' Ali therefore gave his consent, that for that time they should omit that title, of which his arbitrator, Abu Musa, as we have seen already, solemnly deprived him. All these things were transacted in the 37th year of the Hegirah, and A.D. 657. As also the revolt of the Karegites, or Separatists, who this year made an insurrection against Ali.

The occasion of their revolt was, that Ali having put his affairs into the hands of two arbitrators, as we have already seen, some of the Irakians told him, that he had done exceeding wrong, in referring that to the judgment of men, which ought to be determined by God alone. That instead of standing to the peace he had made, he ought to pursue his enemies, who also were the enemies of God, without quarter. Ali answered, ' That having once passed his word, he was obliged to keep it ; and that in this he followed what the law of God prescribed.' These people answered him, 'That there was no other judge or arbitrator between him and Moawiyah but God alone : that what he had done was a sin, and that he ought to repent of it.'

Ali remonstrated to them with a great deal of vigour, ' That the sin lay at their door, in shewing so much inconstancy and stubbornness. That they ought to remember, that when Moawiyah caused the Alcorans to be carried at the head of the two armies, he gave them notice that it was only a trick of their enemies, yet nevertheless they had left off fighting without his order ; and that in short, it was very injurious in them, to press him to the breach of the treaty, which they themselves had obliged him to sign.'

The rebels, not at all satisfied with these reasons, chose for their captain Abdollah, the son of Waheb, who appointed Naharwan (a town between Bagdad and Waset, four miles east of the river Tigris) for the place of their rendezvous. Thither came all Ali's mal-contents, whereof there was a great number from Cufah, Basorah and Arabia.

Ali took little notice of them at first, his thoughts being more taken up about Moawiyah, whom he considered as the much more formidable enemy ; but being informed that they were already increased to the number of 25,000 men, that they condemned all men as impious that did not fall in with their sentiments, and that they had already put to death several Muslemans, for refusing to comply with their measures; he resolved in fine to exterminate a sect, which tended to the subversion of the very foundations of Muslemanism. However he chose rather to gain them by gentleness, and bring them back to their duty by good advice ; but that means proving too weak, he employs the forces of a considerable army, at the head of which he presented himself to their view. Nevertheless he made use of this artifice before he began the battle ; namely to plant a standard without the camp, and make proclamation with sound of trumpet, that whosoever should come under it should have good quarter ; and if any of them would retire to Cufah, they should there find a sanctuary.

This stratagem succeeded well for Ali. For the army of the Karegites dispersed itself in a very little time of its own accord ; and Abdollah, the son of Waheb, found himself reduced to 4000 men only. However this arch-rebel was resolved, with his small number of men, to signalize his bravery by a desperate attempt. For he attacked Ali's army, notwithstanding the inequality of his forces. But his rashness was duly punished, he and all his men were cut to pieces, nine only excepted, which was the same number that Ali had lost in all.

A little before this fight, Ali had foretold to his friends what would be the event. ' You see,' says he, ' these people who make profession of reading the Alcoran, without observing its commandments, they will quit the profession which they make of their sect, as quick as arrows fly from the bow when they are shot off.'

This victory, which was gained in the 38th year of the Hegirah, having reunited all the Arabians under the government of Ali ; there remained nothing else to be done, but to reduce the Syrians. Ali was for marching against Moawiyah immediately after the victory. But some of his great men represented to him, that it would be proper to give his army some refreshment, that every one might make preparation for the war, which it was plain would be more long winded than the former. Ali followed their advice, and formed his camp at Nakilah, not far from Cufah, where he made proclamation, that during the time of his encampment in that place, any one that had any business to do in town, might go for one day, and return the next ; that they might be the sooner in a readiness for their expedition into Syria. The effect of the publication of this order was, that the camp was entirely forsaken ; and the general finding himself left alone, was obliged to go back to Cufah too, as well as the rest.

Ali, at the beginning of his caliphate, had conferred the government of Ægypt upon Saad the son of Kais ; who acquitted himself of his charge with abundance of prudence. For there being in Ægypt a great faction of Othman's partisans, he knew how to accommodate the time, and managed them with great address. This conduct of Saad furnished Moawiyah with an occasion of publishing it all abroad, that this governor was his friend, and acted in concert with him. These reports he spread round about, on purpose to raise a suspicion of him in Ali, who nevertheless had no better friend belonging to him. To forward the matter, Moawiyah forged a letter in Saad's name directed to himself; wherein was insinuated, that the reason why he had not attacked the party of Othmanians, was because he was entirely in his measures.

The device of Moawiyah had its desired effect ; for as soon as the news reached Ali's ears, he recalled Saad from his government, and sent in his room Mahomet the son of Abubeker, the first Caliph, which was the cause of new troubles in that country ; for Mahomet had no sooner set foot in Ægypt, but he began to chase out of it all those who pretended to have had any tye of friendship with Othman, or to preserve any respect for his memory.

Wherefore after his arrival, there was nothing but dissensions and civil wars, and these disorders grew to such a height, that Ali was obliged to send Malec Shutur, who is sometimes called Ushtur Malec, to restore his authority there. But Moawiyah, who had notice of the sending of this new governor, dealt with a countryman that lived upon the confines of Arabia and Ægypt, and at whose house Ushtur Malec was to lodge, to give him poison in the entertainment which he had prepared for him.

This man, an old friend of Moawiyah's, punctually executed his orders, and gave him some poisoned honey to sup ; of which he died before he stirred out of the house. As soon as Moawiyah heard it, he said, ' Verily God hath armies of honey !' Then he despatched Amrou Ben Alas with 6000 horse to take possession of the government of Ægypt in his name ; who made such speed that in a few days he came up to the capital city ; there he joined Ben Sharig, the chief of Othman's party ; and they two marched together to engage Mahomet, the son of Abubeker, who as yet retained the name and authority of governor for Ali. Mahomet was routed, and fell into his enemies hands alive ; who quickly killed him, and inclosing his dead body in that of an ass, burnt him to ashes. As soon as Ayesha heard of the death of her brother Mahomet, she took it extremely to heart, and kneeled down, at the end of all her prayers, to beg a curse upon Moawiyah and Amrou, and took Mahomet's domesticks and dependants into her care. Ali was very much concerned and said, ' We shall reckon for him before God.' All this year there was a continued succession of incursions made into Ali's territories, who was all this while daily employed in making eloquent speeches, and moving his army to go against Moawiyah, but could make no impression upon them to the purpose.

Ali being informed of all this bad news, sent for Abdollah, the son of Abbas, from Basorah, where he was governor, that he might comfort himself with his conversation, and they might take such resolutions together as were most convenient for the bad condition of their affairs. Abdollah having first constituted Ziyad his lieutenant in Basorah, came to Ali, and once again promised him inviolable fidelity. Moawiyah, who was always watchful to make his advantage of all opportunities, was no sooner informed that Ben Abbas had left Basorah, but he sent one Abdallah, surnamed Hadrami, with 2000 horse to seize that place.

Ziyad, who had not troops sufficient to stand against Abdallah, left the city to him, and informed Ali of the pressing necessity he was under of having speedy succours sent him, that at least he might be able to keep the field. Ali sent him some under the command of Hareth, who arrived so seasonably that Abdallah was beaten and killed in the battle, which was fought near Basorah. Upon this the city surrendered itself to Ali's government, who immediately sent back Abdollah Ben Abbas, to take the command of it as he had done before. This was in the 38th year of the Hegirah.

The next year passed over without any considerable adventures, for the Syrians, weary of the war, enterprised nothing against the Arabians, and the Arabians had enough to do to preserve themselves. In the beginning of this year, Abdollah Ben Abbas, lieutenant of Basorah, sent Ziyad, to take upon him the government of Persia, which was put into great disorder upon the account of these commotions between Ali and Moawiyah. He behaved himself so well in that post, and managed so much to the satisfaction of the people, that the Persians said they had never met with any administration since the days of Anusherwan, equal to that of this Arabian. This Anusherwan was surnamed the Just, he was the son of Hormisdas, king of the Persians, and reigned contemporary with Mauritius and Phocas. Mahomet was born in his reign, as he says himself, in the Alcoran, ' I was born in the days of the Just King.'

This was but a short cessation, for in the beginning of the 40th year Moawiyah began to rouse, and sent Ben Arthah with 3000 horse towards that province of Arabia called Hejaz, to seize upon its two principal towns, Meccah and Medinah, where he had always kept a correspondence ever since Othman's death, and by this means to open himself a way into Yemen, or Arabia the Happy. Ali's two governors quitted each of them their respective charges upon his approach, for want of forces sufficient to make a defence. So that Ben Arthah made the inhabitants take the oath of allegiance to Moawiyah. He shed some blood at Medinah, which gave the people an aversion to Moawiyah's government, and proceeded in his march to Arabia Fælix, where he put some thousands to the sword.

All this while Moawiyah was in Syria at Damascus, and Ali at Cufah. Ali always prayed publicly for Moawiyah, Amrou and Dehoc. Moawiyah, on the other side, prayed for Ali, Hasan, and Hosein.

Abdollah foreseeing very well that he should be visited by Ben Arthah, made the best preparation he was able, but to no purpose. He made a shift to escape himself, but left two little boys behind him, both which Ben Arthah barbarously murdered. This cruelty not only occasioned great grief to the father, but raised a just abhorrence in everybody else. Ali was extremely touched, and cursed the author of such a horrible outrage, begging of God to take away his senses and understanding. They say that towards the latter end of his days he did really turn fool, and was always calling for his sword, which his friends perceiving, gave him one made of wood, and another hollow one full of air ; and that this poor wretch imagined that so many blows as he struck with his wooden sword against the other, he killed so many men.

However, Ali did not omit the sending Jariyah to pursue Ben Arthah with 4000 horse : but he had scarce set out towards Yemen, when the other was returning into Syria. At the same time, another great calamity befel Ali, for his brother Okail went over to Moawiyah, who received him with open arms, and assigned him large revenues. Okail alledged no other pretence for his desertion, but only that his brother Ali had not entertained him according to his quality.

A little after the battle of Naharwan, three Karegites of those that were the most zealous for the advancement of their sect, met together at Meccah, and making frequent mention among themselves of those that were killed in the battle, magnified their merit and bewailed their loss. These three men, Abdarrahman the son of Melgem, Barak the son of Abdollah, whom some surname Turk, and Amrou the son of Beker, said one to the other, ' If Ali, Moawiyah, and Amrou, the son of Aasi, these erroneous Imams, were dead, the affairs of the Muslemans would be in a good condition. Immediately the first of them said to his companions, ' For my part, if you will, I will give you a good account of Ali.' The second hearing this discourse, said he would undertake to make a good riddance of Moawiyah ; and the third promised the other two, to kill Amrou Ben Aasi. These three men that were thus devoted to execute their design unanimously, pitched upon a Friday (the day of the solemn assembly of the Muslemans) which fell upon the seventeenth of the month Ramadan : and after having poisoned their swords, every man took his road ; the first that to Cufah, the second that to Damascus, and the third that to Ægypt.

Barak, one of the three devotees, being arrived at Damascus, struck Moawiyah in the reins, but the wound was not mortal. The surgeon that was called to see him, after having searched and considered it, gave him his choice, either to be cauterised, or drink a portion that should render him incapable of generation. Moawiyah, without any hesitation, chose the latter, and did in reality remain the rest of his days without having any other children besides those which were born to him before he received his wound.

The assassin, who was instantly seized, discovered the conspiracy which he had made with his two comrades, and was condemned to have his hands and feet cut off, and be suffered to live. He did live, and it is said he married afterwards. But one of Moawiyah's friends being informed of it, said that it was by no means reasonable, that that assassin who had hindered Moawiyah from having children, should have any of his own ; and so killed him with his own hands.

Amrou Ben Beker, the second of the conspirators, was in Ægypt, on Friday, the 17th of the month Ramadan, the day appointed to strike his blow ; Amrou Ben Aasi was then (fortunately for him) troubled with a fit of the cholic, which hindered him from performing the office of Imam in the mosque that day. Wherefore he appointed another, who supplied his place, and fell down dead with the blow, which the assassin, who mistook him for Amrou, gave him. This same assassin, as he was led to execution, said, without any concern, 'I designed Amrou, but God designed another.' Other authors say that when he was brought before Amrou, he asked who that was. They told him Amrou. 'Whom then,' said he, 'have I killed ?' They answered 'Charijah.' Then Amrou said to him, 'You meant Amrou, but God meant Charijah.'

The third of these conspirators, Abdarrahman, had better success in the execution of his wicked design against Ali, than his other two companions. For being arrived at Cufah, he took up his lodgings at a woman's house, whose nearest relations had been killed at the battle of Naharwan, and who, for that reason, retained in her heart a strong desire of being revenged upon Ali. Abdarrahman, finding this woman in a disposition so favourable to his design, used his utmost efforts to gain her favour, at the same time making her some overtures of marriage, to which she answered : 'The dowry which I will have of the man that marries me, shall be 3000 drachms of silver, a slave, a maid, and Ali's head.' Abdarrahman instantly accepted the conditions. And at the time when he undertook to put his design in execution, she joined two other men with him, whose names were Derwan and Sheith, to bear him company.

Ali, during all this month of Ramadan in which he was killed, had several presages of his death, and used between times to let drop some words to that purpose when he was in private among his friends. He was heard once to say, after he had undergone a great deal of uneasiness ; 'Alas ! my heart, there is need of patience, for there is no remedy against death !' In short, Friday the seventeenth of this month being come, he went out of his house early in the morning to go to the Mosque, and it was observed that a great number of household birds made a great noise as he passed through his yard ; and that one of his slaves having thrown a cudgel at them to make them quiet, he said to them, let them alone, for their cries are only lamentations foreboding my death.

As soon as he came into the Mosque these three villains, who waited for him, pretended to quarrel among themselves, and drew their swords.

Derwan made a blow at Ali, but missed him, and the blow fell upon the gate of the Mosque. Abdarrahman struck him upon the head, just in the same place where he had received a wound before in the battel of Ahzab, which was fought in Mahomet's time, and that stroke was mortal. The three assassins had time to make their escape, without being apprehended. Derwan crept home; where a man who had seen him with the sword in hand against Ali, went and killed him. Shabib betook him to his heels, and ran so well, that he was never taken. Abdarrahman concealed himself for some time; and when Ali was asked who was the author of such an enormous attempt against his person, he answered, 'You shall soon hear tidings of him. In short, a Musleman having found Abdarrahman hid in a corner, with his sword in his hand, asked him if it was not he that had wounded Ali; the assassin, willing to deny it, was constrained by his own conscience to confess it; and was instantly brought before Ali. Ali delivered him in custody to his eldest son Hasan, with orders to let him want nothing, and that if he died of his wound, he should execute his murderer at one stroke only. Hasan punctually obeyed his father's orders, who died the 19th, or 20th, or 21st of the same month, that is, the third, fourth, or fifth day after he was wounded. This is the account that the learned D'Herbelot gives of the death of that murderer out of his Persian authors, as I suppose. Tabari and Abu'lpheda authors of great account among the Arabians, relate it after a quite different manner: Abu'lpheda says, ' That his hand was cut off first, ' and then his foot on the opposite side: next they put out his eyes ' with a red hot iron, then cut out his tongue, and afterwards burnt ' him,' to which he adds, 'the curse of God be upon him.' This account I take to be much the more probable, considering the heinousness of the crime, and the temper of that people. For though it is not at all improbable that Ali might give such orders, yet I can by no means be induced to believe that they were ever so mercifully executed. After what manner soever he was put to death, the hereticks look upon him as a martyr.

As to Ali's age authors differ, some say he was 63, others 66, and some 59. The time of his caliphate was 5 years bating three months; they are not agreed as to the place of his burial; some say he was buried opposite to the Mosque in Cufah; others in the royal palace; others say, that his son Hasan conveyed him to Medinah, and laid him by his wife Phatemah. The most probable opinion is, that he was buried in that place which is visited by the Muslemans to this day as his tomb, where there are a great many oblations left by the devotees.

As to his person, he had a very red face, large eyes, a prominent belly, a bald head, a large beard, very hairy upon the breast, rather short than middle-sized; of a very good look, florid and youthful, frequently smiling. He had in all nine wives, the first of which was Phatemah, Mahomet's daughter, during whose life he married no other. By her he had three children, Hasan, Hosein and Mohassan ; this last died in his infancy.

The second was Omm-al Nebiyin, by whom he had four children, Abdollah, Abbas, Othman and Jaasar, who were all four killed at the battle of Kerbelah.

His third wife, named Asimah, was the mother of Jahya and Aoun.

The fourth, whose name was Omm-habibah, was the mother of Omar.

The sixth, whose name was Caulah, was the mother of Mohammed Ben Haniphiyah, of whom we shall give a further account in the sequel of the history.

I find no further particular mention of the names of the rest of his wives ; there are three more sons, Mahomet the younger, and Amrou, who were born of some one or other of them.

Though there are but fourteen sons mentioned here, it is certain he had fifteen, whereof only five left any posterity behind them : namely, Hasan, Hosein, Mohammed Ben Haniphyah, Abbas and Amrou. As for the number of his daughters they reckon eighteen.

This particular account of his family may seem superfluous to some, but not to those that consider what great changes and revolutions have been made by it in the several succeeding generations of the Muslemans, and of what importance it is throughout the whole course of their history.

They report strange things of Ali. One thing very particularly observable is, that his mother was delivered of him in the very temple itself of Meccah ; which never happened to any one else. The name that his mother gave him first, was Caid ; but Mahomet his cousin-german changed it into Ali.

Among the surnames, or honourable titles, which the Muslemans bestow upon Ali, there are two principal ones ; the first of which is Wasi, which signifies in Arabick, legatee, mandatary, executor of a man's will, and heir, that is of Mahomet. His second title is, Mortada, or Mortadi, which signifies beloved by, or acceptable to God. They called him even whilst he was alive Esed Allah algalib, the victorious lion of God ; to which may be added Haidar, which also in the Arabick language signifies a lion. The Shii, who are his followers, or rather, his adorers, frequently call him Faid alanwar, the distributor of lights or graces. And in Persian Shah Mordman, the king of men, and Shir Khoda, the lion of God.

The greatest part of the Muslemans pretend, that Ali was the first that embraced that religion. And according to their tradition he was indeed a very early Musleman, for it seems he made profession of that religion in his mother's womb. For all the time that she was big of him he hindered her of prostrating herself before her idol which she used to worship. The form of benediction, or blessing, which they always add when they name him, is ' God glorify the face of him.' They say, moreover, that Mahomet, talking of him, said, ' Ali is for me, and I am for him ; he stands to me in the same rank as Aaron did to Moses ; I am the town in which all knowledge is shut up, and he is the gate of it.'

However, these great elogies did not hinder his name and that of his family from being cursed, and their persons excommunicated through all the mosques of the empire of the Caliphs of the house of Ommiyah, down from Moawiyah to the time of Omar Ebn Abdalaziz, who suppressed this solemn malediction. There were besides several of the Caliphs of the house of Abbas, who expressed a great aversion to Ali and all his posterity—such as Motaded and Motawakkel, to whom he is reported to have appeared in their sleep, and threatened with his indignation. On the contrary, the Fatemite Caliphs of Ægypt made his name to be added to that of Mahomet in the publication of the times of prayer, which they made on the turrets of the mosques.

It is said that the sepulchre of Ali was kept hid during the reign of the family of Ommiyah, and not discovered till the reign of the Abbasides, which is not credible. Adhaudedaulet, in the year 367 (of Christ 977), built a sumptuous monument over it, which the Persians generally call Konbud Faid alanwar—the dome of the dispenser of lights and graces. Now, notwithstanding the sepulchre of Ali is so very well known near the city of Cufah, there are some of his sect who believe him to be still alive, and affirm that he shall come at the end of the world and fill the earth with justice. There are some among them so extravagant as to make him a divine person. The more moderate say that he is not truly God, but that in a great many things he partakes of the divine nature.

Ali has a great reputation for wisdom among all the Mahometans. There is extant of his a Centiloquium, or a hundred sentences, which have been translated out of Arabick into Turkish and Persian. There is likewise a collection of verses, under the title of ' Anwar Alokail.' We have in the Bodleian library a large book of his sentences, a specimen whereof we shall annex to this history. But the most celebrated piece of all is intituled ' Jefr we Jame '—it is written upon parchment, in mysterious characters, intermixed with figures, wherein are couched all the grand events that are to happen from the beginning of Muslemanism to the end of the world. This parchment is deposited in the hands of those of his family, and even to this time nobody has decyphered it in any sort of manner but Jaafer Sadek. For, as for the entire explication of it, that is reserved for the twelfth Imam, who is surnamed, by way of excellence, the Mohdi, or Grand Director.

Besides these books which we have been speaking of, we find in

authors several sentences and apophthegms under the name of Ali.
The author of 'Rabi alakyar' quotes this, which is one of the most instructive—' He that would be rich without means, powerful without subjects, and subject without a master, hath nothing to do but to leave off
sinning and serve God, and he will find these three things.' One of his
captains having asked him one day, with impudence enough, what was
the reason that the reigns of Abubeker and Omar, his predecessors,
were so peaceable, and that of Othman and his own were so full of
troubles and diversions, Ali answered him very wisely, ' The reason is
plain : it is because Othman and I served Abubeker and Omar during
their reign, and Othman and I found nobody to serve us but you, and
such as are like you.'

Somebody told him one day that Moawiyah said that Ali and those
of his house distinguished themselves by their bravery, Zobeir and his
family made a noise with their magnificence, but that for his own part
and his family's, they did not pretend to distinguish themselves from
others, or by anything but their humanity and clemency. Ali answered
those that told him, that it looked as if Moawiyah had made use of
artifice in this discourse—as if he had a mind to spur on Zobeir and
him with their magnificence and bravery, to the end that the one throwing himself into a vast expense, and the other into hazards, they might
be in a condition to oppose his usurpation, and he would gain the affections of the people by boasting of the sweetness of his temper.

There is besides in this book, intituled ' Rabi alakyar,' another maxim
of Ali, which is very memorable and very contrary to the conduct of
those who vaunt themselves upon the account of their being of his sect—
' Take great care,' said he, ' never to separate yourselves from the fel-
lowship of the other Muslemans : for he that separates himself from them
belongs to the devil, as the sheep that leave the flock belong to the
wolf. Therefore give no quarter to him who marches under the standard of schism, though he has my turbant upon his head, for he carries
along with him the infallible mark of a man that is out of the way.' It
should be remarked here, by the way, that those of the sect of Ali have
not only a turbant made after a particular fashion, but that they also
twist their hair after a manner quite different to the rest of the Muslemans.

Hosain Waez also recites this passage of Ali, in his ' Paraphrase and
Commentary upon the Alcoran '—' God hath given men two Imams,
that is to say, two pontifs or mediators between him and them. The
first is the prophet who is gone, and is no more among them ; the
second, which remains and shall continue always with them, is the
prayer, which they make to obtain pardon of sins.'

Ali's sectaries are called by the Muslemans (who intitle themselves
Sonnites—that is, observers of the tradition, or orthodox) by the scandalous name of Shii, a name that is formed from that of Shiyah, which

signifies, properly, a scandalous reprobate sect. For a sect that follows approved opinions, is called by the Arabs Medheb; but these sectaries of Ali, of whom we are speaking, do not call themselves by that name. On the contrary, they apply it to their adversaries, and call their own sect Adaliyah, which signifies the religion of them that follow justice and the right side.

There have been some of these partisans of Ali dispersed throughout all the countries of the empire of the Muslemans, who have from time to time raised very great disturbances. They have possessed several estates, both in Asia and Africa—at this day, all the great empire of the Persians, and one-half of the princes of the Uzbeckzs, whose dominions lye beyond the river Gihon, and some Mahometan kings of the Indies, make profession of this sect.

These are the principal memoirs relating to that great Caliph, who, laying aside all those impertinent, fabulous stories which they tell of him, was, if he be considered with regard to his courage, temper, piety, and understanding, one of the greatest men that was ever born in that nation. The inscription of his seal was, ' The kingdom belongs to the only mighty God.'

H A S A N,

THE FIFTH FROM MAHOMET.

AFTER Ali had received his mortal wound, and there was no room left for any hopes of recovery, his friends that were about him enquired of him whom he would nominate for his successor. He told them, that he intended, with regard to that affair, to follow the example of the apostle of God, who did not nominate any successor; that if it did please God to favour them, he would undoubtedly unite their judgments in the making a good choice. So it fell, of course, without any scruple, to his eldest son Hasan, a man who inherited more of his father's piety than his courage; and was reverenced not only upon the account of his near relation to Ali, but because he was very studious of the practical part of religion, and accounted by all a very good man.

As soon as his father Ali was dead, Hasan, it belonging properly to him, as eldest son, to perform that office, stood up and said to the people—' You have killed a man (meaning his father) on that same night in which the Alcoran came down from heaven, and Isa (Jesus) upon whom be peace, was lifted up to heaven, and in which Joshua, the son of Nun, was killed; by God, none of his predecessors exceeded him, nor will any of his successors ever be equal to him.' After this, they proceeded to his inauguration, which was begun by Kais in this form : Stretch out your hand, as a token that you will stand by the book of God and the tradition of the apostle, and make war against all opposers. Hasan answered, ' As to the book of God and the tradition of the apostle, they will stand.' Then the rest came in, with whom he stipulated that they should be subject and obedient to him, and be at peace with his friends and at war with his enemies. But some of the Irakians, who were quite weary of the Syrian war, hesitated at that condition, and said, ' This man will never serve you for a master, we are for no fighting.'

'Tis said that, notwithstanding the remissness of the greater part, forty (and some say sixty) thousand of Ali's men had bound themselves in an association before he was murdered to stand by him to death, and that he was making preparation to march at the head of them. With this trusty body of his father's troops, Hasan was perswaded, contrary to his own inclination, to insist upon his right, and renew the dispute with Moawiyah, who had Syria, Palestine, and Ægypt in his possession, and was proclaimed Caliph in those countries, even before Ali was killed, and refused to acknowledge Hasan's title, because he accused him of having been an accomplice in the murder of Othman.

Hasan was by no manner of means qualified for such an under-taking, being naturally of a most peaceable disposition, and who looked upon the effusion of Muslemans blood with the greatest horror imaginable ; but over-perswaded he set upon his march, having sent Kais before him with 12,000 men. Moawiyah was already upon his march towards them, and after a skirmish between Kais and the Syrians, they rested in expectation of Hasan's arrival. When Hasan came to Madayan, there happened a tumult in his army, occasioned by the sudden murder of one of his men, which was no sooner proclaimed, but the whole host was in such an uproar, that without any regard to his distinction, he was not only justled from his seat, but received a wound. Upon this, he retired into Madayan castle, where the govern-our's nephew proposed to his uncle to put him in irons, and make a present of him to Moawiyah. His uncle gave him an hearty curse, and said, ' What, would you betray the son of the daughter of the apostle of God ?' Hasan perceiving the people divided, and himself ill used and almost deserted by the Irakians, weary of fatigue and dis-turbance, wrote to Moawiyah, proffering to resign the Caliphate to him upon certain terms.

Hosein, his younger brother, was utterly against Hasan's abdication, as being a reflection upon, and disparagement to the memory of their father Ali ; but Hasan, well apprised of Moawiyah's resolution on the one side, and the fickleness of his own Irakians on the other, persisted in his determination, and as it is said, had written to Moawiyah before this last battle, and proposed some conditions. That before Moawiyah had received his letter, he sent him a blank paper signed at the bottom, and bad him write what terms he pleased in it, and he would take care to see them punctually performed. Hasan took the paper and doubled the conditions which he had mentioned in his letter, and when he and Moawiyah came together, he insisted upon the conditions written in the blank paper: which Moawiyah refused, and told him that it was reasonable he should be contented with those he had expressed in his letter, since it was his own proposal. The articles that Hasan proposed were these: 1. That Moawiyah should give him all the money in the treasury of Cufah. 2. The revenues of a vast estate in Persia. 3. That Moawiyah should make no reproachful reflection upon his father Ali. Moawiyah would not consent to the last article. Then Hasan desired that at least he would forbear doing it in his hearing; which Moawiyah promised him, but did not perform.

The conditions agreed upon, Hasan and Moawiyah went into Cufah together, when Amrou Ebno'l Asi gave Moawiyah a hint, that he thought it proper for him to order Hasan to stand up and testify his abdication. Moawiyah did not approve of that motion; but, overcome with Amrou's importunity, he commanded Hasan to do it. Then Hasan stood up and said, having first praised God, ' O people ! God, whose name be magnified and glorified, directed you the right way by the help of the first of our family, and hath prevented the effusion of your blood by the means of the last of us. Moawiyah contended with me concerning a matter to which I had a better pretension than him; but I chose rather to restrain the people from fighting, and surrender it to him. But even this affair also hath a time prefixed for its duration, and the world is liable to changes.' Which last words, as presaging a revolution, Moawiyah so disrelished, that he immediately commanded Hasan to sit down, and chid Amrou severely for having pressed him to it; nay, some authors go so far as to say that he was so exasperated against him, as never to be heartily reconciled as long as he lived: for he knew very well that it was superfluous for Hasan to acquaint the people with what they were all eye-witnesses of: and that if he did speak at all, it was more than probable that he would leave a sting behind him. Hasan, before his departure, stood up and told the Irakians that he had three things to lay to their charge: the murder of his father, the affronts offered to his own person, and the robbing him of his goods. Now, though Moawiyah had promised him the treasury of Cufah, they refused to let him have it, insisting upon its being their property, and therefore could not be alienated without their consent.

However, that was no hindrance to him, for Moawiyah possessed of the Caliphate, which was the only thing he aimed at, never grudged him any revenue whatsoever. He assigned him about £150,000 a year, besides large presents. He and his brother Hosein retired and lived privately at Medinah. He spent most of his vast revenue in deeds of charity. So little was he attached to the things of this world, that

22

twice in his life-time he stript himself of all that he had : and three other several times he divided half his substance among the poor.

His seal or motto during his Caliphate was : ' There is no God but God, the true and manifest king.'

They differ as to the precise time of his reign ; but most assign him about six months, or a little over.

Upon his coming to Medinah, he was blamed by some of his friends there for having so tamely and easily resigned ; but the followers of Ali, Hasan and Hosein to this very day look upon it as a singular demonstration of his excellent disposition, and tenderness over the people, upon which account he had been before recommended by the prophet.   To those that asked him what induced him to resign so easily ; he answered that he was weary of the world : besides that the Cufians were such a faithless people, that never a man of them ever trusted another, but he was a sufferer by it : that never two of them concurred in their opinion and desire of the same thing : nor had they any regard either to good or evil : besides that their behaviour towards his father had quite turned his thoughts from entertaining the least hopes of rectifying any thing that was amiss through their assistance ; and to sum up their character, that they were the most thievish, mischievous people in the world.

Though this is the true character of the Cufians, yet they expressed a great reverence for him ; for when, as soon as he entertained thoughts of his resignation, he made this speech to them : ' We are your commanders and your chiefs, and we are the family of the house of your prophet, from which God hath removed pollution, and whom he hath purified ;' there was not a man present in the congregation but wept so loud that you might hear him sob ; besides they expressed their concern with tears at his departure from Cufah to Medinah.

Whilst he lived at Medinah, some of the Karegites, those hereticks that gave his father so much disturbance, made an insurrection against Moawiyah, who wrote to Hasan to go out against them.   Hasan desired to be excused ; and told him that he had left off all publick affairs on purpose to avoid it ; and that if he had cared for fighting at all, it should have been against him.

At last, in the 49th year of their date, which falls in with the 669th of ours, he died at Medinah, poisoned by his wife, who was suborned to commit that wickedness by Yezid, the son of Moawiyah, upon promise of marrying her afterwards ; but instead of that, she was forced to be contented with a good sum of money, which Moawiyah gave her for her pains ; for Yezid was not so mad as to trust himself in her embraces.

When the time of his death drew near, his physician, as he was walking backwards and forwards about the room, and eyeing him narrowly, said that his bowels were eaten up with poison.   Hosein, his brother, begged of him to tell him who it was that gave him the draught, and swore that he would be revenged on him, if he could reach him, before his burial. If not, he would send somebody that should. Hasan answered, ' O brother! the life of this world is made up of nights which vanish away; let him alone till he and I meet together before God.' And refused to mention the person. Some say that Moawiyah suborned some of his servants to poison him.

He was born at Medinah, in the middle of the month Ramadan, in the third year of the Hegirah. There is an infinity of traditions concerning him and his brother Hosein; and no wonder, considering they were the grandchildren of one reputed an inspired prophet by his only daughter. Of Hasan they relate, that he was very much like his grandfather Mahomet, who, when he was born, spit in his mouth, and named him Hasan. He used to express his fondness of him in his infancy after such a loathsome manner as cannot be repeated. When he was at prayers, little Hasan used to come and clamber upon him, and Mahomet to humour him would hold him on, and prolong the prayers on purpose.* Nay, sometimes in the midst of a discourse to the people, if he saw Hasan and Hosein coming towards him, he would come down to them and embrace them, and take them up with him into the pulpit; then, making a short apology in behalf of their innocency and tender age, proceed in his discourse.

My author says, ' That the Syrians indeed set up Moawiyah at ' Jerusalem, because there was none to oppose them, and the Irakians ' set up Hasan against him, and had undoubtedly succeeded in their ' attempt; if their mismanagement and divisions among themselves ' had not frustrated it. But had they understood aright, they would ' have magnified the mercy of God, in giving them the apostle's grand- ' son. What we find in the book intituled, " The Demonstrations of ' Prophecy," from the tradition of Sephinah, who was a servant or freed ' man of the apostle of God, is a proof that he was the right successor. ' Mahomet said, " The Caliphate shall continue after me 30 years, ' and after that shall be a kingdom." Now Mahomet died in the 11th ' year of the Hegirah, and Hasan's abdication was in the 40th: from ' whence it is plain, not only that Mahomet is a prophet, but that ' Hasan is his rightful successor. That Mahomet had praised him, for ' this his relinquishing the present perishing world, and desiring that ' other which is permanent, and sparing the effusion of the blood of ' this people: that Mahomet one day mounted the pulpit, and Hasan ' sat by him, which he frequently used to do; and Mahomet looked ' sometimes upon him, and sometimes upon the people: after a pause, ' he said, " O people! this son of mine is lord, and God shall unite by

---

* The Mahometans say their prayers prostrated, so that their foreheads touch the ground, though not all the while. And so we are to understand it in the old Testament, when it is said of anyone, 'he fell down and worshipped;' for the same word that signifies worship is used for a Mahometan's saying his prayers.

' his means two great contending parties of the Muslemans." ' This last is from Albochari, the great collector of the traditions of Mahomet.

I have not yet been able to find out who this author is from whom I have taken this last argument, because the book is imperfect both at the beginning and the end, and I could never find any other copy of him: but he hath been of singular use to me throughout the whole course of this history to the life of Merwan, the son of Hakem, where the copy fails. I find in another passage, that he was himself the author of the book of the 'Demonstrations of Prophecy,' which he mentions. He also affirms that he wrote another treatise to prove that it was impracticable for Mahomet to marry Abu Sophyan's daughter, of which more afterwards. Whosoever he was, it is certain he was a great Imam.

A woman once having presented him with a bunch of fine herbs, he asked her if she was a free woman; the woman told him she was a slave, but that the present she had made was rare and curious. Hasan gave her her liberty, and said to those that were present, 'We have received this instruction from God himself, that we ought to give to those that make us presents something of more value than that which they give us;' meaning, that this moral instruction is couched in the Alcoran, which the Muslemans, blind as they are, look upon as the Word of God.

They relate a wonderful instance of the MODERATION of this Caliph. A slave having spilled a dish of scalding broth upon him as he sat at table, threw himself down instantly at his knees, and repeated to him these words of the Alcoran, 'Paradise is open to those that govern their passion.' Hasan answered him, 'I am not at all in a passion.' The slave went on, 'And to those that pardon offences.' 'I pardon you yours,' said Hasan. The slave went on to the end of the verse, which says, 'God loves those above all who do good to them that have offended them.' Hasan concluded too, 'Since it is so, I give you your liberty and four hundred drachms of silver.'

There is an author, who, treating concerning Hasan's death, says, that it was contained in the treaties between him and Moawiyah, that Moawiyah should never declare a successor so long as Hasan lived, but should leave the election in the hands of a certain number of persons, of which Hasan was to have the nomination, as Omar had done before. But that Moawiyah, desirous of leaving the Caliphate to his son Yezid, thought he could not bring his design about so long as Hasan was alive.

He had twenty children, fifteen males, and five daughters. Though his wives were all of them remarkably fond of him, yet he was apt very frequently to divorce them and marry new ones. There are some among the sectaries of Ali who draw the line or descent of the Imams from Abdollah, one of his children, who had a son named Yahya; but the Persians will have the succession to pass from Hasan to his younger brother Hosein.

The Muslemans quote this sentence of Hasan—'The tears which are let fall through devotion should not be wiped off, nor the water which remains upon the body after legal washing; because this water makes the face of the faithful shine when they present themselves before God.'

He died at the age of 47 years, in the month Sefer. He left directions in his will for them to bury him near his grandfather Mahomet; but to prevent any disturbance, and lest he should be carried to the common burial-place, he thought it proper to ask Ayesha's leave, which she granted. But when he was dead, Said, who was governour of the town, and Merwan, the son of Hakem, and all the whole family of the house of Ommiyah, that were then at Medinah, opposed it. Upon which the heats between the two families arose to a great height. At last, Ayesha said that it was her house, and that she would not allow him to be buried there; wherefore they laid him in the common burying-place. When Moawiyah heard of Hasan's death, he fell down and worshipped.

The CALIPHS *of the family of* OMMIYAH, *which are* 14 *in all; the first of which is*

MOAWIYAH,

THE SON OF ABU SOPHYAN, BEING THE SIXTH FROM MAHOMET,

An. Heg. 41. cœpit Maii 6, A.C. 661.

ALL opposition removed, Moawiyah takes entire possession of the Caliphate. The family of Hashem, of which were Mahomet and Ali, lay like coals raked up in embers, not able to stir. The hearts of the people were entirely in the interest of Hosein, the younger brother of Hasan, but Moawiyah had possession and the army. He was indeed a man of great abilities and steady conduct—but before we proceed to give an account of his government, it will not be amiss to enquire a little into his original.

His father, Abu Sophyan, was one of the heads of the noble tribe of the Coreish, of which was Mahomet; and as soon as Mahomet took up arms, not so much for the defence as for the propagation of his pretendedly inspired religion, Abu Sophyan was made generalissimo of the infidels against him; and, after the battle of Beder, he stood very fair for the headship of that tribe. He wanted nothing to recommend him—his courage, his gravity, and his immense riches, set him above all competition. But at last* he was convinced—as it should seem, by a signal victory gained by Mahomet over his enemies—of the truth of his pretensions. This was no small accession to Mahomet's interest, who had been sufficiently galled and harassed by the Coreish. Moawiyah and his wife came in the same day. Abu Sophyan, after his conversion to Mahometanism, begged three things of Mahomet. The first was, that to make amends for former offences, as he had commanded the forces of the infidels against the true religion, he might now have the honour of having the command of the army of the faithful against the infidels, which was granted. His second petition was that his son, Moawiyah, might be his secretary, to which Mahomet assented. The third was that the apostle would vouchsafe to marry his second daughter Gazah, for which Mahomet begged his excuse. Our author says it was not lawful, but forbears the reason, because he says, as we have observed before, he hath written a particular treatise relating to that affair.

Moawiyah was no sooner settled in his government, but the Karegites—enemies to all government, both ecclesiastical and civil—began to infest him. They always were of opinion that the person who was to preside in spirituals should not be one of man's making nor descend by any succession, but whose spirituality should recommend him to the approbation of the godly. Upon Hasan's refusal to take up arms, Moawiyah sent the Syrians against them. But the Separatists beat the Syrians, so he applied himself to his new subjects the Cufians, and the inhabitants of all those parts of Babylonia, and told them that now was their time to give him proof of the sincerity of their obedience—that he should have no security of their loyalty, unless they vigorously opposed this rebellion. They having taken arms, the Separatists would have persuaded them to desist, and asked them whether or no Moawiyah was not their common enemy. Let us alone, said they, to make war upon him : if we kill him, we have ridded you of your enemy—if he kills us, you are rid of us. The Cufians did not think it proper to hearken to their advice, and the war was soon ended by the suppression of the rebels.

We meet with little worth observing after this till the three and fortieth year, which was remarkable for   death of the famous Amrou, of whom it is reported by tradition, that Mahomet said, ' There is no truer Musleman, nor more steadfast in the faith than Amrou.' He was in the wars of Syria, where he behaved himself with singular courage and resolution. Always excellent in his advice, and steady in the execution. Afterwards Omar sent him into Ægypt, which he conquered, and was made lieutenant there. Othman continued him in that post four years, and then removed him : upon which he retired and lived privately in Palestine. After Othman's

* *Yaumal phethi.* The day of victory.

death, he went over to Moawiyah upon his invitation; and had a great share in all that controversy between Ali and Moawiyah, who continued him in the lieutenancy of Ægypt till his death, allowing him all the revenues of that rich country, upon condition that he should maintain the forces that were kept there.

He was justly reckoned one of the most considerable men among the Arabians, both upon the account of the quickness of his natural parts, his valour and good judgment. Before he turned Mahometan, he was one of those three poets that used to write lampoons upon Mahomet, in which he excelled. There are some fine proverbs of his remaining (they are my author's words, for we never saw them), and good verses. His dying speech to his children is pathetic and masculine. If I had had a more perfect copy of it, I would have inserted it. He laments in it very much, his ever having exercised his wit in exposing the prophet.

The same year died Abdollah Ben Salem, a Jewish rabbin, who had turned Mahometan betimes: he used to say that when Mahomet came first to Medinah, he used to press amongst the crowd to get a sight of him; and that at the first glance he perceived that he had nothing in his countenance that looked like an impostor.

We have before observed that Ziyad was in Ali's reign made lieutenant of Persia. Which office he discharged very much to his own reputation, and the advantage of the people. He was a man of incomparable parts, and prodigious greatness of spirit. He was Moawiyah's brother by the father's side, but a bastard; and old Abu Sophyan durst not own him for fear of Omar's severity. He was born in the year of the Hegirah, and as he grew up quickly distinguished himself, by his great abilities and masterly eloquence, to such a degree, that once in the reign of Omar at a meeting of the companions, he was so much taken notice of, that Amrou said, 'Had the father of this youth been of the family of the Coreish, he would have driven all the Arabians before him with his walking-stick.' Moawiyah was resolved to secure him in his interest; and he thought no way so proper, as by owning him publickly to be his brother. Ziyad in Omar's time was made a Cadi or judge; and when witnesses came before him, accusing Almogeirah of incontinency, whether out of favour, or because they failed in their proof, he dismissed Almogeirah, and scourged the witnesses severely. This endeared him to Almogeirah for ever after. Ziyad having been placed in the lieutenancy of Persia by Ali, upon Hasan's resignation to Moawiyah, he kept at a distance, and refused to acknowledge his government. This gave Moawiyah no small uneasiness, who was extremely afraid that Ziyad should strike in with the family of Hashem, and embroil his affairs by renewing the war. Moawiyah had given the lieutenancy of Cufah to Almogeirah; who, making him a visit in the forty-second year, Moawiyah acquainted him with the causes of his uneasiness ; who asked his leave to go to him, to which he consented, and sent a civil letter by him with a kind invitation. Mogeirah made so good use of his friendship with Ziyad, that he never ceased importuning him till he had prevailed upon him to go along with him to Moawiyah. Where he was no sooner arrived, but he immediately acknowledged him Caliph. Soon after which, Moawiyah owned him to be his brother by his father's side, which was done by producing the evidence of the conversation between Ziyad's mother and Abu Sophyan.

Abu Sophyan, in the days of ignorance, before drinking wine was made a sin by the *Alcoran*, travelling in Thayef, refreshed himself at a publick house ; where he lay with this Ziyad's mother, who was then married to a Greek slave. The old man that kept the house was yet alive ; and Moawiyah, to own Ziyad in as publick a manner as might be, upon a set day in a full assembly, examined him touching the conversation of Abu Sophyan with Somyah. The old man gave in such a strong evidence, as would have passed for a very good proof in the case of impotency. Ziyad was angry, and said that he was called for to bring proof, and not scandal. However, by this means he was acknowledged to be a true Arabian, of the noble blood of the family of the Coreish ; which though illegitimate, was a greater honour than he could ever otherways have obtained to : for let his achievements have been never so great, he must still have undergone some reflection upon the account of the baseness of his original.

It is observed that this is the first time that ever the law, that is the *Alcoran*, was openly violated in a judicial way of proceeding. For the child belonged to his legal father, the Greek slave that married his mother : and Mahomet had left it as a decision in such cases ; ' The child to the blankets, and the whore to the stone.' That is, ' Bring up the child, and stone the whore.' Moawiyah's relations stormed, and were quite out of patience, they said that he had not only introduced a son of a whore into the family, to the disparagement of all their kindred ; but had raked into the ashes of old Abu Sophyan, his father, who had lived and died with a good reputation. Moawiyah could bear all their complaints very patiently. He knew he had gained his point, and secured entirely in his interest the greatest man of the age.

Abdollah, the son of Amar, was at this time governor of Basorah ; whom Moawiyah removed as unequal to that charge, because of the too great gentleness of his disposition : for the country was quite overrun with thieves and murderers for want of discipline. He for his part never cared to punish any, but inclined rather to win them by the sweetness of his temper, and a gentle behaviour. The people, insupportably afflicted with this grievance, made their complaint to Moawiyah ; who put in Hareth for a little time : but quickly after made them amends for Abdollah's lenity, by sending them Ziyad, who drew the sword and chastised their insolence with exemplary punishments. When he came to Basorah things were in such a bad condition that there was hardly any walking the streets ; but especially in the night, which was always full of disorder and bloodshed. He made a very severe speech to them, at which he had an excellent talent, -being reckoned the best orator next to Ali, who never had any equal. One of the polite Arabians used to say, ' That he never in his life heard a man speak well, but he wished he would have done, being in pain for him, lest he should fall beneath himself and speak worse ; Ziyad only excepted, for the more he spoke the more he excelled.' In this speech he acquainted them that he was very well apprised of the lamentable condition they were in, upon the account of these disorders : and that he was resolved to put an end to them. He next published an order, forbidding any person of what quality soever to be found abroad in the streets, or in any publick place, after the hour of evening prayer upon pain of death. And to put his order in execution, he appointed a strong watch to go the rounds, and put to the sword every one they met out of their houses after that hour. There were 200 persons killed the first night, but five the second, and no blood at all shed in the third.

Besides the lieutenancy of Basorah, Moawiyah gave him those of Chorasan, Sejestan, India, Bahrein and Amman. Not unadvisedly : for the more committed to his care, so much the lighter to himself was the burthen of his government. The very name of Ziyad made all the villains within the precincts of his government tremble. He was not savage nor cruel in his temper : but strictly just, and absolute in his way of governing : impatient of the least neglect of his commands ; and one that would not abate an ace of his authority. But notwith-standing all his greatness, he met with a rebuff in this five and fortieth year ; which it is uncertain how he would have resented, if the person that offered it had lived a little longer.* He had sent Hakem, the son of Amar, to take a place called Mount Ashal ; Hakem suc-ceeded very well in the enterprise, killed a great number of the 'enemy, and brought off all the riches of the place. Upon this Ziyad sends him word that he had received a letter from Moawiyah, the Emperor of the faithful, commanding him to lay apart all the white and yellow, mean-ing the silver and gold, belonging to this spoil, that it might be put into the treasury. Now as to this particular, there is a decisive rule in the *Alcoran :* there being a chapter made on purpose,† occasioned by a mutiny among Mahomet's soldiers, about the division of the spoil. That is, that after any victory there shall first be taken out a fifth part of the spoils to be reserved for the treasury ; and the rest be divided

* MS. *Hunt.* Numb. 495.
† *Surat' alanphal.* The chapter of spoils ; which is the eighth,

among the soldiers. Hakem stuck close to the text of the *Alcoran,* and sent Ziyàd word that the authority of the book of God was superior to that of the Emperor of the faithful's letter ; and that hath it thus, ' Though the heavens and the earth conspired together against a servant of God, who put his trust in him, he would find him a secure place of refuge, and a means of deliverance.' Then he laid aside the fifth part according to the text ; and divided the spoil among the soldiers. After this (for he expected no mercy), he said, ' O God ! if I be in thy favour take me.' His request was granted ; and he died quickly after.

This same year Zeid the son of Thabet, one of Mahomet's secretaries when he dictated the Alcoran, died. He wrote that copy which was used by the Caliphs or Imams at the command of Othman, the son of Affan.

My author had seen it, and adds, that all he had seen of his writing was an extraordinary fair strong hand. Zeid learned Hebrew in 15 days, so as to be able to read the books of the Jews. He learned Persian of one of Cosroes his ambassadors in 18 days ; and he learned Ethiopick, Greek, and Coptick of one of Mahomet's slaves. He was 15 years old at the battel of ' the ditch.' He was the most pleasant facetious man in the world at home, and the most reserved when he went abroad. Once he saw the people coming from prayers, and he made what haste he could to get out of the way of them, like one that did not care to be seen. He used to say, ' He that doth not reverence men will not reverence God.'

This year Merwan the son of Hakem went on pilgrimage to Meccah ; he was governor of Medinah.

The next year Abdorrahman son of Caled the great was poisoned in Syria : occasioned by Moawiyah's jealousy. For the soldiers, those especially who had been witnesses of his father's valour and conduct, to whom he appeared no way inferior, favoured him to that degree that Moawiyah was afraid of him ; and during his absence upon an expedition against the Greeks, tampered with a Christian servant of his to poison him, upon promise not only to remit him his own tribute, but to give him the lieutenancy of Hems. Upon Abdorrahman's return, the conditions were punctually performed on both sides ; but he did not long enjoy the reward of his perfidiousness ; for Caled the son of Abdorrahman receiving information of it, came into Syria, and revenged his father's death upon that wicked slave : upon which Moawiyah imprisoned him for a time ; and made him pay him the money for the expiation of murther : afterwards he dismissed him and returned to Medinah.

Not long after this, happened the death of a very great man among the followers of Ali. His name was Hejer, a person remarkable for his singular abstinence, piety, and strictness of life, constant purification according to the Mahometan law, and exactness in observing the hours of devotion. He lived at Cufah. It was the custom of Moawiyah and his lieutenants every Friday in their harangues to the people to exceed in the praise and commendation of Othman, and rail and revile Ali. This was done byAlmogeirah when he was lieutenant of Cufah, more out of complaisance to Moawiyah, than any inclination of his own. As he was one day pronouncing these reproaches against Ali, Hejer and his company stood up, and interrupted him, and returned the ill language back again upon himself: but Mogeirah passed it by and forgave them, without taking any further notice. Ziyàd was not so gentle upon the same provoking occasion. He used to divide the year into two equal parts : six months he resided at Cufah ; the other six at Basorah. Coming according to his custom to Cufah, in his harangue he called Ali by the name of Abu Torah, which signifies in Arabick, ' Father of dust, or dusty ' (for it is common with the Arabians to use the word father in such cases). This was the most acceptable nick-name to Ali in the world, having been given him by Mahomet himself. Hejer, resolved to affront him, stood up and said, he seems to have designed a compliment to Ali. This provoked Ziyàd to such a degree that he immediately seized him, and thirteen more of his companions, and sent them in chains to the caliph, Moawiyah.

But though this was the end of it, there were several preceding provocations. For before this, Hejer being so popular for his piety, and such an avowed enemy to Moawiyah, and friend of Ali and his party ; Ziyàd would have carried him along with him to Basorah from Cufah ; for fear he should make any disturbance. Hejer said that he was indisposed. Ziyàd answered angrily, that he knew he was indisposed as to his religion, heart and understanding, adding with an oath that if he dared to raise any commotion, he should have an eye over him. Another time when Ziyàd was making a speech to the people, he stood so long that the hour of prayer was come. Hejer, who was the strictest man alive in all things belonging to the exercise of religion, cryed out ' Salat, to prayers :' Ziyàd took no notice of it, but still went on with his discourse. Hejer, fearing lest the time should be past, began the prayers in the congregation himself, upon which Ziyàd was forced to break off, and come down and joyn with them. This affront he never forgave, looking upon it as a great diminution of his character, but wrote a long letter to Moawiyah, aggravating the matter, and desiring that he might put him in irons, and send him to him. This last time Ziyàd was forced to take a journey on purpose from Basorah to Cufah, upon information that Hejer and the company had refused to acknowledge his lieutenant there, and used to throw dust at him when he was in his pulpit. This obliged Ziyàd to come back to Cufah, where, cloathed in a silk cassock, and a vest of gold brocade, he went into the pulpit himself, and made a severe speech to the people, telling them, he should make but a very insignificant figure in his post if he suffered his authority to be thus set at nought and trampled upon, without making an example of Hejer. In his oration he frequently, as occasion served, used these words, ' And it belongs to the emperor of the faithful ;' at which Hejer took up an handful of dust and flung at him, with these words, ' God curse thee, thou lyest :' Whereupon Ziyàd came down and went to prayers among the people, then retiring to the castle he sent for Hejer, who refusing to come, he sent a party to fetch him, between whom and Hejer's friends there was a little skirmish with stones and cudgels, so that they did not carry him off that time ; but he was taken soon after and sent to Moawiyah, attended with a sufficient number of witnesses to testify against him, that he had spoken reproachfully of the Caliph, affronted the Emir (Ziyàd) and affirmed, that the government did not belong to any of right, but only to the family of Ali. Moawiyah sent some officers with orders to put them to death, and authors differ as to the circumstance of their being admitted into his presence or not. Gadrah, a village on the back-side of Damascus, was the place appointed for their execution ; and during their stay there, Moawiyah advised with his friends how they should be disposed of. Some were for putting them to death, others for dispersing them through the several territories of his vast dominions. Ziyàd sent him word, that if he had any occasion for the kingdom of Irak, they must dye. The chief men of the court begged off six of them. When Hejer was come near the place of execution, he desired space to wash himself, which he always punctually observed, after which he said two short prayers, and rising up, said, ' If I had been afraid of death I could have made them longer ;' but when he saw his grave digged ready for him, his winding sheet spread out, and the executioner's sword drawn, he was observed to tremble. Whereupon, being asked if he did not say that he was not afraid : he asked again, how should it be possible not to be moved at such a prospect ? The executioner bad him stretch out his neck streight : he answered he would not be assistant to his own death. Then his head was immediately struck off ; his body was washed, and he was buried in his chains according to his own directions.

Ayesha had sent a messenger to intercede for him, who arrived too late. Afterwards when Moawiyah went to Medinah, he visited Ayesha, who said to him from behind the curtain, ' What was become of your compassion, Moawiyah, when you killed Hejer and his companions ?' ' I lose that, mother,' said he, ' when I am absent from such persons as you are.'

About the latter end of the eight and fortieth year, Moawiyah sent his son Yezid with a powerful army to besiege Constantinople ; our authors give us no account of the particulars of that siege, but only mention three or four of the most eminent of the companions, whose zeal, notwithstanding their great age, prompted them to undergo such fatigue and hazard. The army suffered the extremity of hardship in their march ; but they had a tradition sufficient to encourage them, it being no less than a plenary indulgence ; Mahomet having said, ' The sins of the first army that takes the city of Cæsar are forgiven.' Here it was that the famous Abu Jyub was killed, who had been with Mahomet at the battels of Beder and Ohud : his tomb is held in such veneration, that to this day the emperors of the Ottoman family go to it to have their swords girt on, on their accession to the throne.

In the fiftieth year died Almogeirah the governor of Cufah. There had been a great plague raging there, which made him retire ; but upon its ceasing he returned and died of it. He was an active man, and of very good parts ; he had lost one of his eyes at the battle of Yermouk, though some will have it that it was with looking upon an eclipse. He was accounted to be of the wrong party, and one of the chief of them ; for thus they reckon ; there are five elders on Ali's side. Mahomet, Ali, Phatemah, Hasan, Hosein ; and their opposites are, Abubeker, Omar, Moawiyah, Amrou and Mogeirah.

The same year Kairwan, the metropolis of that province which is properly called Africa, was built, though not finished till the fifty-fifth year. It lies 33 leagues distant from Carthage, towards the N.E., and 12 from the sea. The account they give of it is, that Moawiyah having constituted Okbah governor of the province of Africa, he put all those to the sword that had revolted from Mahometanism ; for it was their custom upon the approach of the Saracen army to make profession of it, and upon their departure to return to their old religion again. The place of the governor's residence before was in Zeweilah and Barca ; wherefore Okbah resolving to have a garrison thereabouts to keep them in awe, pitched upon Kairwan ; and because his march had been interrupted and perplexed by the woodiness of the country, which was full of wild beasts and serpents ; he felled all the trees round about in that neighbourhood, and bestowed them in the building. This city was of great use to them for keeping the country in subjection ; and it being remote from the sea, and bordering upon the desert, rendered them secure from the invasions of the Sicilian and Roman navies ; so that afterwards it became a flourishing city, considerable not only for its publick and private buildings, riches and the like, but also for the study of the sciences and polite literature.

This same year is remarkable for the death of one Rahya, who was one of the earliest professors of Mahometanism ; he was not present at the battle of Beder. Mahomet used to say to him, ' That of all the men he had ever seen, Rahya did most resemble the angel Gabriel.' The year after Saed Ben Zend died ; he was the last of those (I think they were ten in all) that had a positive promise of Paradise.

About this time Moawiyah, who kept his constant residence at Da-mascus, had a fancy to remove Mahomet's pulpit thither from Medinah. He said, ' That the walking-stick and pulpit of the apostle of God should not remain in the hands of the murderers of Othman. Great search was made for the walking-stick, and at last they found it. Then they went, in obedience to his commands, to remove the pulpit ; when immediately to their great surprize and astonishment, the sun was eclipsed to that degree that the stars appeared.   This put them all into a great conster-nation, for they looked upon it as a manifest indication of the divine displeasure, for their presuming to lay hands upon the apostle's pulpit, in order to remove it from the place where he had set it himself.   This made them desist from their enterprize, and the Medinians were left in the peaceable possession of this holy relic ; till some years afterwards, Abdolmelik had a mind to it ; but one of the Medinians said to him, ' For God's sake do not attempt such a thing, for Moawiyah did but move it once and the sun was eclipsed !'   He urged besides a tradi-tion from Mahomet, who had said, ' Whosoever shall swear upon my pulpit falsely, hell shall be his mansion.'   ' And,' added he, ' will you go and take it away from the Medinians, when it is the decision of their controversies ?'   Upon this representation Abdolmelick forbore and never mentioned it again.   After this Alwaled in his pilgrimage made the same attempt, but when he sent for it, his messenger received this answer, ' Bid your master fear God, and not expose himself to the divine displeasure ;' with which answer Alwaled remained very well satisfied.   Afterwards when Solyman, the son of Abdolmelik, came on pilgrimage that way, Amrou, the son of Abdolaziz, was mentioning these things to him ; ' I do not love,' answered Solyman, ' to hear these things mentioned either of the Emperor Abdolmelik, or of Waled, what have we to do with it ? We have taken possession of the world, and it is in our hands, and we will stand to the determination of the Musle-man doctors.'

And now the famous Ziyàd's time was come.   He died of the plague on the third day of the month Ramadan, in the fifty-third year of the Hegirah, which was his age.   A little before he died he wrote a letter to Moawiyah, acquainting him that he had reduced all Irak into per-fect subjection to him from north to south, and begged of him to give him the lieutenancy of Arabia Petræa.   It is superfluous to add that it was granted, for it was not in Moawiyah's power to deny him anything, shall I say, or rather that it was his interest to have him employed everywhere if possible.   As soon as the Arabians heard of it they were under the greatest concern in the world, for fear he should exercise his tyranny over them as he had done before upon the poor Irakians. Upon the first news of it, the son of Amer, rose up and went to the temple of Mecca to deprecate his coming amongst them, and the people prayed in faith.   Ziyàd, struck with the plague, felt such an

intolerable pain in his hand that he consulted a cadi, in point of conscience, whether it were better to cut it off or not. The Cadi told him,
' That he was afraid, if his time was come, he should go before God
without that hand, which was cut off to avoid the appearing before him,
and if it was not come, he would remain lame among men, which would
be a reproach to his child* ; wherefore he was of opinion, that live or
die he had better let it alone ;' and so left him. However, notwithstanding this grave decision, Ziyàd, impatient of the pain which increased
every moment, was resolved to have it cut off ; but when he saw the
fire, and the cauterizing irons, his heart failed him. It is said that he had
about him no less than 150 physicians, three of which had belonged to Cosroes, the son of Hormuz, king of Persia, but it was not in their power to re-
verse the sealed decree, nor the thing that was determined. He had
been Moawiyah's lieutenant over Irak five years. He was buried near
Cufah, which he passed by in his journey towards Arabia, in order to
take possession of his new government there. When Abdollah, the
son of Amer, heard of the death of Ziyàd, he said, ' Go thy way thou
son of Somyah ; this world did not stay with thee, neither hast thou
attained to the other.'

Upon Almogeirah's death, Moawiyah, who could never do enough
for his brother Ziyad, or rather for himself, added the lieutenancy of
Cufah to all those vast territories he had entrusted him withal before.
He was the first that joyned those two great trusts of Basorah and
Cufah together. When he came first to Cufah, having left Basorah to
the care of Samrah, in his first speech he told the Cufians that he once
had thoughts of bringing along with him 2,000 of his guards, but recollecting that they were honest men, he had brought no other attendance
but only his own family. They threw dust at him, upon which he sat down
and gave private directions to some of his domesticks to seize the doors
of the mosque ; then he commanded every man to seize his next neigh-
bour, without pretending to excuse himself by saying he did not know
who he was. This done, he placed himself upon a seat near the door,
and had them brought before him four by four ; he made every one of
them swear distinctly it was none of us four that threw dust. Those
that took the oath he dismissed ; they that refused it were bound and
laid aside. When he had thus gone through the whole congregation,
there remained thirty, and some say fourscore, that could not take the
oath, whose hands were immediately cut off upon the place.

Not long after he entered upon his government, he issued out an
order that every citizen should leave his door open all night, engaging
to be responsible for all the damage that every particular person should
receive that way ; and it happening one night that some cattle getting

---

* There is nothing more common among the Arabians than to nick-name children from
the imperfections of their parents, as to call such an one the Son of the Lame, or the Son
of the Blind.

into a shop, had put some things out of order ; as soon as Ziyàd was informed of it, he gave everyone leave to have a hurdle or rake at his door, which continued in use ever after, not only in Basorah but in a great many other towns of Irak, of which he was governour.

One night his archers that were upon the watch, having met with a shepherd coming through the town with his flock, carried him before Ziyàd. The shepherd excused himself upon the account of his being a stranger, and ignorant of the order which he had caused to be pub-lished. Ziyad said to him, 'I am willing to believe that what thou tellest me is true ; but since the safety of the inhabitants of this town depends upon thy death, it is necessary that thou shouldest die,' and instantly commanded his head to be cut off.

Now though Ziyàd was so strict in seeing his orders punctually exe-cuted, and severe in inflicting exemplary punishment, yet his behaviour was gentle in respect of that of Samrah, his lieutenant at Basorah, who was abhorred by all men for his cruelty. Ziyàd himself was ashamed of it, for during Ziyàd's six months' absence at Cufah, Samrah had put to death no less than 8,000 persons at Basorah. Ziyad asked him if he was not afraid lest in such a number he might have put to death one innocent man. He answered that he should be under no concern, if at the same time that he had killed them he had killed so many more. Abu Sawar said that he had killed 47 of his men one morning, every one of which had got the Alcoran by heart.

Once, as Samrah's horse went out, they met with a countryman, and one of them struck him through with his lance. They went on, and Samrah, coming up after them, found the poor man wallowing in his own blood : enquiring what was the matter, he was answered that the man meeting the front of his horse, they had killed him. All that Samrah said to it was only by repeating this verse—' When you hear we are mounted, beware of our lances.'

When Ziyàd came to Cufah, he enquired which was the most reli-gious man there. They recommended to him one Abulmogeirah. He sent for him, and told him that if he would keep within his own doors, and not go out, he would give him as much money as he desired ; the religious told him that if he would give him the empire of the whole world he would not omit going out to say his prayers on the Congrega-tion Day (*Yaumo'l Jom-ah—i.e.*, Friday). Well, then, says Ziyàd, go to the congregation, but do not talk about anything. He said he could not help 'Encouraging that which is good, and reproving that which is evil.' For which answer, Ziyàd commanded him to be beheaded.

A little before his death he gathered the people together, and filled both mosque, and street, and castle with them, in order to impose upon them the renunciation of Ali. Whilst they were full of vexation and perplexity, waiting for the event, one of his servants came out and told them that they might go about their business, for his master was not at leisure. The plague had just then seized him, and they all looked upon it afterwards as a providential deliverance.

A famous Persian historian reports that a letter written by Ziyad to Moawiyah, when he asked him for the lieutenancy of Arabia, was expressed in these terms—' My left hand is here employed in governing ' the people of Irak : all the meantime, my right hand remains idle. ' Give it Arabia to govern, and it will give you a good account of it.'

He adds, with some little variation from my Arabick author abovementioned, that Moawiyah having granted him this government, the principal inhabitants of Medinah, who were afraid of his rough and violent temper, were very much alarmed, and that Abdollah, the son of Zobeir, who was one of them, made this publick prayer to God—' Allahomma ectaphi yemin ziyadihi. O God ! satisfy this right hand, which is idle and superfluous to Ziyad.' There is in these words a very elegant allusion to the name of Ziyad, which signifies, in Arabick, abundant and superfluous. And they say that immediately after this prayer there was a pestilential ulcer in one of his fingers of his right hand, of which he died a few days after.

There was afterwards a dynasty of princes of his posterity in Arabia Fælix, who reigned under the name of the Children of Ziyad.

There were several persons, both of the sect of Ali and of the Karegites, or hereticks, that endeavoured to disturb Ziyad's administration, but these commotions were soon extinguished by his excellent conduct. The particulars are to be found at large in our historians, but I have purposely omitted them, because they would only interrupt the thread of our history, and contribute nothing either to the character of any great man, or the giving light to the customs and genius of the people.

This same fifty-third year, Jabalah, the son of Ayham, the last king of the tribe of Gasan, who were Christian Arabs, and of whom we have already given a large account, died.

We now return to Moawiyah, who, in the fifty-fourth year, deposed Saed from the government of Medinah, and restored Merwan, the son of Hakem, to it again. Then he wrote to Merwan to demolish Saed's house, and to seize all his effects that were in Hejaz. Merwan came to execute the Caliph's command, and brought his mule along with him to carry away whatsoever he found of most value. Saed was surprized, and told him he hoped he would not serve him so. Merwan answered it must needs be so ; adding, if Moawiyah had commanded you to have pulled down my house, when you were governour, you would have done it. Upon this, Saed produced a letter of the Caliph's to himself, when he was governor, commanding him to demolish Merwan's house, which, out of friendship, he had ventured to disobey, and by so doing incurred the displeasure of the Caliph. Merwan was sur-

23

prised at this, and readily acknowledged the superior generosity of Saed's temper. They both easily perceived that this was only a contrivance of the Caliph's to set them at variance, but it proved the occasion of uniting them in a stricter friendship. Merwan never left interceding with Moawiyah, till he desisted from urging the execution of that unjust command. Moawiyah was himself afterwards ashamed of his ungenerous dealing, and asked their pardon.

This year Moawiyah deposed Samrah, who was Ziyàd's deputy over Basorah. As soon as Samrah heard the news, he said, ' God curse Moawiyah. If I had served God so well as I have served him, he would never have damned me to all eternity.' One of my authors tells this without any reserve—another seems to scruple the truth of it.

Ziyàd being dead, Obeidollah, his son, came to pay his duty to Moawiyah, who received him very courteously, and enquired of him concerning the characters and behaviour of his father's deputies in their respective provinces. He gave him such a satisfactory account, that he made him lieutenant of Chorasan, when he was but 25 years old. He went to his charge, and passed over the river as far as the mountains of Bochara ; there he encountered the Turks, and having fought them bravely, he put them to such precipitate flight, that the Turkish queen had only time to put on one of her buskins, and left the other behind her to the Arabians, who valued it at 2,000 pieces of gold.

Obeidollah, the son of Ziyad, did not continue long in his lieutenancy of Chorasan, but was removed to Basorah, instead of Abdollah, the son of Amrou, who was there before. The occasion was this : a leading man of one of the tribes of the Arabs threw dust at him while he was preaching. He followed Ziyad's example, and commanded his hand to be cut off. Upon this, some of the same tribe came to Abdollah and told him that if the emperor of the faithful should know that he had cut off the man's hand for such an action, he would deal with him, and all that belonged to him, as he had done by Hejer and his companions. Wherefore, added they, give it us under your hand that you did it indiscreetly. This he foolishly complied with, imagining to pacify them by doing it, whom he knew to be sufficiently provoked. They kept the paper by them for a time, and went with it afterwards to Moawiyah, complaining that his deputy over Basorah had cut off their master's hand upon an uncertainty, and desired of him to execute the law of retaliation upon him. Moawiyah said they could have no retaliation against his deputy, but a mulct they should have, which was accordingly paid out of the treasury; and Abdollah, to satisfy them, was deposed from his lieutenancy, and Obeidollah, the son of Ziyad, substituted in his room. Obeidollah left Chorasan to one Aslam, a worthless man, who did nothing in the place that deserves notice. This same year Merwan, the son of Hakem, and governor of Medinah, conducted the pilgrims to Meccah.

The next year Moawiyah made Saed, who was Othman's grandson, lieutenant of Chorasan, who passing over the river Jihon, formerly Oxus, went to Samercand (afterwards the capital of the great Tamerlane), and Sogd. Having there routed the idolaters he went to Tarmud, which surrendered to him.

Hitherto the government had been elective; but Moawiyah designed if possible to secure the succession in his own family, and make it hereditary. For this end he used all the means imaginable to oblige the people to declare his son Yezid his heir and successor. He entertained some thoughts of it formerly in the days of Almogeirah. It seems Almogeirah had come to Moawiyah, to beg leave to resign the lieutenancy of Cufah; which Moawiyah granted him in consideration of his great age and infirmities; and designed to put Saed the son of Aas into his place. When Almogeirah heard this, he repented himself of what he had done; and advised Yezid to go to his father, and desire him to nominate him his heir. Upon his coming with this advice, Moawiyah asked him who bad him do so. He told him Almogeirah; which surprised Moawiyah, and he restored him immediately to his lieutenancy of Cufah. However this proposal wrought upon Moawiyah's thoughts so, that he wrote to Ziyad to ask his advice about it; who did not approve of it by any means, because he knew that Yezid was a profligate young fellow wholly given up to sporting, gaming, and drinking. Wherefore he sent an intimate friend of his to Damascus, to divert both the father and the son from this project. This friend first applied himself to Yezid, and satisfied him that it would be much better to desist, at least for the present: afterwards he talked with Moawiyah; till at last they concluded to lay it aside. Thus it rested so long as Ziyad lived, till now in his fifty-sixth year, Moawiyah, who was always fond of it, from the time it was first mentioned to him, received it again in good earnest, and wrote circular letters about it to all the provinces. The Syrians and Irakians came in to it. Malec, who was then governor of Medinah, would have had him proclaimed in that city heir apparent to his father: but Hosein the son of Ali, Abdollah the son of Amer, Abdorrahman the son of Abubeker and Ayesha's brother, and Abdollah the son of Zobeir, absolutely refused it. Their refusal kept the people back. Moawiyah, to encourage the matter with his presence, went in person to Medinah, with 1000 horse. He had a conference with Ayesha about it, and the result was, that the people in general of the province of Hejaz came in; but those four before mentioned with their adherents stood it out to the last; though Moawiyah blustered in the mosque, and would have terrified them if he could; they stood their ground resolutely, and let him see by their answers that they despised his threats; and though he was vehemently angry, he durst not offer any violence, for they were too considerable, and too popular to suffer any compulsion.

After this Moawiyah (or Moawie) took an opportunity of saying to his son Yezid, ' Look you, you see I have made the way plain before ' you : there is none that refuses to come in, except only these four. ' Hosein has the Irakians in his interest, who will never let him rest at ' quiet till they draw him out into the field : remember he is your near ' relation, and a man of perfect merit, wherefore if he comes under ' your power let him go.   Abdollah the son of Amer is a man wholly ' given up to devotion ; and when no body else stands out he will come ' in.   As for Abdorrahman, he is a man that is guided wholly by ex- ' ample, what he sees other people do, that he does too.   He minds ' nothing but women and play.   But the man that will attack thee with ' the strength of the lion, and the subtilty of the fox, is Abdollah the ' son of Zobeir ; if you get him into your power, cut him to pieces.'

In the fifty-eighth year died Ayesha, Abubeker's daughter, who had that name from her ; for Becr in the Arabick signifies a girl, and Abu, father.   Mahomet marrying his daughter Ayesha when she was very young, his name was changed into Abubecr, that is the father of the girl.   She survived her husband Mahomet a long time, who died in the eleventh year of the Hegirah.   She was always treated with the ut- most respect, except only that time when she exposed herself in that expedition against Ali.   Sometimes she was called Prophetess, and generally when any one spoke to her, he qualified her with the title of Mother of the Faithful.   Her brother Abdorrahman, one of those four that withstood Yezid's inauguration, died this same year.

The next year died Abu Hureirah, that is the 'father of the cat ;' so nick-named by Mahomet, because of his fondness of a cat, which he always carried about with him.   He was called so constantly by this name, that his true name is not known, nor his pedigree.   He was such a constant attendant upon Mahomet, that there are a great many tra- ditions go under his name.   So many, that the multitude of them make people suspect them : though others receive them all, as of an un- doubted authority, without the least hesitation.

I find nothing worth remarking between this great attempt of Moa- wiyah, in changing an elective monarchy into an hereditary one, and his death.   Great it may very justly be called, considering not only the strength of Ali's party, who though kept under for the present, would be sure to fall into any measures opposite to Moawiyah their mortal enemy ; but also that there were several left of the old society of the apostle, who expected the dissolution of Moawiyah, with no less impa- tience than the papable cardinals long for the possession of the apos- tolick chair.   Besides that Yezid's character was so obnoxious, that whatsoever it might seem in his father's eyes, his uncle Ziyad, who had both capacity and experience enough to understand men, and courage enough to govern them, thought it too unpopular to be proposed to the provinces.   Yet notwithstanding all these difficulties, Moawiyah so managed the matter, that the son was more secure of succeeding the father, than could have been supposed, considering the very attempt was a perfect imposition and innovation, and there was such a vigorous opposition to be expected. As soon as it was over, Yezid sat and gave audience to his ambassadors, who were sent from all the countries round to proffer their allegiance, and congratulate him. Among the rest came old Alahnaph, who was Yezid's uncle. Moawiyah, who was very fond of his son, bad Alahnaph discourse him ; and to give him a fair opportuity of trying his parts, left them some time alone. When Alahnaph came out, Moawiyah asked him what he thought of his nephew. The old man very gravely answered, ' If we lye we are afraid of God, if we speak truth we are afraid of you. You know best both his night and his day : his inside and his outside : his coming in and his going out : and you know best what you design to do : it is our business to hear and obey : yours to give counsel to the people.'

It was part of the agreement between Moawiyah and Hasan, that after Moawiyah's decease, the government should return to Hasan ; but he being dead, Moawiyah's thoughts were entirely bent upon his own son Yezid ; and there really either was in him, or else paternal tenderness made him fancy it, something so grand and majestick, and a capacity so well fitted for the government of a mighty empire ; that his father grew every day more fond of him ; ant though in other respects, Moawiyah was a wise and prudent man, yet could not help frequently expressing in conversation the great opinion he entertained of his abilities. It is said, that once in one of his harangues to the people after this business was over, he said, ' O God ! if thou knowest that I have settled the government upon him, because according to the best of my judgment I think him qualified for it, confirm it to him ! But if I have done it out of affection confirm it not.'

The last speech he made in publick, when he perceived himself in a weak condition, was to this purpose : ' I am like the corn that is to be ' reaped, and I have governed you a long time till we are both weary ' of one another ; both willing to part. I am superior to whosoever ' shall come after me ; as my predecessors were superior to me. Who- ' soever loves to meet God, God loves to meet him. O God ! I love ' to meet thee ! do thou love to meet me ?' He had not walked far after this before he was taken very ill. When he perceived death approaching, his son Yezid being absent, he called the captain of his guards to him, and another faithful servant, and said to them, remember me to Yezid, and tell him this from me, ' Look upon the Arabians ' as your root and foundation, and whenever they send you any ' ambassadors treat them with courtesy and respect. Take care of the ' Syrians, for they are entirely in your interest, and you may depend ' upon them whenever you are insulted by your enemies : but if ever

' you have occasion to make use of them out of their own country, as
' soon as they have answered your purpose send them home again ;
' for they alter for the worse with being abroad. Oblige the Irakians,
' though they were to ask you for a new deputy every day.; you had
' better in such a case part with the dearest friend you have in the
' world, than have 100,000 swords drawn upon you. I am not in fear
' for you of any of the Coreish but three, Hosein, Ben Amer, and
' Abdollah the son of Zobeir. (Here he repeated the characters given
' of them before.) If Abdollah appears against you oppose him ; if he
' offers you peace accept it, and spare the blood of your people as
' much as lies in your power.'

He reigned 19 years, 3 months and 27 days, from the time that the
government came entirely into his hands upon Hasan's resignation.
There are different reports concerning his age ; some say 70 years, and
others 75. When he was dead, Debac the son of Kais went into the
mosque, and stept up into the pulpit with Moawiyah's winding-sheet
in his hand ; where having made an encomium upon him, and satisfied
the people that he was dead, and that that was his winding-sheet, he
said the burying prayers over him. Yezid was then absent at a town
called Hawarin, belonging to the territory of Hems. They wrote to
him and desired his presence ; but he did not come till after his father
was buried, and then went and prayed at the tomb.

Moawiyah embraced the Mahometan religion at the same time with
his father, which was in the ' year of the victory.' Mahomet made
him his secretary, and Omar gave him the lieutenancy of Syria four
years of his reign. Othman continued him in that post during the
whole space of his reign, which was about 12 years. Four years more
he kept Syria in his own hands by force, whilst he held up arms
against Ali. So that taking all together he had possession of Syria,
either as governor or Caliph, nearly 40 years.

He was of a merciful disposition, couragious, of a quick capacity,
and thoroughly skilled in the administration of government. His
good nature prevailed over his anger, and the sweetness of his
temper exceeded its fierceness. He was easy of access, and very
obliging in his behaviour.

There is a tradition that goes under the name of one Hasan a Ba-
sorian, of great authority among the traditionists. He said that there
were four things to be objected against Moawiyah, every one of which
merited his destruction. 1. That he took the Caliphate upon him by
dint of sword, without having first consulted the people, amongst whom,
besides the companions of the apostle, there were a great many persons of merit and distinction. 2. His leaving the Caliphate by way of
inheritance to his son Yezid, a man of a scandalous character, a
drunkard, a lover of musick, and one that wore silk. 3. His scandalous manner of proceeding in the business of Ziyad, when he owned

him for his brother, notwithstanding the determination of Mahomet with relation to such matters. 4. His cruelty to Hejer and his companions. Shaphei reports, that he put Ali Rebiyah in chains, because there were four of his companions whose testimony he rejected, viz., Moawiyah, Amrou, Almogeirah and Ziyàd.

Once there came before him a young man, and repeated a copy of verses to him, expressing his present condition. Moawiyah was very well pleased with the verses. The Arabians delight in charity, and to address the severest tyrant of them all after that manner with something that is fanciful and pungent, is the securest way in the world either for a man to gain his point, or if necessity requires it, to save his neck. The young man's case was, he had married a fair Arabian lass purely for love, and out of mere fondness had spent all his substance, which was very considerable, upon her. She was charmingly beautiful ; and the governor of Cufah cast his wanton eyes upon her, and ravished her from her husband's bosom by force. He, to whom the loss of his substance, though it had been all the world, was nothing in respect of her ; pierced to the very heart, and ready to die with sorrow and vexation, made his application to Moawiyah. Moawiyah resolved to do him justice, and sent an express to the governor to resign the woman. The governor who had not the most absurd taste in the world, told the express, 'That if the Caliph would be pleased to give him leave to enjoy her one twelve-month, he would be contented to have his head struck off at the end of it.' But the Caliph rigidly insisted upon her being delivered up, and had her brought before him. He was very much surprised at her beauty, but much more at the politeness and elegancy of her expression. He that had received so many embassies, and always conversed with the greatest men of his country, never in his life heard such a torrent of eloquence as flowed from the mouth of that charming Arabian. The Caliph asked her jocosely, whether she would have him, or the governour, or her husband. She answered him in verse, with the modesty that became her sex, and I forbear to translate her answer, because I despair of coming up to the spirit of it ; but the sense is, that though what a person in his eminent station was able to do for her, was beyond her merit or expectation, yet it could not be put into the balance against everlasting damnation. She begged of him, if he designed her any favour, to restore her to her own dear husband ; which he very generously performed, and presented her with a very rich equipage and plenty of gold, to repair the shattered circumstances of her husband, who had spent a good fortune upon her.

He was always very munificent. He made a present to Ayesha of a bracelet worth 100,000 pieces of gold, which she accepted. He presented Hasan with 300,000 pieces, and Abdollah, the son of Zobeir, with 100,000. He used to bid those that came to see him, take anything they had a mind to. He presented Hosein with 100,000 pieces, who divided them among ten of his acquaintance. An 100,000 more he gave to Abdollah, the son of Jaafar, who gave them to his wife at her request. He presented Merwan, the son of Hakem, afterwards Caliph, with 100,000 pieces, who divided half of them amongst his friends. At another time he presented Hasan with four millions.

It happened that Sapor, who had seized Armenia by force of arms, sent an ambassador named Sergius, to Moawiyah, desiring his assistance against the Grecian emperor, who, at the same time, sent one Andrew, an eunuch, a great favourite. Moawiyah told them that they were both equally enemies, and that he would assist that side that offered him most. There was some altercation between the two ambassadors ; Sergius reproached the eunuch with the loss of his virility ; the other in return called him Sodomite. But after their audience was over, Andrew the eunuch was revenged upon his antagonist, for he gave directions to the officers upon the frontiers, who seized him in his return, castrated him, and then dismissed him with his testicles about his neck.

Moawiyah was the first Caliph that introduced the Meksourah into the mosque, that is a place raised above, and separate from the rest, where the Caliph, who was as well chief pontiff in religious, as sovereign in civil affairs, began and chanted the prayers, which are, as one may say, the public office of the Muslemans ; and it was in the same place that he made the Cotbah to the people, which is a sort of homily or preachment, and used, before his time, always to follow the prayers, but he began with it first for fear he should forget that which he had prepared to say.

He was the first Caliph that obliged the people to swear allegiance to his son : the first that laid post-horses upon the roads : the first that made a Meksourah : and the first that spoke to the people sitting.

An Arabian robber being once condemned to have his hand cut off, Moawiyah pardoned him for the sake of four very ingenious verses that he made and repeated to him in the field. They remark that this was the first sentence pronounced among the Muslemans that was not put in execution, the Caliphs not having as yet, till Moawiyah, taken the liberty of showing favour to those whom the ordinary judges had condemned.

Abulpheda records this following account of him, as a remarkable instance of his patience and clemency. Arwah the daughter of Hareth, the son of Abdolmutaleb, the son of Hashem, came to make him a visit : she was his aunt, a very old woman, and of Ali's branch of the family ; as soon as Moawiyah had saluted her, she began to reproach him, ' O nephew,' said she, ' you have been very ungrateful and injurious to your cousin, who was a companion (of the apostle), and you called yourself by a name that was none of your own, and took possession of what you had no right to. And our family exceeded all men in sufferings for this religion, till God took his prophet to reward his labours, and to exalt his station: and then you insulted us, and we were amongst you like the children of Israel in the family of Pharaoh: though Ali, after the prophet, was as Aaron was to Moses.' Amrou, who was then present, had no patience, but took her up and said, ' Hold your tongue, old woman, and do not talk thus like one out of your wits.' ' What,' says she, ' do you prate, you son of a whore, when your mother was the most notorious and cheapest strumpet in all Meccah ; and when she was examined concerning five of the Coreish, she confessed that she had lain with them all ; and that you must belong to him whom you resembled most ; you proving most like old Aasi, he was forced to father you.' Moawiyah only said to her, ' God forgive what is past, what would you have ?' She answered, ' Two thousand pieces to buy an estate for the poor of our family ; and 2000 more to marry our poor relations ; and 2000 more for myself to secure me in time of extremity.' Which was all, by Moawiyah's command, paid down to her immediately.

This Caliph was buried in Damascus, where he had established the seat of the Caliphate, and that city always preserved that prerogative so long as the Ommiades, or defendants of Moawiyah reigned there, till the time of the Abbasides, who transferred it to Anbar, Haschemyah and Bagdad. The inscription of his seal was, ' Every work hath its reward,' or as others say, ' There is no strength but in God.'

The second CALIPH *of the house of* OMMIYAH *(being the seventh from* MAHOMET *).*

Y E Z I D,

THE SON OF MOAWIYAH.

An. Heg. 60, cœpit Oct. 12, A.C. 679.

YEZID, the son of Moawiyah, was inaugurated Caliph on the new moon of the month Rejeb, of the 60th year of the Hegirah, which falls in with the 7th day of April, A.D. 680. He was 34 (lunar) years old when he was saluted emperor. He was forthwith acknowledged lawful Caliph in Syria, Mesopotamia, Ægypt, and Persia, and all the other Mahometan countries, except the cities of Meccah and Medinah, and some others of Chaldea, that refused to submit themselves to him: and among the great ones there were none but Hosein, and Abdollah the son of Zobeir, that disputed the Caliphate with him to their death.

He kept all his father's lieutenants and officers in their places, without so much as removing one of them. The governor of Medinah was Waled the son of Otbah ; of Cufah, Nooman the son of Bashir ; of Basorah, Obeidollah the son of Ziyad ; of Meccah, Abdollah Amrou. As soon as he came to the government, he had nothing so much at heart as the bringing in those that had opposed his being nominated his father's heir and successor. Concerning this affair he wrote a letter to Waled, his governor in Medinah, as follows :—' In the name of the most merciful God. From Yezid Emperor of the Faithful to Waled the son of Otbah. Moawiyah was one of the servants of God, who honoured him, and made him Caliph, and extended his dominions and established him. He lived his appointed time, and God took him to his mercy. He lived beloved, and he died pure and innocent. Farewell. Hold Hosein and Abdollah the son of Amer, and Abdollah the son of Zobeir close to the inauguration without any remission or relaxation.' Waled, upon the receipt of this letter, sent for Merwan the son of Hakem, and consulted him concerning the contents of it. Merwan was of opinion that he should send for them and tender them the oath before they were apprised of the Caliph's death, and upon their refusal should strike their heads off. Either this was not so closely concerted but they received some private intelligence, or else they suspected it themselves : which way soever it was, when Waled's messenger came to them, who found them at the mosque, they sent him back with this answer, ' That they were coming.' After a short deliberation, Hosein went to the governor's house, attended with a sufficient number of his friends and domestics, whom he placed about the door, with orders to come in if they should hear any disturbance. The governor having acquainted him with Moawiyah's decease, invited him to own his allegiance to Yezid. He answered, ' That men of his distinction did not use to do things of that nature in private ; neither did he expect that he would ever have desired it of him ; that he thought it better to stay till all the people were met together, according to the custom upon such occasions, and do it unanimously.' Waled consented : but Merwan, who could easily see through this excuse (as the governor did too), said to the governor, ' If he does not do it now before he goes away, there will be a great deal of blood shed between you and him ; wherefore hold him close, and do not let him go out till he hath given his allegiance, otherwise strike his head off.' Hosein leaped out, and having first reproached Merwan for his advice, went to his own house. Merwan swore to the governor that he was never like to see Hosein any more. The governor told him he did not trouble himself about it ; adding, that he had everything he desired in this world, and that he did not believe that that man's balance would be light in the next that should be guilty of the murder of Hosein. It is an article of the Mahometan faith, that at the last day

there shall be a balance supported by the divine power, that shall extend to the utmost limits of heaven and earth, in which the most
minute actions of mortal men shall be weighed; and he whose evil
deeds outweigh his good ones, shall be damned; on the contrary, he
whose good deeds overbalance his evil ones, shall be saved. For this
reason Waled said, 'That his balance would not be light (meaning
that wherein his evil deeds were put), that should kill Hosein.' Then
Waled sent for Abdollah the son of Zobeir, who put him off for the
space of four-and-twenty hours; and taking along with him all his
family, and his brother Jaafar, departed for Meccah; Waled sent a
party of horse to pursue him, but to no purpose. Whilst Waled was
thus taken up with Abdollah, he had little time to take notice of Hosein,
who, whenever he sent for him, put him off with an excuse, and in the
meantime made all the secret preparation he could to follow Abdollah.
He left none of all his family behind him except his brother Mahomet
Hanifiyah, who, before they parted, expressing the most tender affection and concern for him that can be imagined, advised him by no
means to venture himself in any of the provinces, but to lie close either
in the deserts or the mountains, till his friends were gathered together
in a considerable body, and then he might trust himself with them.
But if he was resolved to go into any town, he should prefer Meccah,
where, if he met with the least appearance of anything that disgusted
him, he should immediately withdraw and retire to the mountains.
Hosein having thanked him heartily for his sincere advice, made the
best of his way to Meccah, where he met with Abdollah.

Yezid, not well pleased with Waled's remissness, removed him from
the government of Medinah, and gave it to Amrou, the son of Said,
who was governour of Meccah. He was a very proud man. He gave
Amer, the son of Zobeir, a commission to march against his brother
Abdollah, whom he hated. Abdollah engaged him in the field, routed
him, and put him in prison, where he kept him till he died.

Now though Abdollah seemed to have interest sufficient to carry his
point, and had beat down all opposition before him, and the Medinians
had openly declared for him, so that his fame was spread round about
the country: yet Hosein's glory outshined him, so that he could not
tell how to propose any thing that he designed to the people, so long
as he was there: who both upon the account of his near relation to
Mahomet, and his own personal qualifications, was reverenced above
all men alive. Moawiyah, so long as he lived, treated him with the
utmost respect: and when Hasan had resigned to Moawiyah, both he
and his brother Hosein used to visit him frequently, and he always
received them courteously, and never failed to dismiss them with noble
presents. After Hasan's death, Hosein used to send to him often, and
paid him a visit once every year, and went with his son Yezid in his
expedition against Constantinople. Hosein was the hopes of all the

Irakians; never were people more overjoyed than they were at the death of Moawiyah, whom they had all along detested as a tyrant and usurper. They thought that now there was a period put to all their slavery, and they should be under the gentle government of a man that was sprung of an almost divine race. The Cufians were so impatient, that they sent message after message to him, assuring him that if he would but once make his appearance amongst them, he should not only be secure as to his own person, but in consideration of the esteem which they had for his father Ali, and his family, they would render him their homages, and acknowledge him for the only lawful and true Caliph. They assured him that there was no manner of difficulty in the matter; all the country being entirely devoted to serve him with their lives and fortunes. The messengers they had sent one after another, came to him all together, pressing him with the utmost vehemency, to what he himself had no aversion to: only he thought it a part of a prudent man to use a little caution and circumspection, in an affair of so great consequence, and attended with so much hazard. Wherefore he first sends his cousin Muslim into Irak, to feel the pulse of the people, and see whether or not they were so unanimously in his interest as had been represented. Ordering him, that if he found it so, he should head a body of them, and beat down all opposition if there should be any: besides he gave him a letter to the Cufians to that purpose. Muslim left Meccah, and passed through Medinah, from whence he took along with him a couple of guides, who led him into a vast desert, where there was no road: one of them perished with thirst, and the other soon after died of the cholick. This unprosperous beginning seemed ominous to Muslim, and discouraged him to that degree, that, having found a place where there was water, he would not stir a step further in his journey, till he had dispatched a messenger to Hosein for further instructions. Hosein ordered him to go on to Cufah by all means, and act pursuant to those directions he had received before. When he came to Cufah, he communicated his business privately to such as he could trust, and the matter was whispered about so dexterously, that they reckoned themselves secure of 18,000, before Yezid's deputy, Noman, had heard one word of it. Muslim, sufficiently satisfied with this success, did not defer acquainting Hosein with it: he wrote to him, and told him that every thing was made plain and easie for him now; and that nothing was wanting but his presence. Upon this notice, he set out upon his journey from Meccah to Cufah.

Noman at last received information of the increasing interest of Hosein, and the forwardness of his party; he was both surprised and concerned; and made a speech to the people, wherein he exhorted them to a peaceful behaviour, and to avoid all manner of strife and contention; assuring them that for his own part he would not be the aggressor, nor meddle with any person, unless he was insulted himself; nor would he take up any man upon suspicion; but he swore by that God, besides whom is no other, that if they revolted from their Imam [Yezid] and withdrew their allegiance, he would fight as long as he could hold his sword in his hand. One that stood by told him that this was a matter that required stirring, but that he talked like one of the weak ones. He answered that, 'He had rather be one of the weak ones in obedience to God, than one of the strong ones in rebelling against him.' And with those words he came down. News of this was carried to Yezid, who sent immediately, and removed Noman from the lieutenancy of Cufah, and gave it to Obeidollah, the son of Ziyad, together with that of Basorah, which he had before. This he did at the instance of Sarchun, the son of Moawiyah: for before that time he was not affected well towards Obeidollah, probably because his father, Ziyad, was against his being declared heir to Moawiyah.

Upon this Obeidollah went from Basorah to Cufah. He rode into the town in the evening, with a black turbant on (which was Hosein's dress), and he could not pass along and salute the crowd, but he was saluted by the title of the son of the apostle; they imagining that it had been Hosein, of whose coming they were in hourly expectation. But to their no small grief and mortification, they were soon undeceived, when some of Obeidollah's retinue said to them, 'Stand off, it is the Emir Obeidollah.' He went directly with his retinue to the castle (they were but 17 horse in all) and began to think of proper means for the extinguishing this sedition. For this purpose, he gives 3,000 pieces for a show to one of his domesticks, whose business it was to pretend that he came out of Syria on purpose to this inauguration of Hosein. Muslim had a house in town, where he polled great numbers every day. Obeidollah's man managed his business so well, that he easily gained credit to his story, and was introduced to Muslim, who took down his vote for Hosein. And to colour the matter, he gave some of his money towards the buying arms, to one that Muslim had singled out for that office, whose business it was to receive all the money that was contributed by the party for that purpose. He continued among them the space of a few days, till he had sufficiently informed himself of all their circumstances, and then made his report to Obeidollah. Muslim had changed his quarters, which at first he had taken up at Hani's house, and removed to Sharik's, who was one of the grand Omeras; Sharik was then sick, and they being informed that Obeidollah designed him a visit, contrived to place Muslim in a corner to kill him. The signal agreed upon was, when the sick man should call for water. Afterwards Obeidollah came, attended by Hani and one servant. They sat down (except the servant) and talked with Sharik a while, but Muslim had not courage enough to stir. The girl that was bringing the water, spying Muslim standing there, was ashamed, and went back with it three times. At last he called out loud, 'Bring me some water, though it kills me.' This made Obeidollah's man suspect that there was something more than ordinary in the matter; so he gave a hint to his master, who leaped forth immediately. When they were gone, Hani and Sharik asked Muslim why he did not kill him. He answered he had heard a tradition of the apostle who had said, ' The faith is contrary to murther : let not a believer murther a man unawares.' Wherefore, he said, ' He durst not kill him in this house.' They told him that if he had done it, no body would have concerned themselves to revenge his death, and they could have secured him in the possession of the castle. Sharik died three days after. As for Hani, upon Obeidollah's commanding the registers to be strictly searched, under the severest penalty, he was found standing upon record, as an old offender, and one that had opposed Obeidollah before. Obeidollah remembered him, and sent some of the Omeras, who would not let him alone till they brought him along with them to the castle. When he came there, Obeidollah asked him what was become of Muslim. He at first pretended to know nothing of him, but being confronted by Obeidollah's servant, who had seen Muslim at his house, and paid him money to buy arms for the service of Hosein, he had nothing else to say for himself, but that Muslim intruded himself upon him into his house, and did not come thither by his invitation. Obeidollah commanded him to produce him. He answered, ' That if he was under his feet, he would not take them off from him.' At this Obeidollah gave him such a blow with his mace, that he wounded him in the face, and broke his nose. Hani had like to have seized one of the swords of the guards, but was prevented. Obeidollah told him he had forfeited his life, and commanded him to be imprisoned in a room in the castle. The people of his tribe came flocking about the castle, imagining that he was murdered ; but the Kadi sent one to tell them that he was detained only to be asked some questions about Muslim, and bad them be at quiet, and go peaceably to their houses, for though the Emir had struck him, it would not affect his life. Muslim having heard this news, mounted his horse, and gave the word, 'Ya Mensour Ommet!'* Which was the signal agreed upon among Hosein's party. Four thousand joined him, and he conducted them towards the castle under two colours, the one red, the other green. Obeidollah was then in the castle prison, discoursing concerning Hani's business, and cautioning them against sedition. The Omeras and chief men sat under him, when the watch came and surprised them all, with the news of Muslim's appearance before the castle. Obeidollah sent several men of note and authority among the people, out of the castle, who rode backwards and forwards disswading them from hazarding themselves upon such an account : and bad those that were with him, look out of the castle, and encourage the loyalists.

* O thou that art helped by the people ! meaning Hosein.

A woman called out to Muslim, and told him he might go about his business, for the people would find him work enough. They considering the event was dubious, began to desert by degrees, till Muslim had no more than 30 men left with him, so he retired in the evening and hid himself. Taking the opportunity of the twilight, he departed from Cufah, without so much as a guide left to shew him the way, or any one to comfort him, or give him shelter. Night came on, and he was upon the road alone in the dark, not knowing one step of the way, nor whither he was going. At last he found a house standing alone in the field, and knocked at the door. There came to him an old woman, one that in the days of her youth and beauty had belonged to a great man, but afterwards had a son by another, whom she expected out of the field. Muslim asked her for some water, which when she had given him, and perceived that he made no haste to go away, she told him that it was not convenient for him to stand there at her door, neither would she allow it. At last he let her understand that it was in her power to do a thing that she should have no reason to repent of. She asked him what it was. He told her his name was Muslim, and that the people of the country had deceived him. She no sooner heard his name, but she readily let him in, and having conveyed him into the most secret and retired part of her house, made the best provision for him she was able. At last her son came home, and observing his mother going backwards and forwards very often, would not rest satisfied, till she had acquainted him with the occasion of it, which, to satisfy his importunity she did, having first enjoyned him secrecy. But he, having heard that Obeidollah had promised a reward to whosoever should discover Muslim, went and informed in the morning: so that before Muslim well knew where he was, he found himself surrounded with 70 or 80 horse. He betook him to his sword, and defended himself bravely, for he beat them thrice out of the house. They pelted him with stones, and put fire upon the ends of canes, and flung at him; then he went out and fought abroad: till at last overpowered with numbers, and grievously wounded in a great many places, particularly both his lips almost cut to pieces, he was seized and disarmed, and bound and mounted upon his own mule. When he perceived that it was quite out of his power to help himself, he wept. One of the men that was present told him that it did not become a man that came about such a great undertaking to weep. He answered, 'That it was not upon his own account, but for the sake of Hosein and his family, who he feared were upon their journey from Meccah to Cufah, and as he supposed, came out either that very day, or the day before. Then turning to Mohammed, the son of Alashat, he begged of him, if it was possible, to send to him in his name, to intreat him to go back: which Mohammed performed, but the messenger did not do his part. When Muslim came to the castle gate, there stood a great many of the Omeras, some of which he knew, and others knew him, waiting for admission to Obeidollah. He was very desirous to drink a draught of water, but one of the men told him he should have no drink till he drank the Hamim, that is, the scalding liquor which the Mahometans feign shall be the drink of the damned in hell. Obeidollah appearing, Muslim did not Salam or salute him ; which when they wondered at, he said, ' If Yezid were there himself, he should not think himself obliged to do it, unless he would give him his life.' Obeidollah told him that he had come thither to make a disturbance, and sow the seeds of division amongst people that were all unanimous, and all agreed upon the same thing. Muslim resolutely answered, ' It is not so : but the people of this province know very well that your father, Ziyad, has killed the best of their men, and shed their blood, and exercised over them the tyranny of a Cosroes or Cæsar ; and we come to govern with justice, and appeal to the determination of the book.' Obeidollah called him rogue, and told him he did not use to appeal to the determination of the book, when he was tippling wine at Medinah. For the truth of which accusation, Muslim appealed to God. Having leave given him to make his will, he whispered one of his friends, and left him 700 pieces ; desiring him to beg his dead body of Obeidollah, and to take care to prevent Hosein's advancing any further in his journey. He was overheard by one that stood by, who told every word he said to Obeidollah. He did not disapprove of any one article in it, and as for Hosein, he said, ' If he would be at quiet no body would meddle with him, but if he was the aggressor, they would not flinch from him.' Muslim was then carried to the top of the castle and beheaded. The head was first thrown down to the bottom, and the body after it. Then Hani was brought forth and beheaded in the street. Both the heads were sent for a present to Yezid, with a letter specifying their several circumstances. This was on the eighth day of the month Dulhagiah in the sixtieth year of the Hegirah.

The earnest and repeated solicitations of the Cufians made Hosein resolve to accept their invitation, and go directly to Cufah. They had sent him in a poll of 140,000 : which, together with their letters, he bundled up, and carried along with him. The wisest of his friends looked upon it as a degree of madness in him to embark himself in such a desperate undertaking. At last they said that if he was resolved to go, it was his destiny that precipitated him. Abdollah, the son of Abbas, told him that there was a report spread of his intended journey to Cufah, and desired to know what he meant by it. Hosein told him that if it pleased God, he was resolved upon it. The son of Abbas answered, ' That indeed if the Cufians had taken arms, killed their Emir [Obeidollah] and taken the whole country into their own hands, and then invited him to come and take the government upon him, there would be something in it, and he should advise him to go :

but that so long as they were under the command of their Emir, whose forces were dispersed throughout all those territories for the security of the country, they had in effect at best only invited him to war; and that he had no security that they would not oppose him, and that they who had been the forwardest in appearing in his interest, might not in the end prove his greatest enemies. Hosein said he would leave the event to God. After this Abdollah, the son of Zobeir, came to make him a visit, and enquire into his design. Among other discourse, he said, 'I do not see any reason why we should leave every thing to the disposal of these men, when we are the sons of the Mahogerins or refugees, and have a better right and claim to the government than they.' Hosein told him that the chief of the nobility had written to him, and that his sect (the Shii) were all ready to stand up for him to a man. To which the son of Zobeir answered, 'That if he had such a sect to stand up for him, he would not omit the opportunity. Hosein easily saw through his meaning; for Abdollah, who was a man of a restless aspiring temper, knew very well that all his own pretensions would be in vain, so long as Hosein was alive, but if any thing should befall him, the way to the Caliphate would be made clear for himself; which Hosein took notice of as soon as he was gone. Abdollah, the son of Abbas, was still very uneasy, and resolved to leave no means unattempted to disswade him from his undertaking. He came to him again, and represented to him the fickle temper of the Irakians, and intreated him to stay at least till they had got rid of their enemy the Emir, and then either to go to them, or else into that part of Hejaz, where there were places of strength: that he should keep himself retired, and write circular letters to all his friends, till they had formed a body, and were capable of appearing for him to some advantage; that then he hoped things would succeed according to his desire. Hosein told him he knew that he advised him as a friend. 'At least,' added the son of Abbas, 'if you be resolved to go, do not take your wives and children along with you, for, by God, I fear your case will be like Othman's, who was murdered whilst his wives and children stood looking on: besides, you have rejoiced the heart of Abdollah, the son of Zobeir, in leaving him behind you in Hejaz: and by that God, besides whom there is no other, if I knew that my taking you by the hair of the head till they came in and parted us, would be a means to detain you in Meccah, I would do it.' Then he left him, and meeting with Abdollah, the son of Zobeir, he told him he had no reason to be sad, and immediately repeated, 'Ya leka ming kobeiratin,' &c., a poem wherein the Arabian poet elegantly addresses himself to the lark, and bids her, whilst the field and season favoured her, enjoy herself and sing, and delight in her young ones, and whatsoever else would entertain her; but let her assure herself she should not escape the nets of the fowler.

24

No advice taking effect with Hosein, though Abdollah, the son of Abbas, had sat up with him all night to no purpose, he set out from Meccah with a competent retinue on the eighth day of the month Dulhagiah, being the very same day on which his cousin Muslim was killed at Cufah, concerning whom he had received no other intelligence than what he had sent him, that all things went well. The Emir Obeidollah was very well appraised of Hosein's approach; who when he came as far as Assheraph met with a body of 1000 horse, under the command of Harro, the son of Yezid, of the tribe of Temimah, a man no way disaffected to Hosein's interest. Hosein's men had been for water at the river, and drawn a great deal for the horses, which he did not make use of for himself alone, but ordered them to water the horses of his enemies. At noon he commanded the people to be called together, according to the custom of the Mahometans, and came out to them with nothing but his vest, his girdle and his shoes, and alleged the invitation of the Cufians as the reason of his undertaking that expedition. Then he asked Harro, if he would pray amongst his men; who answered, that after him he would. They parted that night and went every man to his tent, and the next day Hosein made a speech to them, wherein he asserted his title, and exhorted them to submit to him, and oppose all that stood against him, who pretended to usurp authority over the people wrongfully. Harro told him, 'That he did not know who had writ to him, nor what it was;' and on Hosein's producing the letter, Harro said, after he had read a little of it, 'We are none of those that had any hand in writing of it, and we are commanded as soon as we meet you to bring you directly to Cufah into the presence of Obeidollah the son of Ziyad.' Hosein told him, 'That he would sooner die than submit to that,' and gave the word of command to his men to ride; but Harro wheeled about and intercepted them; which provoked Hosein to say, 'May your mother be childless of you' (Arab. *Thacolátka Ommoka*), a common curse among the Arabians. 'What do you mean?' Harro answered, 'If any man but your self had said so much to me, I would have had satisfaction, but I have no room to mention your mother without the greatest respect.' Then speaking to his men they retreated and he told Hosein, '.That he had no commission to fight with him, but he was commanded not to part with him till he had conducted him to Cufah.' But he bad him chuse any road that did not go directly to Cufah, or back again to Medinah; 'and do you,' says he, 'write to Yezid or Obeidollah, and I will write to Obeidollah, perhaps it may please God I may meet with something that may bring me off, without my being exposed to any extremity upon your account.' Hosein upon this turned a little out of the way that leads to Adib and Kadisia, and Harro told him, 'That it was his opinion, that if he would be the aggressor and first set upon the Cufians, he might gain his point; but if he suffered himself to be attacked he would perish.' Hosein asked

him, ' If he thought to terrify him with death.' When they came to
Adib they met with four horsemen, who turned out of the way to come
up to Hosein. Alharro would have rode between them and Hosein,
but he would not permit it. Thirmah was their guide, whom as soon
as they came up Hosein asked ' What news ?' Thirmah answered, ' All
the nobility are against you to a man ; as for the rest their hearts are
with you, but to-morrow their swords will be drawn against you.'   Hosein asked him if he could tell any tidings of his messenger Kais (one
that he had sent before him to prepare the way) : Thirmah said, ' As
for your messenger Kais he was brought before Obeidollah, who commanded him to curse you and your father Ali ; instead of which he
stood up and prayed for you and your father, and cursed Obeidollah
and his father Ziyad, and persuaded the people to come into your assistance, and gave them notice of your coming.   For which Obeidollah
commanded him to be thrown down headlong from the top of the
castle.'   At this news Hosein wept, and repeated this verse of the
Alcoran, ' There are some of them who are already dead, and some of
them that stay in expectation and have not changed.'   He then added,
' O God ! let their mansions be in paradise, and gather us and them
together, in the fixed resting place of thy mercy, and the delights of thy
reward.' Then says Thirmah to him, ' I do not think these people that
' are along with you a sufficient match for those that are against you.
' How is it possible, when all the plains of Cufah are full of horse and
' foot ready to meet you ? I beg of you, for God's sake, if it be possible,
' do not go a span's breadth nearer to them ; but if you please, I will
' conduct you to our impregnable mountain Aja, in which God hath
' secured us from the kings of Gasan and Hamyar, and from Nooman*
' the son of Almundir, and from both the black and the red.   And if
' any calamity befalls us, you may retire thither, and then send to the
' tribe of Tay, and stay among us as long as you please ; for I believe
' there will be no less than 10,000 of that tribe with their swords ready
' at your service, and by God, no body shall ever get at us.'   Hosein
said, ' God reward thee ;' but still persisted in his resolution of going
forwards, and Thirmah took his leave.

When night came on, he ordered his men to provide as much water
as they should have occasion for, and continued his march in the night.
As he went on he nodded a little, and waking on a sudden, said, ' We
belong to God, and to him we return.   I saw a horseman, who said,
" Men travel by night, and the destinies travel by night towards them."
This I know to be a message of our deaths.'   In the morning after the
prayers were over he mended his pace, and taking the left hand road
came to Nineve (not the ancient, but another town of the same name),
and as he rode with his bow upon his shoulder, there came up a person
who saluted Alharro, but took no notice of him.   He delivered a letter

* Concerning him see Socrates Hist. Ecclesiast, lib. III. cap. 18.

to Alharro, containing orders from Obeidollah, to lead Hosein and his men into a place where there was neither town nor fortification, till his messengers and forces should come up. This was on Friday the second day of the month Moharrem, in the 61st year of the Hegirah, that is on October 1, A.D. 680.

The day after Amer the son of Saed came up with 4000 men, which Obeidollah had ordered to Deilam. They had pitched tents without the walls of Cufah, and when they heard of Hosein's coming, Obeidollah commanded Amer to defer his intended march to Deilam, and go against Hosein. Amer begged his pardon, and when Obeidollah threatened him upon his refusal, he desired time to consider of it : every one that he advised withal disswaded him from it; insomuch that his nephew said to him, ' Beware that you do not go against Hosein, and rebel against your Lord, and cut off mercy from you ; by God, you had better be deprived of the dominion of the whole world than meet your Lord with the blood of Hosein upon you.' He seemed to acquiesce and be overruled, but upon Obeidollah's renewing his threats, he marched against him, and met in the place above-mentioned, and sent to enquire of him what brought him thither. Hosein answered, ' That the Cufians had wrote to him, but since they had rejected him he was willing to return to Meccah.' Amer was glad to hear it, and said, ' He hoped in God he should be excused from fighting against him.' Then Amer wrote concerning it to Obeidollah, who sent him this answer, ' Get between him and the water, as he did by Othman the innocent and righteous, the injured emperor of the faithful, and propose to him and his companions to acknowledge their submission to the government of the emperor of the faithful, Yezid; when they have done that we shall consider of further measures.' From that time Amer's men began to hinder Hosein's men from getting any water, the name of the place where they intercepted him was called Kerbela. As soon as Hosein heard it, he said, ' Kerb and Bala, that is, trouble and affliction.' At last Hosein proposed a conference with Amer between the two armies ; they came each of them attended by 20 horse, who kept their due distance whilst they discoursed. The contents of their conference were (according to Abulpheda and some others) that Hosein proposed that they might be admitted to one of these three conditions ; either that they might go to Yezid, or else have leave to return back to Arabia, or else be placed in some garrison where he might fight against the Turks. Amer wrote word of this to Obeidollah, who seemed at first to look upon it as a reasonable proposal ; till Shamer stood up and swore, that he ought to be admitted to no terms till he had surrendered himself, adding, that he had been informed of a long conference between him and Amer. This changed Obeidollah's mind quite. There is a tradition from one that attended Hosein all the way from Meccah, and overheard this conference which says, ' That Hosein did not ask

of him either to be sent to Yezid, or to be put into any of the garrisons,
but only either that he might have leave to return to the place from
whence he came or else have his liberty to go where he would about
the country, till he should see which way the inclinations of the people
would turn.'

Obeidollah, who was resolved not to venture Hosein too near Cufah,
for fear of an insurrection, sent Shamer to Amer with orders that if
Hosein and his men would surrender themselves, they should be received; if not, that he should first propose to Amer to fall upon them
and kill them, and trample them under their horses' feet; and upon
his refusal, to strike his head off and command the forces himself,
Obeidollah gave a letter of protection and security to four of Ali's sons
—Abbas, whom he had by Obeidollah's aunt, Abdollah, Jaafar, and
Othman—which they refused to accept, saying that the security of
God was better than that of the son of Somyah. Obeidollah had sent
a chiding letter to Amer because of his remissness, which made him
undertake to fight against Hosein himself when Shamer proposed it to
him, without knowing that his refusal was to cost him his head. Amer
drew up his forces in the evening, on the ninth of the month, Moharram, and came up to Hosein's tent, who was sitting in his door, just
after evening prayer. He and his brother Abbas desired of them to
give him time till the next morning, and he would answer them to anything they desired of him. This was granted, and one of Amer's men
said that if a Deilamite (a nation which they mortally hated) had asked
such a small request, it ought not to have been refused. At their first
advancing, he was leaning upon his sword and nodding. His sister
came and waked him, and, as he lifted up his head, he said, 'I saw the
prophet in my dream, who said " Thou shalt rest with us."' Then she
struck her face, and said, 'Woe be to us!' He answered, 'Sister, you
have no reason to complain—God have mercy upon you, hold your
peace.' In the night she came sighing to him again, and said, 'Alas
for the desolation of my family! I wish I had died yesterday, rather
than have lived till to-day. My mother, Phatemah, is dead; and my
father, Ali; and my brother, Hasan. Alas for the destruction that is
past, and the dregs of it that remain behind!' Hosein looked upon her,
and said, 'Sister, do not let the devil take away your temper.' Then,
beating her face and tearing open her bosom, she fell down in a swoon.
Hosein, having recovered her with a little cold water, said, 'Sister, put
' your trust in God, and depend upon the comfort that comes from him;
' and know that the people of the earth shall die, and the people of the
' heaven shall not remain; and everything shall perish but the presence
' of God, who created all things by his power and shall make them
' return, and they shall return to him alone. My father was better
' than I, and my mother was better than I, and my brother was better
' than I—and I, and they, and every Musleman, has an example in the

'apostle of God.' Then, charging her not to use any such behaviour after his death, he took her by the hand and led her into her tent. He told his friends that these men wanted nobody but him, and desired them to shift for themselves, and get away, if possible, to their respective habitations. But Alabbas told him they would not, and said, 'God forbid we should ever see the time wherein we should survive you.' Then he commanded his men to cord the tents close together, and put the ropes through one another, that the enemy might not get between them. They made a line of their tents, and Hosein, in the night, ordered a trench to be digged at one end of it, into which they threw a good quantity of wood and cane, which they set on fire, to prevent their being surrounded, so that they could be attacked only in the front. They spent all that night in hearty prayer and supplication, whilst all the while the horse of the enemies guard were riding round about them. The next morning both sides prepared themselves for battel ; and Hosein put his small forces, which amounted to no more than 32 horse and 40 foot, into good order. Amer, having drawn up his men and delivered the flag to one of his servants, came very near.

In the meantime, Hosein went into a tent, and having first washed and anointed, he perfumed himself with the larger sort of musk— several of the great men did the like. One of them asking what was the meaning of it, another answered, 'Alas ! there is nothing between us and the black-eyed girls, but only that these people come down upon us and kill us.' Then Hosein mounted his horse, and took the *Alcoran* and laid it before him, and coming up to the people, invited them to the performance of their duty, adding, ' O God, thou art my confidence in every trouble, and my hope in all adversity.' He set his son, Ali, on horseback, the eldest of that name, for there were two of them, but he was very sick. Then he cryed out, hearken to the advice that I am going to give you ; at which they all gave attention with profound silence. Then, having first praised God, he said, ' O men ! if you will ' hearken to me and do me justice, it will be better for you, and you will ' find no handle of doing anything against me : but if you will not ' hearken to me, bring all that are concerned with you together, that ' your matter be clear, and then make report of it to me without delay. ' My protector is God, who sent down the book (*i.e.*, the Alcoran), and ' he will be the protector of the righteous " (*c. x., v.* 72).

As soon as he uttered these last words, his sisters and daughters lift up their voices in weeping ; at which Hosein said, ' God reward the son of Abbas'—meaning, because he had advised him to leave the women behind him. Then he sent his brother Alabbas and his son Ali to keep them quiet. He next reminded them of his excellency, the nobility of his birth, the greatness of his power, and his high descent, and said, ' Consider with yourselves whether or no such a man as I am ' is not better for you—I who am the son of your prophet's daughter,

'besides whom there is no other upon the face of the earth : Ali was
'my father ; Jaafar and Hamzah, the chief of the martyrs, were both
'my uncles ; and the apostle of God, upon whom be peace, said both
'of me and my brother, that we were the chief of the youth of paradise.
'If you will believe me what I say is true—for, by God, I never told a lye
'in earnest since I had my understanding, for God hates a lye. If you
'do not believe me, ask the companions of the apostle of God [here he
'named them], and they will tell you the same. Let me go back to
'what I have.' They asked what hindered him from being ruled by
the rest of his relations. He answered, ' God forbid that I should set
my hand to the resignation of my right after a slavish manner. I
have recourse to God from every tyrant that doth not believe in the
day of account.'

Just upon this a party of about 30 horse wheeled about, and came up
to Hosein, who expected nothing less than to be attacked by them.
Harro, that had met with Hosein first, was at the head of them. He
came to testify his repentance, and proffer his services to Hosein,
declaring that if he had once thought it would ever have come to that
extremity, he would never have intercepted him, but have gone with
him directly to Yezid ; and to make the best amends for his mistake
that his present circumstances would admit of, was resolved to die
with him. Hosein accepted his repentance. And Harro stood forth,
and called to the people (to Amer, in particular), ' Alas for you ! Will
'you not accept those three articles, which the son of the apostle's
daughter offers you?' Amer told him that if it lay in his power he
would, but Obeidollah was against it, and had been chiding and re-
proaching the Cufians for expressing the least inclination to hearken
to them. Then said Harro, ' Alas for you ! You invited him till he
'came, and then deceived him ; and this did not satisfy you, but you
'are come out to fight against him—nay, you have hindered him, and
'his wives, and his family, from the water of Euphrates, where Jews,
'and Christians, and Sabians drink, and hogs and dogs sport them-
'selves ; and he is like a prisoner in your hands, uncapable of doing
'himself either good or hurt.' Then Amer said to the slave to whom
he had given the flag, ' Bring up the colours.' As soon as they came
up to the front of the troops, Shamer shot an arrow, and said, ' Bear
witness that I shot the first arrow.' The battel thus begun, they exchanged arrows apace on both sides. Two of Amer's men went out,
and offered themselves to single combat—their names were Yaser and
Salem. Abdollah, the son of Amer, having first asked leave of Hosein,
answered them, and killed Yaser first, and Salem next, though Salem
had first cut off all the fingers of his left hand. The next that offered
himself came close up to Hosein, and said to him, ' Hosein, you are
just at hell.' To whom Hosein replied, ' By no means : alas for thee,
I go to a merciful Lord, full of forgiveness, easy to be obeyed—but
you are more worthy of hell.' As he turned about, his horse ran

away with him, and he fell off : his left foot hung in the stirrup, and as he passed by, one of Hosein's men lopped off his right leg. His horse continuing his speed, his head was all the way dashed against the stones, till he died. There were several single combats fought, in all which Hosein's men were superior, because they fought like men that were resolved to die. This made some of the leading men advise Amer not to expose his men any longer to the hazard of single combats. Then Amrou, the son of Hejage, who commanded the right wing, gave an onset, with these words in his mouth—'Fight against those who separate from the religion and from the Imaum [Yezid], and from the congregation.' 'Alas !' said Hosein, 'what do you encourage your men against us—are we the men that separate from the religion, and you those that keep to it ? When your souls are separated from your bodies, you will know which of us deserve hell fire most.' In this attack, Muslim, the son of Ausajah, was killed—he was the first that died on Hosein's side, and Hosein went and commiserated him at his last gasp. Hobeib said to him, having first told him that he was near paradise, 'If I was not sure that I should soon follow you, I would fulfil your will, whatsoever it was.' To whom Muslim answered, in a very low voice, 'This is my will (pointing to Hosein)—that you die for him.'

Then Shamer gave an onset with the left wing with such violence, that they came very near to Hosein, but Hosein's horse repulsed them bravely ; so that they sent to Amer for some archers, who ordered them above 500. As soon as they came up, they let fly their arrows so thick amongst Hosein's horse, that they were all immediately reduced to foot. Harro perceiving his horse wounded, leaped off from him with his sword in his hand, as eager as a lion.

Amer perceiving that they were inaccessible every where, but in the front, commanded his men to pull down the tents ; but that not succeeding, for Hosein's men killed those that went about it, Shamer, God confound him, called for fire to burn Hosein's tent (having first struck his javelin into it) with all that were in it. The women shrieked and ran out of it. 'How,' said Hosein, 'what wouldst thee burn my family ? God burn thee in hell-fire.' One of the great men came to Shamer, and represented to him how scandalous, and how unbecoming a soldier it was to scare the women : he began to be ashamed of it, and was thinking of retreating, when some of Hosein's men attacked him, and drove him off the ground with the loss of some of his men. It was now noon, and Hosein bad some of his friends speak to them to forbear till he had said the prayers proper for that time of day. One of the Cufians said, 'They will not be heard ;' Habib answered, 'Alas for you, shall your prayers be heard, and not the prayers of the apostle's family, upon whom be peace !' Habib fought with great courage till he was killed. Then Hosein said the noon prayers

amongst the poor remainder of his shattered company, and to the rest
of the office he added the 'prayer of fear,' never used but in cases of
extremity.   During the time of the fight he said several prayers, in one
of which there is this pathetical expression, ' Let not the dews of
heaven distil upon them, and withhold thou from them the blessings
of the earth, for they first invited me and then deceived me.'   After
the prayers were over the fight was renewed with great vehemency on
both sides, till they came up close to Hosein, but his friends protected
him : one of them killed ten besides those he wounded ; at last he was
taken, both his arms being broken, and Shamer struck off his head.
Hosein's party were now almost all cut off, and his eldest son Ali was
first wounded with a lance and afterwards cut in pieces.   The rest
were most of them singled out by the archers and shot.   Hosein staid
a long time and nobody came to him, but he turned back again, for
hardly any of them could find in his heart to kill him.   At last one
came and struck him with a sword upon the head and wounded him,
so that his head-piece was full of blood, which he took off and flung
away, saying, that he had neither eat nor drank out of it, and bound
up his head in his turbant.   Quite tired out, he sat down at the door
of his tent, and took his little son Abdollah upon his lap, who was
presently killed with an arrow.   Hosein took his hand full of the
child's blood, and throwing it towards heaven said, ' O Lord !   If
thou withholdest help from us from heaven, give it to those that are
better, and take vengeance upon the wicked.'   At last he grew extremely thirsty, and whilst he was drinking, he was shot in the mouth
with an arrow.   He then lift up his hands to heaven, which were both
full of blood, and prayed very earnestly.   Then Shamer encouraged
some of the stoutest of his men to surround him : at the same time a
little nephew of his, a beautiful child, with jewels in his ears, came to
embrace him, and had his hand cut off with a sword : to whom
Hosein said, ' Thy reward, child, is with God, thou shalt go to thy
pious forefathers.'   Then they surrounded him, and he threw himself into
the middle of them, charging sometimes on the right, and sometimes
on the left, and which way soever he turned himself, they flew off as
so many deer before a lion.   His sister Zeinah, the daughter of
Phatemah, came out and said, ' I wish the heaven would fall upon the
earth ;' then turning to Amer, she asked him if he could stand by and
see Hosein killed : whereupon the tears trickled down his beard, and
he turned his face away from her.   No body offered to meddle with
him, till Shamer set them on again, with reproaches and curses, one
of them, for fear of Shamer, threw a lance at him, but made it fall
short, because he would not hurt him.   At last one wounded him
upon the hand, a second upon the neck, whilst a third thrust him
through with a spear.   When he was dead, they cut his head off.
When he was searched there were found upon him three and thirty

wounds, and four and thirty bruises.   Shamer intended to have killed
Ali the youngest son of Hosein, that was afterwards called Zein Alabe-
din, i.e., 'The ornament of the religious,' who was very young and
very sick, but one of his companions disswaded him from it.   They
took Hosein's spear, and the rest of the spoil, and divided all his
riches, and his furniture, even so far as to take away the women's
richest cloaths : and though Amer forbad their going near the women,
and had given express command, that whosoever had taken anything
from them, should return it again ; yet they were never the better, for
there was nothing restored that they had lost.   Hosein's 72 men were
killed (17 of which were descended from Phatemah) ; and on the other
side, there were 88 killed, besides the wounded.   Then they rode their
horses over Hosein's body backwards and forwards so often, that they
trampled it into the very ground.   Haula, who had his head, went away
post with it to Obeidollah ; but finding the castle shut, he carried it
home to his own house, and told his wife, that he had brought her the
rarity of the world.   The woman was in a rage, and said, 'Other
men make presents of gold and silver, and you have brought the head
of the son of the apostle's daughter ; by God the same bed shall never
hold us two any more ;' and immediately leaped out of bed from him
and ran away.   He procured another of his countrywomen to supply
her place, who reported afterwards that she was not able to sleep all
that night, because of a light which she saw streaming up towards
heaven from the place where Hosein's head lay, and white birds continually hovering about it.   Haula the next morning carried the head
to Obeidollah, who treated it reproachfully, and struck it over the
mouth with a stick ; upon which Zeid, the son of Arkom, said to him
'Take away this stick, for I swear by him, besides whom there is no
other God, I have seen the lips of the apostle of God (upon whom be
peace) upon these lips.'   Obeidollah told him, that if he was not an old
man, and out of his wits, he would strike his head off.

   Zeinab, Ali's sister, put on her worst cloaths, and, attended by some
of her maids, went and sat down in the castle.   Obeidollah asked
thrice who she was, before any one told him : as soon as he knew her,
he said, 'Praise be to God, who hath brought you to shame, and hath
killed you, and proved your stories to be lyes.'   She answered,
'Praise be to God, who hath honoured us with Mahomet (upon
whom be God's peace) and hath purified us, and not [dealt with us] as
you say, for [none but] the wicked is brought to shame, and the lye is
given [to none but] to the evil one.'   He replied, 'Do not you see, how
God hath dealt with your family ?'   She answered, 'Death was decreed
for them, and they are gone to their resting place ; God shall bring
both you and them together, to plead your several causes before him.'
This put him into a rage, but one of his friends bad him remember
that she was a woman, and not take anything amiss that she said.

Obeidollah told her, that God had given his soul full satisfaction over their chief (Hosein) and their whole rebellious family. Zeinab answered, ' You have destroyed all my men, and my family, and cut off my branch, and tore up my root : if that be satisfaction to your soul, you have it.' He swore she was a woman of courage, adding that her father was a poet, and a man of courage. She answered, that courage was no ingredient in a woman's character, but she knew how to speak. Then looking upon Ali, Hosein's son, he commanded him to be searched, for he said, he believed he was arrived at man's estate : being informed that he was, he commanded him to be beheaded. Here Zeinab all in tears embraced her nephew, and asked Obeidollah, if he had not yet drunk deep enough of the blood of their family ; and intreated him, if he was resolved to kill the lad, to give her leave to die along with him. Young Ali begged of him, for the sake of the near relation that there was between him and the women, that he would not send them away without so much as one man to attend them in their journey. Obeidollah pausing awhile, and looking sometimes upon her, and sometimes upon the people, was astonished at her tenderness, and swore he believed she was in good earnest, and had rather die with him, than survive him. At last he dismissed him and bad him go along with the women ; which they looked upon as a very providential deliverance, and said that Obeidollah would have killed Ali, but God diverted him from it.

Obeidollah went from the castle to the great mosque, and going up into the pulpit, said, ' Praise be to God, who hath manifestly shown the truth, and those that are in the possession of it, and hath assisted Yezid the governor of the faithful, and his party, and killed the liar, the son of the liar Hosein, the son of Ali and his party.' This provoked Ali's party to the last degree ; several of them rose up in great indignation, and amongst the rest, there was one who was blind of both his eyes, which he had lost in two several battles, and used to continue in the mosque praying from morning to night. He hearing Ziyad's speech, he cried out, ' O son of Merjanah (that was his mother's name), the liar, the son of the liar, are you and your father, and he that gave you your commission, and his father. O son of Merjanah ! you kill the sons of the prophets, and speak the words of honest men.' Every man, even of his own party, blamed him for his rashness, fearing that he had not only brought destruction upon himself, but upon them too. He was seized by Obeidollah's order, but upon his crying out he was rescued by his party, there being about 700 of them at that time in town ; but notwithstanding his escape for the present, he was killed soon after, and hung upon a gibbet on the heath for an example.

Hosein's head was first set up in Cufah, afterwards carried about the streets, and then sent to Yezid at Damascus, along with the women and young Ali. When Obeidollah's express came to Yezid, and wished him joy of his success, and the death of Hosein, Yezid wept and said, 'I should have been very well pleased without the death of Hosein: God curse the son of Somyah; if I had had him in my power, I would have forgiven him: God loved Hosein, but did not suffer him to attain to anything.' Ali travelled with a chain about his neck; Shamer and Mehphar conducted them with a body of men, but Ali would not vouchsafe to speak one word to them all the way. 'Tis said that whilst they were upon the road, Yezid advised with his courtiers how he should dispose of them. One of them said, 'Never bring up the whelp of a cur; kill Ali the son of Hosein, and extinguish the whole generation of them.' At which Yezid held his peace. Another of a milder temper said, 'O emperor of the faithful, do with them as the apostle of God would do if he were to see them in this their condition.' This moved him to compassion. When he saw Hosein's head, he said, 'O Hosein, if I had had thee in my power I would not have killed thee!' Then sitting down, he called in the chief of the Syrian nobility, and ordered Hosein's wives and children to be brought before him; but he was very angry when he saw the women appear in such a mean condition, and said, 'God curse the son of Somyah, surely if he had ever been related to these women, he could never have treated them after this scandalous manner.' Then turning to Ali, he said, 'This was your father, who set at nought my right, and jostled me out of my government, and God hath disposed of him as you see.' Whom Ali briskly answered with this verse in the Alcoran, 'There is no calamity befalls you, either in the earth, or in your own selves, but it was in a book before we created it' (*chap. lvii.*, 22). Yezid, turning to his son Caled, bade him answer him; but Caled was young and ignorant, and had nothing to say. Then said Yezid, 'What calamity hath befallen you, is what your own hands have drawn upon you, and he pardoneth a great many' (*chap. xlii.*, 29). One of the Syrians would have begged Phatemah, Ali's daughter; she was but a little girl, and could not tell but it might be so, and in a great fright laid hold upon her sister Zeinab's cloaths, who knew very well that it was contrary to the law to force any one out of their own sect, and said, 'He lies: by God, though I die, it neither is in your power nor his.' At which Yezid was angry, and told her that it was in his power, and he would do it if he pleased. She told him it was not in his power to force them out of their own religion, at which he started up in a passion and said, 'Is this the language that you come before me withal? it was your father and your brother that went out from the religion.' 'Then,' said she, 'you and your father and grandfather were all in the right!' This provoked him to say, 'Thou liest, thou enemy of God.' 'How,' said Zeinab, 'you the governor of the faithful, and reproach us unjustly, and make an ill use of your power!' At which he blushed and held his peace. The Syrian petitioning again for Phatemah, Yezid cursed him, and bade ɲim be quiet. He then ordered them to be conducted to the hot-bath, and sent them cloaths and all provisions necessary for their refreshment after the fatigue of their tedious journey. He entertained the women with all possible respect in his palace ; and Moawiyah's wives came, and kept them company the space of three days, mourning for Hosein. So long as they staid, he never walked abroad but he took Ali and Amrou, Hosein's two sons, along with him ! Once he asked Amrou, who was very little, whether he would fight with his son Caled. Amrou immediately answered, ' Give me a knife, and give him one.' An enemy to the family of Ali, a court flatterer, said upon this, ' Depend upon it always that one serpent is the parent of another.'

After they had taken a competent time for their refreshment, and were resolved upon their journey to Medïnah, Yezid sent for his wives and children, to take their leaves, and commanded Nooman, the son of Bashir, to accommodate them with all necessary provisions, and send them home with a safe convoy. When he dismissed them, he said to Ali, ' God curse the son of Marjanah. If your father had fallen into ' my hands, I would have granted him any condition he would have ' desired, and done whatsoever lay in my power to have saved him ' from death, though it had been with the loss of some of my own chil- ' dren. But God hath decreed what you see. Write to me : whatso- ' ever you desire shall be done for you.'

The person to whose care Yezid had committed them, behaved himself so civilly and respectfully to them all the way (for they travelled in the night as well as in the day, and he was very vigilant over them), that Phatemah said to her sister Zeinab, ' Sister, this Syrian hath behaved himself so kindly to us, do you not think we ought to make him a present ?' ' Alas !' said Zeinab, ' we have nothing to present him withal, but our jewels.' ' Then,' said the girl, ' let us give him them.' She consented, and they took off their bracelets and sent them to him, with an apology, begging of him to accept of them as a token of their respect for his courtesy. He modestly refused them, with this generous answer—' If what I have done had been only with regard to this world, ' a less price than your jewels had been a sufficient reward ; but what ' I did was for God's sake, and upon the account of your relation to the ' prophet : God's peace be upon him.' When they came to Medinah, there was such lamentation made between them and the rest of the family of Hashem, as is not to be expressed.

There are different reports concerning Hosein's head : some say it was sent to Medinah, and buried by his mother ; others, that it was buried at Damascus, in a place called the garden-gate, from whence it was removed to Ascalon, and afterwards, by the Caliphs of Egypt, to Grand Cairo, where they interred it and erected a monument over it, which they called the sepulchre of Hosein the martyr. Those Ægyptian Caliphs, who called themselves Phatemites, and had possession of Ægypt from before the year 400, till after the year 660, pretend that Hosein's head came into Ægypt after the year 500 of the Hegirah; but the Imams of the learned say that there is no foundation for that story of theirs, but that they only intended by it to make their pretence to the nobility of their extraction pass more current—since they called themselves Phatemites, as being descended from Mahomet's daughter, Phatemah.

Some pretend to shew his burying-place near the river of Kerbela; others say that there are no footsteps of it remaining. The first sultan of the race of the Bovides built a sumptuous monument there, which is visited to this very day, with great devotion, by the Persians. This sultan called his edifice by the name of ' Kunbud Faiz,' which signifies in the Persian language ' The Magnificent Dome ;' but they now commonly call it, in Arabick, 'Meshed Hosein'—'The Sepulchre of Hosein the Martyr.'

The Caliph Almotawakkel, who began to reign in the year 232, persecuted the memory of Ali and his family to that degree, that he caused Hosein's sepulchre (called by the Persians ' the holy, sublime, and pure place') to be quite razed and destroyed, and to obliterate entirely the least remainder of it, was resolved to draw a canal of water over it; however, he was frustrated in his attempt, for the water would never come near the tomb, but kept its distance out of respect, from whence that water was called ' Haïr,' which signifies ' astonished and respectful'—a name which hath since passed to the sepulchre itself, upon the account of such a miracle. But there is one Naim, who used to be angry with anyone that pretended to know the place of his burial.

The two titles which they generally give Hosein in Persia are that of ' Shahid, the martyr,' or that of ' Seyyid, the lord ;' and by the word ' Alseidani,' which signifies ' the two lords'—without adding anything more, they always understand the two eldest sons of Ali, who were Hasan and Hosein.

They report that amongst other acts of piety which Hosein practised, he used every 24 hours to make a thousand adorations or prostrations before God, and that at the age of 55 he had gone 25 pilgrimages on foot, whereas a good Musleman is not obliged to go above once in his whole life.

Yezdi, in a treatise concerning the divine love,* relates that Hosein having one day asked his father Ali if he loved him, and Ali having answered that he loved him tenderly, Hosein asked him once more if he loved God, and Ali having also answered that question affirmatively, Hosein said to him, ' Two loves can never meet in the same heart— neither hath God given a man two hearts.' At these words Ali's heart was moved, and they say he wept.

Hosein, touched with his father's tears, resumed the discourse, and

* The title is *Resalat phi biyani'l mehabbat.*

said to him, to comfort him, ' If you had your choice between the sin of infidelity towards God, or my death, what would you do?' Ali answered, ' I would sooner deliver you up to death than abandon my faith.' ' Then you may know by this mark,' replied Hosein, ' that the love you have for me is only a natural tenderness, and that which you bear towards God is a true love.'

He was killed on the tenth day of the month Moharram,* in the year of the Hegirah 61. This date is so celebrated amongst the Persians, that to this very day they call it ' the day of Hosein, Yaum Hosein, Rus Hosein.' The memory of, and mourning for, this death, are still annually celebrated among them ; and it is this anniversary weeping and extravagant lamentation, that still keeps up the aversion of this nation to all the Muslemans that are not in the same sentiments with themselves, so that it causes for that time an implacable hatred between the successors of the family of Ommiyah and Aubas, and all those that do not look upon Abubeker, Omar, and Othman, to have been usurpers, and Ali the only rightful and lawful successor of Mahomet.

My anonymous author is very severe upon the sect of Ali, both upon the account of the many fables they have invented concerning Hosein, and their superstitious observation of the day of his death. Let us hear him in his own words—' The sect of Ali,' says he, ' have forged a ' multitude of abominable lyes upon this occasion : they say that the ' sun was eclipsed upon this day, so that the stars appeared at noon ' day ; that you could not take up a stone, but there was blood under ' it ; that the sides of the heavens were turned red, and when the sun ' rose the beams of it looked like blood ; that the heavens looked ' like clotted blood ; that the stars struck one against the other ; ' that the heavens rained red blood, and that before this day ' there was no redness in the heavens ; that when Hosein's head ' was brought into the palace, the walls dropt with blood ; that the ' earth was darkened for the space of three days ; that nobody could ' touch any saffron or juniper all that day but it burnt his fingers ; that ' there was never a stone taken up in Jerusalem, but there was clotted ' blood under it ; and that when one of Hosein's camels that was killed ' was boiled, the flesh of it was as bitter as coloquintida—besides innu-' merable other lyes, without any manner of foundation. But this is ' true, that they that had a hand in his death dwindled away and came ' to nothing, but soon fell sick, and most of them died mad. In the ' time of the government of the family of the Bowides, they used to ' keep this day as a solemn fast, and throw dust and ashes about the ' streets of Bagdad, and cloathe themselves with black sackcloth, ' and express the highest degree of sorrow and lamentation. A great ' many of them would drink no water, in conformity to Hosein, who

---

* October 19, A.D. 680. Though the English reader must not suppose that they keep the ninth of our October, but the tenth of Moharrum, according as it falls, because theirs is the lunar year.

' was killed when he was thirsty—all which are abominable inventions
' and vile practices, contrived on purpose to cast an aspersion upon the
' government of the house of Ommiyah, because he was killed in their
' time. Now they that killed him urge against him that he came to
' depose a person that was set over them by the consent of the people,
' and to make a division amongst them, which was first begun by
' Muslim ; but some of the doctors caution against this with the utmost
' indignation, as a pernicious and dangerous way of arguing. They
' determine thus : if a certain number did interpret [the law] against
' him and kill him, they had nothing to do to kill him, but it was their
' duty to have accorded to him one of his three proposals ; and if a
' party of insolent fellows find fault with a whole people, and rise against
' its prophet (upon whom be God's peace), the matter is not to be
' [determined] according to their practice and example, but according
' to the majority of the nation, both ancient and modern. Those that
' were concerned in Hosein's death, were only a small handful of
' Cufians (God confound them), and the greatest part of them had
' written to him, and brought him into their pernicious counsels and
' designs ; neither did all the army [that went against him] approve of
' that which fell out ; nor did Yezid, the son of Moawiyah, the gover-
' nour of the faithful, at that time approve of his death (though God
' knows) nor had any aversion to him. What appears most probable
' is, that if he had had him in his power before he was killed, he would
' have spared his life, according to his father's direction, as he said he
' would himself.

' Now every Musleman ought to be concerned at this accident of
' his death (God accept him) for he was one of the lords of the Musle-
' mans, and one of the learned men of the society, and the daughter's
' son of the Apostle of God, who was the most excellent of his daughters,
' and he was devout, couragious and munificent ; yet notwithstanding
' all this, what these people do in making an outward shew of sorrow,
' which perhaps is the case of most of them, is not at all becoming.
' His father was a better man than him, yet they did not keep the day
' upon which he was murdered, as they do that of Hosein ; and Ali
' was killed as he went out to morning prayer, on the seventeenth of
  the month Ramadan in the fortieth year : and Othman the son of
' Assan was a better man than Ali, according to those that follow the
' tradition and the Church ;* and he was killed after he had been be-
' sieged in his own house, in the hot days of the month Du'lbagiah, in
' the thirty-sixth year ; and he was cut from one jugular vein to the other ;
' and yet the people never kept his day. And so in like manner Omar,
' the son of Alchitab, was a better man than Othman ; he was killed as

---

* What the Jews call *Edah*, the Greeks ἐκκλησία, and we in English, Church, the Arabians
call *jemáah*, and mean the very same thing by it, *viz.*, the congregation of the faithful
united under their lawful Imam, or head : and they denominate, as we do, those that separate
from them, according to their particular tenets or opinions.

'he was saying the prayers in the Imam's desk, and was. reading the
'Alcoran ; and his day was never kept. And Abubeker was a better
'man than he, but the day of his death was never observed. And the
'Apostle of God, upon whom be peace, who is absolute lord of all the
'sons of men, both in this world and that which is to come ; God took
'him to himself, even as the prophets before him died ; yet the Musle-
'mans never made such a stir about the observation of the day of his
'death as a solemn day, as these fools do about the day in which Hosein
'was killed.' Thus far my author in his own words.

This same year Yezid made Salem, the son of Ziyad, lieutenant of
Sejestan and Chorasan, when he came ambassador to him ; he was
then 24 years of age. As soon as he came to his charge he gathered
together a select number of forces, and the best horses that could be
found, in order to make an invasion upon the Turks. He carried his
wife along with him (the first Arabian woman that ever passed over
that river), who was brought to bed of a son in that part of the country
which is called the Sogd of Samarcand, being the neighbouring plains
and villages that lie round about that city, from whence he was
afterwards surnamed Sogdi, that is, the Sogdian. When she lay in,
she sent to the duke of Sogd's lady, to borrow her jewels ; she sent her
golden crown, that was full of them, which she had not the good manners to restore again, but carried it along with her upon the return of
the Arabians. Salem sent Mohalleb to Chowarezm, the chief city of
the Turks, who were willing to purchase peace at any rate ; he assessed
them and their cattle at so much a head, that the sum arose to fifty
millions : Salem having taken out of it what he thought fit, sent the rest
to Yezid. He then marched forwards towards Samarcand, the inhabitants whereof made their peace with a vast sum of money. This same
year, in the beginning of the month Du'lhagiah, Yezid made Waled, the
son of Otbah, governor of Medinah, who headed the people on pilgrimage to Meccah both this and the following year. Basorah and Cufah
were still in the hands of Obeidollah.

Hosein being removed, Abdollah, the son of Zobeir, who had never
submitted to Yezid's government, began now to declare publickly against
him, and deposed him at Medinah. The inhabitants of Meccah and
Medinah, perceiving that Yezid did all that lay in his power to suppress
the house of Ali, rebelled against him, and proclaimed Abdollah for
their caliph. As soon as he had taken their suffrages, to strengthen
his interest by popularity, he made long speeches to the people,
wherein he aggravated all the circumstances of Hosein's death to the
last degree, and represented the Irakians in general, and the Cufians
in particular, as the most perfidious villains upon the face of the earth :
how they had invited him first, and basely betrayed him afterwards :
what a scandalous proposal they had offered a person of his dignity,
either of surrendering himself into the hands of the son of Ziyad, or

25

else fighting them at so great a disadvantage : how heroically he had behaved himself, in preferring an honourable death to an ignominious life. He magnified his merits, and reminded them of his exemplary sanctity, his frequent watchings, fastings and prayers ; in a word, whatsoever might contribute towards the endearing his memory, and stir up in the people a desire of revenge, and an utter abhorrence and detestation of that government which was the cause of his death. The people, who were always well affected to Hosein, heard these discourses with delight, and Abdollah's party grew very strong. When Yezid heard of his progress he swore he would have him in chains, and accordingly sent a silver collar for him to Merwan, then governour of Medinah, with orders to put it about his neck and send him with it to Damascus, in case he persisted in his attempts ; but Abdollah ridiculed both them and their collar.

There was at this time one Abdollah, the son of Amrou, in Egypt, a person of great repute for his profound understanding : he used to study the prophet Daniel. Amrou, the son of Said, governour of Meccah, sent to him to know what he thought of this man, meaning Abdollah, the son of Zobeir : he answered, that he thought of him no otherwise than as a man that would carry his point, and live and die a king. This answer from a man of his character gave great encouragement to Abdollah and his party, for it had a great influence upon the generality of the people. Amrou, the son of Said, the governour of Meccah, was in his heart a mortal enemy to Abdollah and his pretensions, yet still he thought it the best way to carry it fair with him. Some of Yezid's courtiers represented to him, that if Amrou had been heartily in his interest, it was in his power to have seized Abdollah and sent him to him ; upon which suggestion Yezid removed him, and put Waled, the son of Otbah, into his place.

As soon as Waled had taken possession of his new government of Meccah, he began to exert his authority by imprisoning 300 of the servants and dependants of his predecessor Amrou. Amrou sent a private message to them, to bid them break the prison at such an hour, promising them that there should be a sufficient number of camels ready for them, kneeling in the street, which they should immediately mount, and repair to him, who was going to wait upon Yezid. This succeeded ; and when Amrou came before Yezid he first received him courteously, and bade him sit down by him, and then began to rebuke him for his remissness in the execution of his commands, and not taking sufficient care to suppress Abdollah. To which he answered, ' Governour of the faithful, he that is present sees more than he that ' is absent. The greatest part of the people of Hejaz and Meccah ' were favourably inclined to his party, and encouraged one another ' as well in publick as in private ; besides, I had no forces sufficient ' to oppose them, if I had attempted it. However, he was always

'upon his guard, and in fear of me, and I carried it fair with him,
'in order to take a proper opportunity of getting him into my power.
'Notwithstanding his interest and caution I streightened him, and
'hindered him from doing a great many things. I placed men round
'about the streets and passages of Meccah, that suffered no man to
'pass till he had written down his own name and his father's, and
'from which of God's countries he came, and what was his business.
'And if he was any of his friends, or whom I suspected to favour his
'designs, I sent him packing; if otherwise, I permitted him quietly to
'go about his concerns; and now you have sent Waled, the son of
'Otbah, who in all probability will give you such an account of his
'administration as will justify my conduct, and convince you of the
'sincerity of my advice.' Yezid was very well satisfied, and told him
'that he wasan honester man than they, that had incensed him against
'him, and that he should depend upon him for the future?' In the
meantime the new governour Waled was imploying all his skill to
ensnare Abdollah, who was always upon his guard, and was still too
cunning for him. There was at the same time upon the death of
Hosein, one Naidah, a Yemamian, that appeared with a body of men,
not against Abdollah, but Yezid; as for Abdollah, he and Naidah were
so familiar, that it was generally believed that Naidah would give him
his allegiance. Quickly after Abdollah sent a letter to Yezid, complaining that he had sent a fool of a governour thither, that was not capable
of such a trust: that if he had sent a man of tractable disposition,
their differences might be compromised, as well for the good of the
publick as their own in particular. Yezid, desirous of peace upon
any terms, indiscreetly hearkens to the advice of his mortal enemy,
removes Waled, and sends Othman, the son of Mahomet and grandson
of Abusophyan. This Othman was by no means qualified for a trust
of that importance, being raw, ignorant, and altogether unexperienced,
not capable of looking into any part of his business. He sent ambassadors from Medinah to Yezid, who received them kindly, and gave
them presents; but they took such offence at his conversation, that
when they returned, they did all they could to inflame the people
against him. They told the Medinians that they were come from a
man that had no religion at all; that he was frequently drunk with
wine, and minded nothing but his tabors, his singing wenches, and his
dogs; that he used to spend whole evenings in talking with vile
fellows and singing girls, and they declared that for their part they
did depose him; in which action they were followed by a great
many; and it is said they gave their allegiance to one Abdollah,
the son of Hantelah. Almundir, who was one of the ambassadors,
did not return with them to Medinah, but went to Obeidollah, to Bassorah, who entertained him in his house with a great deal of friendship, for they were old acquaintance. As soon as Yezid was informed

25—2

how the rest of the ambassadors had used him at Medinah, he wrote to Obeidollah to bind Almundir, and keep him close till further orders. Obeidollah looked upon this to be a breach of the rules of hospitality, and instead of obeying the order, shewed it to Almundir, advising him, when the people were come together, to pretend very urgent business, and in the presence of them all to ask leave to be gone. This granted, away goes Almundir, full of resentment, to Medinah, and there confirms all that the other ambassadors had said before to the reproach of Yezid ; adding, that though he confessed that Yezid had presented him with 100 pieces, yet that could not influence him so far as to hinder him from speaking what he was a witness of, relating to his drunkenness, idle conversation, and neglecting the prayers oftener than any of his men. Yezid was informed of all, and vowed to be revenged on him for his ingratitude.

Then Yezid sent Nooman, the son of Bashir, to Medinah, to quiet the people, and persuade them to return to their duty and allegiance : when he came there, he represented to them the folly of their proceedings, and the danger they exposed themselves to by such seditious practices ; assuring them that they were not a match for the forces of Syria. One of them asked him what motive induced him to come upon such an errand, and make division among them after they were agreed? Nooman told him, ' Because he was loath there should be any blood shed between the two parties, and see these poor creatures (meaning the Ansars or inhabitants of Medinah) killed in their streets, and mosques, and in the doors of their own houses.' They would not be ruled by him, and he left them ; but what he gave them fair warning of, they found afterwards too true.

The Medinians in their obstinacy having renounced all allegiance to Yezid, set over the Koreish, Abdollah, the son of Mothi, and over the Ansars, Abdollah, the son of Hantelah, a noble person of excellent endowments, very religious, and very much reverenced by all: he had eight sons went along with him on the embassy. Yezid presented him with 100,000 pieces, and every one of his sons with 10,000, besides their vests. In the beginning of the year 63 they broke out into open rebellion, after this manner: When they were gathered together in the mosque round about the pulpit, one of them said, ' I lay aside Yezid as I lay aside this turbant, throwing his turbant against the ground.' Another said, ' I put away Yezid as I put away this shoe ;' which examples were followed till there was a great heap of shoes and turbants. The next step they took was to turn out Yezid's lieutenant Othman, and banish all the family of Ommiyah, together with all their friends and dependants, from Medinah. They being about 1,000, took refuge in Merwan, the son of Hakem's house, where the Medinians besieged them so closely that they sent word to Yezid, ' That unless they received speedy relief they must inevitably perish.' Yezid wondered, when he heard they were so many, that they should suffer themselves to be so confined without making the least resistance, and asked Amrou, the son of Said, whom he thought the fittest person to be sent upon this expedition, offering it at the same time to him. Amrou excused himself, and told him, ' That he had done him all the service he could there before, and he was pleased to remove him from his government ; now since the blood of the Coreish was to be poured upon the dust, he begged that somebody not so nearly related to them as he was, might be employed in that business.' Upon this he sends for Meslem, the son of Okbah, who, though very ancient and infirm, was willing to undertake the command of the forces, consisting of 12,000 horse and 5000 foot. Meslem told Yezid that those 1000 men that suffered themselves to be so distressed without fighting, did not deserve any assistance ; that they had neither shewn personal courage nor loyalty to their sultan ; that they ought to be let alone till they had exerted themselves, and deserved encouragement. But Yezid told him that his life would do him no good if they were not safe. Yezid rode about with his sword by his side, and an Arabian bow over his shoulders, viewing the troops, and giving directions to his general Meslem ; particularly, that he should take care of Ali, the son of Hosein, concerning whom he had been informed that he was not at all in the measures of the rebels, nor any of his family, wherefore he commanded him to shew him respect, and place him next him. That as for the town, he should summons it three days successively, and if they did not surrender themselves upon the summons, after he had taken it he should leave it for three days entirely to the mercy of the soldiers.

The Medinians refused to surrender, and the general made prepa· rations for a storm. He was advised to make his assault on the east side, that the besieged might have the sun in their faces ; this proved of service to him. The Medinians made a vigorous defence; they had made a large ditch round about the city, and held out a considerable time, till in the end most of the Ansars and considerable men being killed ; they finding themselves pressed, would have surrendered, but Meslem, from whose hands they refused peace at the beginning of the siege, would not receive them but at discretion.

Then entering the city with sword in hand, he first sent for Ali and treated him with respect, and to quiet all his apprehensions of fear, and dismiss him honourably, he called for his own camel, and sent him home upon it ; then they put all to the sword that they met, plundered every thing that was valuable, and got a thousand of the women with child. Without any reverence to its being the burying-place of the prophet they sacked it for three days, and those that escaped the edge of the sword Meslem took under the protection of the government, but only on this condition, ' That they should own themselves slaves and vassals to Yezid ; upon which account he purchased the name of Musriph, which signifies in Arabick, ' extravagant, exorbitant,' because he had exceeded in the execution of his orders.   This battle was fought when there were three nights left of the month Dulhagiah.

Meslem having thus severely chastised the insolence of the Medinians, marched directly with his army towards Meccah, but died by the way, in the month Moharram of the year 64.   Upon his death, Hosein took upon him the command of the army, and besieged Abdollah in Meccah the space of 40 days, during which time he battered it so roughly that he beat down a great part of the temple, and burnt the rest ; and this city had run the same fortune with Medinah, if the news of Yezid's death had not recalled Hosein into Syria.

Abdollah heard of Yezid's decease before the Syrian army had received any intelligence of it, and called out to them from the walls, and asked them what they fought for, for their master was dead.   But they would not believe him, but continued their siege with great vigour, till they received further information.   Hosein having heard that news, told Abdollah that he was of opinion that it would be the best way to forbear shedding any more blood, and proffered him his allegiance, if he would accept of the government, assuring him that all his army, wherein were the leading men of all Syria, would be in his interest, and that there was no fear of any opposition ; but he durst not trust him.   As they were talking together, just where the pidgeons that flew from the temple of Meccah were pecking something upon the ground, Hosein turned his horse aside, which Abdollah taking notice of, asked him the reason ; he said he was afraid his horse should kill the temple pidgeons.   Abdollah asked him how he could scruple that, and at the same time kill the Muslemans ?   Hosein told him that he would not fight against him any more, and only desired that they might have leave to go round the temple of Meccah before their departure, which was granted.   Some say that that temple was not set on fire by the engines, but that Abdollah, hearing in the night a shouting from the mountains of Meccah, put fire upon the end of a spear, to see if he could make any discovery ; which, being wafted with the wind, the sparks laid hold first on the hangings, and then took the wood-work.   Abdollah afterwards, when it was too late, repented his refusal of Hosein's proffer ; and those of the house of Ommiyah, that were in Medinah, accompanied Hosein into Syria.

Yezid died in Hawwarin, in the territories of Hems, when four nights were passed of the first Rebiyah, in the 64th year of the Hegirah, in the 39th year of his age, after he had reigned 3 years and 6 months.   He was a man of a ruddy complexion, with curled hair, black eyes, pitted with the small-pox : he had a handsome beard, and was a thin tall man : he left behind him several children of both sexes.   His son Caled is reported to have been skilled in the art of alchemy, and his son Abdollah to have been the most exact archer of all the Arabians in his time. His mother's name was Meisun, of the family of the Kelabi ; she was an excellent poetess, and had pleased Moawiyah's fancy to that degree with some of her verses, that he made her go back into the desert amongst her own relations, and take her son Yezid along with her, that he might be brought up a poet too. This part of his education succeeded, for he was reckoned to excell that way, though his chief talent consisted in making a drunken catch.

It is observed of him that he was the first Caliph that drank wine publickly, and was waited upon by eunuchs; besides they reproach him with bringing up, and being fond of dogs, which the more scrupulous Mahometans have in abomination.

But the greatest vices of this Caliph were his impiety and covetousness, which occasioned a certain author to say, that to make the empire of the Muslemans flourish, it ought to be in the hands of princes either pious, such as were the first four Caliphs, or liberal, as Moawiyah ; but when it was governed by a prince that had neither piety nor generosity, such a one as Yezid, all would be lost.

The Mahometan doctors look upon Yezid's allowing the soldiers to commit such abominable outrages in the city of the prophet, and suffering it to be so prophaned, as a very wicked action. They do not scruple to say that he did it, imagining to preserve his life and government ; but God dealt with him as a tyrant, and the being cut off in the flower of his age, was a judgment inflicted upon him for that presumption. They quote this saying of Mahomet, 'Whoever injureth Medinah shall melt away, even as salt melteth away in the water.'

All the Persian authors never mention him but with abomination, and ordinarily add this imprecation to his name, 'Laanabullah,' that is, 'The curse of God be upon him ;' which they do not do upon the account of his vices, but because of the death of Hosein, the son of Ali, whom he attempted to destroy by poison, and whom he afterwards caused to be killed with all his family on the plains of Kerbelah.

Under his Caliphate, the Muslemans conquered all Chorasan and Chowarezm, and put the estates of the prince of Samarkand under contribution. The motto of his seal was, 'God is our Lord.'

The third CALIPH *of the house of* OMMIYAH (*being the eighth from* MAHOMET*).*

MOAWIYAH II.,

THE SON OF YEZID.

An. Heg. 64, cœpit Aug. 29, A.C. 683.

As soon as Yezid was dead, his son Moawiyah was proclaimed Caliph at Damascus ; he was near 21 years of age, a religious young man, and of a very weak constitution ; he was of the sect of the Alcadarii (who are a branch of the Motazeli, and differ in their opinions from the orthodox Muslemans, in that they deny God's decree, and assert free-will ; affirming that the contrary opinion makes God the author of evil), and his favourite master was Omar Almeksous.   Him he con-sulted to know whether he ought to accept the Caliphate or not.   His master told him that if he found himself able to administer justice exactly to the Muslemans, and to acquit himself of all the duties of that dignity, that he ought to accept it ; otherwise that he ought not to charge himself with it.

This Caliph had scarce reigned the space of six weeks, but he found himself too weak to sustain the weight of the government, and took a resolution to lay it down.   To this end he called a council of the great-est men of the court, and told them ' That when he first entertained the thought of abdicating himself, he designed to follow the example of Abubeker, and nominate a successor as that first Caliph had done his; but that he had not found, as he had done, men like Omar upon whom to settle his choice.'   Then he told them, ' That he had also a design of imitating Omar, and naming six persons upon one of which the choice should fall by lot ; but that he had not found so many among them capable of it, and therefore could not determine himself to fix upon that number.'

' I am therefore resolved,' added he, ' to leave the choice entirely to your disposal ;' upon which the principal statesmen having told him, ' That they had nothing to do but to chuse that person amongst them that he should please, and that all the rest would obey him.' Moawiyah answered them in these terms : ' As I have not hitherto enjoyed the advantages of the Caliphate, it is not reasonable that I should charge my self with the most odious part that belongs to it ; therefore I hope that you will not take it amiss if I discharge my conscience towards you, and that you judge for yourselves who is most capable amongst you to fill the place.'

As soon as Moawiyah had made his abdication in so good form, they proceeded to the election of a Caliph, and the choice fell upon Merwan the son of Hakem, who was the fourth of the Caliphs of Syria ; Abdollah the son of Zobeir having been declared Caliph in Arabia, Irak, Chorasan, Ægypt, and a great part of Syria.

Moawiyah had no sooner renounced the Caliphate but he shut himself up in a chamber, from whence he never stirred till he died, some say of the plague, others by poison, not long after his abdication ; and they say that the family of Ommiyah was very much irritated at his proceeding, that they made their resentment break out upon the person of Omar Almeksous, whom they buried alive, because they supposed that he had advised Moawiyah to depose himself. This Caliph was nick-named Abuleilah, that is to say, the Father of the night, because of his natural weakness and want of health, which hindered him from appearing much abroad in the day time. The inscription of his seal was, 'the World is a Cheat.'

We must now look backwards a little towards the eastern parts of the empire. As soon as Obeidollah heard of Yezid's death, he acquainted the Basorians with it in a set speech, wherein he represented, ' the near relation that he had to them, that the place of his nativity ' was amongst them, that, as appeared by the books, he had since his ' government over them destroyed 140,000 of their enemies ; that there ' was no person left of any consideration whom they need to fear, but ' what was already in their prisons ; that they were every way the most ' considerable nation in the empire, both with regard to their courage, ' number and extent of country ; that they were very well able to sub- ' sist independent on any help, but that the rest of their provinces were not ' able to subsist without them ; that there was a faction in Syria, and ' till that was appeased, he thought it advisable for them to chuse a ' person duly qualified to be the protector of their state ; that after that ' was done, if the Muslemans agreed upon a successor that they ap- ' proved, it would be well ; if otherwise they might continue as they ' were, till they did.' The Basorians approved of his proposal, and told him that they knew no person so well qualified for such a trust as himself ; he refused it several times, affectedly as may be supposed by his speech, but accepted it at last, overcome by their importunity ; so they gave him their hands to be subject to him till all things were settled, and the Muslemans were agreed upon an Imam or Caliph. This done he sent a messenger to the Cufians, to persuade them to follow the example of the Basorians ; the Cufians received the message with indignation, and were so far from complying with it, that they flung dust upon their governor. Though the Cufians did not follow the example of the Basorians, yet the Basorians followed theirs ; for perceiving the repulse he met with at Cufah, they revoked their subjection to him ; and the faction ran so high, that finding Basorah too warm for him, he made the best of his way into Syria.

There was at that time in the treasury of Basorah sixteen millions of money, part of which he divided among his relations ; the remainder he carried along with him. He would have persuaded the Najari, which are a tribe of the Arabian Ansars, to have fought for him, but they refused it, as did also all his own relations ; for he had rendered himself so obnoxious by his cruelty, that he was dreaded and abhorred by all, beloved by none. His brother Abdollah told the Basorians, that since they had promised their subjection, he and his brother Obeidollah would not fly away from them, but stay and be killed, and leave it as a reproach upon them till the day of judgment. Obeidollah lay concealed in woman's cloaths in Mesoud's house, who advised him to scatter money liberally among the people, and oblige them to renew their oath. Abdollah his brother tryed his utmost with 200,000 pieces, and Mesoud stirred for him as much as he was able, till at last he was killed in the tumult, though upon an old grudge. Obeidollah was at last constrained to fly, and as soon as he was gone, they plundered his effects, and pursued him. He had 100 men with him, that were left him by Mesoud. In the night-time he grew weary of riding upon his camel and exchanged it for an ass. One of his friends observing him riding in that manner with his feet dangling down to the ground, began to reflect upon the uncertainty of human affairs, and say to himself : ' This man was yesterday governor of Irak, and is now forced to make his escape upon an ass.' Then riding up to him (for he had been silent a long time) he asked him if he was asleep ; he said, ' No, he was talking to himself ;' the other told him, ' He knew what it was that he talked to himself, and that was I wish I had not killed Hosein.' Obeidollah told him ' He was mistaken, for he chose rather to kill Hosein, than to be killed by him ;' then having first mentioned some part of his substance, and how he intended to dispose of it, he said, ' What he was sorry for, and what he was speaking to himself was, that he wished he had fought the Basorians at the beginning of their revolt, and struck their heads off for their perjury ; but if he had attempted it he might have lost his own, for the Caregites, who were his mortal enemies, were got to a great head, and resolved either to kill him, or to drive him from Basorah.'

We leave him therefore riding upon an ass, and talking to himself, and return to Hosein, who was come back much about this time from the siege of Meccah to Damascus. He gave an account in what posture he had left matters on that side of the country, and how he had proffered his allegiance to Abdollah, who had refused to accept it, at least to come into Syria ; he told Merwan, and the rest of the family of Ommiyah, that they would do well to look about them in time, their affairs being at this time in a confused perplexed condition ; that they ought to settle the government, before faction, which is both deaf and blind, should overwhelm them ; Merwan was for submitting to Abdollah, but Obeidollah told him that it was a shame for a person of his distinction, who was the head of the noble family of the Coreish, to think of any thing so mean. The people of Damascus had constituted Dehac, the son of Kais, their protector, till the Muslemans should be agreed upon an Imam. Dehac favoured Abdollah, and Hasan the son of Malec was in that part of Palestine that lay near Jordan, and was of the party of the house of Ommiyah. The Basorians were altogether in tumult and confusion, and could not agree about a governor ; during the interregnum, they set up first one, and then another, till at last they wrote to Abdollah, to take the government upon him.

The Ninth CALIPH, *from* MAHOMET ; *(he was not of the house of* OMMIYAH*).*

ABDOLLAH,

THE SON OF ZOBEIR.

An. Heg. 64. cœpit Aug. 29, A.C. 683.

THERE being two Caliphs at the same time will of necessity occasion the repetition of a few circumstances, which will give no offence to an ingenious reader. Though Abdollah was proclaimed before in the days of Yezid, yet this is the place that our Arabian authors assign him in their histories, because he seemed now to be fully settled and established, all the territories of the Muslemans being entirely under his command, Syria only excepted ; but whenever we speak of the entire subjection of the Mahometan countries, we must not be understood of the hereticks and schismaticks, the Caregites and Motazeli, for they, as we have observed already, would never be subject to any ; but upon the least prospect of a favourable opportunity, used their utmost efforts to break from off their necks the yoke of all government whatsoever.

As soon as Yezid was dead, the people of Meccah stood up for Abdollah, the son of Zobeir : Merwan the son of Hakem (who was of the house of Ommiyah) was then at Medinah, and was preparing himself to go to Abdollah, and acknowledge him ; for all took it for granted that interest was so powerful, that it would be to no purpose to oppose him ; when on a sudden there was a report spread, that Abdollah had sent word to his deputy in Medinah, to leave never a man alive there of the house of Ommiyah : instead of which, if he had gone along with Hosein, as he would have persuaded him, or had he caressed Merwan and the house of Ommiyah : he had been immoveably fixed in the government. 'But there is no reversing what God hath decreed.' When they proclaimed him at Meccah, Obeidollah was at Basorah, from whence he fled into Syria, as we have seen before : the Basorians, Irakians, Hejazians, Yemanians and Ægyptians, all came into Abdollah, besides he had a strong private party even in Syria itself, and in Kinnisrin and Hems : in short they were very near coming in universally, but he wanted some qualifications necessary for such a juncture : he was brave and courageous enough, and exemplarily religious, but he wanted both capacity and generosity.

The fourth CALIPH *of the house of* OMMIYAH ; *(Being the tenth from* MAHOMET*).*

MERWAN,

THE SON OF HAKEM.

An. Heg. 94. cœpit Aug. 29, A.C. 683.

UPON this rumour of Abdollah's thus severely threatning the house of Ommiyah, Merwan made haste into Syria, where his friends came about him, and resolved to stand upon their own defence, proclaimed him Caliph ; so that Syria was divided into two factions ; Hassan and the Yemanians in Syria stood for Merwan, and Dehac the son of Kais for Abdollah : this Dehac was a man of great note ; he had been at the first siege of Damascus, and in the 54th year Moawiyah made him his deputy over Cufah ; and because the general's father's name was Kais, the party that followed him were called the Kaisians : there were a great many parleys between them, which it would be too tedious to relate ; at last they brought it to a decisive battle in the plains or meadows of Damascus ; the issue was, that the Kaisians were most shamefully beaten, and Dehac himself killed, and there was a great slaughter amongst the horse. When the Kaisians were routed, Merwan sounded a retreat, and would not suffer his men to pursue. There were killed with Dehac no less than 80 of the nobles of Syria. When Dehac's head was brought to Merwan, he expressed some concern and said, ' That I who am an old man, whose bones are wasted, and am next to nothing, should bring armies together to break one another to pieces !'

He then went into Damascus, and took up his lodging at the house where Moawiyah used to reside ; and there he married Yezid's widow, because it was agreed that Merwan should not transfer the government to his own posterity, but leave it to Yezid's son Caled, who was then a minor, and of whom the people had some expectation : wherefore his friends thought it most secure for him to marry Caled's mother, and take upon him the guardianship of the child, than run the risque of standing upon the sole foundation of his own interest.

When the news of the defeat of the Kaisians and the death of

Dehac came to Emessa, which was under the command of Nooman the son of Bashir, he fled away with his wife and family; and the Emessians pursued him, cut off his head, and brought it together with his wife and family to Emessa.

Merwan after this marched towards Ægypt, and sent before him Amrou the son of Saed, who going into Ægypt turned out Abdollah's lieutenant, and brought the Ægyptians to own Merwan for their sovereign: as he was upon his return towards Damascus, news was brought him that Abdollah had sent his brother Mus'ab, against him with an army; wherefore he turned back and routed Mus'ab before he entered into Damascus.

This year the people of Chorasan chose Salem the son of Ziyad, who was their governour before, for their protector, till the Muslemans should be agreed in the choice of an Imam; he continued in that post about two months: the people of the country never had any governour that they loved so well; they respected him to that degree, that in those few years that he governed them, there were more than 20,000 children named Salem purely out of love to his name.

This year the sect of Ali began to stir in Cufah, in order to rendez-vous in Nochailah in the next year following, that they might march into Syria to revenge the death of Hosein, and sent circular letters to their friends round about the country concerning it: the occasion was this; when the Cufians after Hosein was killed came to reflect coolly upon that matter, their consciences accused them of not having dealt with him so generously as they were obliged both in honour and duty, and they thought there could be no atonement made for such a crime but the taking up arms to revenge his death: They therefore applied themselves to five leading men of the sect, Solyman the son of Sorad who was one of the companions; and Mosabbib the son of Nahbah, one of the choicest friends of Ali: Abdollah the son of Said; Abdollah the son of Wali; and Rephaah the son of Shadad. These all met together in Solyman's house, besides a great many others of the chief men of the sect, to whom Mosabbib made a speech wherein he aggra-vated the heinousness of their neglect 'in having deserted Hosein ' after so solemn an invitation, and having received so many letters ' and messages from him; that they had neither assisted him with ' their hands, nor spoke for him with their tongues, nor supported him ' with their money, nor looked out for any assistance for him. What ' excuse must they have when they should come to appear before God, ' or how should they be able to look his prophet in the face, when ' by their means his son was killed, and his beloved and his offspring ' and his posterity cut off! That there was no way to atone for this ' but by revenging his death upon his murderers, which was no hard ' matter, provided they chose a proper general, one that the people ' would be willing to fight under.' This was seconded by Rephaah.

who added, 'that as to a general, his opinion was, that they should choose the chief of the sect, a person reverenced by all for his years, dignity, piety and experience, Solyman the son of Sorad.' Solyman having first made a speech suitable to the occasion, accepted the command ; and when some other persons arose and made speeches to urge on the matter (for there were above 100 of the chief men amongst them) he told them, that there was enough said already, and the next step they ought to take should be to put what each of them designed to contribute into the hands of Abdollah the son of Wali, to be distributed among the poorest of the sect. The contents of Solyman's circular letter were as followeth :—

'In the name of the most merciful God.

'From Solyman, the son of Sorad, to Saed the son of Hodaiphah,
' and whosoever is with him of the Muslemans ; peace be to you.   The
' present world is a mansion upon which everything that is good turneth
' its back, and to which everything that is bad draweth near (or turneth
' its face), and treateth persons of uprightness ill. The chosen servants
' of God have resolved to leave it, and to sell the little of the present
' world that remaineth not, for the great reward that is with God and
' shall never fail.   The friends of God, your brethren of the sect of the
' family of your prophet, have considered with themselves the trial
' they have undergone in the business of the son of the daughter of
' your prophet, who was called and answered, and called and was not
' answered, and would have returned but was detained, and asked for
' security but was hindered ; and he let the people alone, but they
' would not let him alone, but dealt injuriously by him and killed him,
' and then spoiled him and stripped him wickedly, despightfully and
' foolishly.   Nor did they act as in the sight of God, neither had they
' recourse to God, "And they that have done evil shall know what
' shall be the end of their actions."   Now, what your brethren have
' seriously considered concerning the events of what they were engaged
' in before is this.   They see they have sinned in deceiving the inno-
' cent, the good, and in the delivering him up, and the omitting the
' healing and helping him.   A great sin ! from which there is no way
' left for them to escape, nor any repentance without killing those that
' killed him, or being killed themselves and resigning their spirits upon
' this account.   Now, therefore, your brethren are bestirring themselves
' in earnest, and your enemy ; therefore do you get together all the
' assistance you are able, and we have fixed a certain time for our
' brethren to meet us at a place appointed.   The time is the new moon
' of the month of the latter Rebiyah, in the 65th year, and the place
' where they shall meet us is Nochailah ; O ye who never cease to be
' of our sect and brethren !   And we determined to invite you to this
' business which God would have your brethren undertake, as they

' say, and they show to us that they repent, and that you are persons
' duly qualified for the search of excellency, and the laying hold of the
' reward and repentance towards your Lord from your sin, though it be
' the cutting off your necks, and the killing your children, and the con-
' sumption of your wealth, and the destruction of your tribes and
' families. "He (God) hath not hurt the couragious religious men
' that were killed, but they are now alive with their Lord, sustained as
' martyrs, they met their Lord enduring (affliction) patiently; they are
' made account of, and God hath given them the reward of good men."
' If it please God, persevere patiently in tribulation and affliction, and
' the day of battle (God have mercy upon you); for it is not fit that
' any of your brethren should persevere in any affliction in seeking his
' repentance, but you are worthy and fit to seek the like reward by the
' same means; neither is it fit that any one should seek the favour of
' God by any means, though it were death itself, but you should seek it
' by the same means. "For the best voyage provision is the fear of
' God in this world, and everything besides shall perish and vanish
' away." Wherefore let your souls be assured of this, and your desire
' be fixed upon the mansion of your safety, and the engaging in the
' holy war against the enemy of God and your enemy, and the enemy
' of the family of the daughter of your prophet, till you come before
' God with repentance and desire. God preserve both us and you to
' the happy life, and remove both us and you from hell, and grant it
' may be our reward to dye by the hands of that part of mankind that
' is the most odious of all to him, and are his most vehement enemies.
' He is the most powerful over what he pleases, and disposeth of his
' friends according to his will. Farewell to you.'

Saed read the letter to all the people, who readily gave their assent,
and dispatched a very encouraging answer to Solyman and his friends.
The truth of the matter is, that the sect of Ali had been contriving this
affair from the time of Hosein's death till the death of Yezid the son
of Moawiyah, and had sent privately to one another, and laid up magazines, and strengthened their party.

Six months after Yezid's death, in the midst of the month Ramadan,
Almochtar came to Cufah, and along with him came Ibrahim, the son
of Mahomet the son of Telha, to take care of the tribute of Cufah on
the side of Abdollah the son of Zobeir: the sect of (Ali) readily joined
themselves to this captain Almochtar, who made use of the authority
of Mohammed, the son of Haniphiyah, who was Ali's son, and the
hopes of the party, he told them he was come to them as a counsellor
and a trusty assistant from the son of Alhanifiyah, which circumstance,
added to their confidence in his known abilities, endeared him to them
exceedingly. He made it his business to disparage Solyman, the son
of Sorad, as a person by no means qualified for the trust he had undertaken, but one that would most certainly destroy both them and

himself, having no manner of experience in warlike affairs. Abdollah, the son of Yezid, was then governor of Cufah, and having received information that the sect had a design to seize the city, he called a congregation ' and told them that these people pretended indeed to seek ' revenge for Hosein's death, but he could not easily be induced to ' believe that that was the bottom of their intention ; that for his own ' part they had no reason to fight against him who was no manner of ' way concerned in the matter, but had been a sufferer upon that ac- ' count, that if they would in good earnest follow those up close who ' were guilty of the death of Hosein, he should be willing to assist ' them.' Then turning to the people he said, ' In short it was the son ' of Ziyad that killed Hosein, and that killed the most valuable men ' amongst you ; and the best thing you can do is to make preparation ' of war against him, who is the greatest enemy you have in the whole ' creation, rather than exercise your force upon one another, and shed ' each others blood.' Ibrahim the collector rose up and bad the people not be deceived with his smooth speeches, and declared, that if any of them rose up in arms they should be put to death both father and son without distinction. As he was proceeding, Mosabbib cut him off short, and asked him, ' Whether he pretended to threaten or terrifie them ? That it was more than lay in his power ; we have,' says he, ' already killed your father and grandfather, and we hope, before you go out of this country, you shall be the third.' Ibrahim threatened him with death, when Abdollah the son of Wali stood up, and asked Ibrahim ' What business he had to intermeddle between them and their governor, telling him that he had no manner of authority over them, but he might get him about his business, and look after his tax.' The sect were wonderfully pleased with Abdollah the son of Yezid's speech, and the people very much offended at Ibrahim's behaviour ; there were high words on both sides till Abdollah the governor came down ; he, being informed that Ibrahim had threatened to write to Abdollah the son of Zobeir, and acquaint him with the contents of his smooth speech to the Cufians, made haste to pay him a visit, and swore that he meant nothing by it but only to appease the people, and keep the peace to prevent their doing any further mischief, with which excuse Ibrahim was very well satisfied. And now Solyman and his party pulled off the mask, and appeared barefaced openly in arms.

At this time the separatists, who had before joined Abdollah the son of Zobeir, and assisted him whilst he was besieged in Meccah, deserted him. The case was thus : Obeidollah, when governor at Basorah, had been always th..r implacable enemy, and exerted his utmost to extirpate the whole generation of them root and branch from off the face of the earth ; distressed by his unmerciful persecution they took the opportunity, when Abdollah, the son of Zobeir, first made his appearance at Meccah, of applying themselves to him ; he, as matters ther stood with him, was no less glad of their assistance than they were of his protection, and embraced them without any scrutiny about principles, or asking any questions for conscience sake. They afterwards began to say to one another, that they had committed an error in engaging themselves in a man's interest whose principles were dubious ; and resolved, before they advanced one step further, to bring him to the test. They had not forgotten how both he and his father Zobeir had persecuted them upon account of Othman's death, and they were resolved to make use of it as a proof of his being in their interest, or the contrary. They came to him accordingly in a body, and told him, ' That hitherto they had assisted him without any previous examination of his principles ; now, for satisfaction, they desired to know what he thought of Othman ?' He understood them very well, but seeing but few of his friends about him, he told them that they were come at an unseasonable time, when he had rather be at rest ; if they would defer it a little, and return in the evening, they should have a satisfactory answer. In the meantime he gathers together a sufficient number of guards, and places them in double ranks round about his house. At last they came, and perceiving how matters stood, and what preparation Abdollah had made for their reception, did not think fit to come to blows ; but one of them, a man of a voluble tongue, eminent for his eloquence, made a speech, wherein he briefly recapitulated the most considerable dispensations of providence towards them, and the several successions of their Caliphs since Mahomet, concluding with hard reflections upon Othman's administration, his partiality in favour of his relations, and in a word justified his being murdered. Abdollah told him, ' That as to what he had said concerning the prophet (which was very great), he was not only what he had said, but above it ; and what he had said of Abubeker and Omar was just enough ; but as for Othman, he had more reason to know him than any man alive ; that he was sure he was murdered wrongfully, and that he never wrote that letter whereof he had been accused ; and that for his own part, he should be a friend of Othman's both in this world and that to come, and a friend of his friends, and an enemy of his enemies.' To this they answered, ' God is clear of thee, thou enemy of God !' Which he echoed back again, ' God is clear of you, ye enemies of God ?' Upon this they parted ; but as for Abdollah, he could the more easily part with them. Some of them went to Yemamah, the rest to Basorah ; those that went to Basorah began to say among themselves, ' Would ' to God some of our people would go out in the way of God, for there ' hath been negligence on our side since our companions went out, and ' our teachers stood up in the earth and were the lights of mankind, ' and exhorted them to religion, and sober and couragious men went ' out and met the Lord, and became martyrs maintained with God ' alive.' Thus they encouraged one another mutually till they had

26

gathered together a body of about 300, just about the time that the Basorians made an insurrection against Obeidollah, and taking the advantage of the hurry of the people they broke open all the jails ; but when Obeidollah was gone into Syria, and all the disturbance was over, they were soon routed and driven away from Basorah.

So many things being transacted in several parts of the empire much about the same time, it was necessary to dispatch these first, to clear the way for Moktar, that great and terrible scourge of the enemies of Ali's family, and because he makes so considerable a figure in this part of our history, it will be necessary to be a little more particular in the account of his affairs.   The sect of Ali had entertained no very favourable opinion of him ever since the time of Hasan, in whose service he was reckoned to be too remiss ; but he recovered his esteem with them when Hosein sent Muslim to Cufah to take the suffrages of the Cufians, for he not only entertained him in his house, but made use of all his interest privately to serve him ; still making his appearance in publick against Obeidollah's men, to prevent suspicion.   Going one morning to wait upon Obeidollah, Obeidollah asked him whether he was come with his men to serve Muslim?   Moktar said that he was not, but had been under the banner of Amrou, the son of Horith, and staid with him all night, which Amrou confirmed ; but this not satisfying Obeidollah, who had good intelligence of his secret practices, he struck him over the face with his stick, and dashed one of his eyes all to pieces, and sent him immediately to prison, where he was detained till after Hosein's death ; at which time, finding means to make proper application to Yezid, the Caliph, he was set at liberty by his express command.   Obeidollah knew that it was his interest not to let him go, but was forced to obey the Caliph, and told Almochtar that he allowed him three days, after which if he took him he was under no obligation.

Moktar made the best of his way to that part of Arabia called Hejaz (which is generally taken by our geographers to be Arabia Petræa) and meeting with a friend, who asked him what his eye ailed, he answered, 'The son of a whore made it so ; but God kill me if I do not cut him all to pieces.'   His friend wondered what he meant, there being no probability of its ever being in his power, and Mochtar enquired of him concerning Abdollah, the son of Zobeir.   He answered him, 'That he had made Meccah the place of his refuge ;' to which Mochtar answered, 'I do not believe that he can make any thing of it, but when you see it come to pass, when you see Mochtar up at the head of his men to revenge the death of Hosein, then, by the Lord, I will kill, upon the account of his murder, as many as were killed upon the account of the blood of John, the son of Zacharias, upon whom be peace.'

For the clearing of which passage it must be understood that the

Mahometans entertain a profound veneration for the memory of St. John the Baptist, upon the account of the honourable mention made of him in the third chapter of the *Alcoran*, in these words, 'Then prayed· Zachariah to his Lord, and said, my lord, give me from thee a good progeny, for thou art the bearer of prayers. And the angels called to him as he stood praying in the oratory, God sends thee the good news of John, who shall confirm the truth of the word from God, and shall be a great person, chast, a prophet, and one of the just, or rather, and one of the just prophets.'

Which Hosein Waês paraphrases in these words : 'John the Bap-
' tist, your son, shall publish and give authority to the faith in the
' Messias Jesus, the son of Mary, who is the word of God, or the word
' proceeding from God ; for he shall be the first who shall believe in
' him. He shall become. chief and high priest by his knowledge, by
' the austerity of his life, and by the sweetness of his behaviour, which
' are three qualities requisite to make a person an Imam or high priest
' of the law of God. He shall abstain from having any thing to do
' with women, and from all the pleasures of sense, and, in short, he
' shall be a prophet descended from good men such as his father
' Zachariah, and his grandfather Saleh had been before him, teaching
' men the ways of justice and salvation.'

They have a tradition of St. John the Baptist having been beheaded by the command of a king of Judæa, the blood which flowed from his body could not be stanched till it was avenged by a very great deso- lation which God sent upon the people of the Jews ; and this is what was meant by Almochtar.

When they parted, Almochtar went to Meccah just at that time when Abdollah began to set up himself for the Caliphate, and told him that all things about Cufah were in the utmost confusion; then, whispering him, he said that he was come to proffer him his allegiance, if he would make him easy. I do not find what answer he received, nor whether or no he received any at all. From that time he was seen no more at Meccah till about a twelve-month after, when, as Abbas, the son of Sahel, and Abdollah happened to be talking concerning him he appeared on one side of the temple. Abbas followed him, to find out which way he stood inclined, and asked him if he had been all that while in Thayef (for he had seen him there himself) he told him in Thayef and in other places, but seemed to make a secret of his business. Abbas told him that he was very private, according to the custom of the Cufians ; that all the noble families of the Arabians had sent some great man or other to offer their allegiance to Abdollah, and that it would be very strange if he should be singular and refuse it. Almochtar answered, 'That he came about it the year before, but receiving no satisfactory answer, it looked as if Abdollah had no occa- sion for his service ; and since he found himself slighted, he thought

Abdollah had more occasion for him than he had for Abdollah.' At last Abbas prevailed upon him so far that he said he would do it after he had said the last evening prayer. They appointed to meet at the stone, and Abbas in the mean time rejoiced the heart of Abdollah with the news. When they were admitted into Abdollah's house, Almochtar told him that he expected if he gave him his allegiance to have access to him upon all occasions before any other person, and that he should make use of him in his most weighty affairs. Abdollah would have had him been content with being governed, 'according to the book of God and the tradition.' Almochtar answered, 'That that was no more privilege than what the farthest man alive enjoyed, and that he would never come in upon any other terms than what he had proposed.' Abdollah's affairs being as yet in an unsettled condition, it was thought most advisable to indulge him in his humour; so he continued with Abdollah during the siege of Meccah, and fought bravely in the defence of it; till, as we have related before, upon the news of Yezid's death, the siege was raised, and the army returned into Syria.

Almochtar continued with Abdollah five months, and some days after the death of Yezid, but perceiving that Abdollah was still shy of him, and did not employ him in any considerable post, nor make any great use of him in his counsels, he always was very diligent in enquiring after the condition of the Cufians, and Ali's friends on that side of the country; at last one informed him that there was only a party supported by some provincialists that were in the interest of Abdollah; and as for the friends of Ali's family, they wanted nothing but a man of their own opinion to head them in order to consume the whole earth. Almochtar swore that he was their man, and that by their assistance he would beat down 'all haughty tyrants.' The other told him, that for his further satisfaction, that he might not be deceived, they had gone so far already as to set one over them, but a person of small experience. Almochtar said he did not intend to call them to sedition, but to the right way, and to the church, and forthwith set forth for Cufah. All the way he went, he made it his business to pay his respects to the congregations of the several mosques, and say his prayers among them, and harangue them, assuring them of success and victory, and a speedy deliverance from all their grievances. When he came to Cufah he called the sect together, and told them that he was come 'from the mine of excellency, the Imam that directs 'the right way; who commanded medicines to be applied, and the 'veil to be removed, and the perfection of gracious works, and the 'killing of their enemies. He then represented to them the incapacity 'of Solyman for such an undertaking, as being altogether unex-'perienced in war, and one that would only destroy both them and 'himself.' This he inculcated so frequently that he persuaded a great many of the sect into his interest, who began every day to favour him more and more in their common discourse, and magnify his merit, and promise themselves great things from him. But notwithstanding all this, Solyman's interest was still superior to any amongst the sect, as being the most ancient, and of the greatest authority. He was resolved to go forwards according to his appointment, with what forces he had, expecting to be joined by a great army of the sect at Nochailah. Almochtar staid behind, waiting for an account of Solyman's success, not doubting in the least, but that if he should miscarry the sole command of the sect would fall inevitably into his hands. He was suspected of having a secret design of seizing the province, upon which account some of Solyman's party surrounded his house, and having surprised him, would have persuaded the governour to have bound him, and made him walk barefoot to prison. The governour answered, 'That he would never do so to a man that had not declared himself an enemy, but was only taken up upon suspicion.' Then they would have had him put in irons, but the governour answered, 'That the prison was restraint enough ;' whither he was conveyed upon a mule, and where for a while we must leave him.

We return now to Solyman and his penitents, for so they were called that confederated under him to revenge the death of Hosein, because of their sorrow for their former neglect of him in his extremity. They set out according to their agreement to meet at their general rendezvous at Nochailah, a place not very far distant from Cufah, in the new moon of the latter Rebiyah. When he came there and had taken a view of the camp, he was very much concerned at the smallness of the number, and dispatched two horsemen post to Cufah, with orders to cry round about the streets in the great · mosque, 'Vengeance for Hosein ;' this alarmed the people, and amongst the rest there was an Arabian married to the greatest beauty of her time whom he doated upon to an excess ; as soon as he heard that proclamation he neither answered them one word, nor went out to them, but put on his cloaths in great haste, and called for his arms and his horse. His wife asked him if he was possessed ; he answered, 'By God no ! but I have heard God's herald calling for revenge for the blood of that man (Hosein) and I will answer him, and I will die for him, or God shall dispose of me as he pleases.' 'To whom,' said she, 'do you leave this child of yours ?' 'To God,' saith he, 'who hath no partner ; O God ! I commend to thee my family and my child ! O God preserve me in them.' This said, he followed them, and left her to bewail him.

Those that were gathered together in the street went to the great mosque, were they found a great many people after the last evening prayer, and repeating the same cry, another, a person of distinction, armed himself and called for his horse ; his daughter asking him the reason of it, he answered, 'Child, thy father flies from his sin to his God !' Then calling his nearest relations together he took his leave, and

arrived at Solyman's camp the next morning. They next looked over
the rolls to see how many had given their hands at first, and found
them 16,000, whereof there were not above 4000 present. One said that
Almochtar had drawn off 2000, so that according to that account there
still remained 10,000 guilty of perjury. At last Mosabbib told Solyman,
'That they who did not come out of an hearty intent would do him no
service.' Solyman and several others of the chief men made speeches
to that small handful they had, telling them, 'That it was not this
world they fought for, that they had neither silver nor gold, but were
going to expose themselves to the edges of swords and the points of
spears.' To which the people answered all round, 'It is not this world
that we seek, neither do we come out for the sake of it.' Then they
deliberated about the most proper method of carrying on the design, one
proposed the marching directly into Syria to be revenged on Obeidollah;
another would have them go and destroy all that had a hand in his
death at Cufah, where there were a great many of the chiefs of the
tribes and several other leading men. Solyman did by no means approve
of this last advice, but said, 'That they ought to take vengeance upon
that individual person that had beset him with armed men, and said to
him, "You shall have no protection from me, unless you render your
self entirely to my disposal;" that wicked wretch, the son of that
wicked wretch is your object!' Besides he did not think it proper by
any means to begin a massacre in their own province, which would
alienate their friends and exasperate the people to see their fathers and
brethren and near relations murdered before their faces ; wherefore he
advised them to leave that matter to be considered afterwards, if it
should please God to grant them a safe return out of Syria.

In the mean time Ibrahim (who, as we have mentioned before, was
sent from Abdollah the son of Zobeir to gather the tribute), and Abdollah the son of Yezid, the governour of Cufah, being informed of Solyman's expedition, entertained some thoughts of joyning forces with
him : they conceived it was both plausible and practicable enough to
secure themselves in that part of the country, under the pretence of
revenging the death of Hosein ; besides that Obeidollah's cruelty had
raised the greatest aversion against him imaginable, in all the provinces that had been under his jurisdiction. They went both to Solyman,
and persuaded him to stay till they could raise forces to assist him, or
else to abide where he was, till Obeidollah should come within their
bounds, which they had very good reason to think would not be long,
after the alarm was taken in Syria. This not prevailing Ibrahim
would have persuaded him at least to stay till he could furnish him
with some money (no less than the tribute of the whole province).
The answer of this last proposal was, 'That their going out was not for
this world.' Thus the conference broke off, and Solyman continued his
march into Syria, and Ibrahim and the son of Yezid returned back to
Cufah.

Obeidollah was not idle all this while, but was upon his march towards them. Solyman's men perceiving that their friends of Madayen and Basorah did not join them according to promise began to murmur; and notwithstanding his endeavours to pacify them, they deserted ; so that when he mustered them at Eksas, upon the banks of the Euphrates, there were 1000 of them wanting : Solyman said to the rest, 'It is a good riddance ; for if they had staid they would have only been a burthen to you ; the Lord did not approve of their going out, and therefore he hath withdrawn them, and held them back for the better, wherefore praise ye your Lord.'

Marching all night they came the next morning to Hosein's burying place, where they staid a night and a day, which they spent in praying for him, and begging his pardon. When they first came to his tomb, they all cried out with one voice, and wept and wished that they had been partners with him in his death : there never was seen a greater day of weeping than that. Solyman said, ' O God ! be merciful to Hosein the martyr, the son of the martyr ; the guide, the son of the guide ; the righteous, the son of the righteous ! O God ! we call thee to witness, that we are in their profession of religion, and in their way, and that we are enemies of those that killed them, and friends of those that loved them.' Another account (not contradictory to the former) says, that when they drew near to Hosein's tomb they cried out unanimously, ' O Lord ! we have deceived the son of the daughter of our prophet ; forgive us what is past, and repent towards us, for thou art the repenter, the merciful ! Have mercy upon Hosein and his followers, the righteous martyrs ! And we call thee to witness, O Lord ! that we are the very same sort of men with those that were killed for his sake, and if thou dost not forgive him to us we must be sufferers.' They did not move till the morning after, but continued bewailing him and his friends at his sepulchre, the sight of which renewed their sorrow. Nay, when Solyman commanded them to march, there was never a man of them would stir till he had first stood over Hosein's tomb, and begged his pardon. One that was present there swears that he never saw such crowding and pressing about the black stone. From thence they marched to Hesasah, from Hesasah to Alambar, from Alambar to Sodud, and from Sodud to Kayyarah.

Whilst they were at Kayyarah, Abdollah the son of Yezid, the governour of Cufah, sent them a friendly letter, admonishing them of the desperateness of their undertaking, in encountering such a multitude as they must expect to meet, with such an handful ; assuring them of his being in the same interest with them, and desiring them to return : he concluded thus, ' Do not set at nought my advice, nor ' contradict my command : come as soon as my letter is read to you : ' God turn your faces towards his obedience, and your backs to the ' rebelling against him.' When the letter was read, and the people had asked Solyman's advice, he told them that he saw no reason for going back, that they were never like to be nearer the two Hoseins than now, and that the meaning of their persuading them to return was, that they might assist Abdollah the son of Zobeir, which he reckoned to be erroneous ; but if they died now, they should die in a state of repentance from their sins. At last he came to Hait, from whence he wrote an answer to the governour of Cufah, wherein he gave him thanks for his kind letter, but told him that his men could not accept of his invitation ; that they were true penitents, and resolved to go forwards and leave the success to God. The governour as soon as he received the letter said, that they were resolved to die, and that would be the next news of them. From Hait they went to Karkisia, from thence to Ainwerdah. They designed to depose both the Caliphs, viz., Abdolmelick the son of Merwan, and Abdollah the son of Zobeir, and restore the government to the family of the prophet. Not to enter into a long detail of the tedious particulars of their march and engagement, in short Obeidollah met them with 20,000 men, and cut them all to pieces.

Not long after, in the month of Ramadan, the Caliph Merwan died. We must here remember, that after Moawiyah's decease Merwan was chose Caliph upon this condition, that Caled the son of Yezid should succeed him, excluding his own children, and that Caled had refused to take the government upon himself because he was so very young ; and that to secure the succession to Caled he married Yezid's widow, who was Caled's mother.

However afterwards, Merwan having altered his mind, was desirous to have the succession pass to his own children exclusive of Caled, and accordingly caused his eldest son Abdolmelik to be proclaimed his lawful and proper successor.

Caled, who always hated him, came to him one day, when there were a great many of the nobility about him in the garden, and reviled him after the most reproachful manner. This moved the old man's choler so that he called him bastard ; Caled went and told his mother all that had passed ; the lady touched to the quick with this affront was resolved to be revenged ; but said to Caled, ' Child, you must have a care of such behaviour, for he will never bear it ; let me alone and I will take care of him for you ;' Merwan coming in soon after asked her if Caled had said anything concerning him ; she told him no, he had more respect for him.

Merwan did not long survive it, some say she poisoned him, others that she laid a pillow upon his face when he was asleep and sat upon it till he was dead, and then told the people that he died on a sudden.

Some say his age was 63, others with more probability 71. He reigned 298 days.

He was called Ebn Tarid, ' the son of the expelled : because Mahomet had banished his father Hakem for divulging a secret. He continued in his exile during the reigns of Abubeker and Omar, and the recalling him was objected to Othman as one of the greatest crimes ; it being reversing the sentence of the prophet ; though Othman, mild and good-natured as he was, thought that since the cause of his banishment, and all the bad effects of it that could possibly happen, were at an end, the punishment ought to cease also.

The fifth CALIPH *of the house of* OMMIYAH *; (Being the eleventh from* MAHOMET*).*

A B D O L M E L I C K,

THE SON OF MERWAN.

An. Heg. 65. cœpit Aug. 17. A.C. 684.

ON the third day of the month Ramadan in the 65th year of the Hegirah, Abdolmelick the son of Merwan was inaugurated Caliph, and succeeded his father in the government of Syria and Ægypt : it is reported, that when the news was first brought to him he was sitting with the Alcoran in his lap : whereupon he folded it up and laid it aside, and said, ' I must take my leave of thee now.'

Abdollah still holding it out against him at Meccah, he was not willing the people should go thither on pilgrimage, and for that reason sent and enlarged the temple of Jerusalem so as to take the stone into the body of the church, and the people began to make their pilgrimages thither.

All this while Almochtar was making the best use of his time in order to compass his designs : during his imprisonment he had found means to keep up his correspondence with the sect ; letters were conveyed to him in the lining of a cap : he was soon informed of Solyman's fate, and thought it a proper time to exert himself. Abdollah the son of Zobeir being still in arms at Meccah against Abdolmelick the new Caliph, Ibrahim the son of Ashtar was courted by the sect, who answered, ' That he would join with them if they would be under his command ; but they told him that that was impracticable because they were already pre-engaged to Almochtar, who at a meeting where Ibrahim was present, producing a letter from Almohdi the son of Mahomet, the son of Ali, who was the head of the sect in a lineal succession, Ibrahim gave him his hand without any more to do, and Almochtar took upon him the sole command of the forces. Not only so, but a great many of them inaugurated him Caliph upon these terms,

'That he should govern according to the contents of the book of God
and the tradition of his apostle, and destroy the murderers of Hosein
and his family.' The first he attempted to seize was Shamer, whom he
overcame and killed. The next was Caula, who carried Hosein's head
to Obeidollah, him he besieged in his house, and killed him and burnt
him.   Afterwards he killed Amer who commanded the army that
killed Hosein, and gave orders that the horse should trample over his
back and breast; he killed his son too, and sent both their heads to
Mohammed ben Hanifiyah.   The sect were afraid lest he should have
pardoned Ali the son of Hathem, and begged of him to let them kill
him ; he told them they might dispose of him as they thought fit. They
took him and bound him, saying, 'You stripped the son of Ali before
he was dead, and we will strip you alive ; and you made a mark of him
and we will make one of you ;' then they let fly a shower of arrows
at him, which stuck so thick over all parts of his body that he looked
like a porcupine.   In short, Almochtar found means to surprize them
whensoever he could get any information where they were, and destroyed them with variety of deaths.

   Abdolmelick had about this time sent an army against Abdollah the
son of Zobeir, who was at Medinah ; Almochtar, who had two such
powerful enemies to deal withal, was resolved to try if he could get rid
of one of them first ; he endeavoured to overreach Abdollah by sending an army pretendedly to his assistance on the following occasion.

   Abdolmelick having sent an army out of Syria towards Irak,
Almochtar was afraid lest they should not only fall upon him on that
side, but that he should at the same time be distressed by Abdollah's
brother Musab, from Basorah on the other.   Wherefore he wrote a
deceitful letter to Abdollah, wherein he told him, that being informed
that Abdolmelick the son of Merwan had sent an army against him,
he would willingly come to his assistance with a competent force.
Abdollah answered him, 'That if he was once assured of the sincerity
of his allegiance he might come ; and in order to give him satisfaction
in that article he desired him to take the votes of his men for him, and
when he had received them he should believe him, and not send any
more forces into his country ; and that in the meantime he should send
his intended assistance with all possible speed against Abdolmelick's
army that lay at Dilkora ; upon this Almochtar called Serjabil the son
of wars to him, and dispatched him with about 3000 men, most of
them slaves, for there were not above 700 Arabs amongst them, and
bad him march directly to Medinah and write to him from thence for
further orders.

   Almochtar's design was, as soon as they came to Medinah, to send
an Emir to command them, whilst Serjabil should go and besiege Abdollah in Meccah.   But Abdollah, who had no great reason to put confidence in Almochtar, did not intend to suffer himself to be surprized,

especially since Almochtar had not given him the security he expected; wherefore he sent Abbas, the son of Sahel, from Meccah to Medinah with 2000 men, ordering him, if he found the army in his interest to receive them ; if otherwise, to use the best of his endeavour to destroy them. When Abbas met Serjabil he found his men all in order of battle, the horse all on the right, and Serjabil himself marching before the foot ; Abbas his men were in no order at all. After they had saluted one another, Abbas took Serjabil aside, and asked him if he did not own himself to be Abdollah's subject? To which question when Serjabil had answered in the affirmative, Abbas bad him march along with him to Dilkora ; Serjabil told him, that he had received no such orders from his master, but only to march directly to Medinah. Abbas told him, 'That his master took it for granted that he was come out for no other purpose but to go to Dilkora ;' the other still insisted that his orders were for Medinah. Abbas perceiving how matters stood with him, concealed his suspicion of him, and told him 'He was in the right to obey his orders, he might do as he thought fit, but for his own part he must go to Dilkora.' Serjabil and his men were almost famished for want of provision in their long march ; Abbas made Serjabil a present of a fat sheep which he had by him ready killed, and sent a sheep to every ten of his men ; the sharpness of their hunger soon sent them on work ; they left their order and ran backwards and forwards for water, and whatsoever else was necessary for dressing their victuals : Abbas in the mean time took about 1000 of his best men and came up to their tents. Serjabil perceiving what danger he was in, cried out to his men to come to his assistance, but there was scarce an hundred of them got together when Abbas was come up close to him, crying out, ' O troop of God ! come out and fight with these confederates of the devil ; you are in the right way, but they are perjured villains !' They fought but a very little while before Serjabil and about 70 of his guard were killed ; whereupon Abbas held up a flag of quarter, which they readily ran to, except 300 who were all afterwards put to the sword. Abbas let about 200 of them go. When Almochtar heard the news he wrote to Mohammed the son of Haniphiyah, acquainting him with the disaster, and proffering him to send a powerful army to his assistance, if he would please to accept of it : Mohammed answered him ' That he was very well assured of the sincerity of his zeal for his service ; that if he had thought fit to make use of arms, he should not have wanted assistance ; but that he was resolved to bear with patience, and leave the event to God, who was the best judge.' When the messenger that brought Almochtar's letter took his leave, Mohammed said to him, ' Bid Almochtar fear God, and abstain from shedding blood :' the messenger asked him if he would not write that to him? Mohammed answered, 'I have already com-
' manded him to obey the great and mighty God ; and the obedience
' of God consists in doing all that is good, and in abstaining from all

' evil.' When Almochtar received the letter he gave it another turn, and said to the people, ' I am commanded to do that which is just, and reject infidelity and perfidiousness.'

This same year the Hoseinians went to Meccah, and performed a pilgrimage there, under Abu Abdollah Aljodali, upon this occasion. Though Mohammed the son of Haniphiyah, and all the rest of Ali's family, behaved themselves very inoffensively at Meccah, and were so far from making any disturbance, that they always persuaded their friends to peace, who were ready to hazard their lives in their service, yet Abdollah easily found by experience, that it would be impossible for him to succeed so long as they were alive, and refused the oath of allegiance. For though they did not stir themselves, they had a very strong party, and a great many other disaffected persons made use of the pretence of revenging the death of Hosein. He therefore resolved to make an end of it all at once, and seized Mohammed and his family, and 17 of the principal Cufians, and imprisoned them in the Zemzem, and set a guard over them, and fixed them a time, in which he threatened them, if they did not come in he would put them to death, and burn them to ashes. The Zemzem is the name of a pit at Meccah which the Muslemans say was made out of that spring which God caused to appear in favour of Hagar and Ishmael, whom Abraham had turned out of his house, and obliged to retire into Arabia ; concerning this well they relate a great many strange things not proper to be inserted in this place. Here they were shut up, but (says my author) God whose name be magnified and glorified, gave to them not to come in, though he should execute all his threats upon them. Whilst they were in this condition, they found means to write to Almochtar, and acquaint him with their circumstances, desiring also of the Cufians not to desert them, as they did Hosein and his family. When he received the letter, he called the people together, and having read the letter, said, ' This is from your guide, and the purest of the family of the house of your prophet, upon whom be peace ; they are left shut up like sheep expecting to be killed and burnt ; but I shall give them sufficient assistance, and send horse after horse, as the streams of water follow one another. Then he sent Abu Abdollah Aljodali with 70 troopers, all men of approved valour. After him a second with 400. Then a third with 100. A fourth with 100. A fifth with 40. And last of all a sixth with 40 more. In all, 750. These went out at several times one after the other, and Abu Abdollah their chief made a halt by the way, till he was joined by the two companies, consisting of 40 each, and with this 150 made haste to the temple of Meccah, crying out vengeance for Hosein. At last they went to the Zemzem, where they arrived in very good time, for Abdollah had got the wood ready to burn his prisoners, and there remained but two days of the appointed time. They beat off the guard, and broke open the Zemzem, and begged of Mohammed to give them leave to use their liberty with the enemy of God, Abdollah the son of Zobeir ; but Mohammed answered that he would not allow any fighting in the sacred place of the most high God. Abdollah said, ' Do you think I will dismiss them unless they swear to me? nay, and you shall swear too.' Abu Abdollah answered, ' By the Lord of this sacred place, thou shalt let them go, or we will cut thee to pieces.' Abdollah despising the smallness of their number, swore that if he should give his men leave it would not be an hour's time before all their heads were off. Mohammed the son of Haniphiyah kept back his friends, and would not let them fight, and Abdollah began to cool, when he saw another captain come up with 100 men, and a second with the like number ; then 200 more in a body with the money, who went all to the temple and cried out, 'Allah Acbar,' vengeance for the death of Hosein. When Abdollah saw them he was afraid of them. They took him prisoner, and intreated Mohammed to give them leave to dispose of him as they thought fit, but he would not suffer them. The money which they brought was distributed amongst four thousand of Ali's friends, and the whole business through the exceeding gentleness of Mohammed's temper was amicably compromised.

Before Merwan's death, Obeidollah was sent towards Cufah with an army, and had leave to plunder it for three days. Against him was sent Yezid the son of Ares, worthy to be mentioned upon the account of his heroick courage and presence of mind ; for when death appeared in his face, and he was forced to be held upon his ass on both sides, he appointed three generals to command the army during the fight successively, if there should be occasion for them. Obeidollah never reached so far as Cufah ; and now in the first month of the 67th year, Almochtar found himself at leisure to send his forces against him. There was one thing very remarkable in his preparation ; he made a throne, and pretended that there was something mysterious in it, telling the people, ' That it was of the same use to them that the ark was to the children of Israel ;' and accordingly in this expedition against Obeidollah, it was carried upon a mule on purpose into the battle. The prayer that they said at this ark was, ' O God, grant us to live long in thy obedience, and help us and do not forget us, but protect us.' And the people answered, ' Amen, Amen.' Almochtar's general was Ibrahim the son of Ashtar ; after a sharp engagement, Obeidollah's forces were beaten and himself killed in the camp. Ibrahim cut off his head and burnt his body. The number of the son of Ziyad's men that were drowned in the flight, was greater than that which was slain in the field. His head with some others were sent to Almochtar. Thus God revenged the death of Hosein by the means of Almochtar, though Almochtar had no good design in it. After the success of this battle, the people had such a reverence for this ark, that they almost idolized it.

This year, Abdollah sent his brother Musab to govern Basorah. Al·
mochtar was sole master of Cufah, where he persecuted all that he could
lay his hands on, who were not of Hosein's party. Musab rode muffled
to Basorah, and when he alighted at the temple, and went up into the
pulpit, the people cried out, ' Emir, Emir,' that is, ' a governour, a governour.' He bad Hareth his predecessor give place, which he
did, sitting one step below him. Then having, according to custom,
first praised God he began with these words of the 28th chapter of the
Alcoran, ' We relate to thee, the history of Moses and Pharaoh with
truth, for (the satisfaction of) those that believe ;' till he came to these
words, ' And was of them that defile the earth ;' and *pointed with his
hand towards Syria. And when he came at these words, ' Who were
weakened in the earth, and we shall make them rulers, and make them
heirs ;' pointing towards Hejaz or Arabia Petræa. And at these words,
' And we shewed Pharaoh and Haman, and their armies what they
most feared,' he pointed again towards Syria. Then he said to the
Basorians, ' I hear that you used to give names to your Emirs ; I have
' named myself Hejaz, that is Arabia.'

Soon after one Shebet came to Basorah, upon a crop-eared, bob-
tailed mule, with his cloaths-rent, crying out as loud as he could, ' Ya
gautha, ya gautha, help! help!' As soon as they had described the
manner of his appearance to Musab, he said he was sure it must be
Shebet, for nobody else would do so but him, and ordered them to give
him admission. He came with a heavy complaint, seconded by a great
many of the chief men of Cufah, who represented the great disorders
committed there, and their sufferings under the administration of Almochtar ; particularly an insurrection of their slaves against them,
begging his assistance, and persuading him earnestly to march with an
army against Almochtar. He was very much inclined to hearken to
their proposal, but was resolved not to stir till Almohalleb his lieutenant over Persia should come to his assistance. He wrote to Almohalleb who made no great haste, not very much approving this expedition ; but he obeyed the second summons, and came to him with large
supplies both of men and money. They joined their forces, and marched
towards Cufah against Almochtar, who was not wanting to his own
defence, but mustered his forces, and gave them battle ; after a bloody
fight Almochtar was beaten, and made his retreat into the royal castle
of Cufah. Musab pursued him and besieged him there, where he continued behaving himself bravely till he was killed, upon which his men
surrendered to Musab at discretion, who put them every man to the
sword. They were in all 7000. Almochtar was then 67 years old.

Thus died that great man, who had beaten all the generals of Yezid,
Merwan and Abdolmelick, all three Caliphs of the house of Ommiyah,

---

* When he pointed towards Syria, he meant Abdolmelick, whom he compares to Pharaoh
and Haman ; and when he pointed towards Arabia he meant his brother Abdollah.

and made himself master of Cufah, and all Babylonian Irak, whereof that city was the capital, and never pardoned any one of those who had declared themselves enemies of the family of the prophet, nor those whom he could believe to have dipt their hands in Hosein's blood, or that of his relations; so that it is said that he killed near fifty thousand of those people, without reckoning those who were slain in the battles which he fought.

This year the sect of Separatists called Azarakites, sworn enemies to all established government, both temporal and spiritual, and particularly to the house of Ommiyah, made an eruption out of Persia, and overran all Irak, till they came near Cufah, and penetrated as far as Madayan. They committed all manner of outrages as they went, destroying all they met, ripping open the women with child, and exercising the utmost cruelty without distinction of sex or age. There was a lady of extraordinary piety as well as beauty, which one of them would have spared, to whom another answered, 'What! thou art taken with her beauty, thou enemy of God, and hast denied the faith;' and killed her. Almohalleb, the governour of Mausal and Mesopotamia, mustered his chosen troops at Basorah, and met them at a place called Saulak, where they fought desperately for eight months, without intermitting one day. This year there was such a famine in Syria, that they could not undertake any expedition, nor lay siege to any town, because of the great scarcity of provision. Abdolmelick encamped in a place called Botnan, near to the territories of Kinnisrin. His camp was very much incommoded by the showers of rain; however, he wintered there, and afterwards returned to Damascus.

In the year 69, Abdolmelick left Damascus to go against Musab, the son of Zobeir, and appointed Amrou, the son of Said, to take care of Damascus, who seized upon it for himself, which obliged Abdolmelick to return. Others say that when he went out, Amrou, the son of Said, said to him, 'You are going to Irak, and your father gave me this government after him, and upon that consideration I fought along with him, and you cannot be ignorant of the pains I took in his service; wherefore give me this government after you.' Abdolmelick would not hearken to his proposal, and Amrou returned to Damascus, whither Abdolmelick followed him close. They skirmished in the streets several days; at last the women came with their children, crying out, 'How long will you fight and destroy one another for the government of the Coreish?' and with much ado parted them; and articles of peace were drawn between Amrou and Abdolmelick.

But standing in competition for a crown is a crime never to be forgiven. Three or four days after Abdolmelick sent for him; he was in company with his wife and two or three friends, who dissuaded him from trusting himself in his hands, but he resolved to venture, and as he went out he stumbled. His wife took the omen, and repeated her

persuasions to stay him, but to no purpose. He put on his sword, and took
100 men along with him. When he came thither, he was introduced himself, but the gates were shut upon his men, and nobody permitted to go
in along with him, but only a little footboy. When he came in Abdolmelick
spoke very civilly to him, and placed him by him on the couch where
he sat. After a long discourse, he commanded a servant to take his
sword off. Amrou expressing some unwillingness to be disarmed.
'What,' said Abdolmelick, 'would you sit by me with your sword on?'
After his sword was off, Abdolmelick told him that when he first
rebelled against him he had taken an oath that if ever he got him into
his power, he would put fetters upon him. Amrou said he hoped he
would not expose him in them to the people. Abdolmelick promised
him he would not, and at the same time pulled the fetters from under
his cushion, which were accordingly put upon his hands and feet.
Then he plucked him so violently against the couch that he beat out
two of his fore-teeth; after which he told him that he would still let
him go if he thought he would continue in his duty, and keep the
Coreish right. 'But,' said he, 'there never were two men in one
country engaged in such an affair as you and I are concerned in, but
one of them expelled the other.' Some say that when Abdolmelick
saw Amrou's teeth drop out, as he was taking them in his fingers, he
said, 'I see your teeth are out, you will never be reconciled to me
again after this;' and immediately commanded him to be beheaded.

The Muezzin at the same time called to evening prayers. Abdolmelick went out to prayers, and left the execution of Amrou to his
brother Adolaziz, the son of Merwan, who, standing over him with his
sword, Amrou begged of him for God's sake not to do that office himself,
but to leave it to some other person that was not so nearly related, whereupon he threw away his sword and let him alone. Abdolmelick made
but short prayers, and when he came back, the people observing that
Amrou was not long ago with him, acquainted his brother John with
the matter, who took with him some of his friends, and 1000 of
Amrou's slaves, and made an assault upon Abdolmelick's house, and
broke open the gates, and killed several of the guards. In the mean
time Abdolmelick wondering to find Amrou alive, asked Abdolaziz the
reason of it, who answering that he had forborn him out of compassion. Abdolmelick gave him reproachful language, and calling for a
javelin, he struck Amrou with it, but it not penetrating, he seconded
his blow, still to no purpose : then feeling upon his arm, he perceived
he had a coat of mail on, at which he laughed, and said, 'Cousin, you
come well prepared !' Then he called for his sword, and having commanded Amrou to be thrown upon his back, he killed him ; but was at
the same time seized with such a trembling, that they were forced to
take him up, and lay him upon his couch. All this while John and his
friends were pressing in, killing and wounding all they met : wherefore

they threw out Amrou's head, to satisfie them that their fighting would be to no purpose ; and Abdolaziz, the son of Merwan, to appease their rage, threw money amongst them in plenty.   When they saw the head and the money, they left fighting and fell to picking it up.   But after the heat was over, it is said that Abdolmelick, such was his covetousness, recalled it all again, and ordered it to be put in the publick treasury.   John was taken prisoner and sentenced to death, but Abdolaziz begged of his brother not to kill two of the Ommian family in one day ; whereupon he was imprisoned for about a month or more, after which he advised with those about him concerning the putting him and his friends to death.   He was answered, ' That it was better let alone ; that they were near relations, and the best way would be to give them their liberty, and let them go, if they would, to his enemy Musab, the son of Zobeir ; that if they were killed in that service, he would be rid of them by the hands of others ; that if they returned and were delivered into his hands again, he might then, without incurring any censure, deal with them according to his own discretion.' This advice took place, and they went to Musab, the son of Zobeir. Then Abdolmelick sent to Amrou's wife for the articles of peace which he had signed to her husband.   She bad the messenger go back, and tell him that she had wrapt them up with him in his winding-sheet that he might plead his cause against him with them before his lord. This was an old grudge between Abdolmelick and his cousin Amrou begun in their infancy, occasioned by an old woman of their own family, whom they visited frequently when they were boys, and she used to dress victuals for them, and give each of them his dish by himself ; and always ordered matters so, as to raise emulation between them, and set them together by the ears.   So that they were either always quarrelling or else so obstinately silent as not to speak one word.   Merwan before he died had received information that Amrou had promised him the government after his decease, which made him make the more haste to lay hold of a proper opportunity of proposing to the congregation to swear to his son Abdolmelick and Abdolaziz after him, with which they readily complied without exception.

In the year 70, the Greeks made an incursion into Syria.   Abdolmelick, who had business enough upon his hands already, between Abdollah, the son of Zobeir, in Arabia, and Musab, his brother, in Irak, was not at leisure to go against them, but agreed to pay the Grecian Emperor 1000 ducats every week.   This same year Musab went to Meccah with prodigious wealth and cattle, and all manner of furniture, which he distributed amongst the Arabians.   Abdollah, the son of Zobeir, went this year on pilgrimage.

Abdolmelick, now resolved upon his expedition into Irak against Musab, put to death the principal persons that had been concerned with Amrou, the son of Said.   He had sent before him one Caled, the

27

son of Asid, who going privately into Basorah, had begun to form a party for him. Musab having received intelligence of his proceedings, went to Basorah in hopes of surprising him ; but he being out of the way, he sent for the chief of the Basorians, and reproached them severally ; one with the meanness of his family ; another with some scandalous action either of his own or some of his relations ; all of them with something ; which behaviour only exasperated them, and made them more averse to his interest. Abdolmelick had in the mean time sent several letters to the leading men full of large promises. Amongst the rest, he sent one to the faithful Ibrahim, the son of Alashtar, who delivered it to Musab sealed up as it came. The contents of it were, that if he would come over to his party he would give him the lieutenancy of Irak. Ibrahim told him that he might depend upon it that he had written much to the same purpose to all his friends, and advised him to behead them ; but Musab did not approve of that expedient, because it would create an aversion in their tribes ; then Ibrahim advised him to imprison them or put them in chains, and set some body over them, who, if he should be conquered, should strike their heads off, but if he got the victory he might make a compliment of them to their tribes. Musab answered, ' I have other business to mind ; God bless Ahubehran, who gave me warning of the treachery of the Irakians as if he had clearly foreseen this very business wherein I am now engaged.'

The Syrian nobility did not approve of Abdolmelick's engaging himself in this expedition ; not that they disliked his design, but they chose rather that he should stay at home with them at Damascus, and reduce Irak by his generals, rather than expose his person to the hazards of war, fearing, least if he should miscarry, their government might be in an unsettled condition, and their affairs embroiled. To this he answered, ' That no body was fit for that undertaking but a man of sense, and perhaps he might send a man of courage that wanted conduct ; that he found himself qualified for it by his abilities in war and his personal courage : that Musab was of a couragious family ; that his father Zobeir had been the most valiant of the Coreish, and that he himself was brave, but did not understand war, and loved an easy life ; and that he had some with him that would be against him, but for his own men he could depend upon their fidelity.'

They joined battle at a place called Masken. The Irakians according to their custom, were resolved to betray Musab before ; for they did not intend to expose their country to be ravaged by a Syrian army for his sake. His faithful friend Ibrahim, the son of Ashtar, gave the first charge, and repulsed Mohammed the son of Haroun, whom Abdolmelick supported with a fresh company ; and at the second charge Ibrahim was killed. Musab's general of the horse ran away, and a great many of the rest stood by and would not obey his command :

then he called out, 'O Ibrahim! but there is no Ibrahim for me to day?' It is said, that when Musab was upon his march against Abdol-melick, Abdolmelick asked 'If Omer the son of Abdollah was with him;' being answered, 'No, for he had made him his lieutenant of Persia;' he enquired next 'If Almohalleb was there,' they told him, 'No, he was lieutenant over Mausal;' he asked the third time 'If Ibad the son of Hossem was there;' being answered in the negative, and assured that he had left him behind him at Basorah, he was exceeding glad and then presaged a certain victory. 'For,' said he, 'he will have no body to help him.'

When Musab perceived his forlorn condition, he persuaded his son Isa to ride with those men he had to Meccah, and acquaint his uncle with the perfidiousness of the Irakians: but Isa (who must be very young, for his father was but 36) would not leave him, but told him 'That his life would do him no good if he survived him, and persuaded him to make his retreat to Basorah, where he would find his friends met together, and from whence he might go to the governour of the faithful, meaning his uncle Abdollah the son of Zobeir:' but Musab said, 'It should never be talked among the Coreish that he ran away, nor that he came into the sacred temple of Meccah routed,' and there-fore bad his son, if he chose it, come back and fight; he obeyed and died in battle, and his father Musab was killed not long after him. It is said, that during the engagement Abdolmelick had sent to Musab and tendered him quarter; but he answered, 'That such men as he was did not use to go from such a place at that (meaning the field of battle) without either conquering or being conquered.' After he was grievously wounded with arrows he was stabbed, and his head cut off and carried to Abdolmelick, who proffered the bearer 1000 ducats, which he refused, saying, 'That he did not kill him in obedience to him, but to revenge his own quarrel, and for that reason he would take no money for bringing the head.' Musab was Abdolmelick's intimate friend before he was Caliph, but marrying afterwards Sekinah, Hosein's daughter, and Ayesha the daughter of Telhah, he was thus engaged by those marriages in the interest of two families that were at mortal enmity with the house of Ommiyah.

As soon as this battel was over Abdolmelick entered into Cufah, and with it took possession of both the Babylonian and Persian Irak. As soon as he signified to the people that he expected they should come in and take the oaths to him, they came unanimously. Soon after he came into the castle he enquired after John the brother of Amrou whom he had killed; and being informed that he was not far off, he would have had his men produce him; which they refusing, unless he would first promise them that he should suffer no harm, he seemed to take it ill at first that they should pretend to capitulate with him, but at last he condescended to promise them, and John made his appear-

ance. When he came into his presence, ' Thou vile wretch,' said Abdolmelick, ' with what face wilt thou appear before thy Lord, after having
deposed me ?' ' With that face,' answered John, ' that he hath created.'
Then he took the oath of allegiance to him, and there was an end of
that business. He ordered vast sums of money to be distributed among
the people, and made a splendid entertainment, to which everybody
that would come was welcome. When he was sat down, Amrou the
son of Hareth an ancient Mechzumian came in ; he called him to him,
and placing him by him upon his sofa, asked him what meat he liked
best of all that ever he had eaten ; the old Mechzumian answered, ' An
asses neck well seasoned and well roasted.' ' You do nothing,' says
Abdolmelick, ' What say you to a leg or a shoulder of sucking lamb,
well roasted and covered over with butter and milk* ? Whilst he was
at supper he said,

> How sweetly we live, if a shadow would last !

After supper was over he took the old Mechzumian along with him
to satisfy him concerning the antiquities of the castle, and when the
answers to all his questions began of course with ' This was,' and
' That was,' and ' He was,' and the· like, it raised a melancholy reflection in the Caliph, and he repeated this Arabick verse out of an ancient
poet :

> And everything that is new (Omaim !) goes to decay, and every one that is to day goes to HE
> WAS.

Then returning to his sofa he threw himself upon it, and repeated these
verses :

> Proceed leisurely because thou art mortal, and chastise thy self, O man !
> For what is past will not *be* when it is gone, as that which is present will be past.

Or

> For what *was* will not *be* when it is past, as what *is* will be *it was.*

When Musab's head was brought to him in the castle, one that stood
by said, ' Now I recollect something very particular of my own observation ; I saw Hosein's head presented in this same castle to Obeidollah, Obeidollah's to Almochtar, Almochtar's to Musab, and now at last
Musab's to your self. The Caliph was surprised and concerned at this
discourse, and commanded the castle to be forthwith demolished to
avert the ill omen.

When the news of Musab's death was brought to his brother Abdollah, the son of Zobeir, he made a speech to the people upon that occasion, as follows : ' Praise be to God to whom belongs the creation and
' the command of all things ; who gives dominion to whom he pleases,
' and takes it away from whom he pleases ; and strengthens whom he
' pleases, and weakens whom he pleases ; only God never weakens him

* Hence I observe that the Arabians had not altered their cookery since Abraham's time,
who made use of butter and milk when he entertained the angels. See *Gen. xviii.*, 8. There
is some obscurity in the Arabick.

' that hath truth on his side, though he stands alone, nor doth he
' strengthen him whose friend is the devil, though all the world should
' join in his assistance. There is news come from Irak which is mat-
' ter both of sorrow and joy to us ; it is the death of Musab, to whom
' God be merciful. Now what rejoiceth us is, that his death is martyr-
' dom to him, and what is matter of grief to us, is the sorrow where-
' with his friends will be afflicted at his departure ; but men of under-
' standing will have recourse to patience, which is of all the most noble
' consolation. As for my own part, if I be a sufferer in Musab, I was
' so before in [my father] Azzobeir : nor was Musab any thing else but
' one of the servants of God and an assistant of mine. But the Irak-
' ians are treacherous and perfidious, they betrayed him and sold him
' for a vile price. And if we be killed, by God we do not die upon
' beds as the sons of Abilasi die : by God there was never a man of
' them killed in fight, either in the days of ignorance or Islam : but we
' do not die but pushing with lances and striking under the shadow of
' swords. As for this present world it diverts from the most high king,
' whose dominion shall not pass away, and whose kingdom shall not
' perish ; and if it (the present world) turns its face I shall not receive
' with immoderate joy ; and if it turns its back I shall not bewail it with
' indecent sorrow. I have said what I had to say, and I beg pardon of
' God both for my self and you.'

Whilst Mohalleb was engaged against the Separatists they received
intelligence of Musab's death, before he and his men knew anything
at all of it. Whereupon they called out to his men, 'What ! will you
not tell us what you think of Musab?' They said, 'He is the Imam
of the right way.' 'And he is,' replied the Separatists, 'your friend
both in this world and that to come.' They answered, 'Yes.' 'And
you are his friends both alive and dead?' 'Yes.' 'And what do you
think of Abdolmelick the son of Merwan?' They said, 'He is the son
of the accursed ; we are clear of him before God, and the shedding his
blood is more free for us than yours.' 'And you are,' continued the
Separatists, 'his enemies both alive and dead?' 'Yes, we are his
enemies both alive and dead.' 'Well,' said the Separatists, 'Abdolmelick hath killed your Imam Musab, and you will make Abdolmelick
your Imam to-morrow, though you wash your hands of him to-day,
and curse his father.' To which the other answered, 'You lye, ye
enemies of God.' But the next day, when they were informed of the
truth of it, they changed their note, and Mohalleb and all his men
took the oath to Abdolmelick ; upon this account they were bitterly
reproached by the Separatists, who said to them, 'Now, you enemies
of God ! yesterday you were clear of him both in this world and the
world to come, and affirmed that you were his enemies both alive and
dead, and now to-day he is your Imam and your Caliph, who killed
your Imam whom you had chosen for your patron. Which of these

two is the right ?' They could not deny what they had said the day before, and were loath to give themselves the lye ; so they answered, ' You enemies of God ! we were pleased with the other so long as he presided over us ; and now we approve of this as we did before of the other.' To which the Separatists answered, ' No, by God, but you are brethren of the devils, companions of the wicked, and slaves to the present world.' This is the account of that conference.

Abdolmelick, now upon his return into Syria, made Bashur his brother governour of Cufah, and Caled the son of Abdollah governour of Basorah. When Caled came thither, he made Mohalleb supervisor of the tribute ; indiscreetly, for Mohalleb was the best general of the age, and in all probability the victory which was gotten by the Azarakites was owing to his absence. They beat Abdolaziz who was sent against them, and took his wife prisoner. As they were talking about what she was worth, and valuing her at about 100,000 pieces, one of the chief of them said, ' What, shall she escape so ? I do not see that this heathen doth anything but cause disturbance amongst you,' and struck her head off. Some that stood by told him they could not tell whether they should praise him or blame him, he answered he did it only out of zeal. Caled wrote a letter to Abdolmelick acquainting him with the loss of the army, and desiring to know his pleasure, who answered him thus. ' I understand by the letter you sent by your ' messenger, that you sent your brother to fight against the Separa ' tists ; and received the account of your slaughter and flight ; and I ' enquired of your messenger where Mohalleb was, who informed me ' that he was your lieutenant over Ehwaz ; God rejected thy counsel ' when thou sentest thy brother, an Arabian of Meccah, to battle, and ' didst keep Mohalleb by thy side to gather taxes, who is a man of a ' most penetrating judgment, and good government, hardened in war, ' and is the son of the grandson of it : see therefore and send Mohalleb ' to meet them in Ehwaz or beyond Ehwaz ; and I have sent to Bashur ' to assist thee with an army of Cufians ; and if thou goest and meetest ' thy enemy, do not undertake any enterprize against him till thou hast ' shown him to Mohalleb, and asked his advice about him if it please ' God. Peace be upon thee, and the mercy of God.' Caled was not well pleased with the contents of the letter, both because he had blamed him for sending his brother to manage the war, and because he had laid him under the restraint of doing nothing without the ad vice of Mohalleb. Abdolmelick ordered Bashur to assist them with 5000 Cufians, and to send a messenger first out of complaisance to Mohalleb, who was a person of too great consideration, not to be treated with the utmost respect.

Their forces being ready, they marched and met the enemy near the city Ehwaz, for the Azarakites were advanced so far, and almost come up to the camp of the Muslemans. There were ships in the river, which Mohalleb advised Caled to seize ; but before that could be put in execution, there came a party of the enemies horse, and set them on fire. As Mohalleb passed by one of his generals, and perceived he had not intrenched himself, he asked him the reason of it. The other swore, he valued them no more than a camel's fart. Mohalleb bad him not despise them, for they were the lions of the Arabians. They remained in their intrenchments about twenty days ; and Caled and Mohalleb fell upon them, and, after as bloody a battle as had been fought in the memory of man, entirely routed them and took possession of their camp. Caled sent David to pursue them, and dispatched an express to Abdolmelick acquainting him with the success, who immediately commanded his brother Bashur to send 4000 horse more to join David and pursue them into Persia : these orders were obeyed till they had lost almost all their horses, and were tired, and almost starved, so that the greatest part of the two armies returned on foot to Ehwaz.

Thus Abdolmelick, in the 72nd year, having brought all the eastern part of the Musleman empire entirely under his subjection, had no opposition left but what was made at Meccah by old Abdollah, the son of Zobeir. Against him Abdolmelick sent Hejage, the son of Joseph, one of the most eloquent as well as warlike captains that flourished amongst them, during the reigns of the Caliphs. One reason among others that inclined him to employ him in that service was, because when Abdolmelick was upon his return into Syria, Hejage said to him, ' I saw in my dream that I had taken the son of Zobeir and flayed him ; wherefore send me against him, and commit the management of that war to my charge.' The Caliph was pleased with the dream, and sent him with a strong body of Syrians to Meccah, whither he had written before, promising them protection and security, upon condition that they should come under his obedience. Abdollah sent out parties of horse against him, but in all the skirmishes they came by the worst. Hereupon Hejage wrote to Abdolmelick to send him sufficient force to besiege Abdollah, assuring him that his fierceness was very much abated, and that his men deserted daily. Abdolmelick wrote to Tharick, the son of Amer, to assist him, who joined him with 5000 men. Hejage came to Thaef (a town lying 60 miles E. of Meccah) in the month Shaaban in the 72nd year, and Tharik came to him in the new moon of Dulhagiah, but he did not go round the temple, nor come near it, because he was under a vow ; but kept himself in his arms, and anointed himself till after the death of the son of Zobeir. Abdollah killed the sacrifice (either camels or oxen) on the (*Yaumolnehri*) killing day, that is the tenth of Moharram ; but neither he nor his friends performed the rights of pilgrimage, because they had not been at mount Arafat, which is necessary in order to the making a true pilgrimage, but they being besieged, could not do it.

This same year Abdolmelick wrote to Abdollah, the son of Hazim, to persuade him to come in, and promised him to give him the revenues of Chosaran for seven years, upon that condition ; who took his proffer so disdainfully, that he told the messenger if it were not for making a disturbance between the two tribes, he would have killed him ; however he made him eat the letter he brought. After this Abdolmelick sent a general against him with sufficient force, and killed him. Others say that he was not killed till after the death of Abdollah, the son of Zobeir, and that Abdolmelick sent Abdollah's head to the son of Hazim, imagining that he would not then stand out any longer ; but it had a quite contrary effect, for as soon as he saw it, he swore he would never come under his obedience as long as he lived ; then calling for a bason he washed the head and embalmed it, and wrapped it up in linen, and prayed over it, and sent it to Abdollah's relations at Medinah ; and made the messenger eat the letter, telling him that if he had not been a messenger he would have struck his head off : and some say that he cut his hands and feet off first, and afterwards his head.

The whole time during which Abdollah was besieged was 8 months and 17 nights. They battered the temple of Meccah with engines, and it thundered and lightened so dreadfully, as put the Syrians into a terrible consternation, and made them give over. At this Hejage struck the corner of his vest into his girdle, and putting one of the stones into it that they used to throw out of the engines, slang it ; his example set them on work afresh. The next morning there came upon them storm after storm, and killed 12 of his men, which quite dispirited the Syrians. Hejage said to them, 'O Syrians, do not dislike this, I am a son of Tehamah : this is the storm of Tehamah : this victory is just at hand : rejoice at the news of it ; their men suffer as much by it as you do. The next day there was another storm, and some of Abdollah's men were killed, which gave Hejage opportunity to encourage his men, and say, ' Do not you see that they are hurt, and you are in a state of obedience, and they of disobedience ?' Thus they continued fighting till a little before Abdollah was killed. His friends deserted from him every day, and ran over to Hejage. The greatest part of the inhabitants of Meccah did so, to the number of 10,000 : nay, his two sons Hamzah and Chobeib left him, and went and procured conditions for themselves. When he perceived himself forsaken on all sides, he went to his mother (who was grand-daughter to Abubeker, the first Caliph, and was then 90 years of age, a woman of a most undaunted spirit) and said to her, 'O mother ! the people have 'deserted me even to my own children and family, and I have but a 'few left with me, and they are such as would hardly be able to stand 'it out an hour's pace ; and these people will give me whatsoever I de- 'sire in this world ; what do you advise me to do ?' 'Son,' said she, 'judge for yourself ; if you know that you are in the right, and pretend 'to be so, persevere in it ; for your friends have died for the sake of it ;

' wherefore be not so obstinately resolved to save your neck as to be-
' come the scorn of the boys of the Ommian family! But if thou
' chusest the present world, alas! bad servant! thou hast destroyed
' thyself, and those that were killed with thee. And if thou sayest I
' stood to the truth, and when my friends declined, I was weakened!
' This is neither a part of an ingenuous nor a religious man. And how
' long can you continue in this world? Death is more eligible.' Then
Abdollah drew near, and kissed her head, and said, ' By God, this is
' the same thought wherein I have persisted to this very day; neither
' did I incline towards this world, nor desire to live in it, nor did any
' other motive persuade me to dissent, but my zeal for God. However,
' I had a mind to know your opinion, and you have added to the view
' which I had before: wherefore, mother, look upon me as a dead man
' from this day: nor let your grief be immoderate, but resign yourself
' to God's command; for your son hath not stood in the footsteps of the
' scandalous, nor done anything worthy of reproach; nor prevaricated in
' the judgment of God, nor dealt treacherously in giving his faith: nor
' supported himself by doing injury to any person that delivered up
' himself or entered into covenant; nor did any injustice done by any
' of my officers ever reach me that I approved of, but always dis-
' couraged it; nor was there anything that I preferred to the doing the
' will of my Lord. O God! thou knowest that I do not say this for the
' justification of myself, but to comfort my mother, that she may receive
' consolation after my decease.' She answered, ' I hope in God, I
' shall have good comfort in thee whether thou goest before me, or I
' before thee. Now go out upon my soul, and see what will be the
' issue.' To which he answered, ' God give thee a good reward, O
' mother! you will not cease praying for me, both before and after.'
She answered, ' That I never shall; others are killed in vain, but thou
' for the truth. O God! be merciful to him for his watchfulness in the
' long nights, and his diligence, and his piety towards his father and
'.me; O God, I resign myself to what thou shalt command concerning
' him; I am pleased with what thou dost decree; give me in Abdollah
' the reward of those that are grateful and persevering.' This was
about ten days before he was killed. The day whereon he was killed
he went into the house of his mother, with his coat of mail on and his
helmet, and took hold on her hand and kissed it. She said, ' This
farewell is not for a long time.' He told her he was come to take his
leave of her, for this was his last day in this life. As he embraced her,
she felt the coat of mail, and told him that the putting that on did not
look like a man that was resolved to die; he said that he had not put
it on, but only that he might be the better able to defend her; she said
she would not be so defended, and bad him put it off. Then she bad
him go out, assuring him that if he was killed he died a martyr; he
said he did not so much fear death as the being exposed after it; to

which she courageously answered, that a sheep when it was once killed never felt the flaying. Before he went out to increase his courage, she gave him a draught with a pound of musk in it. At last he went out, and defended himself to the terror and astonishment of his enemies, killing a great many with his own hands, so that they kept at a distance, and threw bricks at him, and made him ·stagger; and when he felt the blood run down his face and beard, he repeated this verse,

"The blood of our wounds doth not fall down upon our heels, but upon our feet :"

meaning, that he did not turn his back upon his enemies. Then they killed him, and as soon as Hejage heard the news he fell down and worshipped. His head was cut off, and his body hung up, and they smelt the perfume of the musk he had drank several days before.

Tharik said to Hejage that never woman bore a braver man. 'How,' said Hejage, 'do you commend a man that was in rebellion against the emperor of the faithful?' 'Yes,' answered Tharik, 'and he will excuse us; do you only consider that we have been besieging him these seven months, and he had neither army nor strong place of defence, nevertheless, whenever we engaged him he was always a match for us, nay, superior to us.' This discourse of theirs reached Abdolmelick's ears, who said that Tharik was in the right.

Abdollah was Caliph nine years, being inaugurated· in the 64th year, immediately afrer the death of Yezid, the son of Moawiyah. He was a man of extraordinary courage, but covetous to the last degree. So that this sentence passed among the Arabians for a sort of a proverb, that there was never a valiant man but was also liberal, till Abdollah, the son of Zobeir. He was in a great repute upon the account of his piety : he is said to have been so fixed and unmoved when he was at prayer, that a pidgeon lighted upon his head, and sat there a considerable time, without his knowing anything of the matter. Abu'lpheda says he wore a suit of clothes 40 years without putting them off his back, but doth not inform us what they were made of. This family of the Zobeirs passed among the Arabians for a half-witted sort of people.

After he was dead, all Arabia acknowledged Abdolmelick for their Caliph, and Hejage took the oaths of allegiance for him. This year Mohammed, the son of Merwan, took Assaphiyah and beat the Greeks ; and it is said that this same year Othman, the son of Waled, fought the Greeks on the side of Armenia with 4000 men, and beat their army consisting of 60,000.

Hejage, now master of all Arabia in the 74th year, pulls down the temple of Meccah, which Abdollah had repaired, placing the stone on the outside of it again, and restoring it to the form it was in before Mahomet's time. He exercised most unmerciful cruelty upon the poor Medinians, and stigmatized them with marks in their necks and hands ; he used frequently to pick quarrels with them without any provocation, and punish them without any crime. He met with one of them once and asked him what was the reason he did not assist Othman, the son of Affan? He answered he did. Hejage told him he lyed, and immediately commanded a stamp of lead to be put upon his neck. Thus he continued plaguing and tormenting them, till the Azarakites raising new commotions in the east, Abdolmelick thought his service necessary in those parts, and made him governor of Irak, Chorasan and Sigistan; upon which he removed from Medinah to Cufah, Abdolmelick's brother Bashur being then dead. He entered into Cufah muffled up in his turbant; the curiosity of the people drew them all round about him, he assured them they should soon know who he was: then going directly to the mosque he mounted the membar or pulpit, where he treated them after a very rough manner, and swore that he would make the wicked bear his own burthen, and fit him with his own shoe; and a great deal more to the same purpose, which increased their terror and aversion. One day, when he went into the pulpit, after a short pause he rose up and said, ' O Irakians! methinks I see ' the heads (*of men*) ripe and ready to be gathered, and turbants and ' beards sprinkled with blood.'

The day after he came to Cufah, hearing a noise in the street, he went directly to the pulpit and made a most reproachful speech to them, swearing that he would make such an example of them by the severity of his punishments, as should exceed all that went before it, and be a pattern for all that should come after it. He then began to give daily instances of his cruelty, and his rage vented itself particularly upon those that had any hand in the murther of the Caliph Othman. From thence he went not long after to Basorah, where he made them a speech much to the same purpose that he had done before at Cufah; and to give them a taste of his discipline, caused one of them to be beheaded upon the place, who had been informed against as being a rebel. This provoked the Irakians to such a degree, that they made an insurrection against him, but to no purpose, for he beat them in a field fight, and having sent eighteen of their heads to Mohalleb returned to Basorah.

The Azarakites appearing with considerable forces, Hejage sent Mohalleb and Abdorrahman the son of Mehneph against them: they had good success at the beginning; but Abdorrahman, thinking it a disparagement to be commanded by Mohalleb, neglected his advice and would not intrench, which gave the enemy an opportunity of taking the advantage of him, and cutting him off. The insurrection of the Basorians against Hejage gave the Azarakites great encouragement at first, who hoped to make the best use of their mutual dissentions; but after that tumult was quelled, they found themselves disappointed.

But the greatest opposition that Hejage ever met with in the whole course of his life, was begun by Shebib a Karegite, and Salehh another sectary, who having been both on pilgrimage at Meccah in the year 75, when Abdolmelick was there, formed a conspiracy against him. The Caliph being informed of it, sent to Hejage to seize them; but notwithstanding his vigilance Salehh staid very secure for a month's space at Cufah, where he concerted measures with his friends, and provided all things necessary for his undertaking. His sect were called the Safrians, and he was the first of them that ever appeared openly in arms; he was a man much given to devotion, and had a great many followers both in Mausal and Mesopotamia to whom he used to read and expound the Alcoran. Some of his auditors desired that he would send them a copy of what they once heard him deliver; he condescended to their request, and it was as followeth.

' Praise be to God, who hath created the heavens and the earth,
' and appointed the darkness and the light; they that deny the faith
' make an equal to the Lord. O God! as for us we will not make any
' equal to thee, nor will we hasten but to thee, nor will we serve any
' besides thee. To thee belong the creation and the government, and
' from thee come good and hurt, and to thee we must go. And we
' testify that Mahomet is thy servant, and thy apostle whom thou hast
' singled out, and thy prophet whom thou hast chosen, and in whom
' thou hast delighted, that he should convey thy message, and thy warn-
' ing to thy servants; and we bear witness that he conveyed the message,
' and admonished the people, and invited to the truth, and stood in right-
' eousness, and helped religion, and made war upon the associators,* till
' God took him, upon whom be peace. I exhort you to trust in God,
' and to abstain from the present world, and to desire the other, and
' frequently to remember death, and to love the believers, and to
' separate yourselves from the conversation of evil doers. For absti-
' nence from the present world increaseth the desire of the servant
' towards that which is with God, and causeth his body to be at
' leisure to obey God; and the frequent remembrance of death
' maketh the servant stand in fear of his lord, so as to be moved with
' love towards him, and to humble himself before him. The separating
' from evil doers, is a law to the Muslemans: God most high saith in
' his book, never pray for any of them that are dead, nor stand at his
' grave, for they denied God and his apostle, and died doing evil
' (Alcoran, chap. ix. 85). And the love of the faithful is a means
' whereby the favour of God is attained, and his mercy and his para-
' dise, (God make us and you of the number of those that bear witness
' to the truth, and persevere). Now it is of the gracious doing of God
' towards the believers that he sent them an apostle of their own, who
' taught them the book and wisdom, and cleansed them, and purified
' them, and kept them in their religion, and was gentle and merciful to
' the faithful, till God took him, the blessing of God be upon him.

* So they called all Idolaters and Christians, as joining partners with God.

' Then the verifier† succeeded him with the good liking of the Musle-
' mans, and governed according to his direction and tradition, till he
' went to God, God be merciful to him. He left Omar his successor,
' and God made him the governor of this flock, and he managed by the
' book of God, and revived the tradition of the apostle of God : neither
' did he cease to do justice to the people committed to his charge,
' nor feared any accusation in the cause of God till he went to him,
' God have mercy upon him. After him Othman governed the Musle-
' mans, and he pursued a shadow, and broke down the bounds, and
' perverted judgment, and weakened the faithful, and strengthened the
' wicked, and the Muslemans went to him and killed him, and God
' and his apostle are clear of him. And after him the people agreed
' to give the government to Ali the son of Abu Taleb, who did not
' make it his business to judge according to the command of God to
' men ; but joined himself to erroneous people, and was fixed amongst
' them and played the hypocrite ; and we are clear of Ali and his
' sectaries. Wherefore prepare yourselves, (God have mercy upon
' you) with alacrity for the holy war, against these jarring people, and
' these erroneous and unjust Imanis ; and for the going out of this
' transitory mansion to the mansion that shall remain ; and for the
' being joined to your brethren the faithful who have certain assurance ;
' who sold the present world for the other, and laid out their substance
' in quest of the favour of God in the latter end. Neither be afraid of
' being killed for the sake of God ; for the being killed is easier than
' death ; and death cometh upon you quicker than thought, and makes
' a separation between you and your children, and your families, and
' your present world, notwithstanding your exceeding aversion to it,
' and your fear of it : wherefore sell yourselves and your substance in
' obedience to God, that you may securely enter into paradise, and
' embrace the black-eyed girls. God make us and you thankful, and
' full of remembrance, such as are directed in the truth, and do that
' which is right according to it.'

Once when he was amongst his friends, he broke out into these
expressions, ' What do you stay for ? How long will you stand still ?
' For, this iniquity hath spread itself, and this injustice is grown to an
' exceeding vast exorbitant height and distance from the truth in
' defiance of the Lord. Wherefore let us come to some resolution,
' and see what is to be done.' In the midst of these speeches there
came a letter from Shebib to Salehh, to acquaint him that since he had
complied with his request, in making an attempt upon the present
powers, he desired to be informed in what condition his affairs were ;
that he thought there was no time to be lost ; that he was not sure he
should not be overtaken by death before he had an opportunity of

† *Arab. Assiddik.* It is the surname of Abubeker, which Mahomet gave him because he
verified or asserted the truth of Mahomet's journey to heaven in the night.

being engaged in a holy war, against these wicked ones. Salehh returned answer, that he waited only for him ; that this delay had raised in him some suspicion ; that they were making all necessary preparations, and staid for nothing but his coming. Shebib gathered together his small company and joined Salehh in Dara'leizirah, over which Mohammed Ben Merwan was governour. They seized some of his horses in a neighbouring village, upon which they mounted their foot. Mohammed soon received intelligence of their march, but despised the smallness of their number (which did not exceed 120) and commanded Adi to go against them with 500 men, who begged his excuse, and told him that he knew that one of their men was as good as 100 of theirs, and that it was unreasonable to send him with such an unequal force ; then Mohammed ordered him 500 more : so he marched from Harrad with this 1000 as unwilling as if he had been led to the place of execution. When he drew near to Salehh, he sent a messenger to let him know that he was not for fighting, and if he would depart out of that territory, and invade some other, he would not oppose him. Salehh said to the messenger ' Go and tell him, that if he is of our opinion it shall be so, but if he be in the measures of the tyrants, and the Imams of enmity, we know what to do.' To which Adi answered, ' that he was not of his opinion, but that he did not come to fight either against him, or any one else. Salehh had no sooner received this answer, but he rode full speed and surprised Adi saying the noon prayers, who suspected nothing of the matter, till he saw the horse coming upon him ; his men were all out of order, and put to the rout without any resistance. He trampled down Adi and his standard as he was at prayers, and moving directly to his camp, took possession of all that was in it. They that escaped carried this sad news to Mohammed, who was very angry, and sent Caled the son of Jora with 1500 men, and Hareth with 1500 more. Calling them both together, he bad them go out against these wicked Separatists, and to add to their speed, told them that he that came up with the enemy first should command the other. Enquiring after Salehh they were informed that he was marched towards Amed ; they kept equal pace, and towards the evening came up with Salehh, who sent Shebib against Hareth, whilst he charged the other general himself. The victory was dubious a long time, notwithstanding the disproportion of the numbers ; for one of the Separatists could beat ten or twenty of the other ; at last Caled and Hareth perceiving that their horse were repulsed, alighted and fought on foot ; this quite altered the condition of the battle ; for by this means they supported themselves with their lances against the enemies horse, and at the same time their archers galled them, and the remainder of their horse trampled them down. Thus they continued fighting till night parted them, at which time Salehh had lost 30 men, and Caled and Hareth more than 70. Both parties were sufficiently weary of one another, for the battle was very sharp the time it lasted, and a great many were wounded on both sides. After they were parted and retired to their respective camps, having said their prayers, and refreshed themselves with such fragments as they had, Salehh asked Shebib his advice, who told him that they were over-matched, and that the enemy would by intrenching themselves prevent any attempt against them. Upon this they decamped under the pro-tection of the night, and marched across over Mesopotamia till they came to Mausil, and from thence to a place called Dascarah, where Hejage having received intelligence of their approach, sent a body of 5000 men against them, under the command of Hareth Alhamdani. Three thousand of them were Cufians of the old soldiers, and the other 2000 were chosen men. Whilst they were marching to Dascarah, Salehh was gone to Jalouta and Catikin ; Alhareth pursued him to a place called Modbage, that lies upon the borders of Mausil, between Mausil and Juchi. There they engaged. Salehh had then with him no more than 90 men, these he divided into three companies, thirty in each : in a short time Salehh was killed. Shebib was beaten off his horse, and fought on foot till he came to the place where Salehh lay dead ; whereupon he called out to the Muslemans to come to him, for they had no commander left, and bad them turn back to back, and make their retreat to a neighbouring empty castle. This they per-formed in exceeding good order, for 70 of them got in safe. Hareth surrounded them in the evening, and bad his men only set fire to the castle-gates, and so leave them there till the morning, where they might be sure to find them. Shebib knew very well that what was to be done must be done by the favour of the night, because it would be absurd to expect that they should be able to defend themselves against such a force in the morning ; and his men having first given him their hands in token of their submission, the gates of the castle being burnt to coals, they wetted their saddle cloths, and spreading them over the coals, stept over. Hareth and his men were in their camp without any apprehension of danger, till about midnight they found Shebib and his men cutting all to pieces in the midst of the camp. Hareth himself was struck down, but his men carried him off the ground, and ran away in the greatest confusion and consternation. This is the first victory that Shebib got ; which added such courage to his party that they daily increased, and became terrible to Hejage himself, who never omitted any endeavour to extirpate them. After a great many battles, wherein Shebib was always superior, whilst Hejage was gone to Basorah he seized the city of Cufah.

This year Mohalleb died, whom Hejage had made governour of Chorasan. He was a person of extraordinary character, both for his abilities and generosity of temper. When he felt death approaching he called his sons about him and gave them a bundle of arrows, to break, which they told him they could not. He asked them next if they could break them singly, they answered affirmatively, he bad them imagine themselves to be like that bundle of arrows.

This year Abdolmelick caused the first money to be coined that ever was in use among the Arabians of their own; for before they used to trade with Greek and Persian money. The occasion was thus. Abdolmelick used to write in the beginning of the letters that he sent to the Greek Emperor, 'Say, God is one.' Or, say, ' There is one God ;' and then mention the prophet with the date of the Hegirah : whereupon the Grecian Emperor sent him word that he had made such and such innovations in his manner of writing, and bad him alter it, or else he would send him some coins with such a mention of their prophet upon them, as they should not very well like. Abdolmelick was angry at this, and said, 'A curse upon their coins;' and from that time began to make money. Hejage stamped some with this inscription, 'Say, there is one God,' which gave great offence to the Muslemans, because the sacred name of GOD would be exposed to the touch of unclean persons of both sexes. Somyor, a Jew, regulated their coinage, which was but rude at first, after whom it received several improvements in the succeeding reigns.

Now though Shebib had beaten the army which Hejage had sent against him, and made such a vigorous opposition, that the Cufians were not able to keep the field ; yet Hejage, resolved not to bear his insults any longer, represented the condition of that part of the country to the Caliph Abdolmelick, who reinforced him with a sufficient number of Syrians, with which he gave Shebib battle near Cufah. Shebib made a noble defence, having in all but 600 men, but was forced at last to give way to the Syrians, whom Hejage was scarce able to hold up against him. At last Shebib's brother was killed and his wife Gazalah, who had attended him when he went first to Cufah, and made a vow to say her prayers in the great temple, and read the Cow and the family of Amram there (they are the second and third chapters of the *Alcoran*) which she had accordingly performed. A body of Syrians pursued Shebib, who killed 100 of them with the loss of only 30 of his own men. Some of them were so tired with their march and the fight, that when they struck with their swords they could not carry an edge; and some of them struck as they sat, because they were not able to rise. In this condition Shebib despairing of doing any thing left them, and passing over the Tigris went towards Juchi : afterwards repassing the Tigris at Waset, he bent his course towards Ehwaz ; from thence into Persia, and so on to Kerman, where he rested and refreshed himself and his men. In the meantime Hejage ordered his wife Gazalah's head to be washed and buried. Soon after Shebib began to advance forwards again, against whom Hejage sent Sophyan, the son of Alabrad, whom Abdolmelick had sent to his assistance out of

Syria. They met at a bridge called Dojail el Ehwaz. Shebib passed the bridge first, and after a sharp encounter was repulsed. Returning again he renewed the battle with vigour, but was beaten back; and when he came to the bridge he made a stand with about 100 men, who fought so bravely till the evening that the Syrians never felt themselves so handled before. Sophyan perceiving that he could do nothing against them, commanded the archers to shoot them, which they did for a while, till Shebib and his men rushed in upon them with their swords and killed above 30 of them; and then wheeling about, he fell upon Sophyan, and they continued fighting desperately till night, and then retreating, Sophyan commanded his men not to pursue them. When Shebib came to the bridge, he commanded his men to go over before him, resolving to renew the fight in the morning. He brought up the rear, and as he was upon the bridge his horse leaped upon a mare that was before him, and loosened the stones of the bridge. Shebib's foot striking at the same time upon the edge of a boat, he was dismounted and fell into the water. When he rose up, he said, 'When God decrees a thing it is done.' Then putting up his head a second time he said, 'This is the decree of the Almighty the Alwise [God!] These were the last words of that great captain, concerning whose mother they relate this remarkable story.

Yezid, the son of Naim, was sent by Othman's command to assist the Syrian Mahometans against the Greeks in the twenty-fifth year of the Hegirah. The Muslemans obtaining the victory, the Christians were exposed to sale. Among the rest he espied a tall, beautiful, black-eyed maid which he bought, and having brought her to Cufah, commanded her to turn Mahometan, and upon her refusal, caused her to be beaten. This only increased her aversion towards him, so that he was glad to let her alone to bring her to a good humour. Afterwards she proved with child of Shebib, and her fondness to her master increasing daily, she turned Mahometan of her own accord; because she knew it would be agreeable to him. So that she changed her religion before Shebib was born, which was on the tenth of the month Dulhagiah, being the day on which the pilgrims kill the sacrifices at Meccah. Awaking out of a slumber, she said, 'I saw, as one that sleeps sees, that there went out from before me a flame which diffused itself round about the heavens, and spread itself to every quarter; after which a coal dropt into a great water and was quenched; now I have brought him forth upon the day wherein you shed blood; and I interpret my dream thus, "That this son of mine will be a man of blood, and that his condition will be exalted to a very high degree in a short time."' Hearing a false rumour once of his being killed, she gave no credit to it, but as soon as she heard he was drowned, she believed it, saying that she knew from the time of his birth that he would come to no other end.

28

His body being drawn up with a net, they cut off his head and sent it to Hejage. When he was opened they found his heart prodigiously firm and hard like a stone.

In the eighty-first year died Mohammed Ben Haniphiyah, the third son of Ali, who because he was not descended from Mahomet as Hasan and Hosein were is not reckoned amongst the Imams, notwithstanding there were several of his followers who secretly owned him to be lawful Caliph after Hosein's death. Some of the sectaries look upon him as a great prophet whom God hath taken and preserved alive in a certain mountain ; and that he shall hereafter appear again and fill the earth with justice and piety, as it is at present full of impiety and wickedness.

From the time of Shebib's death, the Saracen empire was free from any disturbance within itself, till the eighty-second year, when Abdorrahman the son of Mohammed raised a very dangerous commotion in the eastern part of it upon this occasion. Hejage, who hated him, sent him with an inconsiderable force against Zentil, king of the Turks, with orders to carry the war into the midst of his country, with a malicious design to destroy him. Abdorrahman received secret intelligence of his barbarous intentions towards him, and soon acquainted his men with the meaning of the expedition they were engaged in. The soldiers were all in a rage to find themselves so basely betrayed, and, under a pretence of going to war, sent on purpose to be murdered, and fall a sacrifice to Hejage's malice against their general. They vowed revenge, and unanimously swore to be true to Abdorrahman, and renouncing all manner of subjection to Hejage, prepared themselves to revenge his perfidiousness. Abdorrahman, having first concluded a peace with the Turk, returned into Irak, and marched directly against Hejage, who being before informed of it, had petitioned Abdolmelick for succours out of Syria, who sent him a considerable army. With these supplies, Hejage marches against him, but being beaten in the first battle, Abdorrahman carries his victorious army to Basorah, where a great many of the citizens throwing off their allegiance to Abdolmelick, took the oath to him, and intrenching themselves on one side of the city, they soon obtained a second victory over their enemies. From thence he went to Cufah, where he was so far from meeting with any opposition that the citizens came out of their own accord to meet him, and took the oath of allegiance. In the mean time Hejage gathered together all the forces he was able ; and Abdorrahman's army on the other side was increased to the number of 100,000 men, among whom were several of prime note among the Basorians, who had conceived an aversion against Hejage upon the account of his cruelty. They encamped near one another ; and in the space of 100 days fought 81 battles. At last Hejage put Abdorrahman to flight, and cut off 4000 of his men. Abdorrahman retreated to Sahan, where, being seized by Hejage's lieutenant, who was going to him, Zentil, the Turk, his friend and ally, having received notice of it, came to his rescue ; but upon his being threatened with a war by Hejage in case he refused to deliver him up, he was forced to part with him. Abdorrahman having now no remedy left, and abhorring the thoughts of falling into the hands of his most implacable enemy, took an opportunity of killing himself by a fall from the top of an high house.

In the eighty-third year Hejage built a city upon the river Tigris which he called Waset, from its lying in the middle between Basorah and Cufah, that being the signification of the Arabick word. The Persian geographer says, that it is situate at an equal distance from Bagdad, Cufah, Ehwaz, and Basorah, that is, about fifty leagues from each of them.

Now though Hejage survived Abdolmelick and managed all the chief affairs for some time under his son Waled, yet since we must terminate this part of our history with the reign of this Caliph (which was designed to have been carried down to the line of the Abbasides) and it being very uncertain whether or no we shall ever have either opportunity or inclination to continue it any farther ; before we take our leave of this great man, by whose vigilance, courage, and conduct the Saracen empire was perfectly quieted and established under the government of the house of Ommiyah, it will not be amiss to relate a few instances illustrating the greatness and singularity of his genius.

One day as he was taking a walk in the field, he met with a wild Arab who knew nothing at all of him, and asked him 'What sort of a man this Hejage was whom they talked of so much.' The Arab answered, 'That he was a wicked man.' Then said Hejage, 'Do you not know me?' The Arab answering, 'No ;' 'I would have you to know then,' said Hejage, 'that it is Hejage you are talking to now.'

The Arab having heard him talk after this manner, without expressing any manner of concern said to him, 'And do you know who I am?' 'No,' answered Hejage. 'I am,' said the Arab, 'of the family of Zobeir, whose posterity all became fools three days in the year, and this is one of them.' Hejage could not forbear laughing and admiring such an ingenious come off as this : so that though he was extremely severe and reckoned cruel, for they say he had put to death 120,000 persons, and when he died had 50,000 in his prisons ; yet he pardoned this Arab, whom he esteemed for his wit and courage.

Now see another accident, wherein Hejage shewed plainly what he was. Having taken a great many officers prisoners in the battle which he gained over Abdorrahman ; he resolved to put them all to the sword. One of the prisoners, just as he was going to be executed, cried out that he had a piece of justice to demand of Hejage.

Hejage, very much surprised at what he said, asked him 'What he had to demand of him?' The prisoner answered, 'It is because when

28—2

our general Abdorrahman railed against you after an extravagant manner, I told him he was in the wrong.' Upon this Hejage asked the prisoner ' If he had any body to witness his saying so?' 'Yes,' answered the prisoner, and shewed him one of his comrades condemned to death as well as himself, who was present when he said it. Hejage being satisfied of the truth of the fact, said to the witness, ' And what is the reason you did not do so as well as your comrade?' This undaunted man answered him fiercely, ' I did not do it because you are my enemy.' Hejage gave them both their lives; the one to acknowledge his obligation; the other for having confessed the truth with so much frankness and courage.

Some people having complained of the cruelty of his behaviour towards his subjects, and set the fear of God before his eyes; he instantly mounted the pulpit to harangue the people, and without any preparation discoursed them after this manner, with his ordinary eloquence : ' God hath at present given me the power over you, and if I ' exercise it with some severity, do not you believe that you shall be ' upon better terms after my decease ! After the manner that you live ' you will always be ill used; for God hath a great many servants, and ' when I shall be dead he will send you another, who may possibly ' execute his commands against you with greater severity. Would you ' have a prince sweet and moderate? Exercise justice among your ' selves and obey his orders. Depend upon it that the behaviour of ' your selves is the principle, and the cause of the good or ill treatment ' which you receive at his hands. The prince may justly be compared ' to a looking-glass; all that you see in the glass is nothing but the ' return of the objects you present it to.'

Once when he was a hunting, he lost his company, and found himself very thirsty in a lonesome place, where an Arab was feeding his camels. As soon as he appeared the camels were scared away, which made the Arab, who was minding something else, lift up his head in a great passion and say, ' Who is this with his fine cloaths that comes here in the desart to scare my camels, the curse of God light upon him.'

Hejage without taking notice of what he said came up to him, and saluted him very civilly, wishing him peace; but he instead of returning his salutation answered him roughly, ' That he neither wished him peace, nor any blessing of God.' Hejage seemed not to understand him, and begged of him some water to drink. The Arab told him, ' That if he had a mind to drink, he might alight and help himself, for he was neither his fellow nor his man :' Hejage did as he bad him, and having drunk asked him this question, ' Whom do you believe to be the greatest and most excellent of all men?' ' It is the prophet sent by God (burst you),' said the Arab. ' And what do you say of Ali?' added Hejage. The Arab answered, ' His excellency cannot be sufficiently expressed in words.' Hejage continuing his discourse asked, ' What he thought of Abdolmelick ?' The Arab made no answer at first, but being pressed he let fall as much as if he took him to be a bad prince. 'Why so ?' answered Hejage. ' Because he has sent us for a governour the wickedest man under the heavens.'

Hejage, knowing that the Arab spoke of him, said no more ; when it happened that a bird flying over their heads made a sort of noise which the Arab had no sooner heard, but he looked steadfastly upon Hejage, and asked him 'Who he was ?' Hejage having asked him 'What was the reason of that question ;' ' It is,' said the Arab, ' because this bird that went by told me that there was a company of people not far off, and that very likely you are the chief of them.' The Arab had no sooner made an end of his discourse, when Hejage his people came up, and received order from him to carry the Arab along with them.

The day after, Hejage called for him, and made him sit down at his table, and commanded him to eat ; the Arab, before he began to eat, said his usual grace, ' God grant that the end of this meal may be as fortunate as the beginning.'

Whilst they were eating, Hejage asked him ' If he remembered the discourse that had passed between them the day before.' The Arab answered him immediately : ' God prosper you in everything, but as for yesterday's secret, take care that you do not divulge it to day.' ' That I will,' said Hejage ; ' but you must choose one of these two things, either to acknowledge me for your master, and then I will retain you in my service ; or else to be sent to Abdolmelick, to whom I shall give an account of all that you have said of him.' The Arab having heard Hejage's proposal answered him instantly : ' There is a third way you may take, which seems to me to be much better.' 'What is that ?' said Hejage. ' It is,' said the Arab, ' to send me home, and that you and I may never see one another any more.' Hejage, as fierce as he was, was pleased to hear the man talk with so much spirit, and gave him 10,000 drachms of silver, and sent him home according to his desire.

It is proper to observe here, upon the occasion of this bird that made it self be understood by the Arabian, that there are folks among the people of Arabia that pretend to know the language of birds. They say that this science has been known amongst them ever since the time of Solomon, and the Queen of Sheba, who had a bird call Hudhud, that is the houp, who was the messenger of their amours.

Kumeil the son of Ziyad was a man of fine wit. He lived in the time of Hejage, and did by no means approve of his conduct. One day Hejage made him come before him, and reproached him, because in such a garden, and before such and such persons, which he named to him, he had made a great many imprecations against him, saying, ' The Lord blacken his face,' that is, ' Fill him with shame and confusion,' and wished that his neck was cut off, and his blood shed.

Kumeil who had a very ready wit, answered him instantly ; 'It is true that I did say these words in such a garden, but then I was under a vine arbour, and was looking upon a bunch of grapes that was not yet ripe, and I wished that they would turn black soon, that they might be cut off and made wine of.' This ingenious explication pleased Hejage so well, that he sent Kumeil home, and re-established him in his favour.

Ebn Corrah, a person celebrated for his piety and his learning, and whose father had been one of the companions of the apostle, was very well acquainted with him.   One day when he was with him, the porter came out and told them, that there was a Kateb or secretary at the gate ; on which Ebn Corrah said, 'These secretaries are the worst of all sorts of people.'   Nevertheless the secretary came in and was well received by Hejage, who after he had dismissed him, said to Ebn Corrah, 'Were it not for the title of Companion of Mahomet that is in your family, I would make your neck be cut off : for the Alcoran says, 'honour the writers.' Ebn Corrah answered him immediately, 'I speak of the secretaries of the Divan, and not of the angels which are called writers of the Alcoran, because they write the actions of men to produce them at the last judgment.'

It is reported that Hejage, to excuse the severity which he exercised over those that were under him, used frequently to say, that the severe or even violent government of a prince, is better than a weak and too indulgent government; because that only doth wrong to some particular persons, whereas this other hurts and injures all the people in general

He also used to say, that the obedience due to princes is more abso- lute and necessary than that which men owe to God; according to the Alcoran, for that speaking of this latter says, 'Obey God as far as you are able:' in which words there is a condition or exception: but of that which concerns princes it is said, 'Hear and obey,' without any exception: 'so that,' said he, 'if I command any one to submit to such or such a thing, and he refuses it, he is guilty of disobedience, and con- sequently worthy of death.'

Some having heard him talk after this manner, said to him: 'Then you are an envious and an ambitious man, because you pretend to have a greater authority than others.'   To which he answered, 'He is still more envious and ambitious than me, who says to God, give me, O Lord, a condition of life which nobody can enjoy after me.'

Having once recommended himself to the prayers of a religious Musleman, he instantly prayed that it would please God to kill him quickly, for, said he, there can nothing fall out better either for him or for the people.

Mircond writes that when he was taken to his bed of his last sick- ness, he consulted his astrologer to know of him, if he did not find in his ephemerides that some great captain was near the end of his days. The astrologer answered him, that a great Lord called Kolaib was threatened, according to his observations, to die quickly. Hejage replied, ' That is exactly the name that my mother gave me when I was a child.' This word signifies in the Arabick, a little dog.

The astrologer, no less imprudent in his discourse than skilful in his art, went on very bluntly, saying, ' Then it is you that must die, you have no room to doubt it.' Hejage, offended at this discourse, said instantly to the astrologer, ' Since I must die, and you are so dextrous in your predictions, I will send you before. me into the other world, that I may make use of you :' and gave order at the same time to have him dispatched.

The same author places the death of Hejage in the 95th year of the Hegirah, and the 54th of his age; and says of him, that he was born shut up at the bottom; so that they were forced to open him with surgeon's instruments.

They say that he was so magnificent in his entertainments, that he had sometimes 1000 tables furnished, and that he used to make such large presents to his friends, as to give 1,000,000 pieces of silver at one time.

Abulpheragius observes, that he fell sick with eating dirt. That dirt is a sort of medicinal clay, called by the Latins terra lemnia, and by the Arabians thin, and thin mechtoum, lutum and lutum sigillatum; this threw him into a consumption, of which he died. Thus much concerning Hejage out of Monsieur D'Herbelot.

In the 86th year of the Hegirah, Abdolmelick died. The physicians had told him that if he drank he would die; but his thirst increased so violently, that he was not able to forbear any longer, but commanded his son Waled to give him some water, which, he refusing, he commanded his daughter Phatemah ; but Waled willing to keep him alive as long as he could, held her, and would not suffer it. Whereupon Abdolmelick told him in a passion, that if he did not let her go, he would disinherit him: so she gave him water, and he quickly expired. He died in the month Shewal : but he was always afraid of the month Ramadan, and used to say he should die in it because he was born in it, and weaned in it, and had learned the Alcoran by heart in it, and in it was saluted emperor.

The inscription of his seal was, ' I believe in God our Saviour.'

Abu'lpheda says, that he was a man of foresight, and of very good capacity and understanding; he was courageous, learned, and wise; but his being made Caliph quite turned him, and spoiled all his good qualities. He died in the 60th year of his age. He was much more powerful than any of his predecessors. He subdued Abdollah, the son of Zobeir, and added Arabia to his dominions; he entirely quelled all the several sorts of sectaries that appeared in arms against him: in his reign India was conquered in the East, and his victorious arms penetrated even as far as Spain in the West.

INDEX.

THE END.